D0780346

Ecology and Evolutionary Biology of Tree Squirrels

Edited by
Michael A. Steele,
Joseph F. Merritt,
and David A. Zegers

Proceedings of the
International Colloquium
on the Ecology of Tree Squirrels

Powdermill Biological Station
Carnegie Museum of Natural History
22–28 April 1994

Virginia Museum of Natural History
Special Publication Number 6
1998

Printed and bound in the United States of America
Virginia Museum of Natural History, Martinsville, Virginia 24112

ISBN 1-88454909-8

Cover and book design by Lisa Perrell
Cover Photos
Front
Top Left—Sciurus vulgaris by M. Andera, courtesy of American Society of Mammalogists.
Top Right—Sciurus niger niger by John Edwards.
Bottom Left—Sciurus alberti by J. L. Koprowski, courtesy of American Society of Mammalogists.
Bottom Right—Glaucomys volans by N. M. Wells, courtesy of American Society of Mammalogists.
Back
Top Left—S. carolinensis by M. Steele.
Top Right—S. niger by J. L. Koprowski.
Bottom Left—Sciurus arizonensis by J. L. Koprowski.
Bottom Right—Sciurus aureogaster by M. Steele

This book is printed on recycled paper.

Ecology and Evolutionary Biology of Tree Squirrels

CONTENTS

POPULATION BIOLOGY:

REPRODUCTION AND MATING:

DIET, HABITAT SELECTION, AND SPACE USE:

EVOLUTIONARY BIOLOGY AND BIOGEOGRAPHY:

SQUIRREL-PLANT INTERACTIONS:

CONSERVATION AND MANAGEMENT:

APPENDIX I:

PREFACE

In 1992 we discussed the possibility of organizing an international conference on tree squirrels at Powdermill Biological Station of the Carnegie Museum of Natural History, the site of many previous scientific meetings, including one in 1990 on the biology of the Soricidae. Responses to our initial invitations were overwhelming; nearly everyone contacted expressed strong support for such a gathering.

We chose to focus on the ecology of tree squirrels, rather than all aspects of their biology, for two reasons. First, because of their visibility and suitability for study, tree squirrels have been the focus of a number of important ecological investigations involving various aspects of behavior, population biology, evolutionary biology, biogeography, plant-animal interactions, and conservation biology. Secondly, as arboreal granivores, tree squirrels occupy an unique ecological niche, and are, as a result, model organisms for testing a variety of ecological questions. It is our goal that this volume will provide a general overview of much of the current research and illustrate the potential for these organisms as subjects for addressing a number of ecological questions. For obvious reasons, we also chose not to limit our coverage to those species that are strictly classified as tree squirrels (*Sciurus*), but instead include research on other sciurids as available and appropriate.

The International Colloquium on the Ecology of Tree Squirrels, held 22-28 April 1994, brought together 45 participants representing 11 countries: Belgium, Canada, Germany, India, Israel, Italy, Mexico, South Africa, Sweden, United Kingdom, and the United States.

In addition to their involvement in many fine oral and poster presentations, participants also took part in workshops and various field excursions, and enjoyed an extensive tour of the mammal collection of the Carnegie Museum.

The relaxed atmosphere and lively exchange during the colloquium, as well as the extensive contacts and collaborations to result from the meeting, made it an immense success for all. The intellectual exchange was further enhanced by a variety of fine culinary delights, several superb social events hosted by friends and neighbors of the Powdermill Biological Station and the exquisite spring days of the Appalachian Mountains of western Pennsylvania, accented of course by the magnificent wildflowers and avian visitors. (MAS, JFM, DAZ)

ACKNOWLEDGMENTS

The International Colloquium on the Ecology of Tree Squirrels was made possible by funds from the Carnegie Museum of Natural History (CMNH), Pittsburgh, PA, Wilkes University, Wilkes-Barre, PA, and Millersville University of Pennsylvania, Millersville, PA. We are especially indebted to Dr. James E. King, former Director (CMNH), for his support of the colloquium.

The success of this colloquium depended on the gracious support and dedication of many individuals. We are especially indebted to our friends, Ingrid and Bill Rea and Theresa and Thomas Nimick for hosting receptions, and to Ingrid and Bill for providing lodging in their homes for several participants, who will always remember their kind hospitality. We also extend a special thanks to three students of Wilkes University, Craig Owens, Michelle Sileski, and Leila Hadj-Chikh, for their tireless efforts in the preparation of conference materials and organization of registration, housing, and travel arrangements during the conference; their efforts were truly spectacular.

The conference ran particularly smoothly due to the fine preparation of facilities by the Powdermill maintenance staff—Gilbert Lenhart, Albert Lenhart, and Lloyd Moore. Robert Leberman and Robert Mulvihill gave freely of their time to provide bird-banding demonstrations for the participants. Terri Kromel, Educational Coordinator, Powdermill Biological Station, worked long hours to ensure that participants' visit to Powdermill was a fulfilling and memorable one. Theresa Gay Rohall, coordinator of technical sessions, made sure that all events ran smoothly. Participants were kept exceptionally well fed by Pat Piper and the staff of Ligonier Country Catering.

The organizers of the meeting also extend a thank you to Kathy Hodder and her colleagues for presentation of the official "Rancid-biscuit award", to John Gurnell and his colleagues from the United Kingdom for the fine, starlight entertainment, and to Gil Pogany for the exquisite atmosphere he provided as the colloquium's official pianist. The close of the colloquium was accented by a superb tour of the mammal collection of the Carnegie Museum of Natural History, for which we are indebted to Duane Schlitter, former Curator of Mammals, and Susanne McLaren, Collections Manager, for their time, expertise, and overwhelming enthusiasm.

Transportation between the field station and the Pittsburgh International Airport was made possible with the loan of several vehicles from Wilkes, Millersville, and Old Dominion Universities. A special thanks is extended to Bob Rose for volunteering his time and effort to coordinate and assist with transportation during the entire colloquium.

For their very rigorous and thorough reviews of the manuscripts, we also extend a sincere thanks for the fine efforts of more than 55 reviewers, 27 of whom did not participate in the colloquium. Their expert suggestions, criticisms, and insight greatly improved the quality of this volume. Several participants and reviewers, too many to name here, also helped to edit a number of manuscripts. We are especially grateful to Troy Best for his thorough review and editorial insights on the completed volume; his efforts contributed immeasurably to improving the quality of the final publication.

Finally, our very special thanks go to Susan Felker, Publications Manager, Lisa Perrell, Graphic Artist, and Donna Greytak, Publications Coordinator, of the Virginia Museum of Natural History, for their invaluable guidance, patience, and sense of humor and their willingness to take on this once-orphaned publication project and complete it to a high standard. (MAS, JFM, DAZ)

MODELING POPULATION RESPONSES OF NORTH AMERICAN TREE SQUIRRELS TO AGRICULTURALLY INDUCED FRAGMENTATION OF FORESTS

ROBERT K. SWIHART AND THOMAS E. NUPP

Department of Forestry and Natural Resources, Purdue University, West Lafayette, IN 47907-1159

ABSTRACT.—Agriculturally induced fragmentation of forests has been extensive in the midwestern United States, resulting in a landscape characterized by fewer and more isolated tracts of woodland. Much of this region is occupied by four species of tree squirrels: *Sciurus niger*, *S. carolinensis*, *Tamiasciurus hudsonicus*, and *Glaucomys volans*. Differences in morphology, ecology, and life history among these species are suggestive of differential sensitivities to forest fragmentation. Qualitative information from Indiana suggests that *S. niger* and *T. hudsonicus* have expanded their ranges in conjunction with increasing fragmentation, whereas *S. carolinensis* and *G. volans* have been negatively affected. Does fragmentation of forests affect species of squirrels differently? Is fragmentation capable of molding community structure at the patch or landscape level? To address these questions, we constructed spatially explicit models of metapopulations for each species of squirrel using demographic data derived from the literature. Model results were qualitatively consistent with data collected via livetrapping in a fragmented landscape in northwestern Indiana. In terms of population size and persistence in fragmented landscapes, the order of performance was *T. hudsonicus* > *S. niger* > *S. carolinensis* > *G. volans*. Isolation and size of fragments both were important determinants of occupancy, especially for *S. carolinensis* and *G. volans*. In highly fragmented landscapes, metapopulation dynamics rather than interspecific competition appear primarily responsible for structuring communities of squirrels.

INTRODUCTION

Agriculture has caused extensive modification of native vegetation on every continent except Antarctica, and these modifications have had important repercussions for native plants and animals (Saunders et al., 1991). One consequence of extensive conversion of land for production of crops is that the remaining native vegetation often occurs in fragmented patches within a predominantly agricultural landscape. Conversion of forest land has been widespread in the midwestern United States. For instance, nearly 80% of forests in Illinois in 1820 had been converted to agricultural use by 1980 (Iverson, 1988).

Theoretical studies generally have concluded that a species is more likely to survive in a continuous tract of habitat than in a habitat that has been fragmented (Burkey, 1989). Fragmentation results in local populations that may be linked by movements of individuals, producing metapopulations (Gilpin, 1987). Most models and field studies of vertebrate metapopulations have focused on birds (e.g., Temple, 1986; Temple and Cary, 1988; Rolstad, 1991; Pulliam et al., 1992), although work with small mammals has been conducted occasionally (e.g., Henderson et al., 1985; Lefkovitch and Fahrig, 1985; Lorenz and Barrett, 1990). Our objective was to model the impact of fragmentation on tree squirrels in the midwestern U.S., to explore interspecific differences in responses to fragmentation, and to assess the potential importance of fragmentation in shaping communities of squirrels at the local and landscape level.

Four species of tree squirrels occur syntopically within the agricultural landscape of the Midwest. In Indiana, historical records suggest that changes

In M.A. Steele, J. F. Merritt, and D. A. Zegers (eds.). 1998. Ecology and Evolutionary Biology of Tree Squirrels. Special Publication, Virginia Museum of Natural History, 6: 320 pp

in land use have had differential impacts on the species within this guild (Mumford and Whitaker, 1982). Fox squirrels *(Sciurus niger)* and red squirrels *(Tamiasciurus hudsonicus)* have expanded their ranges in conjunction with increasing fragmentation, whereas gray squirrels *(Scuirus carolinensis)* and southern flying squirrels *(Glaucomys volans)* presumably have been negatively affected. Two likely explanations exist for these phenomena, the first related to competitive interactions and the second related principally to species demography. If competition among species is intense and fragmentation has a greater negative impact on gray and southern flying squirrels, it is possible that the observed responses of fox and red squirrels could be a consequence of competitive release induced by fragmentation, or at least changes in competition coefficients favoring fox and red squirrels over gray and southern flying squirrels. Alternatively, structural or vegetative changes in woodlands and the surrounding landscape caused by agriculturally induced fragmentation could combine with interspecific differences in behavior and demography to elicit the observed responses.

Competition seems likely among species exhibiting considerable overlap in habitat requirements and food habits, yet little documentation of competition exists for the species of tree squirrels considered. Manipulation of densities of female fox squirrels by Brown and Batzli (1985*b*) had little effect on abundance of gray squirrels, although some negative interactions were suggested by altered dispersion patterns of gray squirrels. Red squirrels are reputed to behave agonistically toward other sciurids (Flyger and Gates, 1982), and reports exist of red squirrels chasing gray and southern flying squirrels (Klugh, 1927; Preston, 1948). The relationship between red squirrels and gray squirrels is unclear at best, because additional observations of nonterritorial red squirrels suggest that interspecific aggression is minimal (Layne, 1954; Ackerman and Weigl, 1970).

Considerably more evidence can be gathered in support of the hypothesis that differential responses to fragmentation are engendered by interspecific differences in behavior and life history attributes. For instance, fox squirrels exhibit evolutionary affinities to open woods and bur oak *(Quercus macrocarpa)* savannahs at the interface of the eastern deciduous forest and the tall grass prairie (Jones and Birney, 1988; Hoffmeister, 1989). Fox squirrels commonly travel away from woodlots along brushy fencerows (Sheperd, 1994), and they are capable of relying upon agricultural crops to a considerable extent (Korschgen, 1981; Hansen et al., 1986). In contrast, gray squirrels make limited use of agricultural crops as a supplemental source of food (Korschgen, 1981) and are more apt to occupy large tracts of mature forest with a well-developed understory (Nixon et al., 1978). Although typically inhabiting coniferous forests, red squirrels appear capable of functioning as habitat generalists. They exhibit phenotypic flexibility in tailoring behavioral traits to specific environments, including presence or absence of territoriality (Layne, 1954; C. C. Smith, 1968; Rusch and Reeder, 1978), larder or scatter hoarding of seeds (Layne, 1954; C. C. Smith, 1968), and use of cavities, leaf nests, or burrows as nest sites (Yahner, 1980). Demographically, the potential for population increase apparently is better developed in red squirrels than in the other three species (Table 1). Southern flying squirrels inhabit mature hardwood forests in the Midwest (Jones and Birney, 1988), where they move by gliding from tree to tree. Although less is known about southern flying squirrels, agricultural landscapes lacking wooded corridors between forest fragments presumably restrict their interpatch movements.

In general, species with broad habitat tolerances, good mobility, and adaptations to disturbance (and the resulting edge habitat) are well adapted to landscapes dominated by agriculture (Saunders et al., 1991; Meffe and Carroll, 1994). Assuming that these generalities hold for tree squirrels, we predict that fox and red squirrels should be least affected by agriculturally induced fragmentation, with greater negative impacts on populations of gray and southern flying squirrels. To examine our predictions in more detail, we developed spatially explicit population models (Dunning et al., 1995) for each of the four species of squirrels. Each model was constructed with the intent of mimicking as nearly as possible the behavioral and demographic characteristics of the species. No competitive interactions were included in the models; the fate of each species was determined solely by its behavioral and demographic characteristics. Consequently, if model results are similar to changes in composition and abundance documented in the field, the most parsimonious explanation is that the observed changes occurred because of behavioral and demographic differences rather than shifts in competitive interactions.

Table 1. *Parameters used in constructing population projection matrices for tree squirrels, as well as resulting stable age distributions and growth rates. Probability of mortality during dispersal also is given, expressed per 100 m.*

Parameter	Age[1]	Species			
		Gray	Fox	Red	Flying
Survival[2]	Juvenile	0.67	0.47	0.52	0.81
	$Subadult_1$	0.79	0.74	0.65	0.44
	$Subadult_2$	0.77	0.83	0.83	0.72
	Yearling	0.77	0.88	0.83	0.68
	Adult	0.77	0.90	0.83	0.78
Proportion of Females Breeding[3]	$Subadult_2$	0.02	0.00	0.02	0.94
	Yearling	0.56	0.23	0.52	0.80
	Adult	0.64	0.54	0.82	0.71
Litter Size[3]	$Subadult_2$	2.43	0.00	3.50	2.66
	Yearling	2.70	2.50	3.85	2.94
	Adult	3.00	2.93	5.03	3.56
Stable age distribution after spring birth pulse	Juvenile	0.33	0.41	0.55	0.55
	$Subadult_2$	0.25	0.09	0.15	0.15
	Yearling	0.13	0.11	0.11	0.14
	Adult	0.29	0.39	0.19	0.16
	Growth rate, λ_s:	1.07	1.08	1.35	1.07
	Dispersal mortality:	0.025	0.010	0.040	0.350

[1]Pre-adult age classes represent 4-month intervals; thus $subadult_1$ squirrels are 4-8 months old, $subadult_2$ squirrels are 8-12 months old, etc.

[2]Probability of surviving a 4-month interval.

[3]If values differed between the first and second birth pulse within an age class, the mean is given.

Sources: Barkalow et al. (1970), Hansen et al. (1986), Harnishfeger et al. (1978), Lair (1985), Layne (1954), Millar (1970), Nixon et al. (1975, 1986), Nixon and McClain (1969), Thompson (1978), Rusch and Reeder (1978), Sonenshine et al.(1979).

DERIVATION OF SPATIALLY EXPLICIT DEMOGRAPHIC MODELS

We constructed age-specific models of population growth for each species of squirrel in fragmented landscapes consisting of patches of suitable forested habitat. Local populations in fragments were linked by dispersal between patches. Stochastic variation in births and deaths was incorporated into the models, along with stochastic variation in production of mast. Mast determined carrying capacity of local patches and influenced rates of reproduction, dispersal, and survival of juveniles, as well as litter size. The following sections detail the models' components.

Reproduction and survival.—For each species, we compiled information on age-specific rates of survival and fertility from the literature (Table 1). Demographic data for gray and fox squirrels were relatively plentiful, whereas data for red and southern flying squirrels were scarce. Thus, we place more confidence in the models constructed for the former species than for the latter. Demographic data were used to construct population projection matrices for the purpose of calculating annual rates of growth, λ_s, and stable age distributions (Caswell, 1989). Because two pulses of births, separated by about 4 months, are common for all four species in the Midwest, we constructed three 4-month projection matrices. These matrices were multiplied together to yield an annual projection matrix. A λ_s value of 1.07-1.08 was shared by gray, fox, and southern flying squirrels. For red squirrels λ_s = 1.35, indicating a much higher propensity for increase.

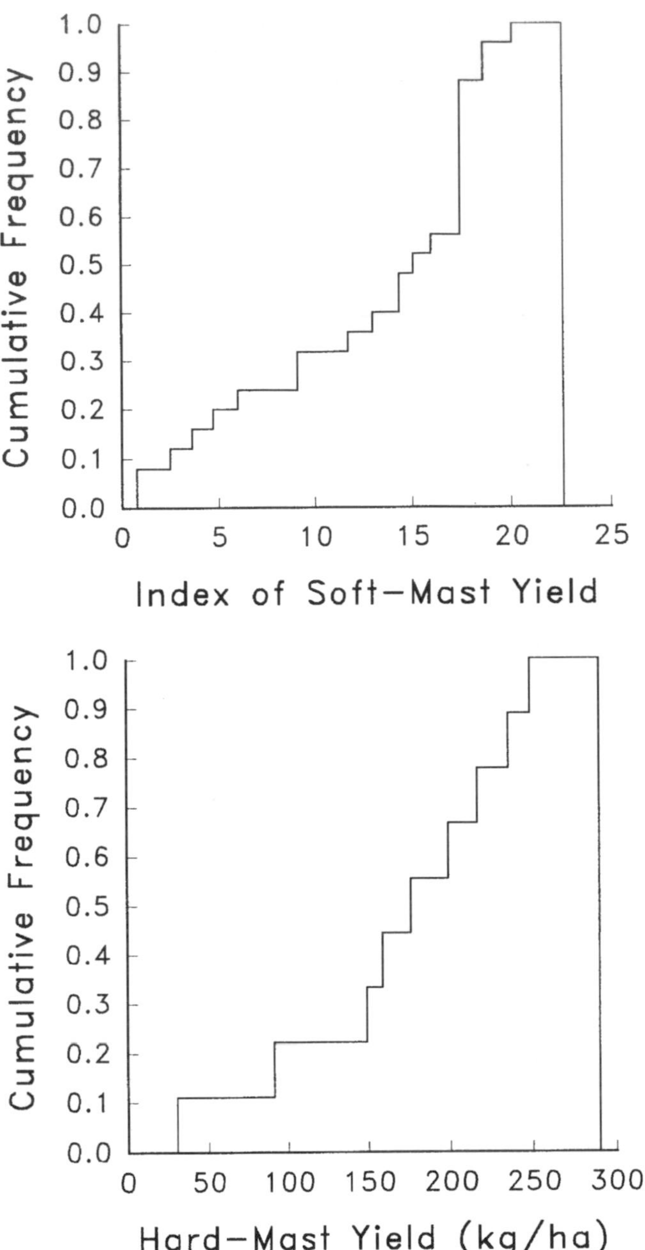

Fig. 1.—Cumulative distribution functions (CDF) used for generating data on production of soft and hard mast. The CDF for soft-mast yield is constructed from data collected by Godman and Mattson (1976), whereas the CDF for hard-mast yield was constructed from data collected by Nixon et al. (1975).

Environmental variation in production of mast.—Each of the tree squirrels in our study relies upon mast as their principal source of food, and variation in the production of mast can influence survival and reproduction (Nixon and McClain, 1969; Nixon et al., 1975; Koprowski, 1991). To enhance realism of the models, we incorporated annual variation in production of soft and hard mast. Cumulative distribution functions (Fig. 1) were constructed from 9 years of data collected for production of hard mast in Ohio (Nixon et al., 1975) and 25 years of data on production of soft mast in Wisconsin (Godman and Mattson, 1976). A mast-yield category was selected randomly using the cumulative distribution function for soft mast, and a particular value within the category was determined by assuming that each value within the interval had an equal probability of occurrence. Selection of hard-mast yield was complicated by the fact that conditions affecting soft-mast yield in spring may affect hard mast-yield in autumn. Thus, yields of soft and hard mast within a year are not necessarily independent. Reports of correlations between production of hard and soft mast within a year varied widely; we used a moderate correlation (r = 0.47) in our simulations. No correlation in yield was assumed between years.

Fragmented landscapes.—Populations occupied a square, 25 km^2 landscape, of which 5% (125 ha) was forest. Non-forested portions of the landscape were presumed to be homogenous and unsuitable for permanent occupancy by tree squirrels. For simplicity, the landscape was constructed using hexagonal cells measuring 1 ha (Pulliam et al., 1992). A patch was defined as a collection of forested hexagons that shared at least one side.

All forested hexagons within a landscape were assumed to be equal in quality, on average. Although spatial variation in, for example, precipitation and temperature precludes a perfectly correlated environment with respect to production of mast, we suspected that patches within a landscape of the size we studied should exhibit a high degree of covariation in production of mast. In other words, if conditions favored a bumper year in one portion of the landscape, chances are that similar conditions occurred elsewhere in the landscape. Accordingly, in our simulations we used a fairly large inter-patch correlation in production of mast within a season (r = 0.77). This correlation was achieved by randomly selecting a yield value for the first patch and then restricting the range of values from which yields were randomly selected for subsequent patches to 45% of the possible range, centered on the initial value.

Thus, autocorrelation in production of mast was evident on a temporal (seasonal) scale as well as on a spatial scale. Although Hanski (1991) termed correlated environmental variation among patches "regional stochasticity," we use the term environmental stochasticity to refer to both temporal and spatial variation in production of mast.

We simulated population dynamics for landscapes (Fig. 2) varying in dispersion of patches (uniform, clumped) and number of patches (4, 25, and 125). Growth of each species was monitored in each landscape, with 10 replications, yielding a 4 x 2 x 3 factorial design. Although viability analysis for a population generally requires a substantially

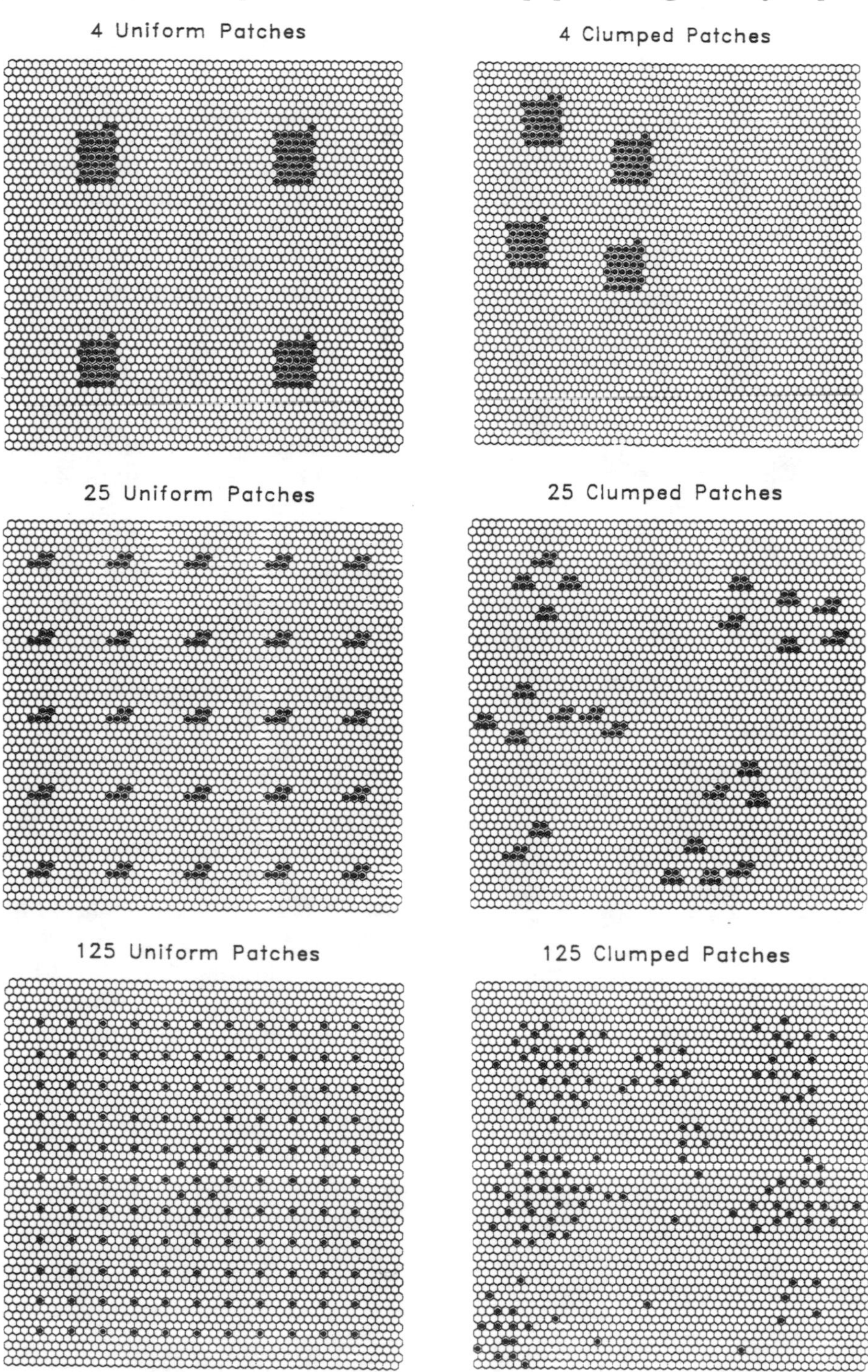

Fig. 2.—Hexagonal landscapes in which dyamics of squirrel populations were simulated. Each hexagon represents 1 ha. Solid circles represent hexagons of forested habitat suitable for use by squirrels, and contiguous forested hexagons are considered forest patches. Note that in the landscapes with four patches, the patch in the upper left is 32 ha, whereas the other three patches are 31 ha.

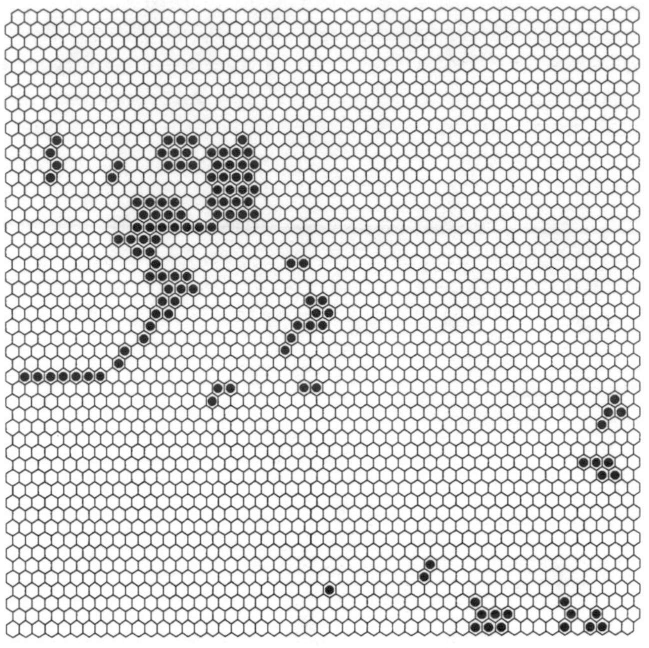

Fig. 3.—The hexagonal landscape representing a portion of Tippecanoe County, Indiana, in which livetrapping of squirrels was conducted. Scale and symbols are as in Fig. 2.

greater number of replicates (Harris et al., 1987), our principal intent was not to conduct a viability analysis, but rather to compare responses of species to fragmentation, as well as factors influencing responses. Small samples tend to reduce the likelihood of detecting subtle differences, thus our results should be viewed as conservative.

To establish baseline levels of performance by populations, we also simulated growth of populations occupying a single 125-ha patch. Habitat heterogeneity within these relatively large expanses of forest was modeled by treating 5-ha blocks of forest as individual patches from the standpoint of production of mast within a season. A 5-ha block size was chosen because it approximates the average size of a patch in the area in which we conduct our fieldwork (see below). This simulation sheds light on the performance of each species in a continuous, albeit somewhat small, habitat as opposed to a landscape consisting of an equal amount of forest scattered among fragments.

Finally, growth of each species was simulated on a landscape in Tippecanoe County, Indiana (Fig. 3). The landscape includes 17 forest patches and is representative of agricultural landscapes throughout much of the upper Midwest. Results of the simulation were compared to the continuous-forest simulation and to data derived from livetrapping during 1991-1993 in and immediately adjacent to the area in question.

Dispersal.—Few data exist on dispersal abilities of tree squirrels, and no data exist on distributions of dispersal distances in fragmented landscapes. We chose to model dispersal in the following manner: a disperser originating from a randomly selected hexagon within a patch was assumed to be capable of detecting any other forested patches within 1 km. Although our choice of detection radius was arbitrary, sensitivity analysis for southern flying squirrels, the least-mobile species, indicated that model results were affected only slightly by changes in the detection radius (see below).

A dispersing squirrel had no prior knowledge of whether any unvisited patches were saturated. If a patch occurred <1 km away, the squirrel moved directly toward the patch (if >1 patch was involved, a random selection was made). Otherwise, the disperser moved in one of six possible directions determined by the midpoints of the sides of the hexagon (Pulliam et al., 1992). If a disperser reached an unsaturated patch, it settled there. Otherwise, it continued searching for a new patch. Squirrels were assumed to have memories adequate to avoid revisiting saturated patches.

Each step in the dispersal process was associated with a certain probability of mortality (Table 1). Values were chosen partly based on allometric considerations of running costs (Taylor et al., 1970) and daily energetic requirements (Nagy, 1987); greater proportional costs (and presumably greater risk of mortality) are incurred by smaller species. The principal rationale for our choice of values relied upon differences in morphology and modes of locomotion, as well as frequency of use of open, non-forested habitat. Fox squirrels are highly mobile animals with documented dispersal distances of several kilometers; they also commonly venture out into the agricultural matrix (Sheperd, 1994). Gray squirrels also are capable of long-distance dispersal in continuous forest, but they rarely are seen crossing agricultural areas. Southern flying squirrels are fairly mobile in continuous forests, but we were unable to find any documentation of movements across agricultural areas. Because of their gliding mode of locomotion, cropland undoubtedly presents a formidable barrier to their movement. We could find no information on dispersal of red squirrels in deciduous forests; hence our value for this species is highly speculative. Based on body size and home-range size, we assigned red squirrels an expected dispersal distance slightly less than that used for gray squirrels. The expected distances at which mortality would occur if dispersal were *across non-forested habitat* were 10 km for fox squirrels, 4 km for gray squirrels, 2.5 km for red squirrels, and 0.3 km for southern flying squirrels. Expected dispersal distances through forested habitat were arbitrarily set an order of magnitude greater for each species.

Dispersal of squirrels in autumn was dictated by hard-mast yield. A linear relationship was assumed between carrying capacity in autumn (k_a) and production of hard mast (m_h). A median carrying capacity in autumn (k^*; all subsequent symbols with an asterisk superscript refer to median values) of 1/ha was used for fox (Koprowski, 1994*a*), gray (Uhlig, 1957; Barkalow et al., 1970), and red (Baumgartner, 1938; Linduska, 1950, in Layne, 1954) squirrels, whereas a value of 4/ha was used for southern flying squirrels (Layne, 1954; Sonenshine et al., 1979). For all species except fox squirrels, failure of a mast crop was assumed to make the habitat unsuitable (i.e., carrying capacity in autumn = 0). Thus, the relationship was of the form $k_a = (k^*/m_h^*)m_h$. Based upon studies of nutrition and food habits (Havera and Smith 1979, Korschgen 1981), we concluded that agricultural crops could support about 15% of the median population of fox squirrels in the absence of hard mast. Thus, for $m_h < m_h^*$, $k_a = 0.15 + ((k^* - 0.15k^*) / m_h^*)m_h$. Production of mast above median values influenced carrying capacity for fox squirrels in the same manner as for the other species.

If the abundance of squirrels in a patch exceeded carrying capacity for the patch in autumn, excess individuals were forced to disperse. Dispersal was hierarchical with respect to age; subadults dispersed first, followed by yearlings, and finally by adults if necessary. We randomized the order in which patches were selected for processing of dispersers.

Dispersal in spring differed from dispersal in autumn in that only subadults born in the previous summer dispersed at this time. Thompson (1978) noted that about 10-20% of subadult gray squirrels dispersed during spring. In models for all four species, we assigned each subadult a dispersal probability of 0.1.

Modeling the annual cycle.—A simulation began immediately after the first birth pulse (Fig. 4). Initially, all patches in a landscape received k^* individuals in each 1-ha cell. Sex ratios were assumed to be 1:1, and individuals were assigned to age classes approximately in accordance with values for stable age distributions (Table 1). Production of soft mast (m_s) was then determined using the data of Godman and Mattson (1976). Survival of juveniles can be reduced by failure of soft mast (Koprowski, 1991); for the 4-month interval between birth pulses, we set our lower limits to juvenile survival as 0.30 for fox, gray, and red squirrels (Barkalow et al., 1970; Koprowski, 1991) and 0.64 for southern flying squirrels. The higher value for flying squirrels reflects the more carnivorous habits of this species (Dolan and Carter, 1977) while maintaining a reduction of the probability of survival equal to that used for fox squirrels (Table 1). Survival of individuals to the second birth pulse was then determined stochastically.

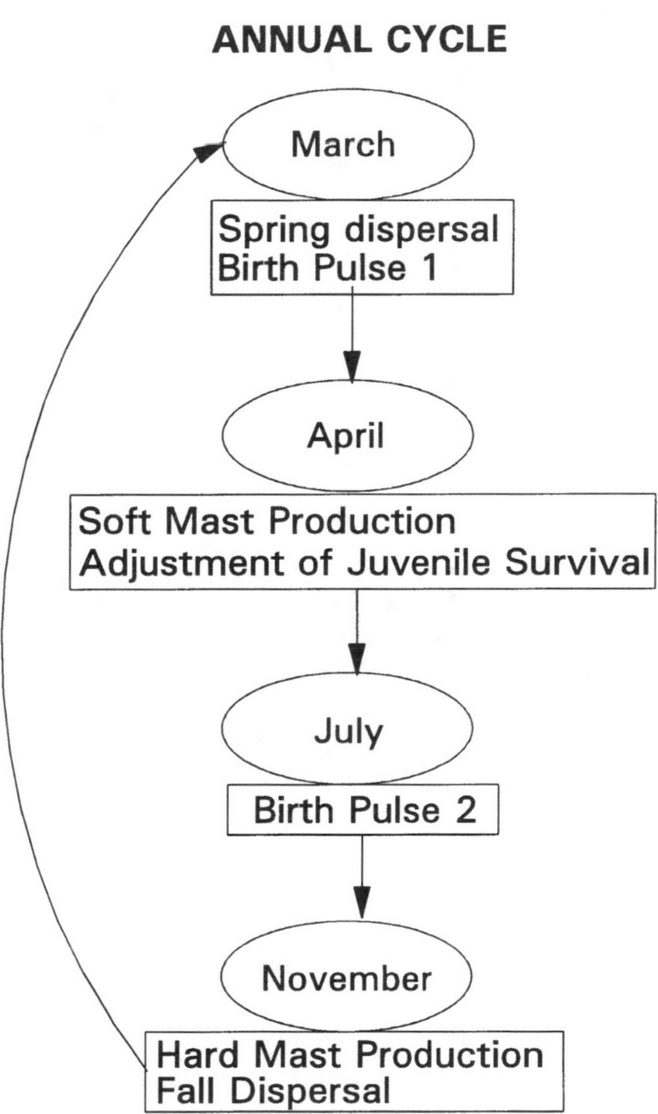

Fig. 4.—Schematic representation of the annual cycle used in modeling dynamics of populations of tree squirrels in fragmented landscapes. Details of the simulation procedure are provided in the text.

Surviving females reproduced with a probability (P_2) dependent upon the soft-mast yield; namely $P_2 = (P_2^*/m_s^*)m_s$, $0 \leq P_2 \leq 1$. Two exceptions to this relationship were assumed: when $m_s < m_s^*$, we used a linear relationship between p_2 and m_s for southern flying squirrels and gray squirrels with intercepts of $P_2 = 0.15$ and 0.10, respectively. In essence, these alterations reflect a slightly reduced reliance by these species on soft mast as the sole factor governing summer reproduction and seem justified based on our review of the literature (Dolan and Carter, 1977; Koprowski, 1994*b*).

After production of young in the second birth pulse, we simulated survival to autumn. Hard-mast yield and k_a were then computed, and autumn dispersal was initiated. After computing overwinter survival, we simulated spring dispersal, followed by reproduction in the first birth pulse (Fig. 4). For the first birth pulse, $p_1 = (p_1^*/m_h^*)m_h$ for all species. For both birth pulses, the number of young per female (y) was computed using minimal and maximal mean litter sizes of the form $y_{min} = 2y^*/3$ and $y_{max} = 11y^*/3$. These values correspond to ranges reported in the literature and were used in conjunction with production of mast (m_i) to estimate y using the linear function:

$$y = bm_i^* + y_{min}, \text{ where } b = (y^* - y_{min})/m_i^* \text{ and } y_{min} \leq y \leq y_{max}.$$

METHODS OF ANALYSIS

Statistical analysis.—Each simulation lasted 100 years or until extinction of the metapopulation occurred (i.e., no individuals remaining). For each run in which a metapopulation persisted, we computed the mean number of squirrels in the landscape during the last 90 years of the simulation, as well as the mean proportion of squirrels dispersing each year and the mean mortality rate of dispersers. We also calculated the mean isolation and size of occupied and vacant patches in a landscape. We computed an index of isolation for a focal patch (I_f) as the sum of distances to all other k-1 patches in the landscape, weighted by the fraction of the total forested area each comprised, exclusive of the focal patch. Mathematically,

$$I_f = \Sigma d_{if}(a_i/(A-a_i)),$$

where d_{if} = distance from the focal patch to patch i (center to center), a_i = area of patch i, and $A = (a_i) - a_f$. Thus, large values of I_f indicate that the majority of remaining forested habitat in the landscape is far away. We prefer I_f to other measures of isolation because, for any given landscape, the use of A ensures that I_f is not dependent upon the size of the focal patch (Gustafson and Parker, 1992).

For the factorial design (species by patch dispersion by patch number and size), mean sizes of population were compared using a three-way analysis of variance, with Student-Newman-Keuls a posteriori comparisons of means. To permit interspecific comparisons of abundance with different values of k^*, we computed the fractional change in abundance relative to the initial size of the metapopulation ($N_0 = 125k^*$) and used this as our dependent variable. Because some cells had missing data, the three-way interaction term and the species-by-number-of-patches interaction were omitted from the analysis. Probabilities of landscape-level extinction by year 100 were compared using logistic regression (Fienberg, 1980; Hintze, 1992), with species, patch dispersion, and patch number as the explanatory variables. For simulations with the Tippecanoe County landscape (Fig. 3), we recorded presence or absence of species in each patch annually, as well as mean abundance and number of successful immigrants and emigrants in each patch. Presence-absence data were used to calculate probabilities of extinction of local patches. The difference in successful immigrants and emigrants at a patch was used as an index of a patch's relative contribution to metapopulation growth. A positive value for this index indicates that a patch served principally as a sink, because immigrants exceeded emigrants. In contrast, a negative value indicates a net contribution to the growth of a metapopulation by virtue of production of emigrants in excess of immigrants. We used each of these dependent variables (mean abundance, probability of patch extinction, and the sink index) to develop multiple-regression models for each species, using area, I_f, and the interaction term area by I_f as explanatory variables. If the interaction term was not significant, it was removed when calculating the final regression model. Mean values of abundance derived from the Tippecanoe County landscape also were compared with values from the 125-ha continuous forest using a two-way ANOVA (species by extent of fragmentation).

Sensitivity analysis.—Because input parameters for our models rely upon data from various sources (e.g., Table 1) as well as educated guesses (especially with respect to dispersal mortality), we evaluated the sensitivity of our simulation results to changes in the values of specific parameters. Sensitivity of population size at year 50, S_N, was measured as

$$S_N = (\Delta N/N)/(\Delta P/P),$$

where $\Delta N/N$ is the fractional change in N resulting from a fractional change in the parameter of interest, P (Jorgensen, 1994). In general, $S_N < 1$ indicates that the model results are insensitive to changes in the parameter value, whereas larger values of S_N indicate increasing sensitivity. For each species, we calculated sensitivity to changes in the probability of dispersal mortality, DM, expressed as the expected dispersal distance in kilometers, i.e., 0.1/DM. We also examined sensitivity of our results for southern flying squirrel, the species with the most-limited mobility (Table 1), to changes in the detection radius.

To determine which rates of age-specific survival and fertility had the greatest effect on population growth, we conducted sensitivity analyses on periodic transition matrices as described by Caswell and Trevisan (1994). Briefly, we divided the annual life cycle of each species into three stages distinguished by the birth pulse in spring, the birth pulse in summer, and dispersal in autumn (Fig. 4). For each stage we constructed a Leslie transition matrix, labelled $\mathbf{B}^{(1)}$, $\mathbf{B}^{(2)}$, and $\mathbf{B}^{(3)}$, respectively. A sensitivity matrix was then calculated for each $\mathbf{B}^{(i)}$. For example, $S_B^{(2)} = [B^{(2)}B^{(3)}]^T S_A^{(2)}$, where the superscript T represents matrix transposition and $\mathbf{S}_A^{(2)}$ is the matrix whose elements a_{ij} are the sensitivities of ${}_s$ to changes in the corresponding entries for $\mathbf{A}^{(2)} = \mathbf{B}^{(1)}\mathbf{B}^{(3)}\mathbf{B}^{(2)}$, the product matrix used to project the matrix through a 1-year interval from stage 2. The elements a_{ij} of $\mathbf{S}_A^{(2)}$ are obtained as $\partial\lambda_s/\partial a_{ij} = v_i w_j/<\mathbf{w},\mathbf{v}>$ (Caswell, 1989), where $\mathbf{w}$ and $\mathbf{v}$ are the stable age distribution and vector of age-specific reproductive values of $\mathbf{A}^{(2)}$, respectively, and the denominator denotes the vector inner product of $\mathbf{w}$ and $\mathbf{v}$. The proportional sensitivities of λ_s to each element of $\mathbf{B}^{(2)}$ are termed elasticities (De Kroon et al., 1986) and are computed as $e_{ij} = (b_{ij}/\lambda_s)(\partial\lambda_s/\partial b_{ij})$. The elasticities measure the proportional contribution of the matrix entries to population growth (De Kroon et al., 1986). After computing elasticity values for $\mathbf{B}^{(1)}$, $\mathbf{B}^{(2)}$, and $\mathbf{B}^{(3)}$, we determined the proportional contribution of each element to annual growth by summing the matrices and dividing by three. For each species, the element contributing the most to annual population growth was then selected for sensitivity analysis in the full stochastic model using the procedures described above for dispersal mortality.

COMPARISON WITH FIELD DATA

We compared results from our simulation models with data on presence-absence of squirrels collected in Tippecanoe County and adjoining sites during 1991-1993. Livetrapping was conducted in 18 forested areas of differing sizes and levels of isolation. At each site trapping was conducted for a minimum of 5 days during spring, and some sites also were trapped in summer and autumn. Grids were established at all sites, with 30 m between adjacent traps. In forested areas <10 ha, the entire area was trapped, whereas grids of 2-3 ha were established in larger forested sites.

RESULTS

Effects of differences in species and landscapes.—For the six fragmented landscapes used in the factorial design, species differed significantly in the mean fractional deviation from N_0 (Table 2). Red squirrels exhibited the greatest relative density, increasing 80.3% above their initial density, followed by fox squirrels with an increase of 35.8%. Gray squirrels declined an average of 33.2% from N_0, and southern flying squirrels declined 55.3%. Values for all species differed significantly ($P < 0.05$).

For all species, both the number and dispersion of patches influenced relative density, but a significant interaction effect (Table 2) precluded interpretation beyond noting that relative density dropped below the initial density only for the four-patch landscape in which patches were uniformly distributed.

Isolation values for occupied and vacant patches varied as a function of species, dispersion, and number of patches (Table 2). Southern flying squirrels differed from the other three species in that vacant patches were more isolated than occupied patches in uniform landscapes rather than in landscapes with a clumped distribution of patches (Table 2, Sp by Pp interaction). In landscapes with 125 1-ha patches, a clumped distribution of patches resulted in a few, highly isolated patches being vacant, whereas vacant patches on average were less isolated than occupied patches when patches were uniformly distributed (Table 2, Pp by Np interaction).

Based on results of logistic regression, probability of extinction of a metapopulation was significantly related to the species involved ($\chi^2 = 32.1$, $P < 0.001$), with a rank order (probability of extinction in parentheses) of southern flying (0.77) > gray (0.65) > fox = red (0). When all species were considered together, no effects of patch dispersion or patch number and size were evident ($P > 0.15$ for both variables). Logistic regressions for each species revealed a significantly elevated probability of extinction for southern flying squirrels occupying landscapes with 125 1-ha patches relative to landscapes with fewer, larger patches ($\chi^2 = 9.1$, $P = 0.002$). No significant effects of dispersion or patch size were evident for the other species.

Table 2.—*Results of analyses of variance for relative density (expressed as a fraction of* k'*) and difference in isolation of vacant and occupied patches as a function of squirrel species (fox, gray, red, southern flying), spatial pattern of forest patches (uniform or clumped), and number of patches (4, 25, 125).*

Response Variable	Source[1]	Degrees of Freedom	Mean Square	*F*	*P*
Density	Sp	3	10.462	695.0	<0.001
	Pp	1	0.085	5.6	0.02
	Np	2	0.728	48.4	<0.001
	Sp x Pp	3	0.027	1.8	0.15
	Pp x Np	2	0.220	14.6	<0.001
	Error	143	0.015		
Patch Isolation	Sp	3	1.489	2.5	0.06
	Pp	1	1.892	3.2	0.08
	Np	2	2.581	4.4	0.01
	Sp x Pp	3	1.715	2.9	0.04
	Pp x Np	2	16.470	27.9	<0.001
	Error	117	0.590		

[1]Sp = species, Pp = pattern of patches, Np = number of patches.

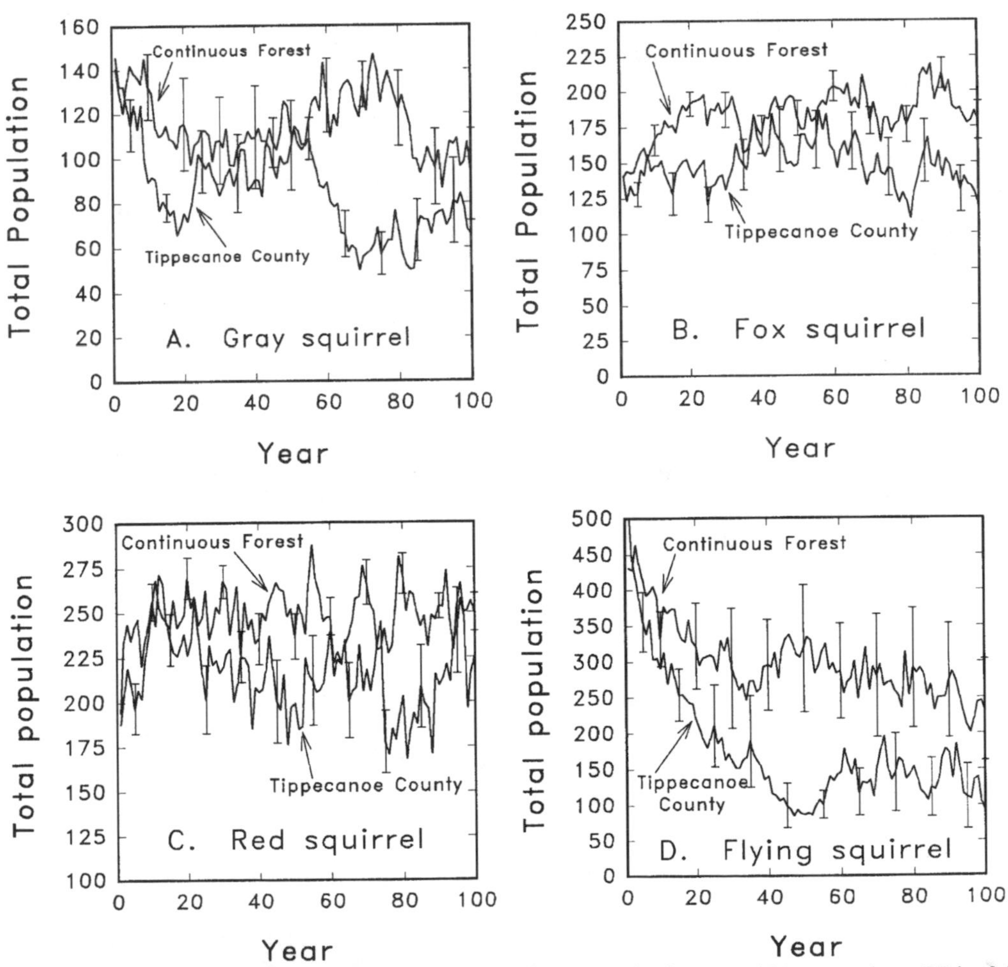

Fig. 5.—Population trajectories simulated for four species of tree squirrels over 100 years in a 25-km^2 landscape. The continuous forest consisted of one 125-ha patch, whereas the Tippecanoe County, Indiana, landscape consisted of 17 patches, ranging in size from 1-69 ha, and totaling 125 ha. Vertical bars at 10-year intervals represent $\pm$1 standard error, with n = 10 replicates. Note that the scale of the ordinates differ for each species.

Table 3.—*Coefficients of multiple regression equations for simulated squirrel populations in a Tippecanoe County, Indiana, landscape. The symbol NS indicates that a regression was not significant (P > 0.05).*

Dependent Variable	Species	R^2	Area[1] (A) Coeff	Area[1] (A) *P*	Isolation (I) Coeff	Isolation (I) *P*	A x I Coeff	A x I *P*
N[2]	Gray	0.80	0.001	0.942	-0.014	0.0001		
	Fox	0.43	-0.045	0.029	-0.005	0.029		
	Red	0.63	-0.102	0.0004	-0.005	0.044		
	Flying	0.38	0.001	0.931	-0.005	0.012		
P_e[3]	Gray	0.92	-9.903	0.0001	1.155	0.0001		
	Fox	0.78	5.077	0.246	0.715	0.003	-0.379	.037
	Red	0.69	10.347	0.050	0.753	0.005	-0.574	.009
	Flying	0.69	-7.526	0.0006	0.555	0.010		
Sink[4]	Gray	0.52	3.348	0.009	0.343	0.015		
	Fox	0.13	NS					
	Red	0.44	10.469	0.018	0.970	0.039		
	Flying	0.57	-9.363	0.001	-0.413	0.118		

[1]Area was subjected to $\log_{10}$ transformation before regression.
[2]Fractional change in abundance relative to N_0.
[3]Probability of extinction at a patch, x 100.
[4]Difference in successful immigrants to a patch and successful emigrants emanating from the patch.

Species differences in "real" landscapes.—Differences in relative density occurred among species ($F_{3,61}$ = 243.8, $P < 0.001$) and between the simulated Tippecanoe County landscape and the simulated 125-ha continuous forest ($F_{1,61}$ = 47.2, $P < 0.001$). The interaction term was not significant ($F_{3,61}$ = 0.1, $P = 0.96$).

Red squirrels achieved the greatest increase in density (86% above N_0), followed by fox squirrels (36% above N_0). Declines in relative density were registered by gray squirrels (18% below N_0) and southern flying squirrels (50% below N_0). All interspecific differences were significant (a posteriori tests, $P < 0.05$).

The fragmented landscape of Tippecanoe County significantly reduced the relative abundance of all species compared with the continuous forest (Fig. 5, $P < 0.05$ for all a posteriori tests), and gray and southern flying squirrels seemed to be particularly susceptible. For instance, persistence of flying squirrels for 100 years dropped from 90 to 50%, and the mean relative density of gray squirrels dropped from near stability (4.5% below N_0) in the continuous forest to a considerably lower level (32.3% below N_0) in the fragmented, Tippecanoe County, landscape (Fig. 5).

Attributes of local populations.—For the Tippecanoe County landscape, isolation (I_f) values were 15.3-38.7, and patch areas were 1-69 ha; correlation between the two variables was small (r = -0.07). Using I_f, area, and the interaction term I_f by area as explanatory variables, multiple regression revealed that increasing area of a patch did not influence relative abundance in a patch for gray and southern flying squirrels but resulted in lower relative abundance for fox squirrels and especially for red squirrels (Table 3).

As isolation of a patch increased, relative abundance within the patch declined for all species, with the greatest negative impact on relative abundance of gray squirrels, followed by flying squirrels, fox squirrels, and red squirrels (Table 3). The probability of local extinction was negatively related to the area of a patch and positively related to isolation for gray and southern flying squirrels. The area-by-isolation interaction was a significant predictor of extinction probability for fox and red squirrels (Table 3), with a marked tendency for local populations in small, highly isolated woodlots to exhibit the greatest probabilities of extinction, whereas populations in the largest and least-isolated tracts exhibited the lowest rates of extinction.

Source-sink dynamics differed greatly among the species. For gray and red squirrels, increased isolation and patch size were associated with an increased influx of individuals, whereas for

Table 4.—*Sensitivity, S_N, of population size at year 50 to changes in parameter values for the expected dispersal distance travelled before mortality (E(Dist)), detection radius (Radius), and survival rates of juvenile (S_J), yearling (S_Y), and adult (S_A) squirrels. Results were obtained for metapopulations simulated on a Tippecanoe County, Indiana, landscape. Initial values of parameters are described in the text, and n represents the number of replicates.*

Parameter	Species	Fractional Change in Parameter	Sensitivity	*n*
E(Dist)	Fox	2	0.0	20
		0.025	0.4	40
	Gray	5	0.0	30
		0.0625	0.7	40
	Red	8	0.0	10
		0.1	0.3	40
	Flying	70	0.0	20
		0.875	0.1	70
Radius	Flying	0.5	0.5	20
S_A	Fox	1.2	1.9	10
	Gray	1.2	8.7	10
	Red	1.2	1.9	10
	Flying	1.2	9.8	10
S_J	Flying	1.2	3.3	10
S_Y	Flying	1.2	2.0	10

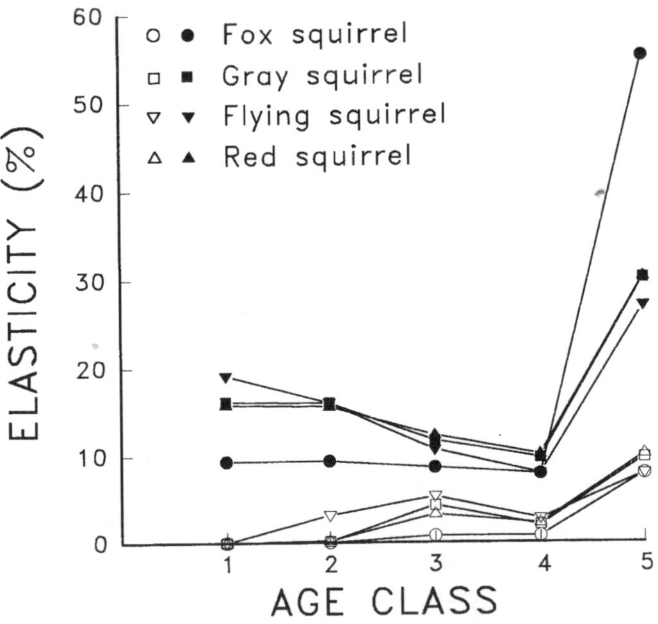

Fig. 6. —Elasticity, the proportional contribution to population growth rate, of age-specific fertility coefficients and probabilities of survival. Filled symbols represent probabilities of survival, whereas hollow symbols represent fertility coefficients.

Table 5. —*Presence of tree squirrels in forested sites in and adjacent to Tippecanoe County, Indiana, classified by area and isolation, and expressed as the number of sites containing squirrels divided by the total number examined within a particular classification. Example: 1/3 indicates presence in one of three sites.*

		Size of Forested Area		
Degree of Isolation	Species	Small	Medium	Large
Small	Fox	1/1	2/2	2/2
	Red	0/1	2/2	1/2
	Gray	0/1	1/2	2/2
	Flying	0/1	1/2	2/2
Medium	Fox	4/4	4/4	1/1
	Red	0/4	2/4	0/1
	Gray	0/4	1/4	0/1
	Flying	0/4	0/4	1/1
Large	Fox	3/3	1/1	
	Red	0/3	1/1	
	Gray	0/3	0/1	
	Flying	0/3	0/1	

southern flying squirrels the opposite was true. Attributes of patches had no effect on source-sink dynamics of fox squirrels (Table 3).

Sensitivity analysis.—Population size was relatively unaffected by changes in the probability of dispersal mortality for all species, with S_N values of 0-0.70 (Table 4). Changes in the radius of detection had little effect on model results for southern flying squirrels (S_N = 0.46).

In contrast, rates of population growth were sensitive to various aspects of survival and fertility, and interspecific differences were apparent. Rates of population growth were most affected by survivorship of adults for all species (Fig. 6). Among species, survival of adults was relatively more important in influencing growth rates of fox squirrels, whereas survival of juveniles had less of an effect on this species (Fig. 6). Elasticity values of fertility coefficients were greatest for adults of all species, with fox squirrels exhibiting the smallest value (Fig. 6).

Values of S_N derived from alteration of parameter values in the full stochastic model confirmed that population size was sensitive to changes in survival of adults, with changes having the greatest impact on gray and southern flying squirrels (Table 4). The reduced sensitivities of fox and red squirrels reflect their superior ability to cope with fragmentation. Because fox and red squirrels exist in simulated fragmented landscapes at densities closer to carrying capacity than either gray or southern flying squirrels (Fig. 5), density dependence limits their ability to respond to changes in survival rates of adults relative to the latter two species.

Livetrapping data.—To permit qualitative comparison with simulation results, data on presence-absence of species at each of the 18 forested areas was cross-classified according to size of woodlot and isolation (Table 5). Fox squirrels were in all forested sites. Red squirrels were less common but occurred in sites irrespective of their degree of isolation or size. Gray squirrels and southern flying squirrels never occurred in small or isolated woodlots.

DISCUSSION

Interspecific differences.—Populations of all four species of tree squirrels were affected negatively by fragmentation of forests in our simulations (Fig. 5), but to varying degrees. In general, populations of red squirrels were least affected. The effects of fragmentation on red squirrels undoubtedly are buffered by the large growth potential of the species (λ_s = 1.35), which permits rapid repopulation of vacant patches.

Fragmentation also seemed to have less of an effect on fox squirrels. Growth potential of fox squirrels (λ_s = 1.08) was lower than red squirrels, making their success all the more remarkable. As a consequence of their well-developed ability to disperse (Table 1), dispersal mortality of fox squirrels typically was low relative to the other species. Because of their use of agricultural crops, fox squirrels also were affected less by variation in production of mast.

Gray squirrels and southern flying squirrels fared poorly in the fragmented landscapes that we modeled. Although flying squirrels are quite mobile in continuous tracts of mature forest, we were unable to find documentation of extensive movements over open ground. If an agricultural matrix is a major impediment to movements of flying squirrels, then clumps of forest patches in close proximity presumably would provide the most innocuous form of fragmentation. Consistent with this prediction, our factorial simulations revealed that populations of flying squirrel fared better in clumped landscapes, due to a reduction in dispersal mortality.

Fragmentation of midwestern forests coincided with declines in abundance of gray squirrels (Nixon et al., 1978), and our model yielded results consistent with these observations. The potential rate of growth of gray squirrels is comparable to that of fox squirrels, and their dispersal ability is seemingly well developed. Our simulations suggest two factors that may contribute to the poorer performance of gray squirrels. First, the stable age distribution of gray squirrels contains proportionately fewer adults than for fox squirrels (Table 1). This discrepancy is even more pronounced after winter and before the first birth pulse, when only 43% of the gray squirrel population consists of adults, whereas 38% are subadults. By comparison, adults and subadults comprise 66 and 14% of fox squirrel populations at this stage of the annual cycle. Following a year in which populations were reduced by a poor mast crop, populations of gray squirrels would recover more slowly because of a relative dearth of adult females. In addition, the stable age structure suggests that because of the relative abundance of subadult gray squirrels, dispersal rates in spring should be higher for gray squirrels than for fox squirrels, and this expectation was borne out by our simulations. Second, gray squirrels are more severely affected by poor production of mast than fox squirrels because they make limited use of agricultural crops as a supplemental source of food (Korschgen, 1981).

Influence of patch size and isolation.—Simulations with the Tippecanoe County landscape indicated that isolation of a patch had the greatest impact on gray squirrels; more-isolated patches exhibited lower relative densities and larger probabilities of annual extinction (Table 3). These results are consistent with data on regional trends in abundance and distribution of gray squirrels. Gray squirrels declined throughout the Midwest in the 1800s as settlers cleared land for increasingly intensive agricultural uses, indicating that loss and fragmentation of extensive tracts of mature forest precipitated the reduction in populations (Nixon et al., 1978). Area of a woodlot dictated occupancy most strongly for gray squirrels (Table 3), with larger woodlots being more likely to contain gray squirrels. Brown and Batzli (1984) examined selection of habitat by gray squirrels and concluded that the size of a forest patch may be an important determinant of occupancy for the species, relative to fox squirrels.

The source-sink dynamics of patches apparently were governed by dispersal ability in our fragmented landscapes (Table 3). Species with poor ability to disperse (i.e., flying squirrels) produced more colonists in large and, to a marginal degree, more isolated patches. Presumably, the size of these patches buffered them against local extinctions, yet their isolation made them relatively inaccessible to potential immigrants. Conversely, species with well-developed dispersal ability (i.e., gray and red squirrels) produced fewer colonists in large, isolated patches. For a given shape and orientation, large patches are easier for a disperser to locate than small patches (Gutzwiller and Anderson, 1992). Thus, dispersers operating with a fixed radius of detection, as in our simulations, would have a greater probability of locating a larger patch, creating an area-dependent "oasis effect." An oasis effect would not occur for southern flying squirrels due to their limited mobility. For fox squirrels, neither isolation nor area of patches correlated with frequency of colonization, indicating that inter-patch movements of fox squirrels were not constrained by these characteristics.

Comparison of simulations with field data.—Our

simulations were consistent not only with findings of previous researchers, but also with our field data. Gray squirrels and southern flying squirrels were captured only in reasonably large forest patches in close proximity to other wooded sites (Table 5). As indicated by our simulations, field data suggest that these species are sensitive to area and isolation effects imposed by fragmentation. Fox squirrels, conversely, were ubiquitous, indicating that the size and isolation of patches have little impact on their distribution in a fragmented landscape such as that encountered in Tippecanoe County. Again, this result was consistent with predictions from our simulations. Red squirrels apparently were not affected by degree of woodlot isolation (Table 5), but they were not distributed as widely across the landscape as predicted by our simulations. This disparity could stem from the relatively recent appearance of red squirrels into the area in conjunction with plantings of *Pinus* (Mumford and Whitaker 1982), although we cannot rule out alternative explanations (see below).

Determinants of guild structure.—Our results suggest that fragmentation of forests strongly influences the structure of this guild of squirrels, and that interspecific differences in demography and behavior are more likely to determine guild structure than interspecific competition. Here, we generate hypotheses, formulated as questions, regarding the effect of biotic and abiotic factors on guild organization at local and landscape levels. We hope that these hypotheses, as well as our tentative predictions, will stimulate further research on this or other guilds in fragmented environments.

To what extent do differences in demography and mobility influence the structure and dynamics of a guild? Our simulations suggest that growth potential can be an important determinant of a species' success in a fragmented landscape. Based on a simulation model, Fahrig and Paloheimo (1988) concluded that species with an enhanced ability to disperse are less affected by fragmentation, and that high local rates of dispersal reduce abundance in the affected patch. Thus, vagile species with good growth potential should fare well in fragmented landscapes, all else being equal. In our models, however, changes in mobility had little effect on population size (Table 4). Pulliam et al. (1992) also found that population size of Bachman's sparrow (*Aimophila aestivalis*) was affected much less by changes in dispersal ability relative to changes in survival of adults. Closer inspection of this prediction will require better demographic data, particularly for survival of adults (Fig. 6). In particular, data on age-specific fertility and survival are scarce for southern flying squirrels and virtually nonexistent for red squirrels in deciduous forests. Moreover, movements of squirrels in fragmented landscapes have not been examined in detail, and no information presently exists on the ability of squirrels to detect distant patches of suitable habitat. Factors influencing movements also are poorly understood.

How does environmental variation in food supply influence population dynamics at local and landscape levels? Guild structure in our model was predicated on interspecific differences in demography and dispersal, within the context of a varying food supply. Spatio-temporal variation in production of mast potentially exerts considerable influence over guild dynamics, and may prevent saturation of local patches. The importance of such variation is determined by several factors, including: 1) the diet breadth of a species, 2) its ability to escape poor conditions via dispersal, and 3) demographic characteristics that govern its ability to rebound locally after poor mast years. In all of these respects, fox squirrels apparently are superior to gray squirrels, resulting in a greater degree of buffering from environmental stochasticity. A poor mast year may spell trouble for local populations of southern flying squirrels in a fragmented landscape, because they are characterized by a slow rate of growth, and their poor ability to disperse limits recruitment from outside the patch. Populations of red squirrels can be decimated by mast failures (M. C. Smith, 1968), but they exhibit a greater propensity for in situ recovery following a decline than the other three species.

The role of competition?—Many of the woodlots we trapped contained less than the full complement of species, and it would be tempting to invoke interspecific competition in a fragmented and variable environment as an explanation for this pattern (Cornell and Lawton, 1992). However, our simulation model assumed that each species functioned entirely independently of other species; i.e., we modeled a non-interactive community (sensu Cornell and Lawton, 1992) with no local biotic interactions. Environmental stochasticity can influence community patterns by reducing the relative importance of competition (Drake, 1990), and our simulation findings for this guild, generated in the absence of competition, reasonably mimic patterns observed in the field. Thus, community patterns in this group of species likely arise from interspecific differences in vital rates and susceptibility to random disturbances (i.e., variation in mast). In fact, environmental stochasticity may be of paramount importance in determining the structure of guilds in a fragmented landscape.

In a constant environment, the niche overlap exhibited by these squirrels suggests that strong competitive interactions would ensue (Preston, 1948; Brown and Batzli, 1985*a*, 1985*b*), and these interactions might determine whether a species absent from a patch could successfully colonize that patch (Case, 1991). However, in the world of granivorous rodents environmental variation in availability of food is the norm (Nixon et al., 1975 Munger and Brown, 1981). Consequently, it is more appropriate to speak in terms of the relative effects of environmental variation on a species. We hypothesize that among species of similar size, richness in local patches is mediated by the triad of demography, dispersal, and breadth of diet. That is, this triad imposes constraints upon responses of a species to local variation in food supply, and fragmentation exaggerates the importance of these constraints for persistence and mean abundance. When constraints imposed by dispersal are relaxed, as in continuous forests, persistence of species should improve, but with a concomitant increase in interspecific interactions. Thus, we predict that fragments should exhibit lower species richness than continuous forests, with local extinctions of gray and southern flying squirrels occurring most frequently. For species that are better able to tolerate fragmentation, such as fox and red squirrels, we predict greater mean population densities in fragments than in continuous forests. In fact, competitive release induced by fragmentation should extend to other granivores occurring in the landscape, such as white-footed mice (*Peromyscus leucopus*) and eastern chipmunks (*Tamias striatus*). Allometric constraints imposed by fragmentation may also become important as the body-size range of the species pool under consideration expands. Small species may achieve release from larger competitors in patches with insufficient areas to support viable populations of the larger species (Nupp and Swihart, 1996). At any rate, we suggest that interspecific interactions are functions of the landscape in which the species occur and are not solely due to intrinsic properties of the species (Danielson, 1991). For the guild considered here, effects of interspecific competition apparently are of lesser importance than intraspecific demographic and ecological responses to environmental stochasticity in determining the structure of local communities.

CONCLUDING COMMENTS

Our metapopulation models for tree squirrels can be improved by refinement of parameters and assumptions, as well as by inclusion of additional biologically relevant information that enables us to view landscapes from a squirrel's perspective (Boyce, 1992; Lima and Zollner, 1996; Milne, 1992). For instance, species composition of patches undoubtedly is influenced by local habitat features in addition to features of the surrounding landscape, and future attempts to predict guild structure should incorporate variables representing each of these scales (Harris and Kangas, 1988; Van Horne and Wiens, 1991). Moreover, patches undergo succession; hence, changes in their suitability over time also must be considered (Holt et al., 1995). Likewise, the landscape matrix in which patches occur is not uniform; in agricultural areas variation in matrix form, and presumably permeability, is manifested spatially as fields with differing crops and temporally as changes in phenology and rotation of crops. Finally, we know little about the spatial correlation of mast production, yet correlated environments can exact a severe toll on the persistence time of metapopulations (Harrison and Quinn, 1989). Given the importance of variation in production of mast to tree squirrels occupying fragmented landscapes, information on the extent of spatial covariation in production is needed.

Anthropogenic influences on the central hardwoods region have had far-reaching impacts on tree squirrels. As we have shown, forest fragmentation can negatively impact all four species, but greatest impacts are on gray and southern flying squirrels. Although the structure of local patches presumably is influenced primarily by demography, dispersal, and breadth of diet (and perhaps by body size; Nupp and Swihart, 1996), the current guild structure at the landscape level reflects historical effects of large-scale disturbances and biogeographic distributions of species (Cornell and Lawton, 1992; Drake et al., 1993). The guild's future structure is less clear. Can corridors mitigate the effects of fragmentation for isolation-sensitive species, such as gray and southern flying squirrels? Will the distribution of red squirrels continue to expand, as predicted by our model? Will an increasing emphasis on conservation tillage ameliorate the effects of agriculturally induced fragmentation? It is becoming increasingly clear that aspects of a species' biology and interactions with other species can be influenced by landscape context. Improving our understanding of landscape-level effects, then, is a necessary step toward improving our ability to predict the consequences of changing landscapes for species and to minimize any negative consequences associated with such change.

ACKNOWLEDGMENTS

We thank A. J. DeNicola and N. A. Slade for constructive comments that improved our modeling efforts. Comments on the manuscript by two anonymous reviewers also were quite helpful. This research was supported by award 93-37101-8702 of the NRI Competitive Grants Program/USDA and is manuscript 94-14527 of the Purdue University Agricultural Research Programs.

LITERATURE CITED

ACKERMAN, R., AND P. D. WEIGL. 1970. Dominance relations of red and grey squirrels. Ecology, 51:332-334.

BARKALOW, F. S., JR., R. B. HAMILTON, AND F. R. SOOTS. 1970. The vital statistics of an unexploited gray squirrel population. The Journal of Wildlife Management, 34:489-500.

BAUMGARTNER, L. L. 1938. Population studies of the fox squirrel in Ohio. Transactions of the North American Wildlife Conference, 3:685-689.

BOYCE, M. S. 1992. Population viability analysis. Annual Review of Ecology and Systematics, 23:481-506.

BROWN, B. W., AND G. O. BATZLI. 1984. Habitat selection by fox and gray squirrels: a multivariate analysis. The Journal of Wildlife Management, 48:616-621.

———. 1985*a*. Foraging ability, dominance relations and competition for food by fox and gray squirrels. Transactions of the Illinois Academy of Science, 78:61-66.

———. 1985*b*. Field manipulations of fox and gray squirrel populations: how important is interspecific competition? Canadian Journal of Zoology, 63:2134-2140.

BURKEY, T. V. 1989. Extinction in nature reserves: the effect of fragmentation and the importance of migration between reserve fragments. Oikos, 55:75-81.

CASE, T. J. 1991. Invasion resistance, species build-up and community collapse in metapopulation models with interspecies competition. Biological Journal of the Linnean Society, 42:239-266.

CASWELL, H. 1989. Matrix population models. Sinauer Associates, Sunderland, Massachusetts, 328 pp.

CASWELL, H. AND M. C. TREVISAN. 1994. Sensitivity analysis of periodic matrix models. Ecology, 75:1299-1303.

CORNELL, H. V., AND J. H. LAWTON. 1992. Species interactions, local and regional processes, and limits to the richness of ecological communities: a theoretical perspective. The Journal of Animal Ecology, 61:1-12.

DANIELSON, B. J. 1991. Communities in a landscape: the influence of habitat heterogeneity on the interactions between species. The American Naturalist, 138:1105-1120.

DE KROON, H., A. PLAISIER, J. VAN GROENENDAEL, AND H. CASWELL. 1986. Elasticity: the relative contribution of demographic parameters to population growth rate. Ecology, 67:1427-1431.

DOLAN, P. G., AND D. C. CARTER. 1977. Glaucomys volans. Mammalian Species, 78:1-6.

DRAKE, J. A. 1990. Communities as assembled structures: do rules govern pattern? Trends in Ecology & Evolution, 5:159-164.

DRAKE, J. A. ET AL. 1993. The construction and assembly of an ecological landscape. The Journal of Animal Ecology, 62:117-130.

DUNNING, J. B., JR., ET AL. 1995. Spatially explicit population models: current forms and future uses. Ecological Applications, 5:3-11.

FAHRIG, L., AND J. PALOHEIMO. 1988. Determinants of local population size in patchy habitats. Theoretical Population Biology, 34:194-213.

FIENBERG, S. E. 1980. The analysis of cross-classified categorical data. The MIT Press, Cambridge, Massachusetts, 198 pp.

FLYGER, V., AND J. E. GATES. 1982. Fox and gray squirrels (*Sciurus niger*, *S. carolinensis*, and allies). Pages 209-229 *in* J. A. Chapman and G. A. Feldhamer, eds. Wild mammals of North America. The Johns Hopkins University Press, Baltimore, Maryland, 1147 pp.

GILPIN, M. E. 1987. Spatial structure and population vulnerability. Pages 125-139 *in* M. E. Soule, ed. Viable populations for conservation. Cambridge University Press, Cambridge, United Kingdom, 189 pp.

GODMAN, R. M., AND G. A. MATTSON. 1976. Seed crops and regeneration problems of 19 species in northeastern Wisconsin. USDA Forest Service, North Central Experiment Station, NC-123. PP.

GUSTAFSON, E. J., AND G. R. PARKER. 1992. Relationships between landcover proportion and indices of landscape spatial pattern. Landscape Ecology, 7:101-110.

GUTZWILLER, K. J., AND S. H. ANDERSON. 1992. Interception of moving organisms: influences of patch shape, size, and orientation on community structure. Landscape Ecology, 6:293-303.

HANSEN, L. P., C. M. NIXON, AND S. P. HAVERA. 1986. Recapture rates and length of residence in an unexploited fox squirrel population. The American Midland Naturalist, 115:209-215.

HANSKI, I. 1991. Single-species metapopulation dynamics: concepts, models and observations. Biological Journal of the Linnean Society, 42:17-38.

HARNISHFEGER, R. L., J. L. ROSEBERRY, AND W. D. KLIMSTRA. 1978. Reproductive levels in unexploited woodlot fox squirrels. Transactions of the Illinois Academy of Science, 71:342-355.

HARRIS, L. D., AND P. KANGAS. 1988. Reconsideration of the habitat concept. Transactions of the North American Wildlife and Natural Resources Conference, 53:137-144.

HARRIS, R. B., L. A. MAGUIRE, AND M. L. SHAFFER. 1987. Sample sizes for minimum viable population estimation. Conservation Biology, 1:72-76.

HARRISON, S., AND J. F. QUINN. 1989. Correlated environments and the persistence of metapopulations. Oikos, 56:293-298.

HAVERA, S. P., AND K. E. SMITH. 1979. A nutritional comparison of selected fox squirrel foods. The Journal of Wildlife Management, 43:691-704.

HENDERSON, M. T., G. MERRIAM, AND J. WEGNER. 1985. Patchy environments and species survival: chipmunks in an agricultural mosaic. Biological Conservation, 31:95-105.

HINTZE, J. L. 1992. Number cruncher statistical system, product 5.3, advanced statistics. Kaysville, Utah, 442 pp.

HOFFMEISTER, D. F. 1989. Mammals of Illinois. University of Illinois Press, Champaign, 348 pp.

HOLT, R. D., S. W. PACALA, T. W. SMITH, AND J. LIU. 1995. Linking contemporary vegetation models with spatially explicit animal population models. Ecological Applications, 5:20-27.

IVERSON, L. R. 1988. Land-use changes in Illinois, USA: the influence of landscape attributes on current and historic land use. Landscape Ecology, 2:45-61.

JONES, J. K., JR., AND E. C. BIRNEY. 1988. Handbook of mammals of the north-central states. University of Minnesota Press, Minneapolis, 346 pp.

JORGENSEN, S. E. 1994. Fundamentals of ecological modelling, Second edition. Elsevier Scientific Publishing, Amsterdam, The Netherlands, 628 pp.

KLUGH, A. B. 1927. Ecology of the red squirrel. Journal of Mammalogy, 8:1-32.

KOPROWSKI, J. L. 1991. Response of fox squirrels and gray squirrels to a late spring-early summer food shortage. Journal of Mammalogy, 72:367-372.

———. 1994*a*. Sciurus niger. Mammalian Species, 479:1-9.

———. 1994*b*. Sciurus carolinensis. Mammalian Species, 480:1-9.

KORSCHGEN, L. J. 1981. Foods of fox and gray squirrels in Missouri. The Journal of Wildlife Management, 45:260-266.

LAIR, H. 1985. Mating seasons and fertility of red squirrels in southern Quebec. Canadian Journal of Zoology, 63:2323-2327.

LAYNE, J. N. 1954. The biology of the red squirrel, *Tamiasciurus hudsonicus loquax* (Bangs), in central New York. Ecological Monographs, 24:227-267.

LEFKOVITCH, L. P., AND L. FAHRIG. 1985. Spatial characteristics of habitat patches and population survival. Ecological Modelling, 30:297-308.

LIMA, S. L., AND P. A. ZOLLNER. 1996. Towards a behavioral ecology of ecological landscapes. Trends in Ecology & Evolution, 11:131-135.

LINDUSKA, J. P. 1950. Ecology and land-use relationships of small mammals on a Michigan farm. Michigan Department of Conservation Game Division Publication, 144 pp.

LORENZ, G. C., AND G. W. BARRETT. 1990. Influence of simulated landscape corridors on house mouse (*Mus musculus*) dispersal. The American Midland Naturalist, 123:348-356.

MEFFE, G. K., AND C. R. CARROLL. 1994. Principles of conservation biology. Sinauer Associates, Sunderland, Massachusetts, 600 pp.

MILLAR, J. S. 1970. Variations in fecundity of the red squirrel, *Tamiasciurus hudsonicus* (Erxleben). Canadian Journal of Zoology, 48:1055-1058.

MILNE, B. T. 1992. Spatial aggregation and neutral models in fractal landscapes. The American Naturalist, 139:32-57.

MUMFORD, R. E., AND J. O. WHITAKER, JR. 1982. Mammals of Indiana. Indiana University Press, Bloomington, 537 pp.

MUNGER, J. C., AND J. H. BROWN. 1981. Competition in desert rodents: an experiment with semipermeable exclosures. Science, 211:510-512.

NAGY, K. A. 1987. Field metabolic rate and food requirement scaling in mammals and birds. Ecological Monographs, 57:111-128.

NIXON, C. M., AND M. W. MCCLAIN. 1969. Squirrel population decline following a late spring frost. The Journal of Wildlife Management, 33:353-357.

NIXON, C. M., AND R. W. DONOHUE. 1975. Effects of hunting and mast crops on a squirrel population. The Journal of Wildlife Management, 39:1-25.

NIXON, C. M., S. P. HAVERA, AND R. E. GREENBURG. 1978. Distribution and abundance of the gray squirrel in Illinois. Illinois Natural History Survey, Biological Notes, 105:1-55.

NIXON, C. M., L. P. HANSEN, AND S. P. HAVERA. 1986. Demographic characteristics of an unexploited population of fox squirrels (*Sciurus niger*). Canadian Journal of Zoology, 64:512-521.

NUPP, T. E., AND R. K. SWIHART. 1996. Effect of forest patch area on population attributes of white-footed mice (*Peromyscus leucopus*) in fragmented landscapes. Canadian Journal of Zoology, 74:467-472.

PRESTON, F. W. 1948. Red squirrels and gray. Journal of Mammalogy, 29:297-298.

PULLIAM, H. R., J. B. DUNNING, JR., AND J. LIU. 1992. Population dynamics in complex landscapes: a case study. Ecological Applications, 2:165-177.

ROLSTAD, J. 1991. Consequences of forest fragmentation for the dynamics of bird populations: conceptual issues and the evidence. Biological Journal of the Linnean Society, 42:149-163.

RUSCH, D. A., AND W. G. REEDER. 1978. Population ecology of Alberta red squirrels. Ecology, 59:400-420.

SAUNDERS, D. A., R. J. HOBBS, AND C. R. MARGULES. 1991. Biological consequences of ecosystem fragmentation: a review. Conservation Biology, 5:18-32.

SHEPERD, B. F. 1994. Ecology and spatial dynamics of fox squirrels (*Sciurus niger*) in fragmented landscapes. M.S. thesis, Purdue University, W. Lafayette, Indiana, 61 pp.

SMITH, C. C. 1968. The adaptive nature of social organization in the genus of tree squirrels *Tamiasciurus*. Ecological Monographs, 38:31-63.

SMITH, M. C. 1968. Red squirrel responses to spruce cone failure in interior Alaska. The Journal of Wildlife Management, 32:305-316.

SONENSHINE, D. E., D. M. LAUER, T. C. WALKER, AND B. L. ELISBERG. 1979. The ecology of *Glaucomys volans* Linnaeus, 1858 in Virginia. Acta Theriologica, 24:363-377.

TAYLOR, C. R., K. SCHMIDT-NIELSEN, AND J. L. RAAB. 1970. Scaling of energetic cost of running to body size in mammals. American Journal of Physiology, 219:1104-1107.

TEMPLE, S. A. 1986. Predicting impacts of habitat fragmentation on forest birds: a comparison of two models. pp. 301-304 *in* J. Verner et al., eds. Wildlife 2000. Modeling habitat relationships of terrestrial vertebrates. University of Wisconsin Press, Madison, 470 pp.

TEMPLE, S.A., AND J. R. CARY. 1988. Modeling dynamics of habitat-interior bird populations in fragmented landscapes. Conservation Biology, 2:340-347.

THOMPSON, D. C. 1978. Regulation of a northern grey squirrel (*Sciurus carolinensis*) population. Ecology, 59:708-715.

UHLIG, H. G. 1957. Gray squirrel populations in extensive forested areas of West Virginia. The Journal of Wildlife Management, 21:335-341.

VAN HORNE, B., AND J. A. WIENS. 1991. Forest bird habitat suitability models and the development of general habitat models. United States Department of the Interior Fish and Wildlife Research Paper, 8:1-31.

YAHNER, R. H. 1980. Burrow system use by red squirrels. The American Midland Naturalist, 103:409-411.

SEX-UNBIASED PHILOPATRY IN THE NORTH AMERICAN RED SQUIRREL: (*TAMIASCIURUS HUDSONICUS*)

KARL W. LARSEN AND STAN BOUTIN

Department of Biological Sciences, University of Alberta, Edmonton, Alberta, CANADA T6G 2E9

Present address of KWL:
Department of Forestry & Natural Resource Science,
The University College of the Cariboo,
P.O. Box 3010, Kamloops, British Columbia CANADA V2C 5N3

ABSTRACT.—Solitary species of animals with promiscuous mating systems hold considerable promise for the study of dispersal, yet they have received little attention. Arboreal squirrels should be of particular interest, because sex-biased dispersal has not been reported in their populations. This makes the group atypical among rodents, and mammals in general. We report on a 3-year study of dispersal in red squirrels (*Tamiasciurus hudsonicus*) in central Alberta, Canada. Using a combination of live-trapping, telemetry, and visual observations, we monitored the movements and settlement patterns of male and female offspring. There was no discernable difference in the movements of male and female offspring prior to acquisition of territory. Similarly, there were no sex-biased differences in distances that offspring settled from their natal territory. Of the major hypotheses put forth to explain dispersal patterns, only the "resource competition" hypothesis predicts unbiased, philopatric dispersal in a promiscuous, solitary species. Because of the philopatric settlement of offspring, inbreeding and intrasexual competition for mates have the potential to develop in the study population. An infrequent overlap of reproductive generations, continuous occupied habitat, and the cost of long-distance dispersal may explain why inbreeding and intrasexual competition for mates have had little, if any influence on the dispersal patterns in our study population.

INTRODUCTION

Greenwood (1980, 1983) rejuvenated the study of dispersal by establishing that female-biased natal dispersal was prevalent in birds, and male-biased natal dispersal was most common in mammals. He suggested that this was a consequence of the predominant mating systems in the two taxa: monogamy in birds and polygyny in mammals. Since his seminal papers, additional reports of sex-biased dispersal among birds and mammals have been published, most of them reaffirming the trends first demonstrated by Greenwood (e.g., Vestal and McCarley, 1984; Rood, 1987; Pärt, 1990).

In recent years, attention has shifted toward theoretical interpretations of sex-biased dispersal (in this study, we use the term dispersal to imply movement and settlement of individuals, particularly offspring). Several reviews (Gaines and McClenaghan, 1980; Pusey, 1987; Johnson and Gaines, 1990) have summarized the numerous evolutionary theories proposed to explain sex-biased dispersal (e.g., Gauthreaux, 1978; Dhondt, 1979; Greenwood, 1980; 1983; Dobson, 1982; Liberg and Schantz, 1985; Johnson, 1986). These theories are variations on three major hypotheses: inbreeding avoidance, intrasexual competition for mates, and resource competition (Johnson and

In M.A. Steele, J. F. Merritt, and D. A. Zegers (eds.). 1998. Ecology and Evolutionary Biology of Tree Squirrels. Special Publication, Virginia Museum of Natural History, 6: 320 pp

Gaines, 1990). The inbreeding-avoidance hypothesis assumes inbreeding is deleterious, and that selection has favored sex-biased dispersal as a means of reducing consanguineous matings. It predicts either sex may be the predominant disperser, depending on mating system. Predictions based on mating systems also have been generated from the intrasexual competition for mates and resource-competition hypotheses. The former states that if competition for mates drives dispersal, then dispersal distances should be biased towards subordinate individuals (usually juveniles) of the sex experiencing greater competition. The resource-competition hypothesis states that philopatry should be stronger in the sex that shows a greater dependency on resources for reproduction. For mammals in general, the argument is that males compete for females, while females compete for resources, hence male-biased dispersal. A detailed discussion of these three hypotheses appears in Johnson and Gaines (1990).

Application of the theory of sex-biased dispersal should involve testing predictions under various mating and social systems, but to date little work has been done with promiscuous systems (pair bonds at most are brief, and both males and females may mate with more than one individual). For example, Anderson (1989) explored the potential causes of sex-biased dispersal in rodents by considering whether selection had acted upon emigrants or residents to produce observed dispersal patterns. However, he did not generate specific predictions for promiscuous mating systems, possibly due to the preponderance of data on polygynous microtine rodents. Similarly, Dobson (1982) chose to jointly consider polygynous and promiscuous systems, and did not present separate predictions for the two systems. Predictions generated for one system will not necessarily be appropriate for the other, as the two may differ markedly in social structure and parent-offspring interactions.

In polygynous 'harem' systems, adult males (sires) may maintain direct contact with adult females after the breeding season, and in doing so, exert potential influence (either ultimately or proximately) on the dispersal of male and female offspring. Conversely, adult males and females in promiscuous systems may become completely disassociated following the mating period (i.e., 'solitary'—Waser and Jones, 1983), with only the females involved with the raising offspring and maintenence of the breeding site. In Table 1, we have used Dobson's and Anderson's works to consider the potential influence of inbreeding, intrasexual mate competition, and resource competition in determining the dispersal pattern of a solitary species that displays a promiscuous mating system (i.e., adult males and females come into contact only during mating, and offspring are raised solely by the mother).

To assess the potential influence of inbreeding on dispersal in promiscuous systems, we assume that recognition (Porter and Blaustein, 1989) will be strong between mothers and offspring, making it possible for mothers and sons to avoid deleterious inbreeding. However, inbreeding avoidance coupled with the presence of the mother will lower the number of potential mates for her male offspring. This should prompt male-biased dispersal as sons emigrate to increase access to potential mates (Table 1). Similar logic applies to the relationship between brothers and sisters: recognition should be strong because of association from birth, but inbreeding avoidance would limit the number of potential mates available to both offspring sexes. In this case, one of the sexes should be the predominant disperser, as a means of increasing access to potential mates (Table 1). One also could argue that both sexes might disperse away from their birth site and one another, in order to improve access to potential mates. If this is the case, then dispersal tendencies could be strong in both sexes, but all offspring (male and female) should leave the natal area (Table 1).

Recognition between fathers and their daughters should be relatively weak in a promiscuous system, since they cannot come into contact until after offspring emerge from the nest, if not later (and this assumes males "know" the litters they have fathered). Thus, an inbreeding avoidance mechanism between fathers and daughters would be unlikely, and daughters should emigrate to reduce the chances of inbreeding. The result would be female-biased dispersal (Table 1).

Intrasexual mate competition should be relatively weak between females in a promiscous mating system, particularly if there is any degree of asynchrony in reproduction. Each female in the population theoretically would have access to each male (spatial constraints notwithstanding), making female competition for mates unlikely. Male competition for mates, however, would be expected to be significantly higher, as all males could try to copulate with a receptive female. Male-biased dispersal should result, as male offspring disperse to reduce competion with related males (Table 1). Resident males also could inhibit settlement of male offspring (Anderson's "Resident Fitness Hypothesis), which also would create male-biased dispersal (Table 1).

TABLE 1.—*Summary of the predictions made by the three major hypotheses that attempt to explain sex-biased dispersal, as applied to a promiscuous mating system where (1) adults are solitary, and (2) only the mother is responsible for raising offspring and maintaining defense of the natal breeding site. See INTRODUCTION for a more detailed outline of the arguments used to generate the predictions.*

Factor	Argument	Dispersal outcome
INBREEDING AVOIDANCE		
Between mother & son	Avoidance mechanism likely prevents inbreeding, but sons disperse to increase access to potential mates.	Male-biased dispersal
Between brother & sister	Avoidance mechanism likely prevents inbreeding, but one or both sexes disperse to increase access to potential mates.	Sex-biased dispersal, or both sexes disperse out of natal area.
Between father & daughter	Avoidance mechanism unlikely, daughters emigrate to prevent inbreeding	Female-biased dispersal
INTRASEXUAL MATE COMPETITION		
	Competition between mothers, daughters, and other related females unlikely; emigration reduces competition between fathers, sons and related males.	Male-biased dispersal
	Resident males prevent male offspring from immigrating	Male-biased dispersal
RESOURCE COMPETITION		
	Mothers should force offspring of both sexes to leave natal territory	Unbiased dispersal
	Resources more important to female reproductive success; females should display greater philopatric tendencies	Male-biased dispersal

Regardless of the mating system, resource competition only should result in sex-biased dispersal if resources are significantly more important to either females or males (Greenwood, 1980; Table 1). Otherwise, unbiased dispersal should occur because neither sex would experience relatively more intense competition for resources by settling in the natal area, and/or the parent(s) would have no adaptive reason to facilitate or impede local settlement of one sex of offspring over the other (Anderson's Relative Fitness Hypothesis). To summarize, we believe unbiased dispersal is predicted in a solitary, promiscuous mammal only if: both sexes of offspring are dispersing away from their natal area, in order to increase access to mates, or resource competition is the chief-determining factor affecting dispersal (Table 1). If both sexes of offspring settle close to their natal area, then the latter hypothesis would seem more likely.

There is some empirical evidence that solitary, promiscuous mammals show no sex-bias in dispersal. Dobson (1982) found that only 16% (9/57) of the studies he surveyed reported an absence of sex-biased dispersal in species with polygynous or promiscuous mating systems. Two of these exceptions were promiscous systems, involving arboreal sciurids (*Tamiasciurus hudsonicus* and *Sciurus carolinensis*). Unfortunately, these studies (Kemp and Keith, 1970; Thompson, 1977; 1978; Rusch and Reeder, 1978) relied on various definitions of 'dispersal', since the researchers were unable to follow offspring directly. Although numerous ecological studies of arboreal squirrels have been published since Dobson's paper (e.g., Tonkin, 1983; Wauters and Dhondt, 1985, 1987, 1989, 1994; Lair, 1985, 1990; Price et al., 1986; Boutin and Schweiger, 1988; Klenner, 1991; Klenner and Krebs, 1991; Boutin et al., 1993;

Larsen and Boutin, 1994), none have re-examined the purported absence of sex-biased dispersal. If it exists, this pattern would be a strong contrast to those normally seen in ground-dwelling squirrels (Holekamp, 1984). If we are to understand the factors that influence dispersal (Table 1), it will be important to study situations where the patterns contravene those normally observed (Pusey, 1987; Ribble, 1992).

Herein we provide an exhaustive test for sex-biased dispersal in a promiscuous, solitary small mammal, the North American red squirrel (*T. hudsonicus*). Red squirrels maintain individual, non-overlapping territories except during the brief estrous period, when females allow males onto their respective territories. In this promiscuous system, only the female parent is involved in raising the offspring and maintaining the breeding site. Unlike most studies, we were able to document the precise origins, movements and settlement patterns of offspring by following individuals from birth through to their first spring and beyond. Thus, we can consider two separate components of dispersal: movement prior to settlement, and settlement itself. Although we were unable to determine paternity of offspring, we assessed the potential for inbreeding and parent-offspring mate competition by measuring the occurence of spatial and temporal overlap of generations. We interpret the patterns of dispersal in this population in light of the factors and predictions outlined in Table 1.

STUDY SITE AND NATURAL HISTORY

This study was conducted in jack pine forest (*Pinus banksiana*) in the Athabasca Sand Hills at Fort Assiniboine, Alberta (54.20°N, 114.45°W), from Spring 1988 to Spring 1991. Squirrels in this area maintain individual non-overlapping territories year-round. Each territory includes a midden, or larder-hoarding site (Gurnell, 1984; Obbard, 1987). Without the midden refuge, and the accompanying winter hoard, it would be virtually impossible for an individual to successfully overwinter (Larsen and Boutin, pers. obs.). Thus, acquisition of a territory is critical to long term survival.

Females in the population normally do not breed until at least their second spring, while males exhibit scrotal testes during their first spring (Becker, 1992). Whether these one-year old males manage to mate successfully is unknown. Estrous females tolerate the presence of males on their respective territories during a one-day estrous period (Becker, 1992) in the spring. During this time, males exhibit considerable movement off of their respective territories (the 'spring shuffle'—

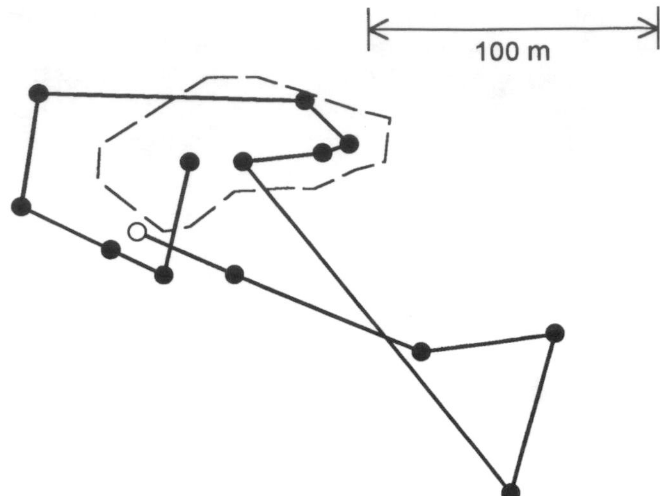

Fig. 1.—Example of the type of forays made by a radio-collared offspring or red squirrels. ○ = initial location recorded at 0800 hr, ● = subsequent locations recorded every 45 min thereafter. The boundary of the natal (mother's) territory is indicated by a dotted line. Similar movements by other offspring are depicted in Larsen and Boutin (1994).

Rusch and Reeder, 1978). Females bear one litter per year, except in very rare cases (4%) in which a litter is lost early enough in the spring to permit a second successful mating. Litter size ranged from 1 to 4 during the study, and did not differ significantly from year to year (Larsen, 1993). Offspring emerge from nests at approximately 90 g (50 days old). When they reach approximately 115 g, they begin making circling forays off the natal territory (Figure 1), apparently as a means of locating a vacant territory. Offspring do not permanently abandon their natal territory until they have claimed a territory of their own (Larsen and Boutin, 1994). Age and body mass are not strongly related to the foray distances of offspring (Larsen and Boutin, 1994). Others details on the natural history of the Fort Assiniboine population appear in Larsen and Boutin (1994, 1995).

METHODS

Baseline data.—This study was conducted on a grid with 30-m intervals, set up in ca.1.75 km^2 of forest. Each Spring (25 April–15 May) and autumn (23 August–1 September) we livetrapped on all the middens in the study area at least once during each day, weather permitting. When possible, trapping of sections of the study area were conducted during the interim summer periods. All squirrels were marked with numbered metal eartags, and females and offspring also were equipped with small, colored-coded tags threaded over the metal eartag. Weight, reproductive condition (Price et al., 1986) and behavior upon release were recorded for each trapped animal. Individuals trapped on their own territory could be identified by their tendency to vocalize ('rattle') aggressively upon release (Lair, 1990), whereas trespassers remained silent or were immediately chased off by the territory holder.

Lactating females were radio-collared and tracked to their respective nests. Approximately three weeks after parturition, each litter was located, and the offspring were eartagged. Offspring emerged from the nest at approximately 90 g, or 50 days of age. Most of the offspring that attained a body mass of 115g (64 days old) were outfitted with radio-collars (Larsen and Boutin, 1994), and these offspring were located at least once every three days. Preliminary information gathered in 1988 indicated that offspring generally were active and moving during the hours of 0800–1100 and 1330–1700 (Larsen, unpubl.), so we focused our collection of telemetry observations within these time periods. Collection of movement data during inclement weather (extreme heat, rain) was avoided. Prior to the analysis described herein, we ran a multiple regression on the data for each year, to determine the effects of time-of-year and time-of-day on the recorded foray distances. The significance of these regressions ($Ps < 0.001$) primarily resulted from the large sample sizes (733, 1153, and 731 observations in 1988, 1989, and 1990, respectively), since the proportion of total variability in the distance measurements attributable to time-of-year and time-of-day was very low (adjusted R^2 values of 0.03, 0.09, and 0.04, respectively). Thus, we felt our location data could be justifiably pooled within each year, without concern for temporal differences.

Fidelity to the same location in conjunction with territorial behavior (Price et al., 1986) was used to determine (within two days) when the offspring had obtained a territory. Only 2 out of 73 offspring were known to relocate after we had judged them as having acquired a territory.

Tests for sex-biased forays.—We recorded the location of all offspring when they were observed using the grid system. We then calculated the distance from each location to the natal midden and to the offspring's previous location. These 'foray' data were calculated only for individuals not holding territories. We also converted foray distances into number of territory increments, using the diameter of an average-sized territory (.65h≈45 m diameter; Larsen, 1993).

We compared differences between male and female offspring using maximum and mean foray distances. Changes in foray distances through time were analyzed using an F-ratio statistic, based on Hotelling's T^2 test (Morrison, 1976). This test is a form of multivariate analysis of variance (F ratio) applicable when one has repeated measures on a series of individuals, and appropriate for determining if the mean of the measurement remains constant over time (Freund et al., 1986).

To control for potential differences due to sibling pressure, we compared the movements of male and female offspring through time, using offspring that only had one sibling of the opposite sex alive during the time of data collection. Male and female siblings normally were located at approximately the same time each day. A Wilcoxon paired-sample test (Zar, 1984) was conducted on foray distances obtained for sibling pairs which met the following criteria: both siblings were collared at approximately the same time (±1 day), both collared siblings were located on the same days, at approximately the same times, no other siblings were alive during the radio-tracking period. The number of data points used for each sibling pair varied, as we only used those locations obtained up to the death of one the siblings and/or the acquisition of a territory by one of the siblings.

We also compared the forays of male and female offspring using an index that we developed. This foray index was calculated for offspring that were collared at approximately the same body mass and age (115 g, 64 days) and subsequently located every third day, for 15 days. The index is the sum of the distance individuals were located from their natal middens, and the distance from each previous location. This procedure takes into account movement away from the natal midden, as well as the distance from the previous location (Fig 2).

Tests for sex-biased settlement.—The territory boundaries of mothers and settled offspring were obtained through telemetry locations, behavioral observation, or by following individuals after they had been released from traps (Larsen and Boutin, 1994). Data for offspring territories sometimes were insufficient (<15 perimeter observations) to plot boundaries, but they did permit us to determine the position of the offspring's territory relative to its mother's. Following our earlier work (Larsen and Boutin, 1994), we assigned offspring territories into one of two categories: Class 1 were territories that lay on or contiguous to the natal (mother's) territory. Class 2 territories had no shared boundaries

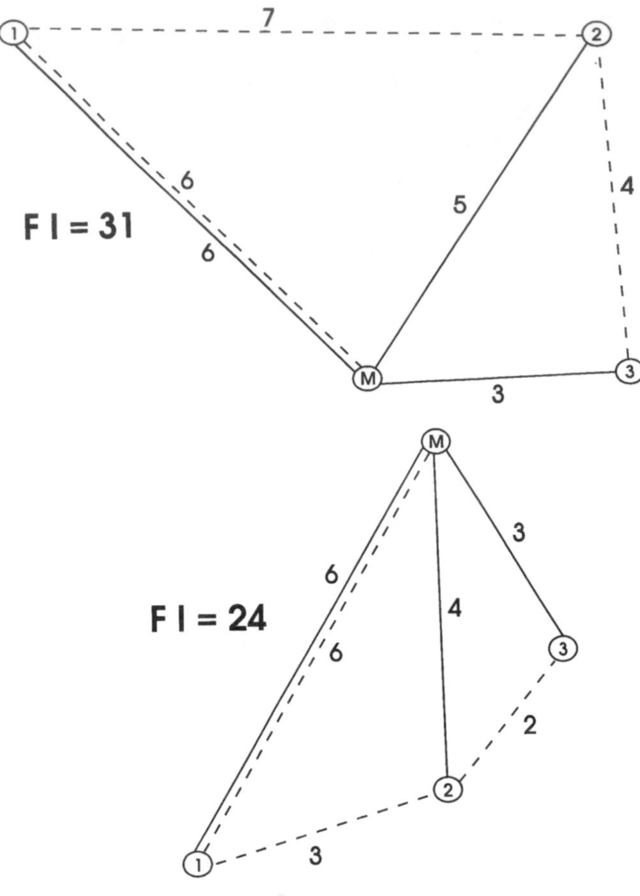

Fig 2.—Diagram showing how the Foray Index (FI) would be calculated for two hypothetical offspring. FI is the sum of the distances individuals are located from their natal middens (the encircled M) and the distances of each location from the previous location. In these two hypothetical examples, each individual has been located three times (①②③). The individual in the top example produces a higher FI because it not only moves further away from the midden than the individual in the lower example, but also it moves in more varying directions. In reality, FI were calculated using eight subsequent locations, and values ranged from 57 to 2271 m.

with the mother's territory, meaning the offspring and its mother had at least one other squirrel living in between them.

Settlement distances were recorded as the distance from the offspring's natal midden to its acquired midden. In cases where the offspring's territory did not encompass an obvious midden-site, we used the arithmetic centre of the locations data. Like our movement data, we converted settlement distances into territory increments.

Experimental removals.—In August 1989, we examined the tendency of breeding females to relocate to vacant territories, by permanently removing neighboring resident squirrels from an experimental grid (Larsen and Boutin, 1995). Some of the vacated territories were claimed by untagged offspring (i.e. originating off the grid); we compared the sex ratio of these settlers with the sex ratio of young born on the grid in the same year.

Potential for inbreeding and competition for mates.—Because we could not assign paternity in our population, we were unable to estimate the amount of inbreeding that occured. However, we assessed the potential for mother/son incest, and daughter/mother competition for mates by noting the occurrence of overlapping, reproductively mature generations. The potential for females to mate with males outside of their immediate area was examined by noting the distances scrotal males were trapped from their territory during the spring period, when females were still entering estrus.

Statistical analysis.—We tested for potential year effects prior to pooling of data across years. In particular, we used log-linear models to test for year effects on all analyses of frequency data. Unless year effects were significant, we present only the results of a simpler, log-likelihood ratio *(G)* test involving only the two factors under consideration. Because litter sizes of 1 and 2 were relatively infrequent during our study (5% and 22%, respectively), we pooled the frequency counts for these two categories in all analyses involving litter size.

RESULTS

TESTS FOR SEX-BIASED FORAYS

Maximum foray of offspring.—Fifty-five radio-collared juveniles (28 females, 27 males) went 12-15 days without obtaining a territory (or being killed), providing 4-5 radio-tracked locations for each individual. The maximum foray observed for each juvenile did not differ between the sexes (normal approximation to Mann-Whitney U, Z=-0.463, P=0.637). This remains true if foray distances are converted to territory increments (Kolmogorov-Smirnov 2-sample test, D=0.12, P=0.98, Fig. 3).

Relative distances of male and female siblings.—There was no significant difference between the mean foray distances recorded for male and female sibling pairs (Wilcoxon paired-sample test, T=85, P=0.299, n=21 pairs of siblings). The number of paired observations used for each pair of siblings varied from two to twenty (= 7.9, SD = 4.81).

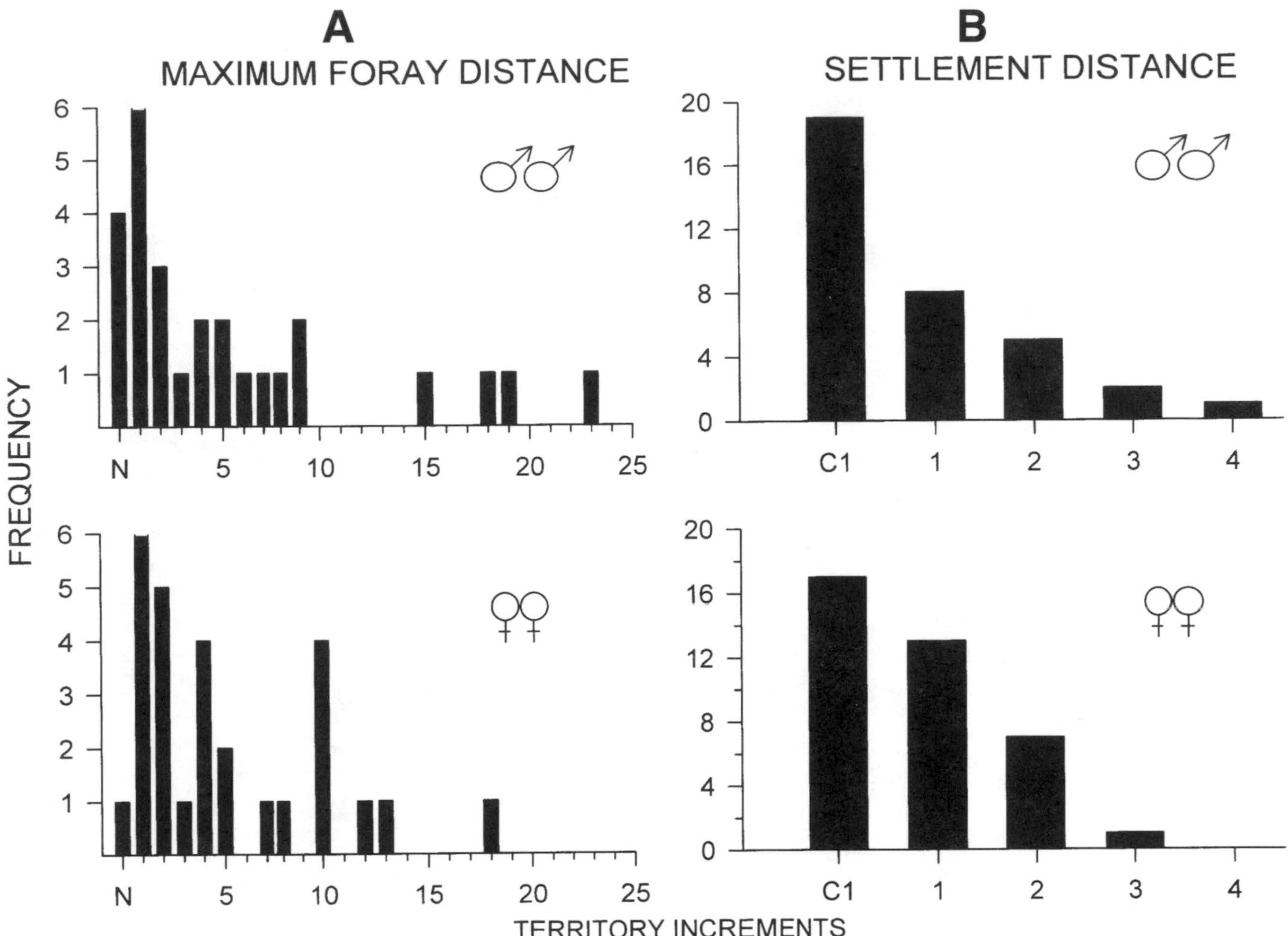

FIG.3.—Absence of sex-biased foray movements (A) and settlement distances (B) recorded for offspring. Maximum foray distances were calculated using the maximum distance from the natal midden recorded for radio-collared offspring that provided four or five locations over a 12-15 day period. The first increment (N) in A includes all maximum distances that occured within the boundaries of the natal territory. For settlement distances, the first increment (C1) represents Class 1 territories (see METHODS in text for definition). Otherwise, distance is given in territory increments, or 90 m intervals, which represents the diameter of a circular territory of 0.65 h (mean territory size).

Actual foray distances of siblings through time.—Although the previous analysis showed that male and female mean foray distances did not differ, this did not eliminate the possibility that the forays of males and females siblings differed through time (i.e., male foray distances increase through time, while female foray distances decrease). To test for this, we used the data from thirteen radio-collared sibling pairs that were located repeatedly every third day, for 21 days. The difference in the distances of each male and female sibling from their respective natal middens did not change significantly over time (F=0.306, $d.f.$=6,7, P=0.915). This can be restated as, the differences in male and female foray distances did not significantly depart from 0 over time.

Sex ratio of untagged juveniles.—The sex ratio of untagged juveniles (i.e. those originating off the study area) trapped on the study area in 1989 and 1990 did not differ significantly from the known ratio of males to females in each year's cohort (binomial test, 1989, 14 males, 12 females, known ratio 0.546, P=0.861; 1990, 11 males, 6 females, known ratio 0.556, P=0.393). The power of these tests to detect departures from the theorized ratio was low, given our small sample sizes.

Foray index.—There was no significant difference in the foray indices obtained for 25 female and 21 male juveniles (normal approx. to Mann-Whitney U, Z=-1.213, P=0.225).

TESTS FOR SEX-BIASED SETTLEMENT

Territory settlement.—Seventy-three offspring obtained territories during the course of our study (38 females, 35 males) with most settling in the immediate vicinity of the natal midden. There was no significant difference in the settlement distances of the two sexes, in terms of actual distance (normal approx. to Mann-Whitney U, Z=-1.01, P=0.31) or in territory increments (Kolmogorov-Smirnov 2-sample test, D=0.0.095, P=0.99, Fig. 3).

Acquisition of natal territory and midden.— Five male and three female offspring assumed complete ownership of their natal midden and territory.

Experimental removals.—The sex ratio of untagged offspring settling on the artifically-vacated territories (4 males:6 females) was not significantly different from that expected (binomial test, known ratio 0.546, P=0.76), although the power of this test was severely limited by the small sample. The lack of immigrants into the removal area, however, does corroborate the short dispersal distances recorded for our study offspring (see above).

Territory classification and offspring sex.—There was no significant difference in the relative proportions of male and female offspring acquiring Class 1 and Class 2 territories, over the three years (H_o*: sex, territory category and year mutually independent* - G=3.08, $d.f.$=7, n=67, P=0.878).

POTENTIAL FOR INBREEDING

Mother/Son.—From 1988 to 1990, 170 males were born in the study area. Thirteen of these males survived to 1 year (sexual maturity), and seven of these had their mother alive at that time. Hence, there was a 0.54 probability that a male surviving to sexual maturity would still have its mother alive.

Father/daughter.—We could not assign paternity, so only potential fathers (i.e. adult males) could be considered. The probability of an adult male living two years (the minimum time required for female offspring to reach maturity) during the course of our study was ca. 0.50 (0.70 annual adult survival[2]). In other words, a female surviving to reproductive maturity had a maximum 50% chance of having its father alive at the time.

Brother/sister.—The probability of an emerging male or female offspring surviving two years was approximately 6% (9% first year survival X 70% annual adult survival). This therefore represents the probability that a male offspring alive at two years would have a sexually-mature sister also alive, and vice versa. This constitutes a very general estimate for the population, i.e., the estimate would be higher for a male offspring born to a litter that also contained three females, etc. Similar provisions could be applied to our other survival-based estimates, but they probably do little to change the magnitude of the probabilities. For example, a more direct assessment of the probability of mature male and female sibling overlap can be drawn from our data: during the course of our study, we documented only one instance of both male and female littermates reaching sexual maturity (1/79 litters).

POTENTIAL FOR MATE COMPETITION

Father/son.—A male offspring surviving to one year of age had approximately a 70% chance of having a living father (i.e. annual adult survival 70%). Conversely, adult fathers had only a 9% chance of having a son alive after one year.

Forays of adult males during breeding season.—We had 644 incidences of scrotal males being trapped off of their respective territories in spring, during the period when females were still entering estrus. These males were trapped as far as 839 m from their respective middens, although 51% of the captures occured on a midden neighboring the male's (n=126, SD=94.4, mode=47).

DISCUSSION

Despite a wide variety of tests, we could not detect a sex-bias in any of our measurements of offspring movement and settlement. We also found extremely limited settlement distances in the population. Even though Class 2 individuals settled on territories spatially removed from their natal territories, the potential for contact between them and their natal territory (and mother) remained. This makes it important that our Class 1 and Class 2 designations are not construed as representing philopatric versus non-philopatric settlement. Other data (Larsen and Boutin, 1994) indicate that movements equal to the maximum dispersal distances recorded here occur frequently; males in particular will travel considerable distances during the mating period. Thus, all offspring that acquired territories during this study should be considered philopatric, for they remained in potential contact with their natal territory and mother.

Why is there unbiased dispersal in the population? The presence of sex-unbiased, philopatric dispersal in the study population is predicted if competition for environmental resources is the major factor influencing dispersal (Table 1; Dobson, 1982). Under the "resource competition" hypothesis, one would expect to see sex-biased dispersal in a promiscuous mating system only if the acquisition of resources is relatively more critical to the reproductive success of one sex. Certainly, in red squirrels it is adult females, not males, that require territories for the successful rearing of offspring. However, the acquisition of a territory prior to the first winter is crucial to the survival of both male and female offspring (Smith, 1968; Zirul, 1970; Rusch and Reeder, 1978; Larsen and Boutin, pers. obs.), much less future reproductive success. Adults, regardless of gender, also require territories for survival. During this study we recorded no instances of overwinter survival by individuals not holding a territory. It is therefore quite reasonable to expect that resource competition should not result in sex-biased natal dispersal in this population.

Deleterious effects from inbreeding either do not occur in our study population, or their impact is equally distributed between the sexes. The models of Waser et al. (1986) suggested that mortality incurred during emigration would be more significant than inbreeding depression. Also, the potential for inbreeding may be minimized by kin discrimination (Hoogland, 1992) or by the death of parents prior to the maturation of offspring (Armitage, 1981; Schwartz and Armitage, 1981). We could not determine if inbreeding between close kin resulted from the strong philopatric tendencies of dispersing offspring (e.g., pikas—Smith, 1987), but the data clearly indicate that emigration is not a viable tactic.

The continuous occupied habitat at Fort Assiniboine should ensure that some level of gene flow occurs despite the philopatric settlement pattern. This situation is considerably different from that of a disjunct ground squirrel colony, or any insular animal population, where emigration over relatively long distances, in sub-optimal habitat, is required to ensure some degree of outbreeding. However, sex-biased dispersal occurs in microtine rodent populations occupying relatively expansive, continuous habitat. Anderson (1989) discussed the evidence for inbreeding costs in rodents, and found it inconclusive. Moore and Ali (1984) have argued that inbreeding has little if any influence on determining dispersal patterns, and Shields (1982, 1984) has suggested that selection should favour consanguineous matings (excepting incestuous pairings) in low fecundity species. In this study, the probability that an offspring reaching sexual maturity still would have its opposite-sex parent still alive was relatively high, so the possibility of direct inbreeding cannot be eliminated. At the same time, offspring appear to be more susceptible to predation while making forays (Larsen and Boutin, 1994), which suggests that even greater movements would carry an increased risk. From these observations, we may conclude that if inbreeding does exist in the study population, it is less costly than attempted long-distance dispersal.

An argument may be made that intrasexual mate competition should be important in determining dispersal patterns in this population, and that male-biased dispersal should be present. Mothers and daughters should experience no significant competition for mates, given the promiscuous mating system and the short, asynchronous estrus periods (Table 1). However, for sex-biased dispersal to occur, the potential for mate competition between a male offspring and its father should increase the closer the offspring settles to its natal territory. This competition should be lessened male offspring emigrate, or if: females mate with males that originate many territories away. The first scenario did not occur at Fort Assiniiboine, but without a knowledge of paternity we cannot determine how female mate choice and spatial and temporal overlap of sires and reproductive sons may affect mate competition. If competition for mates exists between male squirrels, regardless of their relatedness, the continuous habitat at Fort Assiniboine suggests a dispersing male offspring is quite unlikely to find an area where older, dominant males do not exist. Thus, emigration is less likely to increase his potential fitness.

Approximately one-half of the dispersing offspring acquired territories on or adjacent to their natal territories. Red squirrel offspring have been known to obtain part or all of the natal territory in more northern populations (Smith, 1968; Zirul 1970, Price et al., 1986; Boutin et al., 1993; Price and Boutin, 1993). Experimental manipulations at Fort Assiniboine indicate this may be a deliberate action on the part of the mother (Boutin and Larsen, in prep), as suggested by these previous studies. Smith (1968) and Zirul (1970) presented evidence that such nepotism was biased towards daughters, but their samples were small, and in the case of the latter, did not take into account the sex ratio of offspring at birth. Complete abandonment of the natal territory has been reported in several species (see review by Waser and Jones, 1983). One notable example is Jones's (1987) study of banner-tailed kangaroo rats, where 32% of dispersing offspring remained on their natal mounds. In that study, neither sex was more likely to acquire the home mound, but such an event did confer survival advantages to the offspring (Jones, 1986). We also found no evidence of sex-biased acquisition of the natal territory, but perhaps more importantly, only 7% of all dispersing offspring acquired a territory through direct maternal abandonment. Price and Boutin (1993) recorded a higher incidence of natal territory acquisition in dispersing red squirrels in the Yukon, but the fate of the mother was unclear.

Offspring attempting to disperse in the Fort Assiniboine population appear more susceptible to predation while away from their mothers' territories, and the costs of longer forays, or alternative search tactics may outweigh any deleterious effects resulting from philopatric settlement (Larsen and Boutin, 1994). We also have found that Class 2 settlers tend to have higher survival, perhap due to the fact that they often acquire large, established middens (Larsen and Boutin, 1994). However, this 'pay-off' for Class 2 settlers likely would not continue to increase in relation to the distance settled, due to the extensive search time and movements. The models of Waser et al. (1986) suggest the costs of emigrating to more distant territories would exceed the costs of inbreeding. The same would likely apply to costs associated with mate competition.

In summary, the red squirrel population at Fort Assiniboine constitutes a promiscuous system of solitary animals where sex-biased dispersal is absent, and offspring dispersal is universally philopatric. Our examination of dispersal revealed no differential behavior or settlement between the sexes. Costs of inbreeding and/or mate competition did not appear significant enough to cause sex-biased dispersal, or to prompt for non-philopatric dispersal. Resource competition likely dictated that offspring settle off of the mother's territory, but male and female offspring appeared to compete equally for all available sites. Waser and Jones (1983) made the point that solitary animals are not necessary asocial, they merely avoid aggregating. The North American red squirrel, like many territorial organisms, responds differently to familiar versus unfamiliar conspecifics. Social benefits accrued by philopatric behavior of offspring (familiar individuals) may act in tandem with the costs of long-distance movement to produce dispersal patterns such as those documented here. Additional studies on the presence or absence of sex-biased dispersal in arboreal sciurids will be valuable, particularly if patterns become apparent across various species, mating systems, and ecological conditions.

ACKNOWLEDGMENTS

We are indebted to the people of Fort Assiniboine, Alberta, for all of the logistical support we received. Particular thanks are due to George Mansoff, Walter and Ansgard Thomson, and the mechanics at Redi-Fast Fixit. We also recognize the dedication of all the research technicians who provided capable and enthusiastic assistance on the ground and in the trees.

This study was financed by grants to K. W. Larsen from The Canadian Circumpolar Institute (formerly The Boreal Institute for Northern Studies) and The Recreation, Parks and Wildlife Foundation, and a Natural Science and Engineering Research Council of Canada (NSERC) operating grant awarded to S. Boutin. Critical manpower and additional funding were provided through contracts with Employment and Immigration Canada, under the Unemployment Insurance Section 25 job-creation program. Research permits were granted by the Fish & Wildlife Division of the Alberta Ministry of Forestry, Lands and Wildlife. Personal support for K.W. Larsen came from an NSERC Postgraduate Scholarship, and an Izaak Walton Killam Doctoral Scholarship.

LITERATURE CITED

ANDERSON, P. K. (ed.) 1989. Dispersal in rodents: a resident fitness hypothesis. Special Publication, The American Society of Mammalogists, 9:1-141.

ARMITAGE, K. 1981. Sociality as a life history tactic of ground squirrels. Oecologia (Berlin), 48:36-49.

BECKER, C. D. 1992. Proximate factors influencing the timing and occurrence of reproduction in red squirrels (*Tamiasciurus hudsonicus*). Ph.D. dissertation., University of Alberta, Edmonton, 161 pp.

BOUTIN, S., AND S. SCHWEIGER. 1988. Manipulation of intruder pressure in red squirrels (*Tamiasciurus hudsonicus*): effects on territory size and acquisition. Canadian Journal of Zoology, 66:2270-2274.

BOUTIN, S., Z. TOOZE, AND K. PRICE. 1993. Post-breeding dispersal by female red squirrels (*Tamiasciurus hudsonicus*): the effect of local vacancies. Behavioral Ecology, 4:151-155.

DHONDT, A. A. 1979. Summer dispersal and survival of juvenile great tits in southern Sweden. Oecologia (Berlin), 42:1183-1192.

DOBSON, F. S. 1982. Competition for mates and predominant juvenile male dispersal in mammals. Animal Behaviour, 30:1183-1192.

FREUND, R. J., R. C. LITTELL, AND C. SPECTOR. 1986. SAS system for linear models. SAS Institute Inc., Cary, North Carolina, 211 pp.

GAINES, M. S., AND L. R. McCLENAGHAN. 1980. Dispersal in small mammals. Annual Review of Ecology and Systematics, 11:163-196.

GAUTHREAUX, S. A., JR. 1978. The ecological significance of behavioural dominance. Pp. 17-54, *in* Perspectives in ethology (P .P .G. Bateson and P. H. Klopfer, eds.). Plenum Publishing Corporation, London, United Kingdom 3:1-263 pp.

GREENWOOD, P. J. 1980. Mating systems, philopatry and dispersal in birds and mammals. Animal Behaviour, 28:1140-1162.

———.1983. Mating systems and the evolutionary consequences of dispersal. Pp. 116-131, *in* The ecology of animal movement (I. R. Swingland and P.J. Greenwood, eds.). Oxford University Press, Oxford, United Kingdom, 311 pp.

GURNELL, J. 1984. Home range, territoriality, caching behaviour and food supply of the red squirrel (*Tamiasciurus hudsonicus fremonti*) in a subalpine lodgepole pine forest. Animal Behaviour, 32:1119-1131.

HOLEKAMP, K. E. 1984. Dispersal in ground-dwelling sciurids. Pp 297-320, *in* The biology of ground- dwelling sciurids. (J. O. Murie and G.R. Michener, eds.) University of Nebraska Press, Lincoln, 459 pp.

HOOGLAND, J. L. 1992. Levels of inbreeding among prairie dogs. The American Naturalist, 139:591-602.

JOHNSON, C. N. 1986. Sex-biased philopatry and dispersal in mammals. Oecologia (Berlin), 69:626-627.

JOHNSON, M. L., AND M. S. GAINES. 1990. Evolution of dispersal: theoretical models and empirical tests using birds and mammals. Annual Review of Ecology and Systematics, 21:449-480.

JONES, W. T. 1986. Survivorship in philopatric and dispersing kangaroo rats (*Dipodomys spectabilis*). Ecology, 67:202-207.

———,1987. Dispersal patterns in kangaroo rats (*Dipodomys spectabilis*). Pp. 119-127, *in* Mammalian dispersal patterns: the effects of social structure on population genetics (B. D. Chepko-Sade and Z. T. Halpin, eds.). The University of Chicago Press, Chicago, Illinois, 342 pp.

KEMP, G. A., AND L. B. KEITH. 1970. Dynamics and regulation of red squirrel (*Tamiasciurus hudsonicus*) populations. Ecology, 51:763-779.

KLENNER, W. 1991. Red squirrel population dynamics. II. Settlement patterns and the response to removals. The Journal of Animal Ecology, 60:974-994.

KLENNER, W., AND C. J. KREBS. 1991. Red squirrel population dynamics. I. The effect of supplemental food on demography. The Journal of Animal Ecology, 60:961-978.

LAIR, H. 1985. Mating seasons and fertility of red squirrels in southern Quebec. Canadian Journal of Zoology, 63:2323-2327.

———,1990. The calls of the red squirrel: a contextual analysis of function. Behaviour, 115:254-282.

LARSEN, K. W., 1993. Female reproductive success in the North American red squirrel, *Tamiasciurus hudsonicus*. Ph.D. dissertation, University of Alberta, Edmonton, 167 pp.

LARSEN, K. W., AND S. BOUTIN. 1994. Movements, survival, and settlement in red squirrel (*Tamiasciurus hudsonicus*) offspring. Ecology, 75:214-223.

LARSEN, K.W., AND S. BOUTIN. 1995. Exploring territory quality in the North American red squirrel through removal experiments. Canadian Journal of Zoology, 73:1115-1122

LIBERG, O., AND T. VON SCHANTZ. 1985. Sex-biased philopatry and dispersal in birds and mammals: the Oedipus hypothesis. The American Naturalist, 126:129-135.

MOORE, J., AND R. ALI. 1984. Are dispersal and inbreeding avoidance related? Animal Behaviour, 32:94-112.

MORRISON, D. F. 1976. Multivariate statistical methods. Second edition, McGraw-Hill Book Company, New York, 338 pp.

OBBARD, M. E. 1988. Red Squirrel. Pp. 265-281, *in* Wild furbearer management and conservation in North America. Ontario Minstry of Natural Resources, 1150 pp.

PÄRT, T. 1990. Natal dispersal in the collared flycatcher (*Ficedula albicolis*): possible causes and reproductive consequences. Journal of Animal Ecology, 58:305-320.

PORTER, R. H., AND A. R. BLAUSTEIN. 1989. Mechanisms and ecological correlates of kin recognition. Science Progress, Oxford, 73:53-66.

PRICE, K., K. BROUGHTON, S. BOUTIN, AND A. R. E. SINCLAIR. 1986. Territory size and ownership in red squirrels: response to removals. Canadian Journal of Zoology, 64:1144-1147.

PRICE, K., AND S. BOUTIN. 1993. Territorial bequeathal by red squirrel mothers. Behavioral Ecology, 4:144-140.

PUSEY, A. E. 1987. Sex-biased dispersal and inbreeding avoidance in birds and mammals. Trends in Ecology & Evolution, 2:295-299.

RIBBLE, D. O. 1992. Dispersal in a monogamous rodent, *Peromyscus californicus*. Ecology, 73:859-866.

ROOD, J. P. 1987. Dispersal and intergroup transfer in the dwarf mongoose. Pp. 85-103, *in* Mammalian dispersal patterns: the effects of social structure on population genetics (B.D. Chepko-Sade and Z.T. Halpin, eds.). The University of Chicago Press, Chicago, Illinois, 342 pp.

RUSCH, D. A., AND W. G. REEDER. 1978. Population ecology of Alberta red squirrels. Ecology, 59:400-420.

SHIELDS, W. M. 1982. Philopatry, inbreeding and the evolution of sex. State University of New York Press, Albany, 245 pp.

———,1984. Optimal inbreeding and the evolution of philopatry. Pp 132-159, *in* The ecology of animal movement (I.R. Swingland and P.J. Greenwood, eds.). Clarendon Press, Oxford, United Kingdom, 311 pp.

SCHWARTZ, O. A., AND K. B. ARMITAGE. 1981. Social substructure and dispersion of genetic variation in the yellow-bellied marmot (*Marmota flaviventris*). Pp. 139-159, *in* Mammalian population genetics (M. H. Smith and J. Joule, eds.). University Georgia Press, Athens, 380 pp.

SMITH, A. T. 1987. Population structure of pikas: dispersal versus philopatry. Pp. 128-142 *in* Mammalian Dispersal Patterns: the effects of social structure on population genetics (B.D. Chepko-Sade and Z.T. Halpin, Z. T., eds.). The University Chicago Press, Chicago, 342 pp.

SMITH, C. C. 1968. The adaptive nature of social organization in the genus of three [sic] squirrels *Tamiasciurus*. Ecological Monographs, 38:31-63.

THOMPSON, D. C. 1977. Reproductive behavior of the grey squirrel. Canadian Journal of Zoology, 59:1176-1184.

———,1978. Regulation of a northern grey squirrel (*Sciurus carolinensis*) population. Ecology, 59:708-715.

TONKIN, J.M. 1983. Activity patterns of the red squirrel (*Sciurus vulgaris*). Mammal Review, 13:99-111.

VESTEL, B.M., AND H. McCARLEY. 1984. Spatial and social relations of kin in thirteen-lined and other ground squirrels. Pp. 404-423, *in* The biology of ground-dwelling squirrels (J.O. Murie and G.R. Michener, eds.). University of Nebraska Press, Lincoln, 459 pp.

WASER, P. M., AND T. W. JONES. 1983. Natal philopatry among solitary animals. The Quarterly Review of Biology, 58:355-390.

WASER, P. M., S. N. AUSTAD, AND B. KEANE. 1986. When should animals tolerate inbreeding? The American Naturalist, 128:529-537.

WAUTERS, L., AND A. A. DHONDT. 1985. Population dynamics and social behaviour of the red squirrel in different habitats. Proceedings of the International Congress of Game Biologists, 17:311-318.

WAUTERS, L., AND A. A. DHONDT. 1987. Activity budget and foraging behaviour of the red squirrel (*Sciurus vulgaris*, Linnaeus, 1758) in a coniferous habitat. Zeitschrift für Säugetierkunde, 52:341-353.

WAUTERS, L., AND A. A. DHONDT. 1989. Body weight, longevity and reproductive success in red squirrels (*Sciurus vulgaris*). The Journal of Animal Ecology, 58:637-651.

WAUTERS, L., P. CASALE, AND A. A. DHONDT. 1994. Space use and dispersal of red squirrels in fragmented habitats. Oikos, 69:140-146.

ZAR, J. H. 1984. Biostatistical analysis. Prentice-Hall, Inc., Englewood Cliffs, New Jersey, 718 pp.

ZIRUL, D. L. 1970. Ecology of a northern population of the red squirrel, *Tamiasciurus hudsonicus preblei* (Howell). M.S. thesis, University of Alberta, Edmonton, 131 pp.

CONFLICT BETWEEN THE SEXES: A REVIEW OF SOCIAL AND MATING SYSTEMS OF THE TREE SQUIRRELS

JOHN L. KOPROWSKI

Department of Biology, Willamette University, Salem, OR 97301.

ABSTRACT.—Social and mating systems frequently are viewed as important in the regulation of sciurid populations. While well described in many of the more conspicuous ground-dwelling squirrels, the social and mating systems of tree squirrels are documented sparsely. A review of the available data on tree squirrels suggests several patterns: 1) communal nesting occurs at least occasionally in nearly all tree squirrels; however, the relative frequency of this behavior is highly variable among species, 2) natal philopatry and kin-directed behaviors occur among adult females in the most highly social species, 3) plasticity appears to characterize tree squirrel ecology, and 4) significant conflict exists between the sexes and is evident in interactions, communal nesting patterns, and mating behavior. The patterns of group formation and sexual segregation exhibited in tree squirrels resemble those exhibited by ground-dwelling squirrels and suggest similar selective forces are responsible for the origin and maintenance of these patterns.

INTRODUCTION

Differential reproductive success is a key requirement for natural selection. Species differences in life-history traits and behavior frequently evoke natural selection as a major force that has shaped the evolution and proliferation of the characteristics of a species. Comparative and long-term studies with additional field and laboratory experimentation have recently shed light upon the actual variation that exists in the reproductive success of individuals (reviewed in Clutton-Brock, 1988*a*). Whereas variation in reproductive success frequently is assumed to be much greater for males than females (reviewed in Hrdy and Williams, 1983), variation among females is also likely to be considerable (Clutton-Brock, 1988*b*). As a result of such variation, significant conflict likely exists among both males and females for limiting resources within local populations.

Since the 1960s, the social systems of group-living organisms have received intensive study stemming from the controversy over the evolutionary significance of group selection (Wynne-Edwards, 1962; Williams, 1966) and the introduction of inclusive fitness theory (Hamilton, 1964) to explain the patterns that exist among group-living animals. The sociality of the ground-dwelling squirrels (Sciuridae: Marmotini) is among the most widely studied of mammals. A diversity of levels of sociality are evidenced among the ground squirrels ranging from species characterized by relatively solitary social systems such as Franklin's ground squirrels (*Spermophilus franklinii*) to those in which individuals share nests and live in colonies such as black-tailed prairie dogs (*Cynomys ludovicianus*; Armitage, 1981). The fundamental social unit of ground-dwelling squirrel societies is the female-female bond (Armitage, 1981; Michener, 1983); increasing levels of sociality result from the retention of daughters near or in natal areas and formation of kin clusters with increasing levels of amicable interactions (Armitage, 1987).

Increased levels of sociality sometimes connotes that group members have equivalent interests; however, the interests of group members frequently are not harmonious. Kinship can influence the interactions of group members (Sherman, 1981; Armitage, 1989; Hoogland, 1986). Matrilines of female yellow-bellied marmots frequently split as individual females attempt to maximize the direct fitness component of their individual fitness (Armitage, 1987) and aggression

In M.A. Steele, J. F. Merritt, and D. A. Zegers (eds.). 1998. Ecology and Evolutionary Biology of Tree Squirrels. Special Publication, Virginia Museum of Natural History, 6: 320 pp

within groups can be intense (Hoogland, 1985, 1986). Perhaps the most striking conflict of interest exists between the sexes in mammals. Male mammals generally can maximize their fitness by increasing the number of females mated while females are committed to progeny through gestation and lactation with the fitness-limiting resource likely related to food, dens, etc. (Downhower and Armitage, 1971; Clutton-Brock and Vincent, 1991). The reproductive effort of the sexes is the sum of parental effort (effort towards provisioning and rearing of offspring) and mating effort (effort dedicated to the acquisition of mates: Alexander and Borgia, 1979). Most (>95%) mammalian species including the ground and tree squirrels are polygynous (Kleiman, 1977; Armitage, 1981; 1988; Michener, 1983; Heaney, 1984), which suggests that the principal component of the reproductive effort of male sciurids is likely to be mating effort while female reproductive effort is composed predominately of parental effort (Koprowski, 1991*a*; Wauters and Dhondt, 1992).

Herein, I review the sparse literature on the social and mating systems of tree squirrels with special reference to home range size, communal nesting, dominance relations, and mating tactics and examine the role of inter- and intrasexual conflict for resources in shaping the behavioral ecology of the tree squirrels.

REVIEW OF SOCIAL AND MATING SYSTEMS: EVIDENCE FOR SEXUAL CONFLICT

Home range size.-Intersexual territoriality is found only in *Tamiasciurus hudsonicus* and *T. douglasii* (Smith, 1968; 1981; Koford, 1982; Gurnell, 1984; Larsen and Boutin, 1994) and appears tightly linked with the defensibility of the seeds of conifers as well as the availability of food (Gurnell, 1987; Wauters and Dhondt, 1992). Home range size decreases significantly with the supplementation of food (Sullivan, 1990; Klenner and Krebs, 1991). Populations of *T. hudsonicus* in mixed and deciduous forests exhibit a system of overlapping home ranges likely due to indefensibility of the food resources (Layne, 1954; Deutch, 1978; Pesce, 1982). Although territoriality appears relaxed in deciduous forests, the ratio of male to female home ranges remains near 1.0 (Table 1).

Members of the genus *Sciurus* typically exhibit overlapping home ranges (Ingles, 1947; Thompson, 1978; Wauters and Dhondt, 1992); however, intrasexual territoriality is suggested due to the use of exclusive core areas by females in many species (*S. vulgaris*—Wauters and Dhondt, 1992; *S. niger*—Havera and Nixon, 1978; Kantola and Humphrey, 1990; *S. carolinensis*—Taylor, 1969; Thompson, 1978; Kenward, 1985; *S. griseus*—

Table 1.—*Ratio of male-to-female home range size in* Tamiasciurus *and* Sciurus.

Species	Ratio (Male:Female)	Source
T. hudsonicus		
Territorial	1.18	Smith, 1968
Non-territorial	0.72 - 1.26	Layne, 1954; Pesce, 1982
T. douglasii	2.19	Koford, 1982
Sciurus aberti	1.20 - 1.97	Farentinos, 1979; Halloran,1993
S. aureogaster	2.56	McGuire and Brown, 1975
S. carolinensis	1.20 - 1.90	Flyger, 1960, Doebel and McGinnis, 1974, Thompson, 1978
S. granatensis	3.3	Heaney and Thorington, 1978
S. griseus	0.96 - 2.3	Ingles, 1947; Cross, 1969; Gilman, 1986; Foster, 1992;
S. niger	1.59 - 2.56	Adams, 1976; Weigl et al., 1989; Kantola and Humphrey, 1990
S. vulgaris	1.26 - 1.57	Wauters and Dhondt, 1992

Gilman, 1986). Home range size of females appears to be consistently smaller than that of males (Table 1) and more stable in females than males (Thompson, 1978; Wauters and Dhondt, 1992). In addition, male home range size appears to be most strongly influenced by mating activities and spacing patterns of females (Kenward, 1985; Wauters and Dhondt, 1992; Halloran, 1993) rather than food availability.

The consistent pattern among the tree squirrels of sexual dimorphism in home range size along with minimal or insignificant dimorphism in body size suggests that the sexes respond to different resources. The potentially more predictable nature, ease of larderhoarding, and defensibility of coniferous seed crops from northerly latitudes in North America appear to permit *Tamiasciurus* to maintain a territorial system of space use; however, the less predictable nature of coniferous seeds in Europe (Wauters and Dhondt, 1992) and the Southeastern United States (Weigl et al., 1989) as well as the extreme variability in the production of deciduous tree seeds likely makes territorial defense inefficient.

Dominance relations.—Age and body size are significant correlates of dominance in many species of tree squirrel (reviewed in Farentinos, 1972*b*; Gurnell, 1987). In all species of tree squirrel in which intersexual dominance has been assessed, males dominate females of similar size and age (Gurnell, 1987). Males commonly dominate females in *S. carolinensis* (Pack et al., 1967; Allen and Aspey, 1986), *S. niger* (Bernard, 1972; Benson, 1980) and *S. griseus* (Cross, 1969). Males should have ready access to food and dens when competing with females; however, the role of site-specific dominance is virtually unknown among tree squirrels because most studies have examined intersexual dominance relations at localized food resources.

Communal nesting.—Communal nesting is the simultaneous sharing of a nest by two or more squirrels. Most species of *Sciurus* are known to nest communally at least occasionally (Table 2), while communal nests are unknown from *Tamiasciurus*. Although nesting group size generally increases in winter, communal nests can be found during all seasons in *Glaucomys volans* (Layne and Raymond, 1994), *S. aberti* (Halloran, 1993), *S. carolinensis* (Taylor, 1969; Koprowski, 1996), and *S. niger* (Christisen, 1985; Koprowski, 1996). In some populations of a species, nesting aggregations are frequently sex-biased (*G. sabrinus*: Maser et al., 1981; *G. volans*: Layne and Raymond, 1994; *S. carolinensis* and *S. niger*: Koprowski, 1996) which further suggests segregation of the sexes as well as potential conflict between the sexes for a limited resource. However, mixed sex groups are the most common assemblage found among species or subspecies in which communal nesting is uncommon (Table 2).

The seasonality of nesting assemblages suggests that a major function of communal nesting may be for thermoregulatory benefits. Nests alone can raise the ambient temperature nearly 30°C (Pulliainen, 1973; Havera, 1979; Pauls, 1981) and huddling can provide significant energetic and survival benefits in other small mammals (Madison, 1984; Andrews et al., 1987). An understanding of why some species commonly nest in groups during winter months while others species do not will likely involve detailed studies of the energetics of individual squirrels.

Natal philopatry and kinship.—Natal philopatry commonly occurs in *S. carolinensis* (Taylor, 1969; Cordes and Barkalow, 1972; Thompson, 1978; Koprowski, 1996) and likely also in *T. hudsonicus* (Smith, 1968; Larsen and Boutin, 1994) and *G. volans* (Layne and Raymond, 1994). Philopatry is heavily female-biased in some populations of *S.*

Table 2.—*Species of tree squirrel for which communal nesting has been documented to occur.*

Species	Frequency of communal nests assemblage	Most common	Source
Sciurus aberti	Uncommon	Mixed sex	Halloran, 1993;Farentinos,1972*a*
Sciurus arizonensis	?	?	Hoffmeister,1986
Sciurus carolinensis	Common	Single sex	Koprowski,1996
Sciurus nayaritensis	Uncommon	Mixed sex	Koprowski, Unpublished
Sciurus niger rufiventer	Common	Single sex (Males)	Koprowski,1996
Sciurus niger niger	Uncommon	Mixed sex	Weigl et al.,1989
Sciurus vulgaris	Uncommon	Mixed sex	Wauters and Dhondt, 1990*a*
Glaucomys sabrinus	?	Single sex	Maser et al.,1981
Glaucomys volans	Common	Single/Mixed sex	Layne and Raymond, 1994

carolinensis (Cordes and Barkalow, 1972; Koprowski, 1996). Kinship does appear to play a significant role in the recruitment of young into a population (Koprowski, 1996; Boutin et al., 1993; Price and Boutin, 1993; Larsen and Boutin, 1994; Layne and Raymond, 1994) and the frequency of amicable versus agonistic behaviors are directly related to the level of relatedness (Koprowski, 1993*c;* 1996). The role of kinship in the social system of tree squirrels is quite similar to that observed in the ground-dwelling squirrels (Armitage, 1987).

Mating behavior.—Mating behavior is remarkably similar among the tree squirrels (reviewed in Gurnell, 1987). Females are in estrus for <1 day and males compete viciously for access to the female (Thompson, 1977; Koford, 1982; Wauters and Dhondt, 1990*b*; Arbetan, 1993; Koprowski, 1993*a*, 1993*b*). Intrasexual competition frequently yields alternative mating tactics with dominant individuals controlling access to the female (Wauters and Dhondt, 1990*b*; Koprowski, 1993*a*, 1993*b*); however, the female is not a passive part of the mating bout. Female tree squirrels will frequently avoid pursuing males and mate in secluded locations with lower risk of attack and injury to the female (Wauters and Dhondt, 1990*b*; Arbetan, 1993; Koprowski, 1993*a*,1993*b*), mate with multiple males (Farentinos, 1972*b*; Koford, 1982; Wauters and Dhondt, 1990*b*; Arbetan, 1993; Koprowski, 1993*a*, 1993*b*), solicit additional matings (Farentinos, 1980; Koprowski, 1993*d*), and remove copulatory plugs which are formed by the semen of most male tree squirrels (reviewed in Koprowski, 1992; *S. griseus*; Koprowski pers. obs.). All of these behaviors by the female are to the detriment of the reproductive success of individual males-a clear indication of the immense sexual conflict that is pervasive in the social and mating systems of tree squirrels.

EVOLUTION OF SOCIAL AND MATING SYSTEMS IN THE SQUIRRELS

Tree squirrels provide insight into the evolution of sociality in the Sciuridae. The tree squirrel lineage diverged from that of the ground squirrels about 30 to 35 million years ago (Hafner, 1984). The common ancestor of tree and ground squirrels was a semiarboreal (Black, 1972) or arboreal (Emry and Thorington, 1982), forest-dwelling squirrel. Although tree squirrels in the genera *Tamiasciurus* and *Sciurus* do not hibernate, species that occupy mixed and deciduous forest of North America and Europe experience great seasonal variation in available energy leading to critical periods in winter (Montgomery et al., 1975) and possibly summer (reviewed in Koprowski, 1991*b*). The annual cycle in available energy parallels that of ground squirrels, with food availability below maintenance requirements in winter and a season of energy surplus in spring and autumn. Most ground squirrels cope with energy limitations by hibernating, while *Sciurus* and *Tamiasciurus* in mixed and deciduous forests scatterhoard high-energy, storable nuts, nest communally, reduce food intake (Short and Duke, 1971), and rely on fat reserves (Merson et al., 1978). Furthermore, *Tamiasciurus* in coniferous forests larderhoard food reserves to survive periods of available energy shortage. These behavioral and physiological adaptations to seasonal food shortages provide an alternative to the direct avoidance strategy of hibernation used by ground squirrels.

Two models were proposed for the evolution of sociality in the ground-dwelling squirrels. Michener (1983, 1984) presented a verbal model, the Association Model, proposing that the proximate mechanism leading to increased levels of sociality was the overlap in active seasons between adults and subadults. Seasonal coincidence is thought to enable the development of social tolerance that promotes the development of groups when group-living has adaptive value. The most highly social species are characterized by greater coincidence in the overlap of adult and subadult active seasons including complete coincidence of the age classes in the highly social black-tailed prairie dog (Michener, 1983). Armitage (1981) proposed the Life-History Tactic (LHT) Model that views sociality as a life-history tactic in ground squirrels that is related to body-size energetics and resource availability. Sociality is predicted by a multiple regression model:

$$\textit{Sociality} = 0.62 + 2.31\ \textit{Age of first reproduction} - 0.84\ \textit{Age at which adult weight is reached;}\quad R^2 = 0.686$$

Therefore, species that reach adult size in the first year of life due to small adult size, high growth rates, or long active season are less social because mature juveniles disperse; most chipmunks (tribe Tamini), among the smallest of the sciurids and small bodied ground squirrels, appear to fit this prediction (Armitage, 1981).

Heaney (1984) first suggested the linkage between tree squirrel and ground squirrel biology. By applying the LHT Model to a hypothetical, typical tree squirrel, Heaney calculated that tree squirrels have a Sociality index = 1.74, suggesting that tree squirrels such as *Tamiasciurus* and *Sciurus* are "individualistic" or "aggregate in favorable habitat but live individually" (Armitage, 1981). This level of sociality appears to correspond well with the scant data on tree squirrel sociality (Heaney, 1984). Although both models of sociality (Armitage, 1981; Michener, 1983, 1984) predict some degree of complex sociality when applied to tree squirrels, the inferred degree of sociality is quite different. While the LHT Model predicts only moderate levels of sociality, the Association Model predicts that all tree squirrels should be highly social because temporal overlap between the active seasons of adults and juveniles is complete. The Association Model is of little predictive value and overestimates the sociality of most tree squirrels. While overlap between successive generations is an obvious requirement for sociality, coincidence between the active seasons of adults and juveniles, in itself, is not likely the most influential variable on the formation of interactive social units.

Behavioral and physiological plasticity appears the rule among tree squirrels. In addition to the incredible variation in home range/territory size that may occur in different habitats, body size and reproductive maturity are especially plastic in the tree squirrels. Age at first reproduction among tree squirrels is extremely variable within a species and depends heavily upon the availability of resources (reviewed in Gurnell, 1987). Although individuals in many populations are capable of reproducing at 1 year of age, delayed reproduction to greater than 2 years of age is not uncommon in high density or poor quality habitats for *Sciurus* (Harnishfeger et al., 1978; Koprowski, 1991*a;* Taylor, 1969) or for some populations of red squirrels (Larsen and Boutin, 1994). In addition, following an excellent mast year, individuals may reproduce as early as 6 months of age (Smith and Barkalow, 1967). The LHT Model as applied by Heaney (1984) predicted low levels of sociality for squirrels, but underestimated the formation of social units in eastern gray squirrels (Koprowski, 1996). However, Heaney (1984) used a liberal estimate of 0.85 for the age of first reproduction. During my 4 year study (Koprowski, 1991*a*), only 2 of 42 female eastern gray squirrels reproduced as early as 1.5 yr old in a high quality woodlot with densities exceeding 10 squirrels/ha; substituting an age of first reproduction of 1.5 yr, the LHT Model predicts that the sociality index of eastern gray squirrels in this population should be 3.25. This result correctly predicts that an increased level of sociality is expected among eastern gray squirrels and that females might share nests as occurs in ground squirrels with a sociality index level of 4. Similarly, the comparatively high levels of sociality that were observed in certain local populations, such as communal nesting of *S. carolinensis* in England (Taylor, 1969) and formation of kin clusters in *T. hudsonicus* (Larsen and Boutin, 1994), were associated with delayed age of first reproduction as the LHT Model predicts.

A difficulty in the application of the sociality index of Armitage (1981) is that the index levels 3-5 incorporate male tactics observed in ground squirrels but do not allow sufficiently for differing levels of sociality among females. For instance, progressing from level 2 to level 3 does not involve any change in the organization of females; however, females begin to share nests in the progression from levels 3-4. Female gray squirrels form interactive social units and share nests; however, because males are not territorial (Taylor, 1969; Thompson, 1978; Gurnell, 1987) and remain socially separate from adult females (Koprowski, 1996), gray squirrels do not fully fit the descriptions of ground squirrel sociality for any level higher than 2 where females aggregate but do not share nests. Armitage (1981) stated that "This sociality index is admittedly a first approximation, but the data available do not permit a more refined index." By excluding males and modifying the sociality index to express the grouping patterns of females with a range from solitary to aggregate to sharing dens to cooperating within groups, the sociality index would more accurately reflect the trends in the fundamental social unit of the Sciuridae (including the tree squirrels), the female-female bond. The LHT Model of Armitage (1981) appears to have the potential for wider taxonomic application to investigating the role of ecological constraints such as marked seasonality on the evolution of sociality. Due to the exceptional plasticity in behavior and ecology that is related to resource availability and the marked sexual conflict in the strategies for reproductive success among the sexes, tree squirrels hold immense potential for providing insight into the evolution of animal social and mating systems.

ACKNOWLEDGMENTS

This paper is dedicated to the memory of the late W.D. Klimstra who fanned my interest in the ecology of tree squirrels and taught me the need to 'know the study organism'. Kenneth B. Armitage provided stimulating discussions on the evolution and classification of sociality in the squirrels. The National Geographic Society (NGS 5176-94), Southwest Parks and Monuments Association, and Atkinson Fund of Willamette University graciously funded portions of my research. Carol Kruse, Alan Whalon, and the staff of the Chiricahua National Monument provided cooperation and logistic support for my studies on *Sciurus nayaritensis*. I thank A. Baty, J. Brouhard, T. Cervenak, M. Corse, S. Hayden, M. Kneeland, N. Koprowski, Z. Koprowski, N. Michel, L. Nelson, and N. Rodriquez for assistance in the field.

LITERATURE CITED

ADAMS, C. E. 1976. Measurement and characteristics of fox squirrel, *Sciurus niger rufiventer*, home ranges. The American Midland Naturalist, 95:211-215.

ALEXANDER, R. D., and G. BORGIA. 1979. On the origin and basis of the male-female phenomenon. Pp. 417-440, *in* Sexual selection and reproductive competition in insects (M. S. Blum and N. A. Blum, eds.). Academic Press, New York, 463 pp.

ALLEN, D. S., and W. P. ASPEY. 1986. Determinants of social dominance in eastern gray squirrels (*Sciurus carolinensis*): a quantitative assessment. Animal Behaviour, 34:81-89.

ANDREWS, R.V., D. PHILLIPS, and D. MAKIHARA. 1987. Metabolic and thermoregulatory consequences of social behaviors between *Microtus townsendii*. Comparative Biochemistry and Physiology, A, 87:345-348

ARBETAN, P. 1993. The mating system of the red squirrel, *Tamiasciurus hudsonicus*. Ph.D. dissertation., University of Kansas, Lawrence, 102 pp.

ARMITAGE, K.B. 1981. Sociality as a life history tactic of ground squirrels. Oecologia (Berlin), 48:36-49.

_____. 1986. Marmot polygyny revisited: determinants of male and female reproductive strategies. Pp. 303-331, *in* Ecological aspects of social evolution (D. S. Rubenstein and R. W. Wrangham, eds.). Princeton University Press, Princeton, New Jersey 551 pp.

_____. 1987. Social dynamics of mammals: Reproductive success, kinship and individual fitness. Trends in Ecology and Evolution, 2:279-284.

_____. 1988. Resources and social organization of ground-dwelling squirrels. Pp. 131-155, *in* Ecology of social behavior (C. N. Slobodchikoff and P. W. Waser, eds.). Academic Press, New York, 429 pp.

_____. 1989. The function of kin discrimination. Ethology Ecology & Evolution, 1:111-121.

BENSON, B. N. 1980. Dominance relationships, mating behaviour and scent marking in fox squirrels (*Sciurus niger*). Mammalia, 44:143-160.

BERNARD, R. J. 1972. Social organization of the western fox squirrel. M.S. thesis, Michigan State University, East Lansing, 41 pp.

BLACK, C.C. 1972. Holarctic evolution and dispersal of squirrels (Rodentia:Sciuridae). Evolutionary Biology, 6:305-322.

BOUTIN, S., Z. TOOZE, and K. PRICE. 1993. Postbreeding dispersal by female red squirrels (*Tamiasciurus hudsonicus*). Behavioral Ecology, 4:151-155.

CHRISTISEN, D. M. 1985. Seasonal tenancy of artificial nest structures for tree squirrels. Transactions of the Missouri Academy of Science, 19:41-48.

CLUTTON-BROCK, T. H. (ed.). 1988*a*. Reproductive Success. The University of Chicago Press, Chicago, 538 pp.

_____. 1988*b*. Reproductive success. Pp. 472-486, *in* Reproductive success (T. H. Clutton- Brock, ed.). The University of Chicago Press, Chicago, 538 pp.

CLUTTON-BROCK, T. H., and A. C. J. VINCENT. 1991. Sexual selection and the potential reproductive rates of males and females. Nature, 351:58-60.

CORDES, C. L., and F. S. BARKALOW, JR. 1972. Home range and dispersal in a North Carolina gray squirrel population. Proceedings of the Southeast Association of Game and Fish Commissioners, 26:124-135.

CROSS, S. P. 1969. Behavioral aspects of western gray squirrel ecology. Ph.D. dissertation., University of Arizona, Tucson, 168 pp.

DEUTCH, R. S. 1978. Seasonal activity budget of the red squirrel (*Tamiasciurus hudsonicus*) in a southern Ohio deciduous forest. M.S. thesis, University of Dayton, Ohio 84 pp.

DOEBEL, J. H., and B. S. MCGINNES. 1974. Home range and activity of a gray squirrel population. The Journal of Wildlife Management, 38:860-867.

DOWNHOWER, J. F., and K. B. ARMITAGE. 1971. The yellow-bellied marmot and the evolution of polygamy. The American Naturalist, 105:355-370.

EMRY, R. J., and R. W. THORINGTON, JR. 1982. Descriptive and comparative osteology of the oldest fossil squirrel, *Protosciurus* (Rodentia: Sciuridae). Smithsonian Contributions in Paleobiology, 47:1-35.

FARENTINOS, R. C. 1972*a*. Nests of the tasseleared squirrel. Journal of Mammalogy, 53:900-903.

———. 1972*b*. Social dominance and mating activity in the tassel-eared squirrel (*Sciurus abertiferreus*). Animal Behaviour, 20:316-326.

———. 1979. Seasonal changes in home range size of tassel-eared squirrels (*Sciurus aberti*). The

Southwestern Naturalist, 24:49-62.

———. 1980. Sexual solicitation of subordinate males by female tassel-eared squirrels (*Sciurus aberti*). Journal of Mammalogy, 61:337-341.

FLYGER, V. F. 1960. Movement and home range of the gray squirrel (*Sciurus carolinensis*) in two Maryland woodlots. Ecology, 41:365-369.

FOSTER, S. A. 1992. Studies of ecological factors that affect the population and distribution of the western gray squirrel in northcentral Oregon. Ph.D. dissertation, Portland State University, Oregon, 154 pp.

GILMAN, K. N. 1986. The western gray squirrel (*Sciurus griseus*), its summer home range, activity times, and habitat usage in northern California. M.S. thesis, California State University, Sacramento, 71 pp.

GURNELL, J. C. 1984. Home range, territoriality, caching behaviour and food supply of the 'red squirrel (*Tamiasciurus hudsonicus fremonti*) in a subalpine pine forest. Animal Behaviour, 32:1119-1131.

———. 1987. The natural history of squirrels. Facts on File, New York, 201 pp.

HAFNER, D. J. 1984. Evolutionary relationships of the Nearctic Sciuridae. Pp. 3-23, *in* The biology of ground-dwelling squirrels (J. O. Murie and G. R. Michener, eds.). University of Nebraska Press, Lincoln, 459 pp.

HALLORAN, M. E. 1993. Social behavior and ecology of Abert Squirrels (*Sciurus aberti*). Ph.D. dissertation, University of Colorado, Boulder, 210 pp.

HAMILTON, W. D. 1964. The genetical theory of social behavior I, II. Journal of Theoretical Biology, 7:1-52.

HARNISHFEGER, R. L., J. L. ROSEBERRY, and W. D. KLIMSTRA. 1978. Reproductive levels in unexploited woodlot fox squirrels. Transactions of the Illinois State Academy of Science, 71:342-355.

HAVERA, S. P. 1979. Temperature variation in a fox squirrel nest box. The Journal of Wildlife Management, 43:251-253.

HAVERA, S. P., and C. M. NIXON. 1978. Interaction among adult female fox squirrels during the winter breeding season. Transactions of the Illinois State Academy of Science, 71:24-38.

HEANEY, L. R. 1984. Climatic influences on the life-history tactics and behavior of North American tree squirrels. Pp. 43-78, *in* The biology of ground-dwelling Squirrels (J. O. Murie and G. R. Michener, eds.). University of Nebraska Press, Lincoln, 459 pp.

HEANEY, L. R., and R. W. THORINGTON. 1978. Ecology of neotropical red-tailed squirrels, *Sciurus granatensis*, in the Panama Canal Zone. Journal of Mammalogy, 59:846-851.

HOFFMEISTER, D. F. 1986. Mammals of Arizona. University of Arizona Press, Tucson, 602 pp.

HOOGLAND, J. L. 1979. Aggression, ectoparasitism and other possible costs of prairie dog (Sciuridae, *Cynomys* spp.) coloniality. Behaviour, 69:1-35.

———. 1985. Infanticide in prairie dogs: lactating females kill offspring of close kin. Science, 230:1037-1040.

———. 1986. Nepotism in prairie dogs (*Cynomys ludovicianus*) varies with competition but not with kinship. Animal Behaviour, 34:263-270.

HRDY, S. B., and G. C. WILLIAMS. 1983. Behavioural biology and the double standard. Pp. 3-17, *in* Social behavior of female vertebrates (S. K. Wasser, ed.). Academic Press, New York, 399 pp.

INGLES, L. G. 1947. Ecology and life history of the California gray squirrel. California Fish and Game, 33:139-158.

KANTOLA, A. T., and S. R. HUMPHREY. 1990. Habitat use by Sherman's fox squirrel (*Sciurus niger shermani*) in Florida. Journal of Mammalogy, 71:411-419.

KENWARD, R. E. 1985. Ranging behaviour and population dynamics in grey squirrels. Symposium of the British Ecological Society, 25:319-330.

KLEIMAN, D. G. 1977. Monogamy in mammals. Quarterly Review of Biology, 52:39-69.

KLENNER, W., and C. J. KREBS. 1991. Red squirrel population dynamics. I. The effect of supplemental food on demography. Journal of Animal Ecology, 60:961-978.

KOFORD, R. R. 1982. Mating system of a territorial tree squirrel (*Tamiasciurus douglasii*) in California. Journal of Mammalogy, 63:274-283.

KOPROWSKI, J. L. 1991*a*. The evolution of sociality in tree squirrels: the comparative behavioral ecology of fox squirrels and eastern gray squirrels. Ph.D. dissertation, University of Kansas, Lawrence, 116 pp.

———. 1991*b*. Response of fox squirrels and gray squirrels to a late spring-early summer food shortage. Journal of Mammalogy, 72:367-372.

———. 1992. Removal of copulatory plugs by female tree squirrels. Journal of Mammalogy, 73:572-576.

———. 1993*a*. Alternative reproductive tactics in male eastern gray squirrels: "making the best of a bad job." Behavioral Ecology, 4:165-171.

———. 1993*b*. Behavioral tactics, dominance, and copulatory success among male fox squirrels. Ethology, Ecology & Evolution, 5:169-176.

———. 1993*c*. The role of kinship in field interactions of juvenile gray squirrels. Canadian Journal of Zoology, 71:224-226.

———. 1993*d*. Do estrous female gray squirrels, *Sciurus carolinensis*, advertise their receptivity? The Canadian Field-Naturalist, 106:392-394.

———. 1996. Natal philopatry, communal nesting, and kinship in fox squirrels and gray squirrels. Journal of Mammology, 77:1006-1016

LARSEN, K. W., and S. BOUTIN. 1994. Movements, survival, and settlement of red squirrel (*Tamiasciurus hudsonicus*) offspring. Ecology, 75:214-223.

LAYNE, J. N. 1954. The biology of the red squirrel, *Tamiasciurus hudsonicus loquax* (Bangs), in central New York. Ecological Monographs, 24:227-267.

LAYNE, J. N., and M. A. V. RAYMOND. 1994. Communal nesting of southern flying squirrels in Florida. Journal of Mammalogy, 75:110-120.

MADISON, D. M. 1984. Group nesting and its ecological and evolutionary significance in overwintering rodents. Pp. 267-274, *in* Winter ecology of small mammals (J. F. Merrit, ed.) Special Publication, Carnegie Museum of Natural History, 10:1-380

MASER, C., R. ANDERSON, and E. L. BULL. 1981. Aggregation and sex segregation in northern flying squirrels in northeastern Oregon, an observation. The Murrelet, 62:54-55.

MCGUIRE, R. J., and L. N. BROWN. 1975. Field ecology of the exotic red-bellied squirrel in Florida. Journal of Mammalogy, 56:405-419.

MERSON, M. H., C. J. COWLES, and R. L. KIRKPATRICK. 1978. Characteristics of captivegray squirrels exposed to cold and food deprivation. The Journal of Wildlife Management, 42:202-205.

MICHENER, G. R. 1983. Kin identification, matriarchies, and the evolution of sociality in ground-dwelling sciurids. Special Publication, The American Society of Mammalogists, Pp. 528-572, *in* Recent advances in the study of mammalian behavior (J. F. Eisenberg and D. G. Kleiman, eds.). Special Publication, The American Society of Mammologists, 7: 1-753.

———. 1984. Age, sex, and species differences in the annual cycles of ground-dwelling sciurids: implications for sociality. Pp. 81-107, *in* The biology of ground-dwelling squirrels (J. O. Murie and G. R. Michener, eds.). University of Nebraska Press, Lincoln, 459 pp.

MONTGOMERY, S. D., J. B. WHELAN, and H. S. MOSBY. 1975. Bioenergetics of a woodlot gray squirrel population. The Journal of Wildlife Management, 39:709-717.

PACK, J. C., H. S. MOSBY, and P. B. SIEGEL. 1967. Influence of social hierarchy on gray squirrel behavior. The Journal of Wildlife Management, 31:720-728.

PAULS, R. W. 1981. Energetics of the red squirrel: a laboratory study of the effects of temperature seasonal acclimatization, use of rest and exercise. Journal of Thermal Biology, 6:79-86.

PESCE, A. 1982. Dynamics of a non-territorial population of red squirrels (*Tamiasciurus hudsonicus*) in southeastern Michigan. M.S. thesis, University of Michigan, Ann Arbor, 58 pp.

PRICE, K., and S. BOUTIN. 1993. Territorial bequeathal by red squirrel mothers. Behavioral Ecology, 4:144-150.

PULLIAINEN, E. 1973. Winter ecology of the red squirrel (*Sciurus vulgaris* L.) in northeastern Lapland. Annales Zoologica Fennici, 10:437-494.

SHERMAN, P. W. 1981. Kinship, demography, and Belding's ground squirrel nepotism. Behavioral Ecology and Sociobiology, 8:251-259.

SHORT, H. L., and W. B. DUKE. 1971. Seasonal food consumption and body weights of captive tree squirrels. The Journal of Wildlife Management, 35:435-439.

SMITH, C.C. 1968. The adaptive nature of social organization in the genus of tree squirrels *Tamiasciurus*. Ecological Monographs, 38:31-63.

———. 1981. The indivisible niche of *Tamiasciurus*: an example of nonpartitioning of resources. Ecological Monographs, 51:343-363.

SMITH, N. B., and F. S. BARKALOW, JR. 1967. Precocious breeding in the gray squirrel. Journal of Mammalogy, 48:328-330.

SULLIVAN, T. P. 1990. Responses of red squirrel (*Tamiasciurus hudsonicus*) populations to supplemental food. Journal of Mammalogy, 71:579-590.

TAYLOR, J.C. 1969. Social structure and behaviour in a grey squirrel population. Ph.D. dissertation, University of London, London, United Kingdom, 217 pp.

THOMPSON, D. C. 1977. Reproductive behavior of the grey squirrel. Canadian Journal of Zoology, 55:1176-1184.

____. 1978. The social system of the grey squirrel. Behaviour, 64:305-328.

WAUTERS, L., and A. A. DHONDT. 1990*a*. Nest-use by red squirrels (*Sciurus vulgaris* Linnaeus, 1758). Mammalia, 54:377-389.

———. 1990*b*. Factors affecting male mating success in red squirrels (*Sciurus vulgaris*). Ethology Ecology & Evolution, 2:195-204.

———. 1992. Spacing behaviour of red squirrels, *Sciurus vulgaris*: variation between habitats and the sexes. Animal Behaviour, 43:297-311.

WEIGL, P. D., M. A. STEELE, L. J. SHERMAN, J. C. HA, and T. L. SHARPE. 1989. The ecology of the fox squirrel (*Sciurus niger*) in North Carolina: implications for survival in the southeast. Bulletin of Tall Timbers Research Station 24:1-93.

WILLIAMS, G. C. 1966. Adaptation and natural selection. Princeton University Press, Princeton, New Jersy, 305 pp.

WYNNE-EDWARDS, V. C. 1962. Animal dispersion in relation to social behavior. Oliver and Boyd, Edinburgh, 653 pp.

THE USE OF DNA FINGERPRINTING IN DETERMINING THE MATING SYSTEM AND REPRODUCTIVE SUCCESS IN A POPULATION OF THE INTRODUCED GRAY SQUIRREL, *SCIURUS CAROLINENSIS*, IN SOUTHERN ENGLAND

ZOË K. DAVID-GRAY, JOHN GURNELL, AND DAVID M. HUNT

School of Biological Sciences, Queen Mary and Westfield College, University of London, Mile End Road, London, E1 4NS, U.K. (ZKD-G, JG) and Department of Molecular Genetics, Institute of Ophthalmology, University of London, Bath Street, London, EC1V 9EL, U.K. (DMH)

ABSTRACT.—Gray squirrels *(Sciurus carolinensis)*, and other species belonging to the same genus, generally exhibit dominance hierarchies among both males and females, and adopt a promiscuous mating strategy. However, little information is available concerning how dominance translates into reproductive success or indeed on the normal levels of genetic variation within a population. Here we report on preliminary studies of gray squirrels in southern England. This species was first introduced to England and Wales from eastern North America in 1876. We used multilocus DNA fingerprinting techniques to concentrate on three particular questions. What is the mean background band-sharing coefficient among unrelated individuals? What is the Mendelian inheritance of bands and band-sharing coefficients between parents and offspring? We investigated this using captive breeding populations established with unrelated individuals in the summer of 1993. Further, we asked, what is the reproductive success of individuals in a free-ranging population over one breeding season? Here, the population living in an oak wood was studied from March to July 1993 using capture-mark-recapture techniques. The spatial distribution of the home ranges of adults and juveniles have been used as an aid to identifying putative mothers and fathers.

INTRODUCTION.

Gray squirrels *(Sciurus carolinensis)* were introduced from North America to England and Wales several times between 1876 and 1929. They subsequently spread throughout much of England and parts of Wales and Scotland (Gurnell and Pepper, 1993). Gray squirrels and other species within the genus *Sciurus*, do not defend exclusive territories but have overlapping home range systems. Range size is affected by population density, food supply and type of habitat (Don, 1983; Gurnell, 1983, 1987; Kenward, 1985), and also by sex, age and season (Thompson, 1978; Don, 1983; Kenward, 1985). Behavioral observations have shown that a dominance hierarchy exists within the social system of squirrels and that social rank is related to weight, sex and age (Taylor, 1966; Pack et al., 1967; Thompson, 1977; Wauters and Dhondt, 1985; Allen and Aspey, 1986). The hierarchies are linear with older heavier males dominant over females and subadult males and older females dominant over subadults of both sexes, although the spatial extent over which one particular hierarchy operates within a forest is not always clear.

This dominance hierarchy means that individuals of lower rank will have reduced access to limited resources such as food and mates. Reproductive behavior for both males and females requires a considerable amount of energy, and apparently female squirrels must reach a weight threshold before they come into breeding condition (Wauters and Dhondt, 1989). Work by Gurnell (1981) on a gray squirrel population in southern England showed that in years with a poor seed crop and consequently a very restricted food supply, no

In M.A. Steele, J. F. Merritt, and D. A. Zegers (eds.). 1998. Ecology and Evolutionary Biology of Tree Squirrels. Special Publication, Virginia Museum of Natural History, 6: 320 pp

breeding occurred. Competition between individuals is affected by age and weight; heavier, older animals are dominant and this status affords them greater foraging efficiency than subordinates (Wauters and Dhondt, 1989). Dominant animals come into breeding condition earlier and are therefore likely to obtain higher numbers of matings (Gurnell, 1987).

If food supplies are plentiful, females will come into estrus and mating will occur between December and February. Gestation lasts for 7 weeks and pregnant females are present in the population between February and April. The duration of lactation is 10 weeks with lactating females appearing between March and June. Juveniles appear in the population between April and June. As juveniles approach weaning, they forage within their mothers' home range. Gull (1977) found that juvenile gray squirrels had a range of 0.45 ha in early summer, increasing to 4 ha by late summer, and that the range overlap between mother and young decreased from 91 to 54% during this period. Dominant male gray squirrels are believed to show high site fidelity, remaining in the same area of woodland for the duration of the breeding season and maybe for life (Gurnell, 1987). It is therefore assumed that fathers of the offspring are likely to be local males, although it is known that males can substantially expand their home ranges during the breeding season, particularly in the summer (Kenward, 1985).

Prior to mating, gray squirrels engage in a mating chase. Field observations by Taylor (1966), Pack et al.(1967) and Thompson (1977), showed the dominant male at the head of the chase with subordinate males behind, and that in almost all cases the dominant male eventually mated with the female. However, recent studies by Wauters et al.(1990) and Koprowski (1993), have shown that this situation is complicated by the presence of satellite males obtaining sneaky matings, and females removing copulatory plugs to mate with multiple males (Koprowski, 1992). Estrus is asynchronous in female gray squirrels and this provides the potential for dominant males to monopolize the matings within the local population. The presence of males in breeding condition seems to be necessary to bring the female into estrus (Webley and Johnson, 1983), whereas olfactory cues from the females elicit pre-chase behavior in males for several days before the onset of estrus (Thompson, 1977). This enables males to determine the time when females come into estrus.

If a dominance hierarchy is operating, how does this translate into reproductive success? The objective of this study was to determine whether all or most of the offspring within the local population were fathered by one male or several different males. The mating system within a species is usually determined by behavioral observations. However, recent studies (Westneat, 1990; Birkhead et al., 1990; Rabenold et al., 1990; Pemberton et al., 1991) have shown that the calculated reproductive success of individuals based on behavioral observations is often incorrect when compared to results from DNA fingerprinting.

The discovery of multilocus DNA fingerprinting in humans (Jeffreys et al., 1985*a,b*) and its subsequent successful application to a wide variety of other species (Burke and Bruford, 1987; Jeffreys and Morton, 1987; Amos et al., 1991; Gilbert et al., 1991; Pemberton et al., 1991; Ribble, 1991) has enabled the parentage of offspring to be accurately determined. DNA fingerprinting technology is based on polymorphisms found within non-coding 'minisatellite' DNA (Jeffreys et al., 1985*a*). Minisatellites consist of a core sequence of 10-15 base pairs repeated tandemly, and are highly polymorphic due to allelic variation in the repeat copy number of the core sequence (Jeffreys et al., 1985*a*). DNA fingerprints have two main properties: (1) the bands are inherited in a Mendelian fashion with each polymorphic band in an offspring present in at least one parent, and (2) the banding pattern is individual specific, such that the probability that two unrelated individuals share the same banding pattern is generally many orders of magnitude smaller than the reciprocal of the population.

In this study, we have used DNA fingerprinting as a tool to infer parent-offspring and sibling or half-sibling relationships. Because behavioral observation data were not available, the conditions under which DNA fingerprinting are used were not ideal. Relatedness between individuals is determined by high band-sharing coefficients; that is, relatives share greater numbers of fingerprint bands than non-relatives. In the absence of segregation data, other studies (e.g., Westneat, 1990; Pemberton et al., 1991; Quinn et al., 1994) have used a band-sharing analysis based on the observed distribution of band-sharing values between relatives and non-relatives. In our study a 2 x 2 chi-squared contingency table, with adjusted expected frequencies based on band-sharing between unrelated individuals, was used to test for significance of band-sharing coefficients

(Quinn et al., 1994). Any individuals in pairwise comparisons which gave high band-sharing coefficients were assumed to be related if the band-sharing coefficient was found to be statistically significantly higher than expected by chance in the study population.

MATERIALS AND METHODS

Study site.—Work was carried out in Alice Holt forest near Farnham, on the borders of Hampshire and Surrey in southern England. The study area was a 9 ha mature oak (*Quercus robur*) woodland with some mature beech (*Fagus sylvatica*), sweet chestnut (*Castanea sativa*), and with a hazel (*Corylus avellana*) and hawthorn (*Crataegus monogyna*) understory (Gurnell, 1996).

Sample methods.—Squirrels were trapped throughout one breeding season from March to July 1993. There were 14 trapping points throughout the compartment. At each point, a Legg multicapture trap was pre-baited for 5 days prior the commencement of trapping, and animals were trapped for one week in every month (March–July 1993) with two trap inspections each day (am and pm). Each animal was weighed, sexed and given a unique toe clip mark. The toe clippings were immediately placed in liquid nitrogen, and then stored in -80°C freezer for later extraction of DNA. A total of 87 animals were captured: 43 adult breeding males, 16 adult breeding females, 15 sexually immature subadults and 13 spring born juveniles (identified by weight and pelage). Throughout the trapping period, the breeding status of each animal was recorded (pregnancy or lactation in females and testes size in males). This information was later used in conjunction with age characteristics, to assess the likelihood of individuals being putative parents.

DNA fingerprint methods.—Genomic DNA was extracted from toe clips by grinding in liquid nitrogen before adding to an extraction buffer (0.025M EDTA,1.5M NaCl). Proteinase K (400µg/ml) and SDS (0.5%/ml) were then added and samples incubated overnight at 50°C. The samples were extracted with phenol (pH 8.0) once, an equal volume of phenol:chloroform-isoamyl alcohol (24:1) twice and chloroform-isoamyl alcohol once. DNA was then precipitated with ethanol and samples dissolved in water. Approximately 10µg DNA was digested with HINF I (Pharmacia) using manufacturer's buffer in the presence of 10mM spermadine (Sigma). Digests were extracted once with phenol:chloroform-isoamyl alcohol, precipitated with ethanol and resuspended in 17µl water. Electrophoresis was carried out in a 20 x 25cm gel tank using 0.8% agarose (Sigma) in TBE buffer (0.0089M Tris, 0.089M Boric acid, 2mM EDTA, pH 8.0) at 40 volts for 40 hours or until the 3kb marker had reached approximately 20cm. Prior to loading samples, 10µg of an internal marker was added to each sample. The internal marker consisted of lambda DNA digested with *Bst* YI (New England biolabs), and allowed for the accurate calculation of 8DNA fingerprint fragment sizes after reprobing the filters with [α^{32}P]dCTP, (6000µCi/mmol, Amersham) labelled DNA. After electrophoresis, gels were depurinated using 0.25M HCl for 7.5 minutes (x2), then denatured using 0.5M NaOH; 1M NaCl for 15 minutes (x2) and finally neutralised using 1M Tris; 3M NaCl pH 7.4 for 15 minutes (x2). Gels were capillary blotted overnight in 20 x SSC (3M NaCl; 0.3M Tri-sodium citrate, pH 7.0) onto Hybond N (Amersham). DNA was bound to the filter by baking at 80°C for 10 minutes followed by UV crosslinking at 70,000 microjoules/cm^{-2} (Amersham). 20ng of the 600 basepair human minisatellite DNA probe, 33.15 (Jeffreys, 1985*a*), was [α^{32}P]dCTP labelled using the random priming method (Feinburg and Vogelstein, 1983). Unincorporated [α^{32}P]dCTP was removed by passing labelled probe through a G50 Sephadex column. Filters were prehybridized overnight at 65°C in 0.25M phosphate buffer, 7% SDS, 0.1mM EDTA, 1% BSA (Church and Gilbert, 1984), then hybridized overnight in the same solution at 62°C. After hybridization, filters were washed at 62°C once for 15 minutes in 0.25M phosphate buffer, 1% SDS, then twice for 20 minutes in 2 x SSC, 0.1% SDS. Filters were exposed to BetaMax Hyperfilm (Amersham) for 3-7 days with intensifying screens at -80°C. After adequate exposure, the probe was removed from the filter by soaking in 0.1% SDS, 0.1X SSC, then rehybridized using [α^{32}P]dCTP labelled lambda DNA.

Band scoring.—The 33.15 probe autorad was overlaid on to the lambda DNA autorad and bands were scored within the 3-23kb range. For each sample, internal lambda DNA markers were used to accurately determine band sizes and avoid the problem of uneven separation of samples in different lanes of the electrophoresis gel. The intensity of the band was visually confirmed before a match was declared.

Segregation analysis.—When attempting parental analysis using DNA fingerprinting, a segregation analysis should be carried out on a large pedigree, with mother, father and 8 or more offspring, in order to establish that bands are independently inherited and that no linkage disequilibrium is occurring (Bruford et al., 1992). To that end, captive breeding colonies of gray squirrels were established in three large, squirrel escape proof enclosures at Alice Holt forest during December 1992. The two smaller enclosures, A and B, were stocked with two females and three males and a larger enclosure, C, was stocked with four males and four females. To ensure that the breeding pairs were unrelated, all male animals were obtained from Thetford Forest, 150 miles north of Alice Holt Forest. Supplementary food was provided using feeding hoppers and each animal had access to its own nest box.

Home range analysis.—The trap points of each animal in the wild population were entered into home range analysis software (Biotrack, Wareham, Dorset), and its home range was determined by plotting a minimum area polygon. The home range analysis provided information of the space use of the population throughout one breeding season. Determination of home ranges and home range overlap amongst neighboring squirrels was used as a parameter on which to identify putative parents.

RESULTS

DNA fingerprint analysis.—It was possible to run 18 samples on each gel, allowing us to compare up to 17 potential parents and 1 offspring on each gel. λDNA *Bst* Y1 size markers were run in the first and last lanes. Scoring was carried out under the assumptions that shared bands are always identical alleles from the same locus, that all bands are in linkage equilibrium and that all bands have equal population frequencies.

Background band-sharing.—Determining the levels of band-sharing between unrelated individuals provides a base line from which expected band sharing between relatives can be calculated. Unrelated individuals are expected to share a proportion of bands due to the finite number of alleles at any given locus (Lynch, 1988). The probability of band-sharing, x, is the proportion of bands in an individual that are present in a second random individual, and this was determined by comparing fingerprints of similar intensity run in adjacent lanes (Burke and Bruford, 1987). X was found as the mean of each pairwise comparison of the proportion of individuals a's bands that were matched by a band of similar size and no more than a two fold intensity difference (i.e., the difference between heterozygous and homozygous) in individual b, using the calculation:

$$x=((Nab/Na)+(Nab/Nb)) / 2;$$

where Nab = number of bands of similar intensity and electrophoretic mobility in individuals a and b, Na = total number of bands in a which could be scored if present in b, and Nb = total number of bands in b which could be scored if present in a (Jeffreys et al., 1985*b*; Burke and Bruford, 1987). This provides an index which ranges from 0, no bands are shared to 1(all bands are shared). By carrying out pairwise comparisons amongst 15 unrelated squirrels (*n* = 105) from Alice Holt using minisatellite fragments greater than 3kb , the mean probability (x) of two individuals sharing a band of similar size and intensity was calculated to be 0.240±0.052. This is similar to that found in other species, such as, red deer 0.31(Pemberton et al., 1991), zebra finches 0.16 (Birkhead et al., 1990), banner-tailed kangaroo rats 0.3 (Keane et al., 1991) and California mice 0.16 (Ribble, 1991).

Assuming all alleles to be of equal frequency, the mean allele frequency (q) is found from $x = 2q-q^2$ hence q = 0.13 (Jeffreys et al., 1985*a*). From the mean number of fragments per individual (n) and the mean band-sharing coefficient (x), the probability that two unrelated individuals would have an identical fingerprint is $x^n = 2 \times 10^{-10}$. (Table 1). Based on the mean band-sharing coefficient, it is possible to calculate the expected band-sharing coefficients for different degrees of relatedness using (r), the coefficient of relatedness (Hamilton, 1964). For first order relatives (parents-offspring and full siblings) with a coefficient of relatedness (r) of 0.5, the band-sharing coefficient is 0.24 + (0.76/2) = 0.62. For second order relatives (grandparents-grandchildren, half siblings), where r = 0.25, the band-sharing coefficient is 0.24 + (0.76/4) = 0.43, and for third order relatives (cousins) where r =0.125, the band-sharing coefficient is 0.24 + (0.76/8) = 0.33.

Table 1.—*DNA fingerprint data for adult gray squirrels from the Alice Holt population. Average number of bands scored (±SD) and approximate size range, allele frequency and mean background band-sharing coefficient between unrelated individuals (±SD) are given. DNA digested with Hinf I and probed with Jeffreys 33.15 probe.*

Mean no. bands/ind	15.5 (±4.3) *n* = 15
Size range (kb)	3 - 23
Allele freq. (q)	0.13
Mean unrelated band—sharing coefficient (x).	0.24 (±0.052) *n* = 30

Mendelian inheritance.—Gray squirrels have small litter sizes, typically 1-5 (Gurnell, 1987), and it is thought that females need the presence of more than one male to stimulate breeding (Hampshire, 1985). Sequential litters from monogamous pairs are therefore unobtainable. It was thought that during the course of the study, several litters of mixed parentage would be produced in the three enclosures enabling limited segregation analysis to be performed. However, only enclosure B maintained an isolated population. Two offspring (F1 and 59) were born in this enclosure during the winter breeding season of 1992–1993. DNA fingerprinting of the original founder stock and the offspring revealed the parentage of these offspring (Fig. 1).

The two juveniles F1 and 59 were identified as siblings with a band-sharing coefficient of 0.88. The mother was identified as female E7 based on a band-sharing coefficient of 0.83 with offspring 59 and 0.77 with offspring F1. All these band-sharing coefficients were statistically significant. The remaining female in this enclosure was excluded as she did not become pregnant during the winter breeding season. Of the three potential fathers, male 47 had a band-sharing coefficient of 0.50 with offspring F1, and 0.42 with offspring 59. These values deviate from the theoretically expected values for first order relatives of 0.62. However, all the non-maternal bands found in both offspring matched up with the bands in male 47 and this result was statistically significant. The probability (p) of a different unrelated male possessing all the diagnostic bands (m) is x^m, where x is the band sharing coefficient (Jeffreys et al., 1985*b*). This calculation is an approximation of the probability of false inclusion where $p = 1.9 \times 10^{-4}$ for offspring F1, and 8×10^{-4} for offspring 59. Both of the other males had band sharing coefficients of 0.27 or lower. This work confirmed that bands are inherited in a Mendelian fashion and that parentage can be determined by this method (Table 2).

Band-sharing analysis of a wild population.—We lack any direct observational data on which to propose putative parents in the wild population. However, we have information on home ranges and the spatial relationships among individuals in the population. Further, we have shown that a captive bred family has band-sharing coefficients which are either within or close to the range expected for closely related individuals. First and second order levels of relatedness can be determined therefore using the expected band-sharing coefficients of each relationship. Statistical testing of band-sharing coefficients separates first and

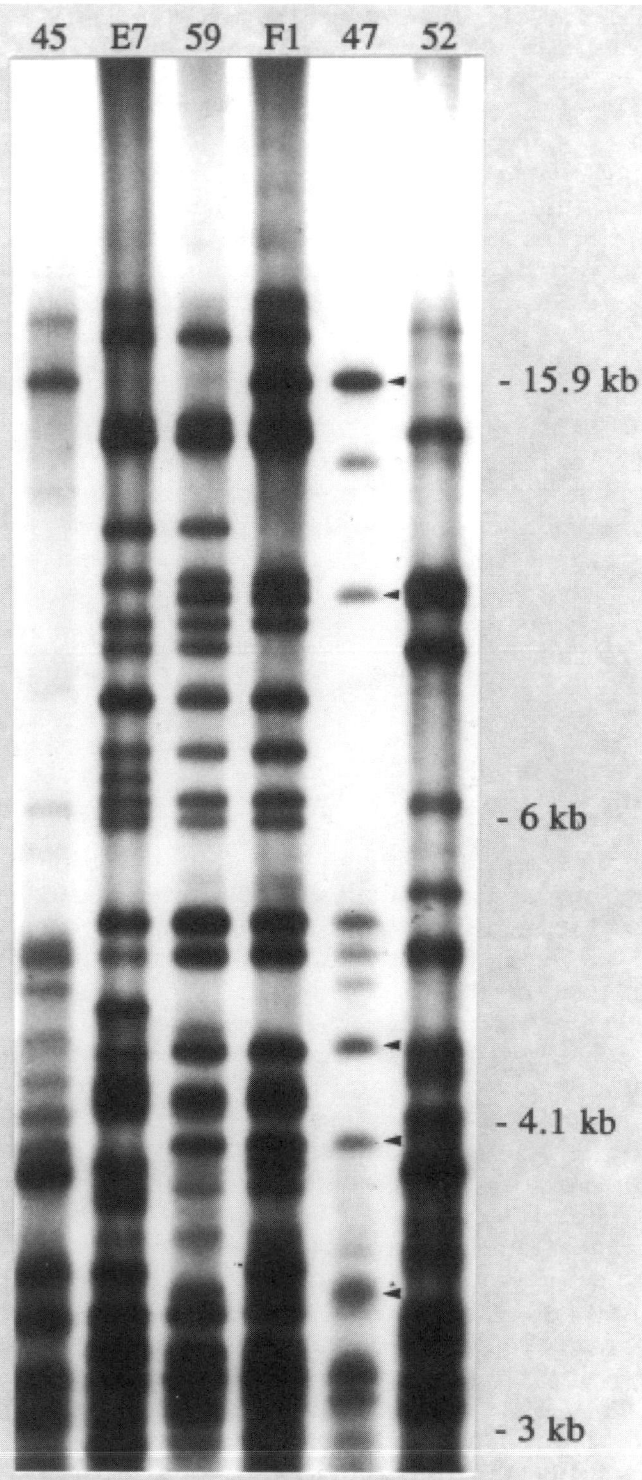

Fig 1.—DNA fingerprints of a captive bred gray squirrel family showing juveniles F1 and 59, female E7 and males 45, 47 and 52. Based on band-sharing coefficients, the juveniles were declared siblings and the female E7 was assigned maternity. Of the three putative fathers, male 47 shared the highest band-sharing coefficients with both juveniles and possessed all the non-maternal specific bands identified in both offspring (arrowed), and was therefore assigned paternity (for band-sharing values see text). DNA was digested with *Hinf* I and probed with Jeffreys 33.15 human minisatellite probe.

Table 2.—*Parentage determination of offspring born in captivity. Band-sharing coefficients between all putative parents and offspring indicate that male 47 and female E7 are the probable parents of juveniles 59 and F1. DNA samples were digested with Hinf I and probed with Jeffreys 33.15 human minisatellite probe. Band-sharing coefficients were derived from pairwise comparisons between individuals as described in methods. The diagonal gives total numbers of bands scored for each individual.*

	Male			Female	Offspring	
	45	52	47	E7	59	F1
45	12	0.26	0.23	0.13	0.065	0.27
52		12	0.13	0.26	0.20	0.20
47			9	0.30	0.42*	0.50**
E7				18	0.83****	0.77****
59					18	0.88****
F1						18

*$P < 0.05$ **$P < 0.025$ ***$P < 0.01$ ****$P < 0.005$

second degree relatives from unrelated animals but it is not possible to distinguish with certainty between first and second degree relatedness, due to the small overlap of band-sharing which has been found between these two groups in other studies (e.g., Westneat, 1990). However, the results of pairwise comparisons between juveniles and potential parents and siblings in this study appear to fit into three distinct classes, those with band-sharing coefficients of ca. 0.60 or over, (6.25% of individuals), those with band-sharing coefficients between 0.43-0.53 (7.5%), and those with band-sharing coefficients below 0.36 (86.25%). There was no overlap between the three groups. The expected band-sharing coefficients represent the number of bands shared on average, and there will obviously be some variation around this value for different degrees of relatedness due to segregation. These groups therefore, approximate well to the expected band-sharing coefficients between 1st order relatives, 2nd order relatives and unrelated animals, respectively.

To date, DNA fingerprint analysis has been completed for 8 of the 13 juveniles and they will be considered here. Using information from home range analyses to determine possible parent-offspring relationships, we ran the 8 juvenile samples on gels with all putative mothers and fathers. The mean number of putative parents overlapping each juvenile was 13.75 (n = 8, SD = 1.85). No adult males had band-sharing coefficients higher than the background band-sharing level (0.240±0.052) with any of the juveniles. This indicates that none of the males whose home ranges overlapped with the juveniles were the fathers. However, juveniles G5 and H2 gave a band-sharing coefficient of 0.61, and female H4 had band-sharing coefficients of 0.70 with juvenile H2, and 0.59 with juvenile G5 (Table 3). These three individuals had band-sharing coefficients either above or very close to the expected range for first order relatives, suggesting that they are mother and two full sibs (Table 3).

Comparisons between juveniles C7, 47 and F6 gave mean band-sharing coefficients of 0.470±0.052 (Table 3). This is above the value expected for second order relatives (0.43), but below that expected for first order relatives (0.62), suggesting they are closely related to each other but are not full sibs. These juveniles, also had mean band-sharing coefficients of 0.480±0.038 with juveniles G5 and H2 who are full sibs to each other. These results would suggest that juveniles C7, 47 and F6 are half sibs to each other and also half sibs of the brother and sister G5 and H2. They must therefore share one parent in common; it cannot be female H4 for three reasons: band-sharing coefficients between female H4 and juveniles C7 and 47 were low (<0.36), implying they were unrelated (no band-sharing coefficient could be calculated between female H4 and juvenile F6 as DNA samples were not run on the same gel): spring litters are the first litters of the year and since all the juveniles are approximately the same age (2-3 months) they cannot be juveniles from a previous litter, and if they were from the same spring litter, the band-sharing coefficients would show that they were full sibs to G5 and H2. This suggests that they are all half sibs related via the same father, who is unidentified. Although they share bands in the range expected of aunts and uncles, their age would preclude them from having that relationship with each other. From this information, we conclude that an unidentified male is the parent of all 5 offspring (Fig 2).

Table 3.—*Band-sharing coefficients between proposed related individuals from the wild study populations. DNA samples were digested with Hinf I and probed with Jeffreys 33.15 human minisatellite probe. Pairwise comparisons were carried out as described in methods. The diagonal gives the total number of bands scored for each individual. N/A = band-sharing coefficient not available.*

	Spring born juveniles								Adult	Subadult
	C7	47	F6	G5	G6	H2	H3	G2	H4	28
C7	14	0.53****	0.45****	0.46**	0.25	0.48****	0.25	0.33	0.34	0.21
47		8	0.43*	0.45****	0.31	0.45****	0.27	0.22	0.36	0.45***
F6			11	0.52*	0.28	0.53*	0.30	0.16	N/A	N/A
G5				12	0.28	0.61***	0.35	0.36	0.59****	0.35
G6					8	0.18	0.19	0.29	N/A	0.52****
H2						10	0.21	0.26	0.70****	0.36
H3							19	0.62**	0.15	N/A
G2								14	0.26	N/A
H4									8	N/A
28										18

$^{*}P < 0.05$ $^{**}P < 0.025$ $^{***}P < 0.01$ $^{****}P < 0.005$.

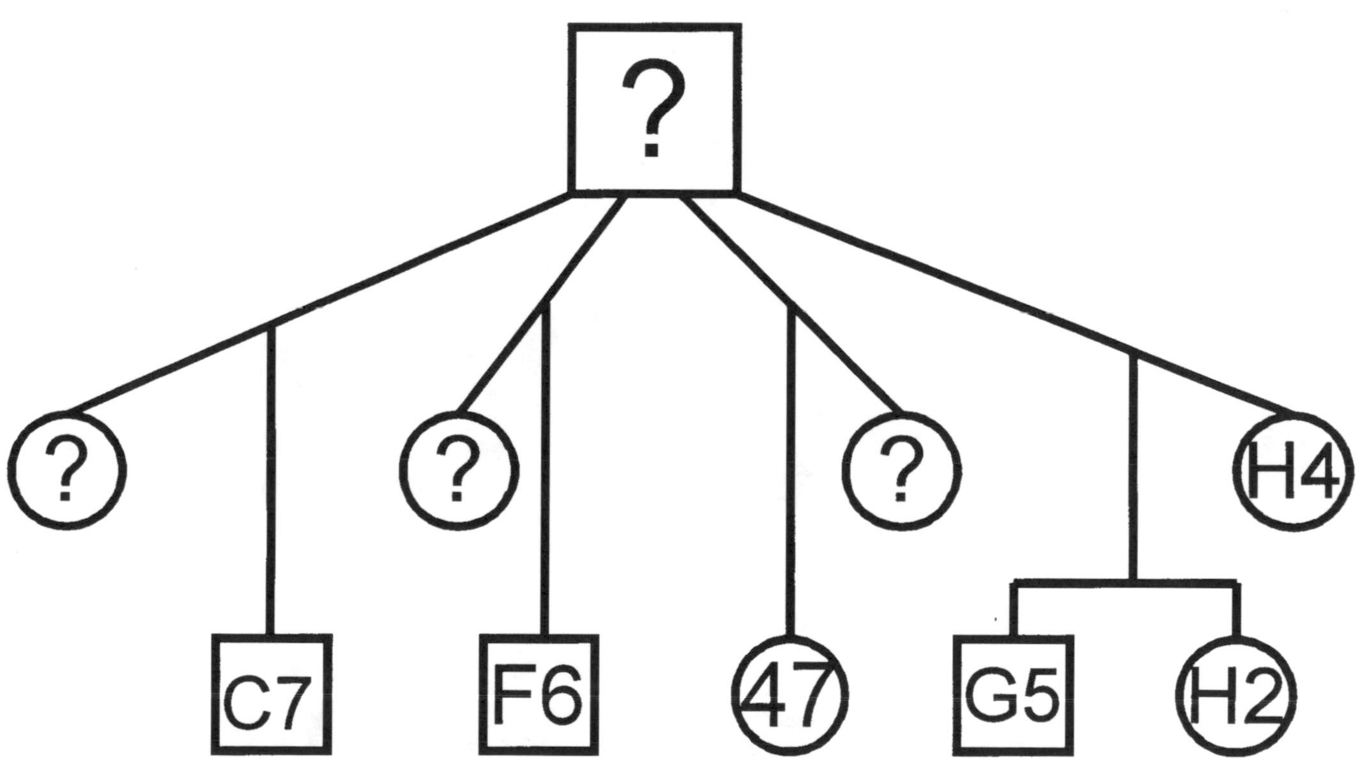

Fig. 2.—Pedigree showing putative half sibling relationships of 5 juveniles in a wild population. Based on band-sharing coefficients, juveniles G5 and H2 were declared full sibs and female H4 was assigned maternity. Juveniles C7, 47 and F6 were declared half sibs to each other and half sibs to juveniles G5 and H2, (for band-sharing values see text). The single putative father and the three putative mothers of juveniles C7, 47 and F6 were not identified.

Of the remaining juveniles investigated, H3 and G2 had a band-sharing coefficient of 0.62 (Table 3), and were considered to be full sibs but were unrelated either to any of the other juveniles, or to any of the other overlapping adults which were included in the analysis. Juvenile G6 appeared to be unrelated to any of the other juveniles or to any of the sexually active males and females. However, this juvenile did have a band-sharing coefficient of 0.52 (Table 3) with subadult female 28. This individual was from a late summer litter of the previous year and had not bred but the band-sharing coefficient suggests that they are related as second order relatives, either as an aunt or as half sibs. Due to the sexual immaturity of this female it would seem unlikely that any of her siblings had become sexually active during the winter breeding season. This means that G6 and female 28 could be half sibs but from different breeding seasons. Juvenile 47 shared band-sharing coefficient of 0.45 with sub adult female 28 but only had a band-sharing coefficient of 0.31 with juvenile G6 (Table 3). So although they both share sufficient bands with 28 to be half sibs, they do not share enough bands with each other to be half sibs; they are therefore unrelated. This situation would arise if the parents of 28 who was born in 1992, mated with different partners in 1993 and from these litters juveniles 47 and G6 were produced. All these proposed relationships between juveniles and adults showed band-sharing levels statistically significantly different from background indicating a high degree of relatedness between these individuals (Table 3).

DISCUSSION

This study demonstrates that populations of introduced gray squirrels in southern England, are genetically highly variable and that DNA fingerprinting is a powerful tool for determining genetic relatedness between individuals. Previously, estimates of individual reproductive success were based on behavioral observation but the methods reported here, provide an independent means of verification and thus increases our knowledge of the variance of mating success found within this species.

By determining the expected band-sharing coefficients for different degrees of relatedness and using chi-square to test for the significance of differences from background, we have been able to show that high levels of band-sharing are not due to chance but are the result of common descent (Quinn et al 1994). Supporting evidence from field data, based on the breeding status of each sexually mature animal and proximity to juveniles, was used as further evidence of the proposed relationship between two individuals. However, in the absence of segregation data, the possibility of linkage disequilibrium among fragments cannot be eliminated (Brock and White, 1991; Hanotte et al., 1992). Furthermore, due to segregation not all individuals who are related will show the theoretically expected band-sharing coefficient and therefore, there are statistical difficulties associated with relatedness based on band-sharing alone (Lynch, 1988; Lynch, 1990; Burke et al., 1991).

Home range overlap was not a good method for identifying putative parents as only one mother of two offspring, female H4 and juveniles G5 and H2, was identified by this method. The ranges of the 5 half sibs, juveniles C7, 47 and F6, had varying degrees of overlap between them (1.9% - 100%), and were localized to one area of woodland. It is possible that the male was local but had a permanent home range in an adjacent area of forest. Adult males have larger home ranges than females and this difference appears to related in some part to breeding activity (Don, 1983). During the breeding season some males can wander well outside their normal home range in search of females in estrus. Kenward (1985) found that males substantially increased their home range size during the summer breeding season. However, this range increase did not always occur during the winter breeding season. This may be attributed to adverse weather conditions restricting foraging behavior. During a mating chase, males from within the local area are attracted to the female by smell, and also by the vocalizations of other males engaged in the chase (Gurnell, 1987). Thompson (1977) found that male gray squirrels are attracted to the mating chase at an average distance of 200m, although one male moved 625m to participate.

Juveniles H3 and G2, who were found to be full sibs had home ranges which overlapped (15%) but had no overlap with any other juveniles. Juvenile G6 had no home range overlap with any other juveniles except subadult 28 (16%), who was thought to be half sibling from the previous breeding season. This provides evidence that different males may be dominant in particular areas of woodland. It is not known over what area of woodland a male may be dominant, and in some species of tree squirrel there appears to be a spatial component to this, with adult males being dominant in some areas of their range but not in others. Koford (1982) showed that in Douglas squirrels, *Tamiasciurus douglasii,* females will mate with animals known to be subordinate to others within her range. However these males exhibited dominance in certain areas within her home range adjacent to their own so they would be dominant in that area but not in others. Farentinos (1972) found that a male was more likely to be dominant if the mating chase was with a female within or near his home range. Work by Wauters et al.(1990), on European red squirrels, *Sciurus vulgaris,* have shown that dominant males at the head of the chase retreated when the chase moved on to a competitors range. The mating chase can be composed of different dominant individuals from the same wood. Some males may therefore be of equal rank (Thompson, 1977). Dominant males may achieve successful matings in some areas but not others; high ranking males who are responsible for most matings therefore have higher reproductive success.

This study also shows that subadult 28 may be related to juveniles 47 and G6 as half sibs but from different breeding seasons. This suggests that the same individual is remaining within the study area and is obtaining matings in subsequent years. However, because the parents are unidentified, it is not possible to determine if they are related via their mother or their father. Although the sample size is small, these results provide further evidence of a polygynous mating system in this species. One male is over-represented as the father of five out of eight juveniles. Although we do not know the ranking of this male, our data support behavioral observations seen in gray squirrels (and other species of this genus), that animals which are dominant within the population obtain significantly higher numbers of matings (Benson, 1980; Koford, 1982, Taylor 1966; Pack, et al., 1967; Thompson, 1977; Wauters et al., 1990).

ACKNOWLEDGMENTS

We would like to thank Harry Pepper and the Wildlife and Conservation section, Forestry Authority, Alice Holt and Tim Venning for all their time and effort in helping establish the captive breeding colonies. Z.K. David-Gray is the recipient of a S.E.R.C. studentship.

LITERATURE CITED

ALLEN D.S., AND W.P. ASPEY. 1986. Determinants of social dominance in eastern grey squirrels (*Sciurus carolinensis)*: a quantitative assessment. Animal Behaviour, 34:81-89.

AMOS, B., J. BARRETT, AND G. DOVER. 1991. Breeding behaviour of pilot whales revealed by DNA fingerprinting. Heredity, 67:49-55.

BENSON, B.N. 1980. Dominance relationships, mating behaviour and scent marking in fox squirrels (*Sciurus niger*). Mammalia, 44:143-60.

BIRKHEAD, T.R., T. BURKE, R. ZANN, F.M. HUNTER, AND A.P. KRUPA. 1990. Extra-pair paternity and intraspecific brood parasitism in wild zebra finches *Taeniopygia guttata,* revealed by DNA fingerprinting. Behavioral Ecology and Sociobiology, 27:315-324.

BROCK, M.K., AND B.N. WHITE. 1991. Multifragment alleles in DNA fingerprints of the Parrot, *Amazona ventralis.* Journal of Heredity, 82:209-212.

BRUFORD, M., O. HANOTTE, J.F.Y. BROOKFIELD, AND T. BURKE. 1992. Single locus and multilocus DNA fingerprinting. Pp. 225-269, *in* Molecular genetic analysis of populations: a practical approach (A. R. Hoelzel, ed.). IRL Press, Oxford, United Kingdom, 315pp.

BURKE, T., O. HANOTTE, M.W. BRUFORD, AND E. CAIRNS. 1991. Multilocus and single locus minisatellite analysis in population biological studies. Pp. 154-168, *in* DNA fingerprinting: approaches and applications (T. Burke, G. Dolf, A. J. Jefferys, and R. Wolff, ed.). Birkhauser Verlag. Basel, Switzerland, 400pp.

BURKE, T., AND M. W. BRUFORD. 1987. DNA fingerprinting in birds. Nature, 327:149-152.

CHURCH, G.M., AND W. GILBERT. 1984. Genomic sequencing. Proceedings of the National Academy of Science, U.S.A. 81: 1991-1995.

DON, B.A.C. 1983. Home range characteristics and correlates in tree squirrels. Mammal Review, 13: 123-132.

FARENTINOS, R.C. 1972. Observations on the ecology of the tassel-eared squirrel. The Journal of Wildlife Management, 36:1234-9.

FEINBERG, A., AND B. VOGELSTEIN. 1983. A technique for radiolabelling DNA restriction endonuclease fragments to high specific activity. Analytical Biochemistry, 132:6-13.

GILBERT, D.A., C. PACKER, A.E. PUSEY, J.C. STEPHENS, AND S.J. O'BRIEN. 1991. Analytical DNA fingerprinting in lions: Parentage, genetic diversity, and kinship. Journal of Heredity, 82:378-386.

GULL, J. 1977. Movement and dispersal patterns of immature gray squirrels (*Sciurus carolinensis*) in east-central Minnesota. M.S. thesis, University of Minnesota, 90 pp.

GURNELL, J. 1981. Woodland rodents and tree seed supplies. Pp 1191–1214, *in* Worldwide Furbearer Conference Proceedings (J. A. Chapman and D. Pursley, eds.). Donnelly, Fals Chard, Virginia, 1552pp.

———. 1983. Squirrel numbers and the abundance of tree seeds. Mammal Review, 13:133-148.

———. 1987. The natural history of squirrels. Christopher Helm, London, United Kingdom

———. 1996. The effects of food availability and winter weather on the dynamics of a grey squirrel population in southern England. Journal of Applied Ecology, 33:325–338.

GURNELL, J., AND H. PEPPER. 1993. A critical look at conserving the British red squirrel, *Sciurus vulgaris.* Mammal Review, 23:125-136.

HAMILTON, W.D. 1964. The evolution of social behaviour. Journal of Theoretical Biology, 7:1-52.

HAMPSHIRE, R. 1985. A study on the social and reproductive behaviour of captive grey squirrels (*Sciurus carolinensis*). Ph.D. dissertation, University of Reading, United Kingdom, 252pp.

HANOTTE, O., M.W. BRUFORD, AND T. BURKE. 1992. Multilocus DNA fingerprints in gallinaceous birds: general approach and applications. Heredity, 68:481-494.

JEFFREYS, A. J., V. WILSON, AND S.L. THEIN. 1985*a*. Hypervariable 'minisatellite' regions in human DNA. Nature, 314:67-73.

———. 1985*b*. Individual-specific 'fingerprints' of human DNA. Nature, 316:76-79.

JEFFREYS, A.J., AND D.B. MORTON. 1987. DNA fingerprints of dogs and cats. Animal Genetics, 18:1-15.

KEANE, B., P.M. WASER, L. DANZL-TAUER, AND D.J. MINCHELLA. 1991. DNA fingerprinting: estimating background band-sharing in banner-tailed kangaroo rats. Animal Behaviour, 42:141-143.

KENWARD, R.E. 1985. Ranging behaviour and population dynamics in grey squirrels. P p . 319-330, *in* Behavioural Ecology (R.M.Sibly and R.H.Smith, eds.). Blackwell Scientific Publications, Oxford, United Kingdom, 493pp.

KOFORD, R.R. 1982. Mating system of a territorial tree squirrel (*Tamiasciurus douglasii*) in California. Journal of Mammalogy, 63:274-283.

KOPROWSKI, J. 1992. Removal of copulatory plugs by female tree squirrels. Journal of Mammalogy, 73(3):572-576.

———. 1993. Alternative reproductive tactics in male eastern gray squirrels: "making the best of a bad job". Behavioural Ecology, 4:165-171.

LYNCH, M. 1988. Estimation of Relatedness by DNA Fingerprinting. Molecular Biology and Evolution, 5:584-599.

———. 1990. The similarity index and DNA fingerprinting. Molecular Biology and Evolution, 7: 478-484.

PACK, J.C., H.S. MOSBY, AND P.B. SIEGEL. 1967. Influence of social hierarchy on grey squirrel behaviour. The Journal of Wildlife Management, 31:721-728.

PEMBERTON, J.M., S.D. ALBON, F.E. GUINNESS, T.H. CLUTTON-BROCK, AND G.A. DOVER. 1991. Behavioural estimates of male mating success tested by DNA fingerprinting in a polygynous mammal. Behavioural Ecology, 3:66-75

QUINN, J. S., R. MACEDO, AND B.N. WHITE. 1994. Genetic relatedness of communally breeding guira cuckoos. Animal Behaviour, 47:515-529.

RABENOLD, P., K.N. RABENOLD, W.H. PIPER, J. HAYDOCK, AND S.W. ZACK. 1990. Shared paternity revealed by genetic analysis in cooperatively breeding tropical wrens. Nature, 348:538-40.

RIBBLE, D.O. 1991. The monogamous mating system of *Peromyscus californicus* as revealed by DNA fingerprinting. Behavioral Ecology and Sociobiology, 29:161-166.

TAYLOR, J.C. 1966. Home range and agonistic behaviour in the grey squirrel. Symposium of the Zoological Society of London, 18:229-35

THOMPSON, D. C. 1977. Reproductive behaviour of the grey squirrel. Canadian Journal of Zoology, 55:1176-1184.

———. 1978. The social system of the grey squirrel. Behaviour, 64:305-28

WAUTERS, L. AND A.A. DHONDT. 1985. Population dynamics and social behaviour of red squirrel populations in different habitats. XVII Congress International Union of Game Biologists, 17: 311-318.

———. 1989. Body weight, longevity and reproductive success in red squirrels *(Sciurus vulgaris).* The Journal of Animal Ecology, 58:637-651.

WAUTERS, L., A.A DHONDT, AND R. DE VOS. 1990. Factors affecting male mating success in red squirrels (*Sciurus vulgaris).* Ethology, Ecology and Evolution, 2:195-204.

WESTNEAT, D. 1990. Genetic parentage study in the indigo bunting: a study using DNA fingerprinting. Behavioral Ecology and Sociobiology, 27:67-76.

WEBLEY, G.E., AND E. JOHNSON. 1983. Reproductive physiology of the grey squirrel (*Sciurus carolinensis*). Mammal Review, 2/3/4:149-154.

THE REPRODUCTIVE CYCLE OF ABERT'S SQUIRREL

GILBERT C. POGANY, W. SYLVESTER ALLRED, AND TONI BARNES

Department of Biological Sciences
Box 5640
Northern Arizona University
Flagstaff, AZ 86011

ABSTRACT.—Evidence is presented which suggests that Abert squirrels can have two reproductive periods in one year. This evidence is based on the collection of actual embryos in early March and June and the lactational status of females in those same months. Preliminary histological examinations demonstrate that spermatogenesis occurs most of the year with a distinct hiatus from July through September. Similar analyses of female tissues indicate that oocyte maturation is continuous throughout the year. There does not appear to be any correlation between the pattern of reproduction with a large number of environmental parameters. The basic mechanism that underlies the dual yearly gestation in Abert squirrels remains unclear.

INTRODUCTION

The specific strategy used by animals to ensure successful reproduction in any given season is essential for the maintenance of their population. Generally, a reproductive pattern is consistent from year to year unless severely perturbed by environmental circumstances at which time it may be altered or even suppressed. In the case of Abert's squirrels (*Sciurus aberti aberti*), knowledge about their reproductive cycle is based upon anecdotal and casual observations. An early hypothesis suggested that, under certain circumstances, Abert's squirrels may have two gestation periods in one year (Hall and Kelson, 1959). However, subsequent observations tended to favor the hypothesis of single breeding seasons (Farentinos, 1972, 1980). No actual data were presented to substantiate these claims.

Yet the role that Abert's squirrels play in their particular environment on the Colorado Plateau is pivotal. They forage on Ponderosa pine trees for food, and utilize the trees for nesting material and shelter (Keith, 1965; Patton, 1975; Allred and Gaud, 1994). They are known to serve as dispersal agents for mycorrhizal fungi by inoculating Ponderosa pine trees with spores (States et al., 1988), thus possibly enhancing nutrient absorption into the roots of trees from a soil understood to be typically impoverished (Kotter and Farentinos, 1984). Pine seed dispersal also is aided by squirrels through buried ovulate cones subsequently left untouched (Bailey, 1932).

In addition to interacting with Ponderosa pine on which they greatly depend, Abert's squirrels also constitute a significant prey item for goshawks (Reynolds, 1963; Reynolds et al., 1992). Hence, the function that characterizes Abert's squirrels within the Ponderosa pine forest ecosystem is that of a primary consumer between plant resources and predators. Therefore, factors affecting their well-being and reproduction are likely to also impact severely on these interactions. Consequently, the squirrel and its reproductive processes could serve as "health indicators" of the Ponderosa pine forest.

A complete evaluation of the adaptation of the squirrels to their environment on the Colorado Plateau requires a detailed knowledge of their reproduction. The present study was intended to provide an in-depth analysis of their reproductive cycle through the histological analysis of their reproductive organs. In addition, we also present evidence that two gestation periods in one year is possible in tassel-eared squirrels. Attempts to unravel some of the prevailing environmental conditions that may be conducive to this reproductive strategy reveal that reproduction by

In M.A. Steele, J. F. Merritt, and D. A. Zegers (eds.). 1998. Ecology and Evolutionary Biology of Tree Squirrels. Special Publication, Virginia Museum of Natural History, 6: 320 pp

Abert's squirrels is independent of photoperiod and temperature. Snow cover, on the other hand, may be a significant factor in determining the specific reproductive strategy used by the squirrels. The case of the Abert's squirrel may, therefore, offer a glimpse into a flexible reproductive pattern designed to accommodate environmental circumstances.

MATERIALS AND METHODS

All animals obtained as roadkills for this study were provided by volunteers and brought to the laboratory for analysis during the sampling period (1992-1994). They were collected within a 50 mile radius and kept frozen until dissected. At that time, the carcasses were thawed overnight at room temperature and measurements were taken. Measurements included, total weight and length, tail, hind foot, ear, and length of tassels. The presence or absence of prominent nipples was also noted as evidence of active lactation.

For both sexes, the reproductive organs were removed and preserved in alcoholic Bouin's for 24 hours. The preserved tissues were processed by means of standard histological procedures (Humason, 1962). The resulting sections were hydrated through an alcohol series and stained with hematoxylin and eosin. All illustrations were made on Plus X Pan film and printed on Ilford RC paper.

When present, embryos were also removed and placed in 70% alcohol and photographed. Their lengths (crown-rump) were determined with calipers (± 0.1 mm).

RESULTS

Embryos were gathered during the months of June and July 1992 and March 1993. Data concerning those embryos are shown in Table 1. All embryos collected were well developed, although their actual age could not be determined. We did not obtain younger embryos than those shown in Table 1.

Evidence of active lactation in females was identified by the presence of conspicuous nipples surrounded by large and clear aureolae. The information concerning their lactational status is presented in Table 2. The preponderance of pregnancies probably occurs during the months of April through July. However, a female with lactating nipples was also observed in March. Assuming a gestation period of 40-45 days (Brown and Yeager, 1945; Brauer and Dusing, 1961) and a lactation period of 8 weeks (Brown and Yeager, 1945), it seemed feasible to speculate that the females may have mated in December and January.

Table 2.—*Numbers and biomass of lactating female Abert's squirrels collected as roadkills within a 50–mile radius of Flagstaff, Arizona.*

Months	No. of lactating females	Weight range (gm)
March	1	752.92
May	4	613.52-767.21
June	3	597.92-701.77
July	4	631.95-812.75
August	1	639.04

Table 1.—*Morphological data collected on squirrel embryos and their date of collection.*

Date	Weight of females (gm)	Length (crown-rump) (cm)*	Number of embryos
6-23-92	724.26	5.45	2
7-07-92	863.18	5.41	2
3-17-93	816.02	5.61	5
3-18-93	695.62	5.51	1
3-30-93	782.46	5.73	3

* The measurements represent the average when multiple embryos are present.

The detailed histological analysis of the testicular and ovarian tissues provided further insight into the reproductive pattern in Abert's squirrels. In males, spermatogenic activity is maintained for a prolonged period of time during the year. The first signs of spermatogenesis were observed during October (Pogany and Allred, 1995; Fig. 1) and were represented by a few meiotic figures within the germinal epithelium. By November, an early wave of spermiation yielded a large number of spermatids being released into the lumen of the epididymis (Fig. 1). Complete spermatogenesis and spermiogenesis were in full swing by March and actively maintained until June (Fig. 2). Testicular regression occurred rapidly and seemed complete by July (Fig. 2) as attested by the collapsed seminiferous tubules and the absence of any lumen. The presence of pyknotic nuclei in unidentifiable germinal cells (Fig. 1) seemed to imply that testicular regression is also being maintained during August. Although male testicular samples for September were lacking, it is assumed that the progressive attrition of testes is either slowed or halted in preparation for the rapid resumption of reproductive activity by October. Even during times of maximal testicular regression, residual meiotic activity could be observed (Fig. 2). This "maintenance meiosis" may serve to retain the germinal epithelium in a state of readiness for the next cycle which is re-initiated as early as the month of October (Pogany and Allred, 1995).

Examination of representative samples of female squirrels revealed a consistent pattern of extensive atresia of follicles in various stages of development (Fig. 3) Mature healthy follicles are few in number and are most preponderant in samples from April. In November, tissues reveal the presence of large quantities of egg nests together with mature follicles undergoing atresion. Characteristically, oocytes within these deteriorating follicles are collapsed, and frequently, only the zona pellucida remains of a follicle that previously underwent atresion. Corpora lutea were only observed in one tissue from November (Fig. 3). This most likely represented recent ovulations thus lending further support for a winter gestation and a biannual pattern of reproduction in Abert's squirrels. However, the histology of ovaries did not display a similar pattern of reproductive activity. Taken together, these observations suggest that follicular growth and maturation are constant throughout the year and that females are in a permanent state of ovarian readiness. Follicular growth is accompanied by extensive breakdown of those follicles that are not destined to be ovulated.

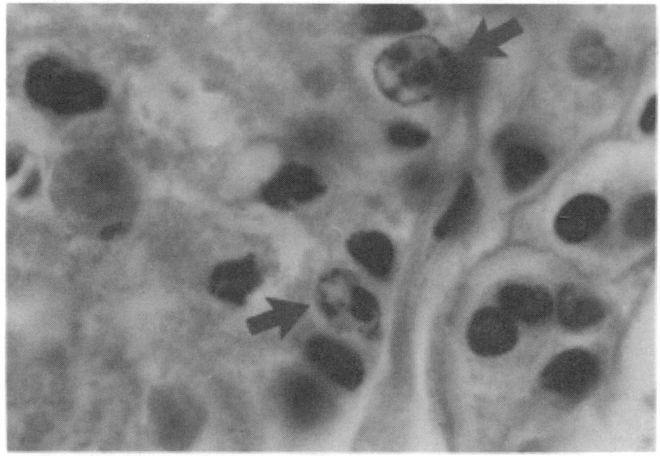

AUGUST

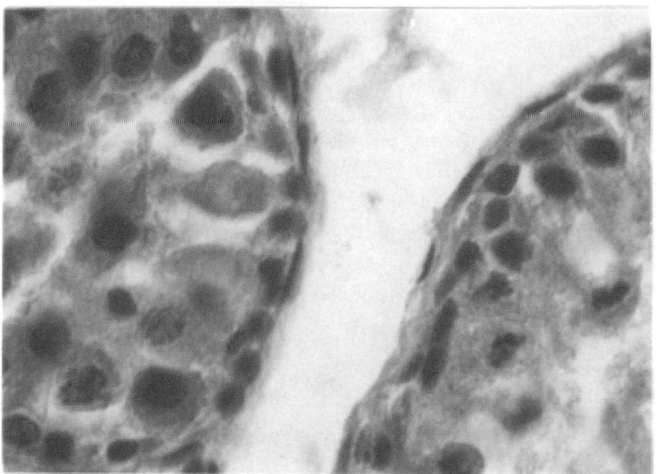

OCTOBER

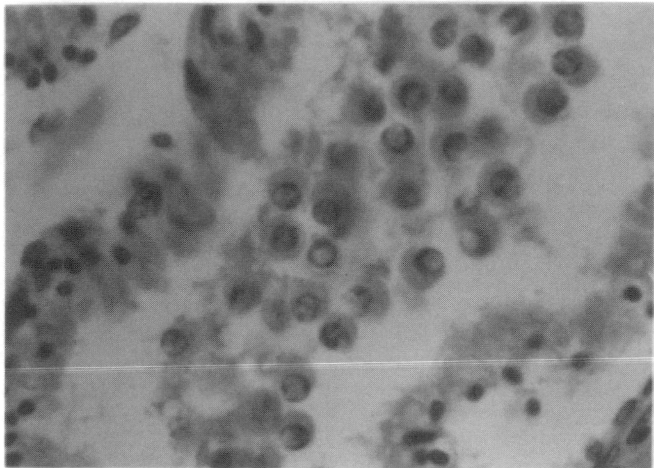

NOVEMBER

Fig. 1.—The testicular status of male Abert's squirrels during the indicated months. Pyknosis of germinal cell nuclei (arrows) suggests that testicular regression is still prevalent. However, by October, recrudescence of testicular activity is evident and is represented by the discharge of spermatids into the lumen of the epididymis (November).

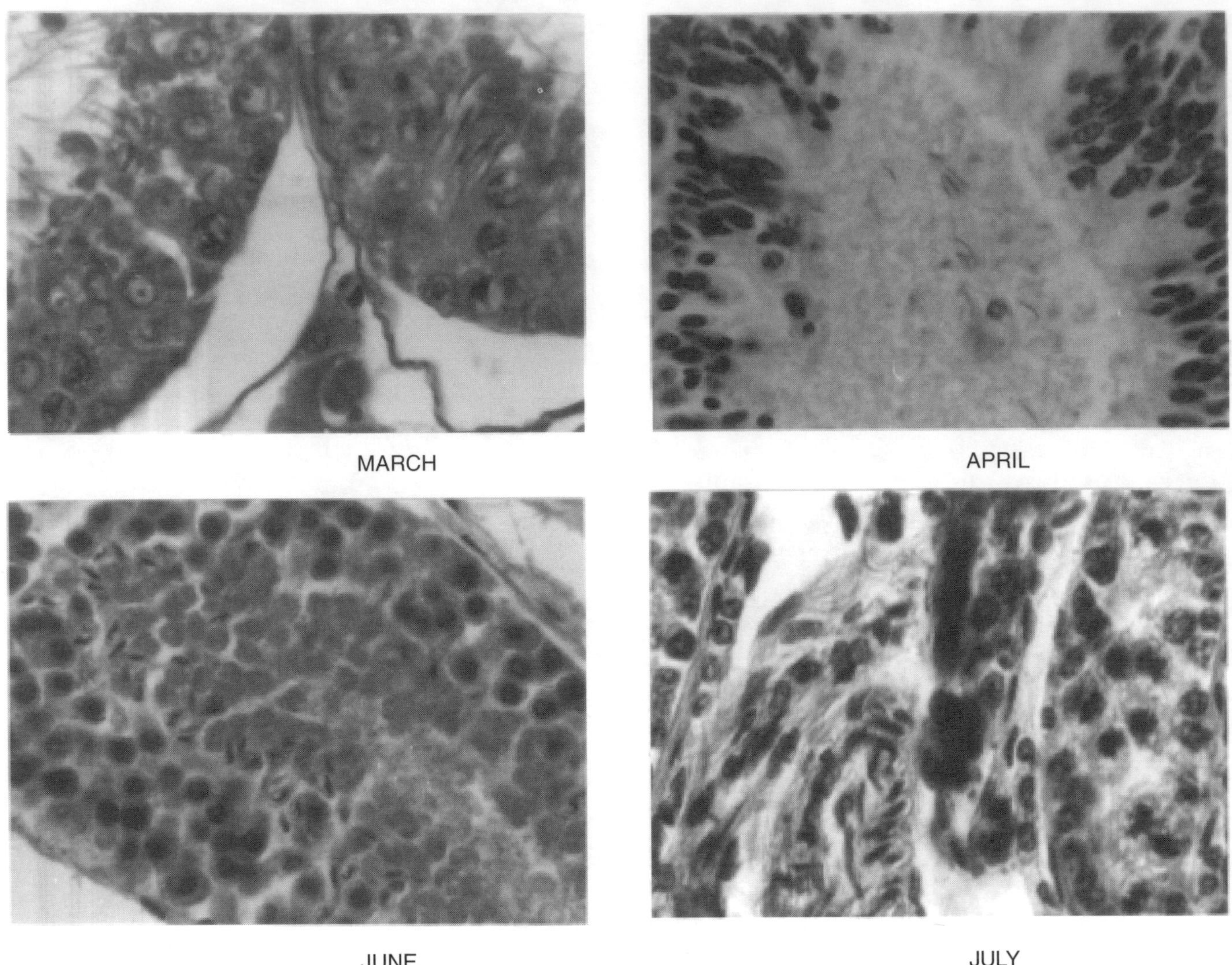

Fig. 2.—The testicular status of male Abert's squirrels during the indicated months. Active spermatogenesis is shown by the presence of mature sperm within the lumen of seminiferous tubules of males collected during the months of March, April, and June. Testicular regression is initiated abruptly in July as the tubules collapse and meiosis is suspended.

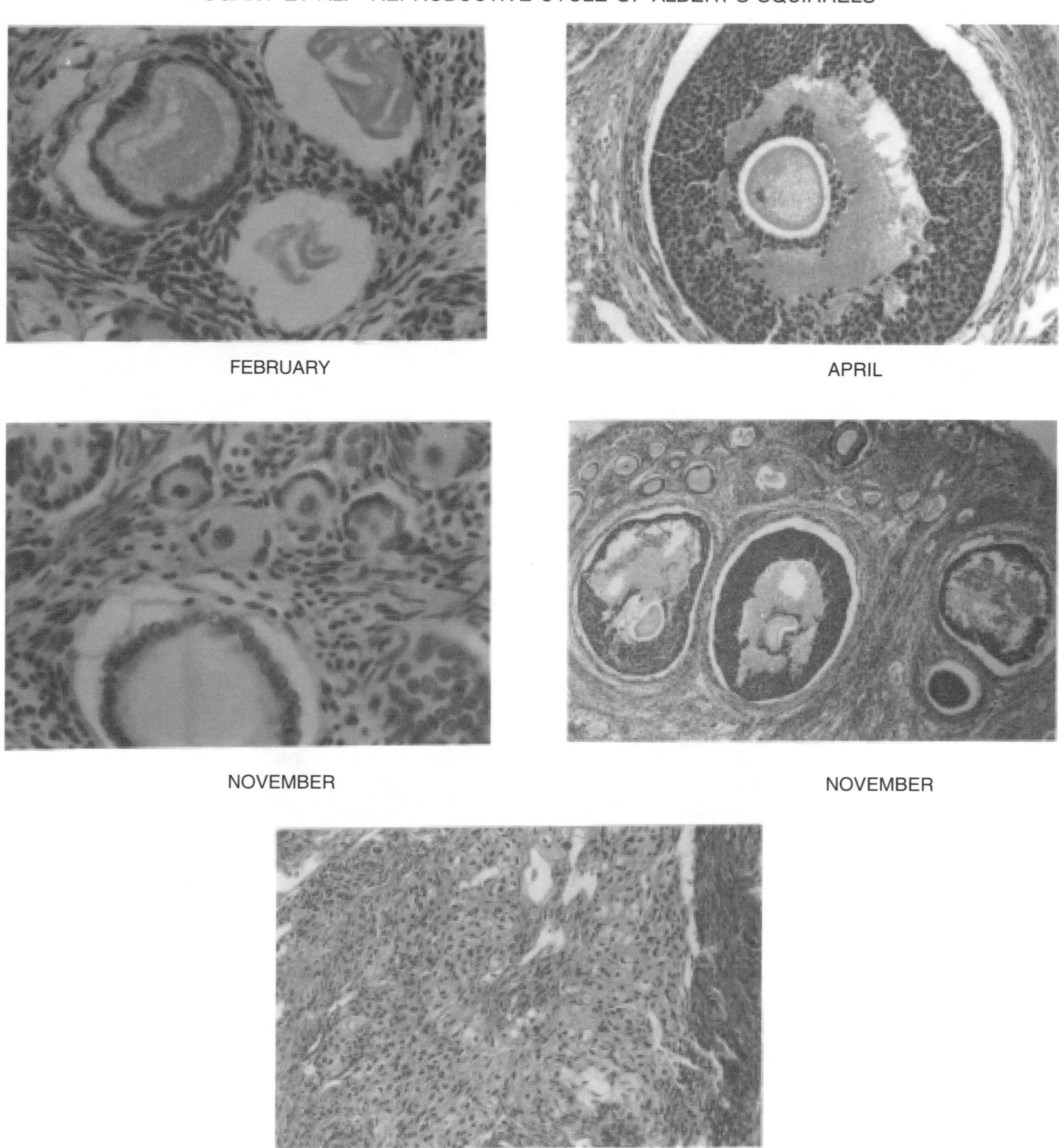

Fig.3.—Representative sections of ovarian tissues collected from road-killed females. Atresia of early follicles is often represented by remnants of the zona pellucida (February). A mature and healthy follicle is shown in an April sample. November samples display a variety of conditions which range from the presence of egg nests to extensive atresia of advanced follicles and also to the presence of a corpus luteum.

Table 3. —*Weather data of collection area within a 50 mile radius from Flagstaff, Arizona. Information provided by the National Weather Service, Pulliam Airport, Flagstaff, Arizona.*

	Snow (inches)			Temperature (°F)*		
Months	1991	1992	1993	1991	1992	1993
January	3.1	63.4	55.7	42.7/18.3	41.7/14.7	42.3/22.0
September	T	2.0	T	76.4/42.8	74.1/40.9	76.3/39.5
October	5.9	24.7	0	68.3/33.2	63.7/30.6	63.1/31.7
November	39.5	40.7	23.0	49.7/24.1	51.0/21.5	49.1/20.9
December	24.0	86.0	13.4	41.5/18.9	43.6/15.9	44.2/16.0

T: trace amounts
* : daily maxima and minima

Attempts to relate the reproduction of Abert's squirrels to specific environmental factors such as snow cover, temperature, and total moisture led us to survey related weather data from months preceding the detection of the winter gestation (Table 3). Quantity of snow showed considerable variation from year to year. However, detection of embryos in March of 1993 seems to imply that insemination of females may have occurred during periods of large snow accumulation in December and January. This is further substantiated by our observations of lactating females as early as in March. Temperature, on the other hand, was remarkably consistent from year to year (Table 3). These observations suggest that this latter environmental parameter does not affect Abert's squirrel reproduction in the winter. Since biannual gestation occurs under widely differing light conditions, there is also evidence that the reproductive activity of Abert's squirrels is independent of photoperiod.

DISCUSSION

The data we report represent the first documented instance of a winter gestation in Abert's squirrels. The combined evidence of actual embryos and lactation strongly suggests that these animals may go through two gestations in one year. This is highly reminiscent of a similar condition previously described for the red squirrel in Wisconsin (Mossman and Duke, 1973). Our results do not necessarily imply, however, that any one female may have two litters in the same year. Possibly, different females, at different times, may be responsible for the dual gestation.

The absence of any evidence of photoperiodic influence on reproduction of Abert's squirrel's suggests that the pattern observed in 1993 may either be inherent or subject to environmental factors not yet resolved. Our attempts to correlate reproductive events with major environmental factors such as snow cover, temperature, and moisture were unsuccessful. Further collections in subsequent years will be essential in establishing the possible causes for the gestations observed in these animals. It is worthy of note that the snow pattern in late 1993 is very similar to that which preceded the 1992 winter gestation. Should our data from the winter of 1994 reveal that large snow cover is related to reproduction, it will be contrary to previous suggestions that snow inhibits reproduction in Albert's squirrels (Stephenson and Brown, 1980). Our data are therefore the first to extend the reproductive season to months prior to March which was previously considered the earliest record (Stephenson, 1975).

Data on female reproduction in tassel-eared squirrels correlate well with our histological analyses of male samples obtained during similar periods (Pogany and Allred, unpublished data). We have observed two peaks of spermatogenic activities: one in late autumn (October-November) and a second one in the spring (Pogany and Allred, 1995). Testicular attrition is conspicuous by July but lasts only until late September. Interestingly, regression is not complete since occasional meiotic divisions have been observed in August and September (Pogany and Allred, unpublished data).

In judging the reproductive pattern of Abert's squirrels, it is important to consider its inherent driving mechanism. Three options are possible. The first would suggest that males only drive the system to which females respond only when ready to do so. In this "male" driven system, spermatogenesis would be extensive and spread over most of the year. The second system would envision the opposite where females would maintain a constant status of sexual preparedness which would only be fulfilled when males are ready. The last mechanism could suggest that both sexes synchronize their pattern so as to conform to the other's preparedness. Further data on the consistency of our observations and the continued analyses of reproductive tissues will be necessary to elucidate this point. In either instance, the question of how spermatogenesis can be maintained during winter months is intriguing and deserves further attention.

The paucity of obvious corpora lutea in most of the female tissues analyzed is surprising. With as many as 5 embryos in one female, well developed corpora lutea had been expected. No explanations are yet available to account for this strange circumstance.

The consistency of this dual reproductive pattern in Abert's squirrels remains to be established. Clearly, such consistency should have considerable influence on the management of Ponderosa pine forests and on current hunting practices. Periods of winter reproduction will have to be taken into consideration when developing new guidelines for such management.

ACKNOWLEDGMENTS

We wish to thank Sharon Malone, Laura Martin, Rayma Sequaptewa for their technical skills; Charles Van Riper, National Biological Service for his financial assistance, Henry Hooper, Vice President, Northern Arizona University for his financial help, and William S. Gaud, chair, Department of Biological Sciences for his encouragement and support.

LITERATURE CITED

ALLRED, W. S., AND W. S. GAUD. 1994. Characteristics of ponderosa pine and Abert squirrel herbivory. The Southwestern Naturalist, 39:89-90.

BAILEY, F. M. 1932. Abert squirrel burying pine cones. Journal of Mammalogy, 13:165-166.

BRAUER, A., AND A. DUSING. 1961. Sexual cycles and breeding seasons of the gray squirrel, *Sciurus carolinensis* Gmelin. Transactions of the Kentucky Academy of Science, 22:16-27.

BROWN L. G., AND L. E. YEAGER. 1945. Fox squirrels and gray squirrels in Illinois. Bulletin of the Illinois Natural History Survey, 123:449-536.

FARENTINOS, R. C. 1972. Social dominance and mating activity in the tassel-eared squirrel. Animal Behaviour, 20:316-326.

———. 1980. Sexual solicitation of subordinate males by female tassel-eared squirrels. Journal of Mammalogy, 61:337-341.

KEITH, J. O. 1965. The Abert squirrel and its dependence on Ponderosa pine. Ecology, 46:153-163.

KOTTER, M. M., AND R. C. FARENTINOS. 1984. Tassel-eared squirrels as spore dispersal agents of hypogeous mycorrhizal fungi. Journal of Mammalogy, 65:684-687.

HALL, E. R., AND K. R. KELSON. 1959. The Mammals of North America. The Ronald Press Company, New York, 1083 pp.

HUMASON, G. L. 1962. Animal Tissue Techniques, W.H. Freeman & Company, New York, 468 pp.

MOSSMAN, H. W., AND K. L. DUKE 1973. Comparative morphology of the mammalian ovary. The University of Wisconsin Press, Madison, 461 pp.

PATTON, D. R. 1975. Abert squirrel cover requirements in south eastern Ponderosa pine. USDA Forest Service Paper Rm-272, 12 pp.

POGANY, G. C., AND W. S. ALLRED. 1995. Abert squirrels of the Colorado Plateau: their reproductive cycle. Pp. 293-305, *in* Proceedings of the Second Biennial Conference on Research in Colorado Plateau Parks (C. Van Riper, ed.). National Biological Service, Information Transfer Center, Fort Collins, Colorado, 305 pp.

REYNOLDS, H. G. 1963. Western goshawk takes Abert squirrels in Arizona. Journal of Forestry, 6:839.

REYNOLDS, H. G., ET AL. 1992. Management recommendations for the northern goshawk in the southwestern United States. USDA Forest Service General Technical Paper Rm-166, Rocky Mountain Forest and Range Experimental Station, Fort Collins, Colorado, 90 pp.

STATES, J. S., W. S. GAUD, W. S. ALLRED, AND W. J. AUSTIN. 1988. Foraging patterns of tassel-eared squirrels in selected ponderosa pine stands. Pp. 425-431, *in* Proceedings of Management of Amphibian, Reptiles, and Small Mammals in North America (R. C. Szaro, K. E. Severson, technical coordinators). USDA Forest Service General Technical Paper Rm-166, Rocky Mountain Forest and Range Experimental Station, Fort Collins, Colorado, 458 pp.

STEPHENSON, R. L. 1975. Reproductive biology and food habits of Abert squirrels in Central Arizona. M.S. thesis, Arizona State University, Tempe, 66 pp.

STEPHENSON, R. L., AND D. E. BROWN. 1980. Snow cover as a factor influencing mortality of Abert squirrels. The Journal of Wildlife Management, 44:951-955.

NEST BOX USE AND REPRODUCTION IN THE GRAY SQUIRREL (*SCIURUS CAROLINENSIS*) IN FLORIDA

JAMES N.LAYNE

Archbold Biological Station, P. O. Box 2057, Lake Placid, FL 33862

ABSTRACT—Patterns of nest box use and aspects of reproduction in the gray squirrel (*Sciurus carolinensis extimus*) were studied from 1973 to 1984 in south-central peninsular Florida near the southern limit of the species' range. Xeric pine-oak habitats predominated in the study area. Adults, subadults, and nestlings comprised 35%, 15%, and 50%, respectively, of original captures. Nest box occupancy was highest from late autumn to early spring due to increased use by adults, many in groups of up to four individuals (mean ± *SE* = 2.16 ± 0.05). Nest boxes in oak phase of sand pine scrub habitat had the highest frequency of use by squirrels, which appeared to reflect high population density attributable to year-round abundance of sand pine cones. Birth dates calculated from estimated ages of nestlings occurred in all months except May, with peaks in January-February and July. Yearly variation in numbers of litters in nest boxes was greater in winter than summer. Litter size (overall mean ± *SE* = 2.77 ± 0.08) varied seasonally, averaging 2.11 ± 0.06 in January-March and 3.34 ± 0.11 in July - September. Two females were known to produce two litters in a year. The overall sex ratio of nestlings was 1.02:1, males:females, and did not vary seasonally. Presently available data on breeding seasons and litter size of gray squirrel populations over a latitudinal range of 44-27^0 suggests a forward shift in the first, and possibly the second, breeding season in the southern part of the range, but no significant trend in either seasonal or overall litter sizes.

INTRODUCTION

The reproductive biology of the gray squirrel (*Sciurus carolinensis*) has been relatively well studied largely because of the species' importance as a small game animal. However, previous studies have been concentrated in the central portion of the range, and less is known about the life history and ecology of populations at or near the northern or southern range limits. I studied nest box use and aspects of reproduction in *S. c. extimus* in south-central peninsular Florida from 1973 to 1984. Objectives of the study were to determine seasonal and habitat relationships in use of nest boxes and to characterize the reproductive characteristics of the gray squirrel near the southern periphery of its range and in habitats in which it has not previously been studied. In addition to its close proximity to the southern range boundary and small body size, approximately 63% of that of northern gray squirrels (Uhlig, 1955*a*), this population also inhabits generally xeric pine-oak uplands rather than more mesic hardwood forests typical of the species elsewhere in its range (Flyger and Gates, 1982).

Based on the decrease in body size of the species in the southern portions of its range (Uhlig, 1955*a*; Barnett, 1977; Heaney, 1984), reduced litter size would be predicted in southern gray squirrel populations. In addition to, or associated with, the factor of body size, the wide variation in climatic conditions from the northern to southern boundaries of the range (44-25° N latitude) also might be expected to be reflected in a latitudinal cline in litter size, timing of the breeding season, or other aspects of reproduction. However, previous studies (Kirkpatrick et al., 1978; Heaney, 1984) have found no obvious latitudinal trends in

In M.A. Steele, J. F. Merritt, and D. A. Zegers (eds.). 1998. Ecology and Evolutionary Biology of Tree Squirrels. Special Publication, Virginia Museum of Natural History, 6: 320 pp

either litter size or breeding seasons. I reexamined the question with the addition of the data from south-central Florida, which extends by 4^0 the latitudinal range for which information on gray squirrel reproduction is available.

METHODS

Description of study area.—The study was conducted on the Archbold Biological Station 12 km S of the town of Lake Placid, Highlands County, Florida (27^{0}10' N lat., 81^{0}20' E long.). The climate of the region is characterized by hot, wet summers and relatively mild, dry winters (Abrahamson et al., 1984). Mean maximum daily temperatures from June to August are 33-34°C, and minimum daily temperatures from December to February average about 9-10°C, with only occasional, brief periods with night time temperatures below freezing. Mean annual rainfall is 1,374 mm, with a pronounced rainy season from June to September.

The vegetation on the study tract (400 ha), last burned in 1929-1930, included the following major associations and phases as described by Abrahamson et al.(1984): southern ridge sandhill, including turkey oak (*Quercus laevis*) and scrub hickory (*Carya floridana*) phases; sand pine scrub, oak phase; scrubby flatwoods, including inopina oak (*Q. inopina*) and sand live oak (*Q. geminata*) phases; flatwoods, palmetto phase; bayhead; and man-occupied, including old field and landscaped phases.

Southern ridge sandhill, sand pine scrub, and scrubby flatwoods comprised most of the study area. These are relatively xeric associations dominated by pines and oaks with well-drained sandy soils. All have a generally dense shrub layer dominated by three or four species of evergreen oaks and a pine overstory, which consists of widely spaced slash pines (*Pinus elliottii*) and sand pines (*P. clausa*) in the sandhill and scrubby flatwoods associations and dense, mature sand pines forming a nearly closed canopy in the sand pine scrub association. Flatwoods and bayhead habitats were restricted to small areas. The flatwoods had an open stand of slash pines and a shrub layer dominated by saw palmetto (*Serenoa repens*) and occurred on poorly drained, often seasonally saturated, sandy soil. Bayhead, a dense forest of broad-leaved evergreen species (*Gordonia lasianthus*, *Persea borbonia*, *Magnolia virginiana*) with a lush understory of ferns, palmettos, and various shrubs, occurred on poorly drained, highly organic soil subject to periodic flooding. The two man-occupied habitats, an old field surrounded by sandhill vegetation and landscaped grounds with scattered large oaks and pines, patches of shrubbery, and mowed grass, comprised about 10% of the study area.

Nest box surveys.—Nest boxes of the design reported by Barkalow and Soots (1965) were placed at heights of from 1.5 to 5.3 m on trees in all habitats. The number of boxes in a given habitat was roughly proportional to the amount of that habitat in the study area. One hundred fifteen boxes in natural vegetation were located on five 2.8-ha grids used in small mammal population studies and along firelanes and trails at intervals of about 120 m. The grids (12 by 12, 15-m intervals) were in typical examples of southern ridge sandhill-turkey oak phase (2 grids), sand pine scrub, scrubby flatwoods-inopina oak phase, and bayhead habitats. Five nest boxes on each grid were placed at the corners and center. Of ten boxes in man-occupied habitats, five were spaced at 100-180-m intervals along the edge of an old field bordered by sandhill habitat, and five were located in a line at 60-90-m intervals through the landscaped area.

Boxes were checked monthly from January 1973 to December 1976 and, except for April 1979, bimonthly (January, March, May, July, September, November) from January 1977 to July 1984. In March 1979, the diameter of the entrance hole of 56 boxes was reduced from 6.4 to 3.2 cm to exclude gray squirrels and encourage use by southern flying squirrels (*Glaucomys volans*), leaving 69 boxes available for gray squirrel occupancy. Nest boxes with the larger holes were checked 9,869 times, with the number of checks in different months varying from 375 in June to 1,215 in January. The number of times individual boxes were examined ranged from 75 to 94 (Table 1). Because of the variation in numbers of boxes in different habitats, schedule of nest box checks, and number of times individual boxes were examined, data relating to nest box occupancy are expressed as frequencies per 100 nest boxes.

Squirrels captured in nest boxes were weighed, sexed, examined for reproductive status, pelage condition, and ectoparasites, and ear tagged. Nestlings too small for ear tagging were toe clipped and ear tagged if recaptured at an older age. Ages of nestlings were estimated from growth data given by Shorten (1951) and Uhlig (1955*b*). As it is probable that growth rates of the larger subspecies studied by these authors differ somewhat from those of the smaller *S. c. extimus* in this study, estimated and actual ages of Florida nestlings may have differed by several days. However, as I only used estimated nestling ages to calculate the month of birth, any effect of this potential error was negligible. Three age classes were recognized based on body weight: nestlings—90 g or less; subadults—91 to 250 g; adults—over 250 g. These categories roughly correspond to ages 0-6 weeks (birth to weaning); 7-12 weeks (weaning to early postweaning), and >13 weeks. Mean weights of 26 adult males (334.2 ± 10.1 g) and 23 adult females (348.2 ±12.7 g) from the study area did not differ significantly (t-test, t = 0.875, $d.f.$ = 47, $P > 0.05$).

RESULTS

Seasonal pattern of nest box use.—A total of 1,321 gray squirrels was handled, including 1,058 original captures and 263 recaptures. Adults comprised 35% of original captures, subadults 15%, and nestlings 50%. Use of nest boxes by squirrels was highest in winter, largely due to an influx of adults other than females with litters, and was lowest in late spring-early summer (Fig. 1). Co-occurrence of adults in nest boxes began in October, reached a peak in February, and declined steeply in spring (Fig. 2). Groups ranged from two to four squirrels, with a mean of 2.16 ± 0.05 (n = 81). Groups consisting of males (48%) and males and females (41%) were more frequent than those comprised of only females (21%) and occurred over a longer period of the year. Male groups consisted of two or three (n = 1) individuals, mixed-sex groups involved a single male with two or three females, and all female groups were of two individuals. Subadult groups, probably littermates in most if not all cases, ranged from two to four, with a mean of 2.56 ± 0.10.

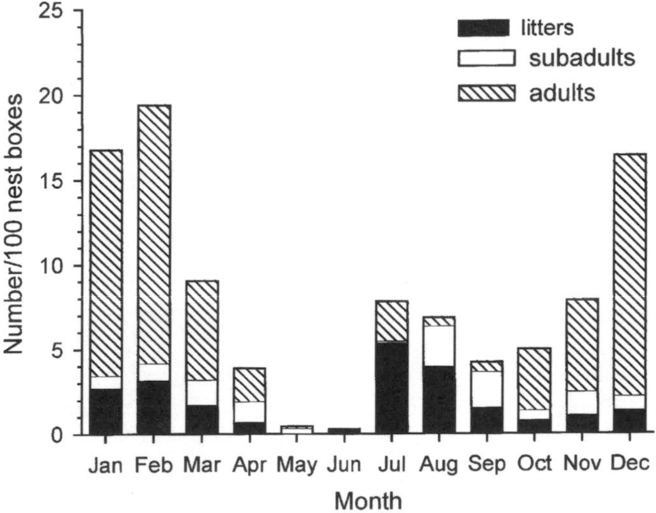

Fig. 1.—Monthly occurrence of litters, subadult, and adult gray squirrels in nest boxes in south-central Florida from January 1973 to July 1984.

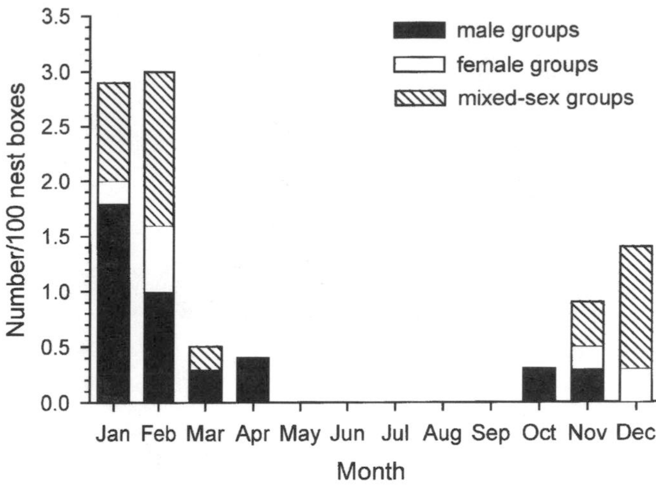

Fig. 2.—Monthly frequencies of aggregations of adult gray squirrels in nest boxes in south-central Florida from January 1973 to July 1984.

The cat-like call termed "mew" by Bakken (1959) and "moan" by Horwich (1972) and considered to be allelomimetic by Hazard (1960) was heard most frequently from September to November when adult groups were beginning to form.

Use of nest boxes in relation to habitat.—Litters occurred in nest boxes in all habitats sampled except bayhead (Table 1), but observed frequencies in different habitats differed significantly from expected frequencies (1.6/100 nest boxes) based on the proportions of boxes available in each habitat and the number of times they were examined (χ^2 = 16.66, $d.f.$ = 7, $P < 0.05$). Nest boxes in turkey oak phase sandhill, sand pine scrub, flatwoods, and old field habitats contained more litters than expected, while numbers of litters in the remaining habitats were less than or the same as expected. In all habitats, there was a marked tendency for the same nest boxes to contain litters in different seasons and years. Use of nest boxes by adults also differed signficantly between habitats (χ^2 = 79.67, $d.f.$ = 8, $P < 0.001$), with greater than expected usage (3.7/100 boxes) in sand pine scrub, turkey oak phase sandhill, and oldfield habitats and less than or equal to expected usage in remaining habitats.

Breeding seasons.—Based on back-dating from estimated ages of litters, births occurred in all months of the year except May, with peaks in January-February and July, indicating two, not very well defined breeding seasons a year (Fig. 3). Assuming a gestation period of 44 days (Webley and Johnson, 1983), peaks in conceptions occurred in November-December and May-June. Ninteen (57%) of 32 mating chases recorded

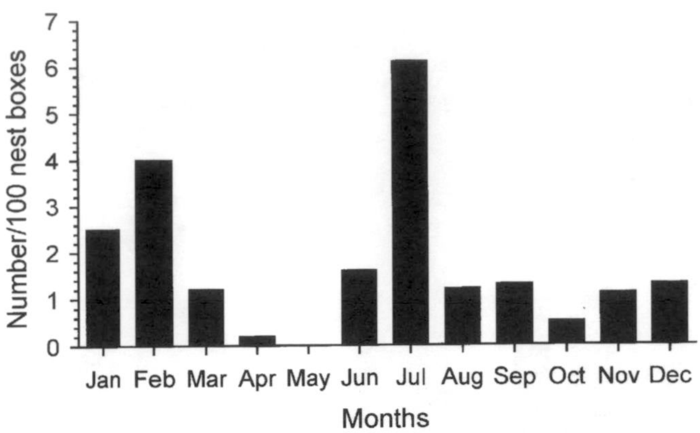

Fig 3.—Seasonal distribution of estimated parturition dates of gray squirrel litters in nest boxes in south-central Florida from January 1973 to July 1984.

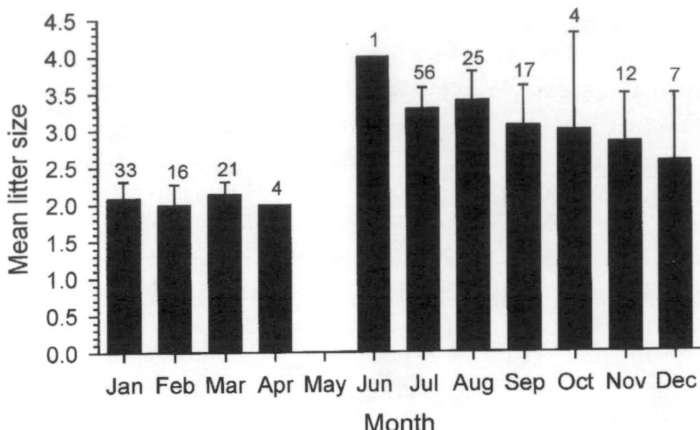

Fig. 4—Monthly mean size of gray squirrel litters in nest boxes in south-central Florida from January 1973 to July 1984. Error bars = 1 SE; sample sizes above bars.

throughout the year with approximately equal observation effort each month also occurred in November-December and May-June, with the remainder in January (1), April (1), July (7), August (3), and September (1). The number of males involved in 20 mating chases for which accurate counts or close estimates of the number of individuals could be made ranged from 2 to 14 (based on actual counts and midpoints of ranges of estimated numbers), with a mean of 5.9 ± 0.7. Copulation was observed once in May and once in November.

Combined frequencies of litters in January and March and July and September, selected to represent the periods of winter-spring and summer-autumn, respectively, were used to compare variation in seasonal breeding activity among years from 1973 to 1983. The frequencies of litters in the two seasons were not significantly correlated ($r = 0.32$, $P > 0.05$), and there were no significant differences between years in frequencies of litters in either season or both seasons combined ($\chi^2 = 6.33$-12.24, *d.f.* = 8-10, $P > 0.05$). However, yearly frequencies of litters in summer-autumn were less variable (*CV* = 49%) than in winter-spring (*CV* = 66%). In addition, no litters occurred in nest boxes in winter-spring in 2 of the 11 years, whereas litters were present in summer-fall of every year.

Litter size and number.—The mean (±*SE*) size of 187 litters in nest boxes from January 1973 through July 1984 was 2.77 ± 0.08 (range = 1-5). Litter size exhibited a strong seasonal trend, decreasing from a peak in summer to a low in winter and spring (Fig. 4). The effect of month on litter size was highly signficant (ANOVA, $F = 8.715$, *d.f.* = 10,185, $P < 0.001$). Overall means of litter size in winter-spring (January, February, March) and summer-fall (July, August, September) from 1973 to 1983 were 2.11 ± 0.06 ($n = 63$) and 3.34 ± 0.11 ($n = 83$), respectively; the difference was significant (*t*-test, $t = 8.86$, *d.f.* = 144, $P < 0.001$). Litters in summer-fall averaged from 17 to 90% larger than litters in winter-spring in each of the nine years with samples for each season. However, there was no significant difference over years in either mean litter size in winter-spring or summer-fall (ANOVA, $F = 1.151, 1.056$, *d.f.* = 9,53, 9,67, respectively, $P > 0.05$). Frequency of litters in nest boxes and mean litter size in different years were not significantly correlated in either winter-spring or summer-fall ($r = 0.40, 0.68$, respectively, $P > 0.05$).

Mean litter size in the three major habitats for January-March and July-September were (summer-fall values in parentheses): turkey oak phase southern ridge sandhill, 2.06 ± 0.17 (3.00 ± 0.36); oak phase sand pine scrub, 2.22 ± 0.15 (3.21 ± 0.19); inopina oak phase scrubby flatwoods, 2.50 ± 0.22 (3.75 ± 0.25). The differences between means for the three habitats were not significant in either season (ANOVA, $F = 1.809, 1.013$, *d.f.* = 2,46, 2,37, respectively, $P > 0.05$).

Only two squirrels were recaptured frequently enough to determine the number of litters produced in a year by individual females. Each had two litters, one in July and November and the other in January and August, giving estimated interbirth intervals of 123 and 183 days, respectively. The first female also gave birth to a third litter the following February (estimated interbirth interval of 98 days).

Sex ratio of litters.—The overall sex ratio of 533 nestlings in all litters combined was 1.02:1, males:females, and was not significantly different from equality ($\chi^2 = 0.05$, *d.f.* = 1, $P > 0.05$). Sex ratios of nestlings also did not vary significantly from 1:1 in any month (January, March, July, August, September, November, December) with sample sizes of five or more individuals of each sex ($\chi^2 = 0 - 0.56$, *d.f.* = 1, $P < 0.05$).

Breeding age of females.—Age at first breeding could be established for only one female of known age. This individual, estimated to be 30 days of age when captured on 30 August, was found with a litter approximately 5-days old on 28 February, giving an estimated age at conception of approximately 5.5 months. This unusually precocious breeding age is comparable to cases reported by Shorten and Courtier (1955), Uhlig (1956) and Smith and Barkalow (1967). Four other females born in July showed no sign of breeding when examined the following December and January at estimated ages of about 5 to 7 months, suggesting that, as in the case of most gray squirrel populations that have been studied, summer-born females do not regularly breed in the following winter-spring period.

DISCUSSION

Nest box use.—Use of nest boxes by gray squirrels in this study exhibited a pronounced seasonal trend, with highest occupancy from late fall to early spring as the result of increased use by adults. There was a high incidence of aggregations in boxes during this period, as in the case of southern flying squirrels (*Glaucomys volans*) in the same study area (Layne and Raymond, 1994). However, flying squirrel groups were much larger, with a mean of 7.2 and maximum of 25 compared with a mean of 2.2 and maximum of 4 for the gray squirrel. The marked difference in size of aggregations of the two sciurids may reflect the difference in their body size in relation to the capacity of the nest box and perhaps local population levels of each species, but interspecific differences in sociality are probably also involved. Aggregations of flying squirrels persisted at a low level during summer months, whereas no groups of gray squirrels were recorded at that time of year. Although the peak in communal nesting of gray squirrels coincided with the peak in winter breeding, the absence of aggregations in nest boxes during the peak of breeding during summer-fall suggests that factors other than reproductive activity influence the behavior.

The seasonal pattern of occurrence of communal nesting of gray squirrels in this study agrees with Horwich's (1972) observations on a captive colony in Maryland, which exhibited an increased tendency to form groups from January to March. Bakken (1959) stated that nesting aggregations could be encountered at any time of year in Wisconsin, but were more apparent during the non-breeding season. Horwich (1972) noted a stronger tendency for the formation of male-female than either male-male or female-female groups. A similar trend was evident in the Florida population.

Of the three major habitats in the study area, nest box use by females with litters and adults combined was highest in oak phase sand pine scrub, intermediate in turkey oak phase sandhill and lowest in inopina oak phase scrubby flatwoods (Table1). Mean numbers of squirrels recorded along transects in these habitats in different seasons from 1969 to 1985 (unpublished data) were 1.2

Table 1.—*Distribution of nest boxes in different habitats (excluding ecotones), number of times checked (number of checks per box in parentheses), and frequency of occurrence of litters and adult gray squirrels in south-central Florida from 1973 to 1984.*

	Nest boxes		Frequency/100 boxes	
Habitat	*N*	*N* checks	Litters	Adults
So. ridge sandhill - turkey oak phase	25	1,925 (77)	2.0	5.9
So. ridge sandhill - scrub hickory phase	11	869 (79)	1.2	3.6
Sand pine scrub - oak phase	33	2,508 (76)	2.0	8.1
Scrubby flatwoods - inopina oak phase	16	1,200 (75)	1.7	2.5
Scrubby flatwoods - sand live oak phase	7	560 (80)	0.5	1.1
Flatwoods - palmetto phase	12	960 (80)	2.9	2.0
Bayhead	2	156 (78)	0	3.2
Man-occupied - old field phase	5	470 (94)	3.0	4.3
Man-occupied - landscaped phase	5	470 (94)	1.7	2.6

individuals/100 m in sand pine scrub, 0.2/100 m in scrubby flatwoods, and 0.1/100 m in sandhill. Based on ANOVA (F = 109.956, *d.f.* = 2,774, P > 0.001) followed by Tukey Unequal N HSD post hoc tests, relative abundance of gray squirrels in sand pine scrub was significantly greater than in either sandhill or scrubby flatwoods (P < 0.001) but did not differ significantly between sandhill and scrubby flatwoods (P > 0.05). These independent data indicate that the high level of use of nest boxes in sand pine scrub reflected population density.

Relative scarcity of natural cavities in the mature sand pine scrub compared with sandhill and scrubby flatwoods associations might also have been a factor in higher nest box use in that habitat. Although suitable natural tree cavities were scarce in all habitats, there were more large pine snags with cavities in sandhill and scrubby flatwoods habitats than in the mature sand pine scrub where leaf nests were most conspicuous. Thus nest boxes might have been more attractive to squirrels in sand pine scrub than in the other habitats.

The higher density of gray squirrels in mature sand pine scrub habitat compared with sandhill and scrubby flatwoods is attributable to the continuous availability and abundance of sand pine cones, as annual production of scrub hickory and oak mast during the period of this study was consistently much lower in the sand pine scrub than the other two habitats: 3.4 ± 0.6 nuts/m^2 in sand pine scrub compared with 16.9 ± 3.1 in sandhill and 7.9 ± 1.2 in scrubby flatwoods (unpublished data). The sand pine has serotinous cones that typically remain sealed for years, many not opening unless the tree is burned. Thus, mature trees have large numbers of unopened cones, which provide gray squirrels a year-round food source.

Reproduction.—The only previous data on reproduction in gray squirrels in Florida are from a one-year study by Jennings (1951) in mesic forests of north-central Florida (Table 2). He found evidence of only a summer-autumn breeding season during that year, but concluded from the presence of two age classes in the population that there were usually two breeding seasons. Mean litter size was 3.43 based on counts of placental scars in 14 females. The short duration and small sample size of Jennings' study preclude detailed comparison of the populations of northern and southern Florida. This study confirms that in Florida gray squirrels normally have two breeding seasons, although in some years they may breed only in summer-autumn; and the means of litter size in summer-autumn in the two regions agree closely. The slight difference in means of litter size in summer-fall (3.43 versus 3.34) between the two populations is probably not significant and may in part reflect the use of placental scar rather than nestling counts in the northern Florida study (Smith, 1967).

Moore (1961) observed that on a world-wide basis tree squirrels as a group appear to show a pronounced trend of decreasing litter size when progressing from north temperate to tropical climates, which is accompanied by a reduction in number of teats. Heaney (1984) also noted latitudinal trends in reproductive characteristics among North American tree squirrels as a group, but the relationships were not evident at the species or even generic levels. Kirkpatrick et al. (1978) compared data on gray squirrel breeding seasons (mating and parturition periods) from 12 localities in North America at latitudes ranging from 42 to 31^0, as well as mean size of litters in winter-spring and summer-autumn from three localities at 36 and 37^0, and found little difference in either breeding season or litter size between the most southern and northern localities. Heaney (1984) compared data on overall litter size for five populations over a latitudinal range of 44 to 31^0 and also found no correlation with latitude. A more comprehensive summary of available data on breeding seasons and litter size of gray squirrels over a latitudinal range extending from 44 to 27^0 with the addition of the data from southern Florida (Table 2) supports the conclusion of Kirkpatrick et al. (1978) and Heaney (1984) that litter size in this species does not exhibit a latitudinal trend. Neither winter-spring, summer-autumn, nor combined mean litter size is significantly correlated with latitude (r = 0.24, 0.44, 0.18, respectively, P > 0.05), and both southern and northern populations have larger litters in summer-fall than in winter-spring. Even in the southernmost population (present study), the first breeding season is occasionally skipped as in northern parts of the range.

Although no north-south trend in litter size is evident, there is some indication that the first breeding season of the gray squirrel is advanced by about a month at the southern extreme of the range. This also may be true of the second breeding season, but the difference is less obvious. Moore (1957) noted that the breeding season of the fox squirrel (*Sciurus niger*) in Florida also was about a month earlier than farther north in Michigan, Ohio, and Illinois. On the other hand, substantial shifts in the breeding season of gray squirrels over a relatively narrow latitudinal range and at different elevations at the same latitude have been documented (Brown and Yeager, 1945;

Table 2.—*Breeding (parturition) seasons and mean litter size of gray squirrel populations at different latitudes. Sources of data: 1, Thompson (1978); 2, Longley (1963); 3, Creed (1957); 4, Wingard (1950); 5, Hoffman and Kirkpatrick (1959); 6. Brown and Yeager (1945); 7. Uhlig (1956); 8, Flyger (1952); 9, Flyger (1955); 10, Flyger and Cooper (1968); 11, Chapman (1939); 12, Nixon and McClain (1975); 13 Packard (1956); 14, Hibbard (1935); 15, Kirkpatrick et al. (1978); 16, Smith (1967); 17, Nupp (1992); 18, Goodrum (1940); 19, Jennings (1951); 20, present study.*

		Birth peaks		Mean litter size				
Locality	Latitude	First	Second	First	Second	Combined	*N*	Source
Ontario,Canada	44			2.95[5]	3.25[5]	3.66[5]	40	1
Minnesota	44	Feb-Mar[1]	Jun-Jul[1]			2.68	19	2
Pennsylvania	41	Mar	Jul	1.50	3[2]	2.00	3	3
Pennsylvania	40	Mar-Apr[1]	Jul-?[1]	2.73[6]	2.00[6]	2.83[6]	32	4
Indiana	40	Mar-Apr[1]	Jul-Aug[1]					5
Illinois (northern)	42	Mar[1]	Aug[1]	2.74[7,8]	2.43[7,8]	2.68[7,8]	34	6
Illinois (central)	40	Mar[1]	Aug[1]					6
Illinois (southern)	38	Feb[1]	Jul-Aug[1]					6
West Virginia	39	Mar	Jul	2.64	2.19	2.52	46	7
Maryland	39	Feb	Aug[2]	2.54	3[2]	2.57	14	8
Maryland	39					2.68	25	9
Maryland	39	Mar	Aug	2.15	3.29	2.69	143	10
Ohio	39	Jan-Feb	sporadic					11
Ohio	39	Feb-Mar[1]	Jul-Aug[1]	2.56[5,7]	3.00[5,7]	2.78[5,7]	14	12
Kansas	39	Mar-Apr[1]	Jul[1]	2.00	2.50	2.25	7	13
Kentucky	37	Feb	Aug	2.36	2.69	2.56	27	14
Virginia (mountains)	37	Mar-Apr	Aug-Sep	2.43[5,7]	3.04[5,7]	2.76[5,7]	13	15
Virginia low elev. (low elevation)	37	Feb-Mar	Jul-Aug	2.35	2.86	2.74[5]	215	15
North Carolina	36	Feb	Jul-Aug	2.47	3.06	2.86	447	16
Alabama	32	Mar[3]	Jul[3]	2.50	2.97	2.92	51	17
Texas	31	Feb-Mar[4]	Sep-Oct[4]			2.7	16	18
Florida	29	none	?		3.43[7]	3.43[7]	14	19
Florida	27	Jan-Feb	Jun-Jul	2.12	3.26	2.77	187	20

[1] Converted from estimates based on females in estrous condition or mating dates by adding 44 days for gestation.

[2] Single record.

[3] Based on median date of mating plus 44 days for gestation.

[4] Based on peak months of pregnancies and adding 22 days on the assumption that gestation averaged half completed during the given month.

[5] Mean calculated from seasonal or monthly means.

[6] Based on counts of young outside nest.

[7] Embryo and/or placental scar counts.

[8] Includes all regions of the state; based on embryos, placental scars, and six litters in nest boxes.

Kirkpatrick et al., 1978). In addition to breeding earlier, gray squirrels in the south may tend to have more prolonged and less well defined breeding seasons than in the north, as suggested by studies in Florida (present study), North Carolina (Smith, 1967) and Texas (Goodrum, 1940) compared with studies in Maryland (Flyger and Cooper, 1968), Illinois (Brown and Yeager, 1945), and Ohio (Nixon and McClain, 1975).

Data from different geographic regions on aspects of the reproductive biology of the gray squirrel other than litter size and timing of the breeding season are nonexistent or too limited for critical analysis for latitudinal trends. Numbers of individuals involved in mating chases in Minnesota (Hazard, 1960) and Wisconsin (Bakken, 1959) ranged from 2-9 (mean = 3.3) and 3-14, respectively, compared with 2-14 (mean = 5.9) in the present study. Even if significant, these differences probably reflect local population density rather than a geographic trend. Sex ratios of litters reported from various parts of the range include: Florida - 1.01:1, males:females (present study); North Carolina - 0.93:1 (Smith, 1967); Kansas - 1.57:1 (Packard, 1956); Illinois - 1.20:1 (Brown and Yeager, 1945); Maryland - 0.94, 1.07 (Flyger, 1952; Flyger and Cooper, 1968); and Minnesota - 0.34: 1 (Longley, 1963). These data do not appear to show any systematic pattern of variation related to geographic location, suggesting that variability of nestling sex ratio reflects local environmental factors.

Although data presently available fail to suggest significant latitudinal variation in any aspect of the reproductive biology of the gray squirrel other than the timing and duration of breeding seasons, the possibility of a latitudinal gradient in litter size and other aspects of reproduction cannot be eliminated. Small sample sizes in a number of cases and differences in methods of determining litter size or breeding seasons in different studies make it difficult to critically compare data from different regions. Additional long term studies in different parts of the range, greater standardization in data collection and analysis, and better controls for the effects of local environmental factors on breeding season, litter size, and other components of reproduction are needed to more definitively evaluate latitudinal gradients in gray squirrel reproduction. It also would be useful to have data on neonatal size, as well as adult body size and litter size, for populations at different latitudes, as absolute or relative litter mass may vary latitudinally even though litter size does not. Unfortunately, the difficulty of breeding the species in captivity (Webley and Johnson, 1983) presumably precludes experimental analysis of geographic variation in the reproductive biology of the gray squirrel, an approach that would greatly aid in factoring out the relative contributions of genetic and environmental factors to variation in litter size and other reproductive traits.

ACKNOWLEDGMENTS

I thank C. A. Winegarner for assistance in checking nest boxes during the entire study, M. A. V. Raymond for aid in analyzing the data, and anonymous reviewers for constructive comments on earlier drafts of the manuscript.

LITERATURE CITED

ABRAHAMSON, W. G., A. F. JOHNSON, J. N. LAYNE, AND P. A. PERONI. 1984. Vegetation of the Archbold Biological Station, Florida: an example of the southern Lake Wales Ridge. Florida Scientist, 47:209-250.

BAKKEN, A. 1959. Behavior of gray squirrels. Pp. 393-407, *in* Symposium on the gray squirrel. (V. Flyger, ed.). Maryland Department of Research and Education Contribution, 162:356-407.

BARKALOW, F. S., JR., AND R. F. SOOTS, JR. 1965. An improved gray squirrel nest box for ecological and management studies. The Journal of Wildlife Management, 29:679-684.

BARNETT, J. 1977. Bergmann's rule and variation in structures related to feeding in the gray squirrel. Evolution, 31:538-545.

BROWN, L. G., AND L. E. YEAGER. 1945. Fox squirrels and gray squirrels in Illinois. Bulletin of the Illinois Natural History Survey, 23:443-536.

CHAPMAN, F. B. 1939. A summary of the gray squirrel investigation in southeastern Ohio. U. S. Department of Agriculture, Bureau of Biological Survey, Wildlife and Management Leaflet, BS-134:1-9.

CREED, W. A. 1957. A study of the northern gray squirrel in Cameron County, Pennsylvania, with emphasis on the beech-birch-maple forest type. M.S. thesis, Pennsylvania State University, State College, 172 pp.

FLYGER, V. F. 1952. A study of the nest box habits and the breeding season of the gray squirrel (*Sciurus carolinensis leucotis*) in Maryland and Pennsylvania. M.S. thesis, Pennsylvania State College, Stage College, 59 pp.

FLYGER, V. F. 1955. The social behavior and populations of the gray squirrel (*Sciurus carolinensis* Gmelin) in Maryland. Sc.D. dissert., Johns Hopkins University, Baltimore, Maryland, 58 pp.

FLYGER, V. F., AND H. R. COOPER. 1968. The utilization of nesting boxes by gray squirrels. Proceedings of the 21st Annual Conference of the Southeastern Association of Game and Fish Commissioners, 1967:113-117.

FLYGER, V. F., AND J. E. GATES. 1982. Fox and gray squirrels. Pp 209-229, *in* Wild mammals of North America: biology, management, and economics (J. A. Chapman and G. A. Feldhamer, eds.). The Johns Hopkins University Press, Baltimore, 1147 pp.

GOODRUM, P. D. 1940. A population study of the gray squirrel in eastern Texas. Texas Agricultural Experiment Station Bulletin, 591:1-34.

HAZARD, E. B. 1960. A field study of activity among squirrels (Sciuridae) in southern Michigan. Ph.D. dissertation, University of Michigan, Ann Arbor, 288 pp.

HEANEY, L. R. 1984. Climatic influences on life-history tactics and behavior of North American tree squirrels. Pp. 43-78, *in* The biology of ground-dwelling squirrels (J. O. Murie and G. R. Michener, eds.). University of Nebraska Press, Lincoln, 459 pp.

HIBBARD, C. W. 1935. Breeding seasons of gray squirrel and flying squirrel. Journal of Mammalogy, 16:325-326.

HOFFMAN, R. A., AND C. M. KIRKPATRICK. 1959. Current knowledge of tree squirrel reproductive cycles and development. Pp. 393-407, *in* Symposium on the gray squirrel. (V. Flyger, ed.). Maryland Department of Research and Education Contribution, 162:356-407.

HORWICH, R. H. 1972. The ontogeny of social behavior in the gray squirrel (*Sciurus carolinensis*). Advances in Ethology, Journal of Comparative Ethology, supplement 8:1-103.

JENNINGS, W. L. 1951. Study of the life history and ecology of the gray squirrel (*Sciurus c. carolinensis* Gmelin) in Gulf Hammock. M.S. thesis, University of Florida, Gainesville, 151 pp.

KIRKPATRICK, R. L., J. L. COGGIN, H. S. MOSBY, AND J. O. NEWELL. 1978. Parturition times and litter sizes of gray squirrels in Virginia. Proceedings of the 13th Annual Conference of the Southeastern Association of Fish and Wildlife Agencies, 1976:541-545.

LAYNE, J. N., AND M. A. V. RAYMOND. 1994. Communal nesting of southern flying squirrels in Florida. Journal of Mammalogy, 75:110-120.

LONGLEY, W. H. 1963. Minnesota gray and fox squirrels. The American Midland Naturalist, 69:82-98.

MOORE, J. C. 1957. The natural history of the fox squirrel, *Sciurus niger shermani*. Bulletin of the American Museum of Natural History, 113:1-72.

MOORE, J. C. 1961. Geographic variation in some reproductive characteristics of diurnal squirrels. Bulletin of the American Museum of Natural History, 122:1-32.

NIXON, C. M., AND M. W. MCCLAIN. 1975. Breeding seasons and fecundity of female gray squirrels in Ohio. The Journal of Wildlife Management, 39:426-438.

NUPP, T. E. 1992. Nest box use and population densities of gray squirrels in southern Alabama. M.S. thesis, Auburn University, Alabama, 108 pp.

PACKARD, R. L. 1956. The tree squirrels of Kansas: ecology and economic importance. Miscellaneous Publications, Museum of Natural History, University of Kansas, 11:1-67.

SHORTEN, M. 1951. Some aspects of the biology of the grey squirrel (*Sciurus carolinensis*) in Great Britain. Proceedings of the Zoological Society of London, 121:427-459.

SHORTEN, M., AND F. A. COURTIER. 1955. A population of the grey squirrel (*Sciurus carolinensis*) in May 1954. Annals of Applied Biology, 43:494-510.

SMITH, N. B. 1967. Some aspects of reproduction in the female gray squirrel *Sciurus carolinensis carolinensis* Gmelin, in Wake County, North Carolina. M.S. thesis, North Carolina State University, Raleigh, 92 pp.

SMITH, N. B., AND F. S. BARKALOW, JR. 1967. Precocious breeding in the gray squirrel. Journal of Mammalogy, 48:328-330.

THOMPSON, D. C. 1978. Regulation of a northern grey squirrel (*Sciurus carolinensis*) population. Ecology, 59:708-715.

UHLIG, H. G. 1955*a*. Weights of adult gray squirrels. Journal of Mammalogy, 36:293-296.

UHLIG, H. G. 1955*b*. The determination of age of nestlings and sub-adult gray squirrels in West Virginia. The Journal of Wildlife Management, 19:479-483.

UHLIG, H. G. 1956. The gray squirrel in West Virginia. Conservation Commission of West Virginia, Division of Game Management, Bulletin, 3:1-83.

WEBLEY, G. E., AND E. JOHNSON. 1983. Reproductive physiology of the grey squirrel (*Sciurus carolinensis*). Mammal Review, 13:149-154.

WINGARD, R. G. 1950. The life history and habitat of the northern gray squirrel in relation to some forest communities in Huntington County, Pennsylvania. M.S. thesis, Pennsylvania State College, State College, 202 pp.

VARIATION IN SPACING BEHAVIOR OF EURASIAN RED SQUIRRELS, *SCIURUS VULGARIS* IN WINTER: EFFECTS OF DENSITY AND FOOD ABUNDANCE

LUC A. WAUTERS AND ANDRE A. DHONDT

Department of Biology, U.I.A., University of Antwerp, B- 2610 Wilrijk, Belgium.

ABSTRACT.—Food, population density and spacing behavior can be related in four ways: spacing behavior is the mechanism relating squirrel numbers to their food, home range size decreases when abundant food leads to high densities (i.e., range size is causally related to density), range size and density are correlated but not causally related, and density is regulated, by territorial behavior, at a fixed level (and no density fluctuations result). We tested the predictions of these hypotheses in two populations of Eurasian red squirrels (*Sciurus vulgaris*) by monitoring changes in density and home range size in winter and food availability over 6 years. Both squirrel numbers and mean winter home range size fluctuated over years. Home range size of both males and females increased when densities were low and decreased when squirrel numbers increased. No significant correlation existed between food availability and mean size of winter home range. Variation in size of core-area followed the same pattern. Our results indicate that in the non-territorial Eurasian red squirrel home range size decreases as a result of increased social pressure at high densities, agreeing with the predictions of the second hypothesis. However, spacing behavior of adults does limit the recruitment of locally born young and immigrants, thereby preventing the depletion of food resources in most years.

INTRODUCTION

The abundance of a certain species can change between habitats, and between years within a specific habitat (Chitty, 1960). In tree squirrels, the importance of food availability as a major factor influencing reproduction, survival and dispersal rate, and thus population size, has been well established (Smith, 1968; Nixon et al., 1975; Gurnell, 1983; Sullivan, 1990; Wauters and Dhondt, 1990; 1995; Klenner and Krebs, 1991; Koprowski, 1991). However, other factors including disease, predation and severe weather might cause a decrease in squirrel numbers below the level set by food (Stephenson and Brown, 1980). Finally, spacing behavior can limit breeding population density and/or juvenile recruitment by preventing immigrants from settling or by forcing locally born juveniles to disperse (Thompson, 1978; Hansen and Nixon, 1985; Price et al., 1986; Wauters and Dhondt, 1993).

Food, density and spacing behavior can be related in four ways. First, spacing behavior can be the mechanism relating squirrel numbers to their food, in which case rich food supplies result in small home ranges, allowing an increase in density. Second, home range size can decrease, as a result of increased social pressure when abundant food leads to high densities. In this case range size is causally related to density. Third, rich food supplies may result in both small home ranges and high density; range size and density are correlated but not causally related (Kenward, 1985). Finally, density can be regulated, by territorial behavior, at a level set by the food available in years with a poor seed-crop. In this case, density does not fluctuate but remains stable over time (Rusch and Reeder, 1978).

These hypotheses can be investigated in two ways: experimentally, by manipulating food supplies (with supplemental food) or density (by removal or addition of animals), monitoring the changes in space use and population dynamics (Boutin, 1990), or by long-term monitoring of changes in food availability, density and home range size in the same population(s) (Kenward, 1985). The first option has been commonly applied in studies on the importance of territoriality in *Tamiasciurus* (Sullivan and Sullivan, 1982; Price et al., 1986; Boutin and Schweiger, 1988; Sullivan,

In, M.A. Steele, J. F. Merritt, and D. A. Zegers (eds.). 1998. Ecology and Evolutionary Biology of Tree Squirrels. Special Publication, Virginia Museum of Natural History, 6: 320 pp

1990; Klenner, 1991; Klenner and Krebs, 1991). The second option has been used to understand the interrelation between food, spacing and density in the non-territorial gray squirrel (*Sciurus carolinensis*) (Kenward, 1985).

In this paper we investigate which of the above hypotheses hold for Eurasian red squirrels (*Sciurus vulgaris*), a species in which spacing behavior differs between males and females, and according to habitat type (Wauters and Dhondt, 1992). We monitored changes of home range size of adults over 6 winters (December - February) in a coniferous and a deciduous woodland. This approach allowed us to test the following predictions:

Hypothesis 1: home range size in winter is strongly inversely correlated with the size of the previous autumn seed-crop;

Hypothesis 2: density in winter is correlated with the size of the seed-crop of the previous autumn; density and size of home range in winter are strongly inversely correlated;

Hypothesis 3: range size and density are inversely correlated; both are correlated with the size of the seed-crop of the previous autumn, and

Hypothesis 4: both range size and density remain stable over years and are not correlated with changes in food availability.

METHODS

The study species.—The Eurasian red squirrel's social behavior differs between habitats and between the sexes (Wauters and Dhondt, 1992). Males have large, strongly overlapping home ranges and a marked dominance hierarchy, while dominant, reproductive females defend exclusive core-areas against other dominant females (intrasexual territoriality). Subordinate females live as floaters or settle along the edges of home ranges of dominant females (Wauters and Dhondt, 1992).

Study areas.—We used two study sites of 30 ha each. One in the 'Merodese Bossen' at Herenthout (Province of Antwerpen, N. Belgium) a mainly coniferous woodland of 212 ha, is dominated by Scots pine (*Pinus sylvestris*) and Corsican pine (*P. nigra*). The south side of the study area is bordered by meadows and by a road that was never crossed by resident squirrels. The west side is bordered by farmland and less suitable patches of woods. Suitable habtitat continues along the north and east side. The second study area lies in the 'Peerdsbos' at Schoten (Province of Antwerpen, N. Belgium) a mainly deciduous woodland of 150 ha. The study plot is dominated by mature oak (*Quercus robur*) and beech (*Fagus sylvatica*) with some chestnut (*Castanea sativa*), and a small plot with Scots and Corsican pine. The study area is bordered by houses and a road on the north side and by meadows and a motorway along the south and south-west side that were never crossed by resident squirrels. On the east side the forest continues.

Trapping and handling squirrels.—Trapping was carried out for at least five days every two months from October 1985 to March 1993. All squirrels were individually marked, weighed, aged, and sexed (Wauters and Dhondt, 1990; 1993). Not all adults present in the winter population could be radiotagged. Therefore, we radiotagged (SR-1 transmitter collars for red squirrels, Biotrack, U.K.) a random subset of adult males and females in each winter (i.e., those that were captured in the beginning of the December trapping session; Table 1).

Table 1.—*The number (%) of adult squirrels radiotagged in each winter.*

Winter	Coniferous area		Deciduous area	
	Males	Females	Males	Females
1985-1986	8 (57)	11 (55)	5 (42)	5 (45)
1986-1987	6 (60)	9 (60)	10 (91)	9 (100)
1987-1988	7 (47)	7 (44)	8 (53)	8 (57)
1988-1989	-	-	6 (35)	7 (41)
1990-1991	11 (58)	10 (67)	7 (23)	8 (29)
1991-1992	8 (31)	9 (53)	9 (45)	8 (53)
1992-1993	9 (43)	10 (71)	-	-

Radio-tracking.—Two point-fixes were taken per day for each radiotagged squirrel, at minimum time intervals of 2 h. From December to February, between 30 and 40 locations were taken, which was sufficient to obtain correct estimates of home range size (Wauters and Dhondt, 1992). For each point-fix, the exact location of the squirrel was recorded using west - east and south - north coordinates. The majority of home ranges were mononuclear (coniferous area, 104 out of 105; deciduous area, 79 out of 89), and size of home range was calculated using the mononuclear range polygon with the recalculated arithmetic mean as range center (Ranges IV; Kenward, 1990). For the multinuclear ranges, multinuclear clustering was used (Ranges IV; Kenward, 1990). Both total size of home range (100% of fixes) and size of core-area (densest 70% of all fixes) were calculated (Wauters and Dhondt, 1992).

Food supply.—Overall food abundance on the study area was calculated by counting fallen seeds (including the remains of food-items consumed before they had fallen) on 34 (coniferous) and 30 (deciduous) 1m^2-plots placed randomly in different age-stands of seed-producing trees. The same plots were sampled each year. Seeds counted were the cones of Scots and Corsican pine in coniferous and deciduous areas, and acorns and beechnuts in the deciduous area. Total energy (kJ/ha) was then calculated from seed abundance and energy content per seed (Wauters et al., 1992).

Data analyses.—Parametric statistics were calculated with SAS (SAS Institute, Inc, 1989). Pearson correlation coefficients were calculated with the PROC COR procedure, ANCOVA models with PROC GLM, and multiple linear regression models with PROC REG (SAS, 1989). For statistical analyses in which study areas were combined, we normalized the values of annual food abundance, mean size of winter home range, and size of core-area in each study area (in a set of normalized data, $\bar{x} = 0$ and $SD = 1$).

RESULTS

There were considerable inter-year differences in mean size of winter home ranges in both habitats (Fig. 1a, b). For males, variation between years was similar in both habitats, ranging from 3.0 to 4.7 ha in the coniferous, and 3.8 to 5.3 ha in the deciduous area (Fig. 1a, b). For females, however, mean size of winter home range varied little in the coniferous area (1.9 to 2.6 ha), while in the deciduous area we found very strong annual variation (1.8 to 4.6 ha, Fig. 1a, b). Similarly, size of core-area varied strongly for both sexes in the deciduous woodland and for males in the coniferous woodland (Fig. 1c, d). Mean female size of core-area in the coniferous woodland, however, remained stable over years (Fig. 1c).

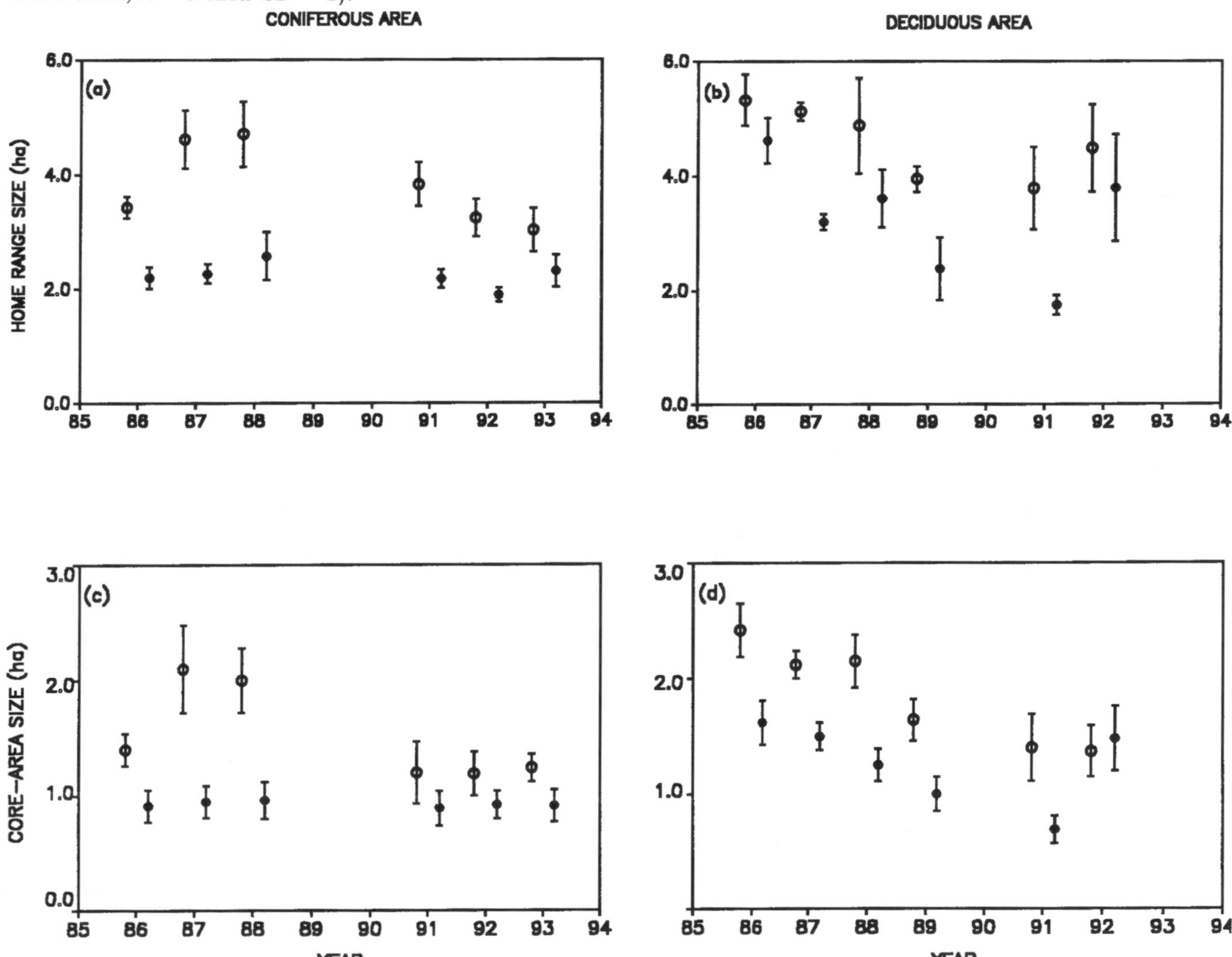

Fig. 1.—Inter-annual variation in size of home range ($\bar{X} \pm 1\ SE_x$) in the coniferous (a) and the deciduous area (b), and in size of core-area ($\bar{X} \pm 1\ SE_x$) in the coniferous (c) and the deciduous area (d), of male (°), and female (•) red squirrels.

We tested the effects of density of the same sex, density of the other sex, food abundance (independent variables), area and sex (classes) on mean home range size, of males and females, with an ANCOVA model. Home range size depended on both area (F = 19.9, *d.f.* = 1, 18, P = 0.0003) and sex (F = 55.9, *d.f.* = 1, 18, P < 0.0001) and varied with density of the same sex (F = 10.4, *d.f.* = 1, 18, P = 0.005). Density of the other sex (F = 1.26, *d.f.* = 1, 18, P = 0.28) and food abundance (F = 1.66, *d.f.* = 1, 18, P = 0.21) were not significantly related with range size. Males had consistently larger home ranges than females (two-tailed Wilcoxon test: P = 0.0022; Fig. 1a, b) and, within each year, ranges were larger in the deciduous than in the coniferous area (two-tailed Wilcoxon test: P = 0.017; Fig. 1a, b).

Because of the different spacing behavior of males and females, data were further analyzed by sex. Areas were combined by using normalized values for size of home range, size of core-area, and food abundance. For both males and females, density was negatively correlated with mean size of home range (Fig. 2), while no correlation existed between range size and food (Table 2a, Fig. 3). The same was true for core-area size (Table 2a). We investigated whether food explained any additional variation in mean size of home range, after density was included in a multiple linear regression model. Since annual variation in numbers of males and females followed the same pattern and were strongly correlated (Pearson correlation coefficient: r = 0.709, n = 12, P = 0.01), only density of the same sex was used in the regression model. For males, mean size of home range and size of core-area in winter decreased with increasing male density, and were larger in winters with richer food supplies (Table 2b). Size of home range and core-area of females decreased when female density increased, although this pattern was less pronounced than in males (Table 2b, Fig. 2). Annual variation in food abundance did not affect either the size of winter ranges, or core-areas of females (Table 2b).

DISCUSSION

The core-area is that part of a squirrel's home range most intensively used (Kenward, 1985; 1990). Therefore, size and overlap of core-area may be more appropriate indicators of the intensity of

Table 2.—*The relationship of normalized mean winter home range size (HR) and core-area size (CA) with the number of males (NM), the number of females (NF) and normalized food abundance (FOOD). a. Pearson correlation coefficients* (n = *12); b. The selected parameters of the multiple linear regression models.*

a. Correlation coefficient (*P*-value)

	Males			*Females*		
	NM	*NF*	*FOOD*	*NM*	*NF*	*FOOD*
HR	-0.772	-0.619	0.01	-0.650	-0.578	0.197
	(0.003)	(0.032)	(0.97)	(0.022)	(0.049)	(0.54)
CA	-0.789	-0.505	0.04	-0.675	-0.707	-0.187
	(0.0023)	(0.094)	(0.91)	(0.016)	(0.010)	(0.56)

b. Selected regression model (*P*-value for partial effects)

Home range size			
NM	F (1, 9) = 25.1 (0.0007)	NF	F (1, 10) = 5.02 (0.049)
FOOD	F (1, 9) = 4.79 (0.056)		
Regression model (R^2 = 0.74)		Regression model (R^2 = 0.33)	
HR = 2.6 - 0.15(NM) + 0.42(FOOD)		HR = 1.9 - 0.12(NF)	
Core-area size			
NM	F (1, 9) = 16.47 (0.0002)	NF	F (1, 10) = 9.97 (0.016)
FOOD	F (1, 9) = 9.17 (0.014)		
Regression model (R^2 = 0.80)		Regression model (R^2 = 0.45)	
CA = 2.7 - 0.15(NM) + 0.49(FOOD)		CA = 2.1 - 0.13(NF)	

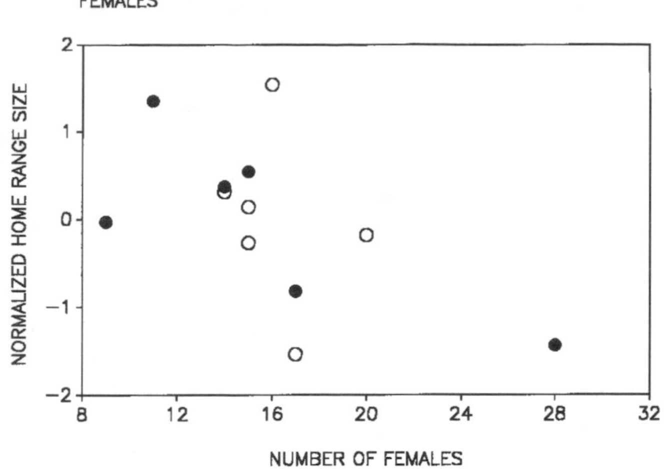

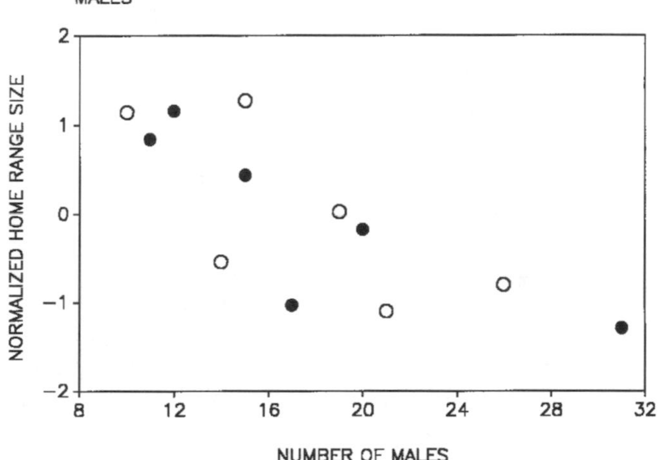

Fig. 2.—The relationship between normalized size of home range and density of the same sex in winter, for males and females in coniferous (○) and deciduous (●) areas.

food abundance (size of the seed-crop produced the previous summer-autumn) should be strongly inversely correlated, as predicted by hypotheses 1 and 3. We found, however, no significant correlations between food and range size, either in males or in females. A positive partial correlation between food and the residual variation in mean size of home range of males, after male density was entered in a multiple regression model, was in the opposite direction of what was predicted. Therefore, we reject hypotheses 1 and 3.

Mean size of winter home range did show strong annual variation, as did winter density. This is in contrast with the predictions of hypothesis 4, which we therefore reject. Variation in both range size and density were large for males and females in the deciduous area, and for males in the coniferous area. In conifer woodland, however, density of females (from 0.47 to 0.67/ha) and mean size of winter home range of females fluctuated

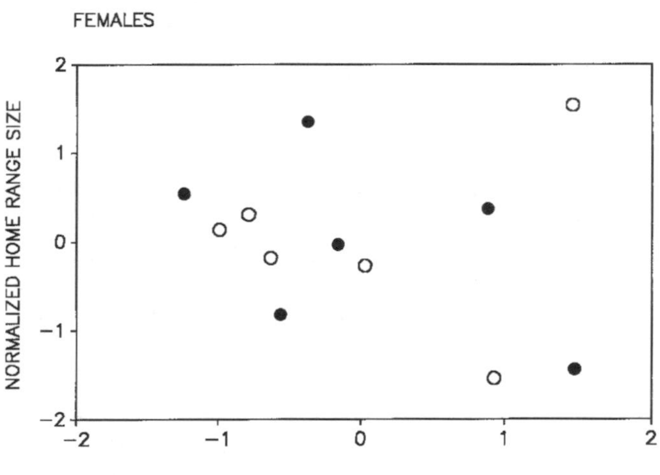

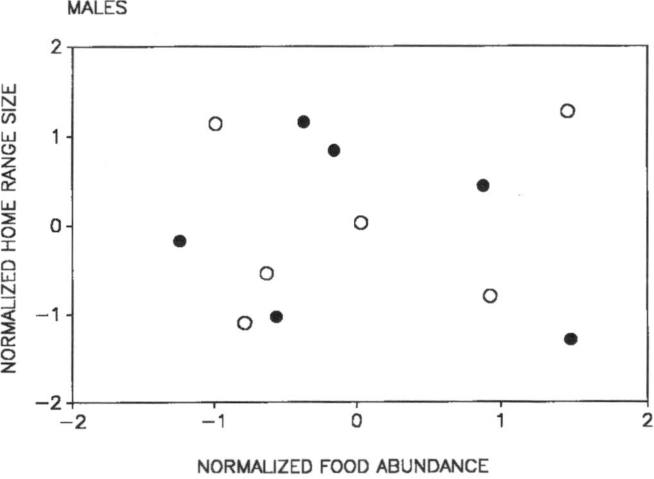

Fig. 3.—The relationship between normalized size of home range and normalized abundance of food in winter for males and females in coniferous (○) and deciduous (●) areas.

intraspecific competition than size and overlap of home range (Wauters and Dhondt, 1992). Our results show similar patterns of annual variation in size of home range and core-area for both male and female red squirrels, with the only exception that size of core-area of females in the coniferous woodland remained stable over years. We therefore feel that variation in total range size is a good measurement of variation in the squirrel's spacing behavior, and use size of home range when discussing the relationship between spacing, density and food.

Winter is the period of the year that red squirrel ranges are most stable and that squirrels feed nearly exclusively on high-energy tree seeds (Wauters and Dhondt, 1987; 1992; Wauters et al., 1992). Thus, if squirrels adjust the size of their home ranges directly to the available food supply, variation in mean size of winter range and overall little. Female red squirrels are the more territorial sex and intrasexual territoriality is most strongly developed in coniferous habitats (Wauters and Dhondt, 1992). Apparently, intrasexual territoriality of females decreases the amplitude of fluctuations in squirrel numbers.

In both descriptive and experimental studies on *Tamiasciurus*, the positive relationship between food abundance and density has been demonstrated (Smith, 1968; Kemp and Keith, 1970; Sullivan, 1990; Klenner and Krebs, 1991). The only study which apparently presents contradicting results is that of Rusch and Reeder (1978). As discussed by Sullivan (1990), the stable densities found by Rusch and Reeder (1978), despite strong fluctuations in the seed-crop, were probably related to the fragmented nature of the habitat where even good spruce habitat did not provide enough food in a mast year to generate population fluctuations. Also Boutin and Schweiger (1988), working on a true island, found that experimental increases in squirrel numbers did not result in an increase of density of territorial squirrels in prime habitat, nor a decrease in territory size. The surplus animals behaved as floaters, or settled in an unoccupied area of poorer quality. On the other hand, decreasing density by removals, did result in an increase of territory size of neighbouring squirrels and in a higher local recruitment of young from females with enlarged territories (Boutin and Schweiger, 1988). This system of a quite stable number of resident squirrels in high quality habitat, with surplus animals behaving as floaters or settling in surrounding marginal habitats, seems typical for populations occupying fragmented landscapes where prime habitat is surrounded by hostile or marginal areas. Sullivan (1990) and Klenner and Krebs (1991) conducting, respectively, long and short term experiments involving addition of food in large, continuous conifer forests, found a two- to four-fold increase in squirrel numbers after food was added. However, availability of excess food at high squirrel density, suggested that factors other than food, apparently territorial behavior, limited population size at high density (Klenner, 1991; Klenner and Krebs, 1991).

Also fluctuating numbers of Eurasian red squirrels in spring and autumn, before dispersal of juveniles, are closely related to changes in the food supply (Wauters and Dhondt, 1990). During a rich seed-crop, reproductive rate and immigration rate increase, and squirrel numbers reach peak densities in October. Density-dependent losses of juveniles and subadults in autumn and early winter, cause a decrease in numbers (Wauters and Dhondt, 1990). Moreover, immigration success, in both males and females, depends on the presence of vacant home ranges (females), or areas of low, intrasexual, density (males, Wauters and Dhondt, 1993). As a result, squirrel numbers in winter are less strongly related to the size of the seed-crop of the previous summer.

The lack of any direct relationship between fluctuations in overall food abundance and mean size of ranges, and the strong correlation between squirrel numbers and size of home range in winter, agree with the predictions of the second hypothesis. We therefore conclude that in red squirrels, as in gray squirrels and *Tamiasciurus* (Gurnell, 1983; Kenward, 1985; Klenner and Krebs, 1991), fluctuations in population size closely follow fluctuations in food abundance. The seasonal decrease over winter, however, is largely density-dependent (Wauters and Dhondt, 1990). When winter densities are high, intra-specific competition for resources and space is intense and squirrels use small home ranges. When numbers decrease, social pressure decreases and squirrels increase the size of their home range. Thus, annual variation in size of home range of non-territorial red squirrels in winter is caused by variation in winter density. Nevertheless, spacing behavior limits local recruitment of juveniles and the number of immigrants that establish residency (Wauters and Dhondt, 1990, 1993), and seems to prevent numbers from becoming too high, thereby preventing the depletion of food resources.

ACKNOWLEDGMENTS

We thank Paola Casale, Rutger De Vos, and Christel Swinnen for helping with the fieldwork. Constructive comments of Giovanni Amori, Michael Steele and an anonymous referee helped to improve the manuscript. This study was made possible with the financial support of the Belgian Institute for the development of Scientific Research in Industry and Agriculture (I.W.O.N.L., grant 840068 to L.W.), the Fund for Collective Fundamental research (F.K.F.O. project to A.D.), Brussels, and the STEP-C-0040 Project from the EC.

LITERATURE CITED

BOUTIN, S. 1990. Experimental additions of food to terrestrial vertebrates: patterns, problems and the future. Canadian Journal of Zoology, 68:203-220.

BOUTIN S., AND S. SCHWEIGER. 1988. Manipulation of intruder pressure in red squirrels (*Tamiasciurus hudsonicus*): effects on territory size and acquisition. Canadian Journal of Zoology, 66:2270-2274.

CHITTY, D. 1960. Population processes in the vole and their relevance to general theory. Canadian Journal of Zoology, 38:99-113.

GURNELL, J. 1983. Squirrel numbers and the abundance of tree seeds. Mammal Review, 13:133-148.

HANSEN, L. P., AND C. M. NIXON. 1985. Effects of adults on the demography of fox squirrels (*Sciurus niger*). Canadian Journal of Zoology, 63:861-867.

KEMP, G. A., AND L. B. KEITH. 1070. Dynamics and regulation of red squirrel (*Tamiasciurus hudsonicus*) populations. Ecology, 51:763-779.

KENWARD, R. E. 1985. Ranging behavior and population dynamics in grey squirrels. Pp 319-330, *in* Behavioral Ecology: Ecological consequences of adaptive behavior (R. M. Sibly and R. H. Smith, eds.). Blackwell Scientific Publications, Oxford, UK 620 pp.

———. 1990. Ranges IV. Software for analyzing animal location data. Institute of Terrestrial Ecology, Wareham, England.

KLENNER, W. 1991. Red squirrel population dynamics. II. Settlement patterns and the response to removals. Journal of Animal Ecology, 60:979-993.

KLENNER, W., AND C. J. KREBS. 1991. Red squirrel population dynamics. I. The effect of supplemental food on demography. Journal of Animal Ecology, 60:961-978.

KOPROWSKI, J. L. 1991. Response of fox squirrels and gray squirrels to a late spring-early summer food shortage. Journal of Mammalogy, 72:367-372.

NIXON, C. M., M. W. MCCLAIN, AND R. W. DONOHOE. 1975. Effects of hunting and mast crops on a squirrel population. The Journal of Wildlife Management, 39(1):1-25.

PRICE, K., K. BROUGHTON, S. BOUTIN, AND A. R. E. SINCLAIR. 1986. Territory size and ownership in red squirrels: responses to removals. Canadian Journal of Zoology, 64:1144- 1147.

RUSCH, D. A., AND W. G. REEDER. 1978. Population ecology of Alberta red squirrels. Ecology, 59:400-420.

SAS INSTITUTE, INC. 1989. SAS/STAT User's guide. Sixth Edition. SAS Institute Inc., Cary, North Carolina, 1028 pp.

SMITH, C. C. 1968. The adaptive nature of social organization in the genus of tree squirrels, *Tamiasciurus*. Ecological Monographs, 39:31-63.

STEPHENSON, R. L., AND D. E. BROWN. 1980. Snow cover as a factor influencing mortality of Abert's squirrels. The Journal of Wildlife Management, 44:951-955.

SULLIVAN, T. P. 1990. Responses of red squirrel (*Tamiasciurus douglasii* populations to supplemental food. Journal of Mammalogy, 71:579-590.

SULLIVAN, T. P., AND D. S. SULLIVAN. 1982. Population dynamics and regulation of the douglas squirrel (*Tamiasciurusdouglasii*) with supplemental food. Oecologia, 53:264-270.

THOMPSON, D. C. 1978. Regulation of a northern gray squirrel (*Sciurus carolinensis*) population. Ecology, 59:708-715.

WAUTERS, L. A., AND A. A. DHONDT. 1987. Activity budget and foraging behavior of the red squirrel (*Sciurus vulgaris*, Linnaeus, 1758) in a coniferous habitat. Zeitschrift für Saugetierkunde, 52:341-352.

———. 1990. Red squirrel (*Sciurus vulgaris* Linnaeus, 1758) population dynamics in different habitats. Zeitschrift für Saugetierkunde, 55:161-175.

———. 1992. Spacing behavior of red squirrels, *Sciurus vulgaris*: variation between habitats and the sexes. Animal Behavior, 43:297-311.

———. 1993. Immigration pattern and success in red squirrels. Behavioral Ecology and Sociobiology, 33:159-167.

———. 1995. Lifetime reproductive success and its correlates in female Eurasian red squirrels. Oikos, 72:402-410.

WAUTERS, L., C. SWINNEN, AND A. A. DHONDT. 1992. Activity budget and foraging behavior of red squirrels (*Sciurus vulgaris*) in coniferous and deciduous habitats. Journal of Zoology, (London), 227:71-86.

SEASONAL CHANGES IN RANGING BEHAVIOR AND HABITAT CHOICE BY RED SQUIRRELS (*SCIURUS VULGARIS*) IN CONIFER PLANTATIONS IN NORTHERN ENGLAND

PETER W. W. LURZ AND PETER J. GARSON

Center for Land Use and Water Resources Research (PWWL)
Department of Agricultural and Environmental Science, University of Newcastle, Newcastle upon Tyne, NE1 7RU, UK (PJG)

ABSTRACT.—The ranging behavior and habitat preferences of over 20 individually radiotagged red squirrels (*Sciurus vulgaris*) have been studied since early 1992 in production conifer plantations consisting of three species exotic to UK: Norway spruce (*Picea abies*), Sitka spruce (*Picea sitchensis*), lodgepole pine (*Pinus contorta*). Feeding activity of squirrels and drey use were monitored by radio tracking, and through recovery of stripped cones along transect lines. These transects also allowed the total annual cone crop to be estimated for the spruce species. Conifer crops differed markedly between 1991 and 1992, and habitat preference by squirrels is shown to correspond to the phenology and size of cone crops in pine and Sitka spruce. A sample of over 70 dreys indicates that they are usually built in the spruces, as opposed to pine. These patterns of habitat use for foraging and drey construction are used to specify design features for commercial forests, consisting of these three commonly grown species, that will benefit this threatened squirrel in Northern England.

INTRODUCTION

In the United Kingdom, the introduced American gray squirrel (*Sciurus carolinensis*) is thought to be better adapted to broadleaved and mixed forest habitats than to conifer woodlands (Gurnell and Pepper 1993; Kenward and Holm, 1993). It is consistent with this view that the native European red squirrel (*Sciurus vulgaris*) has only persisted in sympatry with gray squirrels in woodlands containing a high proportion of conifers (Kenward and Holm, 1989; Usher et al., 1992). Despite this, the red squirrel has become extinct over most of England and Wales, and from parts of Scotland, since the introduction of the gray squirrel a little over a century ago (Middleton, 1930).

The only large area of continuous red squirrel distribution remaining in England covers the northern counties of Cumbria and Northumberland, adjacent to the Scottish border. In this region extensive areas of open upland habitat have been planted with non-native conifers for timber production. The largest single block of this man-made habitat is Kielder Forest, covering an area of about 50,000 ha. Forest Enterprise, the UK government organization responsible for the management of Kielder, has identified a 6,000 ha block (called Spadeadam Forest) as a special conservation area for the red squirrel (McIntosh, 1995). However, our knowledge of its ecology in non-native conifer forests is still very limited, making it difficult to manage such an area effectively for squirrels.

Over the last two years, we have studied the effects of changes in food availability on space use by red squirrels at Spadeadam. In particular, we wanted to determine: 1) how the cone crop varies between tree species and years; 2) whether red squirrels change their pattern of habitat use in parallel with any marked variations in food abundance; and 3) whether squirrels select certain trees for drey-building. In conclusion, we attempt to translate our initial findings on these questions

In M.A. Steele, J. F. Merritt, and D. A. Zegers (eds.). 1998. Ecology and Evolutionary Biology of Tree Squirrels. Special Publication, Virginia Museum of Natural History, 6: 320 pp

into forest management recommendations suitable for implementation in this squirrel conservation area, or other areas like it.

METHODS

Study Site.—As a whole, Kielder Forest is planted with 70% Sitka spruce (*Picea sitchensis*), 12% Norway spruce (*Picea abies*) and 9% lodgepole pine (*Pinus contorta*). Our study area in Spadeadam Forest, located at the southwestern edge of Kielder, contained plantations of all 3 species of cone-bearing age (> 30 years), as well as a small 7 ha block of Omorika spruce (*Picea omorika*).

Cone crop abundance was measured by the use of cone transect lines. A transect was the area between two rows of trees, which was cleared, measured and marked out for a length of up to 70 m. In each case, these lines were walked once a month and all cones were collected and counted. A total of 25 lines (10 Norway spruce, 11 Sitka spruce, 4 lodgepole pine; total length: 1414 m) were established at the start of the project in February 1992. All comparisons of cone crops are standardized and given as densities (i.e., total annual cone count/cone transect area). The total crop reaching the ground for each year is based on the period between 1 October to the following 30 September. Cone counts on a sample of Norway spruce trees that were felled adjacent to the study area in late September 1992, showed that the majority of the 1991 cones had fallen to the ground in the preceding 12 months. The number of cones retained on these trees (n=40) was equivalent to 1% of the total annual crop per tree estimated from two Norway spruce cone transect lines in the nearby study area, representing the area under 65 trees. Our finding for Sitka spruce was equivalent in that the number of cones retained in a sample of 12 felled trees was equivalent to 3% of the 1991 crop estimated from cone transects under 76 trees in an adjacent stand.

In lodgepole pine, by contrast, our observations indicated that the majority of cones counted on transect lines had been stripped by squirrels (see RESULTS), whilst a significant but unknown proportion of cones were retained by the trees beyond 12 months. Thus total cone counts from transects under lodgepole pine are a better indicator of the extent of cone harvesting by squirrels than of the annual cone crop size.

Trapping procedure.—Squirrels were live-trapped in baited Mink (*Mustela vison*) traps (Fuller Engineering, Felcourt, UK) fitted with a wooden nest box in which captured animals could shelter. Squirrels were fitted with radiotransmitter collars (Biotrack, Wareham, UK) containing a thermistor which caused the signal repeat rate to vary directly with temperature. Thus we could easily distinguish an actively foraging individual from an animal in a drey, or one which had died.

Home ranges of squirrels and patterns of habitat use were determined by radio-locating individuals three times a day over 10-day periods (Kenward, 1985). On each occasion ('fix'), the tree species occupied, and the squirrel's position to the nearest 10 m on a mapped grid, were recorded by walking up to the tree containing the squirrel without disturbing it. If the squirrel was detected to be moving during this procedure, the fix was rejected. The location of each drey used by any squirrel (usually 1-4 dreys per individual) was only used once for calculating home range size and shape, in order to avoid artificial clustering of fixes (Kenward, 1985; Wauters and Dhondt, 1992). Minimum convex polygons (MCP) and 70% core home range areas were derived for 6 males and 46 females monitored between February 1992 and January 1994, using the mononuclear range area analysis with the recalculated arithmetic mean as range center in the RANGES IV software (Kenward, 1987, 1990). Biases in habitat utilization in 3 time periods (March and September 93, January 94) were determined by compositional analysis, a technique for making statistically valid comparisons of the proportion of radio locations by individual squirrels in each habitat type with the proportions of these habitats present in the whole study area (Aebisher et al., 1993*a*, 1993*b*). For this purpose the extent of the study area was defined by the outer perimeter of the superimposed MCP ranges of all the squirrels monitored during each period. As the compositional analysis technique can not accept zero as a numerator or denominator in the log-ratio transformation required, 0.001 was substituted for zero proportions of any particular habitat type which was available in the study area but not utilized by an animal.

RESULTS

Variations in cone crops and squirrel feeding preferences.—Cone production by both Norway and Sitka spruce fluctuated strongly between years (Table 1). For instance, cone densities representing the 1992 crops were only 3 and 5% respectively of the figures for the previous year. During the 12 months after the autumn of 1991, the squirrels stripped cones from both Norway spruce and lodgepole pine almost to the exclusion of Sitka spruce, despite the abundance of cones produced

Table 1.—*Cone densities on transect lines beneath Sitka spruce (SS), Norway spruce (NS) and lodgepole pine (LP) for three years with the percentage of cones stripped by squirrels given in brackets.*

Species/Transect (m^2) (No. lines)		Mean Cones m^{-2} ±1 S.E. 1991	S.E.	1992	S.E.	1993	S.E.
SS	772 (11)	4.64	1.35 (1%)	0.26	0.09 (1%)	1.15	2.3 (51%)
NS	712 (10)	4.85	1.07 (40%)	0.14	0.04 (41%)	0.04	0.04 (0%)
LP	259 (4)	2.53	0.27 (74%)	5.22	2.0 (92%)	0.76	0.7 (89%)

*1 October 1991 - 30 September 1992

by this species. In the following year (1992-1993) the same proportion of available Norway spruce cones were stripped, despite cone production being extremely low and less than that for Sitka spruce. Following the fall of 1993, Sitka spruce and lodgepole pine cones were stripped, while squirrels apparently took none of that year's minute crop of Norway spruce cones. Taken together, these results suggest that: 1) lodgepole pine cones provided most of the conifer seed food for this squirrel population in these three years; 2) the preferred diet contains spruce seed of one or other species in addition to pine, and 3) given an abundant crop of cones from both spruce species in one year, Norway is preferred over Sitka spruce.

Range size, location and habitat utilization.—Males tended to have larger MCP and 70% core home range areas than females. The mean MCP range size (±1 *SD*) for males (n=6) was 20.2±14.2 ha (range: 8.9-47 ha), with a mean 70% core area of 7.1±5.8 ha (range: 2.3-18.1 ha). The equivalent values for females (n=46) were 8.7±3.9 ha (range: 3.6-24.7 ha) and 3.5±2.4 ha (range:0.5-8.1 ha). A Mann-Whitney U test for both the MCP estimates and 70% core areas indicated that the range size differences between the sexes were significant ($d.f.$=5; P<0.004 and P<0.05 respectively).

The sexes also differed in their fidelity to particular home range locations. In June and July 1992 seven radio-tagged animals (5 males, 2 females) left the study site, after some of them had been tracked whilst making excursions of up to 1 km from their night dreys. During the same period of time an additional three squirrels (1 male, 2 females) travelled regularly between two discrete areas within their home ranges, only one of which had also been used in March. This had the effect of increasing the proportion of lodgepole pine in the total home range of the two females from 2% and 1% in March to 13% and 12% respectively in July. Insufficient data were available to make a similar comparison for the male. We also have data on the locations of six further animals (1 males, 5 females) for March and July 1992, although they are insufficient to calculate home ranges. The animals occupied an area of forest containing 18% of lodgepole pine and none of them apparently shifted their range during this period.

The changes in range composition that we observed in June-July 1992 occurred just when stripped green pine cones were first encountered on the transect lines. The association between dispersal out of areas containing little lodgepole pine, in some cases into areas with more, together with evidence of cone stripping at the same time, are highly suggestive of a causal link between changes in ranging behavior and food supply. Overall, the tendency to leave rather than to remain in an area of forest was significantly greater in males than in females (Fisher Exact P = 0.035; n = 16).

Increased numbers of radio-collared individuals were available for tracking during the remainder of this study, so that it was possible to make statistically robust comparisons of the proportions of radio-locations in each habitat for each animal with the proportions of these habitats available in the study areas as a whole (Fig. 1). This was carried out using a multivariate analysis of log-ratio differences (Aebischer et al., 1993*a*, *b*). In each of the three time periods, the squirrels showed significant overall departures from random habitat use (March 1993, χ^2 = 19.599, P<0.001; September 1993, χ^2 = 30.935, P<0.001; January 1994, χ^2 = 18.263, P<0.001; $d.f.$=3 in all cases).

Negative values in the matrix given in Table 2 imply avoidance of the numerator habitat type by comparison with the denominator habitat type, whilst positive values imply selection. The statistical significance of these individual comparisons can be assessed by computing t values (mean/$s.e$; df = no. of squirrels in sample).

This procedure showed that in March 1993 there was significant selection of lodgepole pine and significant avoidance of Norway spruce (Table

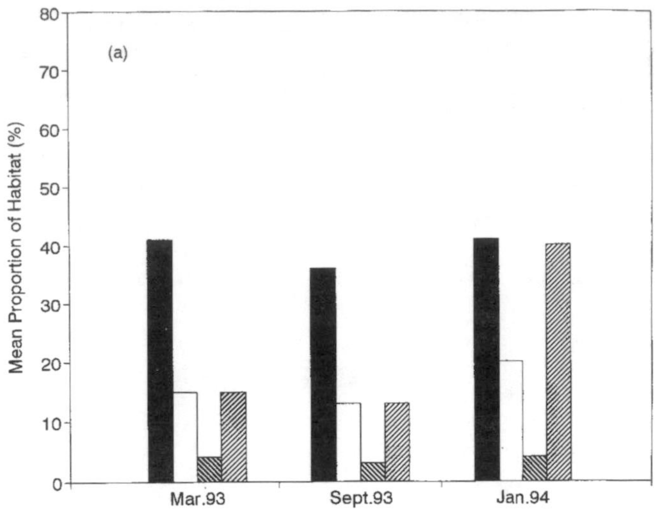

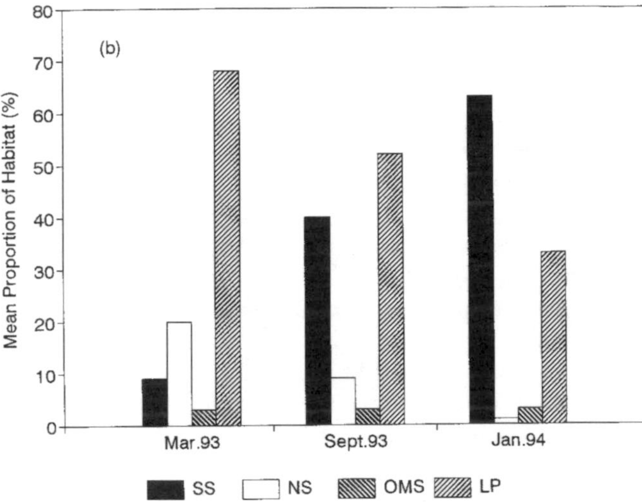

Fig. 1.—The proportions of four forest habitats available during three time periods to radio-collared squirrels at Spadeadam. Section (a) indicates the amount of habitat available for Sitka spruce (SS), Norway spruce (NS), Omoriksa spruce (OMS) and lodgepole pine (LP). Section (b) represents the extent of habitat used by squirrels for each species.

2a), giving a rank order of preference for the four habitat types of: LP > (SS = OMS = NS). In September 1993 there was significant selection of lodgepole pine and Sitka spruce whilst Norway and Omorika spruce were significantly avoided (Table 2b), giving a rank order of (LP = SS) > (OMS = NS). In January 1994 squirrel habitat utilization resembled that seen in September 1993. There was clear selection for Sitka and lodgepole pine over Omorika and Norway spruce (Table 2c), so giving a rank order of (SS = LP) > (OMS = NS).

Drey use.—A total of 73 dreys were found after locating radio-collared individuals. A comparison of the proportion of these dreys in spruce and pine relative to the areas of each tree genus available showed a clear preference for spruce ($\chi^2 = 16.66$, $df = 1$, $P < 0.001$). This was also true for the location of breeding dreys. Ten females that were known from recaptures to be lactating, used one particular drey nearly every night and were presumed to be sleeping with their young (Wauters and Dhondt, 1990). All these presumed breeding dreys were situated in spruce trees (Fisher Exact $P = 0.016$; $n = 10$).

DISCUSSION

Cone crops and feeding preferences.—The data collected from the cone transect lines indicated large variations in cone and therefore presumably in seed abundance between tree species and years. Cone crop cycles have been documented in some conifer species (e.g. Anderson, 1965; Hagner, 1965; Andren and Lemnell, 1992) and large crops of Norway spruce, for example, seem to occur in Kielder Forest on average every 6-8 years, of which the latest was recorded in 1990 (Petty et al., 1995). In intervening years, such as those in this study, seed food supply for squirrels from spruce species fluctuates but is generally very low. This may explain why the size of home ranges for red squirrels in Kielder is much greater than those reported from other studies of this species. For example, male ranges were on average 4 times larger and female ranges 3 times larger than those of a Belgian red squirrel population in a coniferous habitat (Wauters and Dhondt, 1992).

The results of our cone transect lines for the three years together suggest that red squirrels preferred lodgepole pine and Norway spruce cones over Sitka spruce cones as sources of seed food. A pilot study of the quality of the seeds of these three species by us suggests that Sitka spruce contains the highest level of tannins, measured as protein precipitation activity (Martin and Martin, 1982), of the 3 species. Nevertheless, squirrels in Kielder Forest do sometimes feed on Sitka spruce seeds. During the autumn of 1993, we found large numbers of stripped Sitka cones, as well as those of pine, on our transects. Overall these observations suggest that when all three food types are available the choice of diet by squirrels may be influenced by levels of secondary compounds in the seeds as well as by cone availability. Norway spruce and lodgepole pine produce larger seeds with lower tannin levels, probably rendering their cones more profitable as sources of food for squirrels than Sitka spruce cones. However, this conclusion takes no account of variations in the handling time required to extract seeds, the seed content of the different cone types or variations in major nutrient content

Table 2.—*Mean log-ratio differences (± 1 SE) between utilized (squirrel radio locations) and available (total study areas) habitat compositions for 3 periods at Spadeadam Forest. Values on the other side of the diagonal are identical but of opposite sign and are therefore omitted.*

Habitat types (numerator)	Habitat types (denominator)			
Table 2a (March 1993, *n*=10)	Sitka	Norway	Lodgepole	Omorika
Sitka				
Norway	-0.523±1.086			
Lodgepole	2.523±0.538**	3.046±1.196*		
Omorika	0.833±1.103	1.356±1.286	-1.69±0.733*	
Table 2b (September 1993, *n*=12)	Sitka	Norway	Lodgepole	Omorika
Sitka				
Norway	-2.895±0.749**			
Lodgepole	0.139±0.291	3.034±0.949**		
Omorika	-2.124±0.705*	0.771±1.023	-2.263±0.606**	
Table 2c (January 1994, *n*=9)	Sitka	Norway	Lodgepole	Omorika
Sitka				
Norway	-4.373±0.636**			
Lodgepole	-1.204±0.872	3.169±0.86**		
Omorika	-2.374±0.706**	1.999±0.897	-1.170±1.264	

*Significant differences (*P < 0.05, **P < 0.01)*

between the seeds from the different species.

Ranging behavior in relation to food supply.—Red squirrels are known to move to different types of habitat in response to fluctuations in food supply. In some instances these movements can be on quite a large scale (Ognev, 1950). The abrupt emigration of 7 radio collared squirrels and substantial range shifts by a further three in June–July 1992, at a time when a new seed food supply (i.e. green pine cones) became available, provides further support for this view. Males seemed more likely to shift than females, perhaps because the latter may have had unweaned young at the time (Gurnell, 1987). However, no data on breeding condition were collected at that time to demonstrate that this was the case.

Habitat utilization was clearly non-random during the three periods in which it was investigated using compositional analysis. Areas of lodgepole pine were selected in March 1993 at a time when there were virtually no cones in Sitka and Norway spruce. In September 1993 and January 1994, areas of Omorika and Norway spruce were almost devoid of cones, and they were avoided by squirrels. During this time, the home ranges of squirrels centered on areas of Sitka spruce and lodgepole pine, both of which had produced appreciable cone crops in the autumn of 1993. Green pine cones were stripped from July 1993 and green Sitka spruce cones were being taken from September 1993. Thus squirrel ranging patterns in Kielder Forest seem to follow spatial and temporal variations in the conifer seed food supply, as has also been found in forests of Scots pine and Norway spruce in Sweden (Andren and Lemnell, 1992).

Drey location.—Red squirrels at Spadeadam selected the much denser crowns of spruce trees for drey-building over the more open crowns typical of lodgepole pine. Squirrels shelter in their dreys during bad weather (Wauters and Dhondt, 1987) and the structure of spruce trees offers much better physical support and shelter from rain than lodgepole pine. The dense crowns of the spruces may also provide better camouflage for dreys, reducing the chance of raids on nests by aerial predators such as crows (*Corvus corone*) which were observed to destroy a nest containing two unweaned young in Belgium (Wauters and Dhondt, 1990).

Forest design.—Habitat management for red squirrel conservation in Britain has recently been discussed in general by Gurnell and Pepper (1993). Specifically on the basis of our findings in upland conifer plantations we would suggest that any red squirrel conservation area in such habitat should contain a minimum of 20% pine (Lurz et al., 1995), with the native Scots pine being preferred over lodgepole pine, not least because it contains larger seeds (Marquiss and Rae, 1994). This would reduce the impact of marked cone crop variations characteristic of the two spruce species present. In addition, the less variable cone production strategy of pine species together with their habit of retaining mature cones and some of their seed would help to prevent complete exhaustion of the food supply in such mixed forests.

Given that Sitka spruce produces small seeds with a relatively high tannin content, which are shed mainly in the autumn (Fletcher, 1992), the proportion of this species in forests managed for squirrels should be kept as low as is economically acceptable to commercial forest managers. The present proportion of Norway spruce (12%) at Spadeadam should if possible be increased and other conifers such as Scots pine, larch and yew, the seeds of which are known to be taken by red squirrels (Moller, 1983; Tonkin, 1984), should also be included. Given the mobility of squirrels (Andren and Delin, 1994), the average block size for major components of the forest mosaic does not appear to be important as long as a significant proportion of the forest consists of cone producing pine and Norway spruce in blocks that are interconnected.

ACKNOWLEDGMENTS

We would like to thank the Northumberland Wildlife Trust for providing the financial support for this project as well as Viscount Ridley the loan of a field vehicle. We are also grateful for much assistance from Forest Enterprise and Royal Air Force staff at Spadeadam, and in particular the help of Warrant Officer R. Thompson. We would also like to thank Luc Wauters, David Zegers and an anonymous reviewer for their helpful comments on an earlier draft of this manuscript.

LITERATURE CITED

AEBISCHER, N.J., P. A. ROBERTSON, AND R. E. KENWARD. 1993*a*. Compositional analysis of habitat use from radio-tracking data. Ecology, 74:1313-1325.

AEBISCHER, N.J., V. MARCSTROM, R. E. KENWARD, AND M. KARLBOM. 1993*b*. Survival and habitat utilisation: a case for compositional analysis. Pp. 343-353, *in* Marked individuals in the study of bird populations (J.D. Lebreton and P.M. North, eds.). Birkhauser Verlag, Basel, 456 pp.

ANDERSON, E. 1965. Cone and seed studies in Norway spruce. Studia Forestalia Sueica, 23:1-197

ANDREN, H., AND P. LEMNELL. 1992. Population fluctuations and habitat selection in the Eurasian red squirrel *Sciurus vulgaris*. Ecography, 15:303-307.

ANDREN, H., AND A. DELIN. 1994. Habitat selection in the Eurasian red squirrel, *Sciurus vulgaris*, in relation to forest fragmentation. Oikos, 70:43-48.

FLETCHER, A. M. 1992. Flower, fruit and seed development and morphology. Pp. 59-70, *in* Seed manual for forest trees (A. G. Gordon, ed.). Forestry Commission Bulletin 83, HMSO, 132 pp.

GURNELL, J. 1987. The natural history of squirrels. Christopher Helm, London, 201 pp.

GURNELL, J., AND H. PEPPER. 1993. A critical look at conserving the British red squirrel. Mammal Review, 23:127-137.

HAGNER, S. 1965. Cone crop fluctuations in Scots pine and Norway spruce. Studia Forestalia Sueica, 33:1-20.

KENWARD, R.E. 1985. Ranging behaviour and population dynamics of grey squirrels. Pp. 319-330, *in* Behavioural ecology (R.M. Sibly and R.H. Smith, eds.). Blackwell Scientific Publications, Oxford.

———. 1987. Wildlife Radio Tagging: equipment, field techniques and data analysis. Academic Press, London, 222 pp.

———. 1990. Ranges IV. Software for analysing animal location data. Institute of Terrestrial Ecology, Natural Environment Research Council, Cambridge, 34 pp.

KENWARD, R.E., AND J.L. HOLM. 1989. What future for the British red squirrels? Biological Journal of the Linnaean Society, 38:83-89.

———. 1993. On the replacement of the red squirrel in Britain: a phytotoxic explanation. Proceedings of the Royal Society of London (B), 251:187-194.

LURZ, P. W. W., P. J. GARSON, AND S. P. RUSHTON. 1995. The ecology of squirrels in spruce dominated plantations: implications for forest management. Forest Ecology and Management, 79: 79-90.

MARTIN, J.S., AND M. MARTIN. 1982. Tannin assays in ecological studies: Lack of correlation between phenolics, proanthocyanidins and protein precipitating constituents in mature foliage of six oak species. Oecologia, 54:205-211.

MCINTOSH, R. 1995. The history and multipurpose management of Kielder Forest. Forest Ecology and Management, 79:1-12.

MARQUISS, M., AND R. RAE. 1994. Seasonal trends in abundance, diet and breeding of common crossbills (*Loxia curvirostra*) in an area of mixed species conifer plantation following the 1990 crossbill 'irruption'. Forestry, 67:31-47.

MIDDLETON, A.D. 1930. The ecology of the American grey squirrel (*Sciurus carolinensis*, Gmelin.) in the British Isles. Proceedings of the Zoological Society of London, 3: 804-842.

MOLLER, H. 1983. Foods and foraging behaviour of red (*Sciurus vulgaris*) and grey (*Sciurus carolinensis*) squirrels. Mammal Review, 13: 81-98.

OGNEV, S.I. 1950. Animals of the USSR and adjacent countries. 4: Rodents. Moscow, Leningrad. SSSR-Israel Program for Scientific Translations (1966), Jerusalem, 486 pp.

PETTY, S.J., I. J. PATTERSON, D. I. K. ANDERSON, B. LITTLE, AND M. DAVISON. 1995. Numbers, breeding performance, and diet of the sparrowhawk *Acipiter nisus* and merlin *Falco columbarius* in relation to cone crops and seed-eating finches. Forest Ecology and Management, 79:133-146.

TONKIN, J.M. 1984. Red squirrels in deciduous woodland. Ph.D. dissertation, University of Bradford, UK, 361 pp.

USHER, M.B., T. J. CRAWFORD, AND J. L. BANWELL. 1992. An American invasion of Great Britain: the case of the native and alien squirrel (*Sciurus*) species. Conservation Biology, 6:108-115.

WAUTERS, L., AND A. A. DHONDT. 1987. Activity budget and foraging behaviour of the red squirrel in a coniferous habitat. Zeitschrift für Säugetierkunde, 52:341-53.

———. 1990. Nest use by red squirrels (*Sciurus vulgaris* L., 1758). Mammalia, 54:377-389.

———. 1992. Spacing Behaviour of red squirrels, *Sciurus vulgaris*: variation between habitats and the sexes. Animal Behaviour, 43:297-311.

USE OF MULTIPLE REGRESSION AND USE-AVAILABILITY ANALYSES IN DETERMINING HABITAT SELECTION BY GRAY SQUIRRELS (*SCIURUS CAROLINENSIS*)

JOHN W. EDWARDS, SUSAN C. LOEB, AND DAVID C. GUYNN, JR.

Department of Forest Resources, Clemson University, Clemson, SC 29634-1003. (JWE, DCG)
Southern Research Station, Department of Forest Resources, Clemson University, Clemson, SC 29634-1003. (SCL)

ABSTRACT.—Multiple regression and use-availability analyses are two methods for examining habitat selection. Use-availability analysis is commonly used to evaluate macrohabitat selection whereas multiple regression analysis can be used to determine microhabitat selection. We compared these techniques using behavioral observations (n = 5534) and telemetry locations (n = 2089) of gray squirrels (*Sciurus carolinensis*) on the Piedmont National Wildlife Refuge (PNWR) in Georgia. Use-availability analysis of stands classified according to their composition of pine and hardwood basal area produced inconsistent results; no pattern of selection was evident because similarly classified stands (e.g., pine/hardwood) received differing levels of use. In multiple regression analysis, tree species that predicted relative use by gray squirrels differed by season. Deciduous holly (*Ilex decidua*), sweetgum (*Liquidambar styraciflua*), water oak (*Quercus nigra*), willow oak (*Q. phellos*), winged elm (*Ulmus alata*), and yellow-poplar (*Liriodendron tulipifera*) explained the most variation in seasonal stand use by gray squirrels; none of the 17 structural variables measured contributed significantly to predictive models. We found poor to moderate concordance (14.3 - 71.4%) between stand use predicted from multiple regression analysis and stand use determined by use-availability analysis. Our findings suggest that examinations of selection at different scales may result in differing interpretations of habitat use and erroneous inferences regarding habitat selection.

INTRODUCTION

Habitat selection is central to the study of animal ecology. Habitat is defined as an area with the resources and environmental conditions that promote occupancy by individuals of a given species and allows those individuals to survive and reproduce (Morrison et al., 1992). Animals may identify and select habitats by responding to composition of plant species, physiographic make-up, resource distribution, and structural attributes (Laundre and Keller, 1984). Factors such as interspecific and intraspecific competition and predation may further affect habitat selection. Selection is inferred when habitats are used disproportionately to their availability (Johnson, 1980). Johnson (1980) defines habitat selection using hierarchial orders of resolution; first-order selection is the geographic range of a species, second-order selection includes the habitats that make up an animal's home range, and third-order selection is the usage made of various habitats within the home range.

Determination of habitat selection is commonly done by comparing habitat use with habitat availability (hereafter referred to as use-availability). This analysis may be done at either the micro- or macrohabitat level, but is usually conducted at the macrohabitat scale (e.g., Neu et al., 1974; White and Garrot, 1990). Use-availability (UA) anaylses assume that a species selects and uses areas that are best able to satisfy its requirements, and as a result, animals use higher-quality habitats in

In M.A. Steele, J. F. Merritt, and D. A. Zegers (eds.). 1998. Ecology and Evolutionary Biology of Tree Squirrels. Special Publication, Virginia Museum of Natural History, 6: 320 pp

greater proportion than their availability (Schamberger and O'Neil, 1986). Reviews of several use-availability analyses found no superior method and suggest that the choice of analysis should be based on the biological question of interest and statistical assumptions (Thomas and Taylor, 1990; Alldredge and Ratti, 1992; Manly et al., 1993). Use of these analyses usually results in classification of habitat use as either greater than, proportional to, or less than that expected on the basis of availability. UA analysis, however, does not address the question of which habitat characteristics are most important in determining selection (Porter and Church, 1987). In UA analysis a habitat must be classified into an exclusive category (e.g., pine, hardwood, open field). This results in a loss of information and may ignore certain variables that may be important (e.g., structural variables or the presence of an important resource at low levels).

An alternative method for determining habitat selection is multiple regression (MR) analysis. MR analysis reveals habitat characteristics which are most associated with observed use and is helpful in assessing both macro- and microhabitat selection, but is particularly effective in determining microhabitat selection. Further, MR models can be used to predict habitat use.

Because UA and MR analyses usually address different levels of selection (i.e., macro versus micro), it is often necessary to reconcile results among studies using different methods and scales. Using telemetry locations and behavioral observations, we tested whether the results and interpretations of gray squirrel habitat selection at the macrohabitat scale using UA were comparable to those using MR at the microhabitat scale.

METHODS

Study Area.—We conducted the study on the Piedmont National Wildlife Refuge (PNWR), located in central Georgia (Jasper and Jones counties). Much of the 14,000-ha PNWR was covered by pine (*Pinus*) and mixed pine-hardwood forests. Loblolly pine (*P. taeda*) was dominant on ridges and upper slopes. Oaks, hickories (*Carya*), sweetgum, yellow-poplar, and blackgum (*Nyssa sylvatica*) dominated lower slopes and along streams. Midstory species included dogwood (*Cornus florida*), persimmon (*Diospyros virginiana*), hornbeam (*Ostrya virginiana*), winged elm, hawthorn, and maple (*Acer*). Broomsedge (*Andropogon*), japanese honeysuckle (*Lonicera japonica*), muscadine (*Vitis rotundifolia*), smilax (*Smilax*), and blueberry (*Vaccinium*) were common understory species (Radford et al., 1968; Petrides, 1972).

Habitat patterns on the PNWR were influenced by aspect, slope, and forest management practices (Brender, 1973). Because of the topography, presence of several drainages, and small stand size, habitats were uniformly available over the study area.

Radiotelemetry.—We captured gray squirrels using Mosby-type box traps (Day et al., 1981) placed systematically (100 by 100 m) over 121 ha (Tappe, 1991; Tappe et al., 1993). Additional animals were captured using 88 nest boxes (modified from Barkalow and Soots, 1965) placed systematically (100 by 100 m) in trees at 8.5 to 9.8 m throughout a 73-ha portion of the study area. Adult animals were removed from traps or nest boxes, restrained in a soft-webbed handling cone (modified from Day et al., 1981), anesthetized with ketamine hydrochloride, and fitted with a radio transmitter-collar unit (Telonics Inc., Mesa, AZ). These procedures were defined under Animal Use Protocol 348 of the Clemson University Animal Research Committee. Transmitters weighed 18-20 g and had an expected battery life of 9-11 months. We estimated squirrel locations by triangulating from 3 of 115 telemetry stations using a three-element Yagi antenna; the geometric center of the triangle formed by the three intersecting azimuths was used as the animal's location. During 1989 and 1990, we obtained locations on radio-collared squirrels every 2 hours between sunrise and sunset, 2 days each week. Sampling intensity was similar within diurnal periods and among seasons (spring = 148, summer = 216, fall = 191, winter = 207 locations). Activity was measured on 4-5 animals each season (n = 19), with 35-48 locations for each animal.

We assessed radiotelemetry accuracy by placing transmitters 5 cm above the ground at premapped locations. Azimuth readings were taken from 8-10 telemetry stations on transmitters placed at six locations unknown to the observer. We determined error arcs for each trial and calculated an average 90% confidence interval, error polygon (Springer, 1979). We conducted testing during August 1990 to simulate "worst-case" signal attenuation caused by maximum foliar coverage and high humidity (Lee et al., 1985; Chu et al., 1988).

Habitat delineation and characteristics.—We delineated stand boundaries using aerial photographs and ground reconnaissance. A stand was defined as a contiguous group of trees sufficiently uniform in species composition, arrangement of age classes, and condition to be a homogeneous and distinguishable unit (Smith, 1962). On a 10 by 40-m (0.04 ha) plot in each stand, we recorded diameter at breast height (dbh) and identified species of codominant and dominant stems (Smith, 1962). On a 5-m by 20-m plot, we recorded dbh and identified species of midstory stems >2.5 cm dbh and >1.4 m in height. Plots were located centrally to typify stand characteristics. Structural measures included: aspect, slope, % overstory composed of pine, % overstory composed of hardwoods, % midstory composed of pine, % midstory composed of hardwoods, overstory hardwood stems per ha (OHSHA), overstory pine stems per ha (OPSHA), midstory hardwood stems per ha (MHSHA), midstory pine stems per ha (MPSHA), overstory basal area per ha, midstory basal area per ha, stand area, and stand perimeter. In addition, a vertical cover index was determined at the plot center using a 3.6-m pole divided into five equal sections and oriented horizontally at each cardinal direction (N,E,S,W). We recorded a hit if any vegetation contacted the pole in a specified segment. Index values were calculated using the ratio of recorded hits over possible hits (20), at heights of 30, 91, and 152 cm.

We assigned vegetation types on the basis of basal area (USDA Forest Service, 1988). Individual stands were assigned to 1 of 4 types: 1) pine (>69% pine), 2) pine/hardwood (51-69% pine), 3) hardwood/pine (51-69% hardwood), and 4) hardwood (>69% hardwood) We further classified stands on the basis of slope position (top, upper mid, lower mid, and bottom).

Habitat use-availability.—We determined boundaries of seasonal home ranges for each squirrel with >39 locations per season using the harmonic mean method (Dixon and Chapman, 1980) for 95% (95HM) and 53-68% ($\overline{x}$ = 61%, CORE) of the animal's use distribution (Program HOMERANGE, Ackerman et al., 1990); the latter determination represents the core area (Kaufmann, 1962) and is defined as the maximum area where the observed utilization distribution exceeds a uniform utilization distribution (Ackerman et al., 1990). This model identifies areas of concentrated use within home-range areas (e.g., core areas) and thus provides a biological approach to analyzing utilization distributions. We also determined a seasonal home-range boundary with a 95% minimum convex polygon (MCP; Michener, 1979). We used the seasonal home-range boundaries of each squirrel to delineate their available habitats. Spatial analyses on animal locations, stand boundaries, home-range area, and availability of habitats were performed using Geographical Information Systems ARC/INFO (Environmental Systems Research Institute, Redlands, CA). We considered the area of available habitats to be known measures and not estimates (Thomas and Taylor, 1990).

We determined the UA of each stand within individual home ranges for each squirrel and then pooled across animals. This eliminated the assumption of equal availability of vegetation types for all individuals. Although pooling of data may mask individual variation in habitat selection (White and Garrot, 1990), we justified pooling because our objective was to examine group rather than individual patterns of habitat selection; and because sample size constraints prevented selection analyses of seasonal home ranges of individual squirrels. We assumed observations among individuals to be independent. Dependence among observations within individuals may result from insufficient time elapsing between observations or from biased spatial patterns of movements (Swihart and Slade, 1987). Time-to-independence for locational observations within animals, based on a mean body mass of 0.6 kg, is 138 min (Swihart et al., 1988); minimal time between successive locations in our study was 120 min.

Chi-square goodness-of-fit analyses were used to test the null hypothesis that vegetation type use was proportional to availability within seasonal home ranges of radio-collared squirrels (Neu et al., 1974; Byers et al., 1984). Categories were pooled so that at least one observation was expected in each, and no more than 20% of the categories contained <5 expected observations (Roscoe and Byars, 1971). We computed Bonferroni confidence intervals (95%) to infer selection of individual stands in those cases in which significant selection was detected (Neu et al., 1974; Byers et al., 1984). If expected frequencies were outside the confidence interval, then we considered the stand to be used greater than expected (+) or less than expected (-); expected frequencies within confidence intervals inferred stand use proportional (P) to availability. We examined levels of selection for each stand, vegetation type, and season.

Behavioral observations.—We conducted direct observations of randomly selected radio-collared individuals of both sexes, 1 day each month, during 1989 and 1990. Observations began 30 min before sunrise and continued until 30 min after sunset. Each day was subdivided into 3-hour sampling periods in which observations (instantaneous sampling) were recorded at 3-min intervals; sampling periods were staggered to avoid observer fatigue. Combined sampling periods conducted during 4 days each month comprised 2 observation days (i.e., 1 dawn-to-dusk observation for each sex). No individual was observed during consecutive sampling periods. Observations included stand number, strata occupied (e.g., canopy, bole, ground) and general behavior (e.g., resting and maintenance, feeding and foraging, vigilance, locomotion). Due to their wariness, we used precautions (e.g., camouflage clothing and/or blinds) when observing the focal animal and each animal was located 30 min prior to the start of the observation period with the aid of telemetry and binoculars. If at any time during the sampling period the focal animal's behavior appeared affected by the observer's presence (e.g., extreme vigilance or barking directed towards the observer), we terminated the session.

Among the 142 stands comprising the study area, we recorded 5534 gray squirrel (n = 25) observations during the 2-year study. Relative use of stands was calculated, for each season as (number of observations within a stand / total number of observations) x 100. Due to a limited number of radio-collared animals, one individual squirrel contributed 23% of the winter observations; no individual contributed >19% of the observations during other seasons. Observations on focal animals among months and sampling periods were considered independent whereas observations within sample periods were not assumed to be independent (Machlis et al., 1985). The 3-min sampling interval allowed the focal animal sufficient opportunity to change behavioral events; 3 min was not sufficient in most instances for an animal to move from one stand to another. We used a Wilcoxon paired-sample test (Mendenhall et al., 1990) to compare relative use in 3-min intervals with that in 3-hour intervals. Relative use in 3-hour periods included only the first observation recorded in the sampling period and was therefore considered independent. We found no differences (P > 0.10) between measures of relative use in 3-min and 3-hour intervals within seasons. Using the same test, we found no differences (P > 0.10) in patterns of stand use between males and females; and relative use of stands by gray squirrels did not differ (P > 0.10) between years. Comparisons within sexes and seasons between years were not possible because of limited paired samples of relative use. Therefore, analyses included all 3-min observations and combined male and female observations.

Regression analyses.—We used multiple stepwise regression (PROC STEPWISE, MAXR; SAS Institute, Inc, 1991) to model relative stand use. Eighty-four independent variables (17 structural, 25 overstory species, 42 midstory species) describing each stand were used to develop predictive models for each season. Structural variables OHSHA, OPSHA, MHSHA, and MPSHA were log10 transformed (Steel and Torrie, 1980). Importance values of overstory and midstory species ranged from 0 to 1. We calculated importance values by summing relative density with relative basal area and dividing by 2. We selected the five-variable model which explained the most variation in relative use by gray squirrels for each season. We used several diagnostic procedures to evaluate and determine that outliers and collinearity were not a problem in the data set (studentized residuals, Dffits, Dfbetas, pairwise correlation, VIF, condition number; SAS Institute, Inc, 1991). Partial regression coefficients were standardized using PROC REG, option STB (SAS Institute, Inc, 1991). Predicted values of relative use for all 142 stands were calculated for each season on the basis of MR models. We categorized the predicted use of stands within seasons as low (L), medium (M), or high (H), using first quartile, second and third quartiles, and fourth quartile of values of predicted use, respectively. We compared selection levels determined by UA analysis to predicted values of relative use by equating (-) with "L", (P) with "M", and (+) with "H". We determined the percent concordance between analyses for each method of home-range estimation and season.

RESULTS

The angular error of 73 trial azimuths, recorded from distances of 110 to 770 m, averaged 10.6° (SE = 0.87°). Most squirrel locations were determined from azimuths <300 m. The angular error of 16 trial azimuths between 200-300 m averaged 7.3° (SE = 1.41°); the 90% error polygon determined from two error arcs intersecting at 90° from a distance of 250 m was 0.78 ha. Mean stand size on the study area was 2.0 ha (n = 142, SE = 0.19 ha). All locations of squirrels were within 50 m of a stand boundary.

Macrohabitat selection (-, P, +) differed, within stands, depending on the method used to determine boundaries of home range (i.e., 95HM, MCP, CORE) and season (Fig. 1). All home-range methods resulted in concordant selection levels in >57% of stands. Mean percent concordance was highest (85.1%) between MCP and CORE estimates.

Macrohabitat selection within vegetation types differed by stands (Table 1). For example, pine and pine-hardwood types (overstory/midstory) received all levels (-, P, +) of selection in spring;

Table 1.—*Seasonal levels of selection of selected stands and vegetation types by gray squirrels on the Piedmont National Wildlife Refuge, Georgia, 1989-1990, on the basis of use-availability analysis. Selection levels were determined on the basis of 95% harmonic mean home ranges; (+) = stand used more than expected; (-) = stand used less than expected; (P) = stand used in proportion to availability.*

			Vegetation type		
Season	Stand	Selection	Overstory	Midstory	Slope position
Spring	21	(+)	Pine	Pine	Upper mid
	50	(P)	Pine	Pine	Top
	66	(P)	Pine	Pine	Upper mid
	36	(-)	Pine	Pine	Lower mid
	72	(-)	Pine	Pine	Upper mid
	30	(+)	Pine	Hardwood	Bottom
	93	(P)	Pine	Hardwood	Lower mid
	99	(P)	Pine	Hardwood	Upper mid
	56	(-)	Pine	Hardwood	Upper mid
	57	(-)	Pine	Hardwood	Top
Summer	52	(+)	Hardwood	Hardwood	Upper mid
	35	(P)	Hardwood	Hardwood	Upper mid
	30	(P)	Pine	Hardwood	Bottom
	31	(P)	Pine	Hardwood	Bottom
	17	(-)	Pine	Hardwood	Upper mid
	18	(-)	Pine	Hardwood	Upper mid
Fall	15	(P)	Pine	Hardwood	Upper mid
	31	(P)	Pine	Hardwood	Bottom
	84	(P)	Pine	Hardwood	Lower mid
Winter	30	(P)	Pine	Hardwood	Bottom
	58	(P)	Pine	Hardwood	Upper mid
	18	(-)	Pine	Hardwood	Upper mid
	32	(-)	Pine	Hardwood	Upper mid

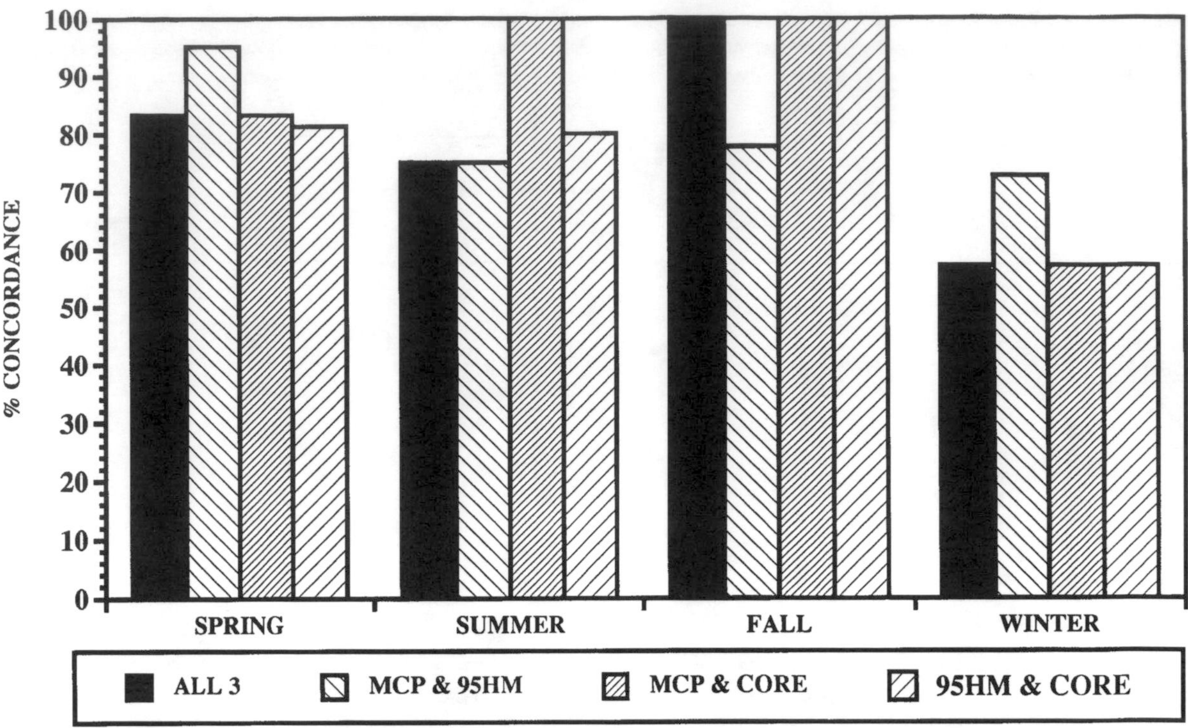

Fig. 1.—Concordance (%) of macrohabitat levels of selection among home-range methods (95% minimum convex polygon [MCP], 95% harmonic mean [95HM], and core area [CORE]), on the basis of use of individual stands by gray squirrels on the Piedmont National Wildlife Refuge, Georgia, 1989-1990.

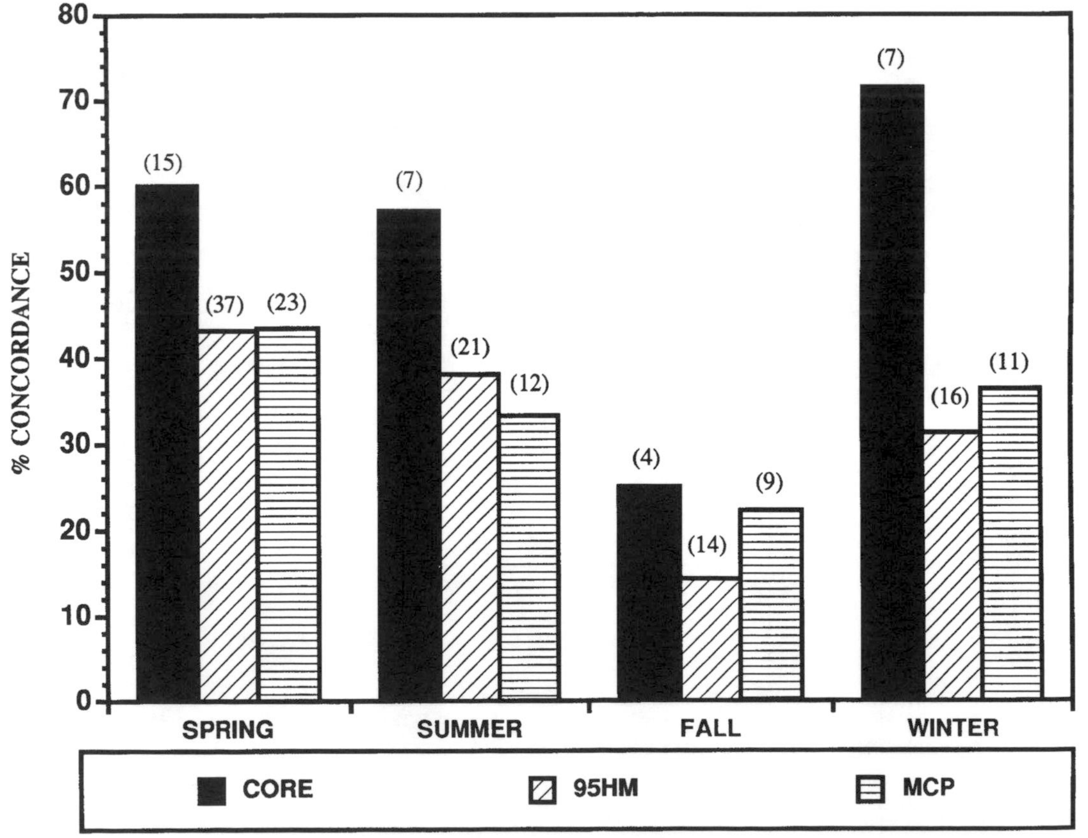

Fig. 2. —Concordance (%) of levels of selection determined by use-availability analysis and those predicted by multiple regression models on the basis of relative use by gray squirrels on the Piedmont National Wildlife Refuge, Georgia, 1989-1990; CORE = core area; 95HM = 95% harmonic mean; MCP = 95% minimum convex polygon. Values in parentheses are numbers of stands.

Table 2.—*Independent variables found to predict microhabitat selection by gray squirrels on the Piedmont National Wildlife Refuge, Georgia, 1989-1990. Relative use was determined on the basis of 1442 observations in spring, 1963 in summer, 920 in fall, and 986 in winter in 18, 29, 22, and 11 stands, respectively.*

Season	Canopy position[a]	Independent variable	Standardized coefficient[b]	*P*[c]	R^2[d]
Spring	Mid	Water oak (*Quercus nigra*)	0.66	<0.01	0.78
	Over	Sweetgum (*Liquidambar styraciflua*)	0.52	0.03	
	Over	Willow oak (*Q. phellos*)	0.51	<0.01	
	Over	S. red oak (*Q. falcata*)	0.27	0.07	
	Mid	Shagbark hickory (*Carya ovata*)	-0.72	<0.01	
Summer	Over	Water oak	0.69	<0.01	0.83
	Over	Willow oak	0.54	<0.01	
	Over	White oak (*Q. alba*)	0.40	<0.01	
	Over	Winged elm (*Ulmus alata*)	0.34	<0.01	
	Over	Overcup oak (*Q. lyrata*)	-0.35	<0.01	
Fall	Mid	Winged elm	0.62	<0.01	0.75
	Mid	Yellow-poplar (*Liriodendron tulipifera*)	0.50	<0.01	
	Mid	Hornbeam (*Ostrya virginiana*)	0.31	0.03	
	Mid	Deciduous holly (*Ilex decidua*)	-0.26	0.06	
	Mid	Poison ivy (*Rhus radicans*)	-0.31	0.03	
Winter	Mid	Deciduous holly	0.84	<0.01	0.99
	Mid	Yellow-poplar	0.67	<0.01	
	Mid	Hawthorn (*Crataegus*)	0.18	<0.01	
	Over	Sweetgum	0.08	0.01	
	Mid	Willow oak	-0.15	<0.01	

[a] Over = overstory; Mid = midstory ; [b] Standardized partial regression coefficient ;

[c] Probability of > | t | ; [d] Coefficient of multiple determination

hardwood types (midstory) received all levels of selection in spring and summer. Stands further classified by slope position also received differing levels of selection.

Habitat variables that predicted gray squirrel microhabitat selection differed among seasons (Table 2). In spring and summer, stand use by gray squirrels was positively correlated with oaks (except overcup oak *Q. lyrata*) and negatively influenced by shagbark hickory (*C. ovata*) and overcup oak. In fall and winter, stand use by gray squirrels was positively correlated with deciduous holly, yellow-poplar, winged elm, and hornbeam, and negatively influence by poison ivy (*Rhus radicans*) and willow oak. Structural variables were unimportant in predicting relative use by gray squirrels in any season.

Concordance among selection levels of stands determined from UA analyses (-, P, +) and predicted levels of use (i.e., L, M, H) from MR models varied from poor to moderate (Fig. 2). Percent concordance differed by season and method of home-range estimation. Percent concordance was higher when the CORE home-range method was used (25.0% - 71.4%) than when the 95HM method (14.3% - 43.2%) or MCP method (22.2% - 43.5%) were used.

DISCUSSION

Studies of macrohabitat selection by radio-collared animals follow a common paradigm: 1) delineate study area boundaries, 2) identify spatial units (e.g., stands) within the study area, 3) classify spatial units into vegetation types on the basis of species composition and structural characteristics (e.g., pine/hardwood bottom), 4) determine availability of vegetation types, 5) quantify location data, and 6) perform UA analysis to determine selection.

One of the most critical aspects of UA analysis is the classification of stands into vegetation types. A problem in identifying vegetation types is the criteria on which they are based. The researcher must identify stand characteristics that best determine a species use (e.g., slope position, species composition, stand age, or seral stage) and then classify stands accordingly. If these criteria are different, too broad, or do not correlate with those of the animal under investigation, then UA analysis may lead to spurious conclusions. This process is made more complex when the different layers (e.g., overstory, herbaceous) of habitats are also considered. Further, stands are usually grouped by vegetation type before analyses are conducted. We found that similarly classified stands often received different levels of selection (see Table 1). Had we grouped stands into vegetation types prior to our analyses, as is commonly done, differences among stands of similar composition and structure would have been masked.

Boundary delineation and subsequent proportional availabilities of stands are also critical steps in UA analysis (Porter and Church, 1987). We restricted our analyses to within home ranges because these boundaries are biologically relevant to the animal and the animal has demonstrated access (availability) to these areas. However, we found macrohabitat selection differed within stands depending on the method of home-range analysis. The choice of which home-range estimate to use is subjective. Because there is no agreement as to which estimate is "best", researchers must choose on the basis of their knowledge of the animal under investigation and their understanding of home-range estimators. Therefore, results of UA analysis are likely to vary depending on which estimator is chosen.

MR analysis is commonly used in wildlife studies to determine which characteristics are most important in predicting animal use (Brown and Batzli, 1984; Bull and Holthausen, 1993; Kotler et al., 1993; Pauley et al., 1993). We found microhabitat selection by gray squirrels most correlated with oak species in spring and summer; sweetgum and shagbark hickory were also important in spring. Midstory, winged elm and yellow-poplar, and deciduous holly and yellow-poplar, were most correlated with squirrel use in fall and winter, respectively. Causal relationships between stand use and species associations are uncertain, however, because occurrences of individual plant species and their contributions in predictive models vary seasonally. On the basis of silvical characteristics (USDA Forest Service, 1990), stand use by gray squirrels was greatest in mesic habitats on lower slopes in all seasons. Because of the mesic conditions in these habitats, midstory hardwoods were abundant in stands used in spring, fall, and winter. We observed squirrels feeding on oak flowers during spring and early summer. Yellow-poplar, hornbeam, and deciduous holly, although providing a food resource in fall and winter, also are indicators of moister stand conditions. These stands on lower slopes provide the greatest availability of oak mast on the PNWR (Edwards et al., 1993). Cavity availability (Edwards and Guynn, 1995), interspecific competition (Edwards, 1995), and predator avoidance also influence stand use and thus, may correlate with stand characteristics. Interpretation of model variables is subjective and based on the researcher's knowledge of the biology and ecology of a species.

UA and MR analyses examine habitat selection at different levels of resolution (vegetation types versus vegetative characteristics). UA analysis provides information concerning selection of vegetation types. Because habitat units (e.g., stands) must be classified into exclusive categories, much information about the vegetative characteristics (composition and structure) as well as other habitat features are lost. In contrast, MR analysis reveals characteristics which are important features in determining habitat use. Our comparisions of these two methods found only poor to moderate concordance between macrohabitat and microhabitat selection in assessing levels of stand use. UA analysis of core areas of use resulted in the highest concordance with MR predictive models. Because core areas represent areas used more intensively than other portions of an animal's home range (Kaufmann, 1962), vegetative characteristics of these areas may be particularly important in determining habitat selection. In our study, both MR models and delineation of core areas and subsequent UA analysis were determined on the basis of intensity of stand use. This similarity, may in part, explain the higher concordance when using boundaries of core area as compared to other methods of home-range determination.

Our findings suggest that examinations of selection at different spatial scales and levels of resolution, although informative, may result in differing interpretations of habitat use and subsequent inferences regarding habitat selection. Where the ecology of a species is well known and the examination of traditional habitat types (e.g., USDA Forest Service, 1988) is important for management decisions, UA analysis (macrohabitat selection) may be a more pragmatic approach. If the goal, however, is to determine which characteristics are most correlated with a species' habitat use, then MR analysis (microhabitat selection) offers a more rigorous approach. We are confident that our MR models more accurately depict stand use by gray squirrels on the PNWR. Interpretation of these models is difficult, however, and their translation into practical guidelines for habitat management is premature. Further research is necessary to test the application of these models.

ACKNOWLEDGMENTS

Support for our study was provided by the USDA Forest Service, Southeastern Forest Experiment Station (Cooperative Agreement 18-409, #110) and the Department of Forest Resources, Clemson University. We thank the staff of the Piedmont National Wildlife Refuge for cooperation in this study. M. L. Morrison and an anonymous reviewer provided many helpful comments.

LITERATURE CITED

ACKERMAN, B., F. LEBAN, M. SAMUEL, AND E. GARTON. 1990. User's Manual for Program Home Range. Forestry, Wildlife and Range Experiment Station Technical Report 15. University of Idaho, Moscow, 80 pp.

ALLDREDGE, J. R., AND J. T. RATTI. 1992. Further comparison of some statistical techniques for analysis of resource selection. The Journal of Wildlife Management, 56:1-9.

BARKALOW, F. S., AND R. F. SOOTS. 1965. An analysis of the effect of artificial nest boxes on a gray squirrel population. Transactions North American Wildlife and Natural Resource Conference, 30:351-359.

BRENDER, E. V. 1973. Silviculture of loblolly pine in the Georgia Piedmont. Georgia Forest Research Council. Report 33, Southeast Forest Experiment Station, Macon, Georgia, 74 pp.

BROWN, B. W., AND G. O. BATZLI. 1984. Habitat selection by fox and gray squirrels: a multivariate analysis. The Journal of Wildlife Management, 48:616-621.

BULL, E. L., AND R. S. HOLTHAUSEN. 1993. Habitat use and management of pileated woodpeckers in northeastern Oregon. The Journal of Wildlife Management, 57:335-345.

BYERS, C. R., R. K. STEINHORST, AND P. R. KRAUSMAN. 1984. Clarification of a technique for analysis of utilization-availability data. The Journal of Wildlife Management, 48:1050-1053.

CHU, D. S., B. A. HOOVER, M. R. FULLER, AND P. H. GEISSLER. 1988. Telemetry location error in a forested habitat. Pp. 188-194, *in* Biotelemetry X: Proceedings of the Tenth International Symposium on Biotelemetry. (C. J. Amlander, Jr., ed.). University of Arkansas, Fayetteville, 733 pp.

DAY, G. I., S. D. SCHEMNITZ, AND R. D. TABER. 1981. Capturing and marking wild animals. Pp. 61-98, *in* Wildlife Management Techniques Manual. (S. D. Schemnitz, ed.). The Wildlife Society, Washington, DC, 686 pp.

DIXON, K. R., AND J. A. CHAPMAN. 1980. Harmonic mean measure of animal activity areas. Ecology, 61:1040-1044.

EDWARDS, J. W. 1995. Resource use by sympatric populations of fox and gray squirrels. Ph.D. dissertation, Clemson University, South Carolina, 66 pp.

EDWARDS, J.W., D. C. GUYNN, JR., AND S. C. LOEB. 1993. Seasonal mast availability for wildlife in the Piedmont Region of Georgia. Research PaperSE-287, Asheville, North Carolina: U.S. Department of Agriculture, Forest Service, Southeastern Forest Experiment Station, 13 pp.

EDWARDS, J. W., AND D. C. GUYNN, JR. 1995. Nest characteristics of sympatric populations of fox and gray squirrels. The Journal of Wildlife Management, 59:103-110.

JOHNSON, D. H. 1980. The comparison of usage and availability measurements for evaluating resource preference. Ecology, 61:65-71.

KAUFMANN, J. H. 1962. Ecology and social behavior of the coati, *Nasua narica* on Barro Colorada Island, Panama. University of California, Publications in Zoology, 60:95-222.

KOTLER, B. P., J. S. BROWN, AND W. A. MITCHELL. 1993. Environmental factors affecting patch use in two species of Gerbilline rodents. Journal of Mammalogy, 74:614-620.

LAUNDRE, J. W., AND B. L. KELLER. 1984. Home-range size of coyotes: a critical review. The Journal of Wildlife Management, 48:127-139.

LEE, J. E., G. C. WHITE, R. A. GARROT, R. M. BARTMANN, AND A. W. ALLDREDGE 1985. Accessing accuracy of a radiotelemetry system for estimating animal locations. The Journal of Wildlife Management, 49:658-663.

MACHLIS, L., P. W. D. DODD, AND J. C. FENTRESS. 1985. The pooling fallacy: problemsarising when individuals contribute more than one observation to the data set. Zeitschrift für Tierpsychologie, 68:201-214.

MANLY, B. F. J., L. L. MCDONALD, AND D. L. THOMAS. 1993. Resource Selection by Animals: Statistical Design and Analysis for Field Studies. Chapman and Hall, New York, 177 pp.

MENDENHALL, W., D. D. WACKERLY, AND R. L. SCHEAFFER. 1990. Mathematical Statistics with Applications, 4th edition. PWS-Kent, Boston, Massachusetts, 818 pp.

MICHENER, G. R. 1979. Spatial relationships and social organization of adult Richardson's ground squirrels. Canadian Journal of Zoology, 57:125-139.

MORRISON, M. L., B. G. MARCOT, AND R. W. MANNAN. 1992. Wildlife-habitat Relationships: concepts and applications. University of Wisconsin Press, Madison, 343 pp.

NEU, C. W., C. R. BYERS, AND J. M. PEEK. 1974. A technique for analysis of utilization-availability data. The Journal of Wildlife Management, 38:541-545.

PAULEY, G. R., J. M. PEEK, AND P. ZAGER. 1993. Predicting white-tailed deer habitat use in northern Idaho. The Journal of Wildlife Management, 57:904-913.

PETRIDES, G. A. 1972. A field guide to trees and shrubs. Easton Press, Norwalk, Connecticut, 428 pp.

PORTER, W. F., AND K. E. CHURCH. 1987. Effects of environmental pattern on habitat preference analysis. The Journal of Wildlife Management, 51:681-685.

RADFORD, A. E., H. E. AHLES, AND C. L. BELL. 1968. Manual of the vascular flora of the Carolinas. University of North Carolina Press, Chapel Hill, 1183 pp.

ROSCOE, J. T., AND J. A. BYARS. 1971. An investigation of the restraints with respect to sample size commonly imposed on the use of the Chi-square statistic. Journal American Statisticians Association, 66:755-759.

SAS INSTITUTE, INC. 1991. SAS User's Guide, version 6. SAS Institute Inc. Cary, North Carolina, 890 pp.

SCHAMBERGER, M. L., AND L. J. O'NEIL. 1986. Concepts and constraints of habitat-model testing. Pp. 5-10, *in* Wildlife 2000; Modelling habitat relationships of terrestrial vertebrates. (J. Verner, M. L. Morrison, and C. J. Ralph, eds.). University of Wisconsin Press, Madison, 470 pp.

SMITH, D. M. 1962. The practice of silviculture, 7th edition. John Wiley & Sons, New York, 578 pp.

SPRINGER, J. T. 1979. Some sources of bias and sampling error in radio triangulation. The Journal of Wildlife Management, 43:926-935.

STEEL, R. G. D., AND J. H. TORRIE. 1980. Principles and Procedures of Statistics: A Biometrical Approach. McGraw-Hill, New York, 633 pp.

SWIHART, R. K., AND N. A. SLADE. 1987. A test for independence of movements as shown by live trapping. The American Midland Naturalist, 117:203-207.

SWIHART, R.K., N. A. SLADE, AND B. J. BERGSTROM. 1988. Relating body size to the rate of home range use in mammals. Ecology, 69:393-399.

TAPPE, P. A. 1991. Capture-recapture methods for estimating southern fox squirrel abundance. Ph.D. dissertation, Clemson University, Clemson, South Carolina, 92 pp.

TAPPE, P.A., J. W. EDWARDS, AND D. C. GUYNN, JR. 1993. Capture methodology and density estimates of southeastern fox squirrels (*Sciurus niger*). Pp. 71-77, *in* Proceedings of the Second Symposium on

Southeastern Fox Squirrels, *Sciurus niger* (N. D. Moncrief, J. W. Edwards, and P. A. Tappe, eds.). Virginia Museum of Natural Histor,y Special Publication, 1:1-84.

THOMAS, D. L., AND E. J. TAYLOR. 1990. Study designs and tests for comparing resource use and availability. The Journal of Wildlife Management, 54:322-330.

U.S. DEPARTMENT OF AGRICULTURE. 1988. Silvicultural examination and prescription field book. Atlanta, Georgia, USDA, Forest Service, Southern Region, 35 pp.

———. 1990 Silvics of North America, conifers volume 1 (675 pp.) and hardwoods volume 2 (875pp.). USDA Forest Service Agriculture Handbook 654, Washington, DC.

WHITE, G. C., AND R. A. GARROT. 1990. Analysis of Wildlife Radio-Tracking Data. Academic Press, New York, 382 pp.

SPATIOTEMPORAL HETEROGENEITY OF FOOD AVAILABILITY AND DIETARY VARIATION BETWEEN INDIVIDUALS OF THE MALABAR GIANT SQUIRREL *RATUFA INDICA*

RENEE M. BORGES

Centre for Ecological Sciences, Indian Institute of Science, Bangalore 560012, INDIA

ABSTRACT.—The variation in daily diets among individual Malabar giant squirrels *Ratufa indica* (Sciuridae) was examined on a monthly basis in two monsoonal forests in western India by quantifying the relative proportions of individual food resources in the food biomass ingested on a daily basis. Data were recorded continuously for entire days on individual, focal animals for a total of 83 days (837 hours) and 59 days (613 hours) at each site respectively, with approximately 10 individual squirrels being followed each month. Rare or clumped tree species, seasonality of fruiting, dioecy, predation on flowers and immature fruit by squirrels, as well as intra- and inter-specific variation in fruiting phenology contributed to spatiotemporal heterogeneity in availability of food resources. In addition, a territorial social organization restricted access by individual squirrels to tree species and individual fruiting trees. The above factors contributed to considerable monthly variation in the composition of daily diets between squirrels, some individuals largely consuming fruit, while others were feeding mainly on resources of low nutritive value such as leaves, pith, bark, and flowers, at the same time. Fruit resources that were major or minor at a population level were identified. Species that were minor fruit resources at a population level were found to be major resources at an individual level owing to the same phenomena.

INTRODUCTION

The spatiotemporal heterogeneity of food resources for arboreal herbivores in tropical forests has been investigated mainly for primates in the Neotropics, Africa, and southeast Asia (e.g., Struhsaker, 1975; Hladik, 1978; Raemaekers et al., 1980; Terborgh, 1983). Some data are available for tropical frugivorous birds (Leighton, 1982; Denslow et al., 1986; Wheelwright, 1986) and bats (Heithaus and Fleming, 1978; Bonaccorso, 1979). Resource availability for tropical, arboreal, herbivorous rodents such as squirrels has scarcely been investigated (MacKinnon, 1978; Payne, 1979; Glanz et al., 1982). A few studies record potential resource competition between primates, birds, and squirrels (Leighton, 1982). Moreover, most studies have described only the average condition of resource availability and utilization for the species or group (e.g., Terborgh, 1983). Some investigators have recorded dietary differences between groups and have related them to intergroup differences in food availability (Sussman, 1977; Richard, 1978; Rudran, 1978; Cheney et al., 1988). Studies on individuals have rarely been attempted (however see Glander, 1981) possibly because of the practical difficulty involved in recognizing and following individuals for extended periods of time in the field.

In this paper, I provide data on: 1) general patterns of spatiotemporal heterogeneity of food resources for a large, arboreal herbivore—the Malabar giant squirrel, *Ratufa indica* (Sciuridae), in two floristically distinct forests in the Indian tropics, 2) variation in resource availability between individual squirrels, and (3) effects of individual variation in resource base on individual variation in diet.

In M.A. Steele, J. F. Merritt, and D. A. Zegers (eds.). 1998. Ecology and Evolutionary Biology of Tree Squirrels. Special Publication, Virginia Museum of Natural History, 6: 320 pp

STUDY SITES

This study was conducted in two monsoonal forests in the Western Ghats of India: Magod (elevation, 665 m)—a moist deciduous patch within the Yellapur Reserve Forest in North Kanara District, Karnataka (January through September, 1985), and Bhimashankar (elevation, 900 m)—an evergreen, seasonal cloud forest within the Bhimashankar Wildlife Sanctuary in Pune District, Maharashtra (January through June, 1986). Further details of the study site are described in Borges (1989). The single wet season at each site was from June through September (Figs. 1 and 2).

METHODS

I continuously timed behavioral transitions from dawn to dusk for individual focal animals (ten individuals per month, one animal per day per month) within a study area of approximately 10 ha at each site gridded at 50 m intervals. The focal animals were habituated, and in most cases, allowed observation from close distances. I estimated the relative contributions of food items to a squirrel's daily diet from feeding rates and average wet masses of the items (per unit item, or per unit volume for bark and pith; see detailed methods in Borges, 1990, 1992, 1993). I mapped all trees used for feeding or nesting by squirrels and determined the spatial distribution of important food tree species by nearest neighbor analysis (Clark and Evans, 1954). In each grid square utilized by the focal squirrels, I counted the number of trees of each species within fruiting, flowering and leafing phenophases every month (within 6.5 ha at Magod and 5.25 ha at Bhimashankar). I counted a tree in more than one phenophase if it had items of different phenophases at the same time.

I defined the core feeding area of a focal animal as that area within which it usually initiated and won aggressive encounters with other individuals. I referred to such an area as a territory following the definition of Noble (1939) who stated that a territory is any defended area. A feeding tree was considered to be outside the territory of an individual if a squirrel: 1) was displaced from it; 2) was alert while approaching, entering, feeding in, and leaving it; 3) left it with a partially consumed food item and proceeded to complete its consumption some distance away because of the entrance into the tree or the proximity of another squirrel; or 4) waited near it for a squirrel currently using the tree to leave before entering the same tree. I called visits to such trees feeding excursions from the territory. I, therefore, approximated each territory by joining the outermost feeding trees considered to be within the territory according to the above criteria (e.g., Jaremovic and Croft, 1987). I estimated territories for only those squirrels that I had observed for three or more months (eleven squirrels at Magod and ten at Bhimashankar). With these data, I estimated the number of trees in different phenophases that were accessible to each individual squirrel on a monthly basis.

RESULTS

Temporal heterogeneity of food resources: general patterns.—The general phenological patterns at the sites are given in Figs. 1 and 2. The overall levels of fruit production were low (e.g., 4.2 and 5.0% of trees with mature fruit at Magod during peaks in fruiting in the dry and wet seasons, and only 1.0% during the one observed peak in fruiting at Bhimashankar). Lean fruiting periods occurred during the early parts of the year at both sites and also during the wet season at Magod.

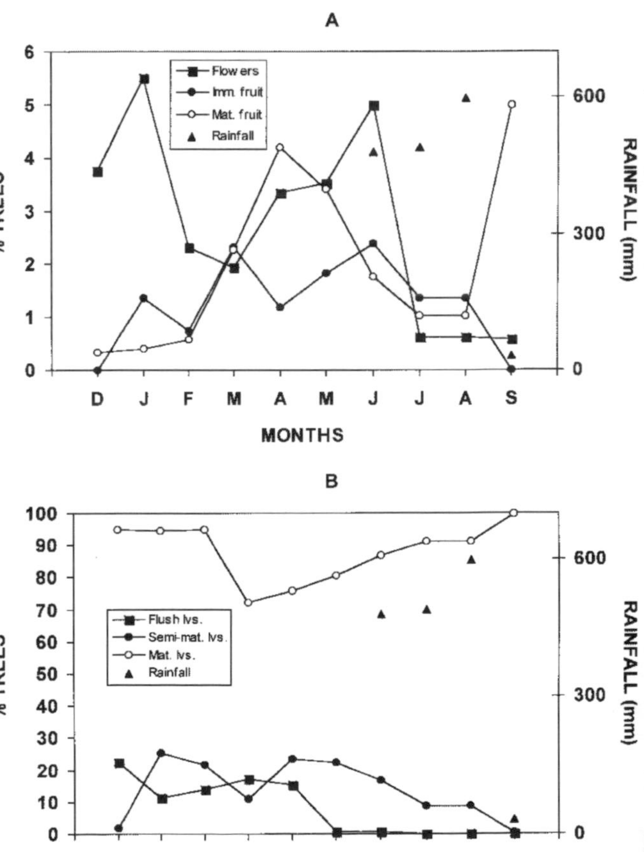

FIG. 1—Phenology of trees in the core observation area at Magod. Points represent the percentage of trees in each phenophase (n = 1761). An individual tree could be recorded in more than one phenophase at the time of a sample. **A**) flowers, immature fruit, mature fruit, **B**) flush leaves, semi-mature leaves, mature leaves. Monthly rainfall also shown.

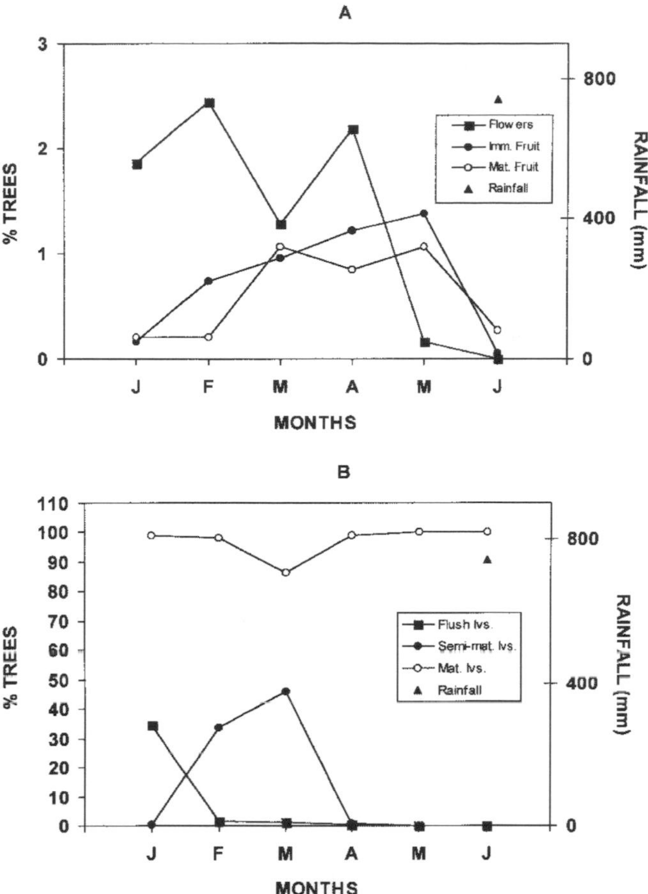

FIG. 2—Phenology of trees in the core observation area at Bhimashankar. Explanation as in Fig. 1 ($n = 1878$). **A)** flowers, immature fruit, mature fruit. **B)** flush leaves, semi-mature leaves, mature leaves. Monthly rainfall also shown.

Food dispersion and availability to individual squirrels.—Fruit was a primary food resource during fruiting seasons and could account for 100% of the daily diet of an individual squirrel. Therefore, the analysis of the spatial distribution of resources was focused on the availability of fruit. Seeds were generally the major fruit component eaten, although only the pulp of a few species was consumed (Tables 1 and 2; Borges, 1989).

I divided fruit species into two categories: 1) major—those that were eaten by seven or more focal squirrels, and 2) minor—those that were eaten by three or fewer focal squirrels in at least one month's observation (Tables 1 and 2). At both sites, some of the major resources were abundantly available while others had low relative abundances. The major resources were also those that generally had the highest maximum daily consumption values at both sites.

At Magod, of the five major fruit resources, *Artocarpus hirsutus* (Moraceae) was found to have a significantly aggregated spatial distribution (Clark and Evans index $R = 0.66$, $Z = -3.3$, $P < 0.01$). Spatial data were not collected for the other major species which, with the exception of *Carallia brachiata* (Rhizophoraceae), were more abundant than *A. hirsutus*. I calculated the total number of flowering and fruiting trees of *A. hirsutus* accessible to each of a set of squirrels over the study period by adding the number of trees of *A. hirsutus* in the core area for each squirrel (i.e., the grid squares within the territory) to the number of trees each squirrel was known to have visited outside its core feeding area (i.e., in territorial excursions) (Fig. 3). Some squirrels had access to a greater number of trees of *Artocarpus* than other individuals. Moreover, two focal squirrels (MFAF, YMPM) never had access to this important resource

TABLE 1.—*Parameters of fruit species use at Magod*

a) Major fruit species i.e. species eaten by 7 or more squirrels in a month's observation

Species	TD	TS	TM	AVE ±	*SD*	MAX	MIN	TT	RA
Aporosa lindleyana#	34	15	4	28.9	21.1	67.2	0.2	397	22.5
*Artocarpus hirsutus**	25	13	5	24.9	21.5	76.3	2.2	29	1.8
Carallia brachiata#	9	7	2	12.7	10.5	29.6	1.2	4	0.2
Olea dioica^	12	15	2	27.6	18.9	52.8	1.3	236	13.4
*Holigarna arnottiana**	26	15	4	44.8	30.5	95.1	3.0	78	4.4
*Vitex alata**	22	15	4	27.0	25.5	81.0	0.1	89	5.1
Gnetum ula+,a	13	15	2	20.4	17.7	64.2	4.5		
b) Minor fruit species i.e. species eaten by 3 or fewer squirrels in a month's observation									
Alseodaphne semicarpifolia^	6	3	2	9.3	10.5	23.9	0.4	6	0.3
Artocarpus heterophyllus#	2	1	2	21.5	20.4	35.9	7.1	3	0.2
Buchanania lanzan^	4	2	2	27.0	10.6	41.0	17.2	9	0.5
Careya arborea#	2	2	1	8.1	5.9	12.3	3.9	51	3.0
Casearia esculenta#	3	3	1	7.1	2.3	9.7	5.5	3	0.2
Cinnamomum macrocarpum#	11	7	2	5.0	4.8	15.8	0.4	79	4.5
*Ficus tsjahela**	10	6	5	15.6	19.3	63.1	0.7	10	0.6
Garcinia indica#	10	6	4	16.7	11.4	38.7	3.6	7	0.6
Randia dumetorum#	1	1	1	(6.9)				50	2.8
Terminalia bellerica^	2	2	1	0.4	0.1	0.4	0.3	9	0.5
Terminalia tomentosa#	14	9	7	0.9	1.2	3.4	0.02	241	13.7
Trichilia connaroides#	2	1	2	7.9	2.1	9.4	6.4	2	0.1
Xantolis tomentosa#	2	2	1	0.4	0.4	0.6	0.1	18	1.0

Column codes: TD = Total number of observation days in which the species was used; TS = Number of individual squirrels that used the species; TM = Number of months in which the species was fed upon; AVE = Mean and standard deviation *(SD)* of species representation in the diet (% of daily diet in terms of wet mass) when the species was included in the diet; MAX = Maximum % recorded usage; MIN = Minimum % recorded usage; TT = Total number of trees of the species in the observation area; RA = Relative abundance (% of total trees). Total number of observed trees in core area (6.5 ha) at Magod (>20 cm DBH) = 1761. Total number of focal squirrels = 15.

* = pulp and seed consumed; ^ = only pulp consumed; # = only seed consumed; + = ovary integument consumed; a = liana.

TABLE 2.—*Parameters of fruit species use at Bhimashankar*

Major fruit species i.e. species eaten by 7 or more squirrels in a month's observation

Species	TD	TS	TM	AVE	± *SD*	MAX	MIN	TT	RA
Olea dioica	12	18	2	16.2	8.7	30.8	1.2	70	3.7
Mangifera indica	33	18	4	48.8	24.4	92.2	8.0	324	17.3
Minor fruit species i.e. species eaten by 3 or fewer squirrels in a month's observation									
Amoora lawii[#]	13	8	4	12.2	12.1	40.1	0.3	39	2.1
Artocarpus heterophyllus[#]	2	2	2	11.3	6.90	16.1	6.4	1	0.1
Carallia brachiata[#]	4	4	2	0.7	0.4	1.0	0.2	4	0.2
Cassine glauca[#]	1	1	1	(1.4)				5	0.3
Diospyros sylvatica[#]	1	1	1	(21.2)				33	1.8
Dyxsoxylum binectariferum[#]	2	2	1	0.6	0.3	0.9	0.4	4	0.2
Syzygium cumini[*]	11	7	3	11.6	11.6	39.2	0.4	98	5.2
Ficus callosa[*]	20	8	6	22.7	21.6	73.4	0.4	9	1.4
Ficus glomerata[*]	18	6	6	21.2	17.5	53.2	0.6	16	1.5
Garcinia talbotii[*]	18	9	4	16.7	13.3	41.7	0.7	58	3.1
Litsea stocksii[#]	3	3	2	20.0	15.2	31.8	2.80	22	1.2
Macaranga peltata[#]	1	1	1	(4.2)				1	0.1
Symplocos beddomei[#]	1	1	1	(9.0)				3	0.2
Xantolis tomentosa[#]	1	1	1	(4.0)				46	2.5
Diploclisia macrocarpa[#,a]	9	7	2	7.3	6.9	19.9	1.30		
Gnetum ula[+, a]	13	10	3	7.6	6.5	22.7	0.04		

Column codes as in Table 1. Total number of observed trees in core area (5.25 ha) at Bhimashankar (>20 DBH) = 1878. Total number of focal squirrels = 18.

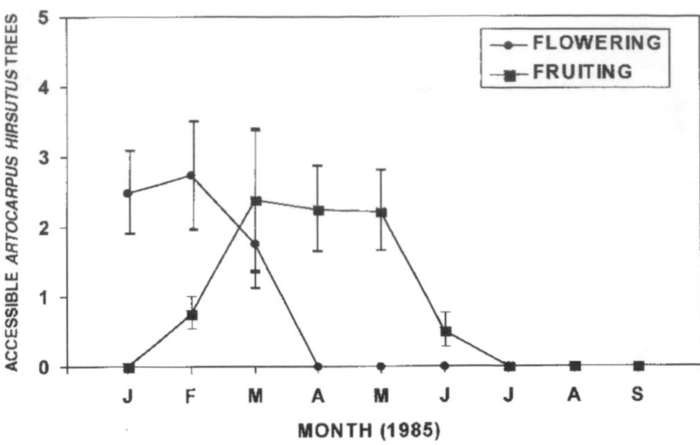

FIG. 3.—The number of trees of *Artocarpus hirsutus* in flower and in fruit that were available to individual squirrels each month at Magod (means and standard errors). Number of squirrels each month: J = 8, F = 8, M = 8, A = 8, M = 9, J = 8, J = 8, A = 5, S = 10.

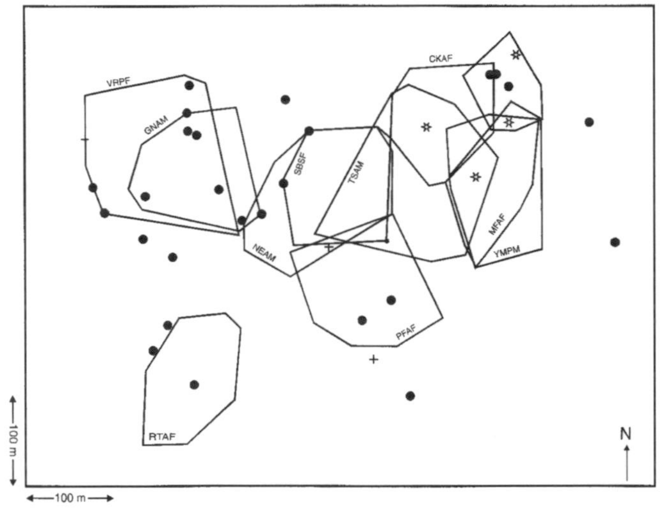

FIG. 4—Distribution of *Artocarpus hirsutus* and *Ficus tsjahela* in the core observation area at Magod relative to the territories of individual squirrels. Each shaded circle (◉) marks the location of *A. hirsutus*, each cross (+) marks the location of non-fruiting *F. tsjahela*, and each asterisk (*) marks the location of fruiting *F. tsjahela*. The 4 letter code (e.g., VRPF) within each territory indicates the identity of the squirrel. The third letter of the code indicates the estimated age class of the squirrel: P = juvenile (one+ year old), S = sub-adult, A = adult. The fourth letter of the code indicates the sex of the squirrel: F = female, M = male. Average territory size = 1.2 ha for males (n = 5) and 1.1 ha for females (n = 6).

(Fig. 4). The flower receptacles of *A. hirsutus* were also an important resource and there was also considerable individual variation in access to the flowers (Fig. 3). The mean number of *A. hirsutus* trees available to a squirrel each month was greatest in March (2.4, SD = 3.0, range = 0 - 8). The variation between individual focal squirrels in the number of flowering and fruiting trees accessible each month was significant (Kruskal-Wallis one-way ANOVA, H = 18.3 for flowers, P < 0.05; H = 55.9 for fruit, P < 0.001; n = 8).

At Bhimashankar, only two species were major fruit resources (Table 2). *Mangifera* (Anacardiaceae) was the most common canopy tree while *Olea* (Euphorbiaceae) was a less common mid-story representative. All focal squirrels (n = 18) had access to these two species.

At Magod and Bhimashankar, 13 and 14 tree species respectively were minor fruit resources (Tables 1 and 2). These were either rare (low relative abundances) and/or patchily distributed. For example, *Garcinia indica* (Clusiaceae) at Magod had an overall clumped distribution (Clark and Evans index R = 0.60, Z = -2.1, P < 0.01). Similarly, *Ficus glomerata* (Moraceae; synonym: *F. racemosa*) and *F. callosa* at Bhimashankar were clumped (Clark

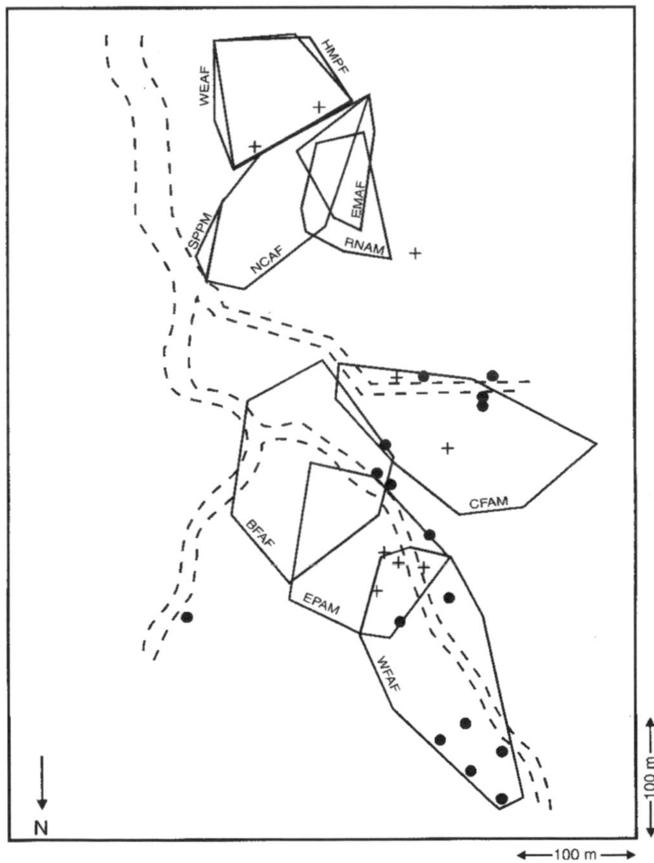

FIG. 5.—Distribution of *Ficus callosa* and *F. glomerata* within the core observation area at Bhimashankar relative to the territories of individual squirrels. Each cross (+) indicates the location of *F. callosa* and each shaded circle (◉) indicates the location of *F. glomerata*. The four letter code within each territory indicates the identity of an individual squirrel. See legend for Fig. 4 for explanation of the code. The dotted lines indicate the course of the river Bhima. Average territory size = 0.7 for both males (n = 4) and females (n = 6).

and Evans index $R = 0.54$, $Z = -3.5$; and $R = 0.60$, $Z = -2.2$ respectively, $P < 0.01$; Fig. 5; see also Borges, 1993). At Bhimashankar, other species also had restricted spatial distributions. For example, *Amoora lawii* (Meliaceae) occurred only on steep slopes adjacent to open rocky cliffs and was unavailable to the riverine squirrels. Conversely, *Syzygium cumini* (Myrtaceae) tended to occur mostly in riverine areas. On the other hand, *Ficus tsjahela* at Magod had an overall random spatial distribution (Clark and Evans index $R = 0.85$, $Z = -0.9$, $P > 0.50$, Fig. 4).

Of the thirteen minor fruit species at Magod, some species such as *Buchanania lanzan* (Anacardiaceae) and *F. tsjahela* were major daily fruit sources for some individual squirrels (see average and maximum daily consumption values in Table 1b). Similar observations were made at Bhimashankar for species such as *A. lawii*, *F. callosa* and *F. glomerata* (Table 2b). At both sites, there were some tree species such as *Randia dumetorum* (Rubiaceae) at Magod and *Cassine glauca* (Celastraceae) at Bhimashankar that were observed to be utilized by only a single focal squirrel. Also, at both sites, lianas such as *Gnetum ula* (Gnetaceae) at Magod and *Diploclisia macrocarpa* (Menispermaceae) at Bhimashankar provided major and minor fruit resources respectively (Tables 1 and 2). The density of lianas, however, was not quantified.

Intraspecific variation in phenology.—Owing to the method by which the phenology data were recorded each month, it was not possible to determine exactly how many individual trees fruited during the study period for many species. However, at both sites, only a fraction of individuals of most species set fruit because they are dioecious or because of unknown causes. For example, at Magod only 57.1% (4/7) of trees of *G. indica* (polygamo-dioecious), 33.3% (1/3) of trees of *Artocarpus heterophyllus*, 33.3% (3/9) of trees of *B. lanzan*, 11.8% (6/51) of trees of *Careya arborea* (Myrtaceae) and 40% (4/10) of trees of *F. tsjahela* bore fruit within the study area. Similarly, at Bhimashankar only 3.0% (1/33) of trees of *Diospyros sylvatica* (Ebenaceae; dioecious), 9.1% (2/22) of trees of *Litsea stocksii* (Lauraceae; dioecious), and 15.5% (9/58) of trees of *Garcinia talbotii* (polygamo-dioecious) fruited during the study period.

Squirrels also reduced fruit production in *C. arborea* and *A. hirsutus* by feeding heavily on the flowers (e.g., mean and maximum daily consumptions of the flowers of *A. hirsutus* during the first fruit shortage were 40.2% [$SD = 32.2$, $n = 18$] and 91.6% respectively), and similarly reduced fruit maturation in *B. lanzan* (by feeding on immature fruit), and in *Terminalia tomentosa* (Combretaceae) (by feeding on the pith of leaf sprays bearing huge clusters of immature fruit). Therefore, at both sites there was also squirrel-induced, intraspecific variation in the size of fruit crops. This, however, was not quantified during the study.

Monthly inter-individual variation in access to fruit sources.—The number of fruiting trees (all species combined) accessible to the focal squirrels at Magod and Bhimashankar over the study period was estimated in the same way that the number of accessible *Artocarpus* trees was estimated (Figs. 6A and 6B). The general pattern of fruit accessibility corresponded to the general fruit phenology of the forest, yet at both sites there was some inter-individual variation in access to fruit each month but this was not significant (Kruskal-Wallis one-way ANOVA, $H = 2.4$ at Magod, $n = 8$; $H = 9.5$ at Bhimashankar, $n = 9$; $P > 0.05$).

Seasonal diet variation between squirrels.—At

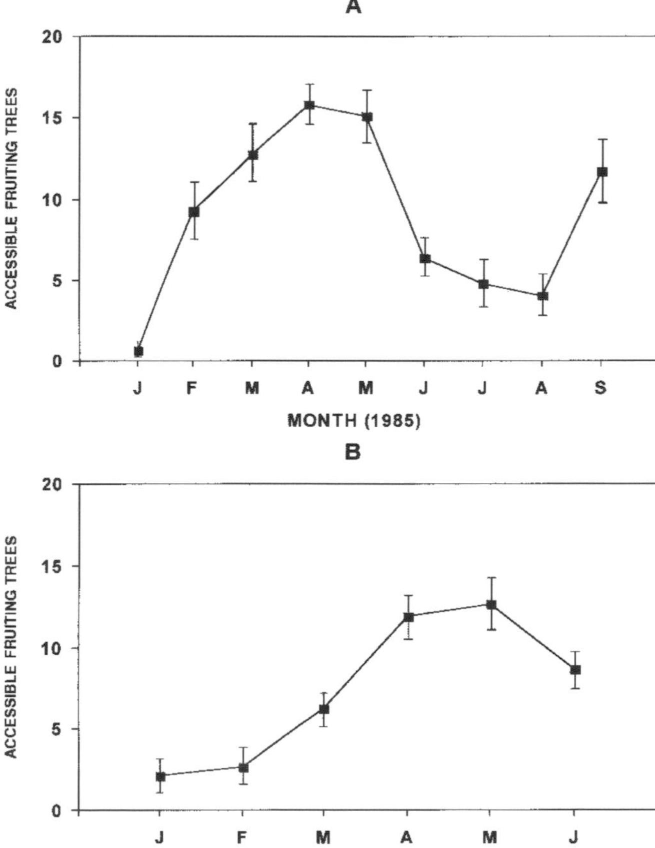

FIG. 6.—The number of fruiting trees accessible to individual squirrels each month (means and standard errors). **A)** at Magod: Number of squirrels each month: J = 8, F = 8, M = 8, A = 8, M = 10, J = 8, J = 9, A = 5, S = 11. **B)** at Bhimashankar: Number of squirrels each month: J = 7, F = 7, M = 8, A = 8, M = 8, J = 8.

Magod, the average daily consumption of fruit calculated over the entire study period was 58.0% ± 34.6% (*SD*) of the diet (n = 83 squirrel days; 837 observation hours) and 48.8% ± 38.6% (*SD*) (n = 59 squirrel days; 613 observation hours) at Bhimashankar. The consumption of fruit tracked the general fruit availability, and therefore, increased steadily to a peak in June at Magod when average fruit consumption was 90.4% (Table 3). At Magod, there was a significant positive correlation between total daily consumption of the major fruit sources and the total number of fruiting trees of these species in the study area (Kendall's τ = .42, $P < 0.0001$). This relationship was not significant at Bhimashankar.

TABLE 3.—*Contributions of item classes to the daily diet (percent wet mass basis) at Magod (means, coefficients of variation and ranges).*

Month	Flush leaves	S. mat. leaves	Mature leaves	Bark	Pith	Flowers	Fruit
Jan '85	33.8	11.9	0.0	8.9	0.0	38.7	6.8
N = 9	92.8	126.4		82.8		66.6	149.9
	0-77	0-37		0-22		5-73	0-32
Feb	3.0	8.0	0.0	3.1	0.0	48.2	37.9
N = 9	264.4	103.0		133.1		76.8	80.6
	0-24	0-21		0-10		0.2-92	4-93
Mar	4.8	11.1	0.04	2.2	0.0	4.9	77.0
N = 9	176.5	76.6	325.0	162.2		85.3	21.0
	0-25	0-23	0-0.4	0-9		0-12	43-91
Apr	6.1	5.8	3.1	1.2	0.0	1.5	82.3
N = 10	104.3	130.8	160.7	183.9		194.1	16.6
	0-18	0-19	0-14	0-7		0-9	62-100
May	2.2	2.5	6.8	0.8	0.03	0.0	87.7
N = 10	184.4	137.3	129.5	276.0	333.3		12.9
	0-12	0-10	0-29	0-7	0-0.3		65-100
Jun	0.5	3.2	5.9	0.0	0.0	0.0	90.4
N = 10	226.1	86.3	106.6				5.5
	0-3	0-7	0.5-21				79-100
Jul	0.0	5.0	32.5	5.6	6.6	0.0	50.3
N = 10		179.1	83.8	215.3	153.1		74.3
		0-26	6-82	0-34	0-28		4-93
Aug	0.0	0.0	62.9	9.3	19.4	0.0	8.4
N = 5			39.9	134.1	111.3		98.1
			21-85	0-28	0-50		0-19
Sept	0.3	1.2	35.9	10.4	0.4	0.0	51.8
N = 11	326.9	213.2	36.2	103.3	269.1		31.9
	0-3	0-7	19-62	0-32	0-4		32-81

Ranges have been rounded to the nearest integer value.

At both sites, however, the inter-squirrel variation in fruit consumption showed a negative (though non-significant) relationship with fruit availability and was highest during lowest fruit availability (Table 3; e.g., *CV* = 150% in January at Magod), and was lowest when fruit availability peaked (Table 4; e.g., in May at Bhimashankar). In the first lean fruiting period at Magod, the range of daily consumption of fruit between squirrels was large (4.2% - 93.4%, $\overline{X}$ = 37.9%), and in the peak fruiting season in June, the range of consumption was small (78.9% - 98.0%). At Bhimashankar, the range of fruit consumption in the lean fruiting period was also large (0% - 54.4%, $\overline{X}$ = 26.2%), and during the peak in fruit availability the variation was smaller (57.0% - 96.6%).

During lean fruiting periods, resources such as bark, leaves, pith, and flowers were consumed (Tables 3 and 4). The variation between squirrels in consumption of foods available in the lean fruiting season was high (Tables 3 and 4). For ephemeral foods such as flush leaves and flowers there was the same general, though non-significant, inverse relationship between inter-squirrel variation in consumption and the availability of the particular resource type, as with fruit at both sites. At Magod, there was also a significant negative relationship between the coefficients of variation of bark and fruit consumption from January to June (Kendall's $\tau = 1.0$, $P < 0.001$). The highest inter-individual variation in bark consumption was

TABLE 4.—Contributions of item classes to the daily diet (percent wet mass basis) at Bhimashankar (means, coefficients of variation and ranges).

Month	Flush leaves	S. mat. leaves	Mature leaves	Bark	Pith	Flowers	Fruit
Jan '86	5.5	4.0	18.8	21.7	0.0	42.0	8.1
N = 9	172.8	205.8	92.5	53.9		78.4	223.7
	0-24	0-22	0-48	4-43		3-95	0-54
Feb	5.0	0.0	12.7	21.7	0.0	57.2	3.5
N = 10	253.0		102.1	55.6		35.1	316.0
	0-40		0-35	10-47		28-84	0-35
Mar	11.6	11.5	4.5	20.0	0.0	3.6	48.8
N = 10	90.2	132.5	147.7	74.6		154.9	64.2
	0-31	0-40	0-21	2-53		0-16	0-89
Apr	4.9	8.2	4.8	4.4	0.1	7.9	64.4
N = 10	76.0	199.2	65.6	91.3	308.3	114.7	40.5
	0-12	0-53	1-12	0-12	0-1	0-24	0-89
May	0.7	0.0	7.0	2.5	0.2	3.7	85.9
N = 10	318.1		95.6	75.7	310.0	230.6	14.7
	0-7		1-23	0.5-6	0-2	0-27	57-97
Jun	0.0	1.4	5.9	1.2	0.0	11.6	79.8
N = 10		86.1	40.9	110.5		170.5	26.1
		0-4	1-10	0-4		0-52	38-95

Ranges have been rounded to the nearest integer value.

associated with low values of variation in fruit consumption (during a period of general high fruit availability in May). This is consistent with the observation that a few individuals were consuming large amounts of bark and other fibrous, filler foods when others had access to higher quality resources (see average values and ranges in Tables 3 and 4). The CVs of mature leaf and bark consumption showed a positive correlation with that of general fruit availability. At Bhimashankar in March for example, when the consumption of fruit was rising (mean consumption was 48.8%), the highest recorded consumption of bark was 53.3%. This was the highest recorded daily consumption of bark at any time during the entire study at either site.

DISCUSSION

During this study in two tropical forests in India, fruit was the most important resource for giant squirrels and could account for 100% of the daily diet of an individual squirrel. The examination of resource patchiness therefore concentrated on fruit. The patterns and causes of variation in fruit resource availability found during this study emphasize that frugivory in the Indian tropics also involves uncertainty of fruit availability at both the temporal and spatial scales (as described by Terborgh, 1986*a*; reviewed by Fleming et al., 1987). My study further showed that access to fruit resources was variable at the level of individual herbivores. Most previous studies have described this variation at the group (Sussmann, 1977; Richard, 1978; Rudran, 1978; Cheney et al., 1988; Dasilva, 1992) or species level (Terborgh, 1983). In this study, territorial interactions between individual squirrels combined with the naturally occurring patchiness of resources to result in considerable inter-individual variation in access to fruit resources with a subsequent effect on inter-individual variation in diet composition.

I observed two lean fruiting periods at Magod and one lean period at Bhimashankar during the study. Even during peak fruiting periods, the overall level of fruit production was low. A low level of fruit production has also been generally observed in the forests of south-east Asia (Terborgh and Schaik, 1987; Schaik et al., 1993). In my study, no measurements are available for fruit production other than the numbers of trees bearing fruit.

Patchiness of resources was a result of patchily distributed tree species, variation in phenology between individual trees of a species, effects of dioecy, and reduction in the crop size of fruit by squirrels feeding on flowers and/or immature fruit. Some of these effects have also been found in other studies. Clumped tree species and fruit resources in the tropics have also been found by Struhsaker (1975), Waser (1977), Rudran (1978), Hubbell (1979), and Hubbell and Foster (1983). House (1992) found that the spatial distribution of males and females in a dioecious tree species can influence patterns of fruit availability. Variation in fruit crop sizes due to extensive predation on the flowers or immature fruit by the consumers has been reported by Waser (1977), Rudran (1978), MacKinnon and MacKinnon (1980), and Leighton (1982). Payne (1979) found that *Buchanania sessilifolia* set less fruit because of predation by *Ratufa affinis* and *R. bicolor* on immature fruit in Malaysia. Leighton (1982) also reported extensive consumption of unripe fruit of *Aglaia* (Meliaceae) and some species of Lauraceae by *Ratufa*.

Lianas were also found to be major fruit resources at both population and individual levels. However, no measurements of their densities were made. The role of lianas in the ecology of arboreal herbivores should be widely investigated as lianas are an important feature of disturbed forest areas. Such areas are becoming increasingly common in the tropics.

At a population level, species that were major fruit resources for squirrels were abundant as well as rare and showed random as well as clumped distributions. Moreover, species that could form minor fruit resources at a population level were important daily resources for some individual squirrels, owing to their spatial distributions relative to the area of access of individual animals. Moreover, in this study, although there was no significant variation between squirrels in the total number of fruiting trees accessible to them (irrespective of the species) at both sites, access to some particular species (e.g., flowering and fruiting trees of *A. hirsutus* at Magod), varied significantly among squirrels. Therefore, the phenology and spatial distribution of individual tree species interact with the areas of access of individual squirrels to produce an individually variable resource base. For example, Borges (1993) found that the importance of figs as a keystone resource was limited by their non-availability to the entire squirrel population during lean fruiting periods.

Although fruit was the most important resource during my study, individual giant squirrels employed dietary flexibility and consumed greater amounts of fibrous plant components such as leaves, bark, pith, and flowers when fruit was not available (see also Borges, 1992). *Ratufa affinis* and *R. bicolor* in Malaysia were also found to consume large amounts of fibrous foods such as leaves and bark during lean fruiting seasons (Payne, 1979; Leighton and Leighton, 1983). In fact, it appears that in south-east Asia leaves and bark are the important resources for frugivores during lean fruiting seasons as opposed to palm nuts, nectar, and small prey in the Neotropics (Terborgh, 1986b).

At a population level, the consumption of fruit by squirrels tracked the general patterns of fruit availability (see also Borges, 1992). In addition, there were general negative relationships between overall fruit availability and inter-squirrel variation in fruit consumption at both sites, as well as inter-squirrel variation in consumption of non-fruit resources such as bark and consumption of fruit at Magod. During periods of fruit abundance, some individuals largely consumed resources other than fruit. Conversely, during periods of fruit scarcity, some individuals were consuming fruit resources that were unavailable to other squirrels.

The observed intra-month variation in diets may be due to the fact that different squirrels were not observed at the same time of the month. However, the patterns of dispersion of tree species and fruit crops, coupled with the utilization of forest space by individuals, indicates that some squirrels had access to resources that were inaccessible to other individuals. Inverse relationships were also observed between monthly inter-individual variation in consumption of ephemeral foods (other than fruit) and their availability. This pattern of variation in resource availability also translated into variation in daily biomass consumption between individual squirrels e.g., as much as a 6-fold difference between maximum and minimum intra-monthly biomass values at both sites resulting from some squirrels feeding on bulky filler foods while others fed on more nutrient-rich items (Borges, 1992). Borges (1989, 1992) has also shown that fruit, especially seeds, at these two sites are a more profitable, easily digestible source of energy and lipid owing to their higher energy, non-structural carbohydrate and lipid content, as well as lower fiber content relative to other types of resources.

Thus different individuals may have experienced different lengths, timings and severities of fruit shortages, and therefore had to cope with nutritional environments of variable quality. This matter requires further investigation especially the long-term effects of differences in nutritional environments on the reproductive success of individuals.

ACKNOWLEDGMENTS

I am grateful to Ted Fleming, Bill Glanz, Carol Horvitz, Doyle McKey, the late Alan Smith, and two anonymous reviewers for valuable suggestions on earlier drafts of this manuscript. I thank Mahadeva, Asawale, Ganpat, Soma and Kisan for superlative assistance in the field. I am especially grateful to Robert Syren for help with data management. Funding for the research was provided by the United States Fish and Wildlife Service and the Chicago Zoological Society.

LITERATURE CITED

BONACCORSO, F. J. 1979. Foraging and reproductive ecology in a Panamanian bat community. Bulletin of the Florida Museum, Biological Sciences, 24:359-408.

BORGES, R. M. 1989. Resource heterogeneity and the foraging ecology of the Malabar giant squirrel *Ratufa indica*. Ph.D. dissertation, University of Miami, Florida, 221 pp.

———. 1990. Sexual and site differences in calcium consumption in the Malabar giant squirrel *Ratufa indica*. Oecologia, 85:80-86.

———. 1992. A nutritional analysis of foraging in the Malabar giant squirrel *Ratufa indica*. Biological Journal of the Linnean Society, 47:1-21.

———. 1993. Figs, Malabar giant squirrels, and fruit shortages within two tropical Indian forests. Biotropica, 25:183-190.

CHENEY, D. L., R. M. SEYFARTH, S. J. ANDELMAN, and P. C. LEE. 1988. Reproductive success in vervet monkeys. Pp. 384-402, *in* Reproductive success: studies of individual variation in contrasting breeding systems (T. H. Clutton-Brock, ed.). The University of Chicago Press, Chicago and London, 538 pp.

CLARK, P. J., and F. C. EVANS. 1954. Distance to nearest neighbor as a measure of spatial relationships in populations. Ecology, 35:445-453.

DASILVA, G. L. 1992. The western black-and-white colobus as a low-energy strategist: activity budgets, energy expenditure and energy intake. Journal of Animal Ecology, 61:79-91.

DENSLOW, J. S., T. C. MOERMOND, and D. J. LEVEY. 1986. Spatial components of fruit display in understory trees and shrubs. pp. 37-44, *in* Frugivores and seed dispersal (A. Estrada, and T. H. Fleming, eds.). Dr. W. Junk Publishers, Dordrecht, The Netherlands, 392 pp.

FLEMING, T. H., R. BREITWISCH, and G. WHITESIDES. 1987. Patterns in tropical frugivore diversity. Annual Review of Ecology and Systematics, 18:91-109.

GLANDER, K. E. 1981. Feeding patterns in mantled howling monkeys. Pp. 231-257, *in* Foraging behavior: ecological, ethological and psychological approaches (A. C. Kamil, and T. D. Sargent, eds.). Garland STPM Press, New York, 533 pp.

GLANZ, W. E., R. W. THORINGTON, Jr., J. GIACALONE-MADDEN, and L.R. HEANEY. 1982. Seasonal food use and demographic trends in *Sciurus granatensis*. Pp. 239-252, *in* The ecology of a tropical forest: seasonal rhythms and long-term changes (E. G. Leigh, Jr., A. S. Rand, and D. M. Windsor, eds.). Smithsonian Institution Press, Washington, D.C., 468 pp.

HEITHAUS, E. R., and T. H. FLEMING. 1978. Foraging movements of a frugivorous bat, *Carollia perspicillata* (Phyllostomatidae). Ecological Monographs, 48:127-143.

HLADIK, A. 1978. Phenology of leaf production in rain forest of Gabon: distribution and composition of food for folivores. Pp. 51-71, *in* The ecology of arboreal folivores (G. G. Montgomery, ed.). Smithsonian Institution Press, Washington,D.C., 574 pp.

HOUSE, S. M. 1992. Population density and fruit set in three dioecious tree species in Australian tropical rain forest. Journal of Ecology, 80:57-69.

HUBBELL, S. P. 1979. Tree dispersion and diversity in a tropical dry forest. Science, 203:1299-1309.

HUBBELL, S. P., and R. B. FOSTER. 1983. Diversity of canopy trees in a Neotropical forest and implications for conservation. Pp. 25-41, *in* Tropical rain forest: ecology and management (S. L. Sutton, T. C. Whitmore, and A. C. Chadwick, eds.). Blackwell Scientific Publications, London, 498 pp.

JAREMOVIC, R. V., and D. B. CROFT. 1987. Comparison of techniques to determine eastern grey kangaroo home range. The Journal of Wildlife Management, 51:921-930.

LEIGHTON, M. 1982. Fruit resources and patterns of feeding, spacing and grouping among sympatric Bornean hornbills (Bucerotidae). Unpublished Ph.D. dissertation, University of California, Davis, 263 pp.

LEIGHTON, M., and D. R. LEIGHTON. 1983. Vertebrate responses to fruiting seasonality within a Bornean rain forest. Pp. 181-196, *in* Tropical rain forest: ecology and management (S. L.Sutton, T. C. Whitmore, and A.C. Chadwick, eds.). Blackwell Scientific Publications, London, 498 pp.

MACKINNON, K. S. 1978. Stratification and feeding differences among Malayan squirrels. Malay Nature Journal, 30:593-608.

MACKINNON, J. R., and K. S. MACKINNON. 1980. Niche differentiation in a primate community. Pp. 167-190, *in* Malayan forest primates (D. J. Chivers, ed.). Plenum Press, New York, 364 pp.

NOBLE, G. K. 1939. The role of dominance in the life of birds. The Auk, 56:263-273.

PAYNE, J. B. 1979. Synecology of Malayan tree squirrels, with particular reference to the genus *Ratufa*. Ph.D. dissertation, Cambridge University, UK, 392 pp.

RAEMAEKERS, J. J., F. P. G. ALDRICH-BLAKE, AND J. B. PAYNE. 1980. The forest. Pp. 21-61, *in* Malayan forest primates (D. J. Chivers, ed.). Plenum Press, New York, 364 pp.

RICHARD, A. 1978. Variability in the feeding behavior of a Malagasy prosimian, *Propithecus verreauxi*: Lemuriformes. Pp. 519-533, *in* The ecology of arboreal folivores (G. G. Montgomery, ed.). Smithsonian Institution Press, Washington, D.C., 574 pp.

RUDRAN, R. 1978. Intergroup dietary comparisons and folivorous tendencies of two groups of blue monkeys (*Cercopithecus mitis stuhlmanni*). Pp. 483-503, *in* The ecology of arboreal folivores (G. G. Montgomery, ed.). Smithsonian Institution Press, Washington, D.C., 574 pp.

SCHAIK, C. P. VAN., J. W. TERBORGH, and S. J. WRIGHT. 1993. The phenology of tropical forests: adaptive significance and consequences for primary consumers. Annual Review of Ecology and Systematics, 24:353-377.

STRUHSAKER, T. T. 1975. The Red Colobus Monkey. University of Chicago Press, Chicago, IL, 311 pp.

SUSSMAN, R. W. 1977. Feeding behaviour of *Lemur catta* and *Lemur fulvus*. Pp. 1-36, *in* Primate ecology: studies of feeding and ranging behaviour in lemurs, monkeys and apes (T. H. Clutton-Brock, ed.). Academic Press, London, 631 pp.

TERBORGH, J. 1983. Five New World Primates. Princeton University Press, Princeton, New Jersey, 260 pp.

———. 1986*a*. Community aspects of frugivory in tropical forests. Pp. 371-384, *in* Frugivores and seed dispersal (A. Estrada, and T. H. Fleming, eds.). Dr. W. Junk Publishers, Dordrecht, The Netherlands, 392 pp.

———. 1986*b*. Keystone plant resources in the tropical forest. Pp. 330-344, *in* Conservation biology: science of scarcity and diversity (M. Soule, ed.). Sinauer Associates, Sunderland, Massachusetts, 584 pp.

TERBORGH, J., AND C. P. VAN SCHAIK. 1987. Convergence vs. nonconvergence in primate communities. Pp. 205-226, *in* Organization of communities: past and present (J. H. R. Gee, and P. S. Giller, eds.). Blackwell Scientific Publications, Oxford, 576 pp.

WASER, P. 1977. Feeding, ranging, and group size in the mangabey *Cercocebus albigena*. Pp. 183-222, *in* Primate ecology: studies of feeding and ranging behaviour in lemurs, monkeys and apes (T. H. Clutton-Brock, ed.). Academic Press, London, 631 pp.

WHEELWRIGHT, N. T. 1986. A seven-year study of individual variation in fruit production in tropical bird-dispersed tree species in the family Lauraceae. Pp. 19-35, *in* Frugivores and seed dispersal (A. Estrada, and T. H. Fleming, eds.). Dr. W. Junk Publishers, Dordrecht, The Netherlands, 392 pp.

CHANGES IN HABITAT PREFERENCE OF THE TREE SQUIRREL *SCIURUS ALLENI* IN A PINE-OAK ASSOCIATION IN EASTERN SIERRA MADRE, MEXICO

JOSE A. GUEVARA G.

Area de Fauna Silvestre
Facultad de Ciencias Forestales, U.A.N.L.
Apartado Postal 41,67700 Linares, N.L. MEXICO

ABSTRACT.—This research deals with aspects of the habitat preference of *Sciurus alleni*, as well as changes in habitat use through the year. The study was conducted in the school forest of the University of Nuevo León (460 ha) in Iturbide, in Eastern Sierra Madre, northeast Mexico. To identify habitat preferences of the squirrels, I used the Modified Electivity Index (MEI) and an 8–Km. transect which was surveyed two times each month, from April 1989 to June 1991. In general, *Sciurus alleni* was observed in all vegetation types included in the transect, except that of *Amelanchier*-bushland. In addition, I found *S. alleni* at significantly lower altitudes in winter and in the dry season. Oak and pine forests always showed the higher MEI values. Besides the *Amelanchier*-bushland (where I never saw squirrels), the most strongly avoided vegetation types were the low forests of oak, juniper and ash. Contrary to what might have been expected, the pine-oak forest had a negative MEI value, suggesting avoidance by the squirrels. Results suggests that food availability has a strong influence on patterns of habitat selection, since most of the encounters with *S. alleni* took place in the areas where food availability was the greatest.

INTRODUCTION

High faunal diversity of Mexico is a result of the variety of climates, vegetation and topography as well as its location in a transition zone between two biogeographic regions (Czihak *et al.*, 1981). This diversity, however, has been drastically reduced in recent years primarily as a result of accelerated destruction of habitats by humans. Tree squirrels are found in all forests of Mexico, except in the southern part of Baja California and some isolated mountains in the north. Some taxonomist recognize two morphologically similar groups for the *Sciurus* genus: the "gray squirrels" (i.e., *Sciurus carolinensis* and *S. aureogaster*) and the "red squirrels"; *S. alleni* and *S. niger* belong to the red squirrels group (Leopold, 1965; Hall, 1981).

An adult *S. alleni* weighs between 400 and 500 g. Its upper parts are grayish brown, darker at the center than at the sides. This species does not exhibit a white spot on the back of the ear like similar species. The tail is dark above and brown or grayish brown below, with a white edge. The ventral parts of the animal are lighter than the dorsal parts.

Although most "red squirrels" live in temperate mountain forests, *S. alleni* can be found in coastal plains, where it has been reported at altitudes ranging from 360 to 2,480 m. However, it seems to prefer the pine-oak forest between 910 and 1,520 m (Leopold, 1965).

Among the 12 recognized species of *Sciurus* in Mexico (Hall, 1981; Ramírez et al., 1983). *S.alleni* has not been well studied. This investigation was conducted to elucidate patterns of habitat preference of *S. alleni* and how this pattern of habitat preference changes through the year by finding the proportion of use of every vegetation type in the study area. This information could be important for the conservation of this endemic squirrel.

In M.A. Steele, J. F. Merritt, and D. A. Zegers (eds.). 1998. Ecology and Evolutionary Biology of Tree Squirrels. Special Publication, Virginia Museum of Natural History, 6: 320 pp

STUDY AREA

This study was conducted in the school forest of the University of Nuevo León in Iturbide. This area (460 ha) is found in the Eastern Sierra Madre, between the 24°42'to 24°45'north latitude and 99°51'to 99°54'west longitude, at an altitude between 1,200 and 1,900 m (Fig. 1). The topography is extremely uneven, with an average inclination between 50 and 70%. The zone shows soils of rendzin, lithosol, and castanozem type.

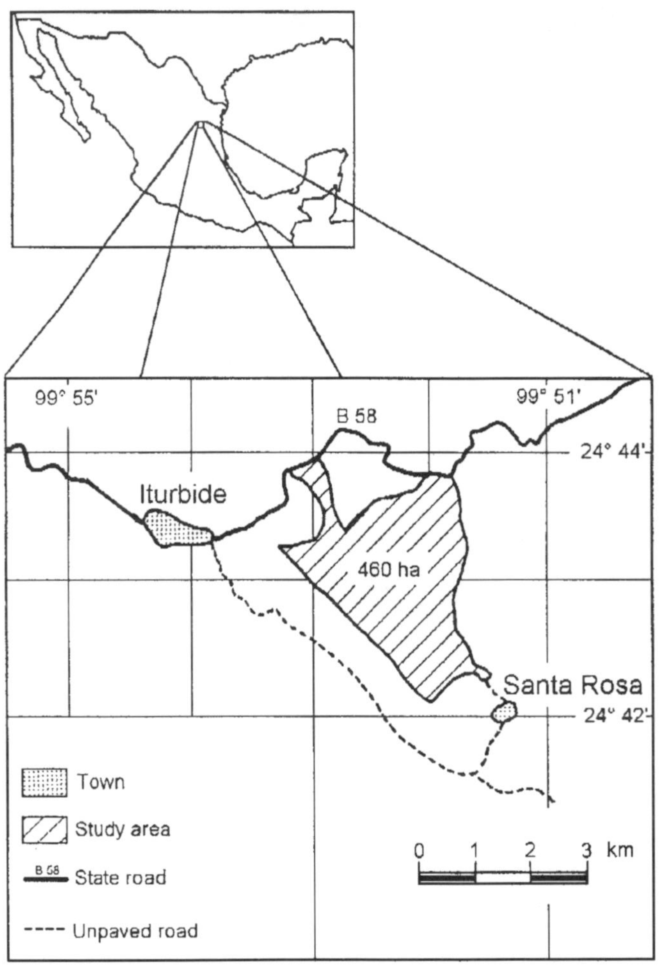

Fig 1.—Location of the study area (northeast Mexico).

Climate is classified as semi-dry, semi-hot with summer rains, and type BS1hw in the Köppen classification adapted to Mexico (Anonymous, 1981). Average mean temperature is 17°C, but temperatures frequently rise above 30°C in summer. In addition, there are typically up to 20 freezing days per year. Average rainfall is 629 mm, with great varibility between years (408 to 963 mm). Average rainfall during the study period (1989–1991) was 658 mm. The area had a wet season from April to October, with 2 peaks: the first in July (119 mm) and the second in September (306 mm). The driest month was January (9 mm). Average temperature was 15.3°C. While May and June were the hottest months (19°C average temperature, 33°C maximum), December and January were the coldest (11°C average temperature, -7°C minimum) (Fig. 2).

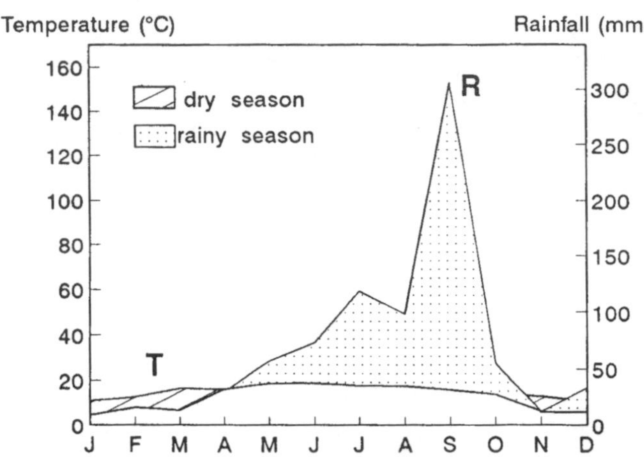

Fig 2.—Climatic diagram. Santa Rosa Station from the study area (Iturbibe, N.L., Mexico) (1989-1991).

Hijweege and Mes (1986) identified 9 vegetation types in the study area (Table 1). The area is dominated by *Quercus canbyi* (Mexican black oak), *Q. glaucoides* (oak, white oak group), *Q. cupreata* (oak, red oak group), *Pinus pseudostrobus* (Mexican white pine) and *Juniperus flaccida* (drooping juniper) with some *Arbutus xalapensis* (madroño), *Fraxinus cuspidata* (fragrant ash), *Ungnadia speciosa* (Mexican-buckeye) and *Carya illinoensis* (pecan). The region's fauna includes both nearctic and neotropical species.

METHODS

To identify habitat preferences of *Sciurus alleni*, an eight km transect was surveyed two times each month, between 0700 and 0730 hrs, depending on the time of the year, from April 1989 to June 1991. This transect covered most types of vegetation in the area, except the "Mosaic", that occupies a minimum part of the study area (Table 1). There was no statistically significant differences between the proportion of the vegetation types in the study area and their proportion in the transect (Wilcoxon $P > 0.40$).

Table 1.—*Vegetation types in the study area with the surface they occupy (in hectares and percent), and the corresponding number of points (availability) and percentages that were covered by the transect.*

Vegetation types	Study area		Transect	
	ha	(%)	Points	(%)
Pine forest	18	3.9	8	5.00
Pine-oak forest	93	20.2	52	32.50
Oak forest	69	15.0	11	6.88
Open oak forest	57	12.4	15	9.37
Low oak-juniper-ash forest	25	5.5	2	1.25
Bush with dispersed trees	64	13.9	50	31.25
Amelanchier-bushland	10	2.2	2	1.25
Bush	111	24.1	20	12.50
Mosaic	13	2.8	00	0.00
TOTAL	460	100.0	160	100.00

All encounters were recorded on a 1:10,000 scale map, noting the place and the number of squirrels observed. Seasons were defined as follows: spring (March to May), summer (June to August), autumn (September to November) and winter (December to February). The rainy season included April to October and December, while the dry season was January to March and November.

The preference of the squirrels for any particular vegetation type was scored by using the Ivlev's electivity index with minor modifications. The Ivlev's electivity index allows one to measure the food preference of a species. Its calculation is based on the ratio of consumption and availability of a certain food item in the animal´s diet (Jacobs, 1974; Krebs, 1989). This index varies between +1 (complete preference) and -1 (complete avoidance). A comparable calculation can be performed to estimate the habitat preferences of a species by using the proportion of animals found in a habitat type Y and the proportion of habitat available in the region (Alonso *et al.*, 1991).

While with Ivlev's formula, habitat avoidance can reach the maximal value of -1 (no animals observed in habitat type Y), a value of +1 could be obtained if habitat type Y does not occur in the area. For this reason, I used a correction of this index, that should be applied to the values in the positive range of the scale. To do so, I calculated the maximal possible value of the index (MVI) in the area, by assigning 100% preference to the habitat with the smallest availability in the region. This value was used as a correction factor. The values calculated with Ivlev's formula were then divided by this factor (MVI) to standardize the results and obtain the modified electivity index (MEI).

Availability of different vegetation types in the area was estimated by noting at each 100-m interval the vegetation present at both sides of the transect (Table 1). Thereafter, the Mann-Whitney *U*-Test was used to detect differences in the number of encounters with the squirrels in the different vegetation types.

RESULTS

Encounters by altitude.—The altitudinal limits of *Sciurus alleni* through the year show a slight variation between 1,790 and 1,820 m and between 1,240 and 1,290 m. Months with highest altitudinal averages were September (1,566 m), November (1,564 m), and May (1,554 m). On the other hand, the months with the lower altitude average were January (1,480 m), March (1,508 m), and December (1514 m) (Fig. 3).

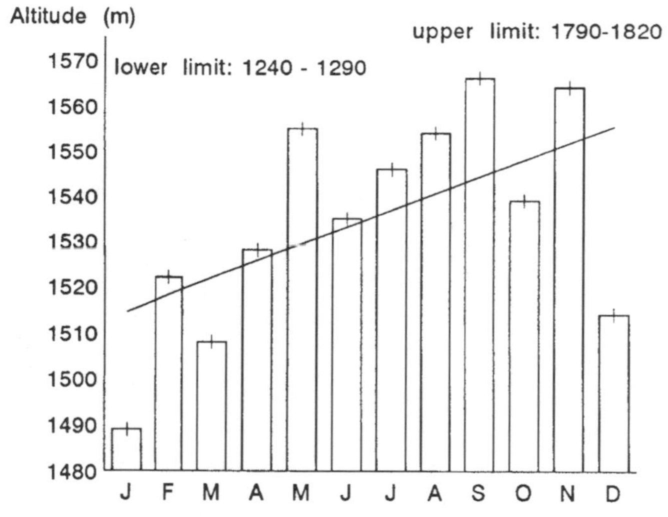

Fig 3.—Monthly average altitude of encounters with *Sciurus alleni* through the year.

Significant differences in altitudinal limits ocurred between summer and winter ($P < 0.037$) and autumn and winter ($P < 0.003$). The lowest altitudinal limits were observed in winter in both cases. Between dry and wet season the altitudinal limits were significantly higher in the wet season ($P < 0.004$).

Encounters by vegetation (modified electivity index). In relation to the Modified Electivity Index (MEI), use is greater than availability (i.e., preference) in the oak forest (+0.5400), the pine forest (+0.4547), and the open oak forest (+0.1455). In contrast, availability is greater than use (i.e., avoidance) in all other vegetation types (Fig. 4).

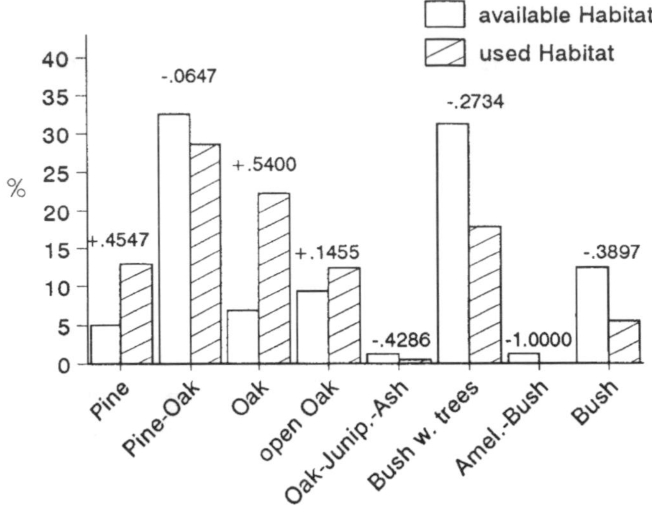

Fig 4.—Use and availability of the vegetation types in the studied area over entire study period. Numbers over the columns show the value of the MEI.

Table 2. — *Monthly preference for the 8 vegetation types in the transect.*

Vegetation types	J	F	M	A	M	J	J	A	S	O	N	D
Pine forest	+	+	+	+	+	+	+	+	+	+	+	+
Pine-oak forest	+		+									
Oak forest	+	+	+	+	+	+	+	+	+	+	+	+
Open oak forest		+	+	+	+	+	+	+	+	+	+	
Low oak-juniper-ash forest												
Bush with dispersed trees												
Amelanchier-bushland												
Bush												

+ = preferences (MEI positive)

The maximum habitat preference was observed in the oak forest (n = 8) and pine forest (n = 4). Both areas showed positive values for the MEI. Avoidance was greatest in *Amelanchier*-bushland (n = 12), low oak-juniper-ash forest (n = 8) and bush (n = 1) which showed the maximum value of -1.0000.

Open oak forests were avoided during two months (December, January), while the pine-oak forests were preferred only during two months (January, March). In this period, squirrels were seen in greater numbers in the lowest parts of the study area, where at that time food availability was greatest (Table 2).

When grouping data by seasons, I observed that preferred vegetation types were always present in lower quantities. In winter only the oak forest and the pine forest showed positive MEI values, supporting the seasonal importance of this vegetation for the squirrels. The oak forest had the maximum preference in the four seasons, followed always by the pine forest. From spring to autumn, the open oak forest was third in preference, while in winter the third-ranked preference corresponded to the pine-oak forest. In spite of this small variation, the oak species in this latter vegetation type tend to produce acorns later (Müller-Using, 1991). Because mature pine cones are an important part of the squirrel diet during winter the pine-oak forest becomes more important for the squirrels in winter in comparison to the open oak forests.

The highest avoidance values were observed in the low forests of oak, juniper, and ash (spring and autumn) and the bush (summer and winter). In addition, the *Amelanchier*-bushland was completely avoided (-1.0000) (Fig. 5).

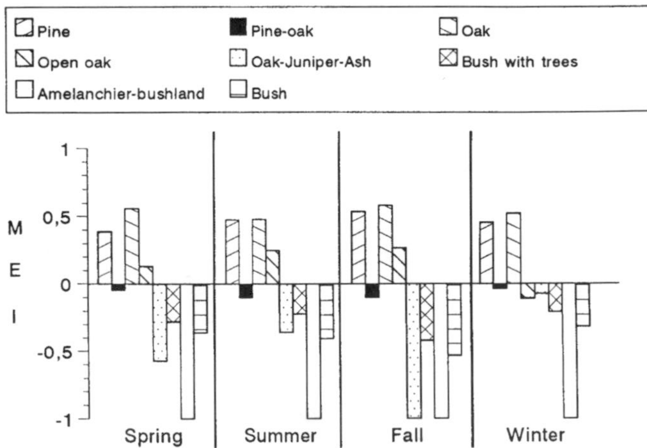

Fig 5.—Seasonal preferences from *Sciurus alleni* for the vegetation types in the study area.

Just as in the analysis by months, the oak forest and the pine forest were preferred by squirrels. Furthermore, the pine-oak forests, the low oak-juniper-ash forests, the bush with dispersed trees, the *Amelanchier*-bushland, and the bush had negative values for the index.

When this study was divided into dry and rainy seasons, squirrels in both seasons show a preference in the pine forests, the oak forests, and the open oak forests. The relative importance of the first two is different, however. The rankings in the rainy season are oak forests (+0.5506), followed by the pine forest (+0.3372). In the dry season, the pine forest is most preferred (+0.5354) followed by oak forest (+0.5294). In both seasons, the open oak forest has the lowest preference value (+0.0539 and +0.2190).

During the rainy season, the low forests of oak, juniper, and ash were the most strongly avoided (-0.6667) next to the *Amelanchier*-bushland (-1.0000). In the dry season the bush (-0.4368) replaces the low forests of oak, juniper, and ash (Fig. 6).

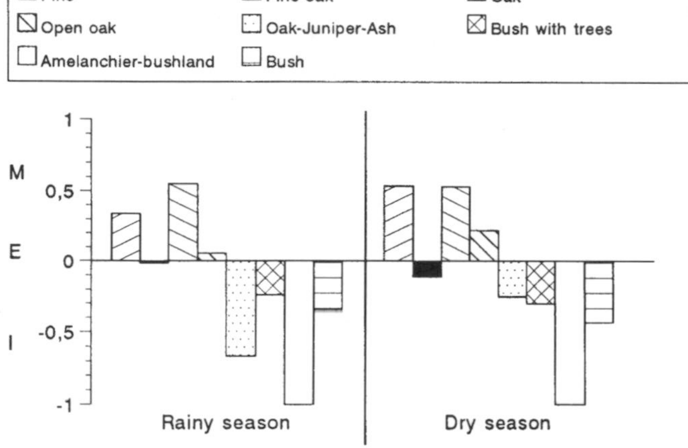

Fig 6.—Use and availability of the vegetation in rainy and dry seasons.

DISCUSSION

Sampling along transects is an efficient and economical way to monitor many animal populations and is recommended for squirrel populations, when monitoring extensive areas (Healy and Welsh, 1992). Because squirrels in the study area do not cease their normal activities as long as human observers do not approach too close, they are easily observed, making them an appropiate subject of investigation for this method of study. Moreover, the fact that the observer does not remain in the same place reduces the danger of counting the same animal twice.

Two disadvantages of this method, however, are that squirrels in dense foliage can easily escape observation, and changes in the activity patterns of the species may result in variation in the number of animals sited (Fagerstone, 1983; Brandl et al., 1991; Healy and Welsh, 1992). I tried to reduce both sources of error by moving slowly and conducting surveys during hours of greater activity.

Seasonal variation in altitudinal limits found between seasons are probably due to changes in the availiability of food in different habitats. For example, seeds of drooping juniper (*J. flaccida*) are an important part of the squirrel's diet during summer. As juniper are found mainly in altitudes over 1,600 m, squirrels are found in greater numbers in the higher altitudinal zones at this time. In winter and spring, oaks offer a greater variety of food (buds, flowers, acorns, bark, butterfly pupae), so squirrels are also found in great numbers in the lower altitudinal zones.

In spite of the slight variation of the altitude limits through the year, squirrels were observed equally at all elevations. This was expected since the altitudinal limits of the region are within those reported for this species (Leopold, 1965; Hall, 1981).

The significant differences found between seasons in certain zones, appear to be a consequence of the vegetation types and the food offered. My results illustrate the importance of the oak forests and the pine forests for these squirrels. It appears that *S. alleni* does not show the seasonal changes in the habitat preference reported for other species of *Sciurus* (Wauters *et al.*, 1992). This is probably because these two vegetation types are the main food source in the study area. On the other hand, *Amelanchier*-bushland, the low forests of oak, juniper, and ash, and the bush were the most strongly avoided.

Contrary to what might have been expected, the pine-oak forest was avoided by the squirrels. This is maybe due to the composition of the pine-oak forest, which has two species of *Quercus*, and only ca. 6% of *Pinus*. Thus this vegetation type can not offer continuity in the food supply throughout the year, whereas the four *Quercus* species in the oak forest tend to produce acorns at different times in the year, creating a continuous food supply for the squirrels. In winter, when the cones are important for the squirrels, the pine forest (over 55% *P. pseudostrobus*) is more preferred than the pine-oak forest. Those vegetation types avoided by the squirrels do not offer any important food resources, although the dense vegetation can reduce the chance of an early detection by predators.

LITERATURE CITED

ALONSO, J. C., J. A. ALONSO, AND L. M. CARRASCAL. 1991. Habitat selection by foraging white stork, *Ciconia ciconia*, during the breeding season. Canadian Journal of Zoology, 69:1957-1962.

ANONYMOUS. 1981. Síntesis Geográfica de Nuevo León. Secretaría de Programación y Presupuesto, México, D.F., 170 pp.

BRANDL, R., E. BEZZEL, J. REICHHOLF, AND W. VÖLKL. 1991. Population dynamics of the red Squirrel in Bavaria. Zeitschrift für Säugetierkunde, 56:10-18.

CZIHAK, G., H. LANGER, AND H. ZIEGLER. 1981. Biologie. Ein Lehrbuch. Third edition, Springer Verlag, Berlin, 944 pp.

FAGERSTONE, K. A. 1983. An evaluation of visual counts for censusing ground squirrels. Pp 239-246, *in* Vertebrate pest control and management materials: fourth symposium (D.E. Kaukeinen, ed.). American Society for Testing and Materials, ASTM STP 817.

HALL, E.R. 1981. The mammals of North America. Second Ed., John Wiley & Sons. Inc., New York 1:1 - 600 + *90*, 2:601 - 1181 + *90*.

HEALY, W. M., AND C. J. E. WELSH. 1992. Evaluating line transects to monitor gray squirrel populations. Wildlife Society Bulletin, 20:83-90.

HIJWEEGE, W., AND G. MES. 1986. Un plan de futuras actividades para el Bosque Escuela en consideración a la situación actual en Iturbide, N.L. Unpublished report. University of Nuevo León, Mexico and University of Wageningen, The Netherlands, 140 pp.

JACOBS, J. 1974. Quantitative measurement of food selection: a modification of the forage ratio and Ivlev's electivity index. Oecologia (Berlin), 14:413-417.

KREBS, C. J. 1989. Ecological methodology. Harper & Row Publishers, New York, 654 pp.

LEOPOLD, A.S. 1965. Fauna Silvestre de México. Aves y Mamíferos de Caza. Editorial Pax México-Librería Carlos Cesarman, Mexico, 605 pp.

MÜLLER-USING, B. 1991. Eichenwälder im nordöstlichen Mexiko. Schriften aus der Forstlichen Fakultät der Universität Göttingen und der Niedersächsischen Forstlichen Versuchsanstalt, 103:1-263.

RAMÍREZ, J., R. LÓPEZ W., C. MÜDESPACHER, AND I. LIRA. 1983. Lista y Bibliografía reciente de los Mamíferos de México. Universidad Autónoma Metropolitana. Unidad Iztapalapa, Mexico, D.F., 363 pp.

WAUTERS, L., C. SWINNEN, AND A. A. DHONDT. 1992. Activity budget and foraging behaviour of red squirrel (*Sciurus vulgaris*) in coniferous and deciduous habitats. Journal of Zoology, 227:71-86.

ARBOREALITY IN TREE SQUIRRELS (SCIURIDAE)

RICHARD W. THORINGTON, JR., AMY M. L. MILLER, AND CHARLES G. ANDERSON

Department of Vertebrate Zoology, Smithsonian Institution, Washington, D.C. 20560 (RWT)
Department of Ecology, Evolution, and Marine Biology, University of California, Santa Barbara, CA 93106 (AMLM)
Department of Zoology, University of Tennessee, Knoxville, TN 37916 (CGA)

ABSTRACT.—The purpose of this paper is to examine the hypothesis that arboreality evolved more than once among extant tree squirrels. The North American fossil, *Douglassia* (formerly *Protosciurus)*, from the late Eocene is considered to have been an arboreal squirrel (Emry and Thorington, 1982). Thus, arboreality may be primitive for squirrels, although the European *Palaeosciurus* from the early Oligocene was probably terrestrial (Vianey-Liaud, 1974). It is unclear how these are related to the Recent tree squirrels, the Sciurini of the Americas and Northern Eurasia, the Ratufini and Callosciurini of Southern Asia, and the Protoxerini and Funambulini, mostly of Africa. Three hypotheses of relationships among Recent squirrels imply a terrestrial origin for some group of tree squirrels: Moore (1959) hypothesized that *Sciurotamias* and *Tamiasciurus* are closely related and that the North American red squirrel is derived from a terrestrial ancestor, Callahan and Davis (1982) hypothesized that *Sciurotamias* and *Ratufa* are closely related and suggested a terrestrial origin for the Asian giant tree squirrels, and Moore (1959) also suggested that the African tree squirrels, Protoxerini and Funambulini, may have evolved from xerine ground squirrels. A review of morphological evidence suggests that *Sciurotamias* is more closely related to chipmunks, the Tamiina, than to either *Tamiasciurus* or *Ratufa*. This contradicts the first two hypotheses cited above and the suggestion that arboreality evolved independently in these two tree squirrels. We cite reasons for doubting the third hypothesis, that African tree squirrels have a terrestrial origin, but do not critically examine it in this paper.

INTRODUCTION

The squirrel family, Sciuridae, includes two radiations of ground squirrels (Marmotini, Xerini) and a larger number of radiations of tree squirrels in South America, North America, Eurasia, and Africa. Formerly, it was presumed that arboreal squirrels evolved from terrestrial squirrels. For example, Black (1963) considered the chipmunks (tribe Tamiini) the basal group from which all other squirrels evolved. Similarly, Moore (1959) thought that the African tree squirrels were derived from the African ground squirrels. However, the earliest fossil squirrel, *Douglassia jeffersoni* formerly *Protosciurus* c.f. *jeffersoni)*, from the late Eocene, 35 Ma, was a tree squirrel (Emry and Thorington, 1982; Emry and Korth, 1996). The earliest chipmunks date from the early Miocene, ca. 25 Ma (Black, 1963; Bruijn, et al., 1980). Thus, it is possible that arboreality is primitive for squirrels and that extant terrestrial squirrels have evolved from tree squirrels once among the Marmotini of North America and Eurasia, independently in the Xerini of Africa and Southern Asia, and also independently in most tribes of tree squirrels. We here examine several hypotheses that arboreality has evolved more than once in the family Sciuridae.

Moore (1959) proposed that *Sciurotamias*, the Chinese rock squirrel, and *Tamiasciurus*, the North American red squirrel, are closely related, and that the red squirrel evolved from a terrestrial rock squirrel ancestor, similar to *S. davidianus*. Callahan and Davis (1982) presented an alternative hypothesis about *Sciurotamias*, arguing that

In M.A. Steele, J. F. Merritt, and D. A. Zegers (eds.). 1998. Ecology and Evolutionary Biology of Tree Squirrels. Special Publication, Virginia Museum of Natural History, 6: 320 pp

it is closely related to *Ratufa*. They explicitly suggested that *Ratufa* evolved from a terrestrial ancestor. Thus, the unresolved phylogeny of *Sciurotamias*, the Chinese rock squirrel, is central to the question of whether arboreality evolved more than once among tree squirrels.

Moore (1959) also suggested that the African tree squirrels evolved from the xerine ground squirrels. This hypothesis has not received careful consideration from subsequent investigators. Moore listed four characters shared by the Xerini and the Protoxerini. One of these is the separation of the buccinator and masticatory foramina. This condition is primitive for rodents (Wahlert, 1991) and therefore does not serve as a good phylogenetic indicator. A second is the prominence of the masseteric tubercle, but this is found in only one genus in the Protoxerini. Therefore, it is likely that it evolved independently in the Protoxerini and the Xerini. This leaves two characters, long orbits and short interorbital width, purportedly supporting Moore's hypothesis. In details the orbits of the Xerines and the Protoxerines are very different, however, especially in the shapes of the lacrimal, jugal, and maxillary bones. On the basis of cranial evidence, Lavocat (1973) considered the earliest fossil squirrels in Africa to be tree squirrels derived from southwest Asia. This also weakens Moore's speculation; but we will not critically examine it in this paper.

In this contribution, we examine and test four hypothesized sister groups: *Tamiasciurus-Sciurus, Tamiasciurus-Sciurotamias, Tamias-Sciurotamias*, and *Ratufa-Sciurotamias* (Fig. 1), challenging the two proposed ground squirrel-tree squirrel hypotheses, each with an alternative hypothesis.

THE STATUS OF THE TAMIASCIURINI

Moore (1959) created a tribe, the Tamiasciurini, for *Tamiasciurus* and *Sciurotamias* because both have three transbullar septa, a rare condition among squirrels. Both Moore (1959) and Black (1963) noted that *Tamiasciurus* is polymorphic for two and three transbullar septa. Corbet and Hill (1992) list two transbullar septa for *Sciurotamias forresti* and three for *Sciurotamias davidianus*. Thus, both genera are polymorphic for number of transbullar septa. Callahan and Davis (1982) showed that *Sciurotamias* lacks the specialized reproductive tract of *Tamiasciurus*. These observations detract from the likelihood that Moore's hypothesis is a good one, but do not test it. The hypothesis would be falsified by finding many derived features shared by *Sciurus* and *Tamiasciurus*, but not by *Sciurotamias*. It is not falsified by showing that proposed synapomorphies of *Tamiasciurus* and *Sciurotamias* are invalid. Bryant (1945) described many osteological and myological similarities between *Sciurus* and *Tamiasciurus*, concluding that *Tamiasciurus* should not be considered a distinct genus from *Sciurus*. He was very careful to distinguish between primitive and derived characters, but he did not study *Sciurotamias*. Similarily, the immunological study by Hight et al. (1974) and the protein electrophoresis study by Hafner et al. (1994) suggested that *Sciurus* and *Tamiasciurus* are closely related, but neither study

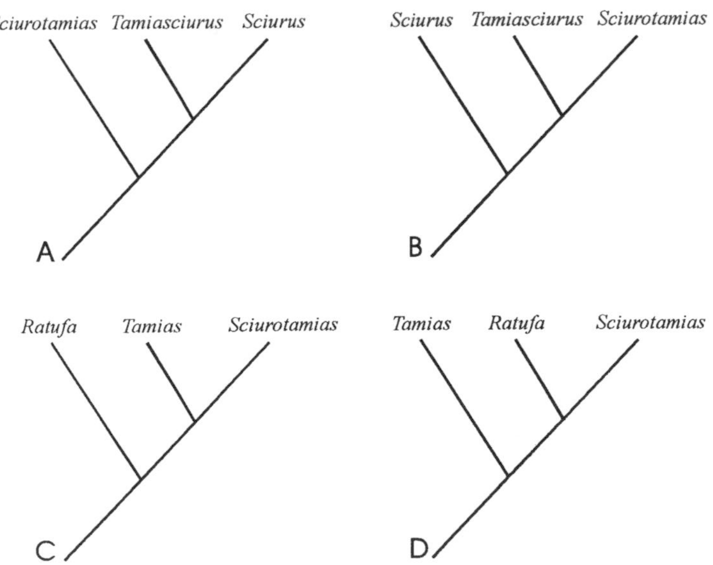

Fig. 1.—Sister-group hypotheses examined: A. Commonly accepted hypothesis that *Sciurus* and *Tamiasciurus* are more closely related to each other than either is to *Sciurotamias,* B. Moore's (1959) hypothesis that *Tamiasciurus* and *Sciurotamias* are more closely related to each other, C. Milne-Edwards' (1871) hypothesis that *Sciurotamias* is closely related to chipmunks, and D. Callahan and Davis (1982) hypothesis that *Sciurotamias* is more closely related to *Ratufa*.

included *Sciurotamias*, so they do not contradict Moore's hypothesis. In spite of the logical weaknesses of these "tests" of Moore's hypothesis, his concept of the Tamiasciurini (*Tamiasciurus* + *Sciurotamias*) has been almost completely abandoned (Hoffmann et al., 1993).

THE STATUS OF THE RATUFINI

Moore (1959) placed the genus *Ratufa* by itself in the tribe Ratufini. Callahan and Davis (1982) described the reproductive tract of *Sciurotamias*, compared it with that of *Ratufa* and suggested that the two genera are closely related and should both be included in the tribe Ratufini. We disagree. In many ways these two genera are remarkably different squirrels. To us, figure 4 of Prasad (1954:479) showing the baculum of *Ratufa* and the glans penis with many ridges and a ventral sulcus, looks very different from figure 3 of Callahan and Davis (1982:45) showing the glans penis of *Sciurotamias* with four simple annuli. Thus, we question the basis for their placement of *Sciurotamias* in the Ratufini. They list the cheek pouch and the hoof-like pollex as supporting evidence. However, *Sciurotamias* has a cheek pouch and *Ratufa* lacks one. Furthermore, we have observed that *Ratufa's* "hoof-like pollex" is supported by a modified first phalanx and a broad, flattened terminal phalanx, but the pollex of *Sciurotamias* is not. Again, these criticisms do not test their hypothesis, which has generally been accepted (e.g., Corbet and Hill, 1992; Hoffmann, et al., 1993). To test it, we compare it with the earlier hypothesis that *Sciurotamias* is most closely related to the chipmunks (Milne-Edwards, 1867; Miller, 1901; Ellerman, 1940; Gromov, et al., 1965; Callahan, 1976).

CHARACTER LIST AND POLARITY ASSESSMENTS

We test the hypotheses of the following sister-groups: *Tamiasciurus-Sciurus*, *Tamiasciurus-Sciurotamias*, *Tamias-Sciurotamias*, and *Ratufa-Sciurotamias*, by re-examining the characters included in studies by Bryant (1945), Moore (1959), and others. We have added other characters from our studies of wrists and ankles. Our polarity assessments are based on the morphologies of *Protosciurus* crania, as described by Black (1963), and postcrania of *Douglassia*, as described by Emry and Thorington (1982), of *Paleosciurus* as described by Vianey-Liaud (1974), and of primitive rodents, as assessed by Wahlert (1985, 1991). We consider the closely related *Douglassia* and *Protosciurus* to be the most primitive sciurids and the best outgroup for all the other sciurids (Emry and Thorington, 1982). Our assessment of the primitive state is listed as (0), different derived states are listed as (1a) and (1b), and sequentially derived states are listed as (1) and (2). We indicate uncertainty of polarities with a question mark (?) and do not use these characters in our assessment.

Character 1. Transbullar septa

(0) Two septa: *Sciurus* (most), *Tamiasciurus* (few), *Sciurotamias forresti, Tamias.*

(0) Three septa: *Sciurus anomalus, Tamiasciurus* (most), *Sciurotamias davidianus.*

(1)No septa: *Ratufa.*

Black (1963) described *Protosciurus condoni* and noted that the type specimen has two and one-half transbullar septa. Therefore, the primitive modal number for squirrels is equivocal and could be two or three transbullar septa. Lack of septa is derived.

Character 2. External auditory meatus

(0) Flange on anterior superior edge; portion of bulla anterior and superior to the meatus not swollen: *Sciurus, Tamiasciurus, Tamias, Ratufa.*

(1) Lacks flange; portion of bulla anterior and superior to it swollen: *Sciurotamias.*

The primitive condition in rodents is an unswollen bulla (Wahlert, 1991). Black's (1963) illustration of *Protosciurus condoni* shows a flange and unswollen bulla. Therefore, the condition in *Sciurotamias* is considered derived.

Character 3. Postglenoid region of the squamosal (Fig. 2)

(?) Pierced by both postglenoid and subsquamosal foramina: *Sciurus* (most), *Tamiasciurus* (most), *Ratufa* (most).

(?) Second foramen posterior to glenoid higher on skull, as if it were a supraglenoid foramen: *Sciurotamias, Tamias.*

The pattern of foramina behind the glenoid is quite variable individually. They are sometimes absent, sometimes fused, and sometimes multiple, particularly in *Sciurus.* The primitive condition in squirrels is not clear and it may also have been variable. This is in agreement with Wahlert's (1974) assessment for primitive rodents.

Character 4. Temporal foramen at squamosal-parietal suture (Fig 2)

(0) Present: *Sciurus, Tamiasciurus, Ratufa affinis* (most).

(1) Absent: *Sciurotamias, Tamias, Ratufa* other species (most).

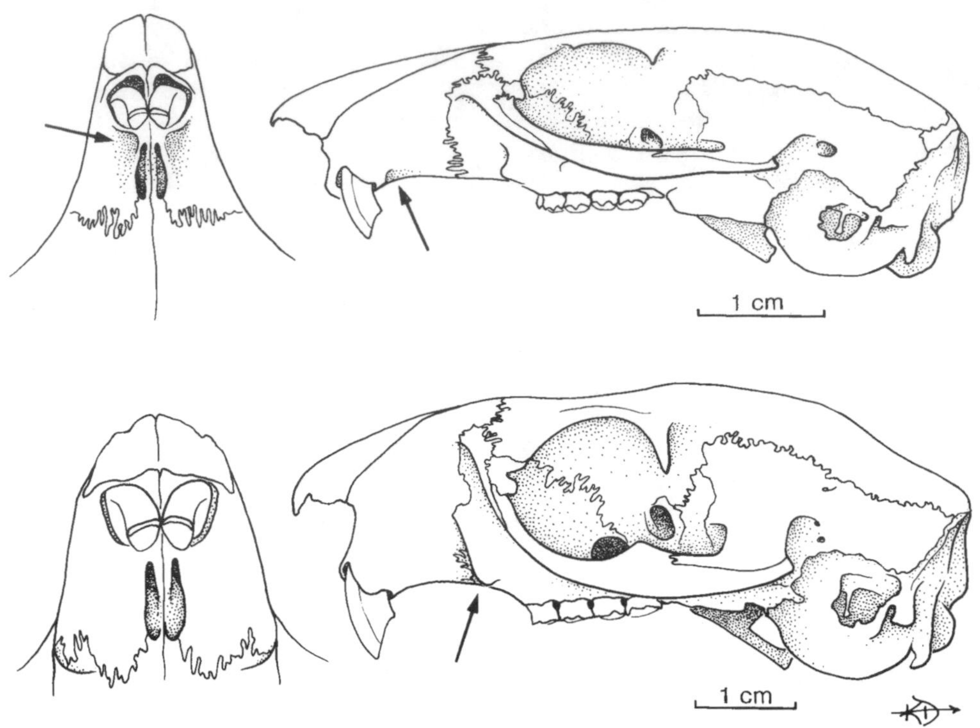

Fig. 2.—Ventral views of rostrum and lateral views of skulls of *Sciurotamias davidianus,* USNM 155219, (above) and *Ratufa bicolor,* USNM 481228, (below). Arrows indicate fossae behind the incisors of *Sciurotamias* and the position of the infraorbital foramen of *Ratufa.* Note also the large sphenopalatine foramen in the orbit and the presence of the temporal foramen in *Ratufa.*

The presence of a foramen at the squamosal-parietal suture is primitive for rodents (Wahlert, 1974), and probably primitive for squirrels (Wahlert, 1991). It is neither mentioned nor figured by Black (1963) in *Protosciurus.*

Character 5. Supraorbital notch (Fig. 2)

(0) Absent or inconspicuous: *Ratufa* (usually).

(1) Open and usually trenchant: *Sciurus, Tamiasciurus, Sciurotamias, Tamias.*

Black (1963) comments on the absence of the supraorbital notch in *Protosciurus condoni,* but it appears to be present in his plate 3, figure 1a. Vianey-Liaud (1974) shows prominent supra-orbital notches in *Palaeosciurus goti.* We have considered its presence to be derived in squirrels, but it is possible that this polarity should be reversed.

Character 6. Sphenopalatine foramen (Fig. 2)

(0) Large, approximately size of sphenoidal fissure: *Sciurus* (most), *Tamiasciurus, Ratufa.*

(1) Sphenopalatine foramen small: *Sciurus granatensis, Sciurotamias, Tamias.*

Black (1963) illustrates the sphenopalatine foramen in *Protosciurus condoni,* showing it to be large. We take this to be primitive for squirrels.

Character 7. Sharp anterior edge of zygomatic arch (Fig. 2)

(0) Does not extend onto the premaxillary bone: *Sciurus griseus* (the anterior masseter extends onto the premaxillary bone but the sharp ridge does not), *Tamiasciurus, Sciurotamias, Tamias* (most).

(1) Extends onto the premaxillary bone: *Sciurus* (most, but barely in *S. anomalus* and *S. granatensis), Tamias* (some), *Ratufa.*

The evolution of sciuromorphy involves the migration of the masseter onto the zygomatic plate and side of the rostrum. The more the masseter musculature extends onto the premaxillary bone, the more derived we consider it.

Character 8. Angle of zygomatic plate (Fig. 2)

(0) More horizontal: *Sciurotamias, Tamias.*

(1) More vertical: *Sciurus, Tamiasciurus, Ratufa.*

Black (1963) describes the evolution of the zygomatic plate from a more horizontal angle to a more vertical angle in his treatments of Miocene *Protosciurus rachelae* and *Sciurus.* The derived condition is associated with the enlargement of the area for origin of the anterior portion of the deep lateral masseter muscle.

Character 9. Length of infraorbital canal (Fig. 2)

(0) Moderately long: *Sciurus, Tamiasciurus.*

(1a) Long, extending to maxillary-premaxillary suture: *Ratufa.*

(1b) Short, barely extending onto the side of the rostrum: *Sciurotamias.*

(2b) Short, not extending onto the side of the rostrum: *Tamias.*

In *Protosciurus*, the infraorbital canal is moderately long, according to Black (1963). The long canal of *Ratufa* is clearly derived. The short canal of *Sciurotamias* and *Tamias* is probably also derived. It is further derived in *Tamias,* because the ventral head of the maxillonasalis muscle passes through the infraorbital foramen to insert on the orbital margin (Bryant, 1945). A large infraorbital foramen and very short canal, like those seen in *Tamias*, are reported in *Spermophilinus bredai* of the middle Miocene (Bruin and Mein, 1968). This is not seen in *Sciurotamias.* Our polarity assessment is in disagreement with Wahlert (1985).

Character 10. Ectopterygoid region

(0?) Lateral pterygoid ridge prominent, parallel to, or diverging slightly from medial pterygoid ridge posteriorly: *Tamias, Ratufa.*

(1a) Lateral pterygoid ridge weak and not diverging: *Sciurotamias.*

(1b) Lateral pterygoid ridge prominent, diverging from medial ridge postero-laterally: *Sciurus, Tamiasciurus.*

In *Tamias,* the pterygoid plate is narrow. The lateral pterygoid ridge terminates posteriorly between the medial side and the middle of the foramen ovale and parallels the medial pterygoid (ectopterygoid) ridge. In *Sciurus* and *Tamiasciurus,* the pterygoid plate is broad. The lateral ridge diverges posteriorly from the medial ridge and terminates on the lateral side of the foramen ovale. In *Ratufa,* the lateral ridge terminates in the middle of the foramen ovale and the wings of the medial pterygoid extend ventrally, not toward the bullae like those of chipmunks and the other tree squirrels. The pterygoid region of *Protosciurus condoni,* as shown by Black (1963), is most similar to that of *Ratufa,* although the wing of the medial pterygoid is unknown, so the other two morphologies are considered to be derived.

Character 11. Posterior edge of palate

(0) Behind M^3: *Sciurus, Tamiasciurus, Sciurotamias, Tamias.*

(1) At the level of M^3: *Ratufa.*

In *Protosciurus condoni*, the posterior edge of the palate is figured as being slightly behind M^3 (Black, 1963: plate 3, figure 1c) and we therefore consider this primitive.

Character 12. Dorsal profile of skull

(0) Flat: *Sciurotamias, Tamias, Ratufa.*

(1) Rounded: *Sciurus, Tamiasciurus.*

The primitive condition for squirrels is the flat profile, as seen in the fossil record (Black, 1963). This feature is allometric, being related to relative brain volume. Therefore, small squirrels have more rounded cranial profiles and large squirrels flatter profiles. For their size, tree squirrels have more rounded profiles than do chipmunks, and *Ratufa* (Fig. 2) appears to have a flat profile because of its large size.

Character 13. Squamosal suture (Fig. 2)

(0) High: *Tamiasciurus, Sciurotamias, Tamias, Ratufa.*

(1) Low, extending less than half way from the root of the zygoma to the notch of the postorbital process: *Sciurus.*

The squamosal almost reaches the postorbital notch in *Protosciurus condoni* according to Black (1963), therefore we consider this to be primitive.

Character 14. Cheek pouches

(0) Absent: *Sciurus, Tamiasciurus, Ratufa.*

(1) Present: *Sciurotamias, Tamias.*

There are fossae anterolateral to the incisive foramina in squirrels with cheek pouches (Fig. 2), for the origin of the dorsal pouch muscle. Therefore, it is possible to document the evolution of cheek pouches in North American fossils. The fossae are absent in *Protosciurus rachelae* of the early Miocene; they are weakly present in *Protospermophilus angusticeps* of the late middle Miocene; and they are deep in *Protospermophilus malheurensis* also of the late Middle Miocene (Black, 1963). They are also present in *Spermophilinus bredai* of the middle Miocene (Bruin and Mein, 1968). Accordingly, we treat cheek pouches as being derived, and assume they date from the Early Miocene, when *Tamias* appears in the fossil record, or slightly earlier. The fossae are also present in *Spermophilopsis* and *Xerus princeps.* This needs further study.

Character 15. Coracoid process of scapula (Fig. 3).

(0) Long: *Sciurus, Tamiasciurus, Ratufa.*

(1) Short: *Sciurotamias, Tamias.*

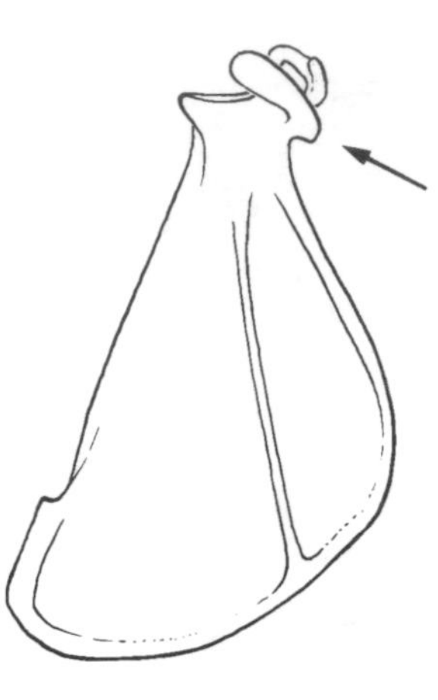

Fig. 3.—Medial views of scapulae of *Sciurotamias davidianus*, USNM 258508, (left) and *Tamiasciurus hudsonicus*, USNM 505581, (right). Note length of coracoid process (arrow) and prominence of fossa for teres major muscle.

The coracoid of *Douglassia* was broken, but it was clearly similar to *Sciurus* and larger than in ground squirrels.

Character 16. Axillary ridge relative to the surface of scapula

(0?) Perpendicular and high: *Sciurus, Tamiasciurus.*

(1a?) Perpendicular and low: *Ratufa.*

(1b?) Perpendicularity intermediate and high: *Sciurotamias.*

(2?) Least perpendicular but high *Tamias.*

Sciurid scapulae are very rare in the fossil record and we know of none that show the axillary ridge.

Character 17. Flange near caudal angle of scapula for teres major muscle (Fig. 3)

(0?) Prominent: *Sciurus, Tamiasciurus, Ratufa.*

(1?) Small: *Sciurotamias.*

(2?) Almost absent: *Tamias.*

Character 18. Subscapular spine (Fig. 3)

(0?) Single: *Sciurus, Tamiasciurus, Sciurotamias, Tamias.*

(1?) Sometimes double: *Ratufa.*

The broken scapula of *Douglassia jeffersoni* shows a single subscapular spine.

Character 19. Metacromion process of scapula

(0?) Less broad and at angle to plane of scapula: *Sciurus, Tamiasciurus, Sciurotamias.*

(1a?) Narrow and abruptly parallel to plane of scapula: *Ratufa.*

(1b?) Broad and most parallel to plane of scapula: *Tamias.*

The metacromion process is unknown for fossil sciurids.

Character 20. Acromion process of scapula

(0?) Broad: *Sciurus, Tamiasciurus, Ratufa.*

(1?) Narrow: *Sciurotamias, Tamias.*

Character 21. Deltoid and pectoral ridges of humerus

(0) Deltoid ridge weak proximally: *Sciurus, Ratufa.*

(1) Deltoid ridge prominent proximally, diverging from pectoral ridge: *Tamiasciurus, Sciurotamias, Tamias.*

In *Douglassia* the deltoid and pectoral ridges are damaged, but appear similar to those of *Sciurus.*

Character 22. Orientation of delto-pectoral crest of humerus

(0) Directed medially with prominent bicipital groove: *Sciurus, Tamiasciurus, Ratufa.*

(1) Directed laterally with less distinct bicipital groove: *Sciurotamias, Tamias.*

This region was broken on *Douglassia* but appeared to be similar to *Sciurus.*

Character 23. Entepicondylar foramen of humerus

(0) Usually present: *Sciurus, Tamiasciurus, Ratufa, Sciurotamias*

(1) Usually absent: *Tamias striatus.*

The entepicondylar foramen is commonly present in rodents, including most Recent squirrels, *Douglassia*, and *Paleosciurus.*

Character 24. Medial epicondyle of humerus

(0) Elongate medially: *Sciurus, Tamiasciurus, Sciurotamias, Ratufa.*

(1) Not elongate: *Tamias.*

The medial epicondyle was elongate in *Douglassia* and in *Paleosciurus.*

Character 25. Extent of the radial notch on ulna

(0) Approximately one-third the width of the semilunar notch: *Sciurus, Tamiasciurus, Ratufa.*

(1) Approximately one-half of the width of the semilunar notch: *Sciurotamias.*

(2) More than one-half of width of the semilunar notch: *Tamias.*

This feature in *Douglassia* is very similar to that in *Sciurus.*

Character 26. Prominent ridge for pronator quadratus muscle on ulna

(0) Present: *Tamias, Sciurotamias.*

(1) Absent: *Sciurus, Tamiasciurus, Ratufa.*

The ridge is prominent in *Douglassia.*

Character 27. Groove on pisiform bone

(0) Pisiform ungrooved: *Sciurus, Tamiasciurus, Ratufa.*

(1) Radial side of pisiform grooved near palmar end: *Sciurotamias, Tamias.*

The pisiform of *Douglassia* is ungrooved, so this is presumed to be the primitive condition. The derived condition is not unique to *Sciurotamias* and *Tamias,* it is also found in *Callosciurus* to which they are not closely related (based on other evidence).

Character 28. Shape of triquetrum

(0) Triquetrum elongate and gracile: *Sciurus, Tamiasciurus, Tamias, Ratufa.*

(1) Triquetrum short and robust: *Sciurotamias.*

The shape of the triquetrum in *Sciurotamias* appears to be unique among squirrels and we think that it is derived.

Character 29. Ventral articulation of metacarpal III and metacarpal IV

(0) Present: *Sciurus carolinensis, S. griseus, S. granatensis, Sciurotamias davidianus, Tamias, Ratufa.*

(1) Absent: *Sciurus niger, Tamiasciurus hudsonicus.*

Loss of this articulation is rare and is presumed to be derived. The presence of the derived condition in *Tamiasciurus* and only part of *Sciurus* can be interpreted in two ways. First, it may be independently derived in the two genera. Second, it may indicate that some species of *Sciurus* are more closely related to *Tamiasciurus* than they are to other species of *Sciurus.*

Character 30. Centrale-greater Multangular articulation

(0) Absent: *Sciurus, Tamiasciurus, Sciurotamias.*

(1) Present: *Tamias, Ratufa.*

Primitively in squirrels the centrale articulates distally with capitate, metacarpal II, and lesser multangular. In several lineages it extends radially, toward the pollex, and also articulates with greater multangular.

Character 31. Articulation of metacarpal III and hamate.

(0) Corner of hamate beveled: *Sciurotamias, Tamias, Ratufa.*

(1) Corner of hamate square: *Sciurus, Tamiasciurus.*

The hamate is slightly beveled in *Douglassia.* The loss of this feature appears to be correlated with the narrowing of the hand and particularly metacarpal III.

Character 32. Lateral iliac ridge

(0) Broad, distinct ridge: *Sciurus, Tamiasciurus.*

(1a) Broad, indistinct ridge: *Tamias.*

(1b) Narrow, distinct ridge: *Sciurotamias, Ratufa.*

The iliac ridge of *Douglassia* is more pronounced than in most Recent squirrels, but is approximated by some *Sciurus.*

Character 33. Dorso-ventral depth of pelvic basin

(0?) Deep: *Sciurus, Tamiasciurus, Ratufa.*

(1?) Shallow: *Sciurotamias, Tamias.*

It is not possible to determine this in *Douglassia.*

Character 34. Pubic symphysis

(0?) Normal: *Sciurus, Tamiasciurus, Sciurotamias, Ratufa.*

(1?) Short: *Tamias.*

The pubic symphysis of chipmunks is shorter than the ascending ramus of the pubis, and the anterior end does not extend cranially to the posterior edge of the acetabulum. This seems to be unique to *Tamias* and is probably derived.

Character 35. Lesser trochanter of femur (Fig. 4)

(0) Directed medially: *Sciurus, Tamiasciurus, Ratufa.*

(1) Directed postero-medially: *Sciurotamias, Tamias.*

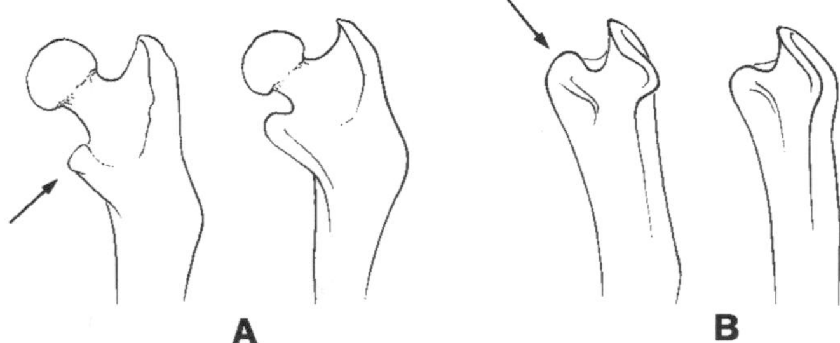

Fig. 4.— (A) Posterior views of proximal ends of femora, and (B) medial views of distal ends of tibiae of *Sciurotamias davidianus*, USNM 258508, (left) and *Tamiasciurus hudsonicus,* USNM 564083, (right). Arrows indicate lesser trochanter of femur and the anterior process of the medial malleolus of the tibia.

The lesser trochanter of *Douglassia* is directed medially. This appears to be the case in *Palaeosciurus goti* as well (Vianey-Liaud, 1974).

Character 36. Popliteal fossa of tibia

(0) Deep with medial and lateral ridges: *Tamiasciurus, Sciurotamias, Tamias.*

(1) Shallow and unridged, sometimes with medial ridge: *Sciurus, Ratufa.*

In *Douglassia,* the popliteal fossa is prominent.

Character 37. Relative lengths of the anterior and posterior processes of the medial malleolus of tibia (Fig. 4)

(0) Anterior process slightly shorter than the posterior process: *Tamias, Sciurotamias.*

(1) Anterior process distinctly shorter than the posterior process: *Sciurus, Tamiasciurus, Ratufa.*

The anterior and posterior processes are approximately the same length in *Douglassia* and *Palaeosciurus goti.*

Character 38. Tarsal foot pads

(0?) Two: *Sciurotamias forresti, Ratufa, Sciurus niger* (rare), *S. vulgaris* (rare).

(1?) One (hallucal): *Sciurus* (most), *Tamiasciurus hudsonicus* (rare).

(2?) None: *Tamiasciurus douglassi, T. hudsonicus* (most), *Sciurotamias davidianus, Tamias.*

We hypothesize that the presence of two tarsal pads is primitive and that loss of one or both is derived. However, in view of the great variation in this character, we are not very confident of this polarity.

Character 39. Two calcaneal facets on astragalus

(0) Separated by a shallow groove: *Ratufa.*

(1) Confluent. *Sciurus, Tamiasciurus, Sciurotamias, Tamias.*

In *Douglassia* the two facets are separated by a groove.

Character 40. Reproductive tract

(0) Large bulbo-urethral glands and presence of penile duct: *Sciurus, Sciurotamias, Tamias, Ratufa.*

(1) Absence of separate bulbo-urethral glands and absence of penile duct. *Tamiasciurus.*

Large, distinctive bulbo-urethral glands occur in the flying squirrels and five tribes of the Sciurinae, as listed below, suggesting that they are primitive for the family Sciuridae.

Pteromyinae (= Petauristinae): *Glaucomys,* Mossman, et al., 1932; Protoxerini: *Heliosciurus* illustrated but misidentified by Kingdon, 1974; 372; Funambulini: *Funisciurus* illustrated but misidentified by Kingdon, 1974; 373; *Funambulus* (in part), Siddiqi, 1938; Ratufini: *Ratufa,* Prasad, 1954; Sciurini: *Sciurus,* Mossman, et al., 1932; Marmotini: *Tamias, Spermophilus,* Mossman, et al., 1932.

Large bulbo-urethral glands and a penile duct are absent in both *Tamiasciurus* (Mossman, et al., 1932) and *Funambulus palmarum* (Prasad, 1954).

Character 41. Shape of baculum

(0?) Baculum nearly symmetric and simple — almost rod shaped, with distal end bent dorsally: *Tamias, Sciurotamias,* and *Ratufa.*

(1a?) Baculum asymmetric and flattened at tip. *Sciurus.*

(1b?) Baculum absent or minuscule. *Tamiasciurus.*

There is no clear evidence on which to base a polarity assessment for the baculum of squirrels. A simple, symmetric baculum would be a good model from which to derive the complex symmetrical bacula of ground squirrels and the complex asymmetric bacula of some other squirrels. Another alternative is that the bacular morphology of *Sciurus* is close to primitive, because it is found in such a diverse group of squirrels as *Sciurillus, Rheithrosciurus,* and *Petaurista.*

A feature not included in our list above is the external morphology of the glans penis, cited by Callahan and Davis (1982) as their justification for placing *Sciurotamias* in the Ratufini. We think that the penile morphologies of *Ratufa* and *Sciurotamias* are both derived but not homologous with one another. The morphology of the glans penis of *Ratufa* is illustrated by Hill (1936, 1940) and Prasad (1954) but interpretation of these drawings is not straightforward. The difference between the illustrations of Hill (1936, 1940) and Prasad (1954) appears to be in their definitions of dorsal and ventral. In comparing the three papers, Prasad (1954) should be viewed upside down. It also seems that the baculum illustrated in Hill (1936) is upside down relative to his illustrations of the penis, but in either orientation it is difficult to visualize how the baculum could fit inside the illustrated penis.

All three publications clearly illustrate 12-23 ridges or folds, with a ventral sulcus on the glans penis of *Ratufa.* According to Callahan and Davis (1982), the ornamentation of the penis of *Sciurotamias* consists of four annuli, three going completely around the penis. No ventral sulcus is shown or described. To us this seems very different from the morphology of *Ratufa*, and we do not consider the two to be homologous.

CHARACTERS SUPPORTING SISTER-GROUP HYPOTHESES

We examined two competing hypotheses (Figs. 5A and 5B) for the phylogenetic placement of *Tamiasciurus*, Moore's hypothesis that *Tamiasciurus* and *Sciurotamias* form a sister group, and the alternative hypothesis that *Tamiasciurus* forms a sister group with *Sciurus*. The more strongly supported hypothesis is that it forms a sister group with *Sciurus*. Two characters, 5 and 39, are shared by both pairs and hence are shown at the base of the tree. The remaining six characters include three in the cranium, two in the forelimb, and one in the hindlimb.

Derived characters shared by *Tamiasciurus* and *Sciurus*:

Character 5: Supraorbital notch present.

Character 8: Vertical angle of zygomatic plate.

Character 10: Posteriorly diverging lateral pterygoid ridges.

Character 12: Rounded skull profile.

Character 26: Reduced ridge on ulna for pronator quadratus muscle.

Character 31: Absence of beveled corner of hamate.

Character 37: Anterior process distinctly shorter than the posterior process of medial malleolus of tibia.

Character 39: Confluent astragalus facets.

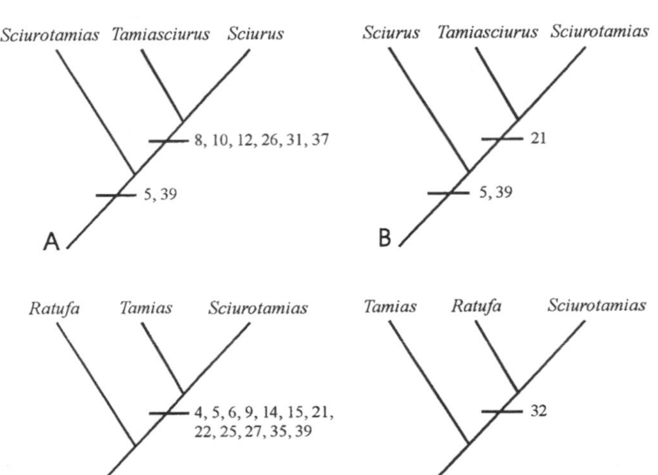

Fig. 5.— Sister-group hypotheses examined. A.-D. as in Fig. 1, but with shared derived characters plotted on them. Numbers correspond to character list in text. Uniquely derived characters not plotted.

Derived characters shared by *Tamiasciurus* and *Sciurotamias:*

Character 5: Supraorbital notch present.

Character 21: Deltoid and pectoral ridges diverge proximally.

Character 39: Confluent astragalus facets.

The hypothesis proposed by Callahan and Davis (1982), that *Sciurotamias* forms a sister group with *Ratufa* (Fig. 5D), is supported by only one character. The original hypothesis of Milne-Edwards (1871), that the Chinese rock squirrel is more closely related to chipmunks (Fig. 5C), is supported by twelve derived characters not shared with *Ratufa*. Nine of these characters are not shared with either *Ratufa* or *Tamiasciurus* -- four of the cranium, four of the forelimb, and one of the femur.

Derived characters shared by *Sciurotamias* and *Tamias*:

Character 4: Temporal foramen absent.

Character 5: Supraorbital notch present.

Character 6: Small sphenopalatine foramen.

Character 9: Short infraorbital canal.

Character 14: Cheek pouch present.

Character 15: Short coracoid process of scapula.

Character 21: Deltoid and pectoral ridges of humerus diverge proximally.

Character 22: Delto-pectoral crest directed laterally.

Character 25: Radial notch on ulna large.

Character 27: Pisiform grooved.

Character 35: Lesser trochanter of femur directed postero-medially.

Character 39: Confluent astragalus facets.

Derived character shared by *Sciurotamias* and *Ratufa:*

Character 32: Narrow, distinct lateral iliac ridge.

The characters we consider to be strongest are those associated with the zygomatic plate, the infraorbital canal, and the cheek pouch. These appear to have evolved early in the evolutionary history of squirrels (Black, 1963) and, based on our personal observations, show little interspecific and intergeneric variation. A smaller number of derived characters supports the tree squirrel hypothesis than the chipmunk-rock squirrel hypothesis. This probably results from tree squirrels retaining more features of the primitive squirrel morphology.

Tamias lacks several derived features of other members of the Marmotini, as described by Bryant (1945): a second subscapular spine, the triangular cross-section of the ilium, and the flaring of the ilium, for example. In these characters *Sciurotamias* is like *Tamias,* appearing to be primitive within the tribe.

DISCUSSION

The taxonomic position of *Sciurotamias,* its behavior, and its use of habitat, are central to the question of whether arboreality evolved more than once among tree squirrels. Moore (1959) placed it with *Tamiasciurus* on the basis of the presence of three transbullar septa. Callahan and Davis (1982) placed it with *Ratufa* on the basis of their perception of the similarity of bacular and penile morphologies. We contend that the similarities in transbullar septa and bacula are primitive and that the features of the penis are not homologous. Our observations lead us to conclude that *Sciurotamias* belongs within the tribe Marmotini. While we contend that the characters shared by *Sciurotamias* and *Tamias* are derived features of the Marmotini, we do not consider them to be derived features linking *Sciurotamias* with *Tamias* within the Marmotini. Thus, we provisionally place *Sciurotamias* within its own subtribe, the Sciurotamiina. Although one species of *Sciurotamias, S. davidianus,* is called a "rock squirrel" and is considered to be terrestrial, the other species, *S. forresti* is described as an arboreal tree squirrel. Unfortunately, little is known about its anatomy or ecology. Similarly, some species of *Tamias* are quite arboreal, and others forage readily in trees. We suspect that this says more about the versatility of small squirrels and their retention of climbing abilities than it does about any independent evolution of arboreality. However, if cheek pouches evolved as an adaptation for terrestrial foraging, then arboreal squirrels with cheek pouches are potentially very interesting. Accordingly, the biology of *Sciurotamias forresti* of southern China deserves study.

We agree with Black (1963) that the Tamiasciurini is not a valid tribe. We concur with his return of *Tamiasciurus* to the Sciurini, but not with his placement of *Sciurotamias* in the Callosciurini. Qiu (1991) also places the *Sciurotamias* lineage in the Callosciurini, although be argues convincingly that *Sinotamias,* a fossil from the upper Miocene of Inner Mongolia, is ancestral to *Sciurotamias* and is closely related to *Spermophilus,* of the Marmotini. We think his evidence better supports our conclusion. Our placement of *Sciurotamias* close to *Tamias* agrees with the earlier assessments of Milne-Edwards (1871), Miller (1901), Ellerman (1940), Gromov et al. (1965), and the initial conclusions of Callahan (1976).

Emry and Thorington (1982) presented evidence that *Douglassia jeffersoni* (of the late Eocene) was an arboreal squirrel. Black (1963) argued that *Protosciurus rachelae* of the early Miocene was a good morphological ancestor of the primitive *Sciurus* of the middle Miocene. Therefore, it is reasonable to contend that the tribe Sciurini has arboreal roots that extend back into the Eocene. The other tribes of tree squirrels probably share ancestry with the Sciurini in the Oligocene. Thus, it is probable that their common ancestor was arboreal, and that arboreality evolved only once in the extant Sciuridae.

ACKNOWLEDGMENTS

We thank V. Louise Roth, Robert S. Hoffmann, and two anonymous reviewers for their helpful recommendations. Special thanks are due to Karolyn Darrow, who assisted with the extensive final revision of the manuscript and prepared all the figures.

LITERATURE CITED

BLACK, C. G. 1963. A review of the North American Tertiary Sciuridae. Bulletin of the Museum of Comparative Zoology, Harvard University, 130:100-248.

BRUIJN, H. DE AND P. MEIN 1968. On the mammalian fauna of the Hipparion beds in the Calatayud-Teruel basin (Prov. Zaragoza, Spain). Part V. The Sciuridae. Proceedings of the Koninklijke Nederlandse Akademie van Wetenschappen, series B, 71:74-90.

BRUIJN, H. DE., A. J. VAN DER MEULEN, AND G. KATSIKATSOS. 1980. The Mammals from the Lower Miocene of Aliveri (Island of Evia, Greece). Proceedings of the Koninklijke Nederlandse Akademie van Wetenschappen, series B, 83:241-261.

BRYANT, M. D. 1945. Phylogeny of Nearctic Sciuridae. The American Midland Naturalist, 33:257-390.

CALLAHAN, J. R. 1976. Systematics and biogeography of the *Eutamias obscurus* complex (Rodentia: Sciuridae). Ph.D. dissertation., University of Arizona, Tucson, 184 pp. (as cited in Callahan and Davis, 1982).

CALLAHAN, J. R., AND R. DAVIS. 1982. Reproductive tract and evolutionary relationships of the Chinese rock squirrel, *Sciurotamias davidianus.* Journal of Mammalogy, 63:42-47.

CORBET, G. B., AND J. E. HILL. 1992. Mammals of the Indomalayan Region. Oxford University Press, New York, 488 pp.

ELLERMAN, J. R. 1940. The families and genera of living rodents. Volume I. Rodents other than Muridae. Trustees of the British Museum (Natural History), London, 689 pp.

EMRY, R. J., AND W. W. KORTH. 1996. The Chadronian Squirrel *"Sciurus" jeffersoni* Douglass, 1901: A new generic name, new material, and its bearing on the early evolution of Sciuridae (Rodentia). Journal of Vertebrate Paleontology, 16:775-780.

EMRY, R. J., AND R. W. THORINGTON, JR. 1982. Descriptive and comparative osteology of the oldest fossil squirrel, *Protosciurus* (Rodentia: Sciuridae). Smithsonian Contributions to Paleobiology, 47:1-35.

GROMOV, I. M., D. I. BIBIKOV, N. I. KALABUKOV, AND M. N. MEIER. 1965. Nazemnye belich'i (Marmotinae). Fauna SSSR, 3:1-467. (In Russian).

HAFNER, M. S., L. J. BARKLEY, AND J. M. CHUPASKO. 1994. Evolutionary genetics of New World tree squirrels (tribe Sciruini). Journal of Mammalogy, 75:102-109.

HILL, W. C. 1936. The penis and its bone in Ceylonese Squirrels; with special reference to its taxonomic importance. Ceylon Journal of Science (B), 20:99-113.

———. 1940. On the penis of *Ratufa macroura melanochra.* Ceylon Journal of Science (B), 22:131-134.

HIGHT, M. E., M. GOODMAN, AND W. PRYCHODKO. 1974. Immunological studies of the Sciuridae. Systematic Zoology, 23:12-25.

HOFFMANN, R. S., C. G. ANDERSON, R. W. THORINGTON, JR., AND L. R. HEANEY. 1993. Family Sciuridae. Pp. 419-465, *in* Mammal Species of the World: a taxonomic and geographic reference, (D.E. Wilson and D.M. Reeder, eds.), Smithsonian Institution Press, Washington, D.C., 1206 pp.

KINGDON, J. 1974. East African Mammals: an atlas of evolution in Africa. Vol. II. Part B (Hares and Rodents). Academic Press, London.

LAVOCAT, R. 1973. Les rongeurs du Miocene d'Afrique orientale. Memoires et Travaux de l'Institut Montpellier, 1:1-284.

MILLER, G. S., Jr. 1901. The subgenus *Rhinosciurus* of Trouessart. Proceedings of the Biological Society of Washington, 14:22.

MILNE-EDWARDS, A. 1867. Description de quelques especes nouvelles d'ecureuils de l'ancien continent. Revue et Magasin de Zoologie, 2:193-232.

———. 1871. Etudes pour servir a l'histoire de la faune mammalogique de la Chine. Pp. 67-229, *in* Recherches pour servir a l'histoire naturelle des mammifers: comprenant des considerations sur la classification de ces animaux, (H.Milne-Edwards and A. Milne-Edwards, 1868-1874). Paris: G. Masson, 394pp.

MOORE, J. C. 1959. Relationships among the living squirrels of the Sciurinae. Bulletin of the American Museum of Natural History, 118:153-206.

MOSSMAN, H. W., J. W. LAWHAH, AND J. A. BRADLEY. 1932. The male reproductive tract of the Sciuridae. American Journal of Anatomy, 51:89-155.

PRASAD, M. R. N. 1954. The male genital tract of two genera of Indian squirrels. Journal of Mammalogy, 35:471-485.

QIU, Z. 1991. The Neogene mammalian faunas of Ertemte and Harr Obo in Inner Mongolia (Nei Mongol), China.-8. Sciuridae (Rodentia). Senckenbergiana lethaea 71:223-255.

SIDDIQI, M. A. H. 1938. The genito-urinary system of the Indian ground squirrel *(Funambulus palmarum).* Proceedings of the National Academy of Science of India, 1:1-10.

VIANEY-LIAUD, M. 1974. *Palaeosciurus goti* nov. sp., ecureuil terrestre de l'Oligocene moyen du Quercy. Donnees novelles sur l'apparition des Sciurides en Europe. Annales Paleontologique (Vertebrata), Paris, 60:103-122.

WAHLERT, J. H. 1985. Cranial foramina of rodents. Pp. 311-332, *in* Evolutionary relationships among rodents: A multidisciplinary analysis (W. P. Luckett and J-L. Hartenberger, eds.). Plenum Press, New York, 721 pp.

———. 1991. The Harrymyinae, a new Heteromyid subfamily (Rodentia, Geomorpha), based on cranial and dental morphology of *Harrymys* Munthe, 1988. American Museum of Natural History Novitates, 3013:1-23.

SPECIMENS EXAMINED (all USNM):

Ratufa affinis—post-crania: 151757, 198121.

Ratufa affinis pyrsonota—skulls: 251673, 257716, 257720.

Ratufa affinis sandakanensis—skulls: 292564, 292565.

Ratufa bicolor—post-crania: 464512.

Ratufa bicolor fretensis—post-crania: 49703.

Ratufa bicolor palliata—penis: 546334.

Ratufa bicolor smithi —skulls: 320803-320807.

Ratufa indica—skulls: 38010, 355785; penis/baculum: 548661. post-crania: 308415.

Sciurotamias davidianus davidianus—skulls: 155110, 155219, 155125-155127, 548431; post-crania: 258505, 258510, 285511, 258516.

Sciurotamias davidianus consobrinus -- skulls: 258511-258513, 544436; post-crania: 258506, 258509.

Sciurotamias forresti—skulls: 255138 (occipital region broken).

Sciurus aberti aberti—skulls: 158892, 159332, 167027.

Sciurus anomalus—skulls: 37412, 152748, 152749.

Sciurus carolinensis carolinensis—skulls: 234368-234370; post-crania: 256047, 397180.

Sciurus carolinensis pennsylvanicus — post-crania: 297850, 505573, 505575, 548048.

Sciurus granatensis—skulls: 318405, 318408, 318409; post-crania: 387805, 540703.

Sciurus griseus griseus—skulls: 43041, 242332, 274351.

Sciurus niger—skulls: 167740, 177744, 177801; skin: 248132 (only one tarsal pad); post c r a - nia: 347957, 397159.

Sciurus vulgaris—skulls: 105106, 105107, 121351; skin: 121351 (juv., has two tarsal pads).

Tamias dorsalis dorsalis—skulls: 23695, 23696, 24882, 32090, 32093.

Tamias dorsalis merriami—skulls: 22723, 22808, 41773, 41776, 41783.

Tamias striatus fisheri—skulls: 62602, 86680, 86686, 86834, 260250; penises/bacula: 2 uncatalogued specimens from Mountain Lake, VA; post-crania: 364947, 396281, 505612, 505613.

Tamias striatus griseus—skulls: 17313, 226948, 227426, 229004, 232129; post-crania: 349628.

Tamias striatus lysteri—skulls: 30225, 30230, 30239, 43415, 96939; post-crania: 500999, 564115.

Tamias striatus ohionensis—skulls: 308622, 308623, 308626, 308636, 308640.

Tamias townsendi ochrogenys—skulls: 96110, 96112, 97146, 97337, 97339.

Tamias townsendi townsendi—skulls: 24423, 24424, 57124, 69373, 69375.

Tamiasciurus douglasii albolimbatus—skulls: 548848, 548849.

Tamiasciurus douglasii douglasii—skulls: 166892, 166893, 231804, 231805.

Tamiasciurus douglasii mearnsi—skulls: 25169, 25171.

Tamiasciurus douglasii mollipilosus—skulls: 23992, 24028.

Tamiasciurus hudsonicus albieticola—skulls: 55796, 50853, 268992, 294450.

Tamiasciurus hudsonicus baileyi—skulls: 66447, 168950, 168951.

Tamiasciurus hudsonicus columbiensis—skulls: 202835, 202836.

Tamiasciurus hudsonicus dakotensis—skulls: 213689, 213690.

Tamiasciurus hudsonicus dixiensis—skulls: 158041, 158042.

Tamiasciurus hudsonicus fremonti—skulls: 48209, 48210; post-crania: 564078.

Tamiasciurus hudsonicus loquax—post-crania: 397070, 397151, 397152, 505579, 505587, 506645, 551803, 564084.

Tamiasciurus hudsonicus hudsonicus—post-crania: 564083.

MORPHOLOGICAL AND PERFORMANCE ATTRIBUTES OF GLIDING MAMMALS

JOHN S. SCHEIBE AND JAMES H. ROBINS

Department of Biology
Southeast Missouri State University
Cape Girardeau, MO. 63701

ABSTRACT.—We compared the morphologies of 141 species of gliding, arboreal, and ground dwelling-mammals, and analyzed the cost effectiveness of gliding locomotion for *Glaucomys volans.* A canonical discriminant analysis revealed that ground dwelling forms have short tails, while gliding and arboreal forms have long tails. Gliders have shorter skulls and shorter upper tooth rows than arboreal forms. Tail length increases with body size more rapidly for gliders than nongliders, presumably because of the allometry of wing loading in large gliders. In spite of their longer tails, large gliders have higher wing loadings, glide faster, and appear to be less maneuverable than small gliders. While gliding conveys an energetic advantage to small animals like *Glaucomys,* it is expensive for *Petaurista.* Gliding is cost effective for *Petaurista petaurista* only if they climb trees rapidly, or if the cost of quadrupedal locomotion is increased.

INTRODUCTION

Recent work by Thorington and Heaney (1981) and Thorington and Thorington (1989) elucidated some of the appendicular adaptations associated with arboreal and glissant locomotion in sciurids. These papers, together with that of Peterka (1936), Polyakova and Sokolov (1965), Oxnard (1968), Bou et al. (1987), and Ando and Shiraishi (1991) constitute the bulk of our knowledge of the skeletal adaptations of gliding mammals. Studies on the myology of gliders (Peterka, 1936; Gupta, 1966; Johnson-Murray, 1987) have illustrated the unique ways in which the plagiopatagia of gliders are constructed and controlled to provide a flight structure. However, very little is known about the diversity of morphological adaptations on a faunal scale or across mammalian orders and families, or how size may have influenced the evolution of gliding.

Some progress has been made in functional research. Studies by Polyakova and Sokolov (1965), Nachtigall et al. (1974), Nachtigall (1979), Scholey (1986), and Ando and Shiraishi (1993) have provided information on the gliding abilities of gliding mammals and their aerodynamic qualities. Scholey (1986) used an energetics approach to study the cost effectiveness of gliding locomotion for *Petaurista petaurista*, but failed to generalize the model to include smaller gliders, or to explore constraints on the evolution of gliding.

Our understanding of the evolution of gliding is limited. Emerson and Koehl (1990) and Emerson (1991) have conducted detailed studies on gliding in rhacophorid frogs, but no such studies have been conducted for mammals. The distribution of gliding vertebrates has been used by Emmons and Gentry (1983) and Dudley and DeVries (1990) to propose several hypotheses about the evolution of gliding. Emmons and Gentry (1983) argued that forest structure, particularly liana densities and the prevalence of palm trees coincides with the diversity of gliding and vertebrates with prehensile tails, while Dudley and DeVries (1990) argued that the great height of oriental forest trees has played a significant role in the evolution of gliding. Other hypotheses for the evolution of gliding include foraging optimization (Norberg, 1985), predator avoidance, and controlled landing (Thorington and Heaney, 1981).

We know too little about the form, function, and ecology of gliders to discriminate between hypotheses for the adaptive significance of gliding locomotion. Also, it is unknown if the selective forces which led to the evolution of the Petauristinae are similar to those which produced the Anomaluridae, or if marsupial gliders have solved the gliding problem in the same way as eutherian gliders. In this paper we analyze some

In M.A. Steele, J. F. Merritt, and D. A. Zegers (eds.). 1998. Ecology and Evolutionary Biology of Tree Squirrels. Special Publication, Virginia Museum of Natural History, 6: 320 pp

basic morphological data on a wide variety of gliding mammals in an effort to add to what is already known about their morphological attributes. We then analyze laboratory and field glides of *Glaucomys volans* to provide a comparison with published data for larger gliders. Finally, we use the results of our glide analyses to evaluate and extend the model of Scholey (1986).

METHODS

We obtained morphological data for terrestrial, arboreal, and gliding sciurids and anomalurids from the literature (Miller, 1912; Allen, 1915; Ognev, 1940; 1947; Hall and Kelson, 1959; Rosevear, 1969; Lekagul and McNeely, 1977; Hoffmeister, 1986, 1989). Data for acrobatids, burramyids, petaurids, and pseudocheirids were obtained at the Australian Museum in Sydney. Skeletal measurements were taken on specimens to the nearest 0.002 cm using dial calipers. External body measurements were taken from the specimen tags. All morphological data were log transformed. The data set included partial information for 155 species of mammals. We maximized sample size for the multivariate analysis by using only six variables: head and body length, tail length, hind foot length, greatest skull length, zygomatic width, and upper tooth row length. Because some of the data from the literature (Lekagul and McNeely, 1977) consisted of ranges rather than means, we used the midpoints of the ranges to estimate species means. For a few species it was necessary to subtract tail length from total length to obtain head and body length resulting in two measures which are not statistically independent. However, the general patterns explored here are probably not influenced strongly by these cases. The resultant data set contained 141 species. These are listed in Appendix I.

A canonical discriminant analysis was used to identify variables which discriminate between terrestrial, arboreal, and glissant mammals and to provide a measure of morphological overlap between the three locomotory modes. This was accomplished by computing mahalanobis distances between the three groups, and using the model of Harner and Whitmore (1977) and Whitmore and Harner (1980) to compute overlap of morphological groups.

The canonical analysis revealed the importance of tail length as a discriminatory variable. Therefore, we explored the allometry of tail length with head and body length and locomotor mode using a stepwise regression analysis with indicator variables (Neter and Wasserman, 1974). The indicator variables were used both as main effects and interaction terms, and enabled us to investigate differences in the intercepts and slopes of flying, arboreal, and ground dwelling mammals. We used the regression model:

$$T_i = ß_0 + ß_1H_i + ß_2X_{1i} + ß_3X_{2i} + ß_4H_iX_{1i} + ß_5H_iX_{2i} + \varepsilon_i,$$

where T = ln(tail length +1), H = ln(head and body length + 1), X_1 is an indicator variable for gliders (gliders = 1, otherwise X_1 = 0), X_2 is an indicator variable for arboreal mammals (X_2 = 1, otherwise X_2 = 0), ß's are regression coefficients and ε_i is an error term. Thus, for a ground dwelling mammal the model is:

$$T_i = ß_0 + ß_1H_i + \varepsilon_i,$$

for gliding mammals,

$$T_i = (ß_0 + ß_2) + (ß_1 + ß_4)H_i + \varepsilon_i,$$

and for arboreal mammals,

$$T_i = (ß_0 + ß_3) + (ß_1 + ß_5)H_i + \varepsilon_i.$$

This approach permitted the use of one regression model to explore three potential relationships, and provided straightforward significance tests for differences between the three groups.

Phylogenetic effects were removed statistically using the regression approach of Miles and Dunham (1992). Indicator variables were used to define orders, and families nested within orders. These variables were then included in the tail length versus head and body length regression, and consequently removed residual variation associated with evolutionary history.

We analyzed glides of *G. volans* in the laboratory and field. The laboratory was an indoor handball court 14 x 7 m with a 7 m ceiling. We erected launching and landing poles consisting of 10.16 cm diameter schedule 40 PVC pipe, covered with astroturf. The launch and landing poles were 6.1 m and 3 m respectively, and each was embedded in a 20 l plastic bucket filled with concrete. The launch and landing poles were separated in the lab at varying distances in an effort to entice the squirrels to glide from one structure to the next. Usually, the animals failed to land on the landing pole and landed on the ground. The horizontal distance of each glide was measured to the nearest cm, and the height of the launch was determined by noting the exact launch point on the pole. In cases where the squirrels landed on the landing pole, the height of the landing point was determined as well. Two observers were used to time the glides and all other performance events. Their times were obtained using digital stopwatches to the nearest .01 sec, and the times averaged to reduce error. We obtained data for 115 glides by eight squirrels in the laboratory. Climbing and running speeds were obtained for 60 climbing and running trials by six squirrels in the lab as well. For these trials the distances were measured directly.

Field glide data were obtained from animals captured in nest boxes on two small mammal trapping grids in the I. R. Kelso Sanctuary, Cape Girardeau Co., Missouri. The site was characterized as a second growth forest dominated by oak *(Quercus alba, Q. stellata, Q. macrocarpa, Q. prinoides, Q. rubra, Q. velutina)* and hickory *(Carya ovata)*. We visited the grids during the autumn of 1993 and spring of 1994, and obtained complete data for 26 glides by 12 animals. Animals were removed from the nest boxes and released on tree trunks. The animals climbed the trees and glided to another tree. We used a clinometer to estimate launch and landing heights (± 0.5 m), and measured horizontal distances of glides (± 5 cm) with a 100 m tape. Glide times were estimated using digital stopwatches to the nearest 0.01 sec.

The parameters for our analysis of Scholey's gliding model (Scholey, 1986) were estimated using linear regression. We regressed vertical drop against horizontal distance, and glide distance against glide time. We attempted to verify Scholey's graphical results using his data for *Petaurista* and discovered several inconsistencies. These were corrected by consulting Scholey's source for the energetics components of the model (Taylor, 1977).

Scholey's glide effectiveness model compares the energetic cost of an animal climbing and then gliding, to an animal using quadrupedal locomotion. The metabolic power consumption of an animal climbing is given as: $P_c = (f + mg/\eta)V_c + aP_b$, where f is a constant defined incorrectly by Scholey (1986) as $10.7^{0.6}$, and correctly by Taylor (1977) as $10.7m^{-0.4}$, and where m = mass, gravitational acceleration = g (9.81 m/s/s), η = climbing efficiency, and V_c = the velocity of climbing. The power of metabolism is defined as P_b, and a = 1.7 (a constant derived from Taylor, 1977). Scholey (1986) defined the power of metabolism as $3.5m^{0.75}$, but this is the basal metabolic rate. Taylor (1977) gives the value as $3.5m^{-.25}$. For our analysis of *G. volans*, we used the relationship determined by Stapp (1992); $P_b = 3.42m^{-.25}$. The energetic cost of climbing, E_c, is simply P_cT_c, where T_c is the time required to climb to a specific height. We obtained this value from direct measures of climbing speed in the lab. The metabolic power consumption of gliding, P_g, is minimal relative to that of climbing, and is estimated by Scholey (1986) as $2P_b$. This figure seems reasonable, and was derived from work by Baudinette and Schmidt-Nielsen (1974, cited in Scholey, 1986) on the herring gull. The energetic cost of gliding, E_g, is $2P_bT_g$, where T_g is the time of gliding. T_g can be derived from the regression analysis of horizontal distance against glide time. The total energetic cost of climbing and gliding, E_t, is $E_c + E_g$. The cost of gliding locomotion is thus: $C_g = E_t/mgD$, where D is the horizontal distance covered by the glide.

The cost of quadrupedal locomotion can be derived in a similar fashion. The metabolic power cost of running is: $P_r = fV_r + aP_b$, where V_r is the velocity of running. Scholey derived this value from estimates for *Callosciurus notatus*. Our values were derived from direct estimates of *G. volans* running in the lab. The energetic cost of running is given as: $C_r = P_r/mgV_r$.

Using the corrected relationships given above, we re-evaluated the results given by Scholey (1986). We then repeated the analysis specifically for *G. volans*. We investigated the effects of climbing efficiencies, climbing speeds, and running speeds on the cost effectiveness of gliding locomotion. Also, we explored the effects of glide ratios and initial drops on the cost effectiveness of gliding. These last two variables, although not independent, were treated as such. The results should be robust within small deviations of initial parameter estimates.

Table 1.—*Total canonical structure for the canonical discriminant analysis of gliding, arboreal, and terrestrial mammals. Coefficients for the morphological variables are correlations of the log transformed original variables on the canonical discriminant functions.*

VARIABLE	CAN 1	CAN 2
Head and body length	0.0102	0.1371
Tail length	0.8221*	0.2204
Hind foot length	-0.1604	0.1848
Greatest skull length	-0.0528	0.3549*
Zygomatic width	-0.0246	0.1751
Upper tooth row length	0.1642	0.3579*
Canonical correlation	0.7997	0.3925
Canonical R^2	0.6396	0.1541
P value	0.0001	0.0013

RESULTS

Morphological Analysis.—Two canonical axes provide significant discrimination between the three modes of locomotion. The first axis is dominated by tail length (Table 1) and discriminates between ground dwelling forms and arboreal/gliding forms. The second axis is correlated most strongly with greatest skull length and upper tooth row length and discriminates between arboreal and gliding mammals. Glissant mammals have the longest tails, short skulls, and short upper tooth rows, while arboreal forms have long tails, long skulls, and long tooth rows (Fig. 1). The greatest morphological overlap occurs between gliding and arboreal mammals (69.28%), while the least occurs between gliding and ground dwelling forms (53.72%). Overlap between arboreal and ground dwelling mammals is 58.62%.

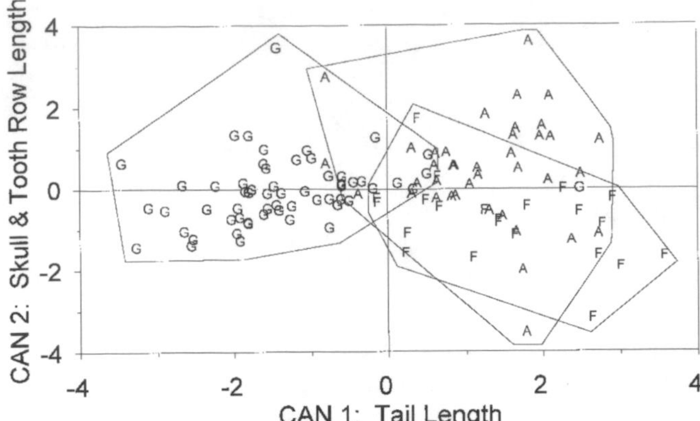

Fig. 1.—The distribution of gliding (F), arboreal (A), and ground dwelling (G) mammals in the canonical discriminant space.

The overall regression of tail length against head and body length is significant (Table 2). Marsupials and eutherians differ significantly in tail length. Within the marsupials, differences exist between four families. Across taxonomic groups, the indicator variable and interaction term for gliding mammals is significant. Thus, the regression line for gliding mammals has a steeper slope than the lines for arboreal and ground dwelling forms (Fig. 2). The regression for the arboreal mammals does not have an intercept different from the ground dwelling mammals. However, the interaction term is significant and thus the slope for the regression line of arboreal species is greater than that for ground-dwelling species, but less than that for gliding species. Overall, small gliders have shorter tails than small arboreal mammals, but larger gliders (head and body length > 172.3 mm) have longer tails than larger arboreal mammals.

Table 2.—*Stepwise regression results for log tail length against log head and body length (HB) and indicator variables for order, family, gliding, arboreal, and ground-dwelling mammals.*

SOURCE	*d.f.*	SS	MS	*F*	*P*
MODEL	8	50.3075	6.2884	30.89	0.0001
ERROR	142	28.9066	0.2036		
TOTAL	150	79.2140			

PARAMETER	$	*SE*	Type II SS	*F*	*P*
INTERCEPT	4.5754				
Order	-3.3416	0.3234	21.7402	106.80	0.0001
Acrobatidae	3.3494	0.4614	10.7296	52.71	0.0001
Burramyidae	2.9048	0.3781	12.0155	59.02	0.0001
Petauride	3.6513	0.3599	20.9488	102.91	0.0001
Pseudocheiridae	3.6460	0.3468	22.5041	110.55	0.0001
Glider	-4.5318	1.2003	6.4964	14.25	0.0002
HB x Glider	0.9986	0.2238	9.0748	19.91	0.0001
HB X Arboreal	0.1195	0.0227	12.5970	27.64	0.0001

R^2 = 0.6351

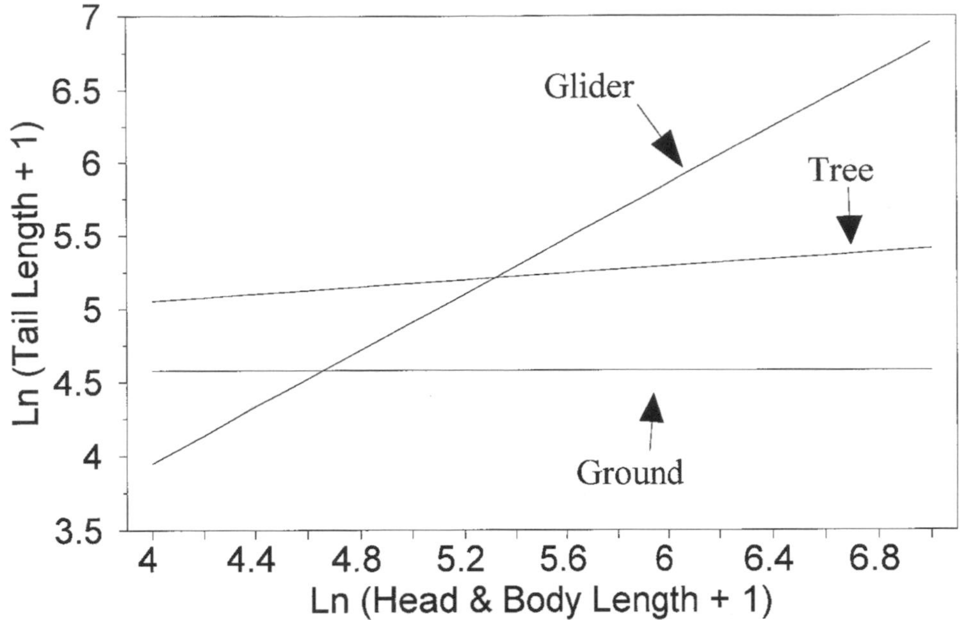

Fig. 2.—Regression lines for log tail length against log head and body length for gliding, arboreal, and ground dwelling mammals.

Performance Analysis.—The regression results of the glide analyses for *G. volans* are presented in Tables 3, 4, and 5. The regression for vertical drop against horizontal distance of the glide is significant and explains 54% of the variance in the glide data. Vertical drop increases with increasing horizontal distance, as expected. The model presented here has a steeper slope than that published by Scholey (1986) for *Petaurista petaurista* (Fig. 3). Thus, for glides greater than 18.62 m, *G. volans* experiences a greater loss in altitude for each additional horizontal m than does *P. petaurista*. The regression also shows that while the initial vertical drop for *P. petaurista* as reported by Scholey (1986) is 7.45 m, that for *G. volans* is only 1.85 m. Thus, *G. volans* appears to reach gliding speed much sooner than does *Petaurista*. *Petaurista* attains a glide speed of about 15.1 m/s in Scholey's analysis, while *Glaucomys* reaches a terminal glide speed of about 8.27 m/s in our study. The minimum glide speed exhibited by *G. volans* was 4.12 m/s and the maximum was 8.85 m/s. Across all glides, the average glide speed, including the launch phase, was 6.37 m/s (*SE* = 0.20).

Table 3.—*Regression results for vertical drop (m) against glide distance (sec) for laboratory and field glides of* Glaucomys volans.

SOURCE	*d.f.*	SS	MS	*F*	*P*
MODEL	1	633.3024	633.3024	95.67	0.0001
ERROR	134	887.0722	6.6199		
TOTAL	135	1520.3746			

PARAMETER	ESTIMATE	*T*	*P*	*SE*	
INTERCEPT	1.8479	3.55	0.0005	0.5206	
TIME	0.5108	9.78	0.0001		0.0522

R^2 = 0.7428

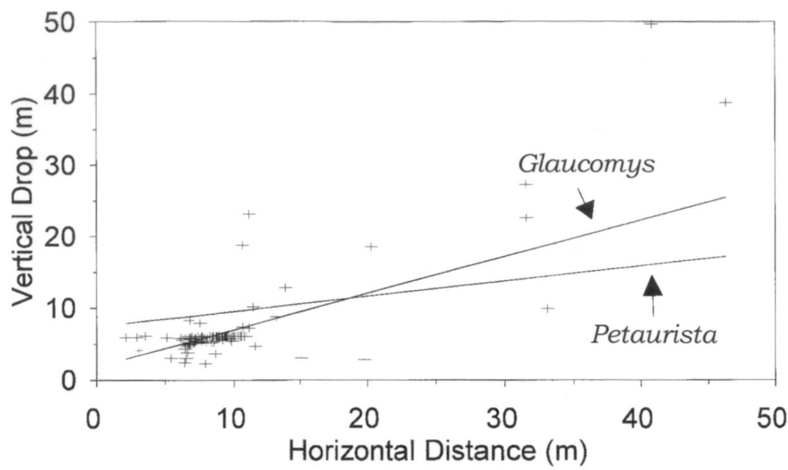

Fig. 3.—Regression line for total vertical drop (m) against horizontal glide distance (m) for *Glaucomys volans*. The line with the shallow slope represents the regression line determined by Scholey (1986) for *Petaurista petaurista*.

The mean glide ratio for *G. volans* in our study is 1.53. That is, the animals travel 1.53 m for every 1 m loss in altitude. The maximum glide ratio is 6.93, and the minimum is 0.36. Clearly, a glide ratio less than one indicates parachuting rather than gliding. These values are based on the direct glide angles. Estimates using actual glide angles would be somewhat higher. Nevertheless, the mean values reported here are lower than those reported by Nowak (1991), and Thorington and Heaney (1981).

The regression of glide distance against glide time is significant (Table 4). The slope for this equation is less than that reported by Scholey for *Petaurista* (Fig. 4). Thus for glides longer than 3.5 seconds, *G. volans* covers shorter distances than does *Petaurista.* There is a significant increase in glide speed with glide distance (Table 5), indicating that *Glaucomys* accelerates throughout the glide. However, the low R^2 for this regression (0.289), together with our observations of repeated glides by individuals (including complete rolls and 180 degree turns), suggests the animals exhibit considerable control over their glides.

Table 4.—*Regression results for glide distance (m) against glide time (sec) for laboratory and field glides of* Glaucomys volans.

SOURCE	*d.f.*	SS	MS	*F*	*P*
MODEL	1	2596.7046	2596.7046	386.90	0.0001
ERROR	134	899.3567	6.7116		
TOTAL	135	3496.0614			
PARAMETER	ESTIMATE	*T*	*P*	*SE*	
INTERCEPT	-3.5420	-4.52	0.0001	0.7842	
TIME	8.0920	19.67	0.0001	0.4114	

R^2 = 0.7428

Table 5.—*Regression results for glide speed (m/sec) against direct glide distance (m).*

SOURCE	*d.f.*	SS	MS	*F*	*P*
MODEL	1	78.2302	78.2302	61.84	0.0001
ERROR	134	169.5155	1.2650		
TOTAL	135	247.7457			

PARAMETER	ESTIMATE	*T*	*P*	*SE*
INTERCEPT	4.4377	18.91	0.0001	0.2347
GLIDE DISTANCE	0.5100	7.86	0.0001	0.0190

$R^2 = 0.3158$

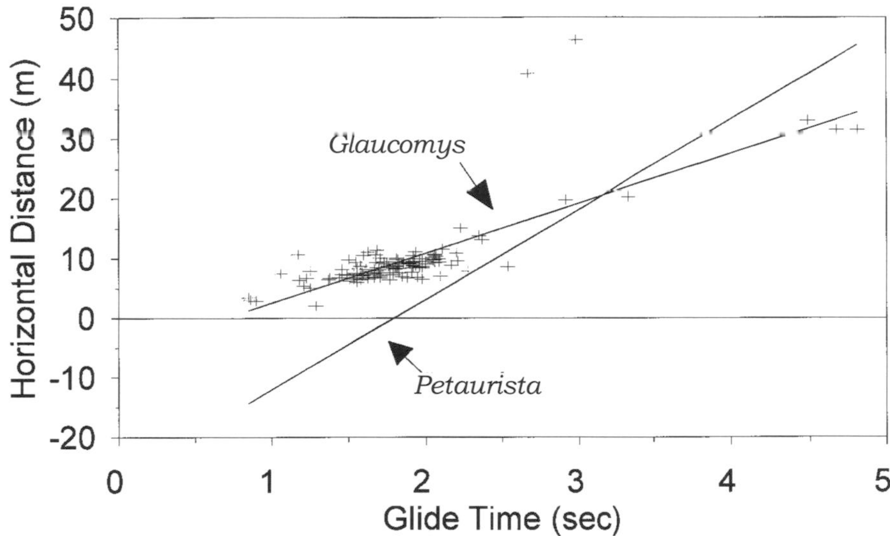

Fig. 4.—Regression line for horizontal glide distance (m) against total glide time (sec) for *Glaucomys volans.* The line with the steeper slope represents the regression line computed by Scholey (1986) for *Petaurista petaurista.*

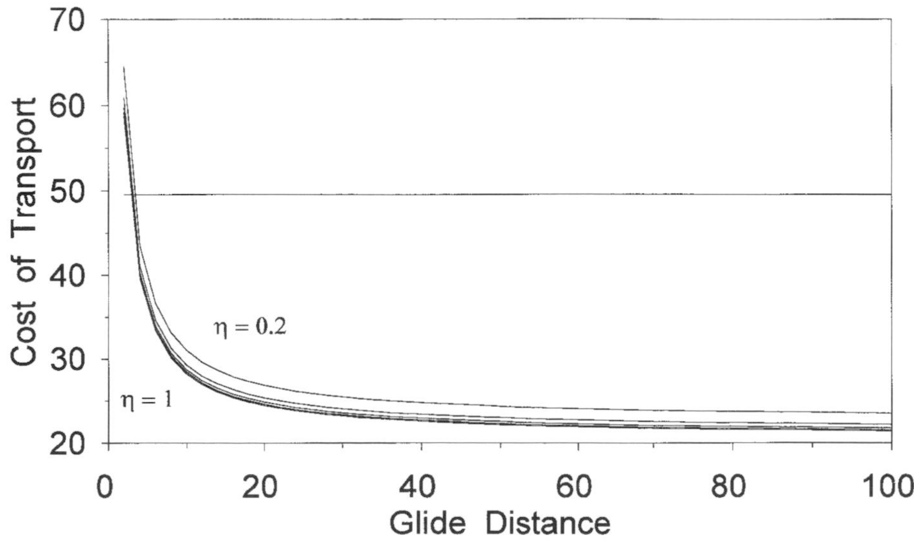

Fig. 5.—Results of the glide cost analysis for *Glaucomys volans.* Increasing climbing efficiencies from 20 to 100% results in a small decrease in the overall cost of the glides. The cost of quadrupedal locomotion is indicated by the horizontal line.

Our reanalysis of Scholey's (1986) work on the cost effectiveness of gliding in *P. petaurista* shows that his results are incorrect. That is, gliding does not become cost effective for *P. petaurista* at horizontal glide distances less than 100 m. This result is based on climbing efficiencies of 0.4 and 0.2, use of metabolic power rather than metabolic rate, and assumptions concerning climbing speeds, and running speeds of *Petaurista* (Scholey, 1986). However, when applied to *G. volans* the Scholey model produces results markedly different from those for *Petaurista*. Glide cost decreases rapidly with horizontal glide distance, especially up to 10 m, and is less than the cost of quadrupedal transport after about 3 m when mean running and climbing speeds are used (Fig. 5).

The distance at which gliding becomes cost effective is dependent on climbing and running speeds. Reducing running speed to 50% of the average for *Petaurista* reduces the cost effective glide distance to less than 40 m. Increasing climbing speed to 200% of the mean reduces the cost effective glide distance to 74 m (Fig. 6). Thus, for gliding to be cost effective in *Petaurista*, the animals must climb quickly and/or run slowly. If quadrupedal locomotion is fast and climbing slow, it is cheaper for *Petaurista* to move quadrupedally than to glide.

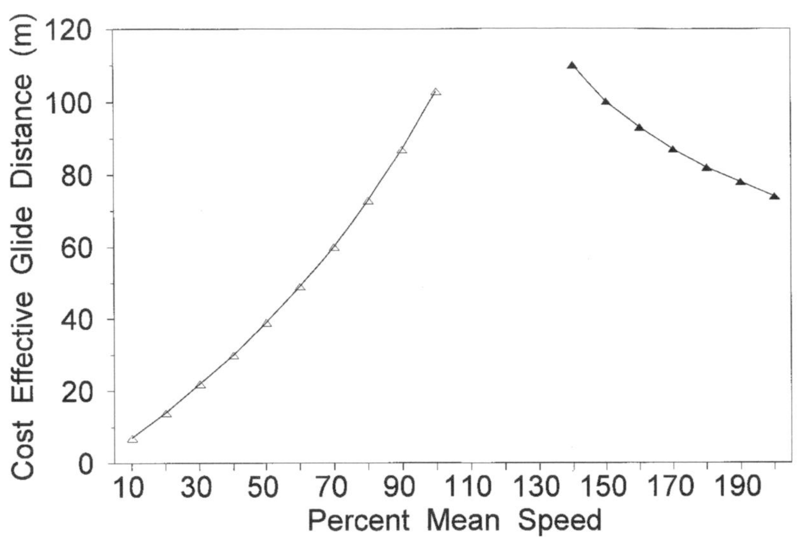

Fig. 6.—The effect of running speeds (open triangles) and climbing speeds (closed triangles) on the distance at which gliding becomes cost effective for *Petaurista petaurista*. Values on the abscissa are percentages of the mean climbing and running speeds (m/sec) reported by Scholey (1986).

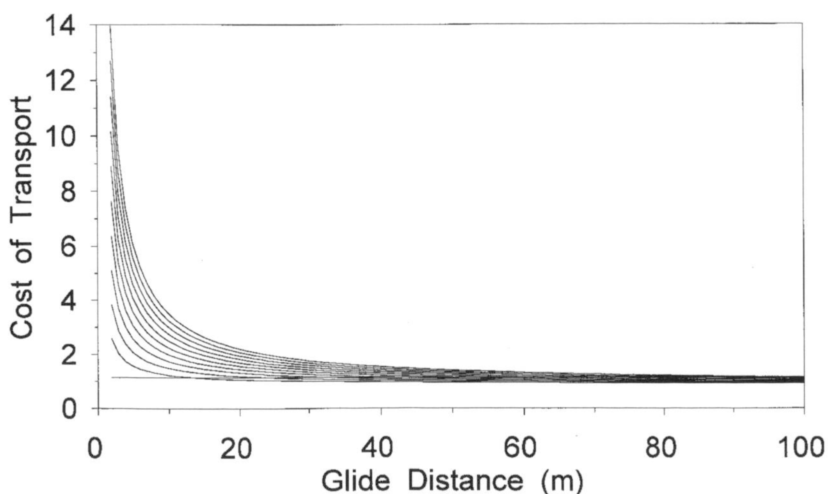

Fig. 7.—The cost of gliding in *Petaurista petaurista* as a function of reductions in the initial vertical drop of the glides. Each lower line represents a 10% reduction in the distance of the initial vertical drop. The cost of quadrupedal locomotion is indicated by the horizontal line.

Two parameters of the vertical drop/horizontal distance regression are subject to selection, and influence the cost effectiveness of gliding. The initial drop and the glide ratio are not independent variables, but we are interested only in the general behavior of the system near the initial parameter estimates. Reducing the initial vertical drop (the intercept of the vertical drop/horizontal distance regression) of a glide by *Petaurista* had the greatest effect on the early portions of the glide (Fig 7), reducing the cost of the glide. During this portion of the glide, the animals accelerate to speeds sufficient to obtain lift for the latter part of the glide. Thus, reducing the initial vertical drop will result in a slower glide with less lift, and consequently, a shorter glide. Increasing the glide ratio (equivalent to decreasing the slope of the regression between vertical drop and horizontal distance) results in reduced glide costs during the later portions of the glides. In fact, increasing the glide ratio by only 20% results in glides which are cost effective relative to quadrupedal locomotion at about 60 m (Fig. 8).

DISCUSSION

Tail length is an important morphological component of gliding. Thorington and Heaney (1981) hypothesized that since the tail is important for steering and balance, flying squirrels should have longer tails than tree squirrels. Based on their sample of 28 squirrels, they rejected the hypothesis, and found that small tree squirrels have shorter tails than small flying squirrels, and that large tree squirrels have longer tails than large flying squirrels. Our larger data set, which includes sciurids, anomalurids, acrobatids, burramyids, petaurids, and pseudocheirids, shows that across gliders in general, their results are not supported. In fact, small gliders have shorter tails than small arboreal mammals, but gliders with head and body lengths greater than 17 cm have longer tails. The slope of the regression for gliders is significantly larger than that for tree squirrels. So although tail length scales with size in both forms, it increases faster in gliding forms. This result supports the initial hypothesis of Thorington and Heaney (1981).

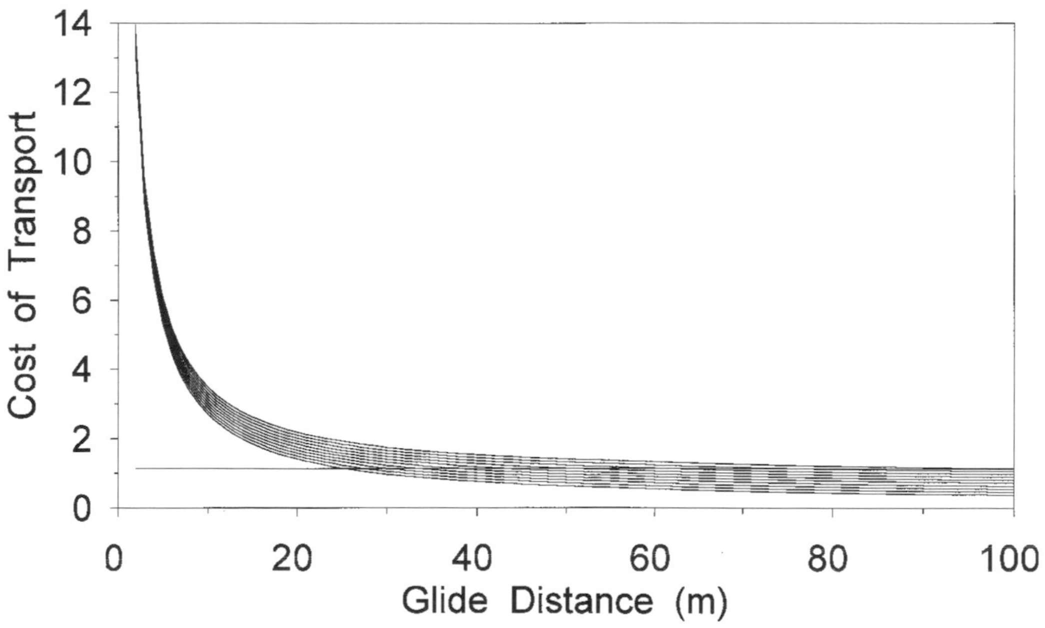

Fig. 8.—The cost of gliding in *Petaurista petaurista* as a function of reducing the slope of the vertical drop/horizontal distance regression. This is the same as increasing the glide ratio. Each lower line represents a percentage increase in the glide ratio. The cost of quadrupedal locomotion is indicated by the horizontal line.

The steering problems of large gliding squirrels are partially a consequence of their increased wing loading. Thorington and Heaney (1981) found wing loadings of the largest forms to be about 3.6 times as large as the smaller forms. They suggested that this would necessitate faster glide speeds for the larger forms. This appears to be the case. Glide speeds reported by Scholey for *P. petaurista* were ca. 15.1 m/s; and Ando (1993) reported glide speeds of 7 to 13.3 m/s for *P. leucogenys*. Our analysis of glides for *G. volans* revealed a mean glide speed of 6 m/s.

Tail shape appears to be related to body size in gliders. Schaller (1984) identified two tail morphologies relevant to gliders: cylindrical tails which act as drag rudders, and flat caudal wings (tails) which act as flow rudders. Small gliders such as *Glaucomys, Pteromys, Hylopetes, Petinomys, Acrobates*, and *Iomys* tend to have flow rudders, while large animals like *Petaurista, Eupetaurus, Petauroides*, and *Anomalurus* have drag rudders. There is some overlap, for example *Petaurus breviceps* has a cylindrical tail. This pattern may be related to the glide characteristics of large and small animals. Flow rudders in small gliders certainly add to the surface area of the wing, but perhaps more importantly may be ideally suited for the control of speed and pitch (Norberg, 1990). This would improve maneuverability in slow flying species. The drag rudders of large gliders may serve to 'orient the body-axis towards the aerial pathway-axis' (Schaller, 1984), perhaps minimizing drag and maximizing speed and lift.

Morphological overlap is greatest between gliders and arboreal mammals, and least between gliders and ground dwelling mammals. Yet, definite differences exist between gliders and arboreal forms. Generally, gliders have shorter tooth rows and shorter skulls than arboreal forms. Analyzing sciurids and anomalurids, Scheibe et al. (1990) found tooth rows in gliding squirrels to be longer than those in nongliding squirrels. They speculated that foraging constraints may have selected for greater efficiency in food processing. Based on our data set, that hypothesis appears to be incorrect. However, marsupial gliders have different dental formulas than sciurids and anomalurids. Additionally, many marsupial gliders are exudivorous, obviating the need for large dental surface areas.

Body size may have a great deal to do with the transition from tree squirrel to glider. The energetic advantages of gliding accrue to a smaller glider much more rapidly than to a large one. Our analysis of Scholey's (1986) model using glide data for *G. volans* reveals that it is energetically cheaper for small gliders to glide than to use quadrupedal locomotion. For large gliders like *P. petaurista*, Scholey (1986) found a glide distance of about 45 m to be necessary before an energetic advantage was realized. In fact, our reanalysis of his model demonstrates that more than 100 m are required for large gliders. Ando and Shiraishi (1993) found the glide distances of *P. leucogenys* to be determined primarily by forest structure and 'learned' glide routes. They reported mean glide distances in five shrine groves to range from 17.5 m to 33.1 m. Using Scholey's (1986) analysis, it would be cheaper for *P. leucogenys* to use quadrupedal locomotion as well. In fact, Ando and Shiraishi (1993) reported the use of quadrupedal locomotion predominated for movements over short distances.

A number of factors can reduce the cost of gliding. These include decreasing the glide angle, increasing the efficiency of climbing, and reducing the initial vertical drop. Increasing the glide angle can be achieved by decreasing wing loading. The fact that styliform and unciform cartilages exist among many forms, and limb lengths of gliders tend to be longer than those of tree squirrels suggests that evolution has resulted in greater patagial surface area. The efficiency of climbing is probably also improved by lengthening of the distal elements of the front appendage. Thorington and Thorington (1991) showed that a wider grasp on a tree trunk increases the normal force of the claws into the trunk, and reduces the tangential force. However, climbing efficiency has a relatively small effect on the cost effectiveness of gliding. Increasing the glide ratio by 10% results in considerably cheaper glides. Increasing the glide ratio through reduced wing loadings is probably difficult for large gliders, and may explain the positive allometry of tail length with head and body length for large gliders. Reducing the extent of the initial vertical drop reduces the glide cost during the initial stages of the glide. However, this results in a slower glide, which may not be possible for large gliders because of the greater wing loadings. Also, slower glides may subject smaller gliders to greater predation risks.

The transition to a gliding morphology is not trivial. Gliders tend to have modifications of the limbs, wrists, and shoulder girdle (Peterka, 1936; Oxnard, 1968; Thorington and Heaney, 1981; Bou et al., 1987) in addition to patagia. If gliding morphologies evolved with the accumulation of modifications, the earliest gliders probably had lower glide ratios and perhaps lower climbing efficiencies than extant forms. This would reduce the hypothesized energetic advantage of gliding. The hypothesis that energetics has driven the evolution of gliding locomotion requires scrutiny.

The hypothesis that gliding conveys some measure of predator avoidance seems suspect for smaller gliders. *Glaucomys* are prey items for many avian, reptilian, and mammalian species (Dolan and Carter, 1977), and form a large portion of the diets of northern spotted owls (Forsman et al., 1984). Smaller gliders may be subject to greater predation pressures because of their slower glide speeds. Also, predation has clearly played a role in the behavior of *G. volans*. Scheibe (in litt) used infrared sensors to study the activity patterns of *G. volans* and determined that the animals exhibit surveillance behavior before emerging from their nest boxes each evening, and follow each evenings activity with surveillance behavior as well. Austad and Fischer (1991) and Holmes and Austad (1994) have argued that gliding mammals live longer than nongliding forms, presumably because of reduced environmental vulnerability (due to arboreal, nocturnal, and nesting habits). However, Stapp (1994) has noted statistical difficulties with the analysis of Austad and Fischer (1991) and Holmes and Austad (1994), and suggests that the data are insufficient to conclude that gliders live longer than tree squirrels.

The fact that gliding has evolved so many times in vertebrates suggests that evolutionarily, it is not difficult to do. The biogeographic distribution and abundance of gliders suggests some relationship between forest structure and gliding. Studies published to date have not provided convincing evidence that gliding provides an energetic advantage over quadrupedal locomotion, nor has any conclusive evidence been published that gliding minimizes predation risks. The scaling of tail lengths and shapes, and limb proportions (Thorington and Heaney, 1981) with glider size, as well as the energetic differences of large and small gliders, suggests a variety of selection regimes. Foraging optimization, predator avoidance, or locomotor efficiency may drive the evolution of gliding, but detailed ecological studies of most gliders are lacking. It seems that a great deal of work is needed before we can understand fully the evolution of gliding locomotion.

ACKNOWLEDGMENTS

We thank J. Dunlap, C. Newhouse, W. Suchland, and D. Dowling for assistance in the field and lab, and D. Figgs and J. Heiland for work during the early stages of the project. We are particularly indebted to T. Flannery, L. Godwin, and the entire curatorial staff of the Australian Museum for their efforts on our behalf. Luba Turchyn graciously provided a translation of the Polyakova and Sokolov (1965) paper. Richard Thorington, R. Goldingay, S. Van Dyke, M. Ando, and S. Ward provided thoughtful comments, ideas, and speculation that encouraged us to pursue this project. Without their insight and experience with gliders, we would have learned much less.

LITERATURE CITED

ALLEN, J. A. 1915. Review of the south American Sciuridae. Bulletin of the American Museum of Natural History, 34:147-309.

ANDO, M., AND S. SHIRAISHI. 1991. Arboreal quadrupedalism and gliding adaptations in the Japanese giant flying squirrel, *Petaurista leucogenys*. Honyurui Kagaku (Mammalian Science), 30:167 181.

———. 1993. Gliding flight in the Japanese giant flying squirrel, *Petaurista leucogenys*. Journal of the Mammalogical Society of Japan, 18:19-32.

AUSTAD, S. N., AND K. E. FISCHER. 1991. Mammalian aging, metabolism, and ecology: evidence from the bats and marsupials. Journal of Gerontology: Biological Sciences, 46:B47-53.

BAUDINETTE, R. V., AND K. SCHMIDT-NIELSEN. 1974. Energy cost of gliding flight in the herring gull. Nature, 248:83-84.

BOU, J., A. CASINOS, AND J. OCANA. 1987. Allometry of the limb long bones of insectivores and rodents. Journal of Morphology, 192:113-123.

DOLAN, P. G., AND D. C. CARTER. 1977. Glaucomys volans. Mammalian Species, 78:1-6.

DUDLEY, R., AND P. DEVRIES. 1990. Tropical rain forest structure and the geographical distribution of gliding vertebrates. Biotropica, 22:432-434.

EMERSON, S. B. 1991. The ecomorphology of Bornean tree frogs (family Rhacophoridae). Zoological Journal of the Linnean Society, 101:337-357.

EMERSON, S. B., AND M. A. R. KOEHL. 1990. The interaction of behavioral and morphological change in the evolution of a novel locomotor type: "flying" frogs. Evolution, 44:1931-1946.

EMMONS, L. H., AND A. H. GENTRY. 1983. Tropical forest structure and the distribution of gliding and prehensile-tailed vertebrates. The

American Naturalist, 121:513-524.

FORSMAN, E. D., E. C. MESLOW, AND H. M. WIGHT. 1984. Distribution and biology of the spotted owl in Oregon. Wildlife Monographs, 87:1-64.

GUPTA, B. B. 1966. Notes on the gliding mechanism in the flying squirrel. Occasional Papers of the Museum of Zoology, University of Michigan, 645:1-7.

HALL, E. R., AND K. R. KELSON. 1959. The mammals of North America. Ronald Press Co., New York, 1083 pp.

HARNER, J. E., AND R. C. WHITMORE. 1977. Multivariate measures of niche overlap using discriminant analysis. Theoretical Population Biology, 12:21-36.

HOFFMEISTER, D. F. 1986. Mammals of Arizona. University of Arizona Press and the Arizona Game and Fish Department, Tucson, 602 pp.

———. 1989. Mammals of Illinois. University of Illinois Press, Urbana, 348 pp.

HOLMES, D. J., AND S. N. AUSTAD. 1994. Fly now, die later: life history correlates of gliding and flying in mammals. Journal of Mammalogy, 75:224-226.

JOHNSON-MURRAY, J. L. 1987. The comparative myology of the gliding membranes of *Acrobates, Petauroides* and *Petaurus* contrasted with the cutaneous myology of *Hemibelideus* and *Pseudocheirus* (Marsupialia: Phalangeridae) and with selected gliding rodentia (Sciuridae and Anomaluridae). Australian Journal of Zoology, 35:101-113.

LEKAGUL, B., AND J. A. MCNEELY. 1977. Mammals of Thailand. Association for the Conservation of Wildlife. Sahakarnbhat Co., Bangrak, Bangkok 5, Thailand, 746pp.

MILES, D. B., AND A. E. DUNHAM. 1992. Comparative analyses of phylogenetic effects in the life-history patterns of iguanid reptiles. The American Naturalist, 139:848-869.

MILLER, G. S. 1912. Catalogue of the mammals of western Europe (Europe exclusive of Russia) in the collection of the British Museum. The British Museum, London, 1019 pp.

NACHTIGALL, W. 1979. Gleitflug des flugbeutlers *Petaurus breviceps papuanus.* II Filmanalysen zur einstellung von gleitbahn und rumpf sowie zur steuerung des gleitflug. Journal of Comparative Physiology, A. Sensory, Neural, and Behavioral Physiology, 133:89-95.

NACHTIGALL, W., R. GROSCH, AND T. SCHULTZE-WESTRUM. 1974. Gleitflug des flugbeutlers *Petaurus breviceps papuanus* (Thomas): flugverhalten und flugsteuerung. Journal of Comparative Physiology, A. Sensory, Neural, and Behavioral Physiology, 92:105-115.

NETER, J., AND W. WASSERMAN. 1974. Applied linear statistical models. Richard D. Irwin, Homewood, Illinois, 842 pp.

NORBERG, U. M. 1985. Evolution of vertebrate flight: an aerodynamic model for the transition from gliding to active flight. The American Naturalist, 126:303-327.

———. 1990. Gliding flight. Pp. 65-75, *in* Zoophysiology 27, Vertebrate flight: mechanics, physiology, morphology, ecology and evolution (S. D. Bradshaw, et al., eds.). Springer-Verlag, New York, 291 pp.

NOWAK, R. M. 1991. Walker's mammals of the world. The Johns Hopkins University Press, Baltimore, Maryland, 1629 pp.

OGNEV, S. I. 1940. Mammals of the U.S.S.R. and adjacent countries. Vol. IV. Rodents. Israel Program for Scientific Translations Ltd., 1966. IPST Cat. No. 1254. S. Monson Binding: Wiener Bindery Ltd., Jerusalem, Israel, 491 pp.

———. 1947. Mammals of the U.S.S.R. and adjacent countries. Vol. V. Rodents. Israel Program for Scientific Translations Ltd., 1963. IPST Cat. No. 745. S. Monson Binding: Wiener Bindery Ltd., Jerusalem, Israel, 662 pp.

OXNARD, C. E. 1968. The architecture of the shoulder in some mammals. Journal of Morphology, 126: 249-290.

PETERKA, H. E. 1936. A study of the myology and osteology of tree sciurids with regard to adaptation to arboreal, glissant and fossorial habits. Transactions of the Kansas Academy of Science, 39:313-332.

POLYAKOVA, R. S., AND A. S. SOKOLOV. 1965. Structure of the locomotor organs in the volant squirrel, *Pteromys volans* L. in relation to its plane flight. Zoological Journal, 44: 902-916.

ROSEVEAR, D. R. 1969. The rodents of west Africa. Trustees of the British Museum (Natural History), London, 604 pp.

SCHALLER, D. 1984. Wing evolution. Pp. 333-348, *in* The beginnings of birds: Proceedings of the International Archaeopteryx Conference, Eichstatt (M. K. Hecht, J. H. Ostrom, G. Viohl, and P. Wellnhofer, eds.). Freunde des Jura-Museums Eichstatt, Willibaldsburg, Germany, 382 pp.

SCHEIBE, J. S., D. FIGGS, AND J. HEILAND. 1990. Morphological attributes of gliding rodents. Transactions of the Missouri Academy of Science, 24:49-55.

SCHOLEY, K. 1986. The climbing and gliding locomotion of the giant red flying squirrel *Petaurista petaurista* (Sciuridae). Biona-report, 5:187-204.

STAPP, P. 1992. Energetic influences on the life history of *Glaucomys volans*. Journal of Mammalogy, 73:914-920.

———. 1994. Can predation explain life-history strategies in mammalian gliders? Journal of Mammalogy, 75:227-228.

TAYLOR, C. R. 1977. The energetics of terrestrial locomotion and body size in vertebrates. Pp. 127-141, *in* Scale effects in animal locomotion (T. J. Pedley, ed.). Academic Press, New York, 545 pp.

THORINGTON, R. W., JR., AND L. R. HEANEY. 1981. Body proportion and gliding adaptations of flying squirrels (Petauristinae). Journal of Mammalogy, 62:101-114.

THORINGTON, R. W., JR., AND E. M. THORINGTON. 1989. Postcranial proportions of *Microsciurus* and *Sciurillus*, the American pygmy tree squirrels. Pp. 125-136, *in* Advances in Neotropical mammalogy (K. H. Redford and J. F. Eisenberg, eds.). The Sandhill Crane Press, Inc., Gainesville, Florida, 614 pp.

WHITMORE, R. C., AND J. E. HARNER. 1980. Analysis of multivariately determined community matrices using cluster analysis and multidimensional scaling. Biometrical Journal, 22:715-723.

APPENDIX I

List of species used in the morphological analyses. Species used in the canonical discriminant analysis are indicated with a C, *and those used in the regression analysis are indicated with an* R. *Numbers indicate replication resulting from different sources, with measurements suggesting geographical or subspecific differences.*

Acrobatidae: *Distoechurus pennatus* (C, R), *Acrobates pygmaeus*, (C, R). Burramyidae: Burramys parvus (C, R), *Cercartetus caudatus* (C, R), *Cercarterus concinnus* (C, R), *Cercartetus lepidus* (C, R), *Cercartetus nanus* (C, R). Petauridae: *Dactilopsila megalura* (R), *Dactilopsila palpator* (C, R), *Dactilopsila tatei* (R), *Dactilopsila trivergata* (C, R), *Gymnobelideus leadbeateri* (C, R), *Petaurus australis* (C, R), *Petaurus breviceps* (C, R), *Petaurus norfolcencis* (C, R). Pseudocheiridae: *Hemibelideus lemuroides* (C, R), *Petauroides volans* (C, R), *Petropseudes dahli* (C, R), *Pseudocheirus canescens* (C, R), *Pseudocheirus forbesi* (C, R), *Pseudocheirus herbertensis* (C, R), *Psedocheirus mayeri* (C, R), *Pseudocheirus peregrinus* (C, R), *Pseudochirops albertisii* (C, R), *Pseudochirops archeri* (C, R), *Pseudochirops corinnae* (C, R), *Pseudochirops cupreus* (C, R). Vombatidae: *Vombatus ursinus* (R). Phascolarctidae: *Phascolarctos cinereus* (R). Sciuridae (Petauristinae): *Aeromys tephromelas* (R), *Belomys pearsonii* (C, R), *Eupetaurus cinereus* (R), *Glaucomys sabrinus* (C, R), *Glaucomys volans* (C, R(2)), *Hylopetes alboniger* (C(2), R(2)), *Hylopetes lepidus* (C, R(2)), *Hylopetes phayrei* (C, R), *Iomys horsfieldi* (R), *Petaurista elegans* (R), *Petaurista petaurista* (C, R), *Petinomys genibarbis* (R), *Petinomys setosus* (C, R), *Pteromys volans* (C, R(2)), *Pteromyscus pulverulentus* (R). Sciuridae (Sciurinae): *Ammospermophilus harrisii* (C, R), *Ammospermophilus insularis* (C, R) *Ammospermophilus interpres* (C, R), *Ammospermophilus leucurus* (C, R), *Ammospermophilus nelsoni* (C, R), *Callosciurus caniceps* (C, R), *Callosciurus erythraeus* (C, R), *Callosciurus finlaysonii* (C, R), *Callosciurus nigrovittatus* (C, R), *Callosciurus notatus* (C, R), *Callosciurus prevostii* (C, R), *Cynomys gunnisoni* (C, R), *Cynomys ludovicianus* (C, R), *Dremomys rufigenis* (C, R), *Epixerus ebii* (R), *Funisciurus anerythrus* (R), *Funisciurus isabella* (R), *Funisciurus leucogenys* (R), *Funisciurus pyrropus* (R), *Funisciurus substriatus* (R), *Heliosciurus gambianus* (R), *Heliosciurus rufobrachium* (R), *Lariscus insignis* (C, R), *Marmota baibacina* (C, R), *Marmota bobak* (C, R), *Marmota camtschatica* (C, R), *Marmota caudata* (C, R), *Marmota marmota* (R), *Marmota monax* (C, R), *Marmota sibirica* (C, R), *Menetes berdmorei* (C, R), *Myosciurus pumilio* (R), *Paraxerus cooperi* (R), *Protoxerus aubinnii* (R), *Protoxerus stangeri* (R), *Ratufa affinis* (C, R), *Ratufa bicolor* (C, R), *Rhinosciurus laticaudatus* (C, R), *Sciurus aberti* (C, R), *Sciurus arizonensis* (C, R), *Sciurus carolinensis* (C, R), *Sciurus nayaritensis* (C, R), *Sciurus niger* (C, R), *Sciurus vulgaris* (C, R), *Spermophilopsis leptodactylus* (C, R), *Spermophilus adocetus* (C(2), R(2)), *Spermophilus alaschanicus* (C, R), *Spermophilus armatus* (C, R), *Spermophilus atricapilus* (C, R), *Spermophilus beecheyi* (C, R), *Spermophilus beldingi* (C, R), *Spermophilus brunneus* (C, R), *Spermophilus citellus* (C, R), *Spermophilus columbianus* (C, R), *Spermophilus dauricus* (C, R), *Spermophilus erythrogenys* (C(2), R(2)), *Spermophilus franklinii* (C, R), *Spermophilus lateralis* (C, R), *Spermophilus madrensis* (C, R), *Spermophilus major* (C, R), *Spermophilus mexicanus* (C, R), *Spermophilus mohavensis* (C, R) *Spermophilus mollis* (C, R), *Spermophilus parryii* (C(3), R(3)), *Spermophilus perotensis* (C, R),

Spermophilus pygmaeus (C, R), *Spermophilus relictus* (C, R), *Spermophilus richardsonii* (C, R), *Spermophilus saturatus* (C, R), *Spermophilus spilosoma* (C, R), *Spermophilus suslicus* (R), *Spermophilus tereticaudus* (C, R), *Spermophilus townsendii* (C, R), *Spermophilus tridecemlineatus* (C, R), *Spermophilus undulatus* (C, R), *Spermophilus variegatus* (C, R), *Spermophilus washingtoni* (C, R), *Sundasciurus hippurus* (C, R), *Sundasciurus lowii* (C, R), *Sundasciurus tenuis* (C, R), *Tamias cinereicollis* (C(2), R(2)), *Tamias dorsalis* (C(2), R(2)), *Tamias minimus* (C, R), *Tamias quadrivittatus* (C(2), R(2)), *Tamias sibiricus* (C, R), *Tamias striatus* (C, R), *Tamias umbrinus* (C(2), R(2)), *Tamiasciurus hudsonicus* (C, R), *Tamiops macclellandi* (C, R), *Tamiops rodolphei* (C, R), *Xerus erythropus* (R). Anomaluridae: *Anomalurus beecrofti* (C, R), *Anomalurus derbianus* (C, R), *Anomalurus pelii* (C, R), *Anomalurus pusillus* (C, R), *Idiurus macrotis* (C, R), *Idiurus zenkeri* (C, R).

ALLOZYMIC VARIATION IN POPULATIONS OF FOX SQUIRRELS *(SCIURUS NIGER)* AND GRAY SQUIRRELS *(S. CAROLINENSIS)* FROM THE EASTERN UNITED STATES

NANCY D. MONCRIEF

Virginia Museum of Natural History,
1001 Douglas Avenue, Martinsville, VA 24112

ABSTRACT.—Allozymic variation was studied in fox squirrels *(Sciurus niger)* and gray squirrels *(S. carolinensis)* by comparing patterns of differentiation within and between these two sympatric species in the eastern portion of their ranges. Allozyme analyses revealed that within each species, there are differences among eastern and western populations, as defined by their geographic location relative to the present Mississippi River channel. The results of this study were broadly consistent with patterns reported in previous allozymic studies of these species. Further investigations are necessary to clarify intraspecific relationships of fox squirrels and gray squirrels in the southeast, midwest, and west.

INTRODUCTION

The most widespread representatives of the genus *Sciurus* in North America, fox squirrels *(S. niger)* and gray squirrels *(S. carolinensis),* occur sympatrically east of ca. 98° W longitude (Hall, 1981). Their ranges are nearly coincident with the distribution of eastern temperate forests. Despite the fact that fox squirrels and gray squirrels are highly visible, important as game species, and widely distributed, very few studies have investigated geographic variation in these species (Barnett, 1977; Havera and Nixon, 1978; Weigl et al., 1989; Moncrief, 1993; Turner and Laerm, 1993). Fox squirrels and gray squirrels are well-suited for a comparative study of geographic variation: their natural history and habitat requirements are extensively documented; they have very similar (if not identical) diets; and they occur sympatrically throughout most of eastern North America. Because of these similarities, patterns of variation in each of these species can be used as a control for assessing geographic variation in the other species, and both species together serve as replicates for studying the biogeographic history of eastern North America. Such wide-ranging surveys of co-distributed species are essential to the study of historical biogeography (Riddle and Honeycutt, 1990; Lamb and Avise, 1992) and are relevant to the understanding of biogenetic diversity (Avise, 1992).

Ten subspecies of *S. niger* and six subspecies of *S. carolinensis* are recognized (Hall, 1981) based on pelage and size characteristics. However, a recent study of fox squirrels (Turner and Laerm, 1993) concluded that pelage characters are too varied and subjective to permit consistent determination of subspecies affinities in the southeastern United States. For this reason, other sources of information must be considered to investigate evolutionary relationships among populations. Biochemical techniques, such as protein electrophoresis, can provide a broadly applicable set of heritable markers to examine genetic structure and interrelationships of populations (Moritz and Hillis, 1990). Moreover, allozyme electrophoresis is among the most cost-effective methods of investigating genetic phenomena at the molecular level (Murphy et al., 1990).

Allozyme variation was studied in fox squirrels and gray squirrels from the lower Mississippi River valley by Moncrief (1993). That study reported differences between eastern and western populations (with respect to the Mississippi River

In M.A. Steele, J. F. Merritt, and D. A. Zegers (eds.). 1998. Ecology and Evolutionary Biology of Tree Squirrels. Special Publication, Virginia Museum of Natural History, 6: 320 pp

channel) in both species. The primary objective of the current study was to investigate allozymic variation in eastern populations of fox squirrels and gray squirrels, expanding the investigations initiated by Moncrief (1993). Results of this study are interpreted in light of Moncrief 's (1993) report as well as subspecific boundaries, which are largely based on pelage and size characteristics.

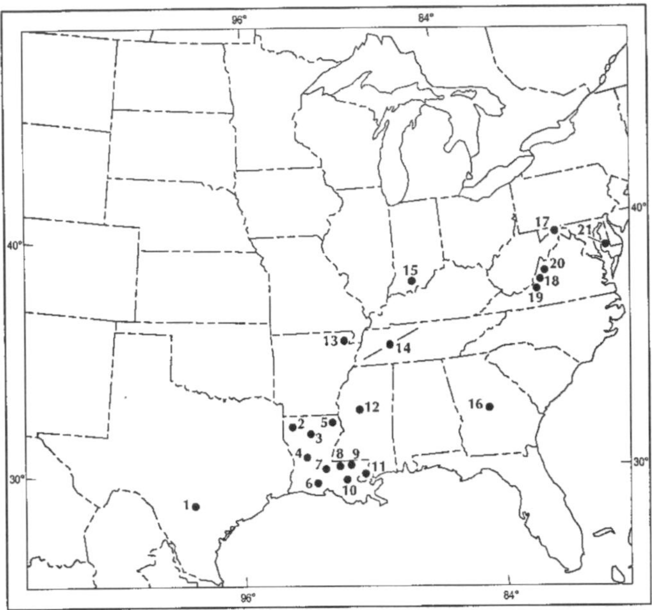

Fig. 1.—Sample localities of *Sciurus niger*. Numerals in bold correspond to sample numbers. Sample sizes are indicated in parentheses, as are locality codes from Moncrief (1993) for samples 1-14. **1**) Texas—Atascosa Co. (1, *NX*); **2**) Louisiana—Bossier Parish (5, *NB*); **3**) Louisiana—Jackson, Bienville, and Winn parishes (11, *NJ*); **4**) Louisiana—Vernon and Grant parishes (7, *NV*); **5**) Louisiana—Madison Parish (7, *NM*); **6**) Louisiana—Acadia Parish (12, *NA*); **7**) Louisiana—Pointe Coupee Parish (4, *NP*); **8**) Louisiana—West Feliciana Parish (3, *NW*); **9**) Louisiana—East Feliciana Parish (6, *NF*); **10**) Louisiana—Ascension, East Baton Rouge, and Iberville parishes (10, *NE*); **11**) Louisiana—St. Tammany Parish (5, *NS*); **12**) Mississippi—Holmes Co. (13, *NH*); **13**) Arkansas—Greene Co. (5, *NK*); **14**) Tennessee—Haywood, McNairy, and Trousdale counties (3, *NT*); **15**) Indiana—Dubois Co. (18); **16**) Georgia—Jones and Jasper counties (40); **17**) Maryland—Allegany Co. (18); **18**) Virginia—Alleghany Co. (6); **19**) Virginia—Craig Co. (8); **20**) Virginia—Augusta Co. (6); **21**) Maryland—Dorchester Co. (34). Specific collecting localities for samples 15-21 are listed in Appendix II.

MATERIALS AND METHODS

Seven samples of *S. niger* comprised of 130 specimens from Indiana, Georgia, Maryland, and Virginia (samples 15-21 in Fig. 1), and five samples of *S. carolinensis* comprised of 94 specimens from Indiana, Georgia, Maryland, and Virginia (samples 11-15 in Fig. 2) were analyzed using standard protein electrophoresis procedures. In addition, selected individuals of each species from Louisiana, Mississippi, Tennessee, and Texas (which were used in Moncrief, 1993; Appendix I) were reanalyzed to allow direct comparison of results from eastern samples with results already reported for samples from the lower Mississippi River valley. Specific collecting localities for the Maryland, Georgia, Virginia, and Indiana samples are listed in Appendix II.

Fig. 2.—Sample localities of *Sciurus carolinensis*. Numerals in bold correspond to sample numbers. Sample sizes are indicated in parentheses, as are locality codes from Moncrief (1993) for samples 1-10. **1**) Louisiana—Bossier Parish (3, *CB*); **2**) Louisiana—Jackson, Bienville, and Winn parishes (12, *CJ*); **3**) Louisiana—Vernon and Rapides parishes (7, *CV*); **4**) Louisiana—Acadia and Lafayette parishes (5, *CA*); **5**) Louisiana—West Feliciana Parish (11, *CW*); **6**) Louisiana—East Baton Rouge Parish (7, *CEP*); **7**) Louisiana—East Baton Rouge Parish (16, *CE*); **8**) Louisiana—St. Tammany Parish (12, *CS*); **9**) Mississippi—Holmes Co. (18, *CH*); **10**) Tennessee—Shelby and Tipton counties (16, *CTS*); **11**) Indiana—Dubois and Orange counties (13); **12**) Georgia—Jones and Jasper counties (40); **13**) Maryland—Allegany Co. (11); **14**) Virginia—Bath Co. (12); **15**) Virginia—Henry Co. (18). Specific collecting localities for samples 11-15 are listed in Appendix II.

Techniques for tissue preparation and staining followed those described in Murphy et al. (1990). Samples of heart, liver, kidney, and skeletal muscle were used to make aqueous extracts of proteins.

Buffer systems, and the enzymes for which they were used are listed in Appendix III. For gray squirrels, 24 enzyme systems that are encoded by 28 presumptive gene loci were assayed (Appendix III); for fox squirrels, 28 enzyme systems that are encoded by 34 presumptive gene loci were assayed (Appendix III). Note that the locus called PGM-1 in Moncrief (1993) is referred to as PGM-2 in this study, and PGM-2 in Moncrief (1993) is called PGM-3 in this study.

For both species, numerous side-by-side comparisons of electromorphs were made to insure correct assessment of relative mobilities. Electromorphs were assumed to represent alleles and were assigned unique letters, with "A" designating the most common allele. The most anodal locus was designated as "locus 1" for enzymes in which the product of more than one gene locus (isozyme) was interpretable. As indicated earlier, 8 *S. niger* and 38 *S. carolinensis* from Moncrief (1993; Appendix I) were included to insure interpretation of results and assignment of letters consistent with previous analyses (Moncrief, 1993). Inclusion of those specimens (Appendix I) allowed direct comparisons with results reported in Moncrief (1993) and complete incorporation of those earlier results into analyses performed in this study.

The BIOSYS-1 program of Swofford and Selander (1981) was used to summarize and to analyze statistically the electrophoretic results for each species. Using this program, allelic and genotypic frequencies and the percentage of polymorphic loci were determined for each sample. Allelic and genotypic frequency data were then used in a series of analyses to estimate genetic variation within and among conspecific populations. Percent polymorphism (*P*) was calculated for each sample using loci for which the frequency of the most common allele was $\leq$95%. For each sample, mean heterozygosity ($\overline{H}$) was calculated as the average proportion of heterozygous individuals at the loci examined (direct-count method), and the expected heterozygosity (H_{exp}, averaged over all loci and assuming Hardy-Weinberg equilibrium) was calculated for each sample using Nei's (1978) formula that corrects for small sample sizes. Genotypic proportions observed at each polymorphic locus were tested for conformation to the proportions expected under Hardy-Weinberg equilibrium. Chi-square tests using Levene's (1949) correction for small sample sizes were used to test for goodness-of-fit between observed and expected numbers of heterozygous individuals at each locus. To assess patterns of divergence among populations, both cladistic and phenetic techniques were employed. First, single-locus techniques (Honeycutt and Williams, 1982; Patton and Avise, 1983; Moncrief, 1993) were used to examine variation at selected individual loci. Relationships of ingroup (conspecific) populations were assessed using individuals of the other species as an outgroup. This technique permitted the identification of ancestral (plesiomorphic) and derived (apomorphic) alleles for interpretation of patterns of variation revealed by subsequent analyses. Allelic distributions at selected loci were superimposed onto maps using pie diagrams to represent allelic frequencies for each sample. With this approach, the distribution of shared-derived (synapomorphic) and shared-ancestral (symplesiomorphic) alleles was portrayed in a geographic context for each species.

Cluster analyses in which differentiation among conspecific populations was considered at all loci combined were then employed using the genetic distance measure of Rogers as modified by Wright (1978). Modified Rogers' distance (Wright, 1978; D_T) was used to examine genetic distances among all samples within each species, which then were clustered using UPGMA (Sneath and Sokal, 1973).

RESULTS

Sciurus niger.—In fox squirrels, 28 of 34 loci were monomorphic for the same allele across all seven samples: ACN-1, ACP, ADH, AK-1, CK-2, FUM, GDA, G3PD, GLUD, GOT-1, GOT-2, G6PD, IDH-1, IDH-2, LDH-1, LDH-2, MDH-1, MDH-2, ME, ODH, PEPA, PEPD, PEPS, 6PGD, PGI, SDH, SOD-1, and SOD-2. Six loci were polymorphic in at least one sample: MPI, NP, PEPB, PEPC, PGM-2, and PGM-3 (Table 1). Percentage of polymorphic loci (*P*) was either 5.9% (Dubois Co., Indiana; Jones and Jasper counties, Georgia; and Dorchester Co., Maryland) or 8.8% (Allegany Co., Maryland; Alleghany Co., Virginia; Craig Co., Virginia; and Augusta Co., Virginia). The average $\overline{H}$ calculated over these seven populations of fox squirrels was 3.3% and ranged from 1.9 (Jones and Jasper counties, Georgia) to 4.4% (Alleghany Co., Virginia). There were no apparent geographically related patterns in levels of genic variation as measured by levels of heterozygosity or polymorphism (Table 1), and these values were comparable to values reported in Moncrief (1993) for 14 samples of fox squirrels from the lower Mississippi River valley.

Table 1.—*Alphabetic designations for electromorphs, mean heterozygosity* ($\overline{H}$), *number of expected heterozygotes* (H_{exp}; *Nei, 1978), and percent polymorphism* (P) *at six polymorphic loci assayed across seven samples of* Sciurus niger. *Allelic frequencies for polymorphic loci are indicated in parentheses. Abbreviations for loci are provided in Appendix III. Sample localities are shown in Fig. 1.*

Sample number	Sample locality	*n*	MPI	NP	PEPB	PEPC	PGM-2
15	Dubois Co., Indiana	18	A(0.97) B(0.03)	A(0.56) B(0.44)	A	A(0.97) B(0.03)	A(0.86) B(0.14)
16	Jones and Jasper counties, Georgia	40	A(0.18) B(0.82)	A(0.75) B(0.25)	A	A	A(0.96) B(0.04)
17	Allegany Co., Maryland	18	A(0.56) B(0.44)	A(0.047) B(0.053)	A	A	A(0.81) B(0.19)
18	Alleghany Co., Virginia	6	A(0.58) B(0.42)	A(0.42) B(0.58)	A	A	A
19	Craig Co., Virginia	8	A(0.56) B(0.44)	A(0.50) B(0.50)	A	A	A
20	Augusta Co., Virginia	6	A(0.83) B(0.17)	A(0.33) B(0.67)	A	A	A
21	Dorchester Co., Maryland	34	A(0.60) B(0.34) C(0.06)	A(0.43) B(0.57)	A(0.97) B(0.03)	A(0.97) B(0.03)	A

Table 1.—continued.

Sample number	Sample locality	n	PGM-3	$\overline{H}$	H_{exp}	P
15	Dubois Co., Indiana	18	A	0.025	0.025	5.9
16	Jones and Jasper counties, Georgia	40	A(0.99) B(0.01)	0.019	0.023	5.9
17	Allegany Co., Maryland	18	A(0.97) B(0.03)	0.041	0.041	8.8
18	Alleghany Co., Virginia	6	A(0.75) B(0.25)	0.044	0.043	8.8
19	Craig Co., Virginia	8	A(0.88) B(0.12)	0.033	0.038	8.8
20	Augusta Co., Virginia	6	A(0.83) B(0.17)	0.029	0.032	8.8
21	Dorchester Co., Maryland	34	A(0.96) B(0.04)	0.037	0.036	5.9

Chi-square tests revealed significant deviation from Hardy-Weinberg expectations in only one sample; there was heterozygote deficiency at PEPC in the sample from Dorchester Co., Maryland. This general absence of departure from Hardy-Weinberg expectations in *S. niger* was consistent with the findings of many allozymic studies of sexually outbreeding organisms (Smith et al., 1981).

Side-by-side comparisons of electromorphs confirmed that *S. carolinensis* and *S. niger* are fixed for alternate alleles at GDA, PGI, PEPD, PEPA (Moncrief, 1993), as well as glutathione reductase (GR, Enzyme Commission Number 1.6.4.2, analyzed using TC7 and TC8).

To assess patterns of divergence among populations, a total of 222 specimens of *S. niger* representing 21 populations (Fig. 1) were analyzed using single-locus techniques as well as cluster analyses. This total included samples from the lower Mississippi River valley reported in Moncrief (1993): ninety-two specimens of *S. niger* representing 14 populations from Texas, Louisiana, Arkansas, Mississippi, and Tennessee (samples 1-14; Fig. 1).

The allozymic analyses revealed that eleven alleles were shared between these two species, in many cases reconfirming results reported in Moncrief (1993). The alleles were designated as follows for *S. niger* and *S. carolinensis*, respectively: ACN-1^A = ACN-1^C, $G3PD^A$ = $G3PD^A$, MPI^A = MPI^A, NP^A = NP^A, NP^B = NP^B, $6PGD^A$ = $6PGD^A$, $PEPB^A$ = $PEPB^A$, $PEPC^A$ = $PEPC^A$, PGM-2^A = PGM-2^B, PGM-2^B = PGM-2^D, and PGM-3^A = PGM-3^A. The locus-by-locus cladistic analysis of *S. niger* (*S. carolinensis* was the outgroup) indicated that alleles MPI^A, NP^A, NP^B, $PEPC^A$, PGM-2^A, PGM-2^B, and PGM-3^A are shared with gray squirrels. These were, therefore, considered ancestral alleles in fox squirrels, and they were discounted in locus-by-locus analyses of relationships within *S.*

a

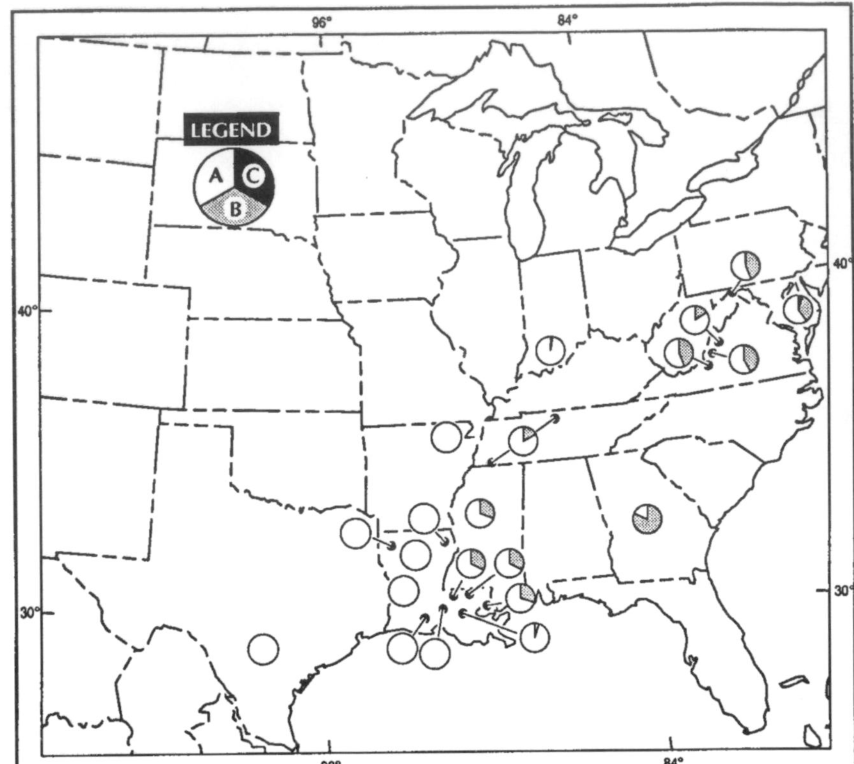

b

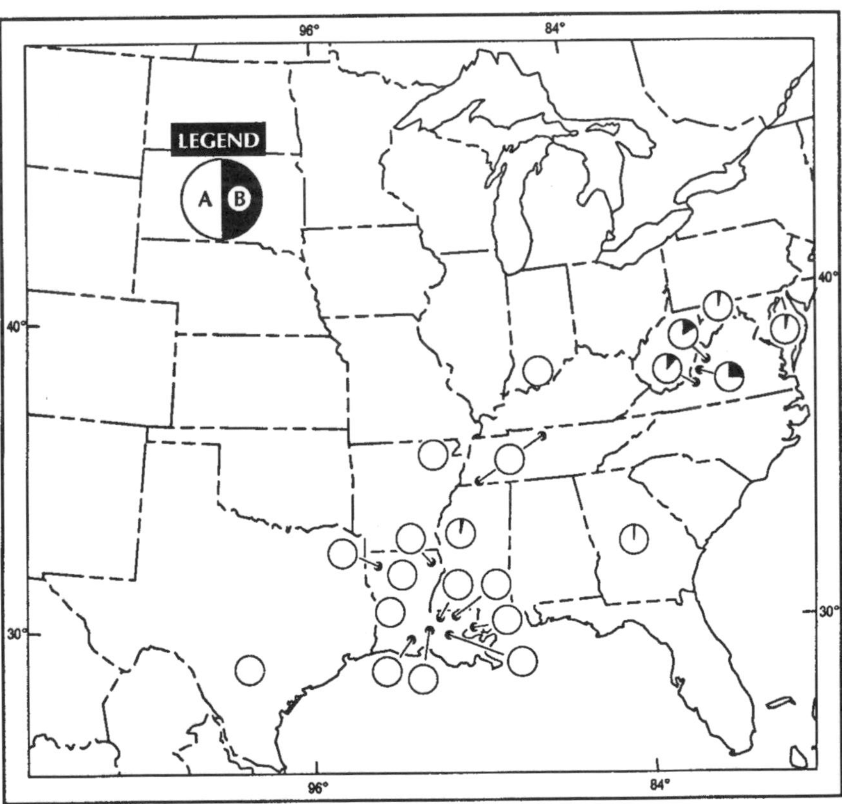

Fig. 3.—Distribution of allelic frequencies at MPI (a), and PGM-3 (b) in *Sciurus niger*.

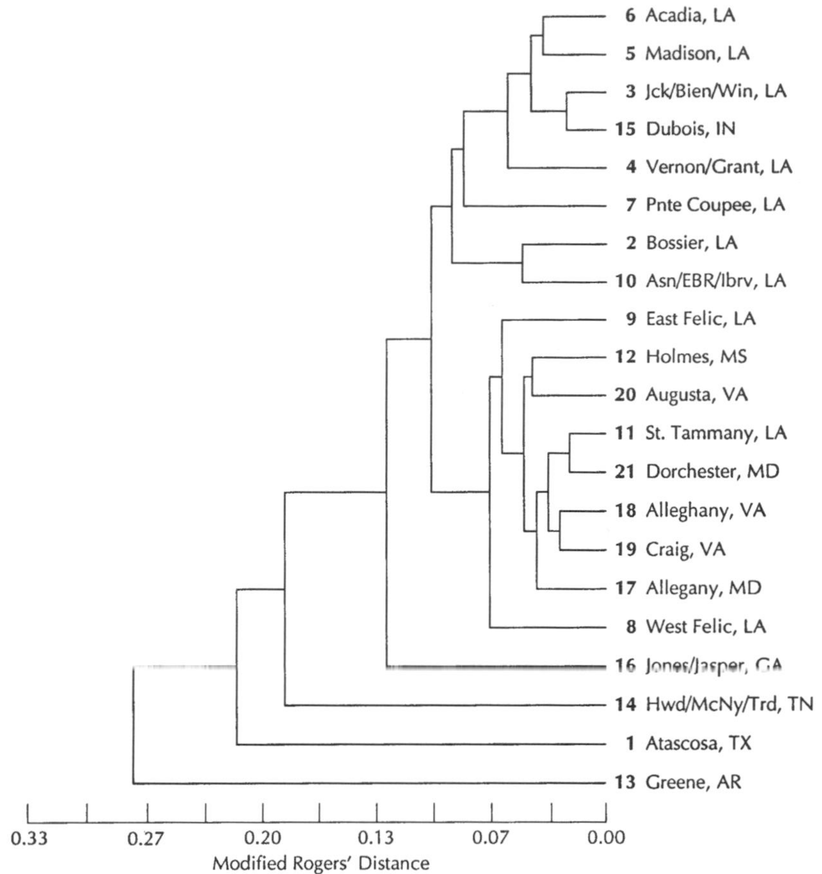

Fig. 4.—Phenogram based on UPGMA cluster analysis of modified Rogers' genetic distance (Wright, 1978) estimated among 21 samples of *Sciurus niger*. Goodness-of-fit statistics are as follows: $F = 2.972$ (Farris, 1972), $F = 11.554$ (Prager and Wilson, 1976), percent standard deviation = 19.809 (Fitch and Margoliash, 1967), and cophenetic correlation = 0.964. Sample localities are indicated in Fig. 1.

niger. Although PGM-2^B was reported in Moncrief (1993) as synapomorphic in *S. niger*, the findings of this study indicated that PGM-2^B was shared with gray squirrels, and was therefore symplesiomorphic. PGM-2^B in *S. niger* was equivalent to PGM-2^D in *S. carolinensis*, and its distribution was discounted in this study.

In fox squirrels, two loci exhibited east-west patterns in their geographic distributions of synapomorphic alleles. At the MPI locus (Fig. 3a), the B allele was present in all samples east of the Mississippi River; it was absent from all western samples, and the MPI^C allele was unique to the sample from Dorchester Co., Maryland (sample 21; Fig. 1). The PGM-3^B allele also occurred only east of the river (Fig. 3b), although it was not present in all eastern samples.

The phenogram resulting from UPGMA cluster analysis of modified Rogers' distance (Wright, 1978) estimates (Fig. 4) reflects a general east-west pattern of differentiation. Seventeen of the 21 samples of fox squirrels fell into two major groups: samples from western Louisiana (samples 2, 3, 4, 5, 6, 7) clustered with one sample from southeastern Louisiana (10) and the sample from Indiana (15); that group then (at the 0.097 level) joined the other eastern and southern samples (8, 9, 11, 12, 17, 18, 19, 20, and 21) included in this study (except the sample from Georgia, 16), which cluster together. The remaining four samples were not associated with either of these two major groupings, and they did not cluster with each other. Rather, each of the following joined the others as a distinct entity: sample 16 (Georgia) joined the two major groups at the 0.126 level, sample 14 (Tennessee) joined at the 0.185 level, sample 1 (Texas) joined at the 0.216 level, and sample 13 (Arkansas) joined at the 0.271 level.

Sciurus carolinensis.—In gray squirrels, 23 of 28 loci were monomorphic for the same allele across all five samples: ACP, AK-1, CK-2, FUM, GDA, GLUD, GOT-2, G6PD, IDH-1, IDH-2, LDH-1, LDH-2, MDH-1, MDH-2, ME, MPI, PEPB, PEPC, PEPD, PEPS, PGI, PGM-3, SDH. Five loci were

Table 2.—*Alphabetic designations for electromorphs, mean heterozygosity* ($\overline{H}$), *number of expected heterozygotes* (H_{exp}; *Nei, 1978), and percent polymorphism* (P) *at five polymorphic loci assayed across five samples of Sciurus carolinensis. Allelic frequencies for polymorphic loci are indicated in parentheses. Abbreviations for loci are provided in Appendix III. Sample localities are shown in Fig. 2.*

Sample Number	Sample locality	*n*	ACN-1	G3PD	NP	6PGD
11	Dubois and Orange counties, Indiana	13	A(0.85) B(0.15)	A	A	A(0.84) B(0.08) C(0.08)
12	Jones and Jasper counties, Georgia	40	A(0.90) B(0.10)	A(0.97) B(0.03)	A(0.99) B(0.01)	A(0.86) C(0.14)
13	Allegany Co., Maryland	11	A(0.95) C(0.05)	A	A	A(0.91) C(0.09)
14	Bath Co., Virginia	12	A(0.92) B(0.08)	A	A	A(0.79) B(0.13) C(0.08)
15	Henry Co., Virginia	18	A(0.97) B(0.03)	A(0.97) B(0.03)	A	A(0.81) B(0.08) C(0.11)

Table 2.—continued.

Sample number	Sample locality	*n*	PGM-2	$\overline{H}$	H_{exp}	*P*
11	Dubois and Orange counties, Indiana	13	A(0.88) B(0.12)	0.019	0.027	10.7
12	Jones and Jasper counties, Georgia	40	A(0.79) B(0.19) C(0.02)	0.026	0.030	10.7
13	Allegany Co., Maryland	11	A(0.65) B(0.35)	0.020	0.027	7.1
14	Bath Co., Virginia	12	A(0.79) B(0.13) C(0.04) D(0.04)	0.021	0.032	10.7
15	Henry Co., Virginia	18	A(0.83) B(0.17)	0.018	0.026	7.1

a

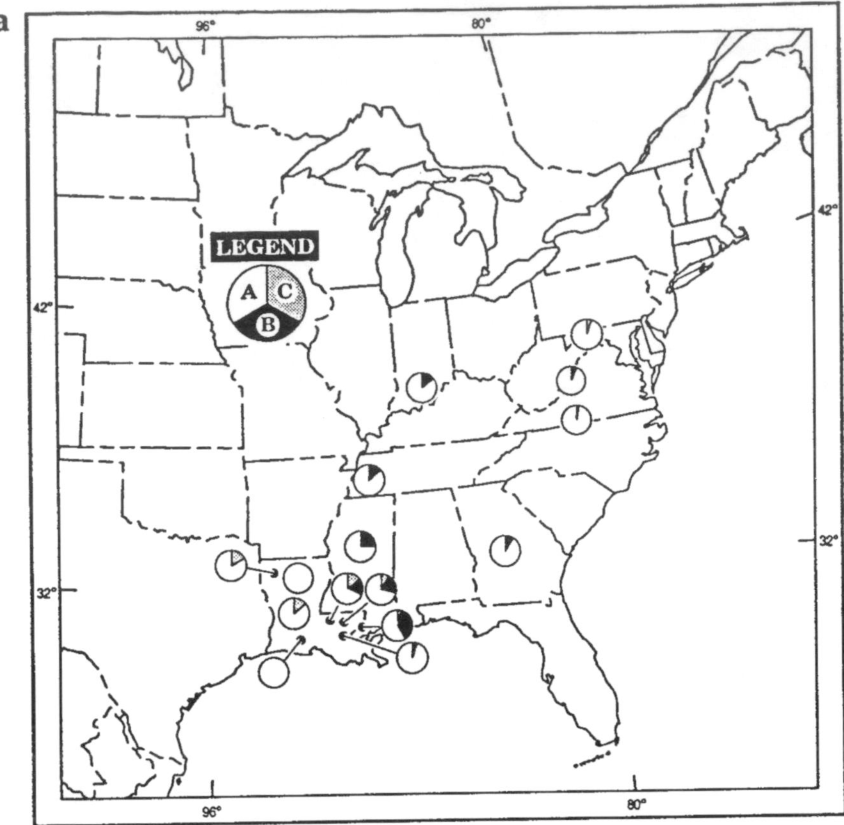

b

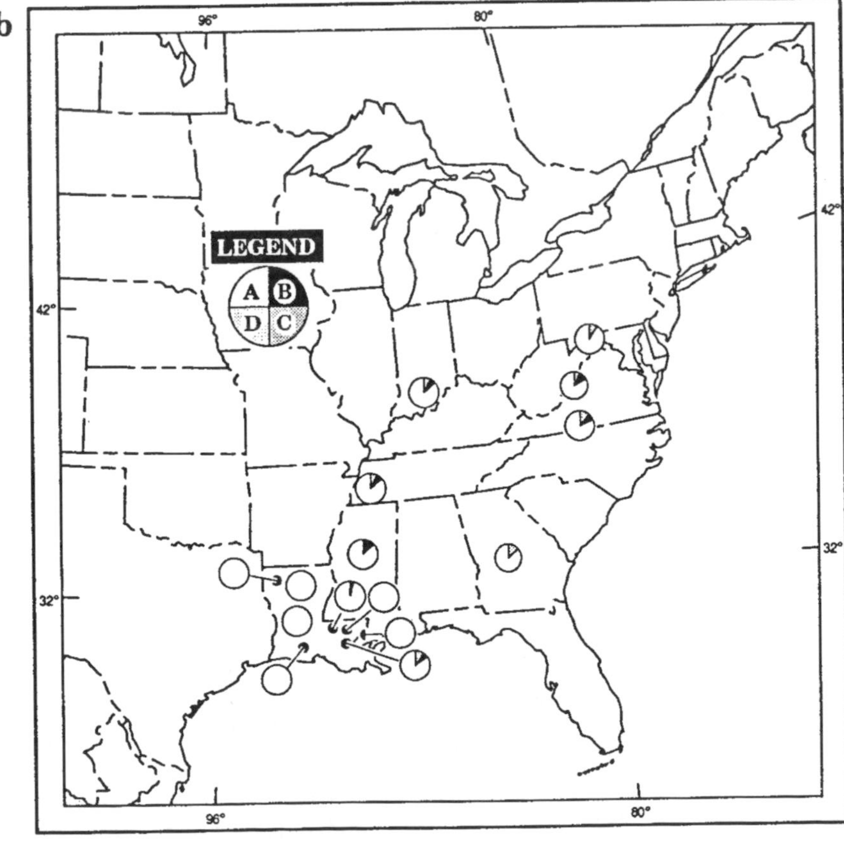

Fig. 5.—Distribution of allelic frequencies at ACN-1 (a), and 6PGD (b) in *Sciurus carolinensis*.

polymorphic in at least one sample: ACN-1, G3PD, NP, 6PGD, and PGM-2 (Table 2). Percent polymorphism was either 7.1 (Henry Co., Virginia, and Allegany Co., Maryland) or 10.7% (Dubois and Orange counties, Indiana; Jones and Jasper counties, Georgia; and Bath Co., Virginia). Average $\overline{H}$ calculated over all samples in this study was 2.1%; values ranged from 1.8 (Henry Co., Virginia) to 2.6% (Jones and Jasper counties, Georgia). There were no apparent geographically related patterns in levels of genic variation as measured by heterozygosity and polymorphism, and as for fox squirrels, the values for $\overline{H}$ and P in gray squirrels (Table 2) were comparable to values reported in Moncrief (1993) for 10 samples of gray squirrels from the lower Mississippi River valley.

Chi-square tests revealed no significant deviations from Hardy-Weinberg equilibrium for these five samples. As with *S. niger*, the agreement between observed and expected numbers of heterozygotes in *S. carolinensis* was consistent with the findings of many allozymic studies of sexually outbreeding organisms (Smith, et al., 1981).

To assess patterns of divergence among populations, a total of 201 specimens of *S. carolinensis* representing 15 populations (Fig. 2) were analyzed using single-locus techniques as well as cluster analyses. This total included samples from the lower Mississippi River valley reported in Moncrief (1993): 107 specimens of *S. carolinensis* representing 10 populations from Louisiana, Mississippi, and Tennessee (samples 1-10; Fig. 2).

As indicated earlier, eleven alleles were shared between fox squirrels and gray squirrels. The following alleles were identified as symplesiomorphs in *S. carolinensis* in the locus-by-locus cladistic analysis: ACN-1^{C}, G3PD^{A}, 6PGD^{A}, and PGM-2^{B}. These alleles were discounted in analyses of relationships among populations of gray squirrels.

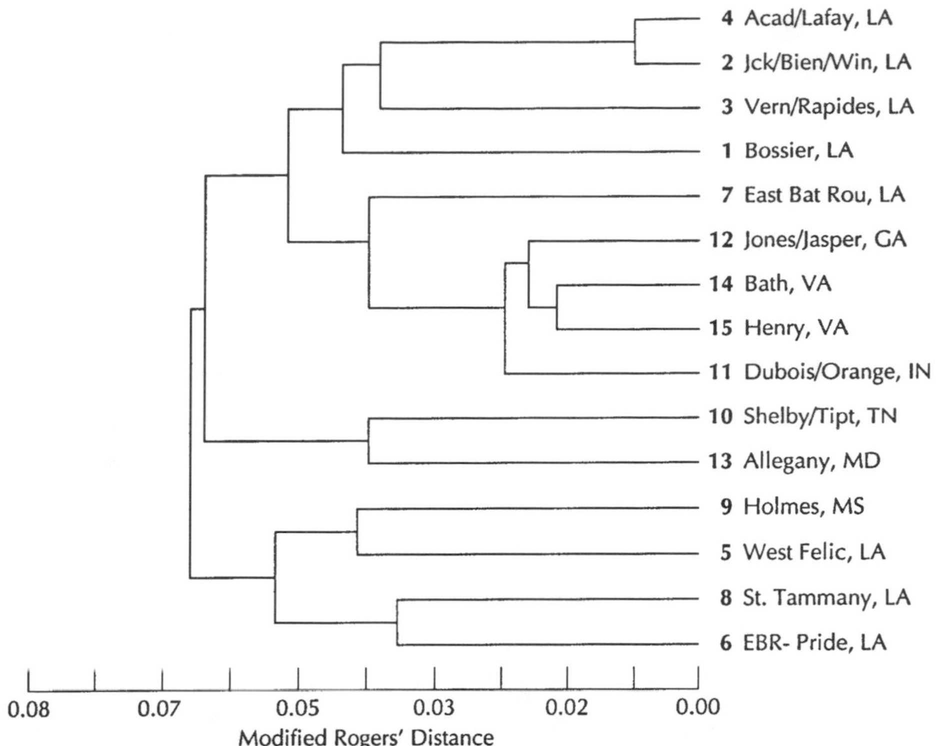

Fig. 6.—Phenogram based on UPGMA cluster analysis of modified Rogers' genetic distance (Wright, 1978) estimated among 15 samples of *Sciurus carolinensis*. Goodness-of-fit statistics are as follows: $F = 0.892$ (Farris, 1972), $F = 15.406$ (Prager and Wilson, 1976), percent standard deviation = 21.367 (Fitch and Margoliash, 1967), and cophenetic correlation = 0.729. Sample localities are indicated in Fig. 2.

In gray squirrels, three loci exhibited east-west patterns in their geographic distributions of synapomorphic alleles. The ACN-1^B allele (Fig. 5a) was absent from all western samples and was present in all samples east of the Mississippi River except Allegany Co., Maryland (sample 13; Fig. 2); the $6PGD^B$, $6PGD^C$ (Fig. 5b) alleles were present only in samples east of the river. In addition, the C allele at PGM-2 (not figured) was present only in eastern samples: Jones and Jasper counties, Georgia, and Bath Co., Virginia (samples 12 and 14; Table 2, Fig. 2), as well as West Feliciana Parish, Louisiana; Holmes Co., Mississippi; and Shelby and Tipton counties, Tennessee (Moncrief, 1993; samples 5, 9, and 10; Fig. 2).

The phenogram resulting from UPGMA cluster analysis of modified Rogers' distance (Wright, 1978) estimates (Fig. 6) depicts four major groups of samples of *S. carolinensis*. Samples from western Louisiana (1, 2, 3, and 4) clustered together and formed a grouping (at the 0.051 level) with a cluster comprised of samples from southeastern Louisiana (7), Indiana (11), Georgia (12), western Virginia (14), and south-central Virginia (15). Next, samples from Tennessee (10) and Maryland (13) formed a pairing and joined the other two groups at the 0.062 level. Finally, samples from central Mississippi and southeastern Louisiana (5, 6, 8, and 9) clustered together and joined the other 11 samples at the 0.063 level as the most distinct group.

DISCUSSION

The single-locus results reported here are consistent with Moncrief 's (1993) findings: both fox squirrels (Fig. 3) and gray squirrels (Fig. 5) exhibited general east-west patterns in allozymic characters that are approximately coincident with the Mississippi River. For example, the B allele at MPI was characteristic of eastern *S. niger* (Fig. 3a) and ACN-1^B was characteristic of eastern samples of *S. carolinensis* (Fig. 5a). Additionally, the PGM-3^B allele of *S. niger* (Fig. 3b) occurred only in eastern samples, and the B and/or C alleles at 6PGD were present in 9 of 11 eastern populations of *S. carolinensis* (Fig. 5b).

When all loci are considered simultaneously, the arrangement of fox squirrel samples (Fig. 4) was broadly consistent with east-west patterns reported in Moncrief (1993). Exceptions to the east-west division of fox squirrel samples included the sample from East Baton Rouge Parish, Louisiana (sample 10; Figs. 1 and 4), which clustered with samples from western Louisiana (2, 3, 4, 5, 6, and 7), as reported by Moncrief (1993). Similarly, the sample from Indiana (15), added to the dataset by this study, clustered with samples from western Louisiana. Both samples 10 and 15 represent populations that are east of the Mississippi River. Moncrief (1993) attributes the placement of sample 10 to fluctuation in the position of the Mississippi River channel. The placement of the Indiana sample (15), which according to subspecific designations should have grouped with samples from Arkansas (13) and Tennessee (14), can not be explained at present.

Most eastern samples of fox squirrels cluster together; samples from western Virginia (sample 20) and western Maryland (21) clustered with central Mississippi (12) and southeastern Louisiana (11), respectively. In contrast to Moncrief 's (1993) findings, samples from Tennessee (14) and Arkansas (13) no longer formed a distinct pairing (Fig. 4). The placement of samples from Georgia (16), Arkansas (13), Tennessee (14), and Texas (1) as outliers (Fig. 4) may indicate that these four samples represent other major groups of fox squirrels. Additional samples from the southeast, west, and midwest are necessary to resolve their relationships.

As in fox squirrels, the UPGMA analyses of gray squirrels (Fig. 6) generally agreed with results reported by Moncrief (1993) and revealed east-west patterns to some extent. All samples of *S. carolinensis* from western Louisiana (samples 1, 2, 3, and 4; Figs. 2 and 6) clustered together, as they did in Moncrief (1993). Most of the eastern samples added to the dataset by this study, Georgia (sample 12), western Virginia (14), south-central Virginia (15), and Indiana (11), clustered together. The exception was the sample from Maryland (13), which formed a pairing with the sample from Tennessee (10); the Tennessee sample did not pair with any other sample in Moncrief (1993). It is interesting to note (Fig. 6) that the Indiana sample (11) clustered with samples from the southeast (12, 14, 15) rather than those samples to which it is closer geographically (samples 10 and 13). Samples from central Mississippi (9) and southeastern Louisiana (5, 6, and 8) clustered together (Fig. 6), but not in the same pattern as in Moncrief (1993). Also in contrast to Moncrief 's (1993) findings, those four samples (5, 6, 8, and 9) are the most divergent grouping (Fig. 6). As in fox squirrels, the position of the sample of gray squirrels from East Baton Rouge Parish, Louisiana (7) is noteworthy. In this study, it clustered with the southeastern samples (12, 14, 15) and midwestern sample (11) rather than (as in Moncrief, 1993) with other samples from southeastern Louisiana (5, 6, 8) and central Mississippi (9). Additional samples of gray squirrels from the southeast, midwest, and west are necessary to further investigate those relationships.

As reported by Moncrief (1993), east-west patterns of divergence in allozymic characters were more profound in fox squirrels than in gray squirrels. Modified Rogers' (Wright, 1978) genetic distance values between populations of fox squirrels ranged from 0.019 (samples 3 versus 15) to 0.305 (samples 13 versus 15), whereas these values ranged from 0.008 (samples 2 versus 4) to 0.094 (samples 8 versus 13) in gray squirrels (data not shown). Cluster analyses of these genetic distance values revealed a more pronounced east-west dichotomy in *S. niger* (Fig. 4) than in *S. carolinensis* (Fig. 6).

For both species, allozymic patterns were consistent with hypotheses of fragmentation and isolation of past populations (Weigl et al., 1989). However, patterns in allozymic variation did not correspond to subspecific boundaries (Hall, 1981). In *S. niger*, the results were broadly consistent with patterns in size and coloration as defined by Weigl et al. (1989): there is a western form, represented in this study by 1, 2, 3, 4, 5, 6, 7, 10, 13, 14, and 15 (Fig. 1) and there is an eastern form, which included samples 8, 9, 11, 12, 16, 17, 18, 19, 20, and 21 (Fig. 1). Similar broadly defined groups have not been identified in *S. carolinensis*. However, the paucity of comprehensive morphological studies of either species precludes definitive comparisons between allozymic patterns and morphological patterns.

Allozymic analyses of samples of both *S. niger* and *S. carolinensis* from other regions (including the southeast, west, and midwest) are necessary to investigate the biogeographical history of these species more completely. Additional genetic information is especially needed for southeastern subspecies of fox squirrels (Loeb and Moncrief, 1993), several of which are threatened or endangered. Additional data will also allow comparisons with patterns documented in, and scenarios proposed for, other species that inhabit southeastern and eastern North America (Avise, 1992; Hayes and Harrison, 1992). Moreover, other biochemical techniques (e.g., mitochondrial DNA restriction site analysis) should reveal additional patterns of intraspecific genetic variation in gray squirrels and fox squirrels, allowing further investigation of "how intricacies of ecological and historical influence [have shaped] associations between geography, morphology, and genetics" (Lamb and Avise, 1992:267) in these species.

ACKNOWLEDGMENTS

I thank the following colleagues for helping me acquire specimens: J. Edwards, M. Fies, W. Giese, T. Mathews, and G. Therres, and I thank M. Hafner and R. Zink (Museum of Natural Science, Louisiana State University) for loaning me tissue samples of individuals used in Moncrief (1993). Specimens of *S. niger cinereus* were collected and are housed under Regional Blanket Permit number 697823 from the U.S. Fish and Wildlife Service. This study was supported in part by contract 50181-0-0811 from the U.S. Fish and Wildlife Service and contract 311208 from the Maryland Forest, Park, and Wildlife Service.

LITERATURE CITED

AVISE, J. C. 1992. Molecular population structure and the biogeographic history of a regional fauna–a case history with lessons for conservation biology. Oikos, 63:62-76.

BARNETT, R. J. 1977. Bergmann's rule and variation in structures related to feeding in the gray squirrel. Evolution, 31:538-545.

FARRIS, J. S. 1972. Estimating phylogenetic trees from distance matrices. The American Naturalist, 106:645-668.

FITCH, W. M., AND E. MARGOLIASH. 1967. Construction of phylogenetic trees. Science, 155:279-284.

HALL, E. R. 1981. The Mammals of North America. Second ed. John Wiley & Sons, New York, 1:1-600 + *90*.

HAVERA, S. P., AND C. M. NIXON. 1978. Geographic variation of Illinois gray squirrels. The American Midland Naturalist, 100:396-407.

HAYES, J. P., AND R. G. HARRISON. 1992. Variation in mitochondrial DNA and the biogeographic history of woodrats *(Neotoma)* of the eastern United States. Systematic Biology, 41:331-344.

HONEYCUTT, R. L., AND S. L. WILLIAMS. 1982. Genic differentiation in pocket gophers of the genus *Pappogeomys*, with comments on intergeneric relationships in the subfamily Geomyinae. Journal of Mammalogy, 63:208-217.

LAMB, T., AND J. C. AVISE. 1992. Molecular and population genetic aspects of mitochondrial DNA variability in the diamondback terrapin, *Malaclemys terrapin.* Journal of Heredity, 83:262-269.

LEVENE, H. 1949. On a matching problem arising in genetics. Annals of Mathematics and Statistics, 20:91-94.

LOEB, S. C., AND N. D. MONCRIEF. 1993. The biology of fox squirrels *(Sciurus niger)* in the southeast: a review. Pp. 1-19, *in* Proceedings of the second symposium on southeastern fox squirrels, *Sciurus niger* (N. D. Moncrief, J. W. Edwards, and P. A. Tappe, eds.). Special Publication, Virginia Museum of Natural History, 1:1-84.

MONCRIEF, N.D. 1993. Geographic variation in fox squirrels *(Sciurus niger)* and gray squirrels *(S. carolinensis)* of the lower Mississippi River valley. Journal of Mammalogy, 74:547-576.

MORITZ, C., AND D. M. HILLIS. 1990. Molecular systematics: context and controversies. Pp. 1-10, *in* Molecular Systematics (D.M. Hillis and C. Moritz, eds.). Sinauer Associates, Sunderland, Massachussets, 588 pp.

MURPHY, R. W., J. W. SITES, JR., D. G. BUTH, AND C. H. HAUFLER. 1990. Proteins I: isozyme electrophoresis. Pp. 45-126, *in* Molecular Systematics (D.M. Hillis and C. Moritz, eds.). Sinauer Associates, Sunderland, Massachussets, 588 pp.

NEI, M. 1978. Estimation of average heterozygosity and genetic distance from a small number of individuals. Genetics, 89:583-590.

PATTON, J. C., AND J. C. AVISE. 1983. An empirical evaluation of qualitative Hennigian analyses of protein electrophoretic data. Journal of Molecular Evolution, 19:244-254.

PRAGER, E. M., AND A. C. WILSON. 1976. Congruency of phylogenies derived from different proteins: a molecular analysis of the phylogenetic position of cracid birds. Journal of Molecular Evolution, 9:45-57.

RIDDLE, B., AND R. L. HONEYCUTT. 1990. Historical biogeography in North American arid regions: an approach using mitochondrial DNA phylogeny in grasshopper mice (genus *Onychomys*). Evolution, 44:1-15.

SMITH, M. W., C. F. AQUADRO, M. H. SMITH, R. K. CHESSER, AND W. J. ETGES. 1981. A bibliography of electrophoretic studies of biochemical variation in natural populations of vertebrates. Institute of Ecology, University of Georgia, Athens, 158 pp.

SNEATH, P. H. A., AND R. R. SOKAL. 1973. Numerical taxonomy: the principles and practice of numerical classification. W. H. Freeman and Company, San Francisco, California, 573 pp.

SWOFFORD, D. L., AND R. B. SELANDER. 1981. BIOSYS-1: a FORTRAN program for the comprehensive analysis of electrophoretic data in population genetics and systematics. Journal of Heredity, 72:281-283.

TURNER, D. A., AND J. LAERM. 1993. Systematic relationships of populations of the fox squirrel (*Sciurus niger*) in the southeastern United States. Pp. 21-36, *in* Proceedings of the second symposium on southeastern fox squirrels, *Sciurus niger* (N. D. Moncrief, J. W. Edwards, and P. A. Tappe, eds.). Special Publication, Virginia Museum of Natural History, 1:1-84.

WEIGL, P. D., M. A. STEELE, L. J. SHERMAN, J. C. HA, AND T. S. SHARPE. 1989. The ecology of the fox squirrel (*Sciurus niger*) in North Carolina: implications for survival in the southeast. Bulletin of Tall Timbers Research Stations, 24:1-93.

WRIGHT, S. 1978. Evolution and the genetics of natural populations, volume 4. Variability within and among natural populations. The University of Chicago Press, Chicago, 580 pp.

APPENDIX I

Individuals from Moncrief (1993)

Field numbers of individuals from Moncrief (1993) included in this study. Vouchers are deposited in the Museum of Natural Science, Louisiana State University, Baton Rouge, Louisiana. Abbreviations in parentheses following a series of numbers indicate sample designations used in Moncrief (1993); numerals in parentheses indicate sample numbers in this study.

Sciurus carolinensis.—LOUISIANA: NDM 955 (CB, 1); NDM 1123, NDM 1124, NDM 1125, NDM 1126 (CJ, 2); NDM 1111, NDM 1108, NDM 1110, JCF 6 (CV, 3); NDM 1058, NDM 1059 (CA, 4); NDM 819, NDM 823 (CW, 5); NDM 721, NDM 834, NDM 839, NDM 912, NDM 1128, NDM 1288 (CE, 7); NDM 880, NDM 993 (CS, 8). MISSISSIPPI: NDM 1075, NDM 1078, NDM 1081, NDM 1085, NDM 1086, NDM 1087, NDM 1089, NDM 1092, NDM 1093, NDM 1095 (CH, 9). TENNESSEE: NDM 831, NDM 833, MJH 127, RVDB 153, CDS 2, CMR 3, PLL 246 (CTS, 10).

Sciurus niger.—LOUISIANA: NDM 953 (NB, 2); MJK 2 (NV, 4); NDM 1005 (NE, 10). MISSISSIPPI: NDM 1082, NDM 1083, NDM 1097, NDM 1102 (NH, 12). TEXAS: NDM 1286 (NX, 1).

APPENDIX II

Specimens Examined

Numerals following each locality indicate the number of specimens examined. Vouchers of all individuals are housed in the Department of Mammals, Virginia Museum of Natural History.

Sciurus carolinensis.—GEORGIA. *Jasper Co.*: 10 km W Round Oak, Piedmont National Wildlife Refuge, Compartment 2 (5); 10 km W Round Oak, Piedmont National Wildlife Refuge, Compartment 8 (1). *Jones Co.*: 10 km W Round Oak, Piedmont National Wildlife Refuge, Compartment 2 (8); 10 km W Round Oak, Piedmont National Wildlife Refuge, Compartment 3 (2); 10 km W Round Oak, Piedmont National Wildlife Refuge, Compartment 4 (9); 10 km W Round Oak, Piedmont National Wildlife Refuge, Compartment 6 (3); 10 km W Round Oak, Piedmont National Wildlife Refuge, Compartment 7 (2); 10 km W Round Oak, Piedmont National Wildlife Refuge, Compartment 8 (2); 10 km W Round Oak, Piedmont National Wildlife Refuge, Compartment 9 (1); 10 km W Round Oak, Piedmont National Wildlife Refuge, Compartment 10 (1); 10 km W Round Oak, Piedmont National Wildlife Refuge, Compartment 16 (3); 10 km W Round Oak, Piedmont National Wildlife Refuge, Compartment 29 (3). INDIANA. *Dubois Co.*: 0.5 km S, 2.5 km E Cuzco, Southern Indiana Purdue Agricultural Center (11); 2.5 km S, 3 km E Cuzco, Southern Indiana Purdue Agricultural Center (2). *Orange Co.*: 11.5 km S, 3.5 km W French Lick (1); 13.2 km S, 5.5 km W French Lick (1). MARYLAND. *Allegany Co.*: Flintstone (1); Oldtown, along Potomac River, above toll bridge (3); Sideling Hill, Sideling Hill Wildlife Management Area (2); Between Spring Gap and Oldtown, along Potomac River (5). VIRGINIA. *Bath Co.*: 2 miles N, 0.25 mile W West Warm Springs, 2 miles E junction VA 39 and VA 621, Cobbler Mountain (12). *Henry Co.*: 0.5 mile N, 0.5 mile W Chatmoss (1); Collinsville, junction Circle Drive and Colonial Drive (1); Jefferson Circle near Hundley Street (1); 1.75 miles N, 0.75 mile E Martinsville, VA 663, 0.5 mile N city limits (1); Martinsville, junction Commonwealth Blvd. and Chatham Rd. (1); Martinsville, junction Commonwealth Blvd. and Fairy St. (1); Martinsville, junction Pine St. and Watts St. (1); Martinsville, junction Thomas Heights and Monroe St. (1); Martinsville, junction Hairston St. and Oakdale St. (1); 0.25 mile S, 5.5 miles W Ridgeway, ca. 0.5 mile SW junction VA 692 and VA 629 (1); Martinsville, Church St. Extended near J. Frank Wilson Park (3); Martinsville, junction Orchard St. and Mulberry Rd. (1); Martinsville, junction Spruce St., Jefferson St., and Mulberry Rd. (1); Martinsville, junction Indian Trail and Spruce St. (1); Martinsville, junction Fairy St. and Commonwealth Blvd. (1); Martinsville, junction Church St. Extended and Bondurant (1).

Sciurus niger.—GEORGIA. *Jasper Co.*: 10 km W Round Oak, Piedmont National Wildlife Refuge, Compartment 2 (2); 10 km W Round Oak, Piedmont National Wildlife Refuge, Compartment 3 (2); 10 km W Round Oak, Piedmont National Wildlife Refuge, Compartment 6 (3); 10 km W Round Oak, Piedmont National Wildlife Refuge, Compartment 7 (4); 10 km W Round Oak, Piedmont National Wildlife Refuge, Compartment 8 (2). *Jones Co.*: 10 km W Round Oak, Piedmont National Wildlife Refuge, Compartment 2 (4); 10 km W Round Oak, Piedmont National Wildlife Refuge, Compartment 3 (5); 10 km W Round Oak, Piedmont National Wildlife Refuge, Compartment 4 (4); 10 km W Round Oak, Piedmont National Wildlife Refuge, Compartment 6 (3); 10 km W Round Oak, Piedmont National Wildlife Refuge, Compartment 8 (3); 10 km W Round Oak, Piedmont National Wildlife Refuge, Compartment 15 (1); 10 km W Round Oak, Piedmont National Wildlife Refuge, Compartment 16 (3); 10 km W Round Oak, Piedmont National Wildlife Refuge, Compartment 25 (1); 10 km W Round Oak, Piedmont National Wildlife Refuge, Compartment 26 (1); 10 km W Round Oak, Piedmont National Wildlife Refuge, Compartment 30 (2). INDIANA. *Dubois Co.*: 0.5 km S, 2.5 km E Cuzco, Southern Indiana Purdue Agricultural Center (10); 2.5 km S, 3 km E Cuzco, Southern Indiana Purdue Agricultural Center (8). MARYLAND. *Allegany Co.*: Oldtown, along Potomac River, above toll bridge (1); Sideling Hill, Sideling Hill Wildlife Management Area (3); Along Potomac River between Spring Gap and Oldtown (15). *Dorchester Co.*: no specific locality (5); Bucktown, Green Briar Road, near Bucktown Store (1); 4 miles S Cambridge, Stone Boundary Road near Schnoor Road (1); ca. 6.5 miles SSW Cambridge, junction Egypt Road and Old Field Road (1); ca. 6.5 miles SSW Cambridge, Egypt Road, 2.6 miles N junction Egypt Road and Key Wallace Drive (2); ca. 9 miles SSW Cambridge, Blackwater National Wildlife Refuge (6); ca. 9 miles SSW Cambridge, Blackwater National Wildlife Refuge, Egypt Road (1); ca. 9 miles SSW Cambridge, Blackwater National Wildlife Refuge, Wildlife Drive (1); ca. 9 miles SSW Cambridge, Blackwater National Wildlife Refuge, Key Wallace Drive (5); ca. 9 miles SSW Cambridge, Blackwater National Wildlife Refuge, S end Egypt Road (1); ca. 9 miles SSW Cambridge, Blackwater National Wildlife Refuge, Visitor Center (1); Between Cambridge and Seward, Maple Dam Road (1); Between Seward and Bucktown, Greenbriar Road (1); 5 miles SW Vienna, Lecompte Wildlife Management Area, Steele Neck Road (1); ca. 3.5 miles SW Vienna, Lecompte Wildlife Management Area, Steele Neck Road (1); ca. 3.5 miles SW Vienna, Lecompte Wildlife Management Area (5). VIRGINIA. *Alleghany Co.*: ca. 0.2 mile SW Callaghan, on VA 600, 0.25 mile W junction VA 600 and VA 159 (1); Callaghan, junction VA 600 and VA 661, confluence of Johnson's and Ogle Creek (1); 3 miles S Covington on VA 18 (1); ca. 2 miles W Covington, on I-64, mile marker 13 (1); ca. 1.125 miles S, 1.1 miles W Falling Spring, near junction VA 666 and VA 641 (1); ca. 0.5 mile SE Nicelytown, 1 mile NNE junction US 60 W and VA 635 N (1). *Augusta Co.*: 1 mile N Centerville on VA 699 (1); 5 miles N Churchville, on VA 42 (2); 5 miles N Craigsville, on VA 42 (1); ca. 5.1 miles S, 1.3 miles W Staunton, on VA 252 between Staunton and Middlebrook (1); 1 mile N Weyers Cave, on US 11 (1). *Craig Co.*: Abbott (1); ca. 1.3 miles S, 1.1 miles W Huffman, 1 mile N Craig Co./Giles Co. line on VA 42 (1); ca. 1.3 miles S, 1.1 miles W Huffman on VA 42 (1); 0.7 mile N, 0.75 mile E New Castle, 5 miles S Alleghany/Craig Co. line (1); 10 miles NE New Castle, near Mill Creek (Fenwick Mines) (3); ca. 7 miles N, 1.75 miles E New Castle, 5 miles S Alleghany/Craig Co. line on VA 617 (1).

APPENDIX III

Buffer Systems and Enzymes

Buffer systems and enzymes used to analyze *Sciurus carolinensis* were as follows: tris-citrate, pH 8.0 (TC8) for peptidase B (leucyl-glycyl-glycine used as substrate; PEPB, Enzyme Commission Number 3.4.11), peptidase C (leucyl-alanine used as substrate; PEPC, 3.4.11), peptidase D (phenylalanyl-proline used as substrate; PEPD, 3.4.13.9), peptidase S (valyl-leucine, leucyl-alanine, or leucyl-glycyl-glycine used as substrate; PEPS, 3.4.11), and phosphoglucose isomerase (PGI, 5.3.1.9); tris-citrate, pH 7.0 (TC7) for acid phosphatase (ACP, 3.1.3.2), adenylate kinase (AK, 2.7.4.3), creatine kinase (CK-2, 2.7.3.2), glutamate dehydrogenase (GLUD, 1.4.1.-), nucleoside phosphorylase (NP, 2.4.2.1), phosphoglucomutase (PGM-2,-3, 2.7.5.1), and sorbitol dehydrogenase (SDH, 1.1.1.14); TC7 and TC8 for aconitase (ACN-1, 4.2.1.3), guanine deaminase (GDA, 3.5.4.3), glutamate oxaloacetate transaminase (GOT-2, 2.6.1.1), glucose-6-phosphate dehydrogenase (G6PD, 1.1.1.49), lactate dehydrogenase (LDH-1, -2, 1.1.1.27), malate dehydrogenase (MDH-1,-2, 1.1.1.37), malic enzyme (ME, 1.1.1.40), mannose phosphate isomerase (MPI, 5.3.1.8), and 6-phosphogluconate dehydrogenase (6PGD, 1.1.1.44); TC8 and tris-maleic EDTA (TM) for fumarase (FUM, 4.2.1.2); TC7, TC8, and TM for glycerol-3-phosphate dehydrogenase (G3PD,

1.1.1.8), and isocitrate dehydrogenase (IDH-1,-2, 1.1.1.42). Buffer systems and enzymes used to analyze *S. niger* were as follows: tris-citrate, pH 8.0 (TC8) for aconitase (ACN-1, Enzyme Commission Number 4.2.1.3), peptidase A (valyl-leucine used as substrate; PEPA, 3.4.11), peptidase B (leucyl-glycyl-glycine used as substrate; PEPB, 3.4.11), peptidase C (leucyl-alanine used as substrate; PEPC, 3.4.11), peptidase D (phenylalanyl-proline used as substrate; PEPD, 3.4.13.9), peptidase S (valyl-leucine, leucyl-alanine, or leucyl-glycyl-glycine used as substrate; PEPS, 3.4.11); tris-citrate pH 7.0 (TC7) for guanine deaminase (GDA, 3.5.4.3), glutamate dehydrogenase (GLUD, 1.4.1.-), lactate dehydrogenase (LDH-1,-2, 1.1.1.27), mannose phosphate isomerase (MPI, 5.3.1.8), nucleoside phosphorylase (NP, 2.4.2.1), octanol dehydrogenase (ODH, 1.1.1.73), phosphoglucomutase (PGM-2,-3, 2.7.5.1); TC7 and TC8 for acid phosphatase (ACP, 3.1.3.2), alcohol dehydrogenase (ADH, 1.1.1.1), glutamate oxaloacetate transaminase (GOT-1,-2, 2.6.1.1), glycerol-3-phosphate dehydrogenase (G3PD, 1.1.1.8), glucose-6-phosphate dehydrogenase (G6PD, 1.1.1.49), isocitrate dehydrogenase (IDH-1,-2, 1.1.1.42), malate dehydrogenase (MDH-1,-2, 1.1.1.37), 6-phosphogluconate dehydrogenase (6PGD, 1.1.1.44), sorbitol dehydrogenase (SDH, 1.1.1.14); TC7 and Poulik (Poul) for fumarase (FUM, 4.2.1.2), and superoxide dismutase (SOD-1,-2, 1.15.1.1); TC8 and Poul for phosphoglucose isomerase (PGI, 5.3.1.9); TC7, TC8, and Poul for adenylate kinase (AK, 2.7.4.3), creatine kinase (CK-2, 2.7.3.2), malic enzyme (ME, 1.1.1.40). Gels made with TC8, TC7, and TM buffers were subjected to 80 milliamperes of current for 4.5 hours; Poul gels were subjected to 150 volts for 6 hours. To enhance resolution, NADP was added to the gel when staining for G6PD, 6PGD, and PGM.

INTERSPECIFIC CORRELATES OF COAT PATTERNS OF SQUIRRELS: ECOLOGY, TAXONOMY, AND BODY SIZE

RICHARD A. KILTIE AND RONALD EDWARDS
Department of Zoology, University of Florida, Gainesville, FL 32611

ABSTRACT.— Squirrels show considerable interspecific variation in coat-pattern features. We used a comparative approach to explore potential causes of this variation. From a worldwide sample of published species depictions, we recorded nominal data describing patterns around the eyes, other facial patterns, dorsal postcranial patterns, presence of agouti or nonagouti pelage, contrast of propodial and epipodial coloration, proximal and distal tail patterns, and presence of white patches on or behind the ears. Predictor variables were nominal (taxonomic genus, activity period, locomotory mode), ordinal (habitat structure, social group size), and interval (head-and-body length, tail length). After transforming the interval variables to categorical ones, multiple correspondence analysis suggested that body size was an important correlate of some coat-pattern features, but that relationships between patterns and predictors otherwise could not be reduced to a few dimensions. Alternatively, we transformed the nominal and ordinal predictors to quantitative ones. Canonical discriminant analyses were then performed for each coat-pattern feature. All analyses except that for proximal tail patterns produced at least one strong discriminant axis. Axes related to size were identifiable for the majority of the pattern variables. These size axes may reflect developmental or functional (camouflage) influences on the expression of coat patterns. Genus, activity period, and locomotory mode jointly contributed to size-independent axes of discrimination for patterns around eyes and for tail-tip patterns; the association with taxonomic membership suggests phylogenetic determinants of these traits. Social group size and habitat structure contributed to discriminant axes for ear patches and for eye-surround patterns; because these associations were independent of size and taxonomy, purely adaptive determinants of those features were implicated.

"The ever-varying squirrels seem sent by Satan himself to puzzle the Naturalists." Rev. J. Bachman, letter to J. J. Audubon, 1839 (quoted in Kingdon, 1974:375.)

INTRODUCTION

As Audubon's coauthor on "The Quadrupeds of North America," Rev. Bachman was probably dead serious in expressing his bedevilment by squirrels, and especially by their coat-color variation and variegation. Bachman undoubtedly shared Linnaeus' goal of understanding God's creation by cataloguing the species in it. As God's adversary who tempts men from their righteous duties, Satan may well have conspired to confuse and frustrate the Reverend, perhaps even to make him doubt whether his labors were worth the trouble. Still, one wonders why the Devil would have chosen squirrels. Since the Devil must be rather busy, one also wonders how much time and effort he could have afforded to spend on these animals just for the sake of puzzling a few naturalists.

For the study described here, our hope was that statistical methods not available in Bachman's time might expose some order underlying interspecific variation in the coat patterning of squirrels. The signs of such order that we sought were interspecific associations between coat-pattern features and other traits of squirrels. Such associations could in turn lead to testable hypotheses of the features' functions. Hence our study was undertaken in the spirit of "exploratory

In M.A. Steele, J. F. Merritt, and D. A. Zegers (eds.). 1998. Ecology and Evolutionary Biology of Tree Squirrels. Special Publication, Virginia Museum of Natural History, 6: 320 pp

data analysis," which puts more emphasis on finding suggestive relationships in data sets than on testing a priori hypotheses. More widespread use of this approach as a preliminary step has been advocated by a number of biostatisticians (e.g., Tukey, 1977, Sokal and Rohlf, 1981, James and McCulloch, 1985).

METHODS

Data Sources

We extracted data on sciurids from Brink (1968), Dorst and Dandelot (1969), Kingdon (1974), Burt and Grossenheider (1976), Askins (1977), Emmons and Feer (1990), and Nowak (1991). For the coat-pattern features, we depended primarily on photographs or paintings; supplemental information on the coat patterns was gathered from text accompanying the illustrations, as were data for the potential predictor variables that we investigated.

The coat-pattern features that we treated are as follows:

Eye: The area directly surrounding the eye was categorized as plain (like the back), striped, black ring, or white ring.

Face: The rest of the face beyond the eye surround was categorized as plain (like the back), blotched, or striped.

Back: The back of the squirrel from the ears to the base of the tail was categorized as plain, blotched, longitudinal dorsal stripes, or lateral stripes.

Agouti: The back of the squirrel from the ears to the base of the tail was categorized as either having substantial nonagouti or all agouti coloration.

Tail: The proximal three quarters of the tail was categorized as plain (like the back), blotched, darker than back, paler than back, or having transverse stripes (rings).

Tail tip: The distal one quarter of the tail was categorized as plain (like the back), darker than the back, or paler than the back.

Propodium: The coat of the proximal portion of the limbs (upper arm or thigh) was categorized as plain (like the back), darker than the back, or paler than the back. (The latter two categories were used if either the front or rear propodia differed from the back.)

Epipodium: The coat of the distal element of the limbs (forearm or leg) was categorized as plain (like the back), darker than the back, or paler than the back. The latter two categories were used if either the front or rear epipodia differed from the back.

Ear patch: The presence or absence of a white mark on or just behind the ears was noted.

We investigated relationships between the coat-pattern variables and the following potential predictors for each species.

Social group size: The species' social habits were classified as solitary, gregarious (i.e., sometimes in aggregations), or colonial. This was an ordinal variable.

Activity period: The typical period of activity was classified as diurnal or nocturnal.

Locomotion: The locomotory mode was classified as arboreal, terrestrial, scansorial (both on the ground and in vegetation), or gliding.

Habitat: The vegetative habitat occupied was classified as open, mixed (intermediate), or closed (forested). This was an ordinal variable.

Head-and-body length (mm): Midpoints were recorded if ranges were given.

Tail length (mm): Midpoints were recorded if ranges were given.

If the author(s) of a source considered intraspecific polymorphism to be significant enough to warrant separate illustrations of the morphs, we treated them as separate "morphospecies." Because Anomaluridae are so similar to flying squirrels, we also included data for them in our data set; exclusion of the anomalurids did not change the qualitative results. Generic assignments followed Wilson and Reeder (1993) and tribal assignments of the Sciurinae followed Moore (1959). The final data set included 172 members of the following tribes (numbers of morphospecies in parentheses): Sciuridae: Callosciurini (44), Funambulini (14), Marmotini (28), Petauristinae (=Pteromyinae, treated as one tribe, 27), Protoxerini (5), Ratufini (4), Sciurini (33), Tamiasciurini (3); Anomaluridae: Anomalurini (6), Xerini (6), Zenkerellini (2). The complete data set can be viewed or downloaded with an internet browser (e.g., Mosaic or Netscape) at http://grove.ufl.edu/~kiltie.

Analyses

Much recent interest in comparative biology has focused on methods to discriminate between adaptive variation among species and effects of shared ancestry ("phylogenetic effects"). These methods require well-documented phylogenies so that independence of sampling units and significance levels can be assessed properly (Harvey and Pagel, 1991). We could not use such methods because no consensus phylogeny exists for squirrel species, and because an excessive number of unresolved branches would have resulted from transforming the available taxonomy into an operational phylogeny. Because our goal was more to develop explanations than to test them formally, the issue of statistical independence of sampling units was not of paramount importance to our study. This exploratory approach lent itself to two multivariate methods representing alternative families of analysis (Gower, 1990): multiple correspondence analysis and canonical discriminant analysis following optimal scoring of nominal variables; the latter can be viewed as a special case of canonical correlation analysis (Gower, 1990).

Multiple correspondence analysis.—The goal of multiple correspondence analysis is to identify associations among sets of categorical variables in a small number of dimensions. It attempts to do so by performing a weighted principal component analysis of a multi-way contingency table and generating scores on each dimension for each state of each variable. Plots of the scores are then examined to identify subjectively the relationships among the categories.

To include head-and-body length and tail length in the correspondence analysis, we had to convert them into categorical variables. We assigned species with head-and-body length (HBL) < 200 mm to the "small" HBL class, those with 200 mm $\leq$ HBL < 299 mm to "medium" HBL, and those with HBL > 299 mm to "large" HBL. The same dimensions were used to recode tail length as small, medium, and large. Taxonomic membership was not included in this analysis because to do so would have made the contingency table too large and sparsely occupied. This analysis was performed using the SAS procedure CORRESP with the MCA option (SAS Institute, Inc., 1989*a*).

Analyses involving optimal scoring of categorical variables.—Our second approach required transforming the categorical predictor variables to quantitative ones. This was accomplished through the SAS procedure PRINQUAL ("principal components of qualitative data," SAS Institute, Inc., 1989b). Nominal variables were transformed by scoring the categories to optimize the covariance matrix (Fisher, 1938; Gower, 1990). Ordinal variables were similarly transformed while preserving their order (Kruskal, 1964).

Head-and-body length and tail length were log-transformed. The PRINQUAL procedure searches for nonlinear transformations of the original nominal variables so as to maximize the variance of a predetermined number of principal components of the covariance matrix. We used transformations optimized over the first three principal components because optimizing over fewer components accounted for less total variance and optimizing over more did not appreciably change the scores.

After the coat-pattern variables were transformed to quantitative ones, we performed nested analysis of variance (NESTED procedure, SAS Institute Inc. SAS, 1989*b*) to investigate what portions of the variances of these variables were attributable to species, genus, and tribe (Harvey and Pagel, 1991). The taxonomic levels were thus treated as random, rather than fixed, variables (Sokal and Rohlf, 1981).

After rescoring the predictor variables, canonical discriminant analysis (CANDISC procedure, SAS Institute Inc., 1989*a*) was applied to investigate the ability of linear combinations of the predictor variables to discriminate among the states of each of the coat-pattern variables. In turn, the relations between a color-pattern variable and predictor variables with high loadings on axes of discrimination for that variable were investigated by contingency table analysis (FREQ procedure, SAS Institute Inc., 1988) if the predictor was categorical or by analysis of variance (GLM procedure, SAS Institute Inc., 1989*b*) for the continuous variables. Our criterion for interpreting dominant contributors to the discriminant axes, and for judging whether the axes represented meaningful variation, was a minimum loading (correlation) of 0.7, which corresponds to a coefficient of determination of about 50%. This criterion generally corresponded to $P \leq 0.05$ for the Wilks lambda statistics generated by the canonical discrimination program. However, such p-values could not be taken literally because discriminant analysis assumes normal distributions among the predictors, which was not true for all of ours, and because we could not assume that all the observations (species) in the analysis were independent observations.

RESULTS

Multiple Correspondence Analysis

The multiple correspondence analysis produced 31 dimensions in total, of which 19 were needed to summarize 90% of the data. The first and second dimensions respectively represented just 15% and 11% of the variance. Plots of these first two axes indicated that small body size and scansorial or terrestrial locomotion were associated with striped patterns on the face and back, medium size and arboreal habits with blotched patterns and paler contrasting extremities, and large size and gliding habits with black eye rings and darker contrasting appendages (Fig. 1). These three associations seemed basically to correspond to chipmunks, tree squirrels and large flying squirrels, but again this result represented a small percentage of the total variation, and subsequent dimensions produced even weaker relationships.

The strongest results of this analysis were the suggestions that: 1) size is an important correlate of some pattern features, but that 2) the

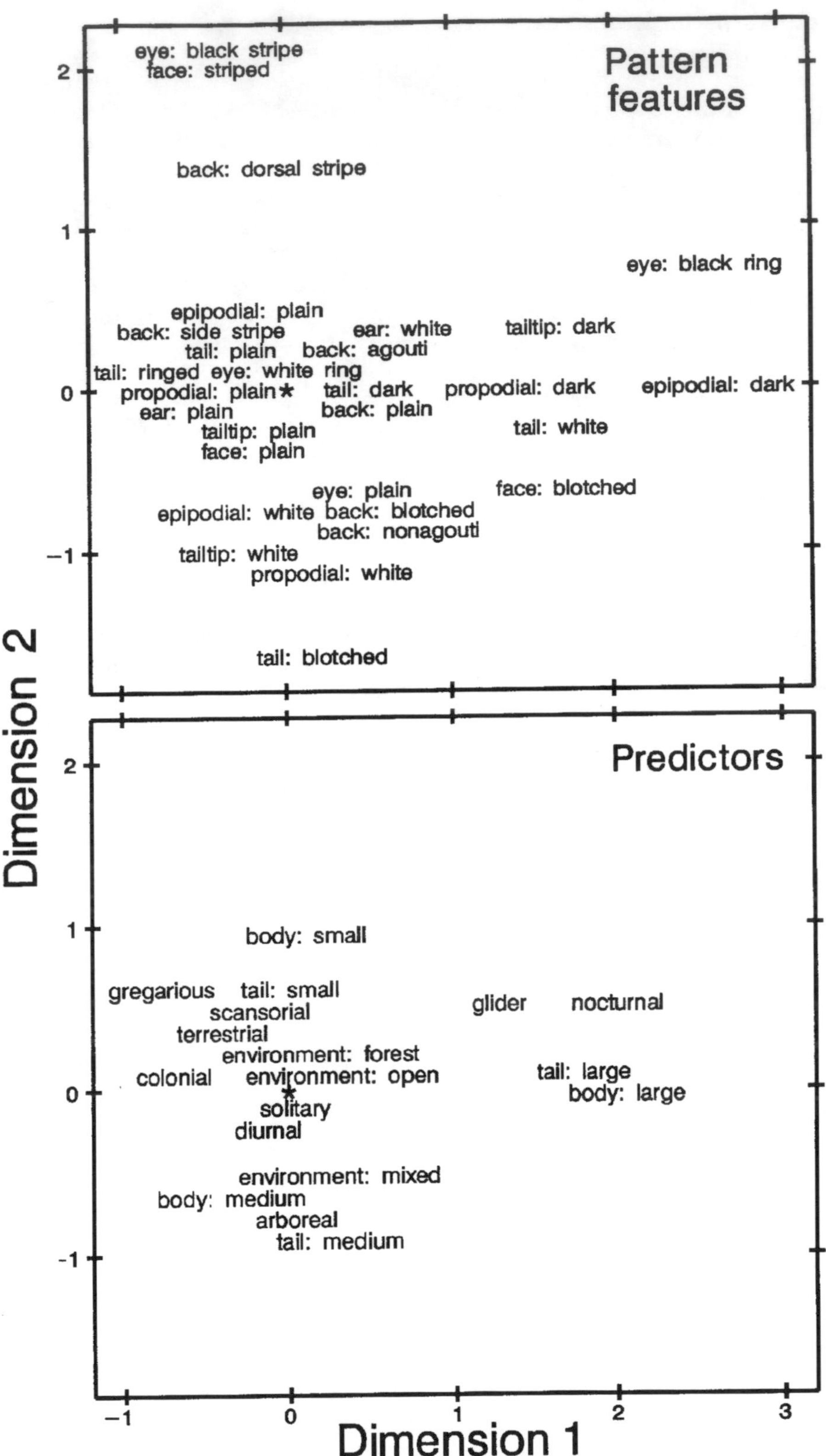

Fig. 1.—Scores of pattern features and predictors on the first two dimensions (15% and 11% of total variance, respectively) from a multiple correspondence analysis. Distance and direction from the origin (*) indicate strength and direction of contributions to the dimensions. Entries with scores between ±0.5 on both dimensions actually clustered more tightly around the origin than shown, but were spread somewhat to improve readability. Features and predictors are plotted separately only to aid readability.

relationship between coat patterns and predictors otherwise cannot be reduced to just a few dimensions.

Optimal Scoring, Nested ANOVA and Canonical Discriminant Analysis

Principal component analysis (after rescoring via the PRINQUAL procedure) indicated that the data could be summarized more concisely than was the case by multiple correspondence. The first six principal component axes of the coat-pattern variables represented 92% of the variance, and the first two axes more than 50% (Table 1). The first axis reflected high correlations among facial pattern, eye pattern and back pattern. The second, independent axis was primarily a function of propodial and epipodial contrast. The subsequent four axes of color-pattern variation represented smaller portions of the total variance and were loaded by agouti pelage, ear patches, proximal tail patterns, and tail-tip patterns, respectively.

The principal component analysis of the rescored predictors revealed three independent axes: One for genus, activity period, and locomotion; a second for social group size and habitat

Table 1.—*Principal components among the coat-pattern variables after optimal PRINQUAL scoring. Entries are loadings (correlations) on each axis. Asterisks denote loadings with absolute values 0.7.*

	Component 1	Component 2	Component 3	Component 4	Component 5	Component 6
Eye	0.87*	-0.23	-0.22	-0.15	-0.05	0.07
Face	0.89*	-0.28	-0.15	-0.11	-0.04	-0.02
Back	0.79*	-0.27	-0.09	0.00	-0.11	-0.09
Agouti	0.24	-0.29	0.77*	-0.11	0.04	0.49
Propodium	0.36	0.74*	0.20	0.19	-0.31	-0.21
Epipodium	0.44	0.73*	0.31	0.14	-0.15	0.02
Tail	0.29	0.51	0.14	-0.49	0.59	-0.21
Tail tip	0.24	0.50	-0.45	0.39	0.30	0.50
Ear patch	0.26	-0.42	0.29	0.66	0.37	-0.30
% Variance	31	23	12	10	8	8
Cumulative % variance	31	54	66	76	84	92

Table 2.—*Principal components among the predictor variables after optimal PRINQUAL scoring. Entries are loadings (correlations) on each axis. Asterisks denote loadings with absolute values ≥ 0.7.*

	Component 1	Component 2	Component 3
Genus	-0.94*	-0.23	0.24
Activity	0.94*	0.25	-0.24
Locomotion	0.94*	0.24	-0.24
Social group	-0.36	0.87*	-0.01
Habitat	0.43	-0.85*	-0.03
Head and body length	0.32	0.38	0.84*
Tail length	0.54	-0.21	0.78*
% Variance	48	26	21
Cumulative % variance	48	74	96

(density of vegetation); and a third for head-and-body length and tail length (Table 2). These accounted for 98% of the variance in the variables after optimal scoring by PROC PRINQUAL.

Nested analysis of variance (Table 3) indicated that the majority of the variance was at the species level for most of the variables. Exceptions were eye pattern, face pattern, and back pattern, whose variances were predominantly at the generic level. Because little or no variance was ascribable to the tribe level, we did not include it in further analyses.

The canonical discriminant analyses generally placed predictor variables with high loadings in groups similar to those identified by the principal component analysis (Table 4). Cases where predictors were not grouped exactly as in the principal component analysis presumably resulted from the fact that optimization criteria are somewhat different in discriminant analysis (i.e., maximizing intergroup variances rather than within-group variances for the axes identified).

Table 3.—*Components of variance (%) attributable to taxonomic levels as determined by nested analysis of variance.*

	Species	Genus	Tribe
Eye	23	77	0
Face	21	79	0
Back	22	78	0
Agouti	76	0	25
Propodium	97	3	0
Epipodium	70	30	0
Tail	90	0	10
Tail tip	75	21	4
Ear patch	55	45	0

Table 4.—*Loadings on the first discriminant axes, except for Eye2 and Eye3, which are loadings on the second and third axes of discrimination for eye-surround pattern. Asterisks denote loadings with absolute values ≥ 0.7. Rightmost column is percent variance explained by each axis (eigenvalue).*

	Genus	Activity	Loco-motion	Group Size	Habitat	H&B Length	Tail Length	Percent variance
Eye	0.96*	-0.96*	-0.96*	0.22	-0.25	-0.39	-0.48	76
Eye2	0.21	-0.22	-0.21	-0.32	0.43	0.56	0.81*	14
Eye3	0.10	-0.07	-0.08	0.63	-0.79*	0.58	0.00	10
Face	-0.44	0.45	0.45	-0.01	-0.05	0.91*	0.79*	95
Back	-0.32	0.33	0.33	0.31	-0.25	0.76*	0.52	76
Agouti	0.17	-0.19	-0.18	-0.40	0.46	0.51	0.84*	100
Propodium	-0.58	0.58	0.58	-0.05	-0.07	0.85*	0.65	77
Epipodium	-0.57	0.58	0.57	-0.12	0.05	0.87*	0.76*	86
Tail	0.52	-0.54	-0.53	-0.43	0.50	-0.17	0.38	59
Tail tip	0.70*	-0.71*	-0.71*	-0.18	0.20	-0.56	-0.20	95
Ear patch	0.57	-0.55	-0.56	0.75*	-0.84*	0.38	-0.15	100

Three independent axes of discrimination among features of eye pattern were identified. The first primarily represented a combination of genus, activity period and locomotory mode. Species in genera having black rings around the eye scored at one extreme of this axis and those with black stripes scored at the other extreme. The former were generally nocturnal gliders and the latter diurnal scansorial or terrestrial species. The second axis ("eye2" in Table 4) primarily discriminated among groups by tail length—species having black eye rings had the longest tails on average, those with plain eye surrounds intermediate tail lengths, and those with white rings or black eye stripes the shortest tails. The dominant variable on the third axis ("eye3" in Table 4) was habitat, and discrimination was between species with black eye stripes and those with white eye rings. Species with white eye rings were associated with open habitats and those with black eye stripes with forested habitats.

The rest of the variables for color pattern produced at most one interpretable axis of discrimination. In the cases of facial pattern, back pattern, presence of agouti pelage, propodial contrast, and epipodial contrast, this axis was primarily correlated with one or the other size variable or with both of them. Although some of the canonical analyses produced discriminant axes having only one of the size variables ≥ 0.7, the analyses of variance for such cases always indicated differentiation in both size variables among classes of the relevant pattern variables.

For back pattern, species with longitudinal stripes averaged the smallest size, those with plain back coloration were intermediate, and those with blotches averaged the largest. Species with some nonagouti pelage averaged larger than those that were all agouti. Species with darkly contrasting propodia and epipodia were larger on average than those with appendages paler than the back or with appendages that were not different from the back.

For proximal tail patterns, Wilks lambda for the first discriminant axis was nominally significant at $P < 0.05$, but none of the predictor loadings were ≥ 0.7. Moderate loadings (0.40 to 0.60) were produced for all the predictors except the size variables.

Distal tail patterns were discriminated by an axis loading on genus, activity period and locomotion. Species in genera with black tail tips were separated from those with plain or white tail tips on this axis. Those with black tips were predominantly nocturnal gliders.

Discrimination of species having pale ear patches from those lacking such patches was primarily on the basis of social group size and habitat. Pale ear patches were associated with solitary behavior and habitats with intermediate vegetative cover.

DISCUSSION

Comparison of Methods

Because most of our variables were categorical and because multiple correspondence analysis is designed for analyzing such variables, it may seem surprising that that approach was not more illuminating than one based on rescoring of the categorical variables as quantitative ones. A couple of factors may have contributed to this result. "The main conceptual difference between PRINQUAL and CORRESP is that PRINQUAL assumes that the categories of a nominal variable correspond to values of a single underlying interval variable, while CORRESP assumes there are multiple underlying interval variables . . . "(SAS Institute Inc., 1989*a*:42). Perhaps the data conformed more to PRINQUAL's assumption than to that of CORRESP. Another consideration is that, in a sense, correspondence analysis stops after assigning scores to the states of the character variables (which are then interpreted subjectively), while our approach with PRINQUAL and discriminant analysis quantitatively investigated the relations of the coat-pattern scores to those of the predictor variables.

Possible Causes of Correlations

Our results indicate that size covaries with many of the coat-pattern features that we investigated. The net effect of most of these associations is that larger species have larger color patches or blotches than smaller species. Selection for camouflage may underlie this trend. Across many animal groups, size of predators is positively correlated with size of their prey (Vézina, 1985). On average, larger predators have larger eyes (Calder, 1984; Vogel, 1988), which should confer greater acuity (Kirschfeld, 1976) and therefore an ability to detect prey at greater distances than smaller predators can. If they are prone to detection at greater distances, larger prey may be selected to match coarser features in their backgrounds. Smaller species, being more prone to smaller predators with smaller eyes and shorter detection distances, might be selected to match finer-scale features in their backgrounds.

Alternative hypotheses can also be offered to explain the size trends we have identified. One alternative is that species of larger body size may be less vulnerable to predators than those of smaller size. Immunity from predators could reduce or eliminate selection favoring camouflage, which in turn might allow greater expression of inter- and intraspecific variation in color patterning.

The work of Murray (1981, 1988) provides another possible perspective on trends with increasing size. Murray has shown that the ontogeny of some mammalian color patterns can be modeled as reaction-diffusion processes. The same underlying ontogenetic process may produce varying degrees of blotchiness in the adult, depending on the size and shape of an animal's body. Such a developmental process could be consistent with an adaptive effect of size-related color patterning if the parameters of the reaction-diffusion process are heritable.

In our data set, generic membership was linked closely to locomotory style and diurnal period of activity. These traits in combination could be used to discriminate species with black eye rings (primarily nocturnal gliders) from those with black eye stripes (*Tamias* and *Paraxerus*). Dark eye rings have been suggested to reduce interference from reflectance in bright habitats, and stripes across the eyes have been suggested to serve as sighting lines or as camouflage of the eye (Burtt, 1981). There are no obvious reasons why the former problem should particularly afflict nocturnal gliders nor why the latter functions should be particularly valuable for squirrels like *Tamias* and *Paraxerus*. Phylogenetic inheritance ("inertia") may be the primary determinant of these traits.

Habitat type and social group size represented additional axes of variation among the predictors that were independent of size and generic membership/locomotory style/activity period. These permitted discrimination of species with white ear patches from those without, such that white ear patches were found more often in species from habitats intermediate between forest and open habitats and whose behavior is also largely solitary. Perhaps under such conditions ear patches provide some form of "startle" protection against potential predators or as flags for young to follow. In addition, we found that white eye rings were associated with open habitats and gregarious or colonial social habits. Again, this is opposite what one might expect if reflectance of bright light into the eye were a problem. Perhaps these eye rings accentuate the eyes in some way that has significance for social interactions in large societies or in open habitats.

We note that nonadaptive explanations for interspecific variation in coat patterning (purely ontogenetic effects, phylogenetic "inertia," or release from predation pressure) must assume that heritable intraspecific variance for coloration is lacking or that the production of pigments entails no cost. The frequent occurrence of albino animal populations in caves and in aphotic parts of the ocean, and perhaps also the prevalence of "countershading" (pale bellies) in animals, suggests that pigment production is costly (Kiltie, 1988). We therefore might expect loss of pigmentation, rather than greater variegation, when coat patterning is not adaptive. As far as we are aware, the only populations of albino squirrels that are not largely maintained by people occur in *Callosciurus finlaysoni bocourti* and *Callosciurus finlaysoni finlaysoni* of Thailand (Askins, 1977). Neither subspecies is unusually large or otherwise distinctive, although the latter is limited to a single island and hence might have been subject to fixation through genetic drift (founder effect). *Callosciurus* in general is a highly variable genus with respect to coloration (Askins, 1977).

Conclusion

With the exception of proximate tail patterns, all the features treated showed interspecific correlations with predictors that hint at functional or phylogenetic determinants. Manipulative experiments (e.g., Kiltie, 1992) will be needed to test the functional possibilities we have raised, and well-supported phylogenies will be needed to evaluate phylogenetic effects. Until then, we hope our results at least allow Rev. Bachman's ghost to rest somewhat easier.

ACKNOWLEDGMENTS

We gratefully acknowledge the hard work of the authors of the compendia from which we extracted the data used in this study. We thank B. D. Patterson and R. W. Thorington, Jr. for helpful comments on the preliminary manuscript.

LITERATURE CITED

ASKINS, R. 1977. Family Sciuridae. Pp. 336-387, *in* Mammals of Thailand (B. Lekagul and J. A. McNeely, eds.). Association for the Conservation of Wildlife, Bangkok, 758 pp.

BRINK, F. H. VAN DEN. 1968. A field guide to the mammals of Britain and Europe. Houghton Mifflin, Boston, Massachusetts, 221 pp.

BURT, W. H., AND R. P. GROSSENHEIDER. 1976. A field guide to the mammals. Third Edition. Houghton Mifflin, Boston, Massachusetts, 289 pp.

BURTT, E. H., JR. 1981. The adaptiveness of animal colors. BioScience, 31:723-729.

CALDER, W. A. 1984. Size, function, and life history. Harvard University Press, Cambridge, Massachusetts, 431 pp.

DORST J., AND P. DANDELOT. 1969. A field guide to the larger mammals of Africa. Houghton Mifflin, Boston, Massachusetts, 287 pp.

EMMONS, L. H., AND F. FEER. 1990. Neotropical rainforest mammals: A field guide. The University of Chicago Press, Chicago, Illinois, 281 pp.

FISHER, R. A. 1938. Statistical methods for research workers. Seventh Edition, Oliver and Boyd, Edinburgh, 356 pp.

GOWER, J. C. 1990. Fisher's optimal scores and multiple correspondence analysis. Biometrics, 46:947-961.

HARVEY, P. H., AND M. D. PAGEL. 1991. The comparative method in evolutionary biology. Oxford University Press, Oxford, United Kingdom, 239 pp.

JAMES, F. C., AND C. E. MCCULLOCH. 1985. Data analysis and the design of experiments in ornithology. Pp. 1-63, *in* Current ornithology, 2 (R. F. Johnston, ed.). Plenum Publishing Co., New York, 364 pp.

KILTIE, R. A. 1988. Countershading: universally deceptive or deceptively universal? Trends in Ecology and Evolution, 3:21-23.

———. 1992. Tests of hypotheses on predation as a factor maintaining polymorphic melanism in coastal-plain fox squirrels. Biological Journal of the Linnean Society, 45:17-37.

KINGDON, J. 1974. East African mammals: an atlas of evolution in Africa. Volume II, part B (Hares and rodents). The University of Chicago Press, Chicago, Illinois, 704 pp.

KIRSCHFELD, K. 1976. The resolution of lens and compound eyes. Pp. 354-370, *in* Neural principles in vision (F. Zettler and R. Weiler, eds.). Springer Verlag, Berlin, 430 pp.

KRUSKAL, J. B. 1964. Multidimensional scaling by optimizing goodness of fit to a nonmetric hypothesis. Psychometrika, 29:1-27.

MOORE, J. C. 1959. Relationships among the living squirrels of the Sciurinae. Bulletin of the American Museum of Natural History, 118:159-206.

MURRAY, J. D. 1981. A prepattern formation mechanism for animal coat markings. Journal of Theoretical Biology, 88:161-199.

———. 1988. How the leopard gets its spots. Scientific American, 258(3):80-87.

NOWAK, R. M. 1991. Walker's mammals of the world, Fifth Ed., The Johns Hopkins University Press, Baltimore, Maryland, 1:1-642; 2: 643-1629.

SOKAL, R. R., AND F. J. ROHLF. 1981. Biometry: the priciples and practice of statistics in biological research. Second ed. W. H. Freeman and Company, San Francisco, California, 859 pp.

SAS INSTITUTE, INC. 1988. SAS Procedures Guide. Release 6.03 edition. SAS Institute, Inc., Cary, North Carolina, 441 pp.

———. 1989*a*. SAS/STAT User's Guide, Version 6. Fourth edition. Volume 1. SAS Institute Inc., Cary, North Carolina, 943 pp.

———. 1989*b*. SAS/STAT User's Guide, Version 6. Fourth edition. Volume 2. SAS Institute Inc., Cary, North Carolina, 846 pp.

TUKEY, J. W. 1977. Exploratory data analysis. Addison-Wesley, Reading, Massachusetts, 688 pp.

VÉZINA, A. F. 1985. Empirical relationships between predator and prey size among terrestrial vertebrate predators. Oecologia, 67:555-565.

VOGEL, S. 1988. Life's devices. Princeton University Press, Princeton, New Jersey, 367 pp.

WILSON, D. E., AND D. M. REEDER (eds.). 1993. Mammal species of the world: a taxonomic and geographic reference. Second ed. Smithsonian Institution Press, Washington D.C., 1206 pp.

GEOGRAPHIC VARIATION IN THE FOX SQUIRREL (*SCIURUS NIGER*): A CONSIDERATION OF SIZE CLINES, HABITAT VEGETATION, FOOD HABITS AND HISTORICAL BIOGEOGRAPHY

PETER D. WEIGL, LORI J. SHERMAN, ADELAIDE I. WILLIAMS, and
MICHAEL A. STEELE AND DAVID S. WEAVER
Department of Biology
Wake Forest University
Winston-Salem, NC 27109 (PDW, LJS, AIW),

Department of Biology
Wilkes University
Wilkes-Barre, PA 18766 (MAS)

Department of Anthropology
Wake Forest University
Winston-Salem, NC 27109 (DSW)

ABSTRACT.—Patterns of morphological and color variation in fox squirrels *(Sciurus niger)* were evaluated by both univariate and multivariate statistical methods on 667 adult specimens from throughout the species range. Two major groups could be recognized: moderately sized, reddish forms occupied hardwood and mixed forests west of the Appalachian Mountains and conformed to Bergmann's rule; large to very large, gray or melanistic (highly variable) animals of the lower Piedmont and eastern coastal plain showed a reversed-Bergmann cline. Discriminant function analysis of size and vegetation type revealed that the smallest squirrels occupied very wet or very dry habitats, intermediate sized forms were found in areas with abundant hardwoods, while the largest animals were from southeastern pine forests. Analyses of mandibular characters associated with masseter function, studies of feeding behavior in the laboratory and extensive field work suggest that much size variation may be explained by food type and food distribution in different habitats. The divergent evolution of the two major groups of fox squirrels is potentially the result of confinement in, and adaptation to, the different conditions of eastern and western refugia during the latter part of the Pleistocene.

INTRODUCTION

The fox squirrel *(Sciurus niger)* is the largest tree squirrel of the western hemisphere (Nowak and Paradiso, 1983) and the most variably colored mammal in North America (Calahane, 1961). Yet, in the 1970s when we initiated studies of this species, little detailed information was available on its morphological variation. In addition, while the populations in the midwestern United States had received extensive ecological study, those in the southeast were largely unknown and were considered rare and even threatened in some areas (Weigl et al., 1989). The major impetus for the present morphological study, however, was a casual examination of the fox squirrel specimens in

In M.A. Steele, J. F. Merritt, and D. A. Zegers (eds.). 1998. Ecology and Evolutionary Biology of Tree Squirrels. Special Publication, Virginia Museum of Natural History, 6: 320 pp

the collections of the U.S. National Museum early in 1976. The incredible array of sizes and colors represented by these specimens from throughout the species' range was totally unexpected and led to questions that became the basis of a long term attempt to describe and explain some of this variation. Specifically, we wanted to know the following: 1) what patterns of morphological variation, especially in size and color, occur over the range of the fox squirrel?, 2) what ecological factors might be associated with such variation? and 3) what historical factors might explain some of this variation?

Over the next fifteen years we investigated many aspects of the biology of this species. Williams (1977) produced a general study of morphological variation in this species, and we subsequently used her work as the basis of a more extensive analysis. On the basis of combined data on 677 specimens of fox squirrels from ten museum collections, ten years of fieldwork with fox squirrel populations in the coastal plain of North Carolina, an array of experimental studies in the laboratory and field (Ha, 1983; Weigl et al., 1989; Gamroth, 1988; Steele, 1988; Secrest, 1990) and ecological information from the literature, we now attempt to address these original questions.

MATERIALS AND METHODS

Morphological measurements were taken from a total of 677 specimens of adult fox squirrels from ten museum collections. For each specimen we noted the coloration of nose, ears, head, dorsum, belly, tail and toes and recorded the following data from the specimen tag: body mass, total length, tail length, ear length and length of hind foot. The following skull characters were measured ($\pm$0.1 mm) (Williams, 1977): occipital nasal length (OC), nasal length (NL), palate length (PL), molar toothrow (TR), post-dental breadth (PD), zygomatic breadth (ZB), mandibular length (MH), mandibular height (ML), length of the coronoid fossa (CF), length of the moment arm of the temporalis (MT) and angle-incisor distance (AID).

Specimens were assigned to different groups according to the questions being addressed. In assessing the relationship between morphological variation and latitude and longitude, animals were grouped by physiography, by dominant vegetation in the area, and by state(s) along east-west or north-south transects. The influence of vegetation was estimated by grouping populations from a single vegetation type or a number of related types as suggested by Braun (1964) and Küchler (1964). Trends and associations observed from analyzing these groups were interpreted in terms of experimental studies (Weigl et al., 1989; Steele and Weigl, 1992, 1993) and pertinent biogeographical information from the literature (Moncrief et al., 1993). Because the fossil record for this species is so limited, tentative explanations of historical influences on fox squirrel morphology have been based on the assumption that these animals occupied similar habitats in the past and on recent data of the probable extent and location of these habitats during late Wisconsin time (Delcourt and Delcourt, 1981, 1987).

Findings of color variation were taken directly from Williams' (1977) analysis of 500 specimens and from subsequent museum and field studies (Weigl et al., 1989). The remaining morphological data were analyzed as follows. Descriptive statistics ($\overline{X} \pm SD$) were prepared for each variable for each group of squirrels. One-way Analysis of Variance (Sokal and Rohlf, 1981) was used to evaluate character and group differences over distance (clines). Cranial measurements were analyzed using Discriminant Function Analysis (P7M, BMDP, 1981, Los Angeles, CA) under standard default parameters to examine multivariate group differences. Pairwise product-moment correlation coefficients were used to examine the relationships between cranial variables, and partial product-moment correlation coefficients (Sokal and Rohlf, 1981) were employed to adjust for the influence of body weight on those pairwise correlations.

RESULTS AND DISCUSSION

The fox squirrel's range currently (or potentially) includes most of eastern North America, from the Canadian border to Florida, southern Texas and northern Mexico and from the eastern coastal plain to the western prairies and along riparian woodlands to the front range of the Rocky Mountains. At one time the species also occupied areas of eastern Pennsylvania, New York and southern New England. Within the present range, Hall (1981) recognized ten subspecies on the basis of size and color characteristics. Fox squirrels seem to prefer open, mature woodland or forest-prairie mosaics, but inhabit predominantly hardwood areas in the western portion of their range and oak-pine forests in much of the east and south. It is clear that the forests that once supported these squirrels before European settlement have been greatly changed in distribution, age structure, species composition and extent. Such habitat modification probably accounts for present reductions in numbers and/ or the fragmentation of the species range. Thus, we are studying remnants of a species in transition (or even decline), and some of our conclusions must remain tentative.

Coloration.—The unusual color polymorphism of the fox squirrel largely accounts for its subdivision into numerous subspecies (Hall, 1981), and has been the subject of an increasing amount of discussion in the literature (Moore, 1956; Lowrey 1974; Kiltie, 1989; Weigl et al., 1989). On the basis of Williams' (1977) study and our subsequent examination of additional specimens, fox squirrel populations can be divided into two fairly distinctive but intergrading groups (Table 1). One group consists of silver, gray, agouti, and melanistic animals often with tan, gold or reddish washes. These animals also usually possess black head markings, white or gray noses and white ears and paws. This group generally occupies pine, oak-pine and wetland forests of the Atlantic and Gulf coastal plain (and some of the adjacent Piedmont), from the Delmarva Penninsula to Florida and from there to the floodplain of Mississippi River. Included in this assemblage are the following subspecies as recognized by Hall (1981): easternmost *S.n. vulpinus, S.n. cinercus, S.n. niger, S.n. shermani, S.n. avicennia,* and *S.n. bachmani.* The other group is characterized by a distinctly reddish, orange or tan agouti coloration and a grizzled or black nose and the virtual absence of white markings on head, feet, or tail. Melanism occurs in a few populations. These animals inhabit hardwood and mixed forest (72%) and forest-prairie mosaics (25%) from southcentral Pennsylvania, the Appalachian Mountains and the uplands of the Gulf states, west to the prairie, the dry lands of Texas, and recently the front range of the Rockies. The subspecies *S.n. rufiventer,* western *S.n. vulpinus, S.n. subauratus S.n. ludovicianus* and *S.n. limitis* can be assigned to this group. Prior to European settlement the range of the fox squirrel probably was more extensive and continuous, and thus the zone of intergradation between these two groups was much larger than at present in the northeast and south of the Appalachian Mountains. The squirrels of New England, New York and central Pennsylvania were reddish or tawny in color (Bangs, 1896; Pool, 1944) and were usually assigned to *S.n. vulpinus.*

Table 1.—*Color variation in populations of fox squirrels based on the predominant color characteristics for particular body regions. Data from eastern and southern coastal plain, coastal plain-upland and western groups demonstrate both regional contrasts and suggest potential extent of gene exchange between eastern and western forms.* (See Fig. 2)

		Eastern and southern coastal plain	Coastal plain and piedmont uplands (Combined)	Appalachian and western areas
Nose				
	white	98%	95%	0
	agouti	1.7%	4.6%	83%
	n	167	197	408
Ears				
	white	94%	90%	2%
	red/orange	4.6%	8%	91%
	n	149	177	382
Toes/paws				
	white	62%	56%	4%
	red/orange	16%	22%	85%
	n	156	186	403
Head				
	black	63%	61%	2.7%
	agouti	5%	10.5%	90%
	n	171	200	408
Belly				
	white	56%	48%	6.6%
	orange	27%	36%	87%
	black	17%	16%	6%
	n	163	191	393

However, it is clear that the animals from eastern Pennsylvania and New Jersey (considered to be *S. n. vulpinus)* represented some sort of intergrade between the reddish animals of the west and the gray and white forms of the Delmarva Peninsula. More extensive interbreeding may have occurred in northern Georgia, Alabama, Mississippi and eastern Louisiana where reddish or tan squirrels have some of the characteristic black and white markings of the more typical coastal plain forms. Clarification of the extent of gene exchange between and within these two groups awaits further genetic and molecular studies like that of Moncrief (1993), but at this point, pelage color indicates plausible groupings and historical influences on the species.

The ecological significance of this color variation has so far remained enigmatic. The distinctive frequency of certain color patterns and markings in small isolated populations and data on parent and offspring coloration suggest a genetic basis for this variation (Weigl et al., 1989), but the factors favoring particular color combinations is unclear. In a series of studies Kiltie (1989, 1992) explored the possibility that the coloration of the southeastern squirrels is cryptic in certain burned and unburned habitats and thus provides protection from visual predators. In North Carolina, Weigl et al. (1989) found that the same three to one proportion of agouti to melanistic forms exists in both adults and litters, suggesting that little selection for or against these morphs has taken place. Clearly, additional longterm studies will be necessary to understand this spectacular color diversity.

Fig.—Geographic variation in the size of the fox squirrel. Both the relative size of eastern and western populations and latitudinal and longitudinal size clines are indicated. Size of dot is roughly proportional to body size.

Size variation.—Analyses of body size characteristics paralleled the findings based on differences in coat color and support the existence of two major groups of squirrels, along with some divergent populations in special habitats. The squirrels we examined from the southeastern coastal plain were the largest tree squirrels on the continent, while those from forests west of the Appalachians are of moderate to large size (Fig. 1). Populations at the southern margin of the range in the wetlands of southern Florida (Moore, 1956) and the Mississippi flood plain as well as in the very dry areas of southern Texas are quite small—about the size of the gray squirrel *(Sciurus carolinensis).*

Of greater interest than general group comparisons is the latitudinal variation exhibited within the two major groups. If one temporarily ignores the populations that occur in wetlands, western fox squirrels clearly display a size cline typical of that predicted by Bergmann's rule, with larger animals in the north and progressively smaller squirrels occupying areas of decreasing latitude (Table 2). On the other hand, the fox squirrels of the Atlantic coastal plain show a reversed-Bergmann cline, with the largest animals inhabiting southern Georgia and northern Florida (Table 3). Longitudinal clines also exist: eastern squirrels are generally larger than those to the west (Tables 4 and 5). Finer analyses, based on one-way ANOVAs of each clinal set and comparisons of means between variables of adjacent populations reveal that the rate of clinal shifts in size varies with morphological character under consideration and discontinuities in physiographic or vegetational conditions. For example, the squirrels in mostly oak forests from Missouri to northern Texas show little variation as a group while those farther north change more rapidly in keeping with vegetational discontinuities. Or, squirrels from the midwest (Ohio to Iowa) show a steady but statistically insignificant decrease in size with longitude, but are distinctly different in size from animals in Pennsylvania forests to the east and prairie animals to the west.

Table 2.—*Latitudinal size cline of western populations of fox squirrels based on analysis of variance of six populations (all* Ps *< 0.0001), showing means, standard deviations, and significant differences between contiguous groups. Groups are from northern hardwood forest; northern oak-hickory (Ohio, Indiana, Illinois, Iowa, Michigan, Indiana, and Wisconsin north of 40° latitude); central oak-hickory (Ohio, Indiana, Illinois, Kentucky, Missouri, and Kansas south of 40° latitude); southern oak-hickory (Tennessee, Arkansas, and Oklahoma); Texas oak (eastern Texas); and xeric woodlands of southern Texas (see Küchler (1964) for vegetation boundaries). Linear measurements = mm; masses = g.*

Skull measurement	Northern hardwoods		Northern oak-hickory		Central oak-hickory		Southern oak-hickory		Texas oak		Xeric woodland
	n = 15		*n* = 94		*n* = 62		*n* = 53		*n* = 8		*n* = 27
OC	66.9 (1.9)	*	66.1 (1.3)	*	65.4 (1.8)	*	64.3 (1.9)	NS	63.6 (2.3)	*	58.9 (1.2)
NL	23.5 (0.8)	NS	23.1 (0.7)	NS	23.0 (1.7)	*	22.5 (0.9)	NS	22.2 (1.1)	*	20.1 (0.7)
TR	11.5 (0.4)	NS	11.4 (0.4)	NS	11.4 (0.5)	*	11.0 (0.4)	NS	11.1 (0.4)	*	10.0 (0.6)
ZB	37.9 (1.3)	P<0.07	37.3 (1.3)	NS	37.2 (1.3)	*	36.3 (1.3)	NS	35.8 (1.5)	*	33.7 (1.1)
ML	30.6 (1.0)	NS	30.0 (1.4)	*	29.4 (1.3)	*	28.5 (1.4)	NS	28.4 (1.7)	*	26.4 (1.2)
CF	25.3 (0.8)	P<0.06	24.7 (1.1)	*	24.4 (1.2)	*	23.5 (1.1)	NS	24.0 (1.4)	*	21.4 (0.8)
MH	23.3 (0.8)	NS	22.9 (0.9)	NS	22.8 (1.0)	*	22.1 (1.0)	NS	22.1 (0.9)	*	20.3 (0.7)
AID	37.1 (1.0)	*P*<0.07	36.5 (1.4)	NS	36.3 (1.1)	*	35.3 (1.3)	NS	35.3 (1.7)	*	32.2 (1.0)
TOTL	536.8 (21.5)	NS	546.6 (25.7)	*	529.8 (31.9)	*	516.2 (45.6)	NS	529.0 (46.9)	*	458.0 (24.1)
WT (g)	843.6 (95.7)	*	790.0 (77.5)	NS	772.1 (92.5)	*	707.5 (104.7)	NS	684.0 (105.7)	*	485.6 (51.5)

* Indicates significant difference between adjacent groups (*P*<0.05); NS = not significant

Table 3.—*Latitudinal size cline of Atlantic coastal plain populations of fox squirrels based on analysis of variance of three groups (all* Ps *< 0.001), showing means and standard deviations of measurements and significant differences between contiguous groups. Delmarva includes animals from the Delmarva Peninsula, mid-south squirrels from North Carolina, South Carolina, and Georgia north of 32° latitude, and deep south group from northern Florida and Georgia south of 32° latitude. Linear measurements = mm, masses = g.*

Skull Measurements	Delmarva		Mid south		Deep south
	n = 15		*n* = 44		*n* = 63
OC	67.8 (1.1)	*	69.1 (1.7)	*	71.6 (2.1)
NL	23.9 (0.7)	*	24.7 (1.2)	*	26.8 (1.2)
TR	11.8 (0.3)	*	12.2 (0.4)	*	13.0 (0.5)
ZB	38.5 (0.6)	*P*<0.07	39.2 (1.2)	*	40.6 (1.5)
ML	30.8 (0.6)	NS	31.0 (1.6)	*	31.9 (1.3)
CF	27.1 (0.6)	NS	25.4 (1.6)	*	26.2 (1.2)
MH	23.6 (0.6)	NS	23.6 (1.1)	NS	23.8 (1.2)
AID	37.5 (0.7)	NS	38.0 (1.3)	*	39.9 (1.2)
TOTL	572.8 (27.9)	*	593.5 (33.2)	*	618.1 (27.8)
WT (g)	897.9 (52.4)	*	961.9 (91.9)	*	1105.9 (130.3)

* Indicates significant difference between adjacent groups (*P*< 0.05); NS = not significant

Table 4.—*Longitudinal size cline of northern populations of fox squirrels based on analysis of variance of four groups (all* Ps *< 0.0001), showing means and standard deviations of measurements and significant differences between contiguous groups. Animals are from northeastern hardwoods (Virginia east of 77° longitude, Pennsylvania, West Virginia, and New York); north central oak-hickory (Ohio, Indiana, Michigan north of 40° latitude); northwestern oak-hickry (Illinois, Iowa, Minnesota, Wisconsin, north of 40° latitude); and northern prairie (also north of 40° latitude). Linear measurements = mm, masses = g.*

Skull Measurement	Northeastern hardwoods			North Central oak-hickory			Northwestern oak-hickory			Northern prairie	
	n = 34			n = 86			n = 8			n = 35	
OC	68.0	(1.7)	*	66.1	(1.3)	NS	65.8	(1.2)	*	63.9	(1.4)
NL	23.9	(0.8)	*	23.1	(0.7)	NS	22.8	(0.7)	*	22.1	(0.7)
TR	11.6	(0.4)	*	11.5	(0.4)	NS	11.4	(0.6)	*	11.1	(0.3)
ZB	38.8	(1.2)	*	37.3	(1.3)	NS	37.1	(0.5)	P<0.06	36.2	(1.0)
ML	31.1	(1.1)	*	30.0	(1.4)	NS	29.9	(0.4)	*	28.4	(1.0)
CF	25.6	(1.3)	*	24.8	(1.2)	NS	24.3	(0.5)	NS	23.8	(0.8)
MH	23.9	(1.0)	*	22.9	(0.9)	NS	23.0	(0.3)	P<0.06	22.4	(0.8)
AID	37.9	(1.3)	*	36.5	(1.5)	NS	36.4	(0.8)	NS	35.7	(1.0)
TOTL	584.9	(37.6)	*	545.8	(24.9)	NS	554.6	(35.1)	*	513.0	(39.0)
WT (g)	919.1	(95.4)	*	790.5	(78.8)	NS	784.7	(65.8)	*	735.8	(154.1)

* Indicates significant difference between adjacent groups (P<0.05); NS = not significant

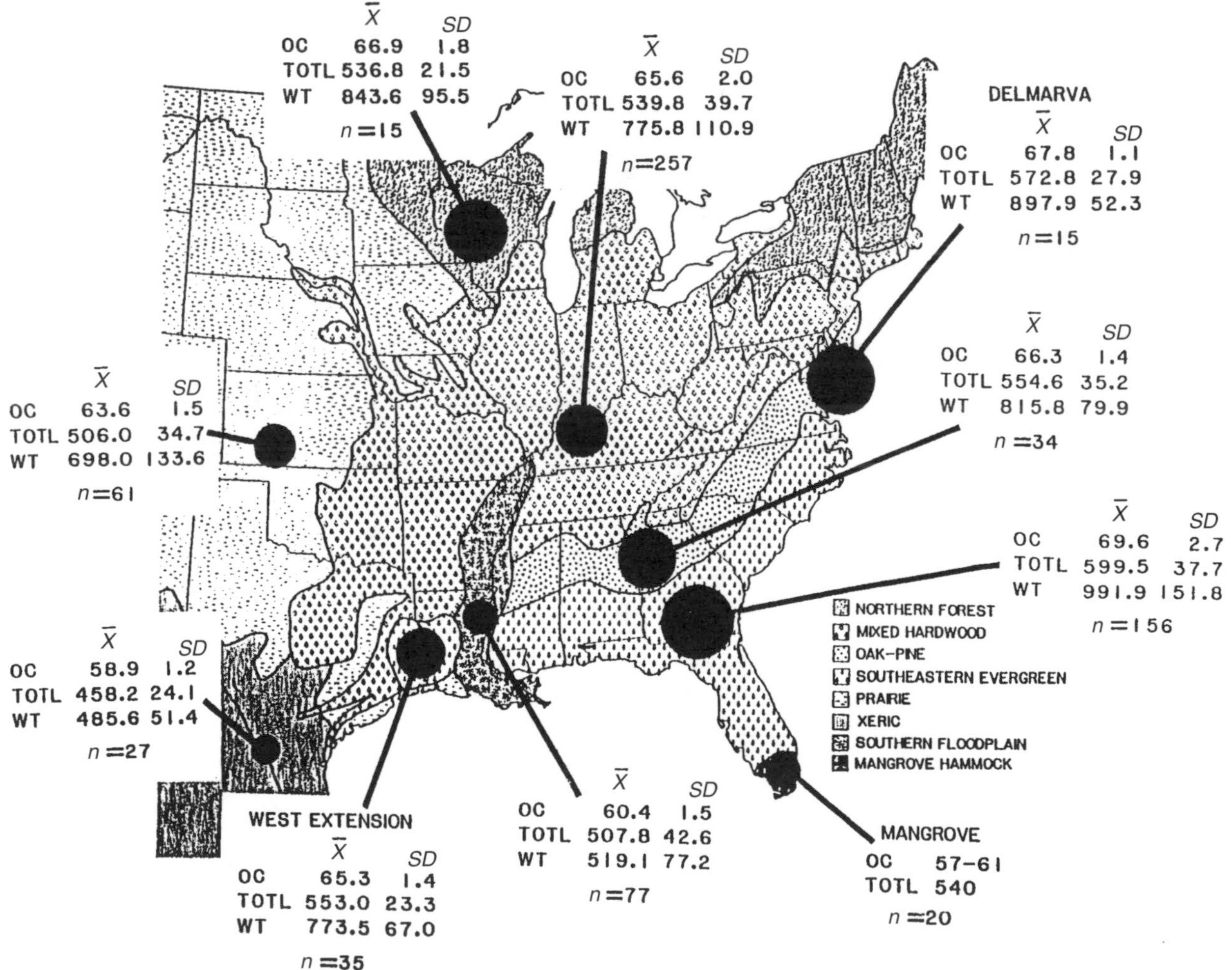

Fig. 2—Size of Fox squirrels and vegetation types in the eastern United States (modified from Braun, 1964 and Kuchler, 1964). Data on mangrove fox squirrel *(S. n. avicennia)* from Moore (1956).

Size and vegetation.—The association between habitat vegetation and body size seems quite obvious when squirrels are grouped and analyzed by vegetation type (Fig. 2). Many of these associations have already been suggested, but Figures 2 and 3 essentially summarize these relationships. The largest squirrels are found in pine and pine oak forests of the Atlantic and Gulf coastal plains. Animals from predominantly hardwood areas are intermediate in size and show the least morphological variation. The smallest squirrels are found in more marginal habitats such as swamp forests, hammocks, mangrove, prairie and semi-desert, and, as would be expected for such an arbitrary grouping, show the most variability in size. Squirrels from mixed vegetation such as the oak-pine of the eastern Piedmont are intermediate in size between populations of the coastal plain and hardwood forests.

Table 5. —*Longitudinal size variation in fox squirrels from southeastern and gulf coastal plain forests, based on analysis of variance of six populations (all Ps < 0.0001), showing means and standard deviations of measurements and significant differences between contiguous groups. Squirrels are from deep south pine forest (southern Georgia and northern Florida); gulf coastal plain (Alabama, Mississippi, and eastern Louisiana); floodplain (Mississippi floodplain); western longleaf pine (western Louisiana and eastern Texas); Texas oak (eastern Texas); and xeric woodland (dry woodlands of Texas). Linear measurements = mm, masses = g.*

Skull	Deep-south measurment			Gulf coastal pine			Floodplain plain			Western longleaf pine			Texas oak			Xeric woodland	
	n = 63			*n* = 49			*n* = 77			*n* = 35			*n* = 8			*n* = 27	
OC	71.6	(2.1)	*	67.5	(2.1)	*	60.4	(1.5)	*	65.3	(1.4)	*	63.6	(2.3)	*	58.9	(1.2)
NL	26.8	(1.2)	*	23.8	(1.4)	*	20.3	(0.7)	*	22.5	(0.8)	NS	22.2	(1.1)	*	20.1	(0.7)
TR	13.0	(0.5)	*	11.8	(0.6)	*	10.5	(0.3)	*	11.4	(0.4)	NS	11.1	(0.4)	*	10.0	(0.6)
ZB	40.6	(1.5)	*	38.3	(1.5)	*	34.4	(1.1)	*	37.3	(0.8)	*	35.8	(1.5)	*	33.7	(1.1)
ML	31.9	(1.3)	*	31.2	(1.2)	*	28.0	(1.2)	*	30.4	(1.6)	*	28.4	(1.7)	*	26.4	(1.2)
CF	26.2	(1.2)	*	24.5	(1.4)	*	21.0	(0.9)	*	23.5	(0.9)	NS	24.0	(1.4)	*	21.4	(0.8)
MH	23.8	(1.2)	*	23.3	(1.0)	*	20.8	(0.7)	*	23.1	(0.8)	*	22.1	(0.9)	*	20.3	(0.7)
AID	39.9	(1.2)	*	37.1	(1.7)	*	32.6	(1.0)	*	35.6	(1.0)	NS	35.3	(1.7)	*	32.2	(1.0)
TOTL	618.1	(27.8)	*	580.9	(42.1)	*	507.9	(42.7)	*	553.0	(23.3)	NS	529.0	(46.9)	*	458.2	(24.1)
WT (g)	1105.9	(130.2)	*	872.3	(111.5)	*	519.2	(77.2)	*	773.5	(67.0)	*	684.0	(105.6)	*	485.6	(51.5)

* Indicates significant difference between adjacent groups (P<0.05); NS = not significant

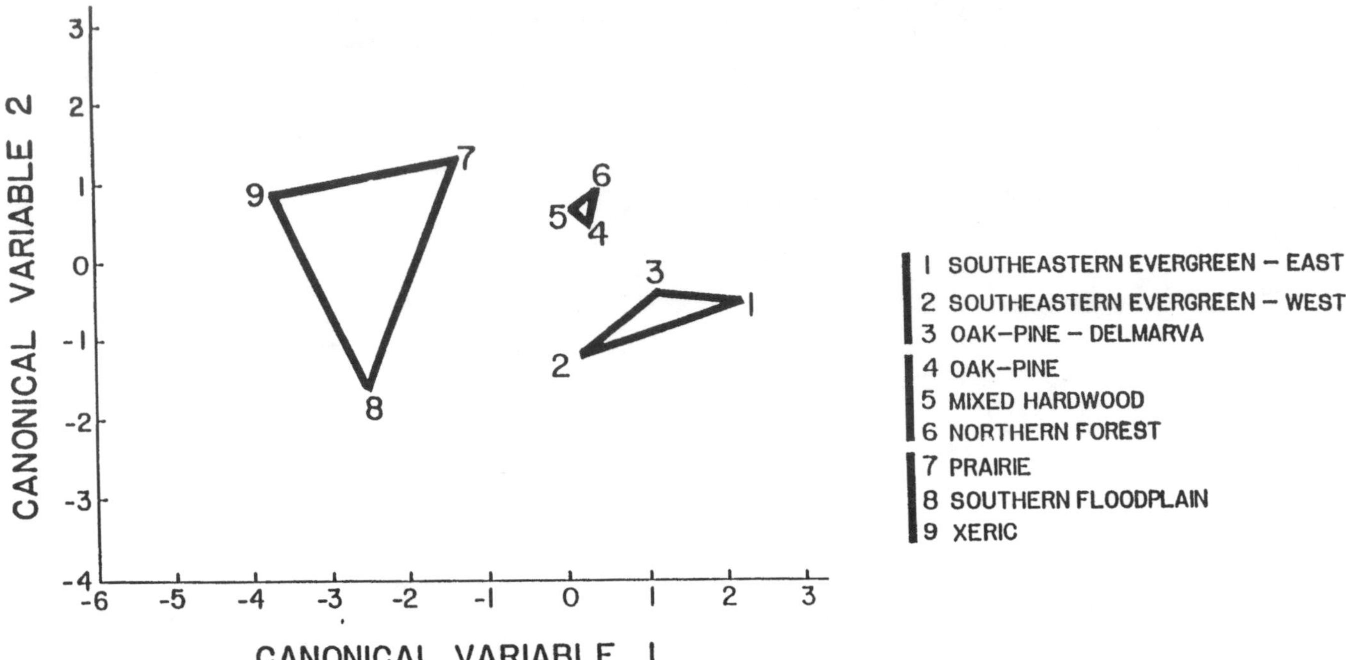

Fig. 3—Discriminant funtion analysis of populations of fox squirrels from different vegetation types. Each triangle represents a vegetational set. Geometric distances between group canonical means are proportional to the degree of similarity between groups. Thus, a large triangle represents greater variability within a vegetational set.

The relationship between size and vegetation is perhaps most evident for the fox squirrels occupying the western extension of the southeastern longleaf pine (*Pinus palustris*) forest in western Louisiana and eastern Texas (Fig. 4, Table 6). For these animals represent a "reddish western" form occupying habitat like that of the southeastern coastal plain. And, they are substantially larger than any neighboring populations. Evidently some factor in this forest type favors larger body size. Taken together the morphological variation in various types of vegetation suggests that some interaction between energy resources and climatic demands might underlie this striking size variation.

Variation in feeding apparatus.—An awareness of a lesser degree of within-group variation in the size characteristics of the reddish, western squirrels compared with eastern animals and information on differences in the food resources of the two groups (Ha, 1983), led to a more detailed comparision of skull and mandibular features, especially those associated with feeding. Accordingly, correlations among skull characters associated with mandibular function were calculated for the two groups (Fig. 5). Except for two correlations (MH: AID and CF:AID), the coefficients for the reddish forms of hardwood forests were significantly greater than those for squirrels from eastern pine forests (*P*s <0.05). Partial correlations that adjusted for clinal variation in body weight (size) showed the same trend (Fig 6.:*P* s <0.05), with the exception of CF:AID. Thus, components of the feeding apparatus in western animals from hardwood forests are apparently more highly correlated with each other and show less clinal variation than those of pine forest animals. In other words, although body size may vary latitudinally among squirrels from hardwood forests, there is relatively less variation in the size of feeding apparatus associated with clinal trends in body size. Selection appears to have led to some sort of "fixation" in the sizes of skull characters associated with feeding (in contrast with those not involved in feeding), perhaps because of the armored nature of major food items in hardwood forests (i.e.,

Table 6.—*Size variation of fox squirrels within and contiguous with the western extension of the longleaf pine-oak forest of western Louisiana and eastern Texas based on analysis of variance of four populations (all* P's *< 0.0001). Shown are the means (+ SD) along with significant differences from the western longleaf population. Southern oak-hickory group include animals from forests in southern Arkansas and northern Louisiana. Linear measurements = mm, masses = g.*

	OC	NL	TR	ZB	ML	CF	MH	AID	TOTL	WT
W. LONGLEAF	65.3	22.5	11.4	37.3	30.4	23.5	23.1	35.7	553.0	773.5
n = 35	(1.4)	(0.8)	(0.4)	(0.8)	(1.6)	(0.9)	(0.8)	(1.0)	(23.3)	(67.1)
FLOODPLAIN	60.4 *	20.3 *	10.5 *	34.4 *	28.0 *	21.0 *	20.8 *	32.6 *	507.9 *	519.2 *
n = 77	(1.5)	(0.7)	(0.3)	(1.1)	(1.2)	(0.9)	(0.7)	(1.0)	(42.7)	(77.2)
S. OAK-HICK	64.7 NS	22.5 NS	11.2 NS	36.6 NS	30.0 NS	23.2 NS	22.7 NS	35.3 NS	542.3 NS	729.0 NS
n = 22	(1.6)	(1.0)	(0.4)	(0.9)	(1.1)	(1.1)	(0.9)	(1.1)	(40.8)	(86.3)
TEXAS OAK	63.6 *	22.2 NS	11.1 N	35.8 *	28.4 *	24.0 NS	22.1 *	35.3 NS	529.0 NS	684.0 *
n = 8	(2.3)	(1.1)	(0.4)	(1.6)	(1.7)	(1.4)	(0.9)	(1.7)	(46.9)	(105.7)

* Indicates significant difference from Western Longleaf ($P<0.05$); NS = not significant

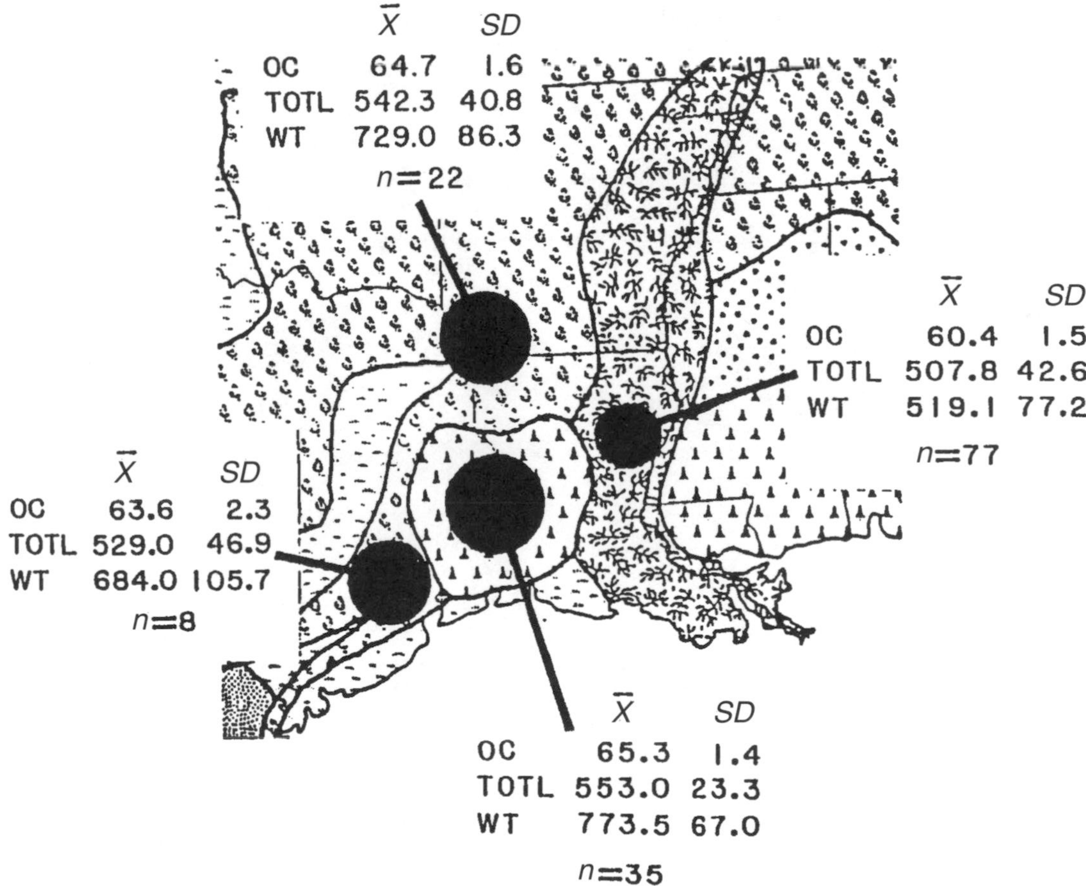

Fig. 4—Variation in body size of populations of fox squirrels in and around the western extension of the longleaf pine-oak forest of Louisiana and Texas. Dot size is proportional to body size.

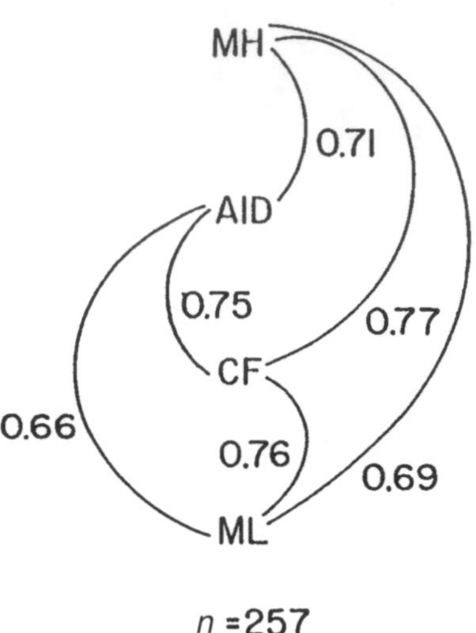

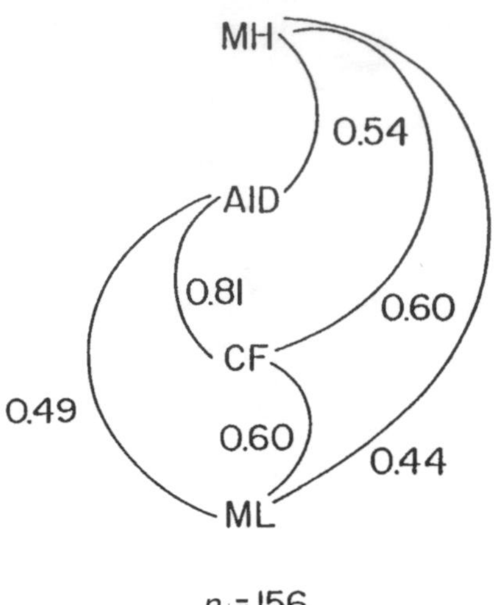

Fig. 5—Correlations among skull characters related to feeding in squirrel from eastern pine forests and western hardwoods. Correlations associated with masseter functions are significantly greater in animals from hardwood forest (P< .005).

hardshelled nuts of the Juglandaceae). In fact, Barnett (1977) postulated just such an evolutionary fixation of feeding characters in a study of clinal variation in the gray squirrel. In contrast, in eastern pine forests where the size and hardness of food items is more variable and food distribution more patchy (Steele, 1988), large body size itself may be more important for handling large food items such as longleaf and other pine cones and for long-distance locomotion among food patches (Weigl et al., 1989). Studies of gray squirrels and both southeastern and midwestern fox squirrels clearly demonstrate the importance of body size, rather than just bite force, in handling and eating longleaf pine cones, a critical resource in these habitats with a low diversity of foods (Fig. 7). Thus, the pattern of variability of feeding structures and other size characteristics in fox squirrels may well reflect the demands of the squirrels' habitual foods and habitat conditions (Weigl et al., 1989).

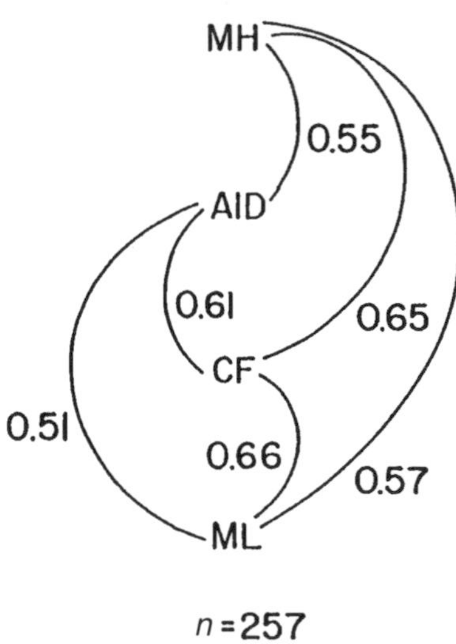

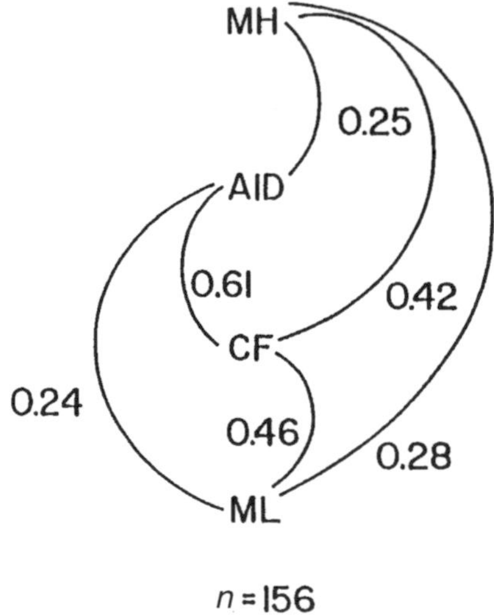

Fig. 6—Partial correlations among skull characters related to feeding (adjusted for clinal variation in body size) in eastern and western populations of fox squirrels. Partial correlations are significantly greater in squirrels from hardwood forests compared to those from pine forest (*P*< 0.05).

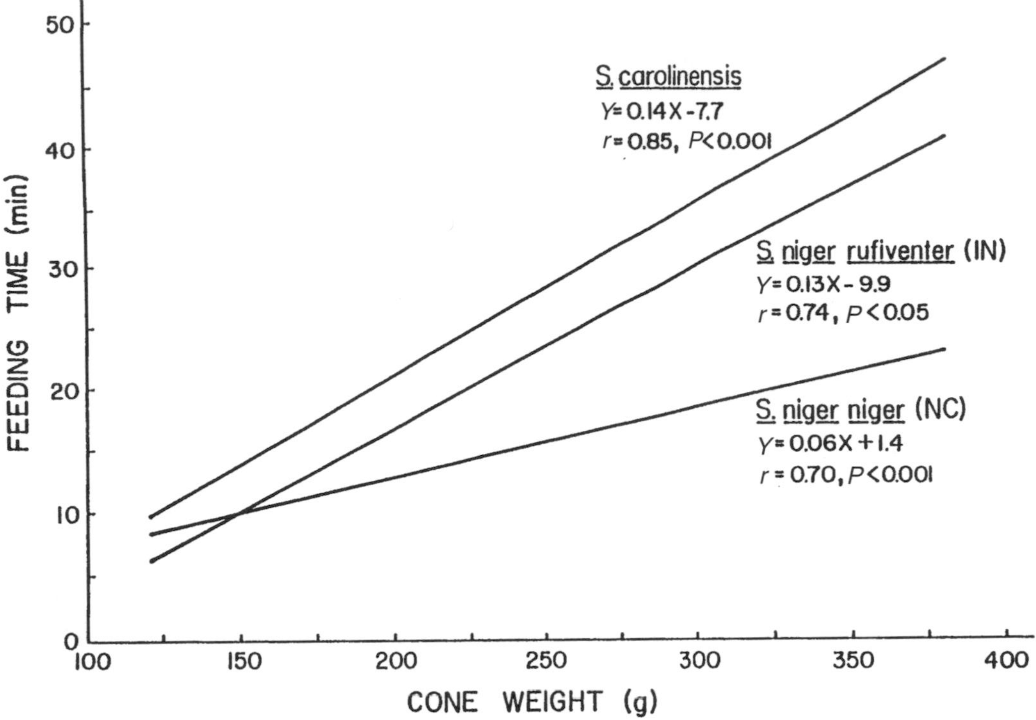

Fig. 7—Feeding time of fox squirrels (eastern versus western) and eastern gray squirrels on different sized cones of longleaf pine trees (Weigl et al.,1989). Cone size has a lesser effect on feeding time in the large eastern fox squirrels.

Historical factors.—The concordance between the data on color and size in defining major fox squirrel groups and the association between these characteristics and latitude, longitude, habitat vegetation and foods raises the question of the origin of such patterns. Since present day conditions provide only a limited basis for explaining the existence of two such distinctive groups, we hypothesize that conditions associated with the late Pleistocene glaciations forced populations of fox squirrels into eastern and western refugia with different habitat conditions. Support for such an assertion, however, does not rest in the fossil record. For, reviews by Kurten and Anderson (1980), Lundelius et al. (1983) and Semken (1983) clearly indicate that the fossil record for the fox squirrel is too fragmentary to reveal much about past populations and their ranges. On the other hand, the vegetation record for the late Pleistocene, especially as found in the studies of Delcourt and Delcourt (1981, 1984, 1987) on late Wisconsin vegetation and of Davis (1976, 1983), on the post-glacial migration of tree species provide a basis for evaluating the idea of separate refugia. If one assumes that the present preference of fox squirrels for open, mature woodland and edge habitats also existed in the past, then the proposed distribution of such forests in Wisconsin times provides evidence for what areas were available at these times. Spruce-fir, jack pine, northern hardwoods and dense, closed-canopy, mixed mesophytic forests usually fail to support fox squirrel populations. Open pine-oak, oak-hickory, oak-chestnut, mixed hardwoods (midwest) and prairie edge are among the more favored habitats. Squirrels in dense southern swamp forests tend to be exceptionally small (stunted). With these habitat data in mind, it is possible to speculate on the biogeographic history of this species using data and maps published by Delcourt and Delcourt (1980).

It is not clear when the proposed division of populations of fox squirrels into eastern and western groups may have originated. Even 40,000 years ago it is likely that the two groups were separated by a wide band of wetland and mesic vegetation in the Mississippi Valley and that they were largely confined to eastern and western regions by northern forests extending across North Carolina and Tennessee. During the slightly warmer conditions of the Wisconsin Interstadial (25,000 BP) suitable hardwood forests increased in area in the southeast making gene exchange between the two groups more likely in the upper Mississippi River Valley. Even this limited interchange would have come to a halt by 18,000 yr BP at the time of the Wisconsin Glacial Maximum. Not only was the area of suitable habitat markedly reduced by boreal forests occupying all of the central United States and possibly by sand dune scrub in Florida, but the small remaining oak-pine forests to the south were divided by a wide barrier of cold-adapted vegetation along the Mississippi River. The divergence of the two groups of squirrels might thus have been accelerated at this time. In spite of improving conditions by 14,000 yr B.P., the two groups probably remained completely isolated. By 10,000 yr B.P., many forests or forest elements had moved north in response to retreating glaciers. The squirrels of the west could have moved north into oak and mixed forests; those of the southeast had access to a newly forested Florida, but may have been prevented from moving north by dense mixed mesophytic forest in the Carolinas and Tennessee. Gene exchange between the two groups still would have been limited by Mississippi River wetland and unsuitable forest types to the north. The warm and dry Hypsithermal Interval (5000 yr B.P.) saw the development of southern pine forests, east and west of the Mississippi River floodplain, and the extension of this and oak pine forest to the north, especially in the eastern coastal plain. Fox squirrels in the west may have resettled hardwood forests in the midwestern United States, as far north as the Great Lakes by this time. Eastern fox squirrels could have extended their range northward into New York and southern New England. Sometime before 5,000 B.P., a small "founder" population of gray and white animals may have settled in the Delmarva area before rising sea levels flooded the intervening lowlands and partially isolated them from other eastern migrants. Gene exchange between eastern and western forms was probably well established south of the Appalachian Mountains by 6500 B.P. At the time of European settlement, fox squirrels would have occupied much of the east, and gene flow north and south of the higher ridges of the Appalachian Mountains would have been fairly extensive, but still limited by the central Appalachian Mountains and the Mississippi River.

The above is a tentative explanation of how and perhaps when the eastern and western groups of fox squirrels became differentiated. Both were isolated for a considerable period; both could migrate north to establish north-south ranges and perhaps clinal trends before appreciable east-west gene exchange was reestablished. Each group inhabited forests which were largely different in species composition and food resources and which differed in maritime versus continental climatic conditions.

In the past few years much has been said about biodiversity: its value, vulnerability and preservation (Wilson, 1993). Such concern has usually focused on the numbers of species living together in a given area. Because of the formerly unexpected level of variability within the single species *Sciurus niger* throughout its range and the apparent relationship between this variability and geographic differences in food type, distribution, quantity and periodicity as well as climate, it might be argued that diversity is conserved only when some array of populations has been evaluated and protected. Without this awareness fox squirrels will cease to exist over much of eastern North America.

ACKNOWLEDGMENTS

We wish to thank the staff of the following museums and collections for permitting us to examine their specimens of fox squirrels : National Museum of Natural History, Washington, D.C.; Museum of Natural History, University of Kansas, Lawrence, Kansas; Museum of Zoology, University of Michigan, Ann Arbor, Michigan; Museum of Natural and Cultural History, Oklahoma State University, Stillwater, Oklahoma; Memphis State University Museum of Zoology, Department of Biology, Memphis State University, Memphis, Tennessee; Louisiana State University Museum of Zoology, Louisiana State University, Baton Rouge, Louisiana ; The Museum, Michigan State University, East Lansing, Michigan; North Carolina State University Mammal Collections, North Carolina State University, Raleigh, North Carolina; North Carolina State Museum of Natural History, Raleigh, North Carolina; Wake Forest University Vertebrate Collection, Wake Forest University, Winston-Salem, North Carolina. Printouts of specimen information can be provided on request but were considered too voluminous to include in this summary paper. We wish to express our gratitude to T.D. Blumenthal and E. Jones for assistance with statistical and computer problems, to V. Flyger, N. Moncrief and an unknown reviewer for helpful comments on the manuscript, to numbers of colleagues, students and North Carolina citizens who provided help and encouragement over a period of many years, and to many family members for their aid and understanding.

LITERATURE CITED

BANGS, O. 1986. A review of the squirrels of eastern North America. Proceedings of the Biological Society of Washington, 10: 145-167.

BARNETT, R. J. 1977. Bergmann's rule and variation in structures related to feeding in the gray squirrel. Evolution, 51: 538-545.

BRAUN, E .L. 1964. Deciduous forests of eastern North America. Hafner Publishing Company, New York, 596 pp.

CAHALANE, V. H. 1961. Mammals of North America. The MacMillan Company, New York, 682 pp.

DAVIS, M. B. 1976. Pleistocene biogeography of temperate deciduous forests. Geoscience and Man 13, 13-26.

——— 1983. Holocene vegetational history of the eastern United States. Pp. 161-181, *in* Late Quaternary Environments of the United States. Vol. II. The Holocene (H.E. Wright, ed.). University of Minnesota Press, Minneapolis, 227 pp.

DELCOURT, H. R., AND P. A. DELCOURT. 1984. Ice age haven for hardwoods. Natural History, 93: 22-28.

DELCOURT, P. A., AND H. R. DELCOURT, 1981. Vegetation maps for eastern North America: 40,000 yr BP to the present. Pp. 123-165, *in* Geobotany II (R.C. Romans, ed.). Plenum Press, New York, 308 pp.

——— 1987. Long-term forest dynamics of the temperate zone: a case study of Late-Quaternary forests in eastern North America. Springer-Verlag, New York, 439pp.

GAMROTH, M. S. 1988. The southeastern fox squirrel (*Sciurus niger*) as a mycophagist: implications for the role of mutualism in perpetuating southeastern forests. M.S. thesis, Wake Forest University, Winston-Salem, North Carolina, 63 pp.

HA, J. C. 1983. Food supply and home range in the fox squirrel (*Sciurus niger*). M.S. thesis, Wake Forest University, Winston-Salem, North Carolina, 32 pp.

HALL, E. R. 1981. The mammals of North America. Second ed., John Wiley & Sons, New York, 1:1-600 + *90*.

KILTIE, R. A. 1989. Wildfire and the evolution of dorsal melanism in fox squirrels, *Sciurus niger*. Journal of Mammalogy, 70: 726-739.

——— 1992. Test of hypotheses on predation as a factor maintaining polymorphic melanism in coastal-plain fox squirrels (*Sciurus niger* L.). Biological Journal of the Linnean Society, 45: 17-37.

KÜCHLER, A. W. 1964. Potential natural vegetation of the coterminous United States. American Geographical Society, New York. 111 pp + map.

KURTEN, B., AND E. ANDERSON. 1980. Pleistocene mammals of North America. Columbia University Press, New York, 442 pp.

LOWREY, G. H. 1974. The mammals of Louisiana and its adjacent waters. Louisiana State University Press, Baton Rouge, 565 pp.

LUNDELIUS, E. L., JR., R. W. GRAHAM, E. ANDERSON, J. GUILDAY, J. A. HOLMAN, D. STEADMAN, AND S. D. WEBB. 1983. Terrestrial vertebrate fauna. Pp. 311-353, *in* Late Quaternary environments of the United States. Volume I. The late Pleistocene (S.C. Porter, ed.). University of Minnesota Press, Minneapolis, 407 pp.

MONCRIEF, N. D. 1993. Geographic variation in fox squirrels (*Sciurus niger*) and gray squirrels (*S. carolinensis*) of the lower Mississippi River valley. Journal of Mammalogy, 74: 547-576.

MONCRIEF, N. D., J. W. EDWARDS AND P. A. TAPPE. 1993. Proceedings of the second symposium on southeastern fox squirrels, *Sciurus niger*. Special Publication, Virginia Museum of Natural History, 1:1-84.

MOORE, J. C. 1956. Variation in the fox squirrel in Florida. The American Midland Naturalist, 55: 41-65.

NOWAK, P. M., AND J. L. PARADISO. 1983. Walker's mammals of the world, Fourth ed. The John Hopkins University Press, Baltimore, 1:1-568, 2:569-1362.

POOLE, E. L. 1944. The technical names of the northeastern fox squirrels. Journal of Mammalogy, 25: 315-317.

SECREST, D. 1990. The olfactory basis of fox squirrel (*Sciurus niger* Linnaeus) foraging on the truffle *Elaphomyces granulatus* Fr.: implications for squirrel habitat mutualism. M.S. thesis, Wake Forest University, Winston-Salem, North Carolina, 89 pp.

SEMKEN, H. A., JR. 1983. Holocene mammalian biogeography and climatic change in the eastern and central United States. Pp. 182-207, *in* Late-Quaternary environments of the United States. Volume II. The Holocene (H. E. Wright, ed.). University of Minnesota Press, Minneapolis, 277 pp.

SOKAL, R. R., AND F. J. ROHLF. 1981. Biometry: the principles and practice of statistics in biological research. Second ed. W.H. Freeman and Company, San Francisco, California, 859 pp.

STEELE, M. A. 1988. Patch use and foraging behavior by the fox squirrel (*Sciurus niger*): tests of theoretical predictions. Ph.D. dissertation, Wake Forest University, Winston-Salem, North Carolina, 220 pp.

STEELE, M. A., AND P. D. WEIGL. 1992. Energetics and patch use in the fox squirrel, *Sciurus niger*: responses to variation in prey profitability and patch density. The American Midland Naturalist, 128: 156-157.

——— 1993. The ecological significance of body size in fox squirrels (*Sciurus niger*) and gray squirrels (*S. carolinensis*). Pp. 57-69, *in* Proceedings of the second symposium on southeastern fox squirrels, *Sciurus niger* (N. D. Moncrief, J. W. Edwards, and P. A. Tappe, eds.). Special Publication, Virginia Museum of Natural History, 1:1-84.

WEIGL, P. D., M. A. STEELE, L. J. SHERMAN, J. C. HA, AND T. L. SHARPE. 1989. The ecology of the fox squirrel *Sciurus niger*) in North Carolina: implications for survival in the Southeast. Bulletin of Tall Timbers Research Station, 24: 1-93.

WILLIAMS, A. I. 1977. Energetic determinants of size in the fox squirrel, *Sciurus niger*. M.S. thesis, Wake Forest University, Winston-Salem, North Carolina, 97 pp.

WILSON, E. O. 1992. The diversity of life. W. W. Norton and Company, New York, 424 pp.

FOOD HABITS AND EVOLUTIONARY RELATIONSHIPS OF THE TASSEL-EARED SQUIRREL (*SCIURUS ABERTI*)

JACK S. STATES AND PETER J. WETTSTEIN

Department of Biology, Northern Arizona University, Flagstaff , AZ 86011 (JSS)
Department of Surgery and Immunology, Mayo Foundation, Rochester, MN 55905 (PJW)

ABSTRACT.—The present distribution of the Abert's, or tassel-eared squirrel, *Sciurus aberti*, is confined to forests dominated by ponderosa pine, *Pinus ponderosa*, in the southern Rocky Mountains and the montane islands of Arizona, New Mexico, and northern Mexico. A review of the current knowledge on the six known subspecies is presented with a focus on the relationship of food habits and foraging behavior to their restricted distribution patterns, genetic diversity, and evolutionary history. Genetic analyses of *S. aberti* resulted in the recognition of a minimum of four subspecies in geographically separated assemblages. Two notable features of foraging behavior common to all subspecies were the strong feeding preference shown for sporocarps of hypogeous fungi and their selective herbivory on the inner bark of ponderosa pine. No other sciurid within the range of Abert's squirrels was found to exhibit this particular year-round foraging pattern. The squirrels appear to play an important ecological role as dispersal agents for the spores which they defecate following consumption of the sporocarps. Upon germination, spores of hypogeous fungi form obligate mutualistic associations with ponderosa pine roots (mycorrhizae), and thereby enhance seedling survival and forest regeneration. Availability of fungi for food appears to be linked to squirrel distribution and abundance. Squirrel feeding preferences for certain pines was found to be related to the terpene composition of resin in the inner bark. A review of literature on terpene-related, selective herbivory of conifers revealed a remarkable coincidence in the geographic distribution of the subspecific assemblages of squirrels relative to the biochemical classification of ponderosa pine host in their particular region, a classification based on the genetically controlled monoterpene composition of xylem resin. These studies are discussed as a putative example of coevolution: adaptation, interaction, and interdependence of Abert's squirrels with ponderosa pine and associated mycorrhizal fungi over a long period of time.

INTRODUCTION

The "tassel-eared" or "Abert's" squirrel, *Sciurus aberti*, is the only arboreal squirrel in North America known to be a strict ecological associate with a single, widespread conifer species, ponderosa pine (*Pinus ponderosa)*. Although ponderosa pine is found throughout mountainous regions from Canada to central Mexico, the modern distribution of this squirrel extends only from the eastern side of the Rocky Mountains, from extreme south-central Wyoming and northern Colorado, south to the Sierra Occidentale in western Durango, Mexico (Hall and Kelson, 1959). The distribution pattern of the Abert's squirrel is discontinuous and confined for the most part to montane "islands" of various size separated by expanses of non-forested and unsuitable habitat.

The geographically isolated squirrel populations exhibit both a wide range of coat coloration and enough morphological variability to justify the recognition of two species and eight subspecies (Hall and Kelson, 1959). *S. kaibabensis* and *S. aberti* were recognized as separate species primarily on the basis of striking differences in coat color and color pattern. The Grand Canyon of the Colorado

In M.A. Steele, J. F. Merritt, and D. A. Zegers (eds.). 1998. Ecology and Evolutionary Biology of Tree Squirrels. Special Publication, Virginia Museum of Natural History, 6: 320 pp

River separates these two populations from one another and their geographic isolation has been considered to be the major factor responsible for speciation by divergence. Although frequently cited in contemporary biology textbooks (Keeton and Gould, 1993) as an example of allopatric speciation via geographic separation, biologists still disagree as to whether the two populations have reached the level of full species. In a comprehensive review of morphometric data of all taxa in the subgenus *Otosciurus*. Hoffmeister and Diersing (1978) recognized as valid only one species, *S. aberti aberti*, and five other subspecies. Compounding this taxonomic debate is strong controversy over theories proposed to account for the modern geographic distribution of Abert's squirrel subspecies and mechanisms of dispersal (Davis and Brown, 1989; Lomolino et al., 1989). The need for explanations regarding the fragmented distribution patterns, the close association with ponderosa pine, and the evolutionary history of the Abert squirrel was the most compelling reason for our current research.

This paper reviews current knowledge on the six subspecies of tassel-eared squirrels, focusing on what the authors and others have researched concerning the relationship of food habits and foraging behavior to their restricted distribution on montane islands of ponderosa pine in the Southwest. Combined with the results of our studies on genetic diversity and divergence in *S. aberti* subspecies, this information is discussed as a putative example of coevolution: Abert squirrel adaptation, interaction, and interdependence with ponderosa pine and its associated mycorrhizal fungi over a long period of time.

DIET COMPOSITION AND FORAGING BEHAVIOR

Much of the ecological and biogeographical literature on tassel-eared squirrels has focused on the identification of factors accounting for their strict ecological dependence on ponderosa pine for food and habitat. Their food habits and foraging behavior are unusual in several respects. Diets of Abert's squirrels invariably include fungi, mycelium and fruiting bodies of hypogeous fungi (truffles) and epigeous fungi (mushrooms) that often approach 100% of the stomach volume in some seasons (Stephenson, 1975; Kotter and Farentinos, 1984*a*; States, 1985). These fungi are known to form obligate, mutualistic symbioses with ponderosa pine rootlets as mycorrhizae (Heidmann and Cornett, 1986; Riffle, 1989). Because the squirrels serve as a dispersal vector for the mycorrhizal fungi they consume, it is also probable that they indirectly influence the distribution of their pine host (Fogel and Trappe, 1978; Kotter and Farentinos , 1984*b*; Molina et al., 1992).

Another significant aspect of foraging behavior that illustrates a unique association of Abert's squirrels with ponderosa pine is their use of inner bark (phloem). Whereas other tree squirrels only occassionally strip or chew the bark from live trees, selecting it as a supplement to their usual diet (Gurnell, 1987), Abert's squirrels consume inner bark on a year-round basis and it constitutes a major portion of their winter diet. They characteristically focus their herbivory on the terminal branches in the upper portions of the canopy. Here, twig segments of variable length and distance from the apical bud are excised and the outer bark is systematically "peeled" away. The thin layer of exposed phloem is separated from the underlying woody xylem, and eaten. The remaining twig, terminal needle cluster, and apical bud is dropped to the ground (sometimes apical buds are also eaten). This pattern of defoliation and the highly visible carpet of clippings and peeled twigs serve as reliable indicators of presence and distribution of the squirrel (Keith, 1965; Hall, 1981).

The squirrels also demonstrate a strong feeding preference for specific trees; selective feeding that often results in the virtual defoliation of the "target" tree tops (Snyder, 1993). Several factors that seem to play a role the in selective herbivory of inner bark include carbohydrate content (Thomas, 1979), ease of peeling (Pederson and Welch, 1985), and the amount and diversity of terpenes in the sap (Farentinos et al., 1981, Zhang and States, 1991). Gaud et al. (1993) observed repetitive feeding to be limited to 25% of the stand and that the likelihood of being a favored tree increased with tree size and reproductive maturity. As a result of selective foraging a significant decline in tree growth and reproductive fitness of target trees has been documented (Snyder, 1993). In ponderosa pine, organic components, such as terpenes, appear to be under genetic control (Smith, 1977), and their presence and diversity has been used to resolve their taxonomy. Thus, Abert's squirrels, through selective herbivory, may serve as an agent in natural selection, and over many years of dependent association, influence the phylogenetic history of ponderosa pine.

Although Abert's squirrels are the only tree squirrel to establish year-round residence in pure stands of ponderosa pine in the Southwest, home ranges of other tree squirrels overlapping ecotones where ponderosa pine is mixed with other conifer and hardwood species. The pine squirrel, *Tamiasciurus hudsonicus*, is occassionally found with Abert's squirrels in areas of higher elevation where Douglas fir is mixed with ponderosa pine. Their diet, principally of seed cones, also includes fruiting bodies of mushrooms and truffles (Smith, 1968) as well as occasional terminal buds and some inner bark (J. S. States, in litt). The Arizona gray squirrel, *Sciurus arizonensis*, occupies woodland and riparian habitats with mixed conifer and deciduous trees at lower elevations and exhibits limited mycophagy (Shewmaker, 1987). The ground-dwelling sciurids which are most frequently encountered in the under-story of ponderosa pine stands include chipmunks, *Tamias*, the golden-mantled ground squirrel, *Spermophilus lateralis*, and the rock squirrel, *Spermophilus variegatus*. These squirrels are known mycophagists (Maser et al., 1978) and although they are potential competitors, their densities are low in stands of ponderosa pine, apparently due to the lack of understory vegetation (Hall and Kelson, 1959).

We examined the stomach contents of four subspecies of Abert's squirrels (*S. a. aberti, S. a. kaibabensis, S. a. chuskensis, S. a. ferreus*) and the three most frequently encountered squirrels foraging within Abert's habitat, as listed above. Samples were collected in the autumn, a period when the highest quantity and diversity of food items are available (Stephenson, 1975, Theobald, 1983). The fidelity of selective herbivory on ponderosa pine and mycophagy on its associated mycorrhizal fungi by Abert's squirrels seems to be more pronounced than that of any other sciurid in its range (Table 1). No recognizable tissues of inner bark were found in any squirrel other than the Abert's subspecies. Hypogeous fungi were consumed by all taxa in greater quantity than epigeous fungi. Although available to all squirrels sampled, fungi were consumed in greater quantity by all four Abert's subspecies, 58% of the stomach volumes, compared to 23% for the other squirrels. Stomach contents of the other squirrels were more diverse and contained many items not consumed by the four subspecies.

As inhabitants of conifer forests, both squirrels consume similar diet items, but a long term diet study of pine squirrels indicated little or no preferential feeding on inner bark (Smith, 1970). This temperance may be explained by observations of apparent difficulty in digestion. In comparative feeding trials where captive squirrels were fed perforce on inner bark, very little of the structural plant tissue was digested by pine squirrels in contrast to its nearly complete reduction by Abert's squirrels (J.S. States, in litt). In addition, pine squirrels typically larderhoard massive caches of cones and aggressively defend them. In striking contrast, Abert's squirrels scatterhoard small caches of pine cones and acorns and exhibit no defensive behavior. Because pine squirrels have been found to occur within ponderosa pine forests outside the geographic range of Abert's squirrels, they could be viewed as habitat generalists, and the separation of the two may be partly due to differences in utilization of food resources. Cone crops of ponderosa pine are highly variable and

Table 1.—*The occurrence of selected food items in the stomachs of Abert's squirrels* (Sciurus) *and associated sciurids collected during autumn in ponderosa pine forests. Values indicate average percent (%) of diet by volume in stomachs. Number of stomachs examined =* (n).

		Food Item (%)					
	n	Seed	Plant matter	Inner bark	All fungi	Hypogeous fungi	Epigeous fungi
S. a. aberti	10	28.7	1.8	7.0	60.2	47.7	12.5
S. a. kaibabensis	10	40.2	1.2	7.8	50.8	45.0	5.8
S. a. chuscensis	10	30.0	1.0	12.0	57.0	57.0	0.0
S. a. ferreus	10	29.7	0.5	5.6	64.2	48.9	15.3
S. arizonensis	10	26.3	64.9	0.0	8.8	5.7	3.1
Tamiasciurus hudsonicus	9	66.5	3.5	0.0	30.0	17.5	12.5
Spermophilus lateralis	3	10.0	62.5	0.0	27.5	22.5	5.0
Spermophilus variegatus	2	2.0	73.5	0.0	24.0	24.0	0.0

unreliable as a food source for both squirrels (Larson and Schubert, 1970). The ability of Abert's squirrels to specially utilize inner bark and hypogeous fungi as alternative food resources may account, in part, for their predominance in ponderosa pine forests.

The importance of fungi in diets of squirrels has been well documented. Austin (1990) found the nutrient content of truffles and mushrooms to be comparable to that of pine seed and inner bark. He concluded that the nutrient levels of fungi should satisfy energetic demands of Abert's squirrels during periods when other primary foods are in short supply. Fruiting bodies of mycorrhizal fungi and inner bark constitute a major portion of their diet on annual basis (Fig. 1). Although total caloric values (kcal\g dry weight) of these fungi are lower (4.4) than pine seed (6.2), they are available in all seasons, and when produced in abundance, contribute to increased body weight (Austin, 1990). In a comparison of biweekly body weights of four, live trapped, free-ranging squirrels through four seasons, States et al. (1988) reported a winter weight loss that paralleled the decrease in availability of fungi, as evidenced by their presence in fecal contents (Fig. 2). Mycophagy has also been reported to be nutritionally advantageous on the basis that fungi are energetically less expensive to consume (Smith, 1970), and they provide higher concentrations of metabolic salts, sodium, potassium, and magnesium, than any other major diet item (Austin, 1990).

Because of their dietary importance, the availability of fungi seems to be critically important in regulating squirrel distribution and abundance. Mortality in Abert's squirrels was related to the depth of snow cover which limited the availability of food resources on the ground (Stephenson and Brown, 1980). States et al. (1988) reported a marked increase in inner bark consumption coincident with increased snow depth, and a corresponding decrease in truffle and availability of seed cones. Also, home ranges of Abert's squirrels were shown to fluctuate in accordance with food supply.

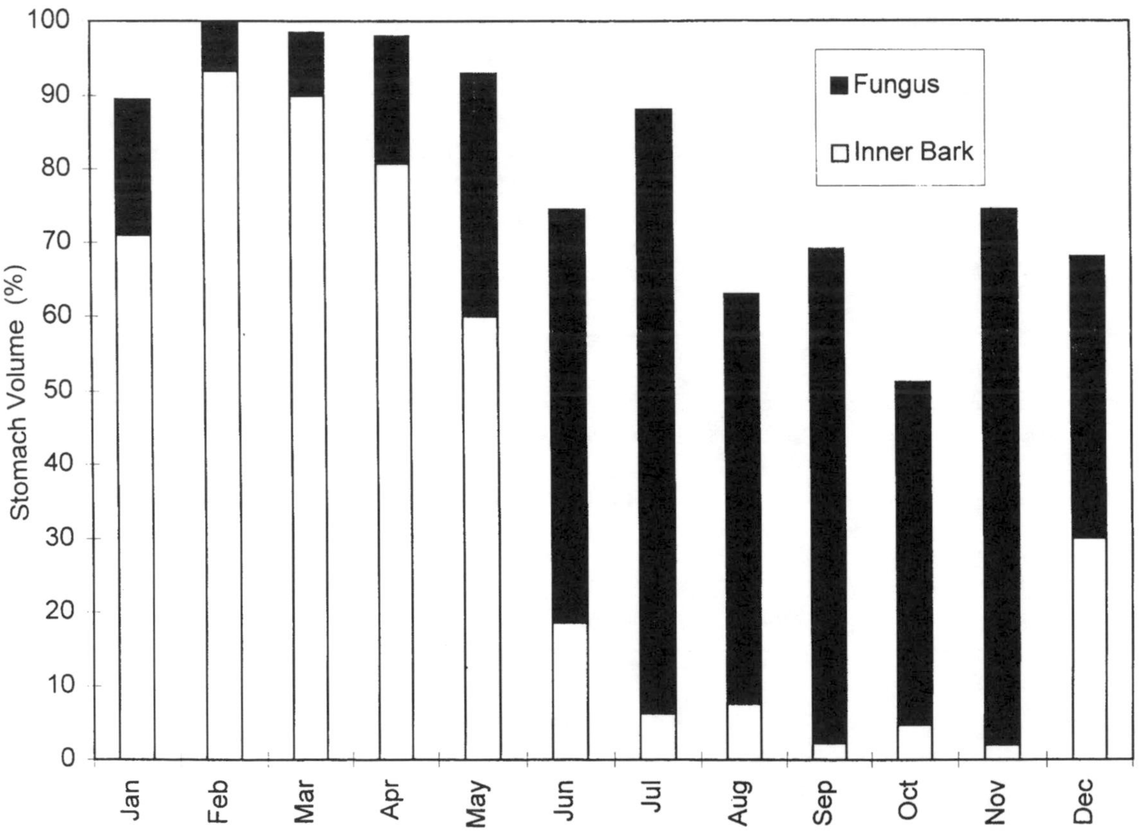

Fig. 1.—Occurrence of fungi and inner bark in stomach contents of Abert's squirrels sampled monthly in a ponderosa pine forest. Values are the monthly averages of the percentage stomach volume occupied by each item in 10 stomach samples.

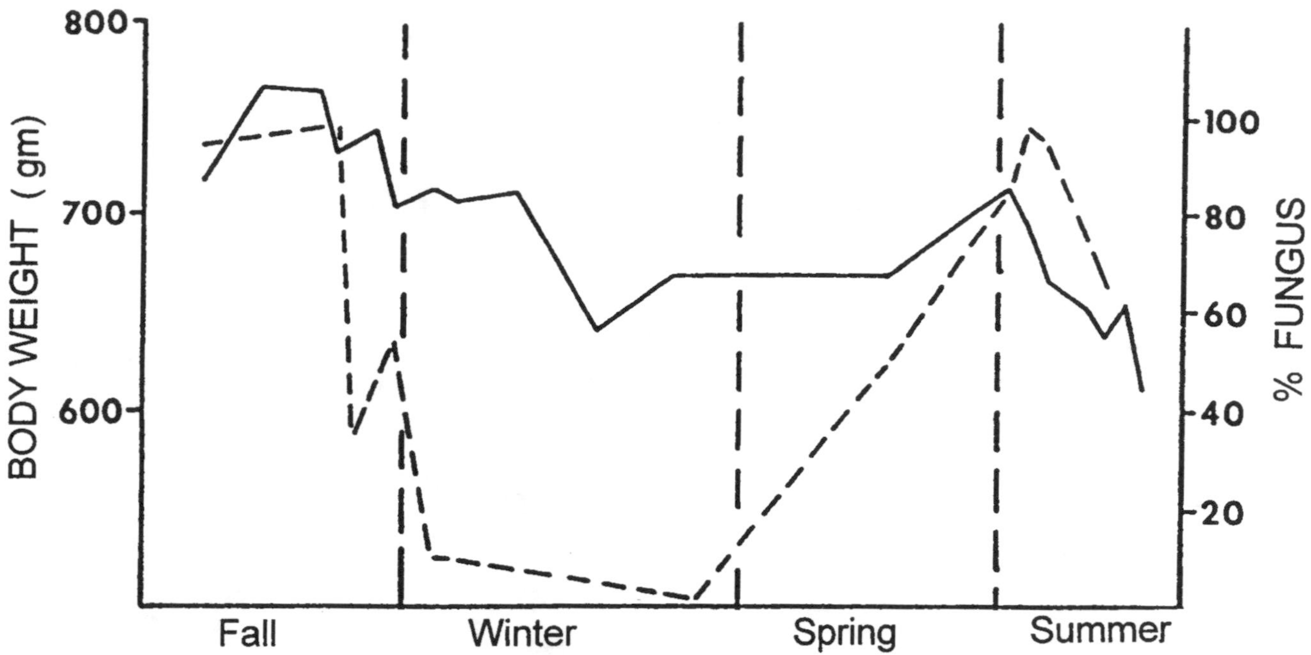

Fig. 2.—Body weights (solid line) of Abert's squirrels compared to fungal content of feces (dotted line) over a year in Coconino National Forest, Arizona (From States et al., 1988).

GENETIC DIVERSITY AND DIVERGENCE

Analysis of genetic relatedness within subspecies of *S. aberti* was conducted early in our research (Wettstein and States, 1986*a*, 1986*b*). We examined the diversity of gene families in the major histocompatibility complex genes and found little evidence to indicate divergence between *S. a. aberti* and *S. a. kaibabensis*. More definitive estimates of divergence using mitochondrial DNA analysis of restriction site polymorphisms (Wettstein et al., 1994), allowed us to recognize, from among the four subspecies present in the United States, two major squirrel assemblages: 1) an *aberti : kaibabensis* group; and 2) a *chuscensis : ferreus* group. Using sequences of the entire cytochrome-*b* gene from samples of all six subspecies of *S. aberti,* we confirmed and extended our previous results in the recognition of three major, geographically separated subspecies assemblages: 1) *barberi*:*durangi* in the western Sierra Madre of Mexico; 2) *ferreus:chuscensis* in the central and southern Rocky Mountains; and 3) *aberti:kaibabensis* in the Colorado Plateau region of Arizona and New Mexico (Wettstein et al., 1995).

Our proposed subspecies groups are in general agreement with the morphological classification and patterns of geographic distribution proposed by Hoffmeister and Diersing (1978). But there are some notable exceptions (Fig. 3). The populations from the San Juan Mountains(Colorado), Santa Fe National Forest (New Mexico), and Manti-LaSal National Forest (Utah) originally designated as *S. a. aberti*, clearly possess mitochondrial DNA of *S. a. ferreus*. Using analysis of neighbor joining and maximum parsimony we identified what appeared to be a level of substructuring of the *S. a. ferreus* population (Wettstein et al., 1995). Consequently, the range of *S. a. ferreus*, depicted in Fig. 2, has been divided into an eastern (E) and a western (W) population geographically separated by low elevation associated with the Rio Grande river drainage (Fig. 3). The high degree of genetic relatedness between *S. a. aberti* and *S. a. kaibabensis* is supportive of the reluctance expressed by Hoffmeister and Diersing (1978) to provide subspecies status for *S. a. kaibabensis* on the basis of morphometric similarities.

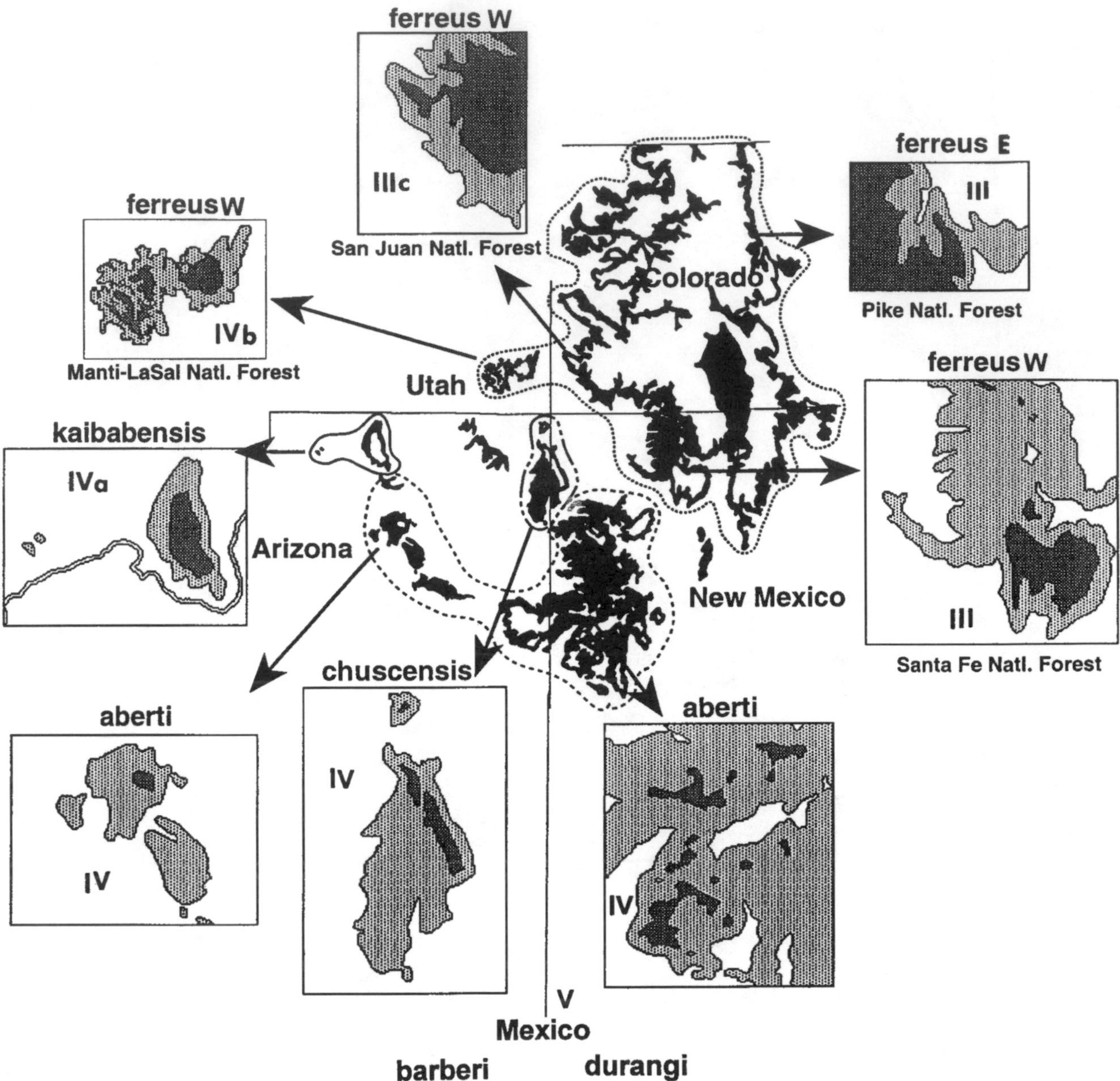

Fig. 3.—Geographic location of subspecies of *Sciurus aberti* and their inferred ranges from an analysis of genetic diversity and divergence. Shaded areas in the full map correspond to ponderosa pine habitat of Abert's squirrels, the light shaded areas in the insert maps indicate high elevation mixed conifer habitat of red squirrels, and the patterned lines encompass subspecies ranges. Roman numerals indicate the biochemical region assigned to ponderosa pines by Smith (1977). Modified from Wettstein et al.(1996).

PATTERNS OF ADAPTATION AND EVOLUTION

In the preceding account we illustrated the relationships that define the ecological "niche" relationships of Abert's squirrels with their pine habitat highlighting the selective nature of their foraging on inner bark of terminal twigs from target trees, pine seeds, and hypogeous fungi, which form mycorrhizal symbionts with pine roots. On the basis of nucleotide divergence, a minimum of four subspecies occupying separate geographc regions were identified and arranged into separate, genetically related assemblages. Based on these analyses, we postulate that the subspecies became genetically distinct sometime before the Wisconsin glacial period about 2 mya (Wettstein et al., 1995). Geographically, the distribution of ponderosa pine far exceeds that of the squirrel populations. However, the subspecies appear to be restricted to well defined montane islands of the southwestern United States and northern Mexico in localities where their host is always present.

In view of a possible historical association of nearly two million years, we are prompted to speculate here on the co-evolutionary relationships that may have developed. Like the squirrels, ponderosa pine is genetically diverse and the species has been separated into several varieties and races (Conkle and Critchfield, 1988). Smith (1977) separates the geographic range of races of ponderosa pine into five chemical regions whose boundaries are defined by the genetically controlled monoterpene composition of xylem resin. There is a surprising coincidence in the geographic distribution of the species assemblages of the squirrels and the monoterpene regions that characterize the host range: *barberi:durangi* = region V;. *aberti;kaibabensis* = region IV; and *ferreus:chuscensis* = region III (Fig. 2). A lesser degree of coincidence for individual subspecies was observed in situations where their host trees contain unique percentages of one or more of the five major monoterpene components. For example, large, possibly sub-regional shifts in terpene ratios within region IV (Smith, 1977), were noted for the north Kaibab plateau occupied by *S. a. kaibabensis* and for the Manti-LaSal forest occupied by *S. a. ferreus* E. We have designated these regions as IVa and IVb in Fig. 3. The selective foraging behavior of Abert's squirrels suggests that they may play a major role as agents of natural selection in their association with their biochemically diverse pine hosts. Farentinos et al. (1981) found amounts of monoterpenes to be significantly lower in twigs collected from trees selected by *S. a. ferreus* for consumption of inner bark. Furthermore, *a*-pinene was the best single predictor of tree selection, i.e. greater concentrations in the inner bark resulted in a higher degree of avoidance by the squirrels.

Trees in biochemical region III have large amounts of 3-carene, moderate amounts of myrcene and *b*-pinene, and small amounts of *a*-pinene and limonene (Smith, 1977). In contrast, inner bark resins of trees in region IV have very high proportions of *a*-pinene and 3-carene, with smaller amounts of *b*-pinene, myrcene, and limonene. Inner bark from trees selected for feeding by *S. a. aberti* contained high amounts of *a*-pinene which did not appear to influence their herbivory. Three monoterpenes present in low concentrations, myrcene, sabinene, and terpinolene, appeared to be the most important feeding deterrents in non-feed trees in *aberti* habitats (Zhang and States,1991).

A parallel example of selective feeding behavior involves the comparative feeding habits of the mountain pine beetle (*Dendroctonus ponderosae*) on two biochemically diverse races of ponderosa pine in California (Region II) and the Rocky Mountains (Region III). In California, Sturgeon (1979) observed marked avoidance of trees with high limonene content resulting larger numbers of pines with high concentrations of limonene and fewer numbers of trees with high *a*-pinene concentrations. This pattern was not detected in pine beetle interactions with the Rocky Mountain population, but there was a significantly higher biochemical diversity of pines in this region (Sturgeon and Mitton, 1986). We suggest that the selective and distinctive feeding habits, documented in both herbivores, help to maintain the characteristic biochemical diversity of the ponderosa pine races with which they are associated.

Hypogeous fungi form obligate, mycorrhizal associations with ponderosa pine and they are dependent on animals, especially squirrels, for spore dispersal. The pines are dependent to a large extent on mycorrhizal fungi for their mineral nutrition and in this regard several hypotheses have been advanced for co-evolution of these fungi with their tree associates (Fogel, 1992). Very little is known regarding aspects of speciation in hypogeous fungi but on an evolutionary scale they exhibit high species diversity and are known to form species specific associations with host trees (Molina et al., 1992). Hypogeous fungi have apparently undergone rapid morphological divergence in response to selective pressures of cold, arid environments (Bruns et al., 1989). The rapid evolution of ponderosa pine before and during the Pleistocene epoch, and its adaptation to strongly seasonal climates and drier sites in western North America was presumably enhanced by mycorrhizal associations which gave them an adaptive advantage over other species in stressful environments (Axelrod, 1986). It can be reasonably assumed that ectomycorrhizal fungi made adaptive responses to the adaptive radiation of the host.

Finally, the putative co-evolution of ectomycorrhizal host trees with ponderosa pine has had an impact on the squirrels as well. Hypogeous fungi make a substantial contribution to the diets of the rodents which disperse their spores. They provide considerable energy and mineral nutrition, and they are clearly favored in *S. aberti* foraging behavior. Their availability during seasons when other food items are in short supply may be a critical factor influencing the distribution and emigration of Abert's squirrels. For example, the relationship between climate and fungus availability may account for the failure of these squirrels to successfully occupy ponderosa pine forests north of the 41st parallel in North America. We conclude that continued study of the apparent interactive relationships among squirrels, pines, and fungi will contribute significantly to an understanding of their evolutionary history.

ACKNOWLEDGMENTS

The authors gratefully acknowledge access to study areas and scientific collecting permits issued by: the U. S. Park Service, Grand Canyon National Park, AZ; the U. S. Forest Service for the Coconino, Coronado, and Kaibab National Forests, AZ; the Arizona Game and Fish Department, Phoenix, AZ.; the New Mexico Department of Game and Fish, Santa Fe, NM; the Navajo Fish and Wildlife Branch, Navajo Nation, Window Rock, AZ; and the Colorado Division of Wildlife, Denver, CO. This research was supported in part by grants GM-41260 and GM-41399 from the National Institutes of Health and by a faculty grant to the senior author by Northern Arizona University, Flagstaff, AZ.

LITERATURE CITED

AUSTIN, W. J. 1990. The foraging ecology of Abert squirrels. Ph.D. dissertation, Northern Arizona University, Flagstaff, 279 pp.

AXELROD, D. I. 1986. Cenozoic history of some western American Pines. Annals of the Missouri Botanical Garden 73:565-641.

BRUNS, T., R. FOGEL, T. J. WHITE, AND J. PALMER. 1989. Accelerated evolution of a false truffle from a mushroom ancestor. Nature, 339:140-142.

CONKLE, M. T., AND W. B. CRITCHFIELD. 1988. Genetic variation and hybridization of ponderosa pine. Pp. 27-43, *in* Ponderosa pine: the species and its management (D. M. Baumgartner and J. E. Lotan, eds.). Washington State Cooperative Extension, Pullman, 281 pp.

DAVIS, R., AND D. E. BROWN. 1989. Role of post-pleistocene dispersal in determining the modern distribution of Abert's squirrel. The Great Basin Naturalist, 49:425-424.

FARENTINOS, R. C., P. J. CAPRETTA, R. E. KEPNER, AND V. M. LITTLEFIELD. 1981. Selective herbivory in tassel-eared squirrels: role of monoterpenes in ponderosa pine chosen as feeding trees. Science, 213:1273-1275.

FOGEL, R., 1992. Evolutionary processes in truffles and false-truffles: evidence from distribution of hypogeous fungi in the Great Basin, USA. Micologiae Vegetazione Mediterranea, 7:13-30.

FOGEL, R., AND J. M. TRAPPE. 1978. Fungus consumption (mycophagy) by small mammals. Northwest Science, 52:1-31.

GAUD, W. S., W. S. ALLRED, AND J. S. STATES. 1993. Tree selection by tassel-eared squirrels of the ponderosa pine forests of the Colorado Plateau. Pp. 56-63, *in* Proceedings of the 1st Biennial Conference on Research in Colorado Plateau National Parks. United States Department of Interior, National Park Service Publication NPS/NRNAU/NRTP-93/10, Flagstaff, Arizona, 186 pp.

GURNELL, J. 1987. The natural history of tree squirrels. Facts on File Publications, New York, 201 pp.

HALL, J. G. 1981. A field study of the Kaibab squirrel *Sciurus aberti kaibabensis* in Grand Canyon National Park, Arizona, USA. Wildlife Monographs, 75:1-54.

HALL, J. G., AND KELSON, K. R. 1959. The Mammals of North America. Vol. I. The Ronald Press Company, New York. 1:xxx + 1-546 + *79*.

HEIDMANN, L. J., AND Z. J. CORNETT. 1986. Effect of various nutrient regimes and ectomycorrhizal inoculations on field survival and growth of ponderosa pine container seedlings in Arizona Tree Planters Notes, 37:15-19.

HOFFMEISTER, D. F., AND V. E. DIERSING. 1978. Review of the tassel-eared squirrels of the subgenus *Otosciurus*. Journal of Mammalogy, 59:402-413.

KEETON, W. T., AND J. L. GOULD. 1993. Biological Science. Fifth edition. W. W. Norton & Company. New York. 1194 pp.

KEITH, J. O. 1965. The Abert squirrel and its dependence on ponderosa pine. Ecology, 46:150-163.

KOTTER, M. M., AND R. C. FARENTINOS. 1984*a*. Tassel-eared squirrels as spore dispersal agents of hypogeous mycorrhizal fungi. Journal of Mammalogy, 65:684-687.

———. 1984*b*. Formation of Ponderosa pine ectomycorrhizae after inoculation with feces of tassel-eared squirrels. Mycologia, 76:758-760.

LARSON, M. M., AND G. H. SCHUBERT. 1970. Cone crops of ponderosa pine in central Arizona including the influence of Abert squirrels. USDA Forest Service Research Paper RM-58, Rocky Mountain Forest and Range Experiment Station, Fort Collins, Colorado. Pp.15.

LOMOLINO, M. V., J. H. BROWN, AND R. DAVIS. 1989. Island biogeography of montane forest mammals in the American Southwest. Ecology, 70:180-194.

MASER, C. J., J. M. TRAPPE, AND R. A. NUSSBAUM. 1978. Fungal small-mammal interrelationships with emphasis on Oregon coniferous forests. Ecology, 59:799-809.

MOLINA, R., H. MASSICOTTE, AND J. M. TRAPPE. 1992. Specificity phenomena in mycorrhizal symbioses: community-ecological consequences and practical implications. Pp. 357-423, *in* Mycorrhizal functioning: an integrative plant-fungal process. (M. F. Allen, ed.). Chapman & Hall, New York.

PEDERSON, J. C., AND B. L. WELCH. 1985. Comparison of ponderosa pines as feed and non-feed trees for Abert squirrels. Journal of Chemical Ecology, 11:149-157.

RIFFLE, J. W. 1989. Field performance of Ponderosa, Scots, and Austrian pines with ectomycorrhizae in prairie soils. Forest Science, 35:935-945.

SHEWMAKER, J. A. 1987. Fungal Consumption by the Arizona gray squirrel (*Sciurus arizonensis*). M.S. thesis. Northern Arizona University, Flagstaff, 50 pp.

SMITH, C. C. 1968. The adaptive nature of social organization in the genus of tree squirrels *Tamiasciurus*. Ecological Monographs, 38:31-63.

———. 1970. The coevolution of pine squirrels (*Tamiasciurus*) and conifers. Ecological Monographs, 40:349-371.

SMITH, R. H. 1977. Monoterpenes of ponderosa pine xylem resin in western United States. USDA Forest Service Technical Bulletin, 1532, 48 pp.

SNYDER, M. A. 1993. Interactions between Abert's squirrel and ponderosa pine: the relationship between selective herbivory and host plant fitness. The American Naturalist, 141:866-879.

STATES, J. S. 1985. Hypogeous mycorrhizal fungi associated with ponderosa pine: sporocarp phenology. p.271, *In* Proceedings of the 6th North American Conference on Mycorrhizae (R. Molina, ed.) Forest Research Laboratory, Corvallis, OR. (abstract).

STATES, J. S., W. S. GAUD, W. S. ALLRED, AND W. J. AUSTIN. 1988. Foraging patterns of tassel-eared squirrels in selected ponderosa pine stands. Pp. 425-431, *in* Management of Amphibians, Reptiles, and Small Mammals in North America. Proceedings of the Symposium (R. Szaro, K. Severson, and D. Patton, eds.). Forest Service- USDA General Technical Report RM-166, Rocky Mountain Forest and Range Experiment Station, Fort Collins, Colorado, 455 pp.

STEPHENSON, R. L. 1975. Reproductive biology and food habits of Abert's squirrels in central Arizona. M. S. thesis, Arizona State University, Tempe, 66 pp.

STEPHENSON, R. L., AND D. E. BROWN. 1980. Snow cover as a factor influencing tassel-eared squirrel mortality. The Journal of Wildlife Management, 44:951-955.

STURGEON, K. B. 1979. Monoterpene variation in ponderosa pine xylem resin related to western pine beetle predation. Evolution, 33:803-814.

STURGEON, K. B., AND J. B. MITTON. Biochemical diversity of ponderosa pine and predation by bark beetles (Coleoptera: Scolytidae). Journal of Economic Entomology, 79:1064-1068.

THEOBALD, D. 1983. Studies on the biology and habitat of the Arizona gray squirrel. M. S. thesis, Arizona State University, Tempe, 49 pp.

THOMAS, G. R. 1979. The role of phloem sugars in the selection of ponderosa pine by the Kaibab squirrel. M. S. thesis, San Francisco State University, California, 62 pp.

WETTSTEIN, P. J., AND J. S. STATES. 1986*a*. The major histocompatibility complex of tassel-eared squirrels. I. Genetic diversity associated with Kaibab squirrels. Immunogenetics, 24:230-241.

———. 1986*b*. The major histocompatibility complex of tassel-eared squirrels. II. Genetic diversity associated with Abert squirrels. Immunogenetics, 24:242-250.

WETTSTEIN, P. J., P. LAGER, L. JIN, J. STATES, T. LAMB, AND R. CHAKRABORTY. 1994. Phylogeny of mitochondrial DNA clones in tassel-eared squirrels *Sciurus aberti*. Molecular Ecology, 3: 541-550.

WETTSTEIN, P. J., M. STRAUSBACH, T. LAMB, J. STATES, R. CHAKRABORTY, L. JIN, AND R. RIBLET. 1995. Phylogeny of six *Sciurus aberti* subspecies based on nucleotide sequences of cytochrome *b*. Molecular Phylogenetics and Evolution, 4:150-162.

ZHANG, X., AND J. STATES. 1991. Selective herbivory of ponderosa pine by Abert squirrels: a re-examination of the role of terpenes. Biochemical Systematics and Ecology, 19:111-115.

ABERT'S SQUIRRELS (*SCIURUS ABERTI*) IN PONDEROSA PINE (*PINUS PONDEROSA*) FORESTS: DIRECTIONAL SELECTION, DIVERSIFYING SELECTION

MARC A. SNYDER
Department of Biology
Colorado College, Colorado Springs, CO 80903 USA

ABSTRACT.—Abert's squirrels are ecologically dependent upon ponderosa pine for food and cover. They are seasonally dependent on ponderosa pine phloem as a primary food source. The squirrels feed preferentially on trees with specific, genetically determined traits, and their feeding activities have dramatic impacts on the fitness of host trees. Because of this, Abert's squirrels are probably agents of directional selection in host stands of ponderosa pine. A comparison of chemical attributes of trees fed upon by Abert's squirrel, the North American porcupine (*Erethizon dorsatum*), the mountain pine beetle (*Dendroctonus ponderosae*), and the parasitic angiosperm, dwarf-mistletoe (*Arceuthobium vaginatum*) shows that trees with different chemical phenotypes are associated with feeding by each of the four species. Since many of the traits associated with differential feeding are under genetic control, and each species reduces the fitness of trees on which it feeds, these species may act in concert to generate multi-directional selection pressures in host stands. Diversifying selection that can result from such multi-directional selection pressures can potentially contribute to the maintenance of genetic variability in host stands. Management strategies developed for ponderosa pine forests should recognize the role that herbivores and parasites may play in generating diversifying selection, since the maintenance of genetically diverse stands is an important aspect of the conservation of forest communities.

INTRODUCTION

Abert's squirrels (*Sciurus aberti*) are highly specialized and selective herbivores that are restricted to stands of ponderosa pine (*Pinus ponderosa*), upon which they are ecologically dependent for food and nest sites. In this paper, I describe specific aspects of the close ecological relationship between the squirrel and the tree: because the squirrels feed selectively on trees with specific, genetically (Dorman, 1976; Squillace, 1976) determined traits, they impose directional selection pressures in host populations of ponderosa pine. I then consider the squirrel-pine relationship in the broader context of multi-species interactions at the community level, and discuss some of the ecological and evolutionary consequences of these interactions: I argue that differential host utilization by different herbivores and parasites can generate multi-directional selection pressures in host populations of ponderosa pine. Finally, I address management and conservation implications of these interactions: the combined impacts of various forest "pests" can potentially contribute to the maintenance of genetic variability within stands.

THE CLOSE ECOLOGICAL RELATIONSHIP BETWEEN ABERT'S SQUIRREL AND PONDEROSA PINE: DIRECTIONAL SELECTION

The geographic distribution of Abert's squirrels is restricted to ponderosa pine stands in parts of Colorado, New Mexico, Arizona, Utah, and extreme southern Wyoming in the United States, and along the Sierra Madre Occidental in Mexico, from northern Chihuahua and Sonora to southern Durango (Hoffmeister and Diersing, 1978). Virtually all aspects of the squirrel's ecology are tied in some way to ponderosa pine.

In M.A. Steele, J. F. Merritt, and D. A. Zegers (eds.). 1998. Ecology and Evolutionary Biology of Tree Squirrels. Special Publication, Virginia Museum of Natural History, 6: 320 pp

Nests of Abert's squirrels, for example, are found primarily in the crowns of live ponderosa pine trees (Farentinos, 1972; Snyder and Linhart, 1994), although they may occasionally be found in cavities of Gambel oaks (*Quercus gambelii)* or in the branches of cottonwoods (Keith, 1965). Nests are usually constructed from twigs clipped from the nest tree and are lined with grasses, pine needles, and other materials that may be available. Most often, nests occur in the upper crowns of large ponderosa pines, on the south side of the main bole, usually at the point where lateral branches join the trunk (Farentinos, 1972; Snyder and Linhart, 1994). Less frequently, nests are constructed in "witches brooms," pathogenic profusions of small branches that can result from infection by dwarf-mistletoes (*Arceuthobium*). Snyder and Linhart (1994) found that nest trees ranged in size from 29.4 to 93.0 cm in diameter measured at ca 1.2 m in height, and that ordinal placement of nests averaged 176° E of N. Ninety-six percent of nests were found in the upper one-half of the tree crown (most in the upper one-third). Nest-height to crown-height ratio averaged 0.68, and nest height ranged from about 7 to about 20 m above the ground. Most nest trees had branches that interdigitated with the branches of neighboring trees (Snyder and Linhart, 1994). Chemical characteristics of nest trees may also play a role in nest-site selection: the squirrels are known to be sensitive to chemical variability of ponderosa pine trees (Snyder, 1992, 1993; Snyder and Linhart, 1993), and in a study conducted in an old-growth stand in northern Arizona, the phloem of nest trees had lower concentrations of copper, iron, and silicon, and higher levels of sodium and nonstructural carbohydrates than phloem of non-nest trees (Snyder and Linhart, 1994). Situating nests in large trees at the junction of the trunk and lateral branches probably maximizes both their structural integrity and protection from abiotic forces such as wind and precipitation. The ordinal placement of nests may be related to solar exposure. Squirrels probably situate nests in trees whose branches interdigitate with those of adjacent trees in order to increase the number and complexity of possible escape routes to the nest, thereby minimizing the probability of successful attack by goshawks and other predators.

The diet of Abert's squirrel varies seasonally with the availability of different food items, but consists almost entirely of tissues from ponderosa pine and other species that occur in close association with it (Keith, 1965; Farentinos, 1972; Hall, 1981; States et al., 1988; Snyder, 1992). Abert's squirrels are therefore considered to be feeding-specialists on ponderosa pine. In spring and summer, the squirrels may utilize a variety of foods including buds, male strobili, and seeds of ponderosa pine, as well as sporocarps of hypogeous fungi, many of which occur in close association with the roots of ponderosa pine.

Pine seeds from developing and mature ponderosa pine cones probably represent the most important and nutritionally valuable food item (e.g., for nitrogen and energy content) during the summer and early autumn. The squirrels eat seeds from the time of early cone development in the spring, throughout the time of cone maturation, generally in early autumn. Individual squirrels may eat seeds from approximately 75 cones per day during this time (Keith, 1965). Ponderosa pine typically masts every 3 to 5 years (Linhart and Snyder, in litt). Because of this, availability of pine seeds can vary dramatically from year to year and from site to site. Even in years when the cone crop is very high, however, seeds are unavailable to the squirrels (except for foraging for individual seeds on the ground) after cones open and seeds are released.

Abert's squirrels are active year-round, but cache little or no food (Keith, 1965). During winter months, they subsist primarily on inner bark tissues stripped from ponderosa pine twigs, since little else of any nutritional value is available during this time. Compared with pine seeds, inner bark (primarily phloem and cambium) is a poor source of nutritionally valuable compounds such as proteins and carbohydrates, as well as specific minerals (Patton, 1974; Snyder, 1992). Reliance on inner bark tissues may be especially prolonged in years when the cone crop is poor or absent.

Abert's squirrels display strong preferences for the inner bark tissues of particular, individual ponderosa pine trees over others, feeding repeatedly (over may years) from these trees, while nearby trees may remain free from herbivory (Keith, 1965; Farentinos, 1972; Hall, 1981; Snyder, 1992). Ponderosa pine trees vary markedly in chemical characteristics, both among populations, and among individual trees within populations (Smith, 1972; Snyder, 1992). In the foothills of the Colorado Rocky Mountains, preferred trees ("target trees") had significantly lower flow rates of xylem oleoresin, and significantly lower levels of both ß-pinene and ß-phellandrene in the xylem oleoresin, compared with closely matched control ("non-target") trees (Snyder, 1992). The phloem of target trees had significantly lower concentrations of iron, and significantly higher concentrations of both sodium and nonstructural carbohydrates, than the phloem of non-target trees (Snyder, 1992). In feeding trials with free-ranging animals, food laced with ecologically realistic concentrations of either ß-pinene or ß-phellandrene were eaten significantly less than control food (Snyder, 1992). Oleoresin characteristics associated with squirrel feeding remained unaffected following five years of simulated herbivory (Snyder, 1992; Snyder, unpublished data), supporting existing evidence (e.g., Dorman, 1976; Squillace, 1976) that these tree traits are under strong genetic control in the genus *Pinus*.

Ponderosa pine trees that are defoliated as a result of feeding on inner bark by Abert's squirrels suffer dramatic reductions in several fitness components including incremental growth, production of male strobili, female cone production and seed quality (Snyder, 1993). Additionally, reproductive output is depressed in trees defoliated experimentally to mimic herbivory by squirrels (Snyder, 1993). Because the squirrels feed preferentially on particular trees, and many of the most important traits that characterize target trees are known to be under strong genetic control (Dorman, 1976), some involving single-gene inheritance (Squillace, 1976), and since target trees suffer dramatic reductions in fitness (e.g., growth and reproduction), Abert's squirrels are thought to be important agents of natural selection in stands of ponderosa pine (Snyder, 1993).

In general, it has been difficult to assess the degree to which mammalian herbivores, including tree squirrels, may generate such directional selection in populations of host plants (Snyder, 1993), primarily because most mammalian herbivores are highly polyphagous. The impacts of herbivory upon plant populations have been investigated most intensively in insect-plant interactions (see Crawley, 1983). The impacts of mammalian herbivores have been more apparent at the community level, as when mammalian herbivores affect the relative abundance of different plant species, or at the ecosystem level, as when mammalian herbivores affect the cycling patterns of particular nutrients.

Studies of interactions between specialized mammalian herbivores such as Abert's squirrels and the plants upon which they feed provide a unique opportunity to assess the potential importance of mammals in generating directional selection in host plant populations, and provide a context for comparison with the apparently more diffuse selection pressures imposed by generalist mammalian herbivores, including most tree squirrels.

COMMUNITY INTERACTIONS: DIVERSIFYING SELECTION?

Ponderosa pine is often the sole tree species in forests that range from 1,500 m to 3,000 m in elevation in the central and southern Rocky Mountains. It is a dominant feature of the biological landscape by virtue of its abundance and size. Because of its apparency, ponderosa pine is the primary source of food for many above-ground herbivores and parasites, many of which focus their feeding activities on inner bark tissues of this tree, primarily phloem. Among its many functions, phloem provides an avenue for the transport of photosynthate throughout the tree, as well as a secondary avenue for the transport of water and dissolved minerals. Phloem is a chemically complex tissue, containing compounds and elements such as nonstructural carbohydrates, amino acids, and minerals including N, P, K, Na, Mg, Ca, Fe, and Mn, all of which potentially can be nutritionally valuable to specific parasites and herbivores. Phloem may also contain a number of compounds and elements which can be deleterious to a variety of herbivores and parasites, e.g., tannins, monoterpenes, Cu and other metals.

Species of herbivores and parasites that rely on phloem of ponderosa pine as a source of nutrition (hereafter "dependent species") can number in the hundreds and represent a broad range of taxa, including mammals, arthropods, angiosperms and others. Among the most important of these dependent species in the southern Rocky Mountains (in terms of impacts upon tree fitness) are Abert's squirrel, the mountain pine bark beetle (*Dendroctonus ponderosae*), the parasitic angiosperm, dwarf-mistletoe (*Arceuthobium vaginatum*), and the North American porcupine (*Erethizon dorsatum*). This taxonomically diverse group of dependent species comprises a guild whose members all feed on phloem of ponderosa pine, yet the four species apparently partition this resource based on tree phenotype: patterns of attack by each species are associated with specific biochemical and physiological tree characteristics that can vary significantly among individual trees (Tables 1 and 2; Snyder, 1992; Linhart et al., 1994; Snyder et al., 1996). This partitioning is related to variability among potential host trees, and to the unique set of life history characteristics, physiology and behaviors associated with the different dependent species (Snyder, 1992; Linhart et al., 1994). The porcupine is a feeding-generalist that will exploit a wide variety of both woody and herbaceous species, although in the Southern Rocky

Table 1.—*Xylem oleoresin characteristics from preliminary analyses of trees utilized by the bark beetle, the dwarf-mistletoe, the porcupine, and Abert's squirrel. For each variable comparisons are made against matched non-target trees (N = 30). The (>) and (<) indicate how quantities compare with non-target trees when differences are significant. Significance levels (ANOVA) are indicated in parentheses. Data for bark beetles, dwarf-mistletoe and squirrels are from trees in a single study site in Boulder County, Colorado. Data for porcupines are from several nearby locations in Boulder County (Habeck, 1990) and therefore are not directly comparable to those for other species. Methods for collection and analysis of xylem oleoresin are modified slightly from Snyder (1992).*

Variable	Beetle	Dwarf-mistletoe	Porcupine	Squirrel
α-pinene	n.s.	(>) (0.045)	n.s.	n.s.
camphene	n.s.	(<) (0.001)	n.s.	n.s.
β-pinene	n.s.	n.s.	n.s.	(<) (0.05)
3-carene	n.s.	n.s.	n.s.	n.s.
myrcene	n.s.	n.s.	n.s.	n.s.
limonene	n.s.	n.s.	n.s.	n.s.
β-phellandrene	n.s.	n.s.	n.s.	(<) (0.01)
terpinene	n.s.	n.s.	n.s.	n.s.
flow rate	n.s.	(<) (0.03)	n.s.	(<) (0.05)

a = not from same study site
n.s.= not significant

Table 2.—*Phloem characteristics from preliminary analyses of trees utilized by the bark beetle, the dwarf-mistletoe, the porcupine, and Abert's squirrel. For each variable comparisons are made against matched non-target trees. The (>) and (<) indicate how quantities compare with matched non-target trees. Significance levels (ANOVA) are indicated in parentheses. Data for bark beetles, dwarf-mistletoe and squirrels are from trees in a single study site in Boulder County, Colorado. Data for porcupines are from several nearby locations in Boulder County (Habeck, 1990) and therefore are not directly comparable to those for other species. Methods for phloem collection and analyses are modified slightly from Snyder (1992).*

Variable	Beetle	Dwarf-mistletoe	Porcupine[a]	Squirrel
Al	n.s.	(<) (0.0007)	n.s.	n.s.
B	(>) (0.02)	(>) (0.0000)	n.s.	n.s.
Ca	n.s.	n.s.	n.s.	n.s.
Cu	n.s.	(<) (0.02)	n.s.	n.s.
Fe	n.s.	n.s.	n.s.	(<) (0.05)
Mg	n.s.	(>) (0.0001)	n.s.	n.s.
Mn	n.s.	(<) (0.001)	n.s.	n.s.
Hg	n.s.	n.s.	n.s.	(<) (0.05)
Mo	(<) (0.08)	n.s.	n.s.	n.s.
P	(>) (0.02)	n.s.	n.s.	n.s.
K	n.s.	n.s.	n.s.	n.s.
Si	n.s.	(>) (0.059)	n.s.	n.s.
Na	n.s.	n.s.	n.s.	(>) (0.01)
Ti	(>) (0.09)	(>) (0.02)	n.s.	n.s.
TNC*	n.s.	(>) (0.005)	n.s.	(>) (0.05)
N	(>) (0.02)	n.s.	n.s.	n.s.
H_20	n.s.	n.s.	(>) (0.02)	N/A

a = not from same study site
n.s. = not significant
* TNC = total nonstructural carbohydrates

Mountains it often focuses on phloem of ponderosa pine during winter months. The other three dependent species are all considered feeding-specialists on pine phloem because it is their primary source of food.

Unlike Abert's squirrels, which typically clip terminal shoots to obtain phloem, porcupines strip off patches of outer bark and feed on the exposed inner bark, often from the upper side of lateral limbs and from the main bole. Consumption of phloem by porcupines can result in girdling of branches or the main bole, which often causes mortality. Preliminary data have suggested that porcupines may utilize certain trees and avoid others because of biochemical differences among trees (Roze, 1989; Habeck, 1990), although a biochemical basis for selectivity has not been demonstrated.

The mountain pine beetle lives almost its entire life beneath the outer bark of ponderosa pine trees. Egg galleries are constructed in the phloem, upon which the larvae feed, then pupate. Adult beetles emerge from the tree for a brief flight period, then bore into the trunk of another tree to continue the life cycle. Tree mortality is common, especially if infestations are heavy. Mortality comes from a combination of damage to phloem by larvae and obstruction of conducting tissues by a blue stain fungus (e.g., *Ceratocystis*). The bases of host selection are poorly known but may include biochemical and physiological attributes of xylem oleoresin, as well as bark thickness, and general features of tree morphology (reviewed in Mitton and Sturgeon, 1982). Oleoresin with high levels of the monoterpene limonene can be toxic to certain species of *Dendroctonus* (Smith, 1966; Sturgeon, 1979). Conversely, the monoterpene myrcene can be attractive to beetles because it is used as a pheromone precursor (Bedard et al., 1969; Mitton and Sturgeon, 1982).

The parasitic angiosperm dwarf-mistletoe (*Arceuthobium vaginatum cryptopodum*) is the primary parasite of ponderosa pine in the central and southern Rocky Mountains and southwestern U.S. Infestation is associated with severe loss of vigor and sometimes death of host trees. Dwarf-mistletoe is an obligate parasite which taps directly into the phloem and xylem tissues of live hosts, which it requires to survive. Though dwarf-mistletoes contain some chlorophyll, they obtain most of their carbohydrates and all their water and minerals from the host tree (Hawksworth, 1978). They can parasitize certain trees very heavily, and adjacent trees lightly or not at all. Patterns of attack are strongly correlated with chemical composition of host trees. The role of tree chemistry in differential attack by *A. vaginatum* is detailed in Snyder et al. (1996).

Although chemical mediation of the use of host trees has been demonstrated only for Abert's squirrel (Snyder, 1992, 1993), the correlative data on host use by bark beetles, dwarf-mistletoes and porcupines (Tables 1 and 2) suggest that these species utilize host trees differentially based at least in part on chemical characteristics of those trees.

Species-specific utilization of phenotypically differentiated host trees by these dependent species can potentially create multi-directional, diversifying selection pressures within stands of ponderosa pine (Linhart, 1989). Abert's squirrels, porcupines, mountain pine bark beetles, and dwarf-mistletoe all reduce the fitness of individual trees upon which they feed, affecting both growth and reproductive capacity and often causing mortality (Fowells, 1965; Mitton and Sturgeon, 1982; Baumgartner and Lotan, 1988; Habeck, 1990; Snyder, 1992, 1993; Linhart et al., 1994; Snyder et al., 1996). Since some of the characteristics associated with attack are known to have at least some genetic component (e.g., Smith, 1972; Dorman, 1976; Squillace,1976) and each dependent species utilizes trees with different phenotypes (Tables 1 and 2), the four dependent species may exert simultaneous, multi-directional selection pressures within stands of ponderosa pine. Diversifying selection that may result from such multi-directional selection pressures can potentially contribute to the maintenance of genetic variability within host stands of ponderosa.

MANAGEMENT IMPLICATIONS

Ponderosa pine is the most widely distributed conifer in North America, ranging from southern British Columbia, throughout much of the western United States and into northern Mexico. The geographic distribution and relative abundance of this tree have had important consequences not only in the context of natural biological communities, but also in the context of human exploitation: ponderosa pine is a major contributor to the volume of lumber cut in North America. Historically, management efforts have focused primarily on attempts to maximize harvestable yields of timber. To this end, species that affect the health and vigor of ponderosa pine (e.g., dependent species described here) have been subject to persistent and often extreme control measures. Although the elimination of "pest" species from stands of trees may have arguably increased short-term harvestable yields in some instances, the long-term consequences of such control measures may be detrimental to the overall health of ponderosa pine forests.

Even though the dependent species in this study all impact individual trees negatively (e.g., reduce growth and reproductive capacity and can cause mortality), in concert they may contribute to the maintenance of genetic variability within forest stands. The maintenance of genetically diverse stands is an important aspect of the conservation of forest vegetation and hence, entire forest communities. Because ponderosa pine is a relatively common feature of the western landscape, the fact that ponderosa pine forests are complex, highly variable systems can be easily overlooked. Ponderosa pine is not simply a homogeneous forest-type that ranges across half a continent. For example, over its geographic range, five races of ponderosa pine are recognized. These races are differentiated on the basis of biochemistry, morphology and physiology (see Smith, 1977; Wang, 1977; Baumgartner and Lotan, 1988; Conkle and Critchfield, 1988). In addition to this large-scale variability, there is also a high amount of within-stand variability in biochemical, physiological, and morphological characteristics (Smith, 1964; Baumgartner and Lotan, 1988; Snyder, 1992; Linhart et al., 1994). In addition, the guild of dependent species and the selective pressures they impose can vary significantly among stands. Management strategies should recognize the inherent value of this variability, and management objectives should include the maintenance of this variability.

It is likely that many recent epidemics or outbreaks of forest pests such as dwarf-mistletoe have resulted from past management strategies that included fire suppression and/or an unintentional reduction in variability among trees within stands. The implementation of forest management strategies designed primarily to maximize the harvestable yield may further decrease this variability by reducing the extent to which diversifying selection operates in forests.

ACKNOWLEDGMENTS

Barbara A. Snyder, Aaron I. Snyder, and Zachary N. Snyder provided field assistance and logistic support. Funding for portions of this work was provided by the U.S. National Science Foundation (BSR 8918478 and DEB 9120065). I thank Boulder County Parks and the USDA Forest Service for allowing field work at Bald Mountain Scenic Area and the Pearson Research Natural Area, respectively. I gratefully acknowledge Yan B. Linhart, Charles H. Southwick, and David M. Armstrong for sharing valuable insights, and Richard H. Smith for performing monoterpene analyses.

LITERATURE CITED

BAUMGARTNER, D. M., AND J. E. LOTAN. 1988. Ponderosa pine: the species and its management. Washington State University Cooperative Extension, Pullman, Washington, 281 pp.

BEDARD, W. D., P. D. TILDEN, D. L. WOOD, R. M. SILVERSTEIN, R. G. BROWNLEE, AND J. O. RODIN. 1969. Western pine beetle: field response to its sex pheromone and synergistic host terpene, myrcene. Science, 164:1284-1285.

CONKLE, M. T., AND W. B. CRITCHFIELD. 1988. Genetic variation and hybridization of ponderosa pine. Pp. 27-44, *in* Ponderosa pine: the species and its management (D. M. Baumgartner and J. E. Lotan, eds.). Washington State University, Cooperative Extension, Pullman, 281 pp.

CRAWLEY, M. J. 1983. Herbivory: the dynamics of animal-plant interactions. Blackwell Scientific Publications, Oxford, United Kingdom, 437 pp.

DORMAN, K. W. 1976. The genetics and breeding of southern pines. U.S. Department of Agriculture, Forest Service Handbook No. 471, 407 pp.

FARENTINOS, R. C. 1972. Observations on the ecology of the tassel-eared squirrel. The Journal of Wildlife Management, 36:1234-1239.

FOWELLS, H. A. 1965. Silvics of forest trees of the United States. U.S.D.A. Forest Service Agricultural Handbook No. 271, 762 pp.

HABECK, S. A. 1990. Winter feeding patterns by porcupines (*Erethizon dorsatum*) in the Colorado Front Range. M. A. thesis, University of Colorado, Boulder, 99 pp.

HALL, J. G. 1981. A field study of the Kaibab squirrel in Grand Canyon National Park. Wildlife Monographs, 75:1-54.

HAWKSWORTH, F. G. 1978. Biological factors of dwarf mistletoe in relation to control. Pp. 5-15, *in* Symposium on dwarf-mistletoe control through forest management, (R. F. Scharpf and J. R. Parmeter, eds). United States Department of Agriculture Forest Service General Technical Report, PSW-31, 190 pp.

HOFFMEISTER, D. F., AND V. E. DIERSING. 1978. Review of the tassel-eared squirrels of the subgenus *Otosciurus*. Journal of Mammalogy, 59:402-413.

KEITH, J. O. 1965. The Abert squirrel and its dependence on Ponderosa pine. Ecology, 46:150-163.

LINHART, Y. B. 1989. Interactions between genetic and ecological patchiness in forest trees and their dependent species. Pp. 393-430, *in* The evolutionary ecology of plants (J. H. Bock and Y. B. Linhart, eds.). Westview Press, Boulder. 600 pp.

LINHART, Y. B., M. A. SNYDER, AND J. P. GIBSON. 1994. Differential host utilization by two parasites in a population of ponderosa pine. Oecologia, 98:117-120.

MITTON, J. B., AND K. B. STURGEON. 1982. Bark beetles in North American conifers. University of Texas Press, Austin, 527 pp.

PATTON, D. R. 1974. Estimating food consumption from twigs clipped by the Abert squirrel. United States Department of Agriculture Forest Service Research Note, RM-272. 4 pp.

ROZE, U. 1989. The North American porcupine. Smithsonian Institution Press, Washington, D.C., 261 pp.

SMITH, R. H. 1964. Variation in the monoterpenes of *Pinus ponderosa* Laws. Science, 143:1337-1338.

———1966. The monoterpene composition of *Pinus ponderosa* xylem resin and of *Dendroctonus brevicomis* pitch tubes. Forest Science, 12:63-68.

———1972. Xylem resin in the resistance of the Pinaceae to bark beetles. United States Department of Agriculture Forest Service General Technical Report PSW-1, Berkeley, California, 7 pp.

———1977. Monoterpenes of ponderosa pine xylem resin in western United States. United States Department of Agriculture Forest Service Technical Bulletin, 1532, 48 pp.

SNYDER, M. A. 1992. Selective herbivory by Abert's squirrel mediated by chemical variability in ponderosa pine. Ecology, 73:1730-1741.

———1993. Interactions between Abert's squirrel and ponderosa pine: the relationship between selective herbivory and host plant fitness. The American Naturalist, 141:866-879.

SNYDER, M. A., B. FINESCHI, Y. B. LINHART, AND R. H. SMITH. 1996. Multivariate discrimination of host use by dwarf mistletoe *Arceuthobium vaginatum* subsp. *cryptopodum*: inter- and intraspecific comparisons. Journal of Chemical Ecology, 22:295-305.

SNYDER, M. A., AND Y. B. LINHART. 1993. Barking up the right tree. Natural History, 102:44-49.

———1994. Nest-site selection by Abert's squirrel: chemical characteristics of nest trees. Journal of Mammalogy, 75:136-141.

SQUILLACE, A. E. 1976. Biochemical genetics and selection composition of volatile terpenes. Pp 167-178, *in* International union of forestry research organizations, joint meeting of working parties on population and ecological genetics, breeding theory, biochemical genetics and progeny testing. Advanced generation breeding. INRA, Cestas, France, 207 pp.

STATES, J. S., W. S. GAUD, W. S. ALLRED, AND W. J. AUSTIN. 1988. Foraging patterns of tassel-eared squirrels in selected ponderosa pine stands. Pp. 425-431, *in* Symposium proceedings, management of amphibians, reptiles, and small mammals in North America (R. Szaro, K. Severson, and D. Patton, eds.). United States Department of Agriculture Forest Service General Technical Report RM-166, Rocky Mountain Forest and Range Experiment Station, Fort Collins, Colorado. 458 pp.

STURGEON, K. B. 1979. Monoterpene variation in ponderosa pine xylem resin related to western pine beetle predation. Evolution, 33:803-814.

WANG, C. W. 1977. Genetics of ponderosa pine. United States Department of Agriculture Forest Service Research Paper, WO-34, 24 pp.

THE EVOLUTION OF REPRODUCTION IN TREES: ITS EFFECT ON SQUIRREL ECOLOGY AND BEHAVIOR

CHRISTOPHER C. SMITH
Division of Biology, Ackert Hall
Kansas State University
Manhattan, KS 66506

ABSTRACT.—The constraints of wind pollination appear to set different optimum flowering patterns and fruit morphology for boreal and termperate forests. For the sake of comparison of selective pressures on reproduction in conifers and angiosperms, I will refer to the structures at the time of pollination as flowers and at the time of seed maturation as fruits and catkins in both groups even though the terms do not apply to conifers. Tree species of boreal forests tend to have wide fluctuations in annual numbers of flowers (mast flowering) and have seeds held in catkins. Temperate forests tend to have uniform annual production of flowers and have fruiting bodies with single seeds. The difference in the reproductive patterns is the result of low probability of cross pollination in temperate forests with their higher diversity of tree species. *Tamiasciurus* is able to form concentrated larder hoards of conifer cones in boreal forests by a system of individual territories because other mammals and birds cannot exploit seeds from closed cones in caches under the snow. *Sciurus* is forced into burying and scatter hoarding individual nuts which could be exploited by larger mammals and birds if the nuts were in a concentrated cache. These scattered caches cannot be defended by a territorial system leaving *Sciurus* with overlapping home ranges and social hierarchies. The causes of lower tree species diversity and prevalence of female catkins in boreal forests are open to speculation.

INTRODUCTION

Cause and effect are very difficult to distinguish in ecological contexts. Jenny (1961) made the distinction in very general terms with state equations he applied to ecosystem studies. He proposed that animals, vegetation, soils, and ecosystem properties (all of which have components resulting from organic evolution) are a function of the original state of the system, energy fluxes in the system, and the amount of time the system has been operating. The latter three features, defined as aspects of the physical environment lacking an evolved biological component, act as independent variables in causing the state of the first four dependent variables in an ecosystem. Levins and Lewontin (1985) in defining evolution and ecology as dialectical processes describe instances where physical environments change because of feedback from changes in the vegetation or other aspects of the living environment. Unlike Levins and Lewontin (1985), I do not find that biological effects on the physical environment negate Jenny's (1961) generality. The physical environment can change independently from changes in the biotic influence of the environment. It did so before life evolved and to a very large extent geological and climatic factors are still independent of biological causation.

Although Jenny (1961) seems to have intended that his state equations be applied in ecological time scales, they should apply equally well in evolutionary time. In studying the interaction between pine squirrels (*Tamiasciurus*) and lodgepole pine trees (*Pinus contorta*) in southwestern British Columbia, I found that Jenny's (1961) ideas were very helpful in understanding the contrast between the situations east and west of the Cascade Mountains outlined in Fig. 1 (Smith, 1970). Because I was studying squirrels at the time, the larger jaw musculature of the red squirrels (*T. hudsonicus*) east of the Cascade Mountains seemed like the obvious cause of the harder lodgepole pine cones in the same area. It was when I started to think about causation in the pine that it became evident that if I treated squirrel jaw musculature as an independent variable in the evolution of cone hardness that I

In M.A. Steele, J. F. Merritt, and D. A. Zegers (eds.). 1998. Ecology and Evolutionary Biology of Tree Squirrels. Special Publication, Virginia Museum of Natural History, 6: 320 pp

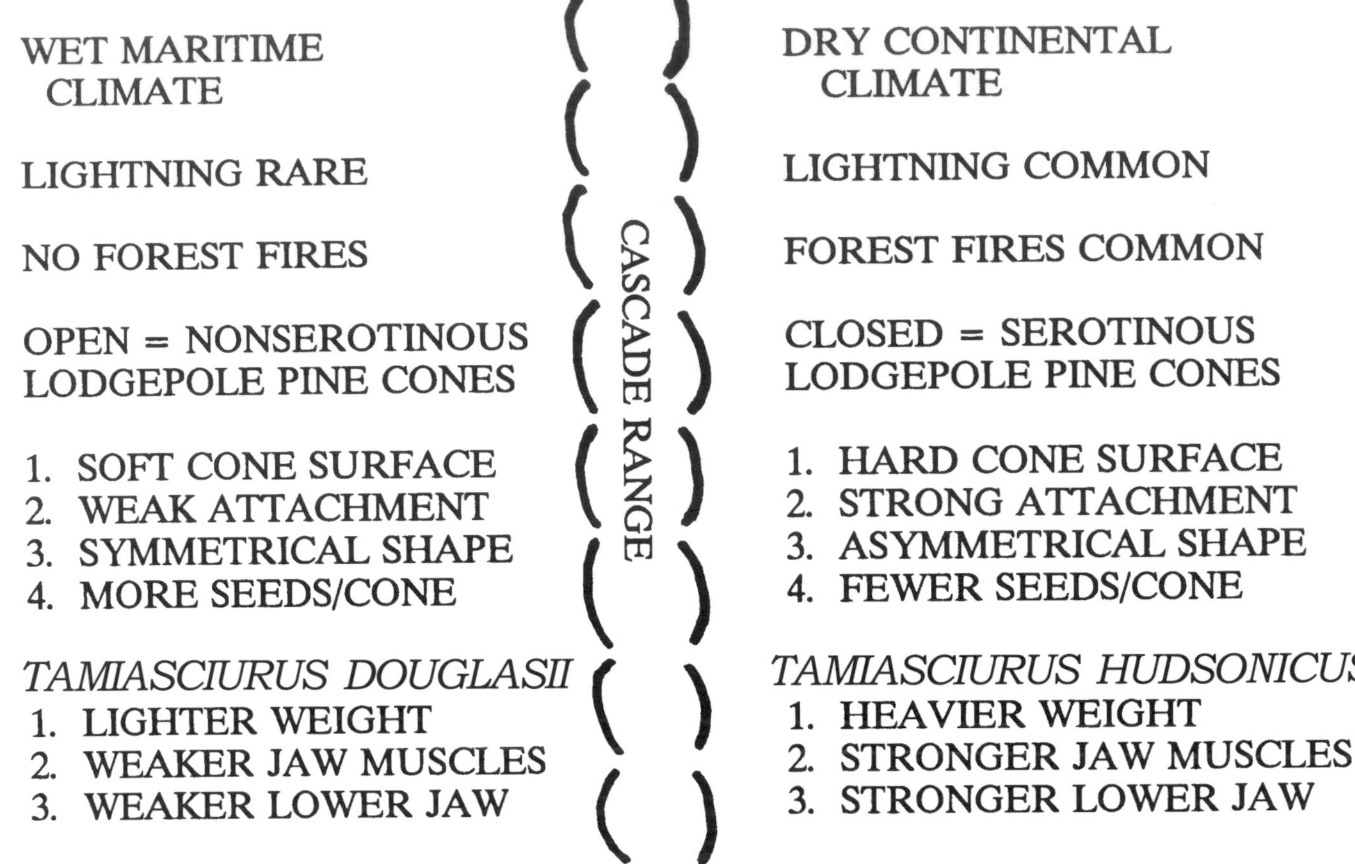

Fig. 1.—Conditions found west and east of the Cascade Mountain Range in southwestern British Columbia. Cause and effect are much more logical going from the top to the bottom of the list of conditions rather than in the opposite direction. In other words, the independent variable is the rain shadow effect of the Cascade Range, not the difference in strength of squirrels' jaws.

would ultimately have to explain the orogeny of the Cascade Mountains on the basis of jaw musculature of squirrels. If the physical environment does act as the independent variable in the evolution of life, that relationship does not exclude extensive feedback between species in the coevolution of community structure. Elliott (1974, 1988) has shown that the feeding choices of squirrels have a marked influence on the evolution of lodgepole pine cones. The physical environment determines at what state the coevolutionary forces between pines and squirrels will be balanced. Where frequent fires selected for serotinous cones, squirrels have a decade or more to extract seeds from a cone while they have only a few months to act as selective agents on cones that open the autumn that they mature. It is logical that where frequent fires select for serotinous cones the balance between selection on pines and squirrels will be at the extreme of hard cones with few seeds and squirrels with powerful jaws.

Here I will attempt to demonstrate how other aspects of the physical environment have influenced the coevolution of tree reproduction and the tree squirrels that eat the trees' reproductive products. In particular I am interested in how wind pollination has led to large differences between the phenology of flowering and flower anatomy in temperate and boreal forests of the Northern Hemisphere. These differences, in turn, influence differences between the behavior and ecology of tree squirrels in the genera *Sciurus* and *Tamiasciurus* in North America. In Eurasia, where *Tamiasciurus* is absent, *Sciurus* may have reached a different balance in its coevolution with tree reproduction.

Patterns of Wind Pollination

Whitehead (1969, 1983) noted the connection between wind pollination and low species diversity in forest communities. He argued that with undirected movement of wind borne pollen, a rare wind-pollinated species would have very low probability of cross-fertilization. Smith et al. (1988, 1990) used lodgepole pine to study the relationship between density of wind borne pollen and seed set in a wind-pollinated species. We found that lodgepole pine set only 16% as many seeds with self pollen as with out-crossed pollen. An individual initiated as many seeds when self-pollinated as when cross-pollinated, but fertilization usually failed with self pollen. After fertilization fails the female gametophyte dies and is reabsorbed leaving empty, but fully developed seed coats. Using the frequency of empty seed coats as an index of self-pollination, Smith et al. (1988) showed that self-pollination occurred more frequently on the leaward side and lower branches of a tree. Although self compatibility ranges from 0 to 100% in different species of conifers (Franklin, 1970), trees as a plant growth form tend to have more polymorphic genetic loci than other plants (Hamrick et al., 1979). Assuming that the polymorphisms are adaptive, self fertilization should have a greater negative effect on trees than other plant growth forms.

Smith et al. (1990) used the density of pollen production and the density of pollen in the air in 17 stands varying from 5 to 100% lodgepole pine in the Front Range of Colorado to demonstrate that long distance pollen movements lead an isolated lodgepole pine tree to have 45% as much conspecific air-borne pollen around it as a tree in a pure stand of lodgepole pine. Lodgepole pine was probably the most common of seven species of trees in the general area. By extrapolating from the relationship between pollen density and seed set in lodgepole pine, Smith et al. (1990) demonstrated that one of the advantages to be derived from the large annual variation in flower production (mast flowering) in most tree species of boreal forests is a higher density of conspecific pollen at the time when most of the flowering occurs. This increased pollen density reduces the probability that individual females will not be pollinated. Although both self and outcrossed pollen are increased proportionately as a result of mast flowering, polyembrony in Gymnosperms and pollen tube competition in Angiosperms increase the probablity of outcrossing in the formation of successful embryos during mast flowering (Willson and Burley, 1983). In conifers, reproductive structures develop by modification of vegetative buds so that mast flowering can be accomplished by hormonal influence of bud development (Allen and Owens, 1972). Separate buds produce male and female catkins in alder (*Alnus*) and birch (*Betula*) and their annual production is facultative in birch (Macdonald and Mothersill, 1987).

The advantage of mast flowering to the tree species of boreal forests results from the packaging of many seeds in a catkin with extensive woody tissue protecting the seeds from predation by insects and vertebrates. The woody tissues of the catkin are produced in an all-or-none fashion; all the tissue is formed or the whole catkin is aborted. This form of development leads to a wide range of seed set within individual catkins. The increase in seed set resulting from mast flowering causes a higher ratio of seeds to woody protective tissue and an increase in fecundity with no increase in the cost of woody protective tissue (Smith et al., 1990). Most conifers have less than 30% of the energy in a catkin in seed tissue and thus more than 70% in woody protective tissue (Smith, 1981). With such catkins, an isolated tree may double its fecundity while increasing its energy outlay to female catkins by less than 10%. The advantage of mast flowering should only apply when the regional density of conspecific trees is great enough to create a regional pollen cloud with enough conspecific pollen to swamp out the effect of self pollen and result in a high frequency of cross-pollinated seeds. Lodgepole pine is one of the few species that does not exhibit mast flowering in boreal forests. In populations that show serotiny, energy held back from reproduction would have a high probability of going up in smoke and mast fruiting would have little effect on seed predators because the seeds are held on the trees for decades. In regions where fire is frequent, lodgepole pine tends to occur in pure stands, thus making mast flowering less needed for high seed set. We used lodgepole pines to show the effect of conspecific pollen density because the density of pollen could be controlled by the frequency of lodgepole pine in mixed-species stands.

The comparison of species diversity in boreal and temperate forests shows that temperate forests hold five to ten times more species in a general region from which a regional pollen cloud would be derived. Using the point at which the border between Ontario and Manitoba bends to the northeast as a sample of the boreal forests and the confluence of the borders of Ohio, Indiana, and Kentucky as a sample of the temperate forest, there is a contrast of 8 to 75 species of trees between boreal and temperate forests (Preston, 1948). None of the boreal forest species are pollinated by animal vectors while at least 18 of those in the temperate forest sample are. The woody plants used were the size of eastern redbud (*Cercis canadensis*) or larger.

Table 1.—*The ratio of larger to smaller crops of reproductive products of trees between successive years near Manhattan, Kansas. The values given are the means of seven ratios derived from eight years (1987-1994). Each species' crop is the sum of the reproductive products on the same two branches on each of 10 trees. The area of branch counted is everything beyond the point at which the diameter of the branch reaches a set value unique for each species.*

Tree species	Male flowers	Female flowers	Fruit
Juniperus virginiana	1.5	2.0	3.3
Juglans nigra	1.7	2.7	6.6
Quercus muehlenbergii	1.7	1.6	2.3
Ulmus americana	2.3	2.3	4.0*
Celtis occidentalis	1.1**	1.1**	∞**
Morus rubra	3.9	2.3	2.4
Fraxinus pennsylvanica	5.5	15.0	135.6***

* Average of three ratios because two crop failures give ∞ as the value of four ratios

** No two successive years were without a seed crop failure. Because flowers were usually killed when the shoot was in the bud, they were impossible to count in successive years except for 5 trees in 1988 and 1989.

*** Average of six ratios because the last crop was a failure giving ∞ as the value for one ratio.

Again extrapolating from data of lodgepole pine (Smith et al., 1990), it is evident that species producing one tenth the conspecific pollen density of lodgepole pine in a regional pollen cloud would cross-pollinate less than 50% of its females, even with widely timed mast flowering. It appears that this low probability of outcrossing is the selective pressure that has led to a different pattern of fruiting in species of temperate forests as opposed to those of boreal forests. Instead of multiseeded catkins typical of boreal forests, trees of temperate forests have each ovule develop in a separate fruit which can be aborted separately at minor energetic cost if it is not well pollinated. Because resources are committed to a fruit only after successful pollination and fertilization, there would be no large increase in the efficiency of producing protective tissue resulting from mast flowering if it were to evolve in temperate forest trees. Indeed, the trees in temperate forests tend to have little variation in annual flower production (Table 1). Many of the genera (*Quercus, Juglans, Carya, Celtis,* and *Morus*) produce flowers along with leaves of the growing stem from an apical spring bud. The proportion of leaves and flowers is characteristic of the individual over years. The variation in seed crops (Table 1) is a result of annual variation in the success of pollination and maturation of the fruit.

The fraction of ovules that result in mature fruit in temperate forests is much lower than the seed set attained in boreal forests during years of mast flowering (Table 2). The pattern for red mulberry (*M. rubra*) is exceptional for trees of temperate forests (Tables 1 and 2). It has many seeds in each 'berry' which is in reality a multiple fruit. Moreover, the success rate for a group of flowers in producing a multiple fruit is close to 100%. The pattern appears to be the result of parthenocarpic seed production because females in this dioecious species have the same number of seeds per fruit whether they are surrounded by males or isolated from them (Table 3). Thus, seed set does not appear to be a measure of the frequency of pollination in mulberries.

If the difference between mast flowering in boreal forests and uniform flowering in temperate forests coupled with the differences in the number of seeds per fruiting body between the two forest types are an evolutionary result of the effect of lower tree species diversity in boreal forests on success of wind pollination, then there are two important questions left unanswered: 1) What limits species diversity in boreal forests? 2) Why are catkins at an advantage over single-seeded fruiting bodies in boreal forests? These two questions are interrelated. Species with single-seeded fruiting bodies should be able to invade areas dominated by species with female catkins because the species with single-seeded fruits can be effectively pollinated when rare relative to species with catkins. However, species with single-seeded fruiting bodies have not invaded the boreal forests. Species with catkins are found in temperate forests only where they tend to form monospecific or low diversity stands on special soil types; *Pinus* on

Table 2.—*Percentage of ovules forming filled seeds. The values for* Morus rubra *and* Juniperus virginiana *are based on number of groups of ovules forming a fleshy fruit. Fruit of* J. virginiana *may have up to four seeds in a fruit and* M. rubra *has approximately 20 seeds in a single multiple fruit. Data for temperate forest species are from 1987 to 1994 near Manhattan, KS.*

Tree species	Mean%	Range	Source
Temperate forest			
Juniperus virginiana	32	10-57	C.C. Smith, in litt
Juglans nigra	15	2-37	C.C. Smith, in litt
Quercus muhlenbergii	13	2-22	C.C. Smith, in litt
Morus rubra	88	71-100	C.C. Smith, in litt
Boreal forest			
Picea sitchensis	54	34-78	Ruth and Berntsen, 1955
Tsuga heterophylla	44	7-72	Ruth and Berntsen, 1955
Pinus contorta	51	34-60	C.C. Smith, in litt
Betula verrucosa	62	11-82	Sarvas, 1952
Betula pubescens	59	29-70	Sarvas, 1952

Table 3.—*Fruit formation in* Morus rubra *in relation to the isolation of female trees from male trees. Each value is the mean for 10 multiple fruits* ± *1* SE.

Flowers per multiple fruit	Seeds per multiple fruit	% seed set
	Isolated females	
17.2 ± 1.33	15.0 ± 1.04	87
17.3 ± 1.13	16.6 ± 1.06	96
	Females surrounded by males	
13.4 ± 1.18	8.1 ± 1.04	60
12.3 ± 0.76	11.2 ± 0.57	91
19.2 ± 0.68	18.5 ± 0.73	96

nutrient-poor, sandy soils leading to dry vegetation that is frequently burned and *Populus, Salix*, and *Betula nigra* on stream alluvium. It would appear that some aspect of the physical environment sets a limit to the narrowness of niche breadth for tree species in boreal forests.

Given low species diversity, why should catkins be an advantage over single-seeded fruits? One possible explanation is that single-seeded fruits are at a disadvantage because they can be more effectively attacked by insects. An ovipositing female insect can easily check a single-seeded fruit for eggs or other signs of earlier visitors and avoid competition for her larval offspring by searching for an unvisited fruit. A catkin should give an insect whose larvae feed on only one seed (some Diptera and Hymenoptera; Keen, 1958) a more difficult problem of determining which seeds have already been attacked. Some indication that insects have problems with multiseeded fruits was discovered in nuts of *Scheelea* palms where bruchid beetles (Family Bruchidae) usually only attacked one seed in a fruit whether the fruit contained one, two, or three seeds. Rodent predators usually attacked all seeds in a fruit, except where the multiseeded fruits were rare (Smith, 1975; Bradford and Smith, 1977).

Some indication that the differences in reproductive patterns of trees between boreal and temperate forests are not just a phylogenetic accident of differences in the evolutionary history of Pinaceae in boreal forests and Angiosperms in temperate forests can be shown by a close look at the family Betulaceae. Catkins of alder and birch in boreal forests contain over 100 seeds each. The bracts subtending the female flowers in alder catkins are quite hard and woody. In birch, the male catkins are initiated before the females and on different shoots. Both types of shoots are facultative in producing terminal catkins in some years (Macdonald and Mothersill, 1987) and there is wide variation in annual flower production resulting in mast flowering similar to most conifers (Sarvas, 1952): Hop hornbeam (*Ostrya*), hornbeam (*Carpinus*), and hazel (*Corylus*) in temperate forests form a graded series showing a decrease in number of seeds per catkin, an opening of the catkin by wider spacing between bracts, an increase in seed size, and an increase in surface area for bracts subtending the seeds although the bracts are thin and papery. Hazel catkins are reduced to so few seeds that individual seeds could be aborted without modifying the structure of the catkin. The reduction of seed number per catkin is consistent with selection for a reduced number of seeds per catkin where assurance of cross pollination is lower.

Tree Fruit Anatomy and Squirrel Behavior

The differences between female catkins as fruiting bodies in trees of boreal forests and the single-seeded fruits of the trees in temperate forests have marked effects on the social organization of squirrels in the genera *Tamiasciurus* and *Sciurus* (Smith, 1995). These two genera are characteristic of boreal and temperate forests, respectively. The whole catkins that *Tamiasciurus* caches in large larders in the center of territories defended be single individuals can not be eaten efficiently by larger animals that might raid the concentrated food supply because less than 30% of the catkins is digestible seeds (Smith, 1970). By placing the catkins in damp soil or the catkin fragments of older cache areas (middens), the squirrels keep the cached cones from drying, opening and releasing their seeds and thus prevent the seeds from being an efficient food resource of nocturnal mice. The main threat to the cached catkins are other *Tamiasciurus*, and their competition is controlled by the evolved conventions of the territorial system (Smith, 1968).

Tamiasciurus is replaced by *S. aberti* in ponderosa pine (*P. ponderosa*) forests at lower elevations in the mountains of southwestern United States and by *S. niger* and *S. carolinensis* in forests with various species of pine in southeastern United States. The failure of *Tamiasciurus* to exploit these habitats is probably related to drier soils and shorter periods of snow cover which would prevent them from keeping cached cones from drying out and losing their seeds. *Tamiasciurus* does cache ponderosa pine cones on the eastern slopes of the Cascade Mountains of Washington and British Columbia in damper habitats (Smith, 1995).

Squirrels in the genus *Sciurus*, in temperate forests, bury nuts in the families Fagaceae (beech, oak, chestnut) and Juglandaceae (walnut, hickory, pecan) individually scattered over each squirrel's home range. These scattered caches tend to center around a squirrel's den tree and overlap relatively little between individuals (Stapanian and Smith, 1978). This pattern of scatterhoarding nuts probably evolved because many of the nuts, like acorns, have a high enough ratio of kernel to shell that they can serve as an efficient diet for large animals, like deer, which cannot remove the shells and thus eat the nuts whole. If squirrels made concentrated caches (larderhoards), they would be unable to defend them from larger competing species. Their pattern of spreading the nuts out and burying them should make the nuts less efficient for other animals to use (Stapanian and Smith,

1978, 1984). When the nuts are spread out, however, individual squirrels cannot effectively watch and defend their caches and a territorial system would be unlikely to evolve when the resources in short supply are indefensible (Brown, 1964).

The absence of *Tamiasciurus* from the boreal forests of Eurasia and its replacement by *Sciurus vulgaris*, which is found in both boreal and temperate forests (Gurnell, 1987), may help to explain the differences between congeneric species of conifers in North America and Eurasia. The ability of *Tamiasciurus* to cut down thousands of catkins in a day and cache hundreds of catkins in a day exerts a very strong selective pressure on conifer cone morphology within and between species (Smith, 1970). *Tamiasciurus* first caches all the cones in its territory belonging to the species with the most seed energy per cone, and continues in order of species with decreasing seed energy per cone. It tends to start to differentiate between trees within a species when it is left with the species that averages the least seed energy per cone. Because food energy per cone for a squirrel is influenced by the size of seeds and number of seeds per cone, and because size of seed is tied to the germination niche of the tree species, the cone character that tends to respond to squirrel selection is the number of seeds per cone (Smith, 1970, 1975). This selective pressure within a community of tree species leads to smaller-seeded species having fewer seeds per cone and larger-seeded species dropping their seeds earlier to escape the caching activity of squirrels. The absence of cone-caching squirrels in Eurasia should help to explain why trees in the same genera in North America and Eurasia tend to differ by having more seeds per cone in Eurasia (Norway spruce—*Picea abies* versus all North American spruce) and hold their seeds in the cone longer into the winter and spring (Scotch pine—*Pinus sylvestris*) versus nonserotinous lodgepole and jack pine (*P. banksiana*).

CONCLUSION

It appears that the constraints of wind pollination set different optimum flowering patterns and fruit morphologies for tree species of boreal and temperate forests. The difference in fruit morphology and conditions for caching fruiting bodies probably led to the differences in social organization in the squirrel genera *Tamiasciurus* and *Sciurus*. There is no strong inference, however, to take the patterns of cause and effect all the way back to the physical environment as an independent variable. The difference in flowering patterns and fruit morphology rest on the difference in tree species diversity in boreal and temperate forests. While that difference is likely to have causes relating to the physical environment, I do not know what they are. Moreover, the idea that catkins have an advantage over single-seeded fruits because they are more difficult for insects to exploit is highly speculative. Finally, a biogeographic accident in the distribution of *Tamiasciurus* and *Sciurus* appears to have an effect on the difference in cone morphology between congeneric species of conifers in North America and Eurasia. The biogeographic distribution of squirrels is likely to have a geological cause as the independent variable from the physical environment, but that cause appears to skip a trophic level to the evolutionary history of squirrels and work back to a lower trophic level of cone morphology. Using the physical environment as the independent variable in explaining the structure of biological nature is probably accurate, but it does not greatly simplify the process of understanding nature.

ACKNOWLEDGMENTS

John Briggs, Ido Izhaki, and Sharon Collinge were of great help in gathering data on tree reproduction. We were able to work in the Nature Conservancy's Konza Prairie Research Natural Area which helped to minimize the disturbance to our trees in riparian forests. Part of the research was supported by National Science Foundation grant DEB-7922190.

LITERATURE CITED

ALLEN, G. S., AND J. N. OWENS. 1972. The life history of Douglas fir. Information Canada, Ottawa, 139 pp.

BRADFORD, D. F., AND C. C. SMITH. 1977. Seed predation and seed number in *Scheelea* palm fruits. Ecology, 58:667-673.

BROWN, J. L. 1964. The evolution of diversity in avian territorial systems. Wilson Bulletin, 76:160-169.

ELLIOTT, P. F. 1974. Evolutionary responses of plants to seed-eaters: pine squirrel predation on lodgepole pine. Evolution, 28:221-231.

———. 1988. Foraging behavior of a central-place forager: field tests of theoretical predictions. The American Naturalist, 131:159-174.

FRANKLIN, E. C. 1970. Survey of mutant forms and inbreeding depression in species of the family Pinaceae. United States Department of Agriculture Forest Service Research Paper, SE-61, 21 pp.

GURNELL, J. 1987. The natural history of squirrels. Facts on File Publications, New York, 201 pp.

HAMRICK, J. L., Y. B. LINHART, AND J. B. MITTON. 1979. Relationships between life history characteristics and electrophoretically detectable genetic variation in plants. Annual Review of Ecology and Systematics, 10:173-200.

JENNY, H. 1961. Derivation of the state factor equation. Soil Science Society Proceedings, 25:385-388.

KEEN, F. P. 1958. Cone and seed insects of western forest trees. United States Department of Agriculture Technical Bulletin No. 1169, 168 pp.

LEVINS, R., AND R. LEWONTIN. 1985. The dialectical biologist. Harvard University Press, Cambridge, Massachusetts, 303 pp.

MACDONALD, A. D., AND D. H. MOTHERSILL. 1987. Shoot development in *Betula papyrifera*. VI. Development of the reproductive structures. Canadian Journal Botany, 65:466-475.

PRESTON, R. J., JR. 1948. North American Trees. Iowa State College Press, Ames, 371 pp.

RUTH, R. H., AND C. M. BERNTSEN. 1955. A 4-year record of Sitka spruce and western hemlock seed fall. United States Department of Agriculture Forest Service, Pacific NW Forestry Range & Experiment Station Research Paper No. 12, 13 pp.

SARVAS, R. 1952. On the flowering of birch and the quality of seed crop. Communicationes Instituti Forestalis Fenniae, 40:1-38.

SMITH, C. C. 1968. The adaptive nature of social organization in the genus of tree squirrels *Tamiasciurus*. Ecological Monographs, 38:30-63.

———. 1970. The coevolution of pine squirrels (*Tamiasciurus*) and conifers. Ecological Monographs, 40:349-371.

———. 1975. The coevolution of seeds and seed predators. Pp. 53-77, *in* Coevolution of animals and plants (L. E. Gilbert and P. H. Raven, eds.). University of Texas Press, Austin, 246 pp.

———. 1981. The indivisible niche of *Tamiasciurus*, an example of non partitioning of resources. Ecological Monographs, 51:343-363.

———. 1995. The niche of diurnal tree squirrels. Pp. 207-225, *in* Storm over a mountain island: conservation biology and the Mt. Graham affair (C. Istock and R. Hoffman, eds.). University of Arizona Press, Tuscon, 291 pp.

SMITH, C. C., J. L. HAMRICK, AND C. L. KRAMER. 1988. The effects of stand density on frequency of filled seed and fecundity in lodgepole pine (*Pinus contorta* Dougl.). Canadian Journal Forest Research, 18:453-460.

———. 1990. The advantage of mast years for wind pollination. The American Naturalist, 136:154-166.

STAPANIAN, M. A., AND C. C. SMITH. 1978. A model for seed scatterhoarding: coevolution of fox squirrels and black walnuts. Ecology, 59:884-896.

———. 1984. Density-dependent survival of scatterhoarded nuts: an experimental approach. Ecology, 65:1387-1396.

WHITEHEAD, D. R. 1969. Wind pollination in the Angiosperms: Evolutionary and environmental considerations. Evolution, 23:28-35.

———. 1983. Wind pollination: some ecological and evolutionary perspectives. Pp. 97-108, *in* Pollination biology (L. Real, ed.). Academic Press, Orlando, Florida, 338 pp.

WILLSON, M. F., AND N. BURLEY. 1983. Mate choice in plants: tactics, mechanisms, and consequences. Princeton University Press, Princeton, New Jersey, 251 pp.

DETECTING THE EFFECT OF SEED HOARDERS ON THE DISTRIBUTION OF SEEDLINGS OF TREE SPECIES: GRAY SQUIRRELS (*SCIURUS CAROLINENSIS*) AND OAKS (*QUERCUS*) AS A MODEL SYSTEM

PETER D. SMALLWOOD, MICHAEL A. STEELE, ERIC RIBBENS, AND WILLIAM J. MCSHEA

Department of Biology, Bryn Mawr College, Bryn Mawr, PA 19010 (PDS)
Department of Biology, Wilkes University, Wilkes-Barre, PA 18766 (MAS)
Biology Department, St. John's University, Collegeville, MN 56321 (ER)
Conservation Research Center, The Smithsonian Institution, Front Royal, VA 22630 (WJM)
Present address of PDS: Department of Biology, University of Richmond, Richmond, VA 23173

ABSTRACT.—For many plant species, animals play a role in dispersing their seeds, but it is often difficult to assess how important the animal agents may be. How (or whether) the animals affect the distribution of the seedlings of these plants is often unclear. Gray squirrels and oak trees present an opportunity to study these questions. Here, we report the results of a series of studies leading from the foraging and storing behavior of gray squirrels to differences in the spatial pattern of seedling recruitment for different oak species within hardwood forests in eastern North America. Previous work has shown that gray squirrels cache acorns of red oak species more often than those of white oak species, and that acorns from the red oak group are carried farther from their source than white oak acorns. There is circumstantial evidence that other mammalian, and even avian dispersal agents exhibit similar behaviors. Assuming these behaviors affect the distribution of oak seedlings, we predict that seedlings of red oak occur further away from their parent trees than those of white oak spp. We mapped adult and seedling oak trees on two 9,000 m^2 plots of second growth forest in northern Virginia. Analyses of these maps using the RECRUITS program (Ribbens et al., 1994) support our predictions. We discuss the implications of differential dispersal of the different oak species, and suggest that other systems might be studied using this approach.

"Plants have an ancient and uneasy relationship with vertebrate animals which . . . either digest or disperse their seeds." Howe (1986)

"In some cases, rodents appear to be the lesser evil." Price and Jenkins (1986)

INTRODUCTION

The successful dispersal of offspring is a component in the life history of all species (Ricklefs, 1990; Gotelli, 1995). As sessile organisms, plants achieve dispersal in a variety of ways, using gravity, wind, water, and animals as dispersal agents. As the quotes above suggest, the relationship between plants and their animal dispersal agents may be complex. Although animal dispersal appears to play an important role for many plant species (see reviews by Howe and Smallwood, 1982; Smith and Reichman, 1984; Vander Wall, 1990), much about this relationship remains poorly understood. For

In M.A. Steele, J. F. Merritt, and D. A. Zegers (eds.). 1998. Ecology and Evolutionary Biology of Tree Squirrels. Special Publication, Virginia Museum of Natural History, 6: 320 pp

example, Price and Jenkins (1986) point out that remarkably few studies include estimates of the proportion of seeds the animal dispersal agents consume, either before or after dispersal. Howe (1986) notes that little is known about the interplay between seed dispersal and seedling mortality.

Oaks and sciurid tree squirrels offer ideal opportunities for the study of the effects of seed dispersal by animals on plant populations. First, there is a diverse array of oak species (although there are controversies in *Quercus* taxonomy, estimates of the number of oak species range into the hundreds; see Kaul, 1985). This permits comparisons of tree species with seeds that are similar in many respects, yet different in certain key aspects hypothesized to affect the behavior of their sciurid dispersal agents. Second, sciurids generally scatterhoard acorns. Vander Wall (1990) points out that scatterhoarded seeds are much more likely than larderhoarded seeds to germinate, survive, and recruit into the plant population. Therefore, scatterhoarded seeds are likely to be important to the dynamics of oak populations. Third, the foraging and caching behaviors of sciurids have been the object of considerable study (e.g., Smith and Follmer, 1972; Lewis, 1982; Fox, 1982; Stapanian and Smith, 1984; Smallwood and Peters, 1986; Steele et al., 1993; Steele and Smallwood, 1994; Hadj-Chikh et al., 1996). Although there is certainly a great deal more to be learned about the caching behavior of sciurids, these studies permit us to make predictions as to how their caching behavior might affect the local distribution of oak trees.

Here, we present evidence that the caching choices made by sciurids (among other vertebrates) affect the distribution of seedlings recruited into oak populations. Our previous studies of the foraging behavior of gray squirrels led us to predict that oaks from the white oak group would show relatively short mean dispersal distances; i.e., that the seedlings appear mostly near to adult, putative parent trees. We predicted that red oak species would show relatively long dispersal distances. Using field data from hardwood forests in Virginia, and a new analysis program designed to estimate mean dispersal distances from parent trees (Ribbens et al., 1994), we tested these predictions. The evidence supports our predictions. Before we present this evidence, we briefly review the relevant background on the caching behaviors of sciurids, and how the differences between oaks affect their caching behaviors.

Oaks (*Quercus*) are often divided into two subgenera (Kaul, 1985): The white oak group (hereafter WO, for the type species, *Q. alba*), and the red oak group (hereafter RO, for the type species *Q. rubra*; sometimes called Black Oak, BO in other papers). Acorns vary in physical and chemical properties, both within and between these subgenera. In general, RO species produce acorns with high lipid content (18-25% by dry wt.), high tannin content (6-10%), and generally require a period of winter dormancy before germinating. WO acorns generally have lower concentrations of lipids (5-10%), lower concentrations of tannins (<2%), and usually germinate in autumn, soon after the seed falls to the ground (Ofcarcik and Burns, 1971; Short, 1976; Fox, 1982).

The early germination of WO acorns constitutes a potential problem for gray squirrels (*Sciurus carolinensis*). Neither gray nor fox squirrels (*S. niger*) will eat the protruding radicle of a germinated acorn (Smith and Follmer, 1972; Smallwood, in litt.) Squirrels bite the protruding radicle off, discard it, and open the acorn to consume the remaining cotyledon. WO acorns often germinate early in the autumn, and by mid-winter have transported most of the reserves out of the cotyledon and into the growing radicle (Fox, 1982); thus they become mostly unpalatable for squirrels. Fox reported on "notching" behavior of gray squirrels, hypothesizing that the behavior was an adaptation for caching WO acorns. By excising the embryo of the acorn ("notching"), squirrels prevent WO acorns from germinating. Pigott et al. (1991) has reported this behavior for gray squirrels, and we have seen circumstantial evidence of this behavior in two other small mammal species.

Smallwood and Peters (1986) hypothesized that gray squirrels may have another, perhaps simpler means of dealing with the early germination schedule of WO acorns. They hypothesized that gray squirrels eat WO acorns immediately to satisfy daily energetic requirements, preferring to store the RO acorns for future use. Notching behavior might then become particularly important in years or locations where only WO acorns are available: when squirrels are forced to rely on WO acorns for both immediate consumption and storage for the winter. Several experiments have now confirmed this prediction for gray squirrel populations in Ohio and Pennsylvania (Fig. 1).

Steele et al. (in litt.) confirmed our behavioral observations with studies of metal-tagged acorns. The metal tags allowed us to locate acorns after dispersal with a metal detector. These studies suggest that in addition to squirrels, other small rodents (e.g., *Peromyscus*) cache RO acorns more frequently, and carry them further distances than WO acorns. Caching birds (e.g., blue jays; *Cyanocitta*

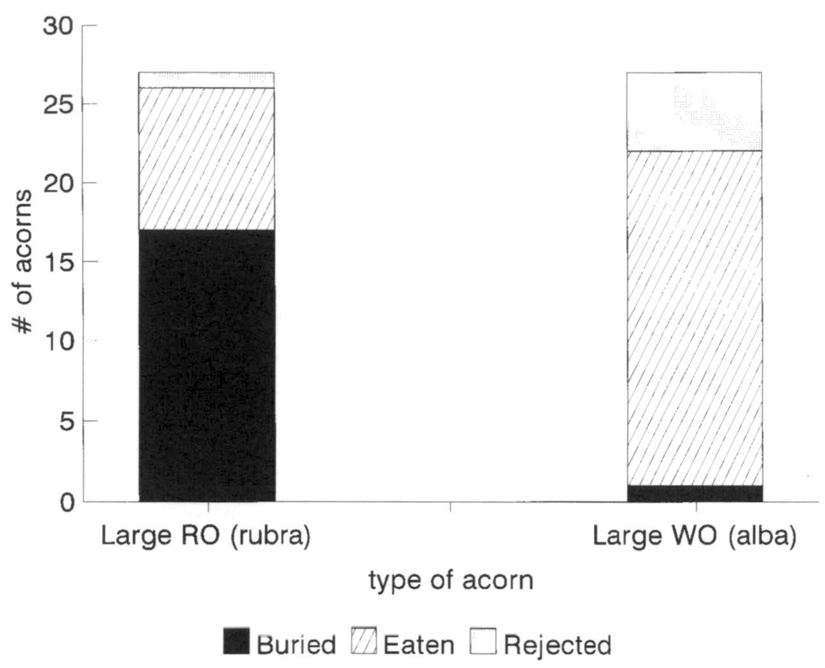

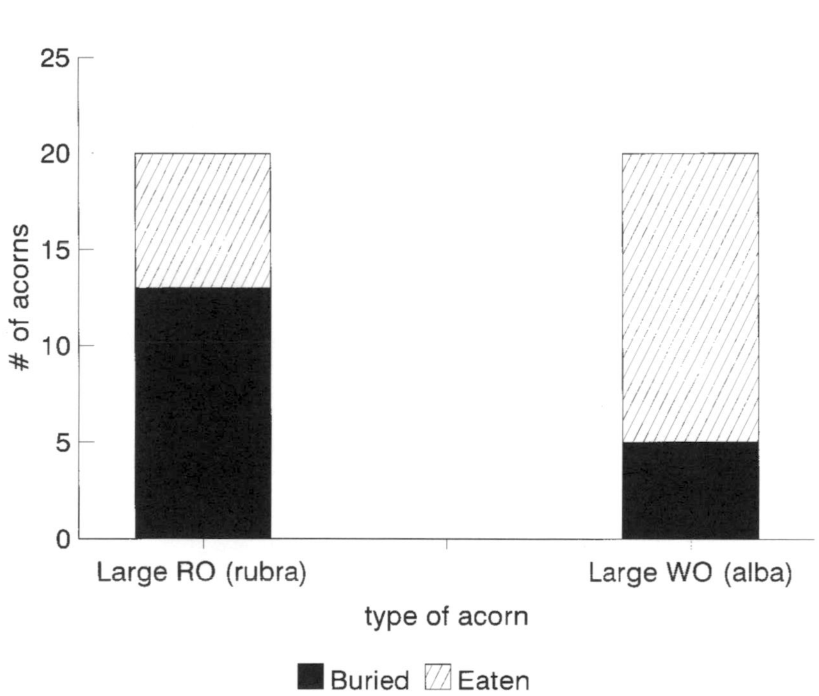

Figure 1.—Frequency of caching versus immediate consumption of RO and WO acorns. In each case, gray squirrels bury acorns of the RO group more frequently, and consume WO acorns immediately. a) from Smallwood (1992) experiments conducted in central Ohio, and b) from Hadj-Chikh et al. (1996) experiments conducted in NE Pennsylvania. In each case, the difference in burial rates between RO and WO acorns is statistically significant by contingency table analyses.

cristata) may behave in a similar fashion: in Virginia, Darley-Hill and Johnson (1981) found blue jays mostly cached two RO species (pin and black oaks, *Q.* paulustris and *velutina*), even though the WO, *Q. alba* was available.

We postulate that the ultimate advantage of this caching preference is to avoid loss of acorns to early germination. There are a number of alternative hypotheses for the ultimate advantage of this behavior to the squirrels (e.g., perhaps the behavior is an adaptation to the higher infestation rate of WO acorns, or perhaps to the lower tannin content of WO acorns). However, for our purposes here, it is sufficient to note that gray squirrels do in fact cache RO acorns far more often and at further distances from the parent tree than WO acorns.

In this study, we sought to determine whether the caching behaviors of gray squirrels (and other scatterhoarders) affect the distribution of seedlings recruited into the oak population. Given that RO acorns are more often cached and WO are more likely to be eaten than dispersed, we hypothesize that seedlings of the RO group will appear more widely distributed than those of the WO group (Smallwood and Peters, 1986; Vander Wall, 1990; Smallwood, 1992). One should note that seedling distributions may be very different from seed distributions (Howe, 1986; Vander Wall, 1990), due to a variety of factors related to post-dispersal mortality. Nevertheless, we begin with the simplest hypothesis: that on a local scale within a forest, the caching of RO acorns results in RO seedlings that are more widely distributed than WO seedlings.

METHODS

Study sites.—In August of 1993, we mapped two study plots in the George Washington National Forest of western Virginia, near Front Royal, USA. Plots were established in a mixed hardwood forest of old (ca. 100 years) second-growth. Oaks were the dominant species of the canopy, and there was relatively little understory on our plots. The rocky soil was well-drained, and exhibited 6 to 7 degree slope to the east. Each plot consisted of a 100 x 60 m rectangle capped at each end by a hemisphere with a radius of 30 m (Fig. 2). Two RO species (*Q. rubra* and *Q. velutina*) and two WO (*Q. alba* and *Q. prinus*) species occurred on our plots. Although several oak species can be found in this area, typical tree communities here are dominated by *Q.*

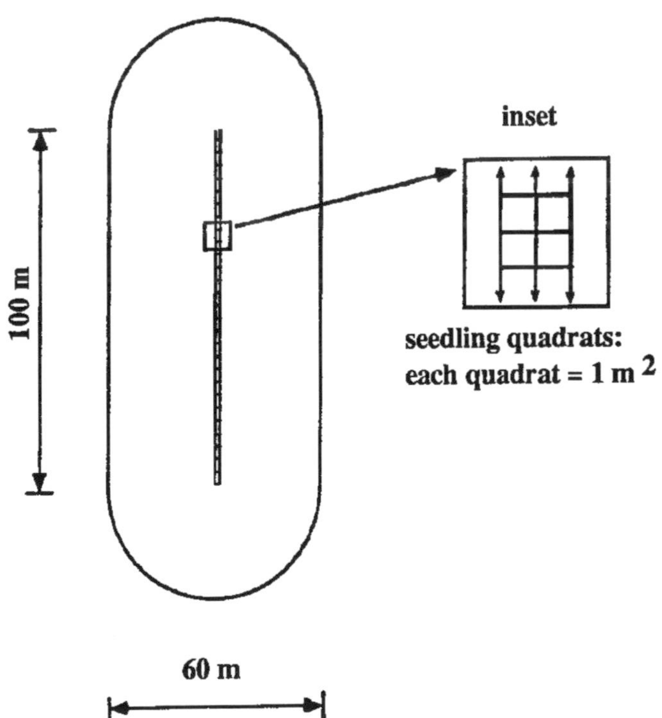

Figure 2.—Plot 1 of two study plots used for field data in this paper. All adult oak trees were mapped throughout the plot. Seedlings were counted in each 1-m^2 quadrat in the narrow strip along the center of the plot. The layout of plot 2 was similar, except that the seedling strip in plot two was eight quadrats wide instead of two, quadrupling the area surveyed for seedlings in plot 2.

prinus and *Q. rubra*, with *Q. alba* and *Q. velutina* frequently co-occurring (Stephenson and Adams, 1991). We mapped the position of every adult oak tree in each plot (±1 m) and measured its diameter (± 0.5 cm) at breast height (dbh), defining "adult" as any tree greater than 15 cm dbh. In plot 1, we counted the number of seedlings of each species in every 1 m^2 quadrat in a strip down the center of the plot. The strip measured 2 x 100 m, yielding 200 quadrats. In order to increase the number of seedlings in our sample, in plot 2 we mapped all the seedlings in an 8 x 100 m strip down the center of the plot (yielding 800 quadrats). Conveniently, the seedlings of these four oak species can be distinguished by leaf shape, texture, and scurfiness (a gritty fuzz found on the leaves of some plants). Of the 616 seedlings found, only three seedlings could not be confidently identified; these were discarded from the analyses.

Analyses.—Ribbens et al. (1994) developed the computer program we use for testing our predictions. Although this analytical tool has been accepted by peer review in the botanical literature, it is likely to be unfamiliar to students of animal behavior. Therefore, some introduction to this program is necessary. Here, we present a nontechnical intuitive explanation of the program. We refer readers to Ribbens et al. (1994) for details.

Ecologists are often interested in parameters that describe the recruitment patterns for their subject species: e.g., the distance from parent plants to seedlings, the number of seedlings produced by a typical parent plant, etc. The program developed by Ribbens et al. (1994—hereafter referred to as RECRUITS program) estimates key recruitment parameters from map coordinates of seedlings and adults. The program is most easily explained using the concept of seed shadows (Janzen, 1971). Imagine a single tree in an open field producing seeds. Barring any special dispersal mechanisms, more seeds will be found closer to the trunk of the tree, and fewer seeds will be found further from the trunk. Janzen (1971) termed this pattern the seed shadow, where the shadow is deeper (more seeds) closer to the parent tree, and thins out as one moves away from the parent tree. This can be expressed as a graph of the density of seeds per square meter as a function of distance from the parent tree. If one wishes to investigate post-dispersal mortality, one can instead investigate seedling shadows, or even sapling shadows (Howe, 1986).

Although conceptually useful, actual measures of seed shadows are often impractical in real landscapes, where several trees may have overlapping seed shadows. Any given seedling (or recruit) might be from the tail end of the seed shadow of a distant tree, or from the proximal end of a nearby tree. One can consider two approaches to quantifying parameters of seedling production, dispersal and survival for trees in real landscapes. First, one may search for isolated trees where the overlap of each seed shadow is likely to be small or absent. While simple in some respects, it is not at all clear that the seed shadows of isolated trees resemble that of trees in forests; the very fact that it is an isolated tree suggests it is not representative. Ribbens et al. (1994) take a different approach: they statistically estimate shadow parameters (numbers of seedlings, mean dispersal distance) from map data, in which the influence of each adult within the neighborhood of the recruit is considered, with influence assumed to decrease with increasing distance from the recruit. By influence, we mean the probability that the adult tree actually produced that seedling recruit. The RECRUITS program uses maximum likelihood statistics to calibrate parameters for a Poisson-based dispersal function, via a searching algorithm that finds those parameters that give the closest fit between the predicted number of seedlings and the actual number found in each square meter of ground where seedlings were counted.

This method works by considering the influence of every tree, scaled by tree diameter at breast height (dbh) and distance from the tree to the recruits (larger trees--larger dbh--yielding more recruits). Thus, the number of recruits (R_i) predicted in quadrat i given T trees, is:

$$\theta \quad R_i = \sum_{j=1}^{T} STR * \left(\frac{dbh_j}{30}\right)^{B} * \frac{1}{n} * \left(e^{-D \cdot m_{ij}^{\theta}}\right)$$

where R_i is the predicted number of seedlings in the ith quadrat; STR (Standardized Total Recruits) is the total number of recruits produced by a tree of 30 cm dbh, dbh_j is diameter at breast height of the jth tree, and n is a normalizer used to decouple the two halves of the equation (see Ribbens et al., 1994 for details). Thus, the first half of the equation models the total number of recruits produced by each adult tree (scaled by dbh_j), without reference to where those recruits might be located.

STR (Standardized Total Recruits) estimates the reproductive success of a tree, and therefore incorporates both the production of seeds and the seed/seedling survivorship. Consistent with Ribbens et al. (1994), we scale STR relative to a 30-cm dbh tree. This standardization enables direct comparisons of STR between species and sites. ß determines the relationship between dbh and number of recruits: ß=1 would indicate a linear relationship, ß=2 would indicate the number of recruits increases as the square of dbh, etc.

The second half of the equation models the effect of distance from adult trees on their contribution to the number of seedlings found in each quadrat. The term m_{ij} is the distance from the ith quadrat to the jth tree. θ and D determine the rapidity of decline of the recruitment intensity as distance from the adult decreases. θ determines the basic shape of the curve relating m_{ij} to number of recruits in a quadrat: $\theta = 2$ would indicate a normal curve, $\theta > 2$ indicates a more square-shaped curve. D is a multiplier, scaling the particular curve determined by θ. A smaller D means that a tree's contribution of recruits to a quadrat falls off more rapidly with its distance from that quadrat.

Based on Ribbens et al. (1994), we fixed ß to 2 and θ to 3, and calibrated (estimated) two parameters: STR and D. Fixing ß to 2 implies that STR increases as tree size increases as the square of the tree diameter. In addition to finding the "best fit" values for D and STR, RECRUITS fits 95% confidence intervals to the parameters, and calculates the product-moment correlation of fit between observed recruits and predicted recruitment distributions as a conservative measure of the ability of the function to track the observed distribution of recruits. Because D is completely correlated with the more intuitively interpretable mean dispersal distance (MDD), we also calculated MDD values, and discuss them instead of D values. MDD is the average dispersal distance from each seedling to its parent tree.

In summary, RECRUITS is an analytical tool. One enters the map coordinates of each adult tree, and an estimate of its size (dbh) from a large study plot into this program. One also enters the location of each seedling from a narrow strip within the larger plot (such that every adult tree that might have contributed seeds to the seedling strip is mapped). From this field data, RECRUITS estimates the parameters of a seed shadow that best account for the actual number and location of seedlings in the study plot. Here, we used RECRUITS to estimate D, a parameter that describes how the number of seedlings/m^2 produced by an adult tree declines as the distance from the adult tree increases. Recalling that D can be transformed into MDD (mean dispersal distance), our a priori prediction is that the seedlings of red oak (*Q. rubra* and *velutina*) have larger MDD's than those of white oak (*Q. alba* and *prinus*).

RESULTS

In plot 1, we mapped 280 adult oak trees, and counted 141 seedlings (recruits) in our seedling quadrats (Table 1). Plot 2 contained more adult oak trees, but like plot 1 it was dominated by the two WO species, *Q. alba* and *Q. prinus*. As expected, we found many more oak seedlings in plot 2 (because our seedling strip was four times as wide, and therefore included four times the number of 1-m^2 quadrats). Curiously, *Q. prinus* seedlings are under-represented in plot 2.

Table 1.—*The total number of adult oak trees and recruits mapped, listed by species and plot. Also given is the mean number of seedlings per quadrat (1-m^2). Note, the area surveyed for seedlings in plot 2 was 4 times the area of that for plot 1--see text.*

Subgenus	WO		RO	
Species	*Q. alba*	*Q. prinus*	*Q. rubra*	*Q. velutina*
Plot 1, adult trees	121	115	22	22
Plot 1, recruits	38	22	39	41
Plot 1, recruits/m^2	0.19	0.11	0.19	0.20
Plot 2, adult trees	220	90	31	15
Plot 2, recruits	141	19	200	116
Plot 1, recruits/m^2	0.17	0.02	0.25	0.14

Recruitment models were constructed for all four species for each plot. Models that did not converge upon a solution and models that did not produce a significant product-moment correlation were discarded. Valid models were obtained from plot 1 for *Q. alba, Q. prinus,* and *Q. velutina*, and from plot 2 for *Q. prinus* and *Q. rubra* (Table 2). The ranking of these species in terms of increasing mean dispersal distances (MDD) is: *Q. prinus* < *Q. alba* < *Q. rubra* < *Q. velutina*; as predicted, the two RO species had the highest MDD values, and the two WO species had the lowest MDD values. Based upon these models, we calculated predicted recruitment profiles for these four species around a tree 30 cm in dbh (Figure 3), and we calculated 95% confidence intervals for the MDD and STR parameters (Table 2). MDD confidence intervals were quite wide for *Q. prinus* in plot 2 and for *Q. velutina,* indicating a greater level of uncertainty in our estimate of the MDD for these species. There was some overlap between the confidence intervals of MDD for the two WO species, but the two RO species were both unique from each other and from the two WO species.

In addition to assessments of the validity of the models (using likelihood and the product-moment correlations), we evaluated the ability of these models to predict recruitment for independent data. For the one species with replicates, we used the parameters for plot 1 to predict the observed data for plot 2, and vice versa. For the other three species, we performed a cross-validation analysis, in which we omitted every third quadrat, calculated new recruitment models, and used these new models to predict recruitment for the quadrats that were omitted. In all cases, there was a significant predictive ability (Table 3). Together these two tests demonstrate the ability of these recruitment models to predict recruitment in quadrats other than those used for calibrating the model.

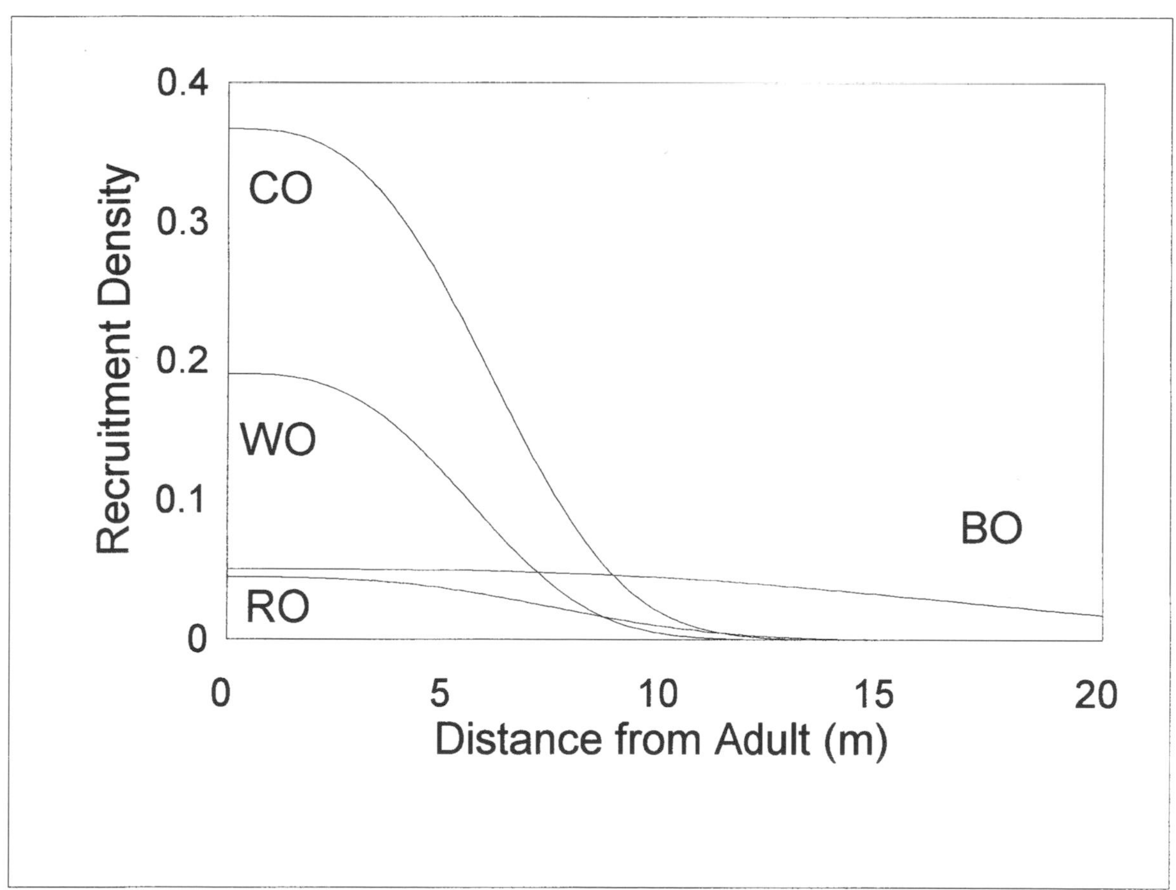

Figure 3.—Predicted recruitment profiles for each oak species. Each line shows the predicted density of recruits (seedlings/m^2) around a 30 cm dbh tree, using the models calibrated for each species. The species displayed here are WO species; *Q. alba* (WO) and *Q. prinus* (CO), and RO species; *Q. rubra* (RO) and *Q. velutina* (BO). Note that the RO species have longer, flatter recruitment profiles, indicating longer dispersal distances.

Table 2.—*Low, maximum likelihood, and high 95% confidence intervals for MDD (Mean Dispersal Distance) values for all species, sorted by MDD. MDD is measured in meters from the parent tree. Also shown are the maximum likelihood estimate for STR (seedlings per adult tree) for each species, and the* r-*value for the correlation between* R_p, *the predicted number of seedlings in each quadrat, and the actual number of seedlings in each quadrat. All correlations were significant* (P<0.05).

Species	Low MDD	Best MDD	High MDD	STR	*r*
Q. prinus, plot 1	3.81	4.72	6.41	22.01	0.53
Q. prinus, plot 2	3.98	5.07	10.89	8.72	0.10
Q. alba, plot 1	4.18	6.41	11.72	8.57	0.14
Q. rubra, plot 2	12.99	14.60	16.60	55.42	0.23
Q. velutina, plot 1	37.51	43.97	51.42	381.14	0.27

Table 3.—*Cross-validation correlations between observed recruits in 1 of every 3 quadrats and expected recruits derived from models calibrated using the remaining quadrats, for* Q. alba, rubra, *and* velutina. *We were able to fit models for* Q. prinus *in each plot separately. This allowed us to validate the model by correlating the observed recruits in one plot with the expected number of recruits predicted by the best-fit parameters from the other plot. All correlations were significant* (P<0.05).

Species	Correlation
Q. velutina, plot 1	.282
Q. rubra, plot 2	.208
Q. alba, plot 1	.162
Q. prinus, plot 1	.540
Q. prinus, plot 2	.106

*significant; *P*<0.05

DISCUSSION

The results above are consistent with our prediction that seedlings of WO species occur nearer to putative parent trees, while RO seedlings are more dispersed. In general, the r^2 values for the correlation between the number of recruits predicted and the actual number of seedlings in each quadrat was low (although significant in every case; Table 2). Animal dispersal agents introduce more variability into seed dispersal than abiotic dispersal agents, e.g., wind (Ribbens, 1995). This, and many other factors not included in this version of RECRUITS (texture of the soil, competitive effects of neighboring plants), may contribute to the low correlations we obtained. Despite this low correlation, we found a clear separation between the MDD's for RO and WO seedlings, in accordance with our prediction. While many seed predator/ dispersers may contribute to this pattern, the prediction was derived from studies of gray squirrel foraging and caching behavior. If our prediction stands the tests of time and replication in other forests, it has many implications for efforts to understand and manage forests.

One should note here that seedling distributions do not always reflect seed dispersal. As Howe (1986) and Vander Wall (1990) note, many post-disperal mortality factors may act to significantly distort the seed shadow before it matures into a seedling shadow. In this case, one might imagine that even though RO acorns are cached much more often, they are also retrieved from caches at a higher rate. If even a few WO acorns are cached intact, they may enjoy a very high survival rate due to their early germination schedule (see the discussion of European jays and acorns below). If that were true, then post-dispersal mortality might compensate for the bias in caching, resulting in no differences in the distributions of

RO and WO seedlings. However, this does not appear to be the case in our study plots. If early germination does increase the effective dispersal of recruits by lowering post-dispersal mortality, it is apparently not enough to offset the lower rates and distances of WO acorn dispersal.

Evidence has accumulated in recent decades that the rates of recruitment for oak species are insufficient to maintain oaks in modern forest. While adult oak trees are producing seeds, their saplings are often rare. This problem appears to be widespread (e.g., *Pennsylvania*—Abrams and Downs, 1990; Smith and Vankat, 1991; *Indiana*—Andersen and Folk, 1993; *Wisconsin*--Hix and Lorimer, 1991; Crow 1992; *southern Appalachians*--Loftis, 1990; *California*—Borchert et al., 1989). Postulated reasons for this lack of recruitment include modern fire suppression (Abrams and Nowacki, 1992), overpopulation of deer (Crow, 1992; McShea and Schwede, 1993), and many others.

Our results suggest that squirrels and other scatterhoarders may significantly affect oak recruitment. If RO acorns are dispersed more widely, then they are more likely to appear in open areas such as gaps, meadows, and recently disturbed habitats. Consistent with this expectation, RO seedlings appear to be less shade-tolerant than WO, and better able to withstand low soil moisture (McCarthy and Dawson, 1990; Kubiske and Abrams, 1992; Kolb et al., 1990; Crow, 1992). Since WO seedlings are more likely to be found near or under their parent tree, we might expect WO species to form "pure" stands (species composition overwhelmingly dominated by one species) more often than RO. Consistent with this, reconstructions of pre-settlement forest composition in Pennsylvania often conclude that many areas were thoroughly dominated by *Quercus alba* (Abrams and Downs, 1990). In contrast, *Q. rubra* stands appear to have been less dominated by the single oak species, often occurring as scattered, large individual trees (Loftis, 1990).

Differences in dispersal distances might lead to differences in the genetic structure of oak populations. Specifically, we would expect RO species to be more outbred, while WO species would exist as more isolated sub-populations. Some researchers have found that populations of a RO species (*Q. rubra*) are separated into small sub-populations, where the sub-populations adapt to local conditions (Kubiske and Abrams, 1992; Sork et al., 1993). However, without similar studies on WO species, we cannot yet say whether RO sub-populations are more or less isolated and subdivided than comparable WO species.

Differences in dispersal distances might also lead to different rates of colonization, and/or migrations for the RO and WO species ranges on longer time scales in response to regional or global climate changes. RO species might be expected to colonize open ground more rapidly than WO, especially if other dispersal agents have the same foraging/caching preferences as gray squirrels. Studies conducted with metal-tagged acorns (Steele et al., in litt.) suggest that other small rodents cache RO acorns more frequently and further from the source than those of WO. Caching by birds (e.g., blue jays; *Cyanocitta cristata*) may be even more important than mammal behavior for oak range migrations, due to the longer dispersal distances involved. In Virginia, Darley-Hill and Johnson (1981) found blue jays concentrated on two RO species (pin and black oaks, *Q. paulustris* and *velutina*), even though the WO *Q. alba* was available. They note large numbers of pin and black oak seedlings were present in their study areas. In Michigan, Harrison and Werner (1984) implicated blue jays as the dispersal agent moving oak seeds into patches of open ground, but they did not distiguish between species of oak seedlings.

It is suggestive to note the very high MDD for *Q. velutina* in our study (Table 2). Darley-Hill and Johnson (1981) note that blue jays generally did not use *Q. rubra* acorns because the acorns were too large for their bills. Instead, the jays used smaller acorns, including *Q. velutina*. Blue jays often carry acorns long distances—much further than small mammals—to cache them (Darley-Hill and Johnson, 1981; Scarlett and Smith, 1991). Perhaps the very large MDD for velutina in our study reflects the dispersal activity of blue jays.

Studies of past range migrations of North American forests have shown that nut-bearing trees were the first to recolonize eastern North America as the glaciers retreated (Graumlich and Davis, 1993). Johnson and Webb (1989) implicate blue jays as a critical dispersal agent making such rapid recolonization possible. Our work here suggests that if the caching preferences of blue jays resemble those of squirrels, RO species were likely the first of the oaks to recolonize after the receding glaciers, with WO species following afterwards. Two caveats should be noted here. First, jays and other birds may be limited in their use of very large acorns (some varieties of *Q. rubra* and *Q. prinus*). Darley-Hill and Johnson (1981) note that blue jays did not use *Q. rubra*, and speculated that the acorns were simply too large for the birds to handle. Scarlett and Smith (1991) similarly report that blue jays in Arkansas rely primarily on oak species with small acorns. Bossema (1979) makes the same observation and speculation for European jays in Great Britain. Second, some jays may store WO acorn species, as their early sprouting may make them easier to retrieve in the spring. Sonesson (1994) reports that the European jay finds *Q. robur* (a WO species) by their shoots, harvesting the cotyledon and leaving the rest of the seedling intact. Thus, it seems that a WO species, *Q. robur*, is gaining a great dispersal benefit from a scatterhoarder. If this behavior is widespread among blue jays and other scatterhoarders in USA, it would counteract the dispersal biases we predict from our studies of sciurid scatterhoarding behavior. Data reported in Darley-Hill and Johnson (1981) and observations by one of us (MAS) suggest that blue jays behave more like our sciurids than European jays, storing RO acorns more often than WO acorns—as long as the acorns are small enough for the birds to handle. Clearly, more work needs to be done in this area.

We hope this approach might be used to study the effects of animal dispersal agents on plant populations in a variety of other systems. For example, various small rodent species have been suggested as agents of seed dispersal in shrub oak invasions of heathlands in Denmark (Jensen and Nielsen, 1986), and have been reported as scatterhoarders of acorns in oak forests in Japan (Kikuzawa, 1988). Scrub jays transport large numbers of acorns in south-central Florida (DeGrange et al., 1989). Berg and Hamrick (1994) report that of the two dominant scrub oaks in the sandhill habitat of costal South Carolina, the white oak (*Q. margaretta*) exhibited a clustered distribution, while the red oak (*Q. laevis*) did not. In all of these systems, animals scatterhoard acorns in areas suitable for germination. These systems, as well as many other animal-dispersal systems, may be profitably studied using the same approach we use here.

CONCLUSIONS

Our understanding of gray squirrel foraging and caching behavior led us to predict that seedlings from the RO subgenus of *Quercus* would be more widely dispersed, and those of the WO group would have shorter dispersal distances. Here, we use field data from study plots in Virgina and the RECRUITS program (Ribbens et al., 1994) to estimate dispersal distances for four species of oaks. The resulting estimates support our prediction; the two RO species have longer Mean Dispersal Distances than the two WO species. Additional study plots in other locations should be studied to see if this pattern is widespread. When considering oak forests in locations beyond midwestern and eastern USA, one must realize that other animal dispersal agents may have foraging and caching preferences different from those of the tree squirrels discussed here. Further, the RO/WO catagorization of oak species may not be as meaningful in other regions of the USA or beyond (e.g., Fleck and Layne, 1990 find that some WO species in south Florida have higher tannin content than RO species).

Mean Dispersal Distances of oak seedlings are important, because they are likely to affect many other aspects of oak ecology: from the genetic structure of oak populations, to patterns of oak recruitment within forests and in open areas of succession, to the range migration of oaks in response to past or future climate changes. Short dispersal distances (such as those found for WO species in this study) can be an important form of recruitment limitation with important implications for post-recruitment community dynamics (Pacala et al., 1996).

ACKNOWLEDGMENTS

We would like to thank the Biology Departments at Bryn Mawr College, Wilkes University, and St. John's University, as well as the Conservation Research Center for supporting this work. We would like to thank EarthWatch for providing the field assistance in mapping out our study plots. Smallwood would also like to thank the Department of Biology at the University of Pennsylvania for support, and the members of the Ecology group there for their challenging questions. We also thank David Zegers, Guy Steucek, and an anonymous reviewer for improving the manuscript.

LITERATURE CITED

ABRAMS, M. D., AND J. A. DOWNS. 1990. Successional replacement of old-growth white oak by mixed mesophytic hardwoods in southwestern Pennsylvania. Canadian Journal of Forest Research, 20:1864-1870.

ABRAMS, M. D., AND G. J. NOWACKI. 1992. Historical variation in fire, oak recruitment, and post-logging accelerated succession in central Pennsylvania. Bulletin of the Torrey Botanical Club, 119:19-28.

ANDERSEN, D. C., AND M. L. FOLK. 1993. *Blarina brevicauda* and *Peromyscus leucopus* reduce overwintering survivorship of acorn weevils in an Indiana hardwood forest. Journal of Mammalogy, 74:656-664.

BORCHERT, M. I., F. W. DAVIS, AND J. MICHEALSEN. 1989. Interactions of factors affecting seedling recruitment of blue oak (*Quercus douglasii*) in California. Ecology, 70:389-404.

BERG, E. E., AND J. L. HAMRICK. 1994. Spatial and genetic structure of two sandhill oaks: *Quercus laevis* and *Quercus margaretta* (Fagaceae). American Journal of Botany, 8:7-14.

BOSSEMA, I. 1979. Jays and oaks: An eco-ethological study of a symbiosis. Behaviour, 70:1-117.

CROW, T. R. 1992. Population dynamics and growth patterns for a cohort of northern red oak (*Quercus rubra*) seedlings. Oecologia, 91:192-200.

DARLEY-HILL, S., AND W. C. JOHNSON. 1981. Acorn dispersal by the blue jay (*Cyanocitta cristata*). Oecologia, 50:231-232.

DEGRANGE, A. R., J. W. FITZPATRICK, J. N. LAYNE, AND G. E. WOOLFENDEN. 1989. Acorn harvesting by Florida scrub jays. Ecology, 70:348-356.

FLECK, D. C., AND J. N. LAYNE. 1990. Variation in tannin activity of acorns of seven species of central Florida oaks. Journal of Chemical Ecology, 16:2925-2934.

FOX, J. F. 1982. Adaptation of gray squirrel behavior to autumn germination by white oak acorns. Evolution, 36:800-809.

GOTELLI, N. J. 1995. A primer of Ecology. Sinauer Associates, Inc., Publishers, Sunderland, Massachusetts, 206 pp.

GRAUMLICH, L. J., AND M. B. DAVIS. 1993. Holocene variation in spatial scales of vegetation patterns in the upper Great Lakes. Ecology, 74:826-840.

HADJ-CHIKH, L. Z., M. A. STEELE, AND P. D. SMALLWOOD. 1996. Caching decisions by gray squirrels: A test of the handling-time and perishability hypotheses. Animal Behaviour, 52:941-948.

HARRISON, J. S., AND P. A. WERNER. 1984. Colonization by oak seedlings into a heterogenous successional habitat. Canadian Journal of Botany, 62:559-563.

HIX, D. H., AND C. G. LORIMER. 1991. Early stand development on former oak sites in southwestern Wisconsin. Forest Ecology and Management, 42:169-193.

HOWE, H. F. 1986. Seed dispersal by fruit-eating birds and mammals. Pp. 123-190 *in* Seed dispersal (D. R. Murray, ed.). Academic Press, Sydney, Australia, 322 pp.

HOWE, H. F., AND J. SMALLWOOD. 1982. Ecology of seed dispersal. Annual Review of Ecology and Systematics, 13:201-228.

JANZEN, D. H. 1971. Seed predation by animals. Annual Review of Ecology and Systematics, 2:465-492.

JENSEN, T. S., AND O. F. NIELSEN. 1986. Rodents as seed dispersers in a heath-oak wood succession. Oecologia, 70:214-221.

JOHNSON, W. C., AND T. WEBB. 1989. The role of blue jays (*Cyanocitta cristata*) in the postglacial dispersal of Fagaceous trees in eastern North America. Journal of Biogeography, 16:561-571.

KAUL, R. B. 1985. The reproductive morphology of *Quercus* (Fagaceae). American Journal of Botany, 72:1962-1977.

KIKUZAWA, K. 1988. Dispersal of *Quercus mongolica* acorns in a broadleaved deciduous forest. Forest Ecology and Management, 25:1-8.

KOLB, T. E., K. C. STEINER, L. H. MCCORMICK, AND T. W. BOWERSOX. 1990. Growth response of northern red oak and yellow poplar seedlings to light, soil moisture and nutrients in relation to ecological strategy. Forest Ecology and Management, 38:65-78.

KUBISKE, M. E., AND M. D. ABRAMS. 1992. Photosynthesis, water relations and leaf morphology of xeric versus mesic *Quercus rubra* ecotypes in central Pennsylvania in relation to moisture stress. Canadian Journal of Forest Research, 22:1402-1407.

LOFTIS, D. L. 1990. A shelterwood method of regenerating red oak in Southern Appalachians. Forest Science, 36:917-929.

LEWIS, A. R. 1982. Selection of nuts by gray squirrels and optimal foraging theory. The American Midland Naturalist, 107:250-257.

MCCARTHY, J. J., AND J. O. DAWSON. 1990. Growth and water use efficiency of *Quercus alba, Q. bicolor, Q. imbricata,* and *Q. paulustris* seedlings under conditions of reduced soil water availablity and solar irradiance. Transactions of the Illinois State Academy of Sciences, 83:128-148.

MCSHEA, W. J., AND G. SCHWEDE. 1993. Variable acorn crops: responses of white-tailed deer and other mast consumers. Journal of Mammalogy, 74:999-1006.

OFCARCIK, R. P., AND E. E. BURNS. 1971. Chemical and physical properties of selected acorns. Journal of Food Science, 36:576-578.

PACALA, S. W., C. D. SAPONARA, J. SILANDER, J. W. KOBE, AND E. RIBBENS. 1996. Forest models defined by field measurements 2. Estimation, error analysis and dynamics. Ecological Monographs, 66:1-43.

PIGOTT, C. D., A. C. NEWTON, AND S. ZAMMIT. 1991. Predation of acorns and oak seedlings by grey squirrel. Quarterly Journal of Forestry, 85:173-178.

PRICE, M. V., AND S. H. JENKINS. 1986. Rodents as seed consumers and dispersers. Pp. 191-236, *in* Seed Dispersal (D. F. Murray, ed.). Academic Press, Sydney, Australia, 322 pp.

RIBBENS, E. 1995. Predicting tree seedling distributions: the role of recruitment in forest community dynamics. Ph.D. dissertation, The University of Connecticut, Storrs, 211 pp.

RIBBENS, E., J. A. SILANDER, AND S. W. PACALA. 1994. Seedling recruitment in forests: calibrating models to predict patterns of tree seedling dispersion. Ecology, 75:1794-1806.

RICKLEFS, R. E. 1990. Ecology. Third edition. W.H. Freeman and Co. New York, 896 pp.

SCARLETT, T. L., AND K. G. SMITH. 1991. Acorns preference of urban blue jays (*Cyanocitta cristata*) during fall and spring in northwestern Arkansas. The Condor, 93:438-442.

SHORT, H. L. 1976. Composition and squirrel use of acorns of black and white oak group. The Journal of Wildlife Management, 40:479-483.

SMALLWOOD, P. D., AND W. D. PETERS. 1986. Grey squirrel food preferences: The effects of tannin and fat concentration. Ecology, 67:168-174.

SMALLWOOD, P. D. 1992 Temporal and spatial scales in foraging ecology: testing hypotheses with spiders and squirrels. Ph.D. dissertation, University of Arizona, Tucson, 124 pp.

SMITH, C. C., AND D. FOLLMER. 1972. Food preferences of squirrels. Ecology, 53:82-91.

SMITH, C. C., AND O. J. REICHMAN. 1984. The evolution of food caching by birds and mammals. Annual Review of Ecology and Systematics, 15:329-351.

SMITH, L. L., AND J. L. VANKAT. 1991. Communities and tree seedling distribution in *Quercus rubra* and *Prunus serotina* dominated forests in southwestern Pennsylvania. The American Midland Naturalist, 126:294-307.

SONESSON, K. L. 1994. Growth and survival after cotyledon removal in *Quercus robur* seedlings, grown in different natural soil types. Oikos, 69: 65-70.

SORK, V. L., K. A. STOWE, AND C. KOCHWENDER. 1993. Evidence for local adaptation in closely adjacent subpopulations of northern red oak (*Quercus rubra* L.) expressed as resistance to herbivores. The American Naturalist, 142:928-942.

STAPANIAN, M. A., AND C. C. SMITH. 1984. Density-dependent survival of scatter-hoarded nuts: An experimental approach. Ecology, 65:1387-1396.

STEELE, M. A., AND P. D. SMALLWOOD. 1994. What are squirrels hiding? Natural History, 10/94:40-45.

STEELE, M. A., T. W. KNOWLES, K. BRIDLE, AND E.L. SIMMS. 1993. Tannins and partial consumption of acorns: Implications for dispersal of oaks by seed predators. The American Midland Naturalist, 130:229-237.

STEPHENSON, S. L., AND H. S. ADAMS. 1991. Upland oak forests of the ridge and valley province in southwestern Virginia. Virginia Journal of Science, 42:371-380.

VANDER WALL, S. B. 1990. Food hoarding in animals. The University of Chicago Press, Chicago, Illinois, 445 pp.

DISPERSAL OF HALF-EATEN ACORNS BY GRAY SQUIRRELS: EFFECTS OF PHYSICAL AND CHEMICAL SEED CHARACTERISTICS

MICHAEL A. STEELE, KIMBERLY GAVEL, AND WENDY BACHMAN
Department of Biology
Wilkes University
Wilkes-Barre, PA 18766

ABSTRACT.—Previous studies have shown that gray squirrels and other acorn predators selectively consume only the basal portion of acorns from many oak species and that these partially eaten acorns often germinate. These and other observations suggest that several acorn characteristics, including tannin distribution, the acorn shell (pericarp), and acorn geometry may induce incomplete consumption and dispersal of acorns. To determine which of these factors influence partial acorn consumption, we conducted a series of experiments in which we presented free-ranging gray squirrels (*Sciurus carolinensis*) with whole acorns, shelled acorns, carved acorns (in which the basal and apical ends were carved to appear as the opposite ends) and artificial acorns to which varying amounts of tannin were added. Pericarp removal did not affect partial consumption; however seed shape significantly affected the part of the seed eaten, and tannin levels significantly affected the amount of the seed eaten. Partial consumption of seeds was also more evident following a food-supplement experiment. Free-ranging squirrels were observed to consume the basal half of acorns of more than 40% of the acorn crops of individual red oak (*Quercus rubra*) and pin oak (*Q. palustris*) trees, and to regularly disperse and scatterhoard apical fragments following consumption. We suggest that tannin levels and acorn shape may interact to promote partial seed consumption and dispersal, especially when food is abundant.

INTRODUCTION

Tree squirrels are widely recognized in both temperate and tropical regions as important selective agents of conifer and nut-bearing trees. They exert both negative and positive influences on plant reproductive success. As seed predators, squirrels can greatly reduce overall plant fecundity, particularly in conifer forests, where seeds and cones are either stored in central larderhoards (where successful recruitment is unlikely—Smith, 1968; Smith, 1970; Gurnell, 1984, 1987), consumed directly in trees prior to dispersal (Smith, 1968; Janzen, 1971; Elliot, 1974, 1988; Benkman et al., 1984; Mollar, 1986; Steele and Weigl, 1992), or indirectly lost as a result of other foraging activities (e.g., twig clipping and bark stripping—Allred et al., 1994; Snyder, 1993). Although a few studies have reported the dispersal or establishment of pine seeds by squirrels (Hall, 1981; Kato, 1985; Miyaki, 1987; see also Vander Wall [1992] for dispersal by chipmunks), most species are regarded as significant predators of conifer seeds.

In contrast to conifers, many other tree species—especially those of the nut-bearing trees—may benefit considerably from the foraging and caching activity of squirrels, especially when seeds are scatterhoarded by these animals (see Price and Jenkins [1986] and Vander Wall [1990] for reviews). It is has been shown, for example, that gray squirrels selectively cache sound acorns (Steele et al., in litt), store acorns in sites suitable for germination (Barnett, 1977), and fail to recover as many as 70% of acorn stores during high mast crops (Barnett, 1977). It is also argued that species of nut-bearing trees exhibit a range of general characteristics (or adaptations) that are thought to enhance seed harvest and dispersal by squirrels

In M.A. Steele, J. F. Merritt, and D. A. Zegers (eds.). 1998. Ecology and Evolutionary Biology of Tree Squirrels. Special Publication, Virginia Museum of Natural History, 6: 320 pp

and other rodents (Vander Wall, 1990). Examples (as reviewed by Vander Wall, 1990) include high lipid content, fleshy pericarps that encourage seed harvest (Smythe, 1978), woody endocarps that limit consumption by predators other than squirrels (Smith and Follmer, 1972; Vander Wall, 1990), seed drop, and mast fruiting (Silvertown, 1980; Lalonde and Roitberg, 1992).

Despite this close association between tree squirrels and their seed trees, the actual mechanisms by which squirrels and other seed hoarders affect plant reproductive success is poorly understood and at best based on a range of untested assumptions. In particular, little research has been directed at the specific adaptations of trees and seeds that influence caching and foraging decisions and the reciprocal effects of these decisions on seed survival.

Recently though, Steele et al. (1993) provided evidence that gray squirrels and several other seed consumers may enhance the reproductive success of oaks via their response to chemical characteristics of acorns. They demonstrated that tannin content (total precipitable phenolics) is highest in the apical portion of red oak acorns (subgenus Erythrobalanus) near the embryo, and lowest in the basal portion, from which the majority of cotyledon is consumed (< 40% of the total mass). Most importantly, they showed that remaining acorn fragments germinate at rates equal to or higher than those of whole acorns.

These observations collectively suggest that a strong link exists between acorn chemistry and seed dispersal, and may indicate a possible adaptation by oaks to promote partial consumption and survival of acorns. They do not, however, demonstrate any causal relationship between tannins, partial seed consumption and seed germination; nor do they address possible alternative explanations for partial consumption of acorns by squirrels and other seed consumers.

Therefore, the objectives of this study were to test three alternative hypotheses to explain the partial consumption of acorns by the eastern gray squirrel. In a series of field experiments, we tested the null hypotheses that partial acorn consumption (i.e., consumption of the basal portion of the seed) is not related to either tannin concentrations in the seed, the ease at which the pericarp can be removed from the basal end of the seed, or the shape (geometry) of the seed. In addition, we made extensive field observations to quantify the degree to which partial acorn consumption by gray squirrels occurs under natural field conditions, to determine the effects of food availability on the behavior, and to assess whether squirrels disperse the remaining apical fragments.

METHODS

Study area and field collections.—We conducted behavioral experiments during the autumns of 1990 and 1991 in Kirby Park, a 48.5–ha, urban park, located in Wilkes-Barre, Pennsylvania. The site is characterized by an open (16.2 ha) stand of mature native northern red oaks (*Quercus rubra*), pin oaks (*Q. palustris*), and silver maples (*Acer saccharinum*), bordered by a mowed field and a dense riparian woodlot (32.2 ha) dominated by an overstory of silver maples. We selected the site because gray squirrels there regularly consumed and cached acorns and were easily observed as a result of their habituation to human activity. All other observations were recorded from oak trees on the campus of Wilkes University, 0.5 km from the Kirby Park site.

In 1990, intensive observations on partial seed consumption were made at three pin oak trees. During autumn seed fall, we collected all acorn fragments under the canopies of each tree and determined whether each seed was consumed from the basal end or any other portion of the seed, and whether the seed was attacked by gray squirrels or any other seed predators (e.g., blue jays, *Cyanocitta cristata*; or weevils, *Curculio*).

To evaluate the relationship between food availability and partial acorn consumption, we followed patterns of partial acorn consumption during the autumn of 1991 as acorn availability in the trees declined. Beginning on September 1, and at weekly intervals thereafter, we collected all acorns and acorn fragments under the canopies of four pin oak and four northern red oak trees. Following each collection, all acorns and fragments (any seed part > 0.25g that contained cotyledon) were returned to the lab and categorized by the damage sustained. Acorn categories included whole acorns, acorns in which only the basal portion had been eaten, and all other acorn fragments. This last group included any acorn fragment not obviously eaten from the basal end and therefore represented a conservative estimate of “other” damage. As evidenced from incisor marks on acorn cotyledon, gray squirrels were the predominant vertebrate seed predators, although blue jays were observed to occasionally feed at one pin oak tree.

Immediately following each collection, a sample of both partially eaten seeds (n = 50) and whole acorns (n = 30) from each sample were dried (at 50°C) to a constant mass and weighed to the nearest 0.01g. The percent of each seed consumed was then calculated by dividing the mass of each partially eaten seed by the mean mass of whole acorns from the same sample. The proportion of acorns remaining in each tree at each collection interval was estimated by subtracting the number of acorns and fragments collected previously from the total number of acorns and fragments collected during the entire season. Spearman rank correlations were then used to evaluate the relationship between the proportion of individual seeds eaten and the proportion of acorn crops remaining in the tree.

Effects of physical characteristics of acorns.—To assess the influence of the pericarp on partial acorn consumption, we first conducted preliminary experiments in 1990 in which we presented free ranging squirrels (n = 16-27) with shelled acorns (from which the pericarps were removed) and whole red oak and pin oak acorns acorns on nine independent trial dates (between November 15 and January 1): three in autumn with pin oak acorns only and six in early winter (each with red and pin oak acorns). For each of the nine trials, squirrels were presented with both whole and shelled acorns of one species, and for each acorn we determined whether the animal consumed the acorn from the apical or basal end.

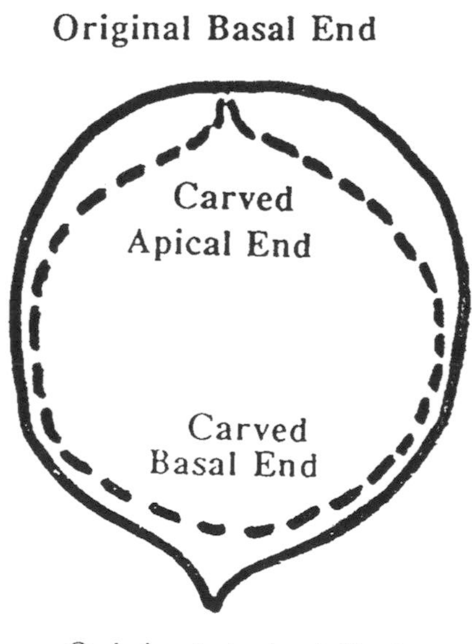

Fig. 1.—Diagram illustrating whole acorn with pericarp removed (solid line) and carved acorn (dashed line) in which the basal and apical ends were carved to reverse the shape of the original seed. As indicated, the entire surface of shelled seeds was scraped in order to control for possible chemical changes (e.g., tannin oxidation) induced by carving the cotyledon.

In autumn of 1991, we conducted more extensive experiments in which we tested the squirrels' responses to whole acorns, shelled acorns, and shelled acorns in which the apical and basal ends were carved to appear as the opposite ends of the seed. Whole acorns served as a control, and the latter two treatments allowed us to test whether partial acorn use was related to either the presence of a pericarp or the geometry of the seed. Carved acorns were prepared by first shelling an acorn, rounding the true apical end of the cotyledon into a rounded edge (resembling that of the true basal end), and then carving the true basal end to resemble an apical tip (Fig. 1.). In addition, the entire surface of the cotyledon was scraped lightly with a knife so that chemical alterations (resulting from oxidation of tannins when cotyledon is cut) would not bias the animals' responses to either end of the seed.

During each daily trial (in both 1990 and 1991), we presented individual squirrels (n = 16-25) with either whole, shelled, or carved acorns and determined whether each seed was partially eaten, and whether it was eaten from the basal end or another part of the seed. For each observation, a squirrel was presented with a single acorn type and then observed until the fate of the seed was established. Independence of observations was maintained within each daily trial by presenting each squirrel with only a single food item per trial (see Smallwood and Peters, 1986; Steele et al., 1996). To control for hunger, all trials were conducted in the early morning hours when animals were least likely to be satiated (<0900 h). Because all experiments were conducted in early morning, squirrels only cached a few whole acorns and these events were not included in further analyses. A random block design was used to establish order of daily trials.

Effects of tannins and food availability.—To test the influence of tannins and food availability on partial consumption of acorns, we conducted two series of feeding experiments in the spring of 1992 in which we presented free ranging gray squirrels with acorns of varying tannin concentrations under conditions of both high and low food abundance. In the first, we presented squirrels with whole pin and red oak acorns, and basal and apical halves of both acorn species. These trials were based on previous results that revealed higher tannin levels in the apical portion of acorns of the red oak subgenus (*Erythrobalanus*; Steele et al., 1993).

In the second set of experiments, we presented artificial acorns made from the cotyledon of red oak acorns, again under low and high food conditions. Red oak seeds from a single tree were shelled, ground to a fine powder, and mixed with varying amounts of laboratory grade tannic acid to produce artificial acorn dough with 0%, 2%, and 6% additional tannin by mass (see Smallwood and Peters, 1986). Each mixture was then molded into acorn-sized doughballs of ca. 5g and stored at 4°C until experiments were conducted.

Prior to presentation of supplemental food, we performed one feeding trial with each treatment involving pin oak and red oak acorns, and two trials with each of the artificial acorn treatments. Then, following completion of these 12 trials, we provisioned study animals with 22 kg of supplemental food (sunflower seeds and pin oak acorns) that we distributed in small piles (0.5 kg) throughout the study site every day for 14 d. We then repeated the same 12 trials, under simulated conditions of high food abundance.

In both pre- and post-supplement trials, only one treatment was conducted per day (n = 15-25 squirrels), and statistical independence of observations was maintained as described for previous experiments. Prior to supplementation, we measured eating times and the proportion of individual seeds consumed; and after supplementation we measured eating times and estimated the proportion of each seed eaten based on reductions in feeding times. All proportions (percentages) were arcsin transformed. Trials involving pin and red oak acorns were each analyzed independently with a Two-way Analysis of Variance without replication and those from trials involving artificial acorns were analyzed with a Two-way Analysis of Variance with replication.

RESULTS

In 1990, we recovered 244, 271, and 315 partially eaten acorns from the three pin oak trees examined, and partial consumption by squirrels accounted for 62.7, 52.7, and 71.1% of these samples, respectively. Greater than 97.5% of all partially eaten acorns were consumed from only the basal half of the seed (Fig. 2). Likewise, during the autumns of 1991, gray squirrels consistently consumed less than 50% and 35% of the basal portion of individual acorns of red and pin oaks respectively (Fig. 3). For both oak species, few acorns (<5% of acorn crops) sustained damage on any part of the seed other than the basal end (Fig. 2).

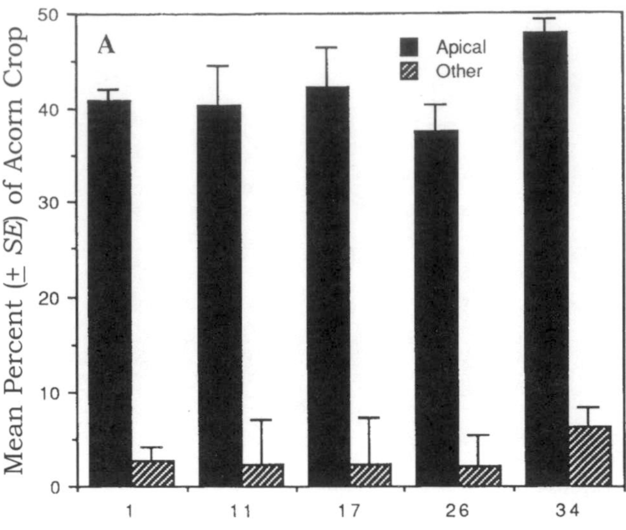

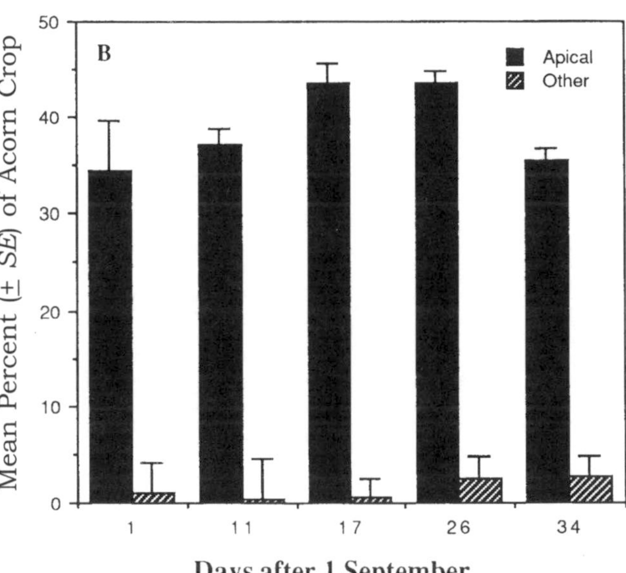

Fig. 2.—Mean proportion of acorn samples from four red oak (*Q. rubra*; A) and four pin oak (*Q. palustris*; B) trees in which individual seeds were only partially eaten by squirrels. Shown are those seeds eaten from only the basal end (apical fragments) along with all other acorn fragments.

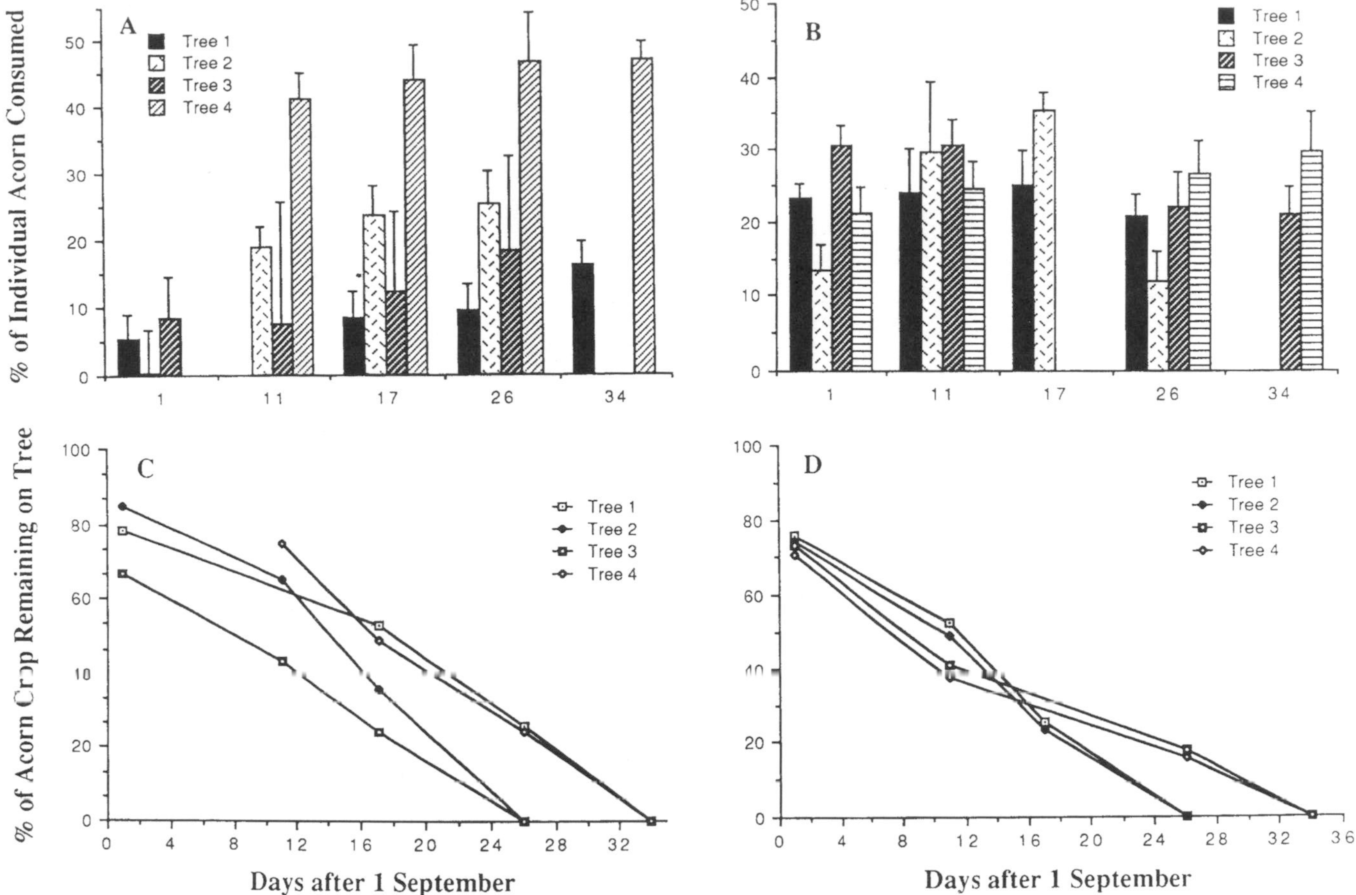

Fig. 3.—The relationship between partial seed consumption and acorn availability. Shown are the the mean proportion (±*SE*) of individual seeds eaten from the basal end of acorns from four red oak (*Q. rubra*; A) and four pin oak (*Q. palustris*; B) trees during five weekly intervals during September 1991. Also shown are the estimated number of acorns remaining in each of the red oak (C) and pin oak trees (D) during the same time intervals.

In 1991, partial consumption of acorns continued until after seed fall in early October, and during this time the proportion of individual seeds eaten remained below 50% for red oak acorns and 40% for pin oak acorns (Fig. 3). In addition, for all four red oaks there was a significant negative correlation between the mean proportion of each seed eaten and proportion of acorn crops remaining in the tree (-8.0 > r_S's > -1.0, Ps < 0.01), suggesting that partial consumption may indeed be affected by food supply. The same pattern, however, was detected in only one of the four pin oak trees (r_S = -1.0, P < 0.001; all other trees, r_S's > -2.0, P_S > 0.50; Fig. 3).

In preliminary feeding experiments in 1990, squirrels fed from the basal portion of both shelled and whole acorns of both tree species. In the three autumn trials with pin oak acorns, all but two shelled (93.1%, n = 29) and two whole seeds (94.7%, n = 38) were consumed from the basal ends. During winter trials, squirrels fed from the basal ends of all shelled (n = 31) and whole (n = 36) pin oak acorns and all shelled (n = 27) and whole red oak acorns (n = 35).

In 1991, squirrels again fed from the basal end of whole pin oak and northern red oak acorns (Table 1); and when the pericarp was removed, the animals still fed from the basal end of the seed. For carved acorns of both red oak (G = 32.3, P = 0.0001) and pin oak (G = 42.2, P = 0.0001), however, the squirrels exhibited a significant reversal in their behavior and fed from the original apical end of the seeds (Table 1). During these feeding experiments, squirrels again consistently consumed only a small portion of the whole and shelled acorns of both oak species (>55% of all observations). In addition, the animals scatterhoarded between 63.6 and 72.7% of these partially eaten seeds (Table 1.).

In feeding experiments in which squirrels were presented with whole and half red oak acorns, squirrels consistently consumed nearly 100% of individual whole acorns, and 100% of the basal and apical halves prior to the food supplement, probably due to the lack of food during spring (Fig. 4a). After presentation of supplemental food, however, squirrels consumed a significantly smaller portion of all three acorn types ($F_{1,105}$ = 1236.6, P < 0.0001). In addition, there was a significant difference in the estimates of the proportion of each seed type consumed following the food supplementation ($F_{2,105}$ = 33.5, P < 0.0001). Results for pin oak acorns paralleled those for red oak acorns; there was a significant effect of food supplement ($F_{2,118}$ = 466.0, P < 0.0001) and acorn type ($F_{1,118}$ = 101.8, P < 0.0001), and both whole seeds and apical fragments were estimated to receive less damage than the basal fragments (Fig. 4b).

Prior to the addition of food, squirrels consumed nearly all of each artificial seed, with the exception of those with an additional 6% tannic acid which sustained significantly less damage (Fig. 4c; $F_{1,96}$ = 29.9.0, P < 0.0001). Following the supplement, an estimated, 50% decrease in acorn consumption was observed in the artificial acorns with 6% tannic acid ($F_{2,96}$ = 429.7, P < 0.0001), while the proportion of other artificial acorns eaten remained relatively constant (Fig. 4c).

Table 1.—*Feeding responses of gray squirrels to whole, shelled, and carved acorns. Shown are the number of acorns eaten from the basal end of the seed, the number of acorns partially eaten, and the number of these partially eaten acorns that were dispersed and cached. Carved acorns were prepared by removing the pericarp and carving the surface of the cotyledon as shown in Figure 1. Values in parentheses represent proportions of total sample. See text for statistical summary.*

Acorn species	Experimental treatment	Total eaten *n*	No. (%) eaten from basal end	No.(%) partially eaten	No.(%) Apical Fragments dispersed and cached
Red oak	Whole	20	19 (95.0%)	13 (65.0%)	9 (69.2%)
	Shelled	17	17 (100.0%)	11 (64.7%)	8 (72.7%)
	Carved	18	4 (22.2%)	7 (38.8%)	4 (57.1%)
Pin oak	Whole	20	20 (100.0%)	17 (85.0%)	11 (64.7%)
	Shelled	20	17 (85.0%)	11 (55.0%)	7 (63.6%)
	Carved	16	0 (0.0%)	11 (68.8%)	6 (54.8%)

DISCUSSION

These results indicate that partial acorn consumption is common under natural field conditions, that this response may account for the fate of more than 40% of the acorn crops of individual oak trees, and that partial consumption of acorns is usually followed by scatterhoarding of apical fragments. Because partially eaten or damaged acorns can still germinate (Beaman, 1981; Steele et al., 1993), we argue that this behavior has the potential to exert a significant impact on dispersal and survival of acorns.

Although Steele et al. (1993) did not demonstrate successful survival of partially eaten seeds beyond germination (plumule emergence), they did observe significantly higher germination rates for these damaged seeds than for whole intact seeds. Furthermore, while it is likely that a reduction in cotyledon mass may ultimately reduce overall seedling survival (Korstian, 1927; Beaman, 1981), or partially eaten acorns may be retrieved more readily, partial seed consumption need only result in successful establishment of a few seeds in order to have adaptive significance for oaks. In fact, it is quite plausible that some oaks invest excess energy per seed as a "bait" for dispersal, thereby increasing the probability of survival of

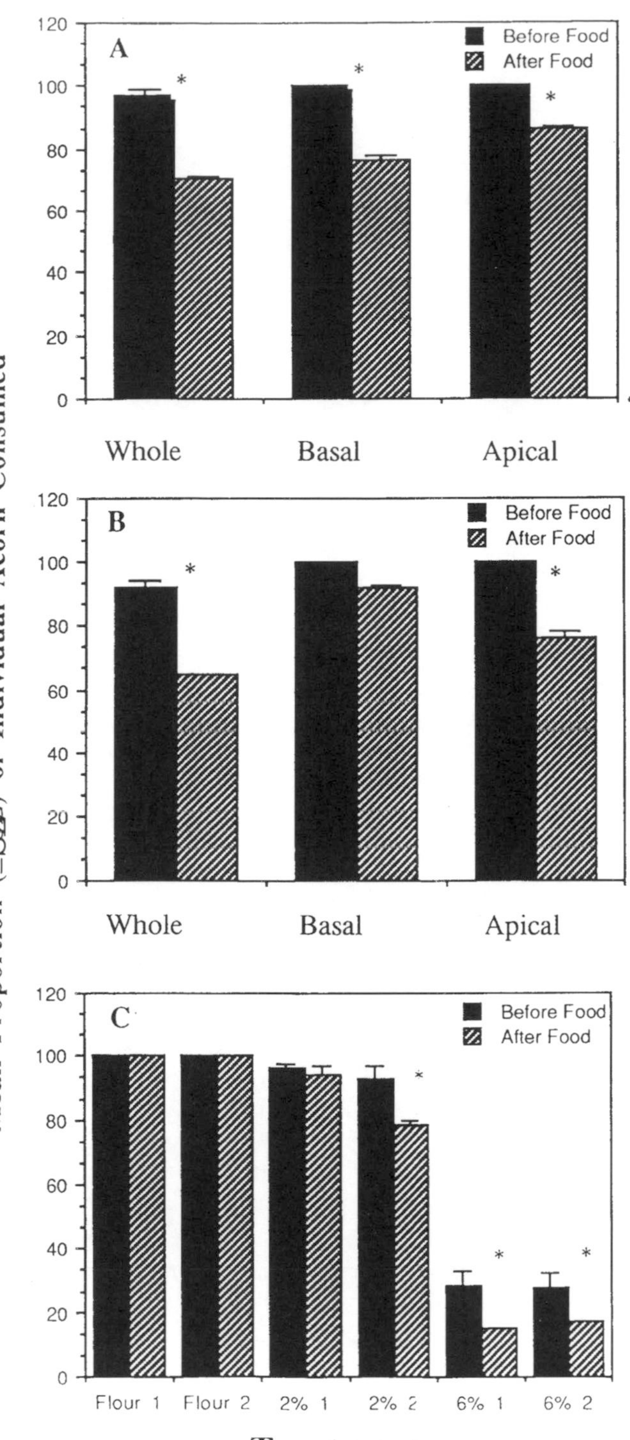

Fig. 4.—Effects of food availabity and tannin concentrations on partial seed consumption. Shown are the proportion of whole and half red oak acorns, (*Q. rubra*; A) whole and half pin oak acorns, (*Q. palustris;* B) and artificial acorns (with varying tannin concentrations; C) eaten by gray squirrels prior to, and following, a two-week food supplementation. Values after supplementation represent calculations of the percent eaten based on reductions in feeding time. * indicates significant difference ($P < 0.01$).

partially consumed acorns. Given the temporal and geographic preponderance of this behavior (Steele et al., 1993), we maintain that this response by gray squirrels and other seed predators may reflect an important reproductive strategy of oaks.

In addition to demonstrating the relative frequency with which this behavior occurs, this study was also designed to determine whether the acorn pericarp, acorn shape, and tannin levels within the seed directly influenced partial seed consumption. Only the pericarp of seeds could be dismissed as a factor contributing to consumption of the basal portion of acorns. In feeding experiments in which squirrels were presented shelled acorns (Table 1), the animals still consistently fed from only the basal portion of the seeds. Thus, it is unlikely that ease of opening the pericarp from the basal end of the seed affects this behavior.

In contrast though, both seed geometry and tannin levels appear to contribute to the response. When shelled seeds were carved so that each end of the seed appeared as the opposite, squirrels reversed their behavior and fed from the carved basal (true apical) ends of acorns. This strongly suggests that seed shape in part explains why squirrels first feed on the basal end of seed. It does not, however, account for consistent consumption of only the top half of the acorns. We argue, instead, that the most plausible explanation for partial acorn consumption is the higher tannin levels in the apical portion of the seed (Steele et al., 1993), and that acorn shape only increases the probability that the animal will begin to feed from this end.

Tannins, a varied group of water-soluble phenolic compounds, are widely recognized as an important class of chemical defenses in most oaks (Howe and Westley, 1988), and are considered antiherbivore agents because of their ability to disable digestive enzymes, and to complex with plant proteins and render them undigestible and unpalatable (Feeney, 1970; Bate-Smith, 1972; Bernays, 1981; Robbins et al., 1987*a*; 1987*b*). In addition, experimental studies have shown that many animals, including gray squirrels (Smith and Follmer, 1972; Short, 1976; Smallwood and Peters, 1986), alter their food preferences in response to tannins. Smallwood and Peters (1986) demonstrated that tannins directly influence acorn preferences in gray squirrels and suggested that tannins may serve as a proximate cue for animals that typically bury red oak acorns and eat the more perishable acorns of white oak.

In our experiments, squirrels appeared to consume significantly smaller amounts of those artificial acorns with higher concentrations of tannins, at least when food was abundant (Fig. 4). It should be noted, however, that because we constructed artificial acorns from the tissue of red oak seeds, those seeds constructed of 6% tannin contained unrealistically high levels of phenolics (see Smallwood and Peters, 1986). Nevertheless, for one trial, calculations indicate that squirrels consumed significantly smaller portions of those artificial acorns with only 2% additional tannin when food was abundant, suggesting that squirrels may be sensitive to relatively small differences in tannin levels.

Steele et al. (1993) reported that, in addition to gray squirrels, a variety of acorn predators, including blue jays, grackles, two species of *Peromyscus*, and insect larvae of the genus *Curculio* selectively consume only the basal portion of several acorn species. Because many of these species exhibit a different technique for attacking and eating acorns, it is unlikely that partial seed consumption is universally related to any single physical characteristic of the seed. Instead, we suggest that the distibution of tannins (and perhaps other chemicals) in the seed is the most plausible ultimate factor(s) directing partial seed consumption. From our results, however, it appears that gray squirrels rely on visual (i.e., shape of the acorn) rather than chemical cues for dealing with this problem.

If it is true that tannins direct this behavior, then this response to the top and bottom halves of individual acorns is analogous to the response that squirrels and other mammalian seed predators show to different species of acorns of the red oak and white oak subgenera (*Erythrobalanus* and *Leucobalanus*, respectively). Squirrels consistently store the dormant red oak acorns (also high in tannin) that overwinter before germinating, and eat the non-dormant white oak seeds that germinate immediately in the autumn (Steele and Smallwood, 1994), or excise the embryos of white oak acorns before caching to prevent early germination and loss of seed caches (Fox, 1982). Experimental evidence suggests that these responses are an attempt to limit perishability of seed caches (Hadj-Chikh et al., 1996) and that tannins may be the proximate cue directing such decisions (Smallwood and Peters, 1986; Smallwood, 1992).

We conclude that a suite of characteristics, including at least tannin levels (and perhaps other chemical gradients not tested in this study) and seed geometry induce partial seed consumption by gray squirrels. Furthermore, we argue that these physical and chemical characteristics interact with overall food availability to influence this behavior in gray squirrels. Finally, we suggest that some of these physical and chemical characteristics of acorns may represent adaptations of acorns that promote partial seed consumption and subsequent dispersal by squirrels and other seed consumers.

ACKNOWLEDGMENTS

We are grateful to the City of Wilkes-Barre for permission to work at Kirby Park and to Travis Knowles and Leila Hadj-Chikh for reviewing earlier versions of the manuscript. This project was funded by the Biology Department of Wilkes University and Grants-in-Aid from the Pennsylvania Academy of Science (to WB) and Sigma Xi (to KG).

LITERATURE CITED

ALLRED, S. W., W. S. GAUD, AND J. S. STATES. 1994. Effects of herbivory by Abert squirrels (*Sciurus aberti*) on cone crops of ponderosa pine. Journal of Mammalogy, 75:700-703.

BARNETT, R. J. 1977. The effect of burial by squirrels on germination and survival of oak and hickory nuts. The American Midland Naturalist, 98:319-30.

BATE-SMITH, E. C. 1972. Attractants and repellents in higher animals. Pp. 45-56, *in* Phytochemical Ecology. (J. B. Harborne, ed.) Academic Press, New York, 272 pp.

BEAMAN, B. A. 1981. Factors affecting the establishment, growth, and survival of white oak (*Quercus alba* L.) in an upland hardwood forest. Ph.D. dissertation, Duke University, Durham, North Carolina, 225 pp.

BENKMAN, C. W., R. P. BALDA, AND C. C. SMITH. 1984. Adaptations for seed dispersal and the compromise due to seed predation in limber pine. Ecology, 65:632-642.

BERNAYS, E. A. 1981. Plant tannins and insect herbivores: an appraisal. Ecological Entomology, 6:353-360.

ELLIOT, P. F. 1974. Evolutionary responses of plants to seed eaters: pine squirrel predation on lodgepole pine. Evolution, 28:221-231.

———. 1988. Foraging behavior of a central-place forager: field tests of theoretical predictions. The American Naturalist, 131:159-174.

FEENEY, P. 1970. Seasonal changes in oak leaf tannins and nutrients as a cause of spring feeding by winter moth caterpillars. Ecology, 51:565-581.

FOX, J. E. 1982. Adaptation of gray squirrel behavior to autumn germination by white oak acorns. Evolution, 36:800-809.

GURNELL, J. 1984. Home range, territoriality, caching behavior and food supply of the red squirrel (*Tamiasciurus hudsonicus fremonti*) in a subalpine forest. Animal Behaviour, 32:1119-1131.

———. 1987. The natural history of squirrels. Christopher Helm, London, 201 pp.

HADJ-CHIKH, L. Z., M. A. STEELE, AND P. D. SMALLWOOD. 1996. Caching decisions by grey squirrels: a test of the handling time and perishability hypotheses. Animal behaviour, 52: 941-948.

HALL, J. G. 1981. A field study of the Kaibab squirrel in Grand Canyon National Park. Wildlife Monographs, 75:1-54.

HOWE, H. F., AND L. C. WESTLEY. 1988. Ecological relationships of plants and animals. Oxford University Press, Oxford, 273 pp.

JANZEN, D. H. 1971. Seed predation by animals. Annual Review of Ecology and Systematics, 2:465-492.

KATO, J. 1985. Food and hoarding behavior of Japanese squirrels. Japanese Journal of Ecology, 35:13-20.

KORSTIAN, C. F. 1927. Factors controlling germination and early survival in oaks. Yale University School Forestry Bulletin, 19:1-122.

LALONDE, R. G., AND B. D. ROITBERG. 1992. On the evolution of masting behavior in trees: predation or weather? The American Naturalist, 139:1293-1304.

MIYAKI, M. 1987. Seed dispersal of the Korean pine, *Pinus koraiensis*, by the red squirrel, *Sciurus vulgaris*. Ecological Research, 2:147-57.

MOLLAR, H. 1986. Red squirrels (*Sciurus vulgaris*) feeding in Scots pine plantation in Scotland. Journal of Zoology (London), 209:61-84.

PRICE, M. V., AND S. H. JENKINS. 1986. Rodents as seed consumers and dispersers, Pp. 191-235, *in* Seed dispersal, (D. R. Murray, ed.) Academic Press Inc., Orlando, Florida, 322 pp.

ROBBINS, C. T., S. MOLE, A. E. HAGERMAN, AND T. A. HANLEY. 1987*a*. Role of tannins in defending plants against ruminants: reduction in protein availability. Ecology, 68:98-107.

———. 1987*b*. Role of tannins in defending plants against ruminants: reduction in dry matter digestion. Ecology, 68:1606-1615.

SHORT, H. L. 1976. Composition and squirrel use of acorns of black and white oak groups. The Journal of Wildlife Management, 40:479-48.

SILVERTOWN, J. W. 1980. The evolutionary ecology of mast seeding in trees. Biological Journal of the Linnean Society, 14:235-250.

SMALLWOOD, P. D. 1992. Temporal and spatial scales in foraging ecology: testing hypotheses with spiders and squirrels. Ph.D. dissertation, The University of Arizona, Tucson, 112 pp.

SMALLWOOD, P. D., AND W.D. PETERS. 1986. Grey squirrel food preferences: the effects of tannin and fat concentration. Ecology, 67:168-174.

SMITH, M. C. 1968. Red squirrels responses to spruce cone failure in interior Alaska. The Journal of Wildlife Management, 32:305-317.

SMITH, C. C. 1970. Coevolution of pine squirrels (*Tamiasciurus*) and conifers. Ecological Monographs, 40:349-371.

SMITH, C. C., AND D. FOLLMER. 1972. Food preferences of squirrels. Ecology, 53:83-91.

SMYTHE, N. D. E. 1978. The natural history of the Central American agouti (*Dasyprocta punctata*). Smithsonian Contributions to Zoology, 257:1-52.

SNYDER, M. A. 1993. Interactions between Abert's squirrel and ponderosa pine: the relationship between selective herbivory and host plant fitness. The American Naturalist, 141:866-879.

STEELE, M. A., L. Z. HADJ-CHIKH, AND J. HAZELTINE. 1996. Caching and feeding decisions by *Sciurus carolinensis*: responses to weevil-infested acorns. Journal of Mammalogy, 77: 305-314.

STEELE, M. A., T. KNOWLES, K. BRIDLE, AND E. L. SIMMS. 1993. Tannins and partial consumption of acorns: implications for dispersal of oaks by seed predators. The American Midland Naturalist, 130: 229-238.

STEELE, M. A., AND P. D. WEIGL. 1992. Energetics and patch use in the fox squirrel, Sciurus niger: responses to variation in prey profitability and patch density. The American Midland Naturalist, 128: 156-167.

STEELE, M. A., AND P. D. SMALLWOOD. 1994. What are squirrels hiding? Natural History, 103: 40-45.

VANDER WALL, S. B. 1990. Food hoarding in animals. The University of Chicago Press, Chicago, Illinois, 445 pp.

———. 1992. The role of animals in dispersing a "wind-dispersed" pine. Ecology, 73:614-621.

AN ECOLOGICAL STUDY ON CONSERVING THE BRITISH RED SQUIRREL, *SCIURUS VULGARIS*

JOHN GURNELL AND TIM VENNING

School of Biological Sciences, Queen Mary and Westfield College, University of London, London E1 4NS England (JG) and Forest Enterprise, Thetford District, Brandon, Suffolk IP27 0TJ England (TV)

ABSTRACT.—An investigation was initiated in Thetford Forest in East Anglia to assess specific conservation tactics for the recovery of red squirrels (*Sciurus vulgaris*). Thetford Forest was first invaded by gray squirrels between 1968 and 1974, and they were found throughout the forest by 1985. Red squirrels are still found within the forest but their population numbers are believed to be low. The study investigates ways of changing the competitive balance between the species in favor of the red squirrel. We tested the removal of gray squirrels (*S. carolinensis*), supplemental feeding of red squirrels and reintroducing red squirrels to boost the remaining population. Our efforts have resulted in sightings of red squirrels within the Reserve and the capture of six animals within 11 months of the start of the study. Three red squirrels were successfully released into the forest.

INTRODUCTION

The British red squirrel (*Sciurus vulgaris*) is becoming increasingly rare in central and southern England and Wales and is also under threat in Northern England and Scotland. Its current status and reasons for its decline have recently been reviewed by Gurnell and Pepper (1993). Loss of suitable habitat and habitat fragmentation are partly responsible for this situation (Verboom and Apledorm, 1990; Bright, 1993). However, the species is particularly threatened by the continued spread of the gray squirrel (*S. carolinensis*), which was introduced from North America on several occasions around the turn of the century and is now a permanent member of the British fauna (Gurnell, 1987).

Several studies are monitoring the distribution and numbers of red squirrels more precisely, and investigating possible conservation tactics (Gurnell and Pepper, 1993). Our study considers a recovery program for red squirrels in Thetford Forest, East Anglia. Gray squirrels started to colonize Thetford Forest in 1968 (Reynolds, 1981) and were firmly established throughout the forest by the mid 1980's (Gurnell, 1966). In recent years red squirrels have become rare although they were still known to be present at the beginning of this study in 1992. Gray squirrels have replaced red squirrels in broadleaf and mixed forests throughout much of Britain, but red squirrels have persisted in Thetford Forest and other large conifer forests. Thus Thetford Forest is a very suitable site to attempt a recovery program.

Maintenance of viable red squirrel populations depends on designing and managing habitats which favor red squirrels and discourage gray squirrels (Gurnell and Pepper, 1991). The recovery program focuses on short-term tactics and has been designed, first to identify reasons for the decline of the population, and second to promote the recovery of the population using reintroductions (Gurnell and Pepper, 1988). The decline of red squirrels at Thetford results from the encroachment of gray squirrels (Gurnell and Pepper, 1993; Gurnell, 1996). Thus, we have been removing gray squirrels from the Reserve. Also, because we believed that exploitative competition for food results in the ecological replacement of red by gray squirrels (Gurnell and Pepper, 1993), food hoppers have been used to selectively provision red squirrels with supplemental food.

METHODS

Field study design.—Thetford Forest was originally planted with Scots pine (*Pinus sylvestris*) between 1925 and 1940. A second rotation crop of Corsican pine (*P. nigra* Maire) is replacing the Scots

In M.A. Steele, J. F. Merritt, and D. A. Zegers (eds.). 1998. Ecology and Evolutionary Biology of Tree Squirrels. Special Publication, Virginia Museum of Natural History, 6: 320 pp

pine. In 1992, a Reserve was designated consisting of 8,044 ha of Scots pine and 7,279 ha of Corsican pine with 1,891 ha of broadleaves, other conifer species and unplanted land. Within the Reserve, four types of sampling were performed: gray squirrel removal, supplementary feeding, red squirrel trapping and transects to quantify signs of feeding.

Beginning in September 1992, between eight and ten multicapture cage traps (Rowe, 1980) were used to capture gray squirrels in selected parts of the forest, especially towards the edge of the Reserve and, where possible, in places that contained broadleaf trees. Traps were prebaited for 1 week and set for 5 days. They were checked twice daily. Captured gray squirrels were removed from the study site and assessed for sex, weight and reproductive condition by post-mortem examination. Eye lenses were removed and stored in 10% formal-saline to estimate age using eye lens weight (Dubock, 1979).

Food hoppers which exclude gray squirrels (Pepper, 1993; Gurnell and Pepper, 1993) were grouped into clusters of three to minimize competition among squirrels. They were evenly spaced in each cluster with 20 m between hoppers. Twenty five clusters were used throughout the Reserve. The hoppers were filled with a mix of maize, sunflower seeds, peanuts and wheat. They were operational beginning in April 1993.

At each hopper cluster, 5 single-capture live traps (Gurnell and Pepper, 1994) were placed on boards fixed to trees 3 to 4m from the ground. One trap was placed in the center of the hopper cluster and 4 were placed around the cluster with 50 m between traps. Captured animals were weighed, ear tagged, and their breeding condition noted. Some were fitted with radiocollars (Biotrack, Wareham, Dorset). Red squirrel trapping started in March 1993. Traps were prebaited for 1 week and set for 5 days. Traps were visited twice daily. Captured gray squirrels were removed from the site.

Two transects (1 x 50 m) were marked within 200 m of each hopper cluster. Cores of cones eaten by squirrels were collected at intervals of 6 weeks. Transect studies were initiated in September 1992 with 13 lines and was increased to 30 lines by November 1993. The transects were used to estimate feeding intensity and habitat utilization.

From April 1993, a regular 6-week cycle of field work involving trapping squirrels, examining hoppers and assessing feeding remains, was established within the Reserve.

Reintroduction.—A 1-ha pre-release pen was erected in the center of the Reserve (Gurnell and Pepper, 1993). A strip of trees (4m wide) was cleared on each side of the fence. Nest boxes, food hoppers, and water stations were placed inside the pen. Two meter-high bridges of pine tree trunks were erected across the fence linking trees inside and outside the pen. Squirrels were allowed to leave the pen at their own volition.

Four adult red squirrels, 1 wild juvenile male (R1), translocated from Kielder Forest in north England together with 3 captive-bred adults from East Anglia (one female R2 and two males, R3 and R4), were placed in the pen in August 1993. The animals were examined for general health prior to release and the adults were fitted with radiocollars. Within the first week, one female (R2) was found dead, evidently killed by a goshawk (*Accipiter gentilis*) or a sparrowhawk (*A. nisus*).

RESULTS

Gray squirrel removal and feeding signs.—Between September 1992 and February 1994, 525 gray squirrels were removed. Most were collected from March to May 1993 (Fig. 1a). Adult males predominated in winter and summer samples, adult females predominated in autumn and spring. Juveniles were captured in each season with peaks in winter and summer.

Feeding signs were high in both winters but declined to a low in mid-summer and autumn (Fig. 1b). Subjective estimates suggest good cone availability throughout the study. Thus, the decline in feeding rate during summer indicated the removal policy was working reasonably well. However, increase in feeding during winter 1993–1994 suggests that gray squirrels were entering and remaining within the Reserves for several weeks. Some feeding may have resulted from red squirrels since it is not possible to distinguish cones used by red and gray squirrels.

Hoppers.— The 75 food hoppers were in place by the end of March 1993. Some food was taken from hoppers in the center of the Reserve 2 weeks later, and others in the southeast, 4 weeks later. Subjective observations indicate red squirrels visited hoppers in these areas regularly. Objective observations beginning in August showed little food was taken from hoppers elsewhere in the Reserve, whereas hoppers in the center and southeast were often empty. Much of the food consumption was attributed to mice (*Apodemus sylvaticus*).

Pilot reintroduction.—Following erection of 12 bridges over the pen walls on 10th September, squirrel R4 was observed leaving the pen on one of the bridges. It was radiotracked and moved north initially, but within 2 days had moved south where

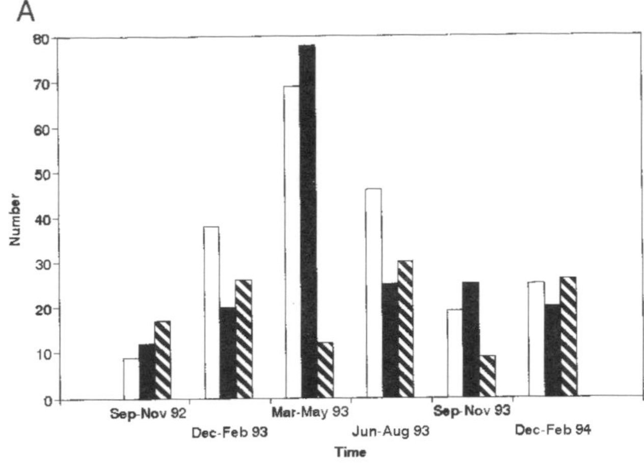

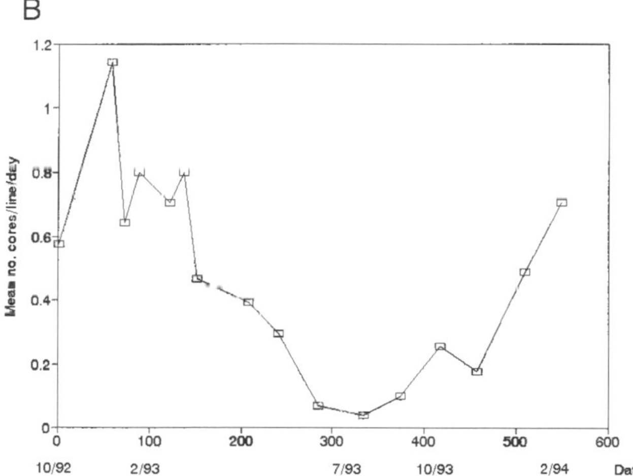

Fig. 1.—(A) The numbers of adult male (open bars), female (solid bars), and young gray squirrels <1 year old (cross-hatched bars) removed from the reserve in each season. (B) Index of signs of squirrel feeding (the mean number of cone cores collected per transect line standardized for the number of days between inspections). Time is in days from the beginning of the study in September 1992 and each point is the median date between inspections. Thirteen lines were set up at the beginning of the study in September 1992 and this increased to 30 lines by November 1993.

it settled in a home range for the following 3 weeks until the radiotracking stopped (Fig. 2). Its radiocollar was found on the ground in December.

Squirrels R1 and R3 were not seen leaving the pen, but R3 remained in the pen until the afternoon of the 12th September. It then settled in a home range near R4 (Fig. 2). Its collar was found on the ground at the end of October. Both R3 and R4 used at least 3 different dreys during this time. Although it was believed that R1 left the pen, it was captured inside the pen at the beginning of December.

Two wild squirrels (R5, a male, and R6, a female) were captured on 31 August in the southeast of the Reserve and fitted with radiocollars. They were monitored at the same time as the released animals. They were > 1,700m from the pen and had partially overlapping ranges (Fig. 2). Both wild squirrels used two different dreys during this time. The ranges of the wild squirrels were slightly smaller than those of the released squirrels (Fig. 2).

Thus three red squirrels were successfully introduced into the Reserve and two are known to have settled into home ranges not far from the pen. They utilized existing dreys. Although squirrels R3, R4 and R5 lost their collars after 4 or more weeks, there is no evidence they died or left the area.

Red squirrels within the Reserve.—The first red squirrel was seen within the Reserve in March 1993 in the south-east. Three additional sightings occurred between April and June in this area. A red squirrel was also seen outside of the pen in September. In addition to the three animals released into the Reserve, 13 wild Thetford red squirrels were captured between June 1993 and March 1994; three in the southeast, four in the center

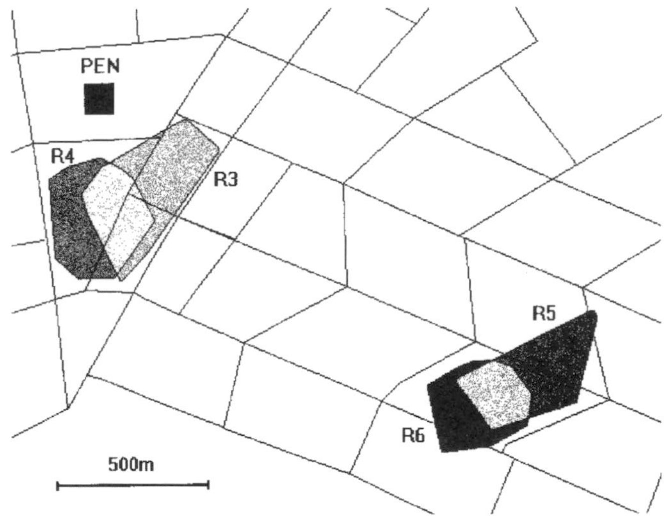

Fig. 2.—Radiotracked home ranges of two male red squirrels (R3 and R4) which were free to leave the pen in the center of the Reserve on 11th September 1993, and two wild red squirrels (R5 male, R6 female). The ranges were monitored concurrently over a three week period. The ranges shown are 80% minimum area polygons (Ranges IV, Biotrack). The 80% range sizes are: R3 - 13 ha, R4 - 11 ha, R5 - 10 ha, R6 - 8 ha. The outline polygons are forest compartments each containing a particular age of Scots or Corsican pine trees.

and six in the pen. Also two tagged red squirrels moved into the pen. One of these was R1, which was released from the pen in September and re-entered in November. The other was a male animal captured in June 1993 and recaptured in the pen in March 1994. Six red squirrels are known to have died. One was killed by a goshawk and two died of parapoxvirus (Keymer, 1983). One died in a trap in the pen and another was found dead in the pen the day after it was captured in December, and may have died as the result of shock or peritonitis associated with capture.

DISCUSSION

Gray squirrel removal.—The removal of >500 gray squirrels from the Reserve over a 15 month period is a low rate of return on effort. If we assume that all the animals captured between September and February at the start of the study were residents, which is unlikely, this represents a density of 1 gray squirrel per 9 ha of forest. Densities of gray squirrels are generally low in conifer forests (Gurnell and Pepper, 1988; Gurnell, 1996), but this is exceptionally low. Further work is required on the suitability of species, age and stocking densities of conifer trees for both red and gray squirrels. Numbers of gray squirrels do increase within conifer stands when the cone crops are good, but they disappear when the crops become depleted or fail (Gurnell, 1996). Feeding signs in 1992 and 1993 suggest that cone crops were good in both years. Constant removal of gray squirrels results in a slow depletion of seed supplies and consequently the Reserve can be considered good habitat for squirrels. It is possible that red squirrels have not used the hoppers extensively because natural food supplies have been good. We expect that they will be used more when cone crops fail.

Reintroductions involve manipulations of genetic variation among populations. For this reason they may not be appropriate. At one time there was a race of red squirrels unique to Britain and Ireland, *S.v. leucourus*. Many introductions of European subspecies of squirrel have taken place, especially during the 18th and 19th centuries. Squirrels were also moved within the UK (Shorten, 1954). It is likely that British red squirrels are now mixed genetically. Thus, it is unclear whether reintroductions and captive breeding programs of red squirrels in Britain should depend on the geographic origin of the animals involved.

The sightings and captures of red squirrels within the Reserve are encouraging. It seems likely that these animals entered the Reserve or became 'more visible' as gray squirrels were removed. Few red squirrels have been captured or recaptured in traps. Perhaps few red squirrels visited the traps because of abundant cones on trees. However, it is odd that the pen seemed to attract squirrels and six of the last seven new animals were captured there.

We hope to continue the study to 1997 and plan to further evaluate the conservation tactics being used. Also we hope to complement these studies with work on captive breeding and health and welfare. In particular, work on parapoxvirus is required since little is known about this disease (Keymer, 1983; Sainsbury and Gurnell, 1995). A GIS model for the Reserve will be used to assess red and gray squirrel population numbers in relation to conservation management.

ACKNOWLEDGMENTS

The study was funded by English Nature (under their Species Recovery Program), the Forest Enterprise, and the Forestry Authority. We are indebted to the many people who supported and assisted with the field work, in particular T. Courage, Z. David-Gray, P. Lurz, W. Marriott, R. Mackintosh, E. Ogilvie, S. Orton, B. Roebuck, H. Pepper, A. Sainsbury, and D. Stapleford.

LITERATURE CITED

BRIGHT, P. W. 1993. Habitat fragmentation - problems and predictions for British mammals. Mammal Review, 23:101-111.

DUBOCK, A. C. 1979 Methods of ageing gray squirrels (*Sciurus carolinensis*) in Britain. Journal of Zoology, (London), 188:27-40.

GURNELL, J. 1987. The natural history of squirrels. Christopher Helm, London. 201 pp.

GURNELL, J., and H. PEPPER. 1988. Perspectives on the management of red and gray squirrels. Pp 92-109, *in* Wildlife management in forests. (D.C. Jardine, ed.). Institute of Chartered Foresters, Edinburgh, 123 pp.

———.1991. Conserving the red squirrel. Research Information Note No. 205, Forestry Commission, Edinburgh, 4 pp.

———.1993. A critical look at conserving the British red squirrel. Mammal Review, 23:127-137.

———.1994. Red squirrel conservation: field study methods. Research Information Note 244. The Forestry Authority, Research Division, Alice Holt Lodge, Farnham, Surrey, 9 pp.

———.1996. Conserving the red squirrel. Pp 132-140, *in* Thetford Forest Park (S. Harris and P. Ratcliffe, eds.). Forestry Commission, Edinburgh, 178 pp.

KEYMER, I. F. 1983. Diseases of squirrels in Britain. Mammal Review, 13:155-158.

PEPPER, H. W. 1993. Red squirrel supplementary food hopper. The Forestry Authority Research Information Note 235, Alice Holt Lodge, Farnham, Surrey, England, United Kingdom, 2 pp.

REYNOLDS, J. C. 1981. The interaction of red and gray squirrels. Ph.D. thesis, University of East Anglia, Norwich, United Kingdom, 230 pp.

ROWE, J. 1980. Grey squirrel control. Forestry Commission Leaflet No. 56, Her Majesty Stationary Offices, London, United Kingdom.

SAINSBURY, A., AND J. GURNELL. 1995. An investigation into the health and welfare of red squirrels, *Sciurus vulgaris*, involved in reintroduction studies. The Veterinary Record, 137: 367-370.

SHORTEN, M. 1954. Squirrels. London, Collins, 212 pp.

VERBOOM, B., AND R. VAN APPLEDORM. 1990. Effects of habitat fragmentation on the red squirrel, *Sciurus vulgaris* L. Landscape Ecology, 4:171-176.

SOUTHEASTERN FOX SQUIRRELS: *r*-OR K-SELECTED? IMPLICATIONS FOR MANAGEMENT

PHILIP A. TAPPE AND DAVID C. GUYNN, Jr.
School of Forest Resources, Arkansas Forest Resources Center, University of Arkansas, Monticello, AR 71656 (PAT)

Department of Forest Resources, Clemson University, Clemson, SC 29634 (DCG)

ABSTRACT.—Life histories of species are often categorized by wildlife biologists using the concept of *r*- and K-selection. This concept has frequently been misinterpreted and overgeneralized. To evaluate a species' survival strategy effectively, an array of determinants must be considered. However, because wildlife management practices emphasize interactions between animals and their habitats, the logistic growth model, and thus density-dependent mechanisms, are widely accepted as valid concepts in the context of wildlife management. Consequently, it is often useful to place a species along the *r*-K continuum, and term it as being more *r*- or K-selected relative to the segment of the continuum under consideration.

Southeastern fox squirrels *(Sciurus niger)* are classified as a small game species by most management agencies. Classification of a mammalian species as small game generally implies that it is thought to be a relatively *r*-selected species and is thus most often associated with relatively liberal bag limits and season lengths. However, recent studies have provided limited data which, when examined collectively in the framework of life histories and compared to other small game species, suggest that southeastern fox squirrels may be more appropriately managed as a relatively K-selected species. The realization that southeastern fox squirrels may be relatively more K-selected than many other species of small game suggests a reevaluation of current harvesting practices and regulations. The determinants of the harvestable surplus of small game species are usually reproductive success and juvenile survival; however, in species such as the southeastern fox squirrel, the number of breeders prior to each breeding season may be the more important criteria. Also, it is critical to be able to manage fox squirrel and gray squirrel (*S. carolinensis*) harvests separately; however, most southeastern states currently lump fox squirrels and gray squirrels under the same regulations, and do not separate squirrel harvest figures by species.

INTRODUCTION

Populations of *Sciurus niger niger* are perceived to be declining in North Carolina (Weigl et al., 1989) and South Carolina (Wood and Davis, 1981). In addition, *S. n. cinereus* is a federally listed endangered species, and *S. n. avicennia* and *S. n. shermani* are considered to be endangered and a species of special concern, respectively, by the State of Florida. Thus, an assessment of the survival strategy of the ecologically and morphologically similar (Weigl et al., 1989) southeastern fox squirrels is essential for effective management.

Life histories, or survival strategies, of species are often categorized by wildlife biologists using the concept of *r*- and K-selection. However, this concept, originally formulated by MacArthur and Wilson (1967), has frequently been misinterpreted and overgeneralized (Boyce, 1984). MacArthur and Wilson described the *r*-K concept using a model of density-dependent selection, with *r*-selection occurring in expanding populations and favoring productivity, and K-selection occurring in crowded populations and favoring efficiency.

Pianka (1970) described an *r*-K continuum, with the *r*-endpoint representing a "quantitative" extreme and the K-endpoint representing a "qualitative" extreme. He characterized extreme *r*-selected organisms as being semelparous and having a high r_{max} (as opposed to logistic r), early

In M.A. Steele, J. F. Merritt, and D. A. Zegers (eds.). 1998. Ecology and Evolutionary Biology of Tree Squirrels. Special Publication, Virginia Museum of Natural History, 6: 320 pp

reproduction, rapid development, and small body size. Additionally, these traits were associated with ephemeral or unpredictable environments, high density-independent mortality, large fluctuations in population density, little competition, and short lifespans. In contrast, he characterized extreme K-selected organisms as being iteroparous and having low r_{max}, delayed reproduction, slow development, and large body size. These traits were associated with constant or predictably seasonal environments, density-dependent mortality, fairly constant population densities near carrying capacity, high competition, and long life spans. After the publication of Pianka's (1970) interpretation of *r*- and K-selection, the term *r*-strategist became synonymous with a small species that could reproduce quickly, and the term K-strategist was equated with a large species that could not. However, Pianka's correlates of *r*- and K-selection may not necessarily be inferred from MacArthur and Wilson's (1967) density-dependent selection model (Boyce, 1984). In addition, some of the associations between life history traits and specific factors as put forth by Pianka (1970) may not always hold true. For example, Stearns (1976) suggested that "bet-hedging" with high juvenile mortality may result in traits differing from those put forth by Pianka (1970) in respect to environmental stability.

Density-dependent mechanisms are only a few of the factors that can influence survival strategies. Other factors affecting survival strategies can be density-independent and/or frequency-dependent mechanisms (e.g., Schaffer, 1974; Southwood, 1977; Stearns, 1977; Boyce, 1988*a*, 1988*b*). Thus, the *r*-K concept is not "all-embracing." To evaluate a species' survival strategy effectively, an array of determinants must be considered. However, because wildlife management emphasizes interactions between animals and their habitats, the logistic growth model, and thus density-dependent mechanisms, are widely accepted as valid concepts in the context of wildlife management. Consequently, comparison of wildlife species along the *r*-K continuum is useful.

Southeastern fox squirrels are classified as a small game species by most management agencies. Classification of a mammalian species as small game generally implies that it will be managed as a relatively *r*-selected species (Bailey, 1984) and is thus most often associated with relatively liberal bag limits and season lengths. However, recent studies have provided limited data which, when examined collectively in the framework of life histories and compared to other small game species, suggest that southeastern fox squirrels may be more appropriately managed as a relatively K-selected species. It is essential for wildlife managers to understand a species' survival strategy, particularly if it is to be harvested (Dasmann, 1981; Bailey, 1984). Although very limited data are available on a few population and environmental factors, a gestalt approach to interpreting the existing data can help provide a reasonable basis for inference in regard to whether southeastern fox squirrels should be managed as a more *r*- or K-selected species. To facilitate this, a short summary of the information available on population parameters will be followed by a breakdown of the available data on various environmental factors that may play important roles in shaping survival strategies of fox squirrels. Finally, the interrelationships between these factors and their possible effects on survival strategies will be examined, and the resulting management implications will be discussed.

POPULATION PARAMETERS

Population Density

Several researchers have reported density estimates of southeastern fox squirrel populations. Though few have been supported by strong empirical data, these estimates indicate that southeastern fox squirrels typically occur at densities much lower than that of other squirrel species. Estimates of densities of southeastern fox squirrels have ranged from 0.1/km^2 to 38/km^2 (Moore, 1957; Williams and Humphrey, 1979; Humphrey et al., 1985; Kantola, 1986; Weigl et al., 1989; Tappe and Guynn, 1990). In comparison, midwestern fox squirrels may have densities ranging from 40 to 80+/km^2 (Baumgartner, 1938; Brown and Yeager, 1945; Nixon et al., 1986; Nixon and Hansen, 1987), and gray squirrel densities frequently exceed 80/km^2 (Brown and Yeager, 1945; Flyger, 1960; Mosby, 1969; Nixon and Hansen, 1987).

Weigl et al. (1989) conducted the only long-term study (>2 years) to date which estimated southeastern fox squirrel densities. Although their density estimates, based on nestbox inspections, may be biased, the resulting population trends may be useful. Density estimates were obtained for 12 different sites over a period of eight years and ranged from 0 to 35/km^2. Ranges of density estimates within sites averaged 3/km^2 for 9 of the sites. Density estimates at the other three sites varied within sites by 15, 22, and 29/km^2. These data suggest that most of the populations may have remained relatively stable over the eight years.

Therres and Wiley (1988) assessed the status of Delmarva fox squirrel populations at 36 sites in Maryland originally surveyed 17 years earlier in 1971 (Taylor, 1976). Their assessments of population changes were based on interviews with landowners, game wardens, and biologists that were familiar with the sites. Of the 36 sites, all but 1 were perceived to have the same or slightly higher populations of fox squirrels. Thus, populations of Delmarva fox squirrels at these sites may have remained fairly stable over the long term, at least since they were listed and protected as endangered species in 1967.

Reproduction

Breeding seasons.—Southeastern fox squirrels have been reported to have two breeding seasons (winter-spring and summer-autumn); however, there is no evidence that any individual female may produce more than 1 litter per year (Weigl et al., 1989). A 44- to 45-day gestation period with a ca. 90-day dependency period has been assumed for southeastern fox squirrels based on data from gray squirrels and midwestern fox squirrels (Moore, 1957; Asdell, 1964; Gurnell, 1987).

Based on examination of 7 litters, Moore (1957) found the winter-spring breeding season of Sherman's fox squirrel in Florida to begin with conception in November or December, with parturition in January and February and weaning in March–May. The summer-autumn breeding season (based on examination of 4 litters) began with conception in May–July, parturition in June–August, and weaning in September–November.

Weigl et al. (1989), studying the southeastern fox squirrel in North Carolina, examined a total of 37 litters over 8 years. They found that during the winter-spring breeding season, conception most often occurred in December–February, parturition in February and March, and weaning in May or June (29 litters). However, during 2 years, additional reproduction (6 litters) occurred in winter with conception in February or March, parturition in April and May, and weaning in July or August. Only 2 litters were observed during the summer-autumn breeding season, both in the same year. Conception was during July and August, parturition in August and September, and weaning in November and December.

Litter size.—Mean litter sizes of southeastern fox squirrels have been reported by Moore (1957) for the Sherman's fox squirrel in Florida as 2.3 (range 1-4, 11 litters), as 2.4 (range 1-4, 12 litters) for the Delmarva fox squirrel in Maryland (Lustig and Flyger, 1975), and as 2.5 (range 1-5, 37 litters) for the southeastern fox squirrel in North Carolina (Weigl et al., 1989). Sex ratios were not significantly different from 1:1 in any of these studies. These values are equal to or below the lowest mean litter sizes recorded for gray squirrels and midwestern fox squirrels (Gurnell, 1983; Weigl et al., 1989).

Mortality

Weigl et al. (1989) suggest that longevity of southeastern fox squirrels may be appreciable after the first year of life. Eisenberg (1981) suggested that in some cases size may be directly related to longevity, whereas fecundity may be inversely related to longevity. If this is the case with southeastern fox squirrels, they may have longer potential lifespans than many other species of squirrels. Adult southeastern fox squirrels (900-1200 g) are approximately twice the size of adult gray squirrels (400-600 g) and a third larger than adult midwestern fox squirrels (600-900 g). However, field data relating size to longevity in squirrels are lacking.

The populations studied by Weigl et al. (1989) appeared to remain relatively stable based on their estimates using nest box surveys. In addition, the observed sex ratios were not significantly different from 1:1 and the age structures were skewed toward the adult age class. These data can be interpreted in many ways. A stable population, coupled with a low recruitment rate, may suggest low adult mortality; however, dispersal of young and bias towards use of nest boxes due to social dominance may also help to explain these data.

Most predators do not appear to regularly prey on adult, southeastern fox squirrels, but may take them opportunistically (Moore, 1957; Flyger and Gates, 1982). Examples of potential predators of southeastern fox squirrels include bobcats (*Felis rufus*), red foxes (*Vulpes vulpes*) and gray foxes (*Urocyon cinereoargenteus*), red-tailed hawks (*Buteo jamaicensis*), and great horned owls (*Bubo virginianus*). The majority of hunting-induced mortality by man also appears to be opportunistic (Weigl et al., 1989); however, Wood (1985) reported that in South Carolina, fox squirrels were of considerable trophy value. A cause of adult mortality that may have a major impact on southeastern fox squirrels is the automobile (Weigl et al., 1989). Nest predators may have a considerable impact on vulnerable nestlings (Weigl et al., 1989); however, data are not available for mortality rates of nestlings. Potential nest predators include raccoons (*Procyon lotor*), opossums (*Didelphis virginiana*), rat snakes (*Elaphe obsoleta*), and pine snakes (*Pituophis melanoleucus*).

ENVIRONMENTAL PARAMETERS

Habitat

Habitat relations are some of the most studied aspects of ecology of southeastern fox squirrels. Primary habitats have been generally characterized as being open, pine-hardwood forests with adjacent hardwood stands (Weigl et al., 1989) and pine forests interspersed with hardwood drains (Edwards, 1986). These habitat characterizations can be examined on 3 levels: 1) composition, 2) structure, and 3) landscape dimensions.

Habitat composition.—Most studies have found that pine-hardwood mixtures, or a close association of pine and hardwood types, are important to southeastern fox squirrels. Longleaf (*Pinus palustris*) and loblolly (*P. taeda*) pine, and several species of oaks (*Quercus*), and other hardwoods have all been preferred (either as pine stands, mixed pine-hardwood stands, or drainages) by southeastern fox squirrels in various studies (Moore, 1957; Hilliard, 1979; Edwards, 1986; Kantola, 1986; Weigl et al., 1989). However, Weigl et al. (1989) suggested that the actual species of pines and hardwoods may not be a major determinant of habitats of southeastern fox squirrels. Taylor (1973) and Dueser et al. (1988) found that when sites occupied by fox squirrels were compared to those with no fox squirrels, species composition had little relationship to habitat quality. In addition, southeastern fox squirrels are sometimes known to exploit areas such as golf courses and low-density, residential areas (Weigl et al., 1989). Thus, species composition may be of little importance to fox squirrels. However, a diversity of resources such as food must be available; for example, more than one "primary" acorn-producing tree species may be desirable to compensate for variable mast production. Also, as of yet no substantive data are available on factors such as optimum mixtures of pines versus hardwoods. Therefore, composition may have much more importance to fox squirrels than previously thought.

Habitat structure.—Besides habitat composition, habitat structure may have major implications for the survival strategy of southeastern fox squirrels. Taylor (1973) and Dueser et al. (1988) compared habitats of Delmarva fox squirrels and gray squirrels and found that habitats of fox squirrels had lower average understory cover (29.7%) than those of gray squirrels (71.5%), a lower percentage of shrub ground cover, and greater percentages of trees $\geq$ 30 cm dbh and of overstory cover. Also, Weigl et al. (1989) used factor analysis to evaluate various components of southeastern fox squirrel versus habitats of gray squirrels in North Carolina. The loading of the first and most important factor indicated that understory characteristics accounted for a majority of the variance (88%) in the model. Important variables included understory density, number of species, and escape routes. The second factor was loaded by overstory characteristics such as density, and the third factor represented moisture conditions. Weigl et al. (1989) concluded that habitat of fox squirrels was typified by open, low diversity mature forest with little understory, and relatively xeric conditions. In contrast, gray squirrel habitat was characterized by a closed canopy, more diverse and dense understory, and relatively moist conditions.

Landscape dimensions.—In addition to habitat structure, dimensions of landscape may also be of considerable importance to survival strategies of southeastern fox squirrels. Dueser et al. (1988) conducted the only study to date that directly measured and tested specific landscape variables. Areas, percentages, and shapes of several different land classes did not significantly differ between sites on which fox squirrels were present and sites on which they did not occur. However, the distance between woodlots was found to be important, thereby suggesting that the degree of isolation may play an important role in habitat selection.

Additional information on landscape dimensions has been indirectly provided by studies investigating habitat utilization. Based on telemetric studies and locations of nests, Edwards (1986) found fox squirrels to prefer ecotone areas, and suggested that the association and juxtaposition of hardwood and pine habitat types in the Coastal Plain of South Carolina were of considerable importance.

Based on nest counts at her study site in Florida, Kantola (1986) also found ecotone areas to be of considerable importance to fox squirrels. The ecotone areas were generally downslope from upland sites of longleaf pine and turkey oak (*Quercus laevis*). Kantola (1986) suggested that, because ecotone areas were associated with higher mast production, more diverse food sources, and occurrence of Spanish moss (for nest insulation), they are important considerations in habitat selection.

Weigl et al. (1989) observed a pattern of ecotone use by fox squirrels in North Carolina that indicated a seasonal aspect to ecotone importance. Based on telemetric locations, fox squirrels apparently spent more time during the summer in moist, cool ecotone areas and bottomland hardwoods than in the sites of upland pine-oak. Shifts back to the pine-oak areas corresponded to cone ripening in late summer.

Resource Requirements

Food habits.—Data on food habits of southeastern fox squirrels are limited to direct observations of feeding squirrels and examination of stomach contents. The diets of southeastern fox squirrels have been found to include a wide assortment of food items including a large variety of mast, pine seeds and buds, hypogeous and epigeous fungi, berries, and insects (Moore, 1957; Ha, 1983; Kantola, 1986; Weigl et al., 1989). However, seeds of loblolly pine, oak acorns, and hickory nuts may be of similar importance in the Piedmont Region.

Acorns are an important food source during autumn, winter, and early spring, and pine cones are a critical food source for 1-2 months during late summer (Moore, 1957; Ha, 1983; Kantola, 1986; Weigl et al., 1989). As with most other species of squirrels, reproduction of southeastern fox squirrels is strongly associated with mast crops (Gurnell, 1983; 1987; Kantola, 1986; Weigl et al., 1989). Weigl et al. (1989) associated changes in recruitment and density with successive seasons of low or high food availability. However, their conclusions were based on subjective measures of food availability. They also suggested that the cone crops of late summer were critical in bridging the season of poor food supply (early summer) and the time of major mast production in the autumn. Thus, variability and patchiness of acorn and cone crops may have major implications for the survival of southeastern fox squirrels.

Nest habits.– Several studies have investigated nest use by southeastern fox squirrels. In the southernmost areas of the fox squirrel's range, leaf nests are utilized significantly more than cavities. Hilliard (1979) in Georgia and Kantola (1986) in Florida both reported that cavities only accounted for about 7% of all the utilized nests in these areas. Edwards (1986) in South Carolina reported that females occupied cavities more often than males (29% versus 7%). In addition, he found that cavity use also varied by season, increasing primarily during the winter months. Weigl et al. (1989) suggested that low availability of cavities due to forestry practices resulted in low use of cavities. Hilliard (1979) and Weigl et al. (1989) suggested that availability of cavities may play an important role in litter survival. Weigl et al. (1989) in North Carolina also observed that nest box use increased during cold or rainy weather and during periods of low food supply. However, Kantola (1986) reported that nest boxes were seldomly used in Florida. Thus, availability of cavities may be much more important in more northern extremes than in more southern areas.

While fox squirrels have been reported to build leaf nests in a variety of tree species (Moore, 1957; Hilliard, 1979; Edwards, 1986; Kantola, 1986), they frequently show a preference for large trees. Edwards (1986) reported a mean dbh of 41.2 cm in South Carolina, and Hilliard (1979) reported a mean dbh of 39.1 cm in Georgia. In addition, fox squirrels are known to utilize several nests. Hilliard (1979) found fox squirrels to use an average of 9 (range, 5-14), and Edwards (1986) observed an average of 5 (range, 1-12) nests. The large variation in numbers of nests used may be related to the variation in the duration of monitoring for each squirrel (Edwards, 1986).

Home range.—Sizes of home ranges of southeastern fox squirrels are significantly larger than those of midwestern fox squirrels (Ha, 1983). Average annual size of home ranges (determined by the minimum convex polygon method [MCP]) for southeastern fox squirrels ranged from 9.0-31.6 ha (Hilliard, 1979; Flyger and Smith, 1980; Edwards, 1986; Kantola, 1986; Weigl et al., 1989). For comparison, average annual size of home ranges (MCP) for midwestern fox squirrels have been reported to range from 0.8 to 7.0 ha (Baumgartner, 1943; Adams, 1976; Harvera and Nixon, 1978). Home ranges of southeastern fox squirrels also appear to vary by sex. Reported home ranges of males (20.0-31.6 ha) are larger than those of females (9.0-19.3 ha).

Social Behavior

Fox squirrels are considered fairly solitary animals, with social interactions generally restricted to mating (Moore, 1957; Weigl et al., 1989). Weigl et al. (1989) rarely found next boxes being used by more than one squirrel, except in the cases of male-female groupings. In addition, data from surveys of nest boxes indicate that close proximity is relatively uncommon, with most occupied nest boxes a considerable distance apart, although fox squirrels are not territorial. Telemetry studies have shown considerable overlap in home ranges of fox squirrels, but there is little evidence of social interaction (Weigl et al., 1989).

Competition

Intraspecific competition.—Although no substantive data are currently available, Weigl et al. (1989) suggest that intraspecific competition may be of some importance, particularly when food supplies are low or when nest cavities are scarce. Because food resources and nest cavities are often limited, they believe that solitary behavior and intolerance may indicate intraspecific competition.

Interspecific competition.—Many other species utilize acorns and nest cavities; however, there is no data to indicate their impact on fox squirrel populations. Weigl et al. (1989) suggest that in open, upland pine-hardwood habitat, competitors may be relatively rare and opportunistic. However, both Taylor (1973) and Weigl et al. (1989) have proposed that habitat modification has resulted in marginal habitat where gray squirrels have a competitive advantage.

INTERRELATIONSHIPS AND EFFECTS OF FACTORS ON SURVIVAL STRATEGIES

Many obvious gaps exist in our current knowledge of the ecology of southeastern fox squirrels. Much research needs to be done to define parameters such as birth and death rates, dispersal, sex and age structure, competition, and resource availability. However, the broad overview of southeastern fox squirrel ecology that has been provided through several recent studies may allow inferences to be drawn to form a "rough draft" of the possible interrelationships of population and environmental factors.

Based on an extension of the available data, southeastern fox squirrels may be typically characterized as having low, relatively stable long-term populations with low, variable recruitment, and limited sources of mortality, particularly when compared to other small game species such as gray squirrels and midwestern fox squirrels. The food supply, along with the composition, structure and landscape aspects of the habitat that produce it, are probably the most important factors affecting population densities, recruitment, and survival of fox squirrels.

Based upon subjective measures of food availability, Weigl et al. (1989) linked food supply to body weight, and associated body weight with reproductive success. In their study, weight varied seasonally with food supply; within seasons, body weight reflected food availability. They reported a significant, positive correlation between body weight and litter size, and found that fox squirrels <960 g reproduced only when food availability was very high. During years of extremely poor food availability, 90% of the reproductively capable females in their study failed to produce litters, whereas in years of good food availability only 12% failed to produce litters. In addition, they found a significant positive association between the number of reproducing females in the spring and the food supplies of the previous autumn. Kantola (1986) also observed evidence of low reproductive activity during years of mast failure of turkey oak.

In addition to litter size and frequency, Weigl et al. (1989) suggested that differential growth rates of nestlings may be associated with low food availability. They reported that weight discrepancies within litters appeared most often in those born later in the spring, and related this to limited or declining food supplies often found in late spring. Thus, reproductive output may be adjusted to food availability in the form of differential growth in order to enhance the fitness of a few young and the mother.

Habitat composition and structure are of substantial importance to southeastern fox squirrels. Although species composition of habitat has been found to vary throughout the range of fox squirrels, adequate food supplies are a necessity. Habitat which includes a variety of mast-producing species may help compensate for variable mast production. Also, the pine habitat component may be very important as a seasonal source of food.

Habitat composition can be very important also in providing nest sites. Although the optimum mixture of pines and hardwoods is not known, this may be a major factor in areas where fox squirrels depend on nest cavities.

Habitat structure may also be an important factor in food production. The "openness" of habitat of fox squirrels may, to some extent, help determine food production. This "openness" may result in larger tree crown sizes and reduced competition for light, nutrients, and water (Goodrum, 1938; Flyger and Gates, 1982), thereby affecting mast production.

Besides food production, the availability of suitable nest cavities and the amount of competition may be influenced by habitat structure. Because of the large size of fox squirrels, large mature trees are needed to provide cavities of suitable size. Also, the large size of fox squirrels has been attributed to its association with open forests of longleaf pine. Weigl et al. (1989) suggest that the large size of southeastern fox squirrels is an advantage in handling large longleaf pine cones, and is beneficial for cursorial locomotion within the open spaces. Habitat characterized by a dense understory may increase the risk of predation on fox squirrels (Taylor, 1973). In addition, an increase in canopy closure and understory density may result in immigration into the area by potential nest and food competitors such as the gray squirrel.

Landscape dimensions play an important role in respect to southeastern fox squirrel distribution and abundance. As suggested by previous studies, the association and juxtaposition of habitat types may be critical factors in habitat selection. Ecotone areas, patches of hardwoods, and pine-hardwood mixtures, have all been repeatedly identified as areas of high use by fox squirrels (Edwards, 1986; Kantola, 1986; Weigl et al., 1989), implying that they may be associated with a relatively high, more diverse food supply than open pine areas, and a critical area for nest sites.

The seasonality of food supplies, low diversity of open pine stands, and asocial behavior may all partially explain the large home-range sizes of southeastern fox squirrels (Weigl et al., 1989), suggesting that large areas of suitable habitat are required. While the large body size and high mobility of southeastern fox squirrels allow for exploitation of patchy habitats, the degree of interspersion and the degree of isolation of important habitat types are certainly important factors affecting the area available for fox squirrel populations.

The habitat in which southeastern fox squirrels probably evolved, large longleaf pine forests and adjacent bottomlands (Weigl et al., 1989), has already been greatly modified, dissected, and destroyed throughout the southeast. This has undoubtedly contributed to the decline of the southeastern fox squirrel (Taylor, 1976; Williams and Humphrey, 1979; Weigl et al., 1989). Similar habitats of the Coastal Plain and Piedmont Regions are mostly of a small, disjunct nature. Because of low densities and large area requirements, further fragmentation of existing habitat could prove highly detrimental to populations of fox squirrels. Continued habitat destruction, land development, and fire suppression will likely result in the expiration of breeding populations, or in small, isolated populations susceptible to inbreeding and homozygosity.

As evidenced by the available data, very little is known about regulation of populations of southeastern fox squirrels. For example, there is a paucity of data on dispersal and social interactions. Gurnell (1987) has stated that the densities of most squirrel populations are highly variable, and regulation over long periods of time is unlikely unless it is finely tuned to food supply. Also, Flowerdew (1987) suggested that populations that are finely tuned to food supply may remain relatively stable at low densities, with these densities being at levels at which a population can survive during periods of poor food availability. Obviously, because habitat composition, structure, and landscape dimensions affect food supply and availability, they may be considered important aspects of regulation for some species. This may be a reasonable hypothesis based on the available data for southeastern fox squirrels.

r- OR K-SELECTED?

The ecology of southeastern fox squirrels is not well known, and much of the available data are largely subjective and lacking empirical basis. However, several factors may support the supposition that southeastern fox squirrels are relatively more K-selected than most small game species, and thus may benefit from being managed from this viewpoint.

In relation to other small game species such as the gray squirrel, southeastern fox squirrels appear to be relatively long-lived, have smaller and fewer litters, lower adult mortality, and lower resource thresholds. Also, population densities may be more relatively stable over the long-term than other small-game species. Bailey (1984) outlined some aspects of management and population dynamics of biotic potential, and associated small game species with a faster rate of population turnover and a higher importance of each year's reproduction to harvestable surpluses. These do not appear to be appropriate characterizations of southeastern fox squirrels when compared to other small game species. Thus, while southeastern fox squirrels are obviously more *r*-selected than many big game species, they exhibit more attributes associated with K-strategists than do many other small game species. Obviously, much research is needed in the area of life table statistics. Information of this kind could shed light on many of the problems of interpreting the survival strategy of southeastern fox squirrels.

MANAGEMENT IMPLICATIONS

The dependence of southeastern fox squirrels on specific habitat characteristics obviously suggests habitat manipulation and prescribed fire as important management techniques. Significant aspects of management of southeastern fox squirrels include size, composition, structure, and arrangement of habitat types. Weigl et al. (1989) suggest that the "island archipelago" model described by Harris (1984) may be an important concept in long-term management of southeastern fox squirrels. This management concept involves the maintainance of suitable habitat through a system of long-rotation islands and dispersal corridors. Thus, the highly mobile, wide-ranging southeastern fox squirrels which require a mosaic of habitats may benefit significantly from such a management system.

Finally, the realization that southeastern fox squirrels may be relatively more K-selected than many other species of small game suggests a re-evaluation of current harvesting practices and regulations. Steen (1944) observed that a large majority of small-game species that are harvested each year are juveniles. Consequently, he suggested that the determinants of harvestable surplus of small game species are primarily reproductive success and juvenile survival. However, in species such as southeastern fox squirrels, the number of breeders prior to each breeding season may be the important criterion for determining harvestable surpluses.

Most southeastern states (except Florida, North Carolina, and Virginia) currently lump fox squirrels and gray squirrels under the same regulations, and do not separate figures of squirrel harvest by species. The "typical" season for fox squirrels opens in mid-October and lasts through January. Bag limits range from no limit in portions of South Carolina to 1/day in North Carolina. The most common daily bag limit is six.

Because southeastern fox squirrels are ecologically different from gray squirrels, it is critical to be able to manage their harvest separately from that of gray squirrels. Careful monitoring and examination of the resulting harvest figures may prove very valuable and enlightening. To support a hunting season, large areas of good habitat and relatively high densities of fox squirrels are required. However, the length of season and bag limits must be evaluated, and most likely shortened and lowered to be more in line with the reproductive potential associated with southeastern fox squirrels in their current habitats. Previously hunted areas containing good habitat but relatively low densities of fox squirrels may benefit from a period of closed seasons followed by open seasons of reduced bag limits. However, in areas of small, disjunct habitat with few dispersal corridors and small populations, it is likely that hunting pressure would have serious detrimental effects.

LITERATURE CITED

ADAMS, C. E. 1976. Measurement and characteristics of fox squirrel, *Sciurus niger rufiventer*, home ranges. The American Midland Naturalist, 95:211-215.

ASDELL, S. A. 1964. Patterns of mammalian reproduction. Second edition. Comstock Publishing Company, Ithaca, New York, 670 pp.

BAILEY, J. A. 1984. Principles of wildlife management. John Wiley & Sons, New York, 373 pp.

BAUMGARTNER, L. L. 1938. Population studies of the fox squirrel in Ohio. Transactions of the North American Wildlife Conference, 4:579-584.

———. 1943. Fox squirrels in Ohio. The Journal of Wildlife Management, 7:193- 202.

BOYCE, M. S. 1984. Restitution of *r*- and K-selection as a model of density-dependent selection. Annual Review Ecological Systems, 15:427-447.

———. 1988*a*. Evolution of life histories: theory and patterns from mammals. Pp. 3-30, *in* Evolution of life histories of mammals. Yale University Press, New Haven, Connecticut, (M. S. Boyce, ed.) 373 pp.

———. 1988*b*. Where do we go from here? Pp. 351-361, *in* Evolution of life histories of mammals. Yale University Press, New Haven, Connecticut, (M. S. Boyce, ed.) 373 pp.

BROWN, L. G., AND L. E. YEAGER. 1945. Fox and gray squirrels in Illinois. Illinois Natural History Survey Bulletin, 23:449-532.

DASMANN, R. F. 1981. Wildlife Biology. Second ed. John Wiley & Sons, New York, 212 pp.

DUESER, R. D., J. L. DOOLEY, AND G. J. TAYLOR. 1988. Habitat structure, forest composition, and landscape dimensions as components of habitat suitability for the Delmarva fox squirrel (*Sciurus niger cinereus*). Pp. 414-421, *in* Management of amphibians, reptiles and small mammals in North America (R. Szaro, ed.) U.S.D.A. Forest Service, Rocky Mountain Forest and Range Experiment Station. Fort Collins, Colorado, 458 pp.

EDWARDS, J. W. 1986. Habitat utilization by southern fox squirrel in coastal South Carolina. M.S. thesis, Clemson University, South Carolina, 52 pp.

EISENBERG, J. F. 1981. The mammalian radiations. The University of Chicago Press, Chicago, Illinois, 610 pp.

FLOWERDEW, J. R. 1987. Mammals, their reproductive biology and population ecology. Edward Arnold, Baltimore, Maryland, 241 pp.

FLYGER, V. F. 1960. Movements and home range of the gray squirrel, *Sciurus carolinensis* in two Maryland woodlots. Ecology, 41:365-369.

FLYGER, V. F., AND J. E. GATES. 1982. Fox and gray squirrels, *Sciurus niger, S. carolinensis* and their allies. Pp. 209-229, *in* (R. Szaro, ed.) Wild mammals of North America. The Johns Hopkins University Press, Baltimore, Maryland, (R. Szaro, ed.) 1147 pp.

FLYGER, V. F., AND D. A. SMITH. 1980. A comparison of Delmarva fox squirrel and gray squirrel habitats and home range. Transactions Northeastern Section of The Wildlife Society Fish and Wildlife Conference, 37:19-22.

GOODRUM, P. 1938. Squirrel management in eastern Texas. Transactions North American Wildlife Conference, 3:670-676.

GURNELL, J. 1983. Squirrel numbers and the abundance of tree seeds. Mammal Review, 13:133-148.

———. 1987. The natural history of squirrels. Facts on File Publishing, New York, 201 pp.

HA, J. C. 1983. Food supply and home range in the fox squirrel (*Sciurus niger*). M.S. thesis, Wake Forest University, Winston-Salem, North Carolina, 32 pp.

HARRIS, L.D. 1984. The fragmented forest. The University of Chicago Press, Chicago, Illinois, 211 pp.

HAVERA, S. P., AND C. M. NIXON. 1978. Interaction among adult female fox squirrels during their winter breeding season. Transactions Illinois State Academy of Science, 71:24-38.

HILLIARD, T. M. 1979. Radio-telemetry of fox squirrels in the Georgia coastal plain. M.S. thesis, University of Georgia, Athens, 113 pp.

HUMPHREY, S. R., J. F. EISENBERG, AND R. FRANZ. 1985. Possibilities for restoring wildlife of a longleaf pine savanna in an abandoned citrus grove. Wildlife Society Bulletin, 13:487-496.

KANTOLA, A. T. 1986. Fox squirrel home range and mast crops in Florida. M.S. thesis, University of Florida, Gainesville, 68 pp.

LUSTIG, L. W., AND V. FLYGER. 1975. Observations and suggested management practices for the endangered Delmarva fox squirrel. Proceedings Annual Conference Southeastern Association of Game and Fish Commissioners, 29:433-440.

MACARTHUR, R. H., AND E. O. WILSON. 1967. The theory of island biography. Princeton University Press, Princeton, New Jersey, 203 pp.

MOORE, J. C. 1957. The natural history of the fox squirrel, *Sciurus niger shermani*. Bulletin American Museum of Natural History 113, 71 pp.

MOSBY, H. S. 1969. The influence of hunting on the population dynamics of a woodlot gray squirrel population. The Journal of Wildlife Management, 33:59-73.

NIXON, C. M., AND L. P. HANSEN. 1987. Managing forests to maintain populations of gray and fox squirrels. Illinois Deptartment of Conservation Technical Bulletin, 5, 35 pp.

NIXON, C. M., L. P. HANSEN, AND S. P. HAVERA. 1986. Demographic characteristics of an unexploited population of fox squirrels (*Sciurus niger*). Canadian Journal of Zoology, 64:512-521.

PIANKA, E. R. 1970. On *r*- and K-selection. The American Naturalist, 104:592-597.

SCHAFFER, W. M. 1974. Optimal reproductive effort in fluctuating environments. The American Naturalist, 108:783-790.

SOUTHWOOD, T. R. E. 1977. Habitat, the templet for ecological strategies? The Journal of Animal Ecology, 46:337-365.

STEARNS, S. C. 1976. Life-history tactics: A review of the ideas. Quarterly Review of Biology, 51:3-41.

———. 1977. The evolution of life history traits. Annual Review of Ecological Systems, 8:145-172.

STEEN, M. O. 1944. The significance of population turnover in upland game management. Transactions North American Wildlife Conference, 9:331-335.

TAPPE, P. A., AND D. C. GUYNN, JR. 1990. Boundary-strip width for density estimation based on telemetric locations. Proceedings Annual Conference Southeastern Association of Fish and Wildlife Agencies, 44:279–283.

TAYLOR, G. J. 1973. Present status and habitat survey of the Delmarva fox squirrel (*Sciurus niger cinereus*) with a discussion of reasons for its decline. Proceedings Annual Southeastern Association of Game and Fish Commissioners, 27:278-289.

———. 1976. Range determination and habitat description of the Delmarva fox squirrel in Maryland. M.S. thesis, University Maryland, College Park, 76 pp.

THERRES, G. D., AND G. W. WILLEY, SR. 1988. An assessment of local Delmarva fox squirrel populations. Maryland Naturalist, 32:80-85.

WEIGL, P. D., M. A. STEELE, L. J. SHERMAN, J. C. HA AND T. L. SHARPE. 1989. The ecology of the fox squirrel (*Sciurus niger*) in North Carolina: implications for survival in the Southeast. Bulletin, Tall Timbers Research Station, 24:1-93.

WILLIAMS, K. S., AND S. R. HUMPHREY. 1979. Distribution and status of the endangered Big Cypress fox squirrel (*Sciurus niger avicennia*) in Florida. Florida Scientist, 42:201-205.

WOOD, G. W. 1985. Trophy value of the fox squirrel and its management inference in South Carolina. Clemson University Forestry Bulletin, 47, 4 pp.

WOOD, G. W., AND J. R. DAVIS. 1981. A survey of perceptions of fox squirrel populations in South Carolina. Clemson University Forestry Bulletin, 29, 6 pp.

BARK-STRIPPING DAMAGE BY GRAY SQUIRRELS IN STATE FORESTS OF THE UNITED KINGDOM: A REVIEW

JACKIE DAGNALL, JOHN GURNELL AND HARRY PEPPER

School of Biological Science, Queen Mary and Westfield College, London E1 4NS (JD, JG) and Forestry Authority, Alice Holt, Farnham, Surrey GU10 4LH (HP)

ABSTRACT.—The range of the North American gray squirrel in Britain continues to expand, which has increased the need to understand and control damage due to bark stripping of commercial tree crops. Squirrel numbers, tree species and stand age are important factors affecting damage levels, and silvicultural factors may operate indirectly by increasing tree quality and susceptibility to damage. Since 1958, the Forestry Commission of Great Britain (FC) has been monitoring damage levels in Forestry Commission forests and has carried out studies on the intensity of damage in monoculture and mixed species plantations. This paper reviews these data, and the current control policy in public-owned forests, and comments on the results of a questionnaire survey of North American forests and wildlife agencies on bark removal damage to trees by squirrels. In Britain, gray squirrels are now controlled in most public forests during the season of most intense damage (April–July). If this was stopped the risk of severe damage and heavy economic losses to the forest industry would be very high. In contrast, and with one or two notable exceptions, bark removal damage by squirrels is not perceived as a problem to forestry in North America.

INTRODUCTION

Two species of tree squirrels inhabit the British Isles, the native red squirrel, *Sciurus vulgaris*, and the introduced North American gray squirrel, *S. carolinensis*. Both species have been implicated in some form of pest activity in Britain: in forest, agricultural and urban settings. However, damage to trees, particularly in the form of bark removal, is considered the most serious (Shorten, 1957). Squirrels cause damage by stripping away outer bark, which is then discarded, and eating the soft inner bark (mainly phloem) underneath (Gurnell, 1987). At the turn of the century, bark-stripping was a recognized habit of red squirrels, occasionally sufficient to warrant their control (Gill, 1992), but red squirrels are now scarce or absent in much of England and Wales (Gurnell and Pepper, 1993) and reports of serious damage by red squirrels are rare in these places. In contrast, bark-stripping by gray squirrels has been a problem in forestry (particularly in England and Wales) for at least 60 years (Middleton, 1930).

In this paper we describe some of the results from 40 years of research into tree damage by gray squirrels, and the current management policy for Forestry Commission forests. Since 1958, the primary source of numerical information has been the Annual FC Squirrel Questionnaire. The Questionnaire is distributed each year to directors of all FC forests in England, Scotland, and Wales. Changes to forestry policy (and organizational restructuring) during the 1960s and early 1970s, have affected the continuity of the data, thus we only present the results from 1973.

The results show that the relative number of forests reporting damage in England and Wales has increased substantially since 1973 (Fig. 1). In Scotland, fewer than 5% of the surveys report gray squirrel damage in any one year (not included in Fig. 1). Current control policy for gray squirrels was developed partly from the findings of the questionnaire, and partly from other research projects conducted by the FC over the last 30 years. We

In M.A. Steele, J. F. Merritt, and D. A. Zegers (eds.). 1998. Ecology and Evolutionary Biology of Tree Squirrels. Special Publication, Virginia Museum of Natural History, 6: 320 pp

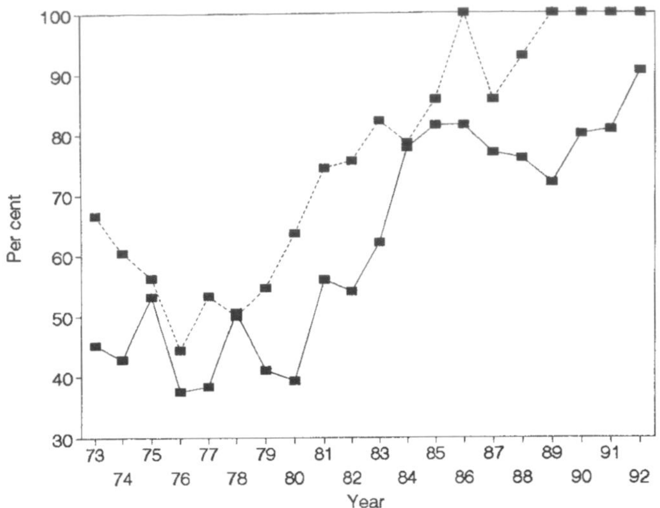

Fig. 1.— Proportion of FC Forest Districts reporting damage since 1973 in England (n=106 forests in 1973 to 21 Forest Districts in 1992) and Wales (n=48 forests in 1973 to 8 Forest Districts in 1992). Compiled from the Annual Squirrel Questionnaires conducted by the Forestry Commission. Solid lines = England, dashed lines = Wales.

assess these data in relation to the control of both damage and squirrel populations, and we consider future research opportunities.

The spread of the gray squirrel in Britain.— The first introduction of the gray squirrel , in Cheshire, England in 1876, involved a single pair of animals (Middleton, 1931). By 1929, a further 31 (known) introductions had taken place, mainly throughout England but also in Scotland and Wales, only one of which was unsuccessful. The changing distribution of gray and red squirrels in Britain since then has been reviewed elsewhere (Lloyd, 1983). The gradual but continual encroachment of gray squirrels from centers of abundance into previously unoccupied areas, closed many of the gaps in their distribution which led to the present position where gray squirrels are ubiquitous over most of central and southern England and Wales (Gurnell and Pepper, 1993).

The history of damage control.—Damage to valuable timber trees by red squirrels in Britain was a problem at the turn of the century, when they were particularly abundant. Thereafter, red squirrel numbers declined. By the 1920s it was clear that gray squirrels were damaging trees and in 1931 a National Anti-Gray Squirrel Campaign began, and continued throughout the 1940s and 1950s. Bark-stripping is characteristically sporadic, serious in some years and places but not others, and control was on a local level, usually carried out by shooting. In 1957, a nationwide survey of public woodland revealed that bark-stripping was widespread and financial losses were likely on a large scale (Shorten, 1957). As a result the Forestry Commission organized widespread control of grays on an annual basis. Research increased accordingly to determine how control could be achieved on a large scale. At that time, little was known about gray squirrel population dynamics in British forests. Over the last 30 years, progress has been made towards understanding bark-stripping, although it is still not possible to predict exactly when and where it will occur. The available evidence points to high population densities, especially of juveniles, and agonistic behaviour during the period of damage as the main contributors to damage (Taylor, 1966, 1969; Mackinnon, 1976; Kenward and Parish, 1986). However, individual site and tree characteristics also affect the severity of the damage incurred (Kenward and Parish, 1986; Gurnell and Pepper, 1988).

CHARACTERISTICS OF DAMAGE

Damage arises in both pure and mixed stands of young trees (10–40 years old), termed Damage-Vulnerable (DV) woodland (Gurnell and Pepper, 1988). Bark-stripping usually starts in May, and peaks in June and July. This is a period of vigorous tree growth, when trees are naturally more 'strippable' because the outer bark adheres less strongly to the wood (Hampshire, 1985; Wästerlund, 1985 Gill, 1992). Occasionally, damage may extend into September, but damage does not occur during autumn or winter (October to February). Damage has also been related to the thickness of the phloem layer (Kenward and Parish, 1986), tree species (Table 1 and see below), and possibly tree provenance (seed origin/parent stock) and growing conditions.

The severity of damage in DV woodlands has been found to increase with the number of squirrels, particularly juveniles, entering during the period of damage (Kenward and Parish, 1986). The density of squirrels in and around DV woods at that time is related to food supply the previous winter (Gurnell, 1983). The better the autumn tree seed supply, the better the survival and the more likely it is that some females will produce two litters during the breeding season, one in early spring and the other in summer (Gurnell, 1983, 1989). Early spring litters result in juveniles being present during the period of damage. In addition, there will be a second period of recruitment from second litters later in the season of damage. There are likely to be more agonistic encounters when population numbers are high and when juveniles enter the

Table 1.–*Tree species damaged by gray squirrels from Squirrel Questionnaire Reports sent out to all Forestry Commission forests 1963-1983 (Rowe and Gill, 1985).*

Common name	Specific name	Numbers of damage incidents per year
Beech	*Fagus sylvatica*	>15 yr-1
Sycamore	*Acer pseudoplantanus*	
Oak	*Quercus*	
Scots pine	*Pinus sylvestris*	
Larches	*Larix*	
Red oak	*Quercus robur*	
Maples	*Acer*	
Western hemlock	*Tsuga heterophylla*	
Lodgepole pine	*Pinus contorta*	1-15 yr^{-1}
Sweet chestnut	*Castanea sativa*	
Norway spruce	*Picea abies*	
Corsican pine	*Pinus nigra*	
Ash	*Fraxinus excelsior*	
Birch	*Betula*	
Lawson cypress	*Chamaecyparis lawsoniana*	
Sitka spruce	*Picea sitchensis*	
Poplar	*Populus* var.	
Hornbeam	*Carpinus betulus*	
Elm	*Ulmus*	
Lime	*Tilia*	
Horse chestnut	*Aesculus hippocastanum*	
Hazel	*Corylus avellana*	
Aspen	*Populus tremula*	
Gean	*Prunus avium*	
Willow	*Salix*	
Robinia	*Robinia pseudoacacia*	
Tulip tree	*Liriodendron tulipifera*	<1 yr^{-1}
Turkey oak	*Quercus cerris*	
Acacia (species not recorded)		
Western red cedar	*Thuja plicata*	
Fir	*Abies*	
Douglas fir	*Pseudotsuga menziesii*	
Cryptomeria		
Redwood	*Sequoia*	
Maritime pine	*Pinus maritima*	
Southern beech	*Nothofagus*	

population (Kenward and Parish, 1986), possibly contributing to higher levels of damage. The juxtaposition of DV woods and mature broadleaf woods is also important. Mature broadleaf woods are good over-winter habitats, and Potentially High Density (PHD) habitats for gray squirrels (Gurnell and Pepper, 1988). Where PHD habitats are near to DV habitats, the amount of damage due to bark stripping in the latter can increase (Kenward et al., 1992). Thus, increasing the isolation of DV woodlands may reduce damage (Kenward et al., 1988*b*, 1992). FitzGibbon (1993) found the distribution of dreys of gray squirrels in small farm woodlands in East Anglia was influenced by both habitat and relative isolation, including the distance to the nearest large wood of at least 5ha in size. All the small woods which contained dreys were less than 450m from other woodlots. Based on known foraging movements recorded for gray squirrels, a buffer zone of at least one kilometer between PHD and DV habitats is recommended (Gurnell and Pepper, 1988).

The relationships among seed supplies, numbers of squirrels and damage could also be compounded by other site-related factors. For example, over-winter food for pheasant provides a supplement for squirrels and may lead to early matings in poor seed years (Kenward et al., 1988*a*). This can increase damage to nearby DV woodland the following summer (Kenward et al., 1992). In contrast, severe winter weather conditions may delay the onset of breeding, especially during years of natural food scarcity, and then damage may be less serious (Gurnell, 1989).

The variation in damage among sites and years means that the management policy must be flexible. Currently, an index of risk is being developed to predict where and when squirrels will damage trees (Gurnell, 1989). This requires an understanding of the factors which contribute to the variation in damage among sites and years. We examine tree and habitat variables below.

EXTENT OF THE PROBLEM

The area of vulnerable broadleaf woodlands (ages 10 to 40 years) has remained fairly constant over the last 20 years, and is considerably less than the area of conifer plantation (Fig. 2a). However, the area of vulnerable conifer in England and Wales has declined slightly in recent years, whereas the area of conifer has increased considerably in Scotland with extensive new plantings in the 1980s.

Fewer forests report damage to conifer plantations than to broadleaf woodland and the number of forests reporting damage to both type of woodlands has generally declined since the 1970s until recently when the number of damage reports seems to have levelled off (Fig. 2b). Currently about 55 reports from broadleaf woodlands in England are received each year, 24 from broadleaf woodlands from Wales, 18 from conifer plantations in

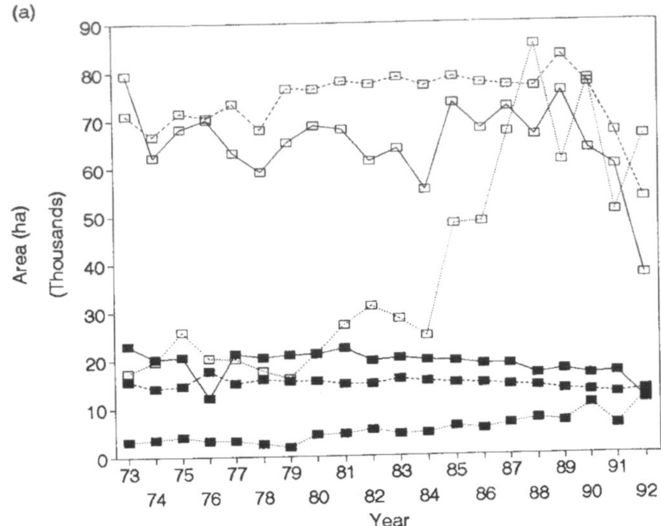

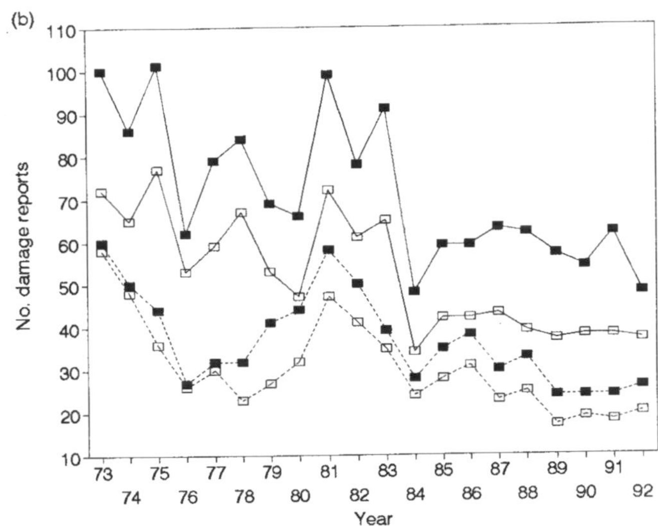

Fig. 2.—(a) Total area of broadleaf (beech, sycamore and including larch) and conifer (excluding larch) forest vulnerable to damage in England and Wales between 1973 and 1992. Compiled from the Annual Squirrel Questionnaires sent out to all FC forests by the Forestry Commission. (b) The number of damage reports to broadleaf (beech, sycamore and including larch) and conifer (excluding larch) forests in England and Wales between 1973 and 1992. Compiled from the Annual Squirrel Questionnaires sent out to all FC forests by the Forestry Commission. The number of damage reports from Scottish forests are very small and are not included. Solid lines = England; dashed lines = Wales; dotted lines = Scotland; solid squares = broadleaf forests, open squares = conifer forests.

England and 17 from conifer plantations in Wales. There is a positive correlation between the number of damage reports to conifers (excluding larch) and broadleaf tree species (sycamore, beech but including larch) in England (r = 0.48, n = 20, P < 0.05) and Wales (r = 0.80, n = 20, P < 0.01). Further, the area of vulnerable broadleaf woodland in England is correlated with the number of damage reports (r = 0.58, n = 20, P < 0.01), and so is the area of vulnerable conifer plantations and the number of damage reports to conifer (r=0.49, n=20, P<0.05). Even so, the area of vulnerable woodland fails to explain 66% and 76% (i.e. coefficients of non-determination) of the variation in the number of damage reports to broadleaf and conifer forests, respectively. Equivalent correlations of vulnerable woodland with reports of damage are higher for Wales where there are no significant correlations in the case of broadleaf (r = 0.32, n = 20, P > 0.05) or conifers (r = 0.25, n = 20, P > 0.05) and comparable coefficients of non-determination are 90% and 94% for broadleaf and conifer forests respectively. To date, there have been few reports of damage to conifers by gray squirrels in Scotland. Thus, other factors are at least partly responsible for the increase in the number of damage reports in England and Wales. The most likely reason is that there has been a real increase in the amount of damage to trees by gray squirrels, and also an increased awareness by foresters of the problem with more detailed reporting of damage incidents. Untangling these two factors retrospectively is not possible.

A particular feature of damage due to bark removal by gray squirrels in Britain is the very wide range of tree species attacked, including both broadleaf and conifer species (Table 1). Therefore, any species of tree may suffer some damage at some time. However, certain species and ages of tree are much more likely to be damaged than others, and we will consider these below in relation to woodland type and woodland age.

Broadleaf woodlands.—In 1985, the number of hardwood species on which squirrel damage had been reported totalled 22 species (Rowe and Gill, 1985). However, several surveys have shown that

Table 2.—(a) *Cumulative distribution of damage by species and age on the Dalkeith Estate in central Scotland in 1979. Damage refers to any bark removal by gray squirrels scored as a presence/absence on any one tree. Total damage as a percentage of trees damaged assessed by nearest neighbour method (Melville et al., 1983) using a minimum number of 100 trees per area assessed (standard deviations in brackets where applicable). Stem damage refers to the proportion of the damaged trees with stem damage. (From Melville, 1980).*

		Oak			Sycamore			Beech	
Age (yrs)	Area (ha)	Mean % trees dam	Stem dam (% of total)	Area (ha)	Mean % trees dam	Stem dam (% of total)	Area (ha)	Mean % trees dam	Stem dam (% of total)
20	10.2	42 (6.5)	100	10.2	61 (7.4)	73	10.2	10 (3.2)	65
40	5.5	8	100	0			5.5	36 (8.2)	0
65	1.7	0		1.7	0		1.7	37 (8.1)	0

(b) *Distribution of damage by species and age on 18 Estates in central Scotland in 1979 (from Melville, 1980). Assessments carried out as in (a) above. There were no significant differences in damage levels in woodland plots of different sizes. There were no significant differences in damage levels according to age in oak and beech but there was a significant difference in damage according to age in sycamore* (F = *12.3,* d.f. = *2.5,* P< *0.001).*

		Oak			Sycamore			Beech	
Age (yrs)	No. woods	Mean area (ha)	Mean % trees dam	No. woods	Mean area (ha)	Mean % trees dam	No. woods	Mean area (ha)	Mean % trees dam
10 - 20	6	5 (5.8)	8 (16.8)	19	5 (6.2)	43 (32.1)	7	4 (3.9)	14 (20.3)
21 - 40	2	3 (1.4)	7 (2.1)	17	4 (5.4)	19 (17.6)	6	2 (1.1)	10 (15.6)
41 - 65	4	6 (2.9)	0	17	6 (5.4)	4 (16.9)	16	6 (4.4)	17 (22.1)

sycamore and beech are particularly susceptible (e.g., Rowe and Shorten, 1957; Melville, 1980; Petamedes, 1983; Rowe, 1984; Gill, 1985; Kenward et al., 1992).

The location of bark damage may vary among tree species. Damage occurring within 1m of the ground is usually termed basal damage. Crown damage is that which occurs on any aerial parts in the main canopy, and stem damage is usually associated with the area of the stem in between the base and canopy. Damage to beech often occurs on the base (Melville, 1979; Petamedes, 1983). In contrast, damage to sycamore and certain other hardwoods (e.g., oak) tends to occur most frequently on the stem and in the crown. For example, in 1979, a survey of damage in Scotland found a higher percentage of stem damage to both oak and sycamore in one particular locality than on beech (Melville, 1980; Table 2). Nevertheless, there was substantially more stem damage to young beech that year than had previously been observed in both FC and private woodlands in the Chilterns, central England (Melville, 1979). The reasons for this are unclear. Petamedes (1983) recorded that 85% of wounds on beech were on the base of the trees, compared to 66% on sycamore from a study in Scotland. However, wounds on the base of beech (11 - 750 cm^2) were larger than those on sycamore (11 - 588 cm^2), whereas wounds on the stem were smaller (12 - 375 cm^2 and 12 - 1250 cm^2, respectively). Although basal damage to beech can be serious, in that it affects the portion of the tree with the largest volume of timber, damage to individual sycamore trees tends to be severe, often with the whole stem stripped from top to bottom. Thus, recording damage as the proportion of trees stripped, as has been done in most surveys, is not indicative of the severity of damage to individual trees.

The location of wounds on a tree is probably related to the ease of bark removal and bark thickness, and hence to growth characteristics of tree species. Beech and sycamore tend to have thin bark whereas oak and conifers tend to have thicker bark. Moreover, damage is likely to occur more frequently in the crown of species such as oak, whose bark becomes thicker with age and is thinnest in the crown (Gill, 1992). Site conditions, such as local climate and soil, may affect tree growth and contribute to variation in damage levels among sites. Squirrel damage is sometimes most severe on the largest trees in a stand and those with the greatest volume of phloem (Kenward and Parish, 1986).

The provenance of trees could be important, as is the case with vole damage to lodgepole pine in Scandinavia (Rousi, 1983*b*). Growing varieties of broadleaves with natural resistance to stripping could be an alternative method of tree protection (Kenward et al., 1992) but needs testing.

Conifer plantations.—Reports of damage to Corsican pine (*Pinus nigra*), maritime pine (*P. pinaster*), lodgepole pine (*P. contorta*), western red cedar (*Thuja plicata*), Japanese larch (*Larix leptolepis*) and Scots pine first appeared in 1954-1955 (Shorten, 1957). Since then, damage has also been reported on western hemlock, Norway Spruce, Lawson cypress, Sitka spruce, and firs (Rowe and Gill, 1985). An unusual occurrence of bark-stripping was reported from Halwill Forest in Devon, England during the late winter of 1975. Between 24% and 35% of lodgepole pines had been damaged on the mainstem and in the crown (Pepper, 1975). This was the only conifer in the area and the damage occurred in February, considerably earlier than normal. Quantitative reports of damage are few. Tee and Rowe (1985) reported damage on a range of age classes and species of conifers at Delamere forest in Cheshire, England including Corsican pine and Scots pine, sufficient to devalue timber from thinnings by up to 2%. Thus, damage of gray squirrels to conifers requires a great deal of further study (Gurnell, 1989).

Mixed species woodlands.—In Britain, the planting of hardwoods in mixtures with a conifer nurse or cash crop has occasionally been associated with an increase in damage to the broadleaf trees (e.g., Aldhous, 1981). This may result from the conifer providing greater cover for the squirrels, thereby affecting their local density and distribution (Kenward et al., 1992). In particular, beech in mixtures has been found to be more heavily damaged than as a monoculture (Table 3). The relative number of trees damaged was especially important in the case of the mixed crops because of the lower stocking density of beech in these areas. More information is required on combinations of tree species in relation to damage in mixed species woodlands.

Age of woodland.—Most of the economically significant bark-stripping occurs to the main stem of trees aged 10 - 40 years (pole stage; Gurnell and Pepper, 1988). The age of susceptibility to attack appears to be species-related. Most species receive the majority of the damage before age 40, although beech can remain vulnerable for a further 20 years (Table 2). Some variation from site to site may result from different management policies for trees and squirrels. One survey of the Chiltern Forest District found that damage tended to be higher in the private plantations in the later life of the crop. Mean damage (± 95% confidence

Table 3.—*Comparison of damage percentage and stocking density* (SD) *of beech in mixtures (with either Corsican pine, Scots pine or Norway spruce) and pure crops in southern England in 1978. Trees were scored as damaged if any bark had been removed by squirrels from the stem, crown, or base, regardless of wound size (Pepper, 1973; Rowe, 1978). Damage percentage was assessed by the Nearest Neighbor Method, after Melville et al., 1983. There was no significant difference between the mean percent damage levels (* F= *1.01,* P>*0.05). Compt. = forest compartment (stand of trees as defined by Forestry Commission boundaries).*

Crop type	Number of compartments surveyed	Mean area compartments (ha) (SD)	Stocking density (no.beech ha^{-1})	Mean damage % (SD)
Pure	10	11.4 (4.12)	2580	29 (15.9)
Mixed	10	15.4 (5.02)	1280	37 (19.1)

intervals) to beech in the 10 to 40 years age class was 41% (± 11.4%) in FC woods and 44% (± 18.3%) in private woods. Mean damage to beech trees over 40 years in FC and private woods (combined) was 53% (± 10.8%). This may result from differences in the level of control between private and FC forests or that more damaged stems are removed during thinning operations in public forests. However, the effect of thinning on reducing the number of damaged stems in the final crop may not be so marked in other circumstances. For example, one survey showed that the percentage of stems damaged in Corsican and Scots pine plantations was not reduced after thinning (Tee and Rowe, 1985).

CONTROL POLICY FOR GRAY SQUIRRELS IN FC FORESTS

Prior to the use of warfarin poison, gray squirrels were controlled by trapping and shooting, the latter sometimes in conjunction with drey-poking. Shooting and drey poking are less effective than trapping, and on their own will not prevent damage (Rowe, 1980). Trapping and shooting still occur at a local scale, especially where the use of poison is not permitted. Since the Squirrel (Warfarin) Order of 1973, warfarin poisoning has been the most widely and only truly effective method of controlling gray squirrels. One study showed that no further damage to a beech plantation occurred after the introduction of warfarin control in 1973, and the old wounds on the beech trees gradually closed over a number of years masking the damage to the trees. Further damage occurred in 1983 after the site was sold and the control stopped. The Control of Pesticides Regulations, 1986, only permits the use of warfarin between 15 March and 15 August each year. Control at any other time is a waste of effort and resources because it does not reduce the number of squirrels in vulnerable woodland in the spring and summer (Gurnell and Pepper, 1988). By law, and for the protection of man and other wildlife, warfarin must be dispensed from food hoppers consisting of a food container reached by means of an entrance tunnel that allow access by only squirrels. Since 1989, poison hoppers incorporate a perspex door in the tunnel, secured by a magnet at the base, which restricts the use of hoppers by non-target wildlife (Pepper, 1989; Pepper and Stocker, 1993).

Warfarin may not be used where red squirrels are present but modifications to food hoppers are continuing. Legislation permitting, the new design will allow warfarin hoppers, which selectively keep out all animals except gray squirrels, to be used in such areas (Gurnell and Pepper, 1993). Geographically, these areas exist at the edge of the red squirrel's range, such as in North Wales and border woodlands between England and Wales. Adopting such a strategy will have the two-fold advantage of reducing inter-specific competition amongst the two squirrel species for food resources, thereby promoting conservation of red squirrels, and preventing damage to trees.

ECONOMIC CONSIDERATIONS OF DAMAGE

Estimates of the costs of damage prevention and losses to timber are difficult to evaluate. The total cost of damage may not be fully realized until the crop is felled. Annual control costs include capital cost equipment, (hoppers and/or traps), consumable materials, (whole wheat and whole

Table 4.—*Estimated costs of two methods of squirrel control: poison hoppers and cage trapping. Details for hoppers are based on figures from the the 1992 season, as revealed by the Annual FC Squirrel Questionnaire. Both estimates are based on the treatment of approximately 20,300 ha of woodland, which was the area of FC woodland over which gray squirrels were controlled by warfarin poisoning in 1992. Costs for cage traps are for comparison only and do not represent actual costs incurred. All prices quoted, except totals, are to the nearest £500. Note that the number of visits to hoppers per two-week period are approximate, and depend on the amount of bait eaten in each locality. N/A = not applicable.*

		Hoppers	Cage-traps
Capital costs	Number	4925	6767
	cost (£)	10,000	34,000
Consumables	Whole maize amount (kg)	1970	11,500
	Cost (£)	250	3,500
	Whole wheat amount (kg)	18137	N/A
	Cost (£)	3,500	
	Warfarin cost (£)	16,000	N/A
Labour	Person-days per damage season	28	20
	Number hoppers or traps visited per person	250	60
	Visits to hopper or trap per two-week period	1-3	>14
	Cost (£)	20,000	81,000
Total cost (£) of consumables and labour		50,000	119,000
Estimated cost (£) per ha controlled		2.46	5.86

maize bait, warfarin concentrate), and labor. Overall, warfarin control is considerably cheaper than trapping (Table 4) because it is less labor intensive.

The mature broadleaf trees now being felled are at least 120 years old and were not at risk of being damaged by gray squirrels 90 - 100 years ago. Therefore, there are few data on the loss of revenue resulting from damage. Dutton (1993) estimated a loss of yield class could cost between £1 to £2.25 ha^{-1} $year^{-1}$, excluding internal degrade. Ultimately, losses in revenue will be greatest for high value crops (see Gurnell and Pepper, 1988). Thus tree protection may not be economically viable when the losses from damage at felling are less than the costs of squirrel control over the 10 - 40 years following planting. Losses to the non-market value of trees (landscaping, conservation) as a result of damage are even more difficult to assess.

FUTURE PROSPECTS FOR DAMAGE CONTROL

Killing animals, especially with poisons, is becoming increasingly unacceptable to the general public in Britain and alternative methods of damage prevention must be found. Manipulating the habitat in a way which makes it unfavorable for grays will probably form the basis of future integrated control programes. Populations of forest rodents are known to respond, sometimes quite markedly, to changes in habitat, especially changes in food and cover (Borrecco, 1976). New planting must be given careful consideration, with the aim of limiting over-winter survival of squirrels as far as possible. This includes reducing the number of available nest sites and sources of both natural and supplemental food (Gurnell, 1987).

Vegetative cover, high pruning and thinning all appear to exert some influence on the amount of damage which occurs at a site. Kenward et al. (1992) found that, as the percentage of ground cover increased in young beech or sycamore woods, the severity of bark-stripping by gray squirrels decreased. Conversely, red squirrels in British Columbia cause more damage in areas of high vegetative cover (Sullivan et al., 1994). The involvement of vegetative cover in damage events in the Britain needs to be further explored as a means of preventing access of squirrels to trees, thereby limiting the amount of basal stripping. Pruning the lower bole of susceptible trees to a height of five to six meters, may reduce mainstem stripping by squirrels, since without branches there is nowhere for them to perch (Evans, 1984). Research is currently underway at the FC to assess the feasibility and effectiveness of such a measure.

Several studies have shown gray squirrel damage to be particularly prevalent on the most vigorous trees (MacKinnon, 1976; Potamodoo, 1983, Kenward et al., 1988*a*). In Britain, the area of bark stripped appears to be related to phloem width (volume per unit area; Kenward and Parish, 1986). Phloem width may increase in the two to three years following a thinning operation, and this may affect the vulnerability of trees to bark-stripping (Kenward, 1989). Thinning requirements would appear to conflict with requirements for preventing damage, since thinning aims to preserve the best formed trees and provide more space, to enhance growth rates (Evans, 1984). Sullivan and Moses (1986) obtained equivocal results from comparing damage by *Tamiasciurus hudsonicus* in thinned and unthinned stands of lodgepole pine at two sites in British Columbia. At one site, damage was significantly reduced in the thinned stand compared with the unthinned stand, whereas at the other site significantly more damage occurred in the thinned stand.

Sterilization, as an alternative to extermination, has been proposed and tested on a variety of mammal pest species, most notably rodents (Davis, 1961; Bowerman and Brooks, 1971; Kendle et al., 1973). Johnson and Tait (1983) reported on investigations into the success of chemical control of reproduction in Britain gray squirrels. To prevent spring breeding, the optimum timing for reproductive control of both males and females would be November to April. Unfortunately, bait acceptance is low when natural seeds are abundant during the autumn and winter (Gurnell, 1996). Hence bait acceptance would be affected by mast production by trees, which tends to vary widely between species, sites, and years (Gurnell, 1993). Current research concerns the development of a vaccine induced immuno-contraceptive for gray squirrels (Moore, pers. comm.). These vaccines work by causing an immune response in the female against unique proteins in the male sperm and are therefore species specific. The immune response prevents fertilization. It may be several years before such vaccines are commercially available.

BARK REMOVAL BY SQUIRRELS IN NORTH AMERICA

In North America, damage to trees by gray squirrels appears very sporadically in the literature and comparisons between Britain and North America have failed to reveal why they are not a pest in their native environment. Kenward (1989) suggested that most broadleaf woodlands of North America regenerate naturally. Phloem widths tend to be low in naturally regenerated trees, and this makes them less vulnerable to damage. Kenward supported this idea by assessing gray squirrel damage to sugar maple, *Acer saccharum*, during the summer. However, most reported damage to sugar maple occurs in winter not summer (Gill, 1992) when squirrels are supplementing their diet. Thus a study on phloem and damage on sugar maple during the winter would be revealing.

Further, replicated studies should be carried out in pure stocks of broadleaf plantations and natural hardwood forests in North America within the range of *S. carolinensis*. Self-seeded forests exhibit a higher degree of genetic variation than plantations, and may show natural resistance to damage. Thus, these studies should consider tree quality, damage and mode of regeneration, and include inventories of other habitat variables such as seed production, tree size and age, canopy closure and field cover.

Another hypothesis of bark-stripping in Britain is that it results from agonistic encounters during the establishment of young in the population, but it is not clear why this behaviour is apparently absent in North America. Observations of squirrels stripping bark are anecdotal, and it is not known which animals in a population or how many are involved in bark-stripping events. Future research should consider radio-tracking and observational studies of squirrels to examine their behavior and the events leading to damage.

In Britain, gray squirrels appear to actively select certain trees for stripping (Gill, 1992). This feeding pattern is similar to that of Abert's squirrels (*S. aberti*) in North America, which feed on certain trees of ponderosa pine to the exclusion of other trees in the same locality (Farentinos et al., 1981). The chemical and nutritive components of outer and inner bark have been studied for their role in tree selection by Abert's squirrels (Pederson and Welch, 1987; also see Gaud et al., 1993), and such studies are needed on both British and North American broadleaf trees to see whether natural feeding deterrents (e.g., tannins) play a part.

Damage to lodgepole pine by red squirrels (*T. hudsonicus*) in Canada is well documented (Sullivan and Sullivan, 1982*b*; Brockley and Elmes, 1987; Sullivan and Vyse, 1987). Some success in reducing the amount of bark stripping by red squirrels has been achieved in British Columbia using supplementary or diversionary feeding. Sullivan and Klenner (1993) observed significantly less damage (11.3%) by *T. hudsonicus* in a plantation to which sunflower seeds (*Helianthus annuus*) were (manually) applied compared to an untreated control stand (57.5%). Replications of this exercise in three other areas proved equally successful in reducing damage, suggesting that damage occurs in these situations because of insufficient food supplies. However, feeding per se is not perceived to be the factor initiating damage in Britain (Kenward 1983; Gurnell 1987; Gurnell and Pepper, 1988). Supplementary feeding in Britain is used as a conservation tactic to maintain *S. vulgaris* populations (Gurnell and Pepper, 1993), but it may increase tree damage caused by gray squirrels. For example, if food hoppers containing poison are placed in DV woodland, they can attract gray squirrels which results in increased local damage. In fact it is better to place hoppers in PHD woodland wherever possible. Thus, the use of diversionary food in DV plantations in Britain is not advocated.

In the autumn of 1993 a postal survey of squirrel damage in North America was initiated by the Forestry Commission (Gill and Dagnall, in litt). Questionnaires were sent to regional offices of the American forest services (USDA, US Fish and Wildlife Service).

Many of the returns were negative; that is, bark-stripping did not occur in those areas, confirming the absence of this behavior in most areas of North America. The positive returns (19 out of 41 completed questionnaires) showed most damage involved *S. carolinensis,* but four other species of tree squirrel were also mentioned: *S. niger, S. griseus, T. hudsonicus and T. douglasii.* Fourteen positive returns described the damage as rare, occasional or very variable (serious in some years and places but not others). In only five cases was damage described as frequent (annual occurrence); two cases concerned *S. carolinensis* and one each concerned *S. griseus*, *S. niger* and *T. hudsonicus*. In 14 cases, the damage had been observed either in plantations or urban "parks," but a small number (seven) indicated damage had also occurred on naturally-regenerated trees. Six respondents replied that damage was serious enough to justify controlling squirrels, and interestingly, four out of the six had observed the damage in plantation forests. The species implicated in the four plantation forests were *S. carolinensis* with *T. hudsonicus*, *S. griseus* with *T. hudsonicus*, *S. carolinensis* and *T. hudsonicus*. Both the natural forests involved *S. carolinensis*.

The occurrence of damage in managed forests reinforced the idea that some aspects of intensive forestry lead to high levels of damage. However, this is contradicted by observations of damage in naturally regenerated stands. Damage to trees in urban "parks" may result from a combination of high densities of squirrels (because of year round abundance of natural and artificial foods) well spaced and managed trees. Further investigation into cases of bark-stripping in the USA, particularly those involving *S. carolinensis*, are necessary.

CONCLUSIONS

Because wounds of trees heal in time, the effects of damage accumulation by squirrels are not revealed until felling. Consequently, the damage caused to trees in Britain before intensive poison control of gray squirrels started in 1973 may not be revealed for many years. Currently most public forests control gray squirrels each year and the risk of severe damage is high if controls are stopped (Gurnell, 1989). Thus gray squirrels are and will remain a major pest species to forestry in Britain. Moreover, together with deer and rabbits, gray squirrels seriously threaten the establishment of new woodland (Gill et al., 1995). The control of gray squirrels in public-owned and private forests is achieved almost entirely by using warfarin poison. However, the widespread use of warfarin may become generally unacceptable, and alternative ways of controlling squirrels or reducing the vulnerability of trees to damage require further research as a matter of urgency.

LITERATURE CITED

ALDHOUS, J. R. 1981. Beech in Wessex - a perspective on present health and silviculture. Forestry, 54:197-210.

BORRECCO, J. E. 1976. Controlling damage by forest rodents through habitat manipulation. Pp. 203-210, *in* Proceedings of the 7th Vertebrate Pest Conference (C. C. Siebe, ed.). University of California, Santa Cruz, 323 pp.

BOWERMANN, A. M., AND J. E. BROOKS. 1971. Evaluation of U-5897 as a male chemosterilant for rat control. The Journal of Wildlife Management, 35:618-624.

BROCKLEY, R. P., AND E. ELMES. 1987. Barking damage by red squirrels in juvenile-spaced lodgepole pine stands in south- central British Columbia. Forestry Chronicle, 63:28-31.

DAVIS, D. E. 1961. Principles for population control by gametocides. Transactions of the North American Wildlife and Natural Resources Conference, 26:160-167.

DUTTON, J. C. F. 1993. Gray squirrel control in Britain - Part 2. Forestry and British Timber, 22:31-35.

EVANS, J. 1984. Silviculture of broadleaved woodland. Forestry Commission Bulletin 62, H e r Majesty's Stationary Office, London, 232 pp.

FARENTINOS, R. C., R. J. CAPRETTA, R. E. KEPNER, AND V. M. LITTLEFIELD. 1981. Selective herbivory in tassel-eared squirrels: role of monoterpenes in ponderosa pines chosen as feeding trees. Science, 231:1273-1275.

FITZGIBBON, C. D. 1993. The distribution of gray squirrel dreys in farm woodland: the influence of wood area, isolation and management. Journal of Applied Ecology, 30:736-742.

GAUD, W. S., W. S. ALLRED AND J. S. STATES. 1993. Tree selection by tassel-eared squirrels of the Ponderosa pine forests of the Colorado Plateau. Pp. 56-63, *in* Proceedings of the First Biennial Conference on Research in Colorado Plateau National Parks (R.G. Rowlands, C. van Ripper III and M. K. Sogge, eds.). United States Department of the Interior National Park Service, Denver, Colorado. 250 pp.

GILL, R. M. A. 1992. A review of damage by mammals in north temperate forests. 2. Small mammals. Forestry, 65:281-308.

GILL, R. M. A., J. GURNELL, AND R. C. TROUT. 1995. Do woodland mammals threaten the development of new woods? Pp. 201-224, *in* The ecology of woodland creation (R. Ferris-Kaan, ed.). John Wiley & Sons, Chichester, Britain, 244 pp.

GURNELL, J. 1983. Squirrel numbers and the abundance of tree seeds. Mammal Review, 13:133-148.

———. 1987. The natural history of squirrels. Christopher Helm, London, 201 pp.

———. 1989. Demographic implications for the control of gray squirrels. Pp. 131-143, *in* Mammals as Pests (R. J. Putman, ed.). Chapman and Hall, Inc., London, 271 pp.

———. 1993. Tree seed production and food conditions for rodents in an oak wood in southern England. Forestry, 66:291-315.

———. 1996. The effects of food availability and winter weather on the dynamics of a grey squirrel population in southern England. Journal of Applied Ecology, 3:325-338.

GURNELL, J., AND H. W. PEPPER. 1988. Perspectives on the management of red and gray squirrels. Pp. 92-109, *in* Wildlife management in forests (D. C. Jardine, ed.). Institute of Cartered Foresters, Edinburgh, 123 pp.

———. 1993. A critical look at conserving the British Red Squirrel *Sciurus vulgaris*. Mammal Review, 23(3/4):127-137.

HAMPSHIRE, R. J. 1985. A study on the social and reproductive behaviour of caprive grey squirrels (*Sciurus carolinensis*). Ph.D. thesis, University of Reading, England, 235 pp.

HAMPSHIRE, R., E. JOHNSON, AND A. J. TAIT. 1983. Prospects for the chemicalcontrol of reproduction in the gray squirrel. Mammal Review, 13:167-172.

KENDLE, K. E., A. LAZARUS, F. P. ROWE, J. M. TELFORD, AND D. K.VALLANCE. 1973. Sterilization of rodent and other pests using a synthetic oestrogen. Nature, 244:105-108.

KENWARD, R. E. 1983. The causes of damage by red and gray squirrels. Mammal R e - view, 13:159-166.

———. 1989. Bark-stripping by gray squirrels in Britain and North America: why does the damage differ? Pp. 144-154, *in* Mammals as pests (R. J. Putman, ed.). Chapman and Hall, Inc., London, 271 pp.

KENWARD, R. E., AND T. PARISH. 1986. Bark-stripping by gray squirrels (*Sciurus carolinensis*). Journal of Zoology, (London), 210:473-481.

KENWARD, R. E., T. PARISH, AND P. A. ROBERTSON. 1992. Are tree species mixtures too good for gray squirrels? Pp. 243-253, *in* The ecology of mixed species stands of trees (M. G. R. Cannell, D. C. Malcolm, and P. A. Robertson, eds.). Special Publication Series of the British Ecological Society, 11. Blackwell Scientific Publications, Oxford, United Kingdom, 312 pp.

KENWARD, R. E., T. PARISH, J. HOLM, AND E. H. M. HARRIS. 1988. Gray squirrel bark-stripping I: The roles of tree quality, squirrel learning and food abundance. Quarterly Journal of Forestry, 82:9-20.

KENWARD, R. E., T. PARISH, AND F. DOYLE. 1988. Gray squirrel bark-stripping II: Management of woodland habitats. Quarterly Journal of Forestry, 82:87-94.

LLOYD, H. G. 1983. Past and present distribution of red and gray squirrels. Mammal Review, 13:69-80.

MACKINNON, K. 1976. Home range, feeding ecology and social behaviour of the gray squirrel (*Sciurus carolinensis* Gmelin). Ph.D. thesis, University of Oxford, Britain, 180 pp.

MELVILLE, R. C. 1979. Assessment of the importance and extent of gray squirrel and *Glis glis* damage within the Chiltern Forest area. Unpublished Forestry Commission report. Forest Research Station, Alice Holt Lodge, Farnham, Surrey, Britain, 3 pp.

———. 1980. Gray squirrel damage in central Scotland. Unpublished Forestry Commission report. Forest Research Station, Alice Holt Lodge, Farnham, Surrey, Britain, 5 pp.

MELVILLE, R. C., L. A. TEE, AND K. RENNOLLS, (1983) Assessment of wildlife damage in forests. Forestry Commission Leaflet No. 82. Her Majesty's Stationary Office, London, 19 pp.

MIDDLETON, A. D. 1930. The ecology of the American gray squirrel in the British Isles. Proceedings of the Zoological Society of London, 1930:809-843.

MIDDLETON, A. D. 1931. The grey squirrel. Sidgwick and Jackson, Ltd., London, 107 pp.

PEDERSON, J. C., AND B. L. WELCH, 1987. Comparison of Ponderosa pines as feed and nonfeed trees for Abert squirrels. Journal of Chemical Ecology, 11:149-157.

PEPPER, H. W. 1973. Assessment of the extent of gray squirrel damage to hardwood plantations using the sample plot method. Unpublished Forestry Commission report. Forest Research Station, Alice Holt Lodge, Farnham, Surrey, Britain, 5 pp.

———. 1975. Report on a visit to Halwill forest, 13 May 1975. Unpublished Forestry Commission report. Forest Research Station, Alice Holt Lodge, Farnham, Surrey, Britain, 3 pp.

———. 1989. Hopper modification for grey squirrel control. Forestry Commission Research Information Note no.153. Forestry Commission, Edinburgh, 4 pp.

PEPPER, H. W., AND D. STOCKER. 1993. Grey squirrel control using modified hoppers. Forestry Authority Research Information Note no. 232. Forestry Commission, Edinburgh, 4 pp.

PETAMEDES, G. S. 1983. A study of bark-stripping by grey squirrels in Dalmeny estate (centralScotland). M.Phil. thesis, University of Edinburgh, Scotland, 120pp.

ROUSI, M. 1983. Vole damage in tree species trials in northern Finland in the winter of 1981/82. Folia Forestalia, 569:1-11.

ROWE, J. J. 1975. Comparative toxicity of 3 anticoagulants to grey squirrels, *Sciurus carolinensis* (Gmelin). Unpublished Forestry Commission report. Forest Research Station, Alice Holt Lodge, Farnham, Surrey, Britain, 7 pp.

———. 1978. Comparison of grey squirrel damage to beech in mixtures and pure crops - February 1978. Unpublished Forestry Commission report. Forest Research Station, Alice Holt Lodge, Farnham, Surrey, Britain, 3 pp.

———. 1980. Grey squirrel control. Forestry Commission leaflet no. 56, 2nd ed., Her Majesty's Stationary Office, London, 17 pp.

———. 1984. Grey squirrel bark-stripping damage to broadleaved trees in southern Britain up to 1983. Quarterly Journal of Forestry, 78:231-236.

ROWE, J. J., AND R. M. A. GILL. 1985. The susceptibility of tree species to bark-stripping damage by grey squirrels (Sciurus carolinensis) in England and Wales. Quarterly Journal of Forestry, 79:183-190.

SHORTEN, M. 1957. Damage caused by squirrels in Forestry Commission areas, 1954-1956. Forestry, 30:151-172.

SULLIVAN, T. P., AND D. S. SULLIVAN. 1982. Influence of fertilisation on feeding attacks to lodgepole pine by snowshoe hares and red squirrels. Forestry Chronicle, 58:263-266.

SULLIVAN, T. P., AND R. A. MOSES. 1986. Red squirrel populations in natural and managed stands of lodgepole pine. The Journal of Wildlife Management, 50:595-601.

SULLIVAN, T. P., AND A. VYSE. 1987. Impact of red squirrel feeding damage on spaced stands of lodgepole pine in the Cariboo Region of British Columbia. Canadian Journal of Forest Research, 17:666-674.

SULLIVAN, T. P., AND W. KLENNER. 1993. Influence of diversionary food on red squirrel populations and damage to crop trees in young lodgepole pine forest. Ecological Applications, 3:708-718.

SULLIVAN, T. P., J. A. KREBS, AND P. K. DIGGLE. 1994. Prediction of stand susceptibility to feeding damage by red squirrels in young lodgepole pine. Canadian Journal of Forest Research, 24:14-20.

TAYLOR, J. C. 1966. Home range and agonistic behaviour in the gray squirrel. Symposium of the Zoological Society of London, 18:229-235.

———. 1969. Social structure and behaviour in a gray squirrel population. Ph.D. thesis, University of London, England, 212 pp.

TEE, L. A., AND J. J. ROWE. 1985. An appraisal of revenue loss from conifer thinnings due to gray squirrel (*Sciurus carolinensis*) bark-stripping damage. Quarterly Journal of Forestry, 79:27-28.

WÄSTERLUND, I. 1985. The strength of bark on Scots pine and Norway spruce trees. Swedish University of Agricultural Sciences, Report No. 167, Garpenberg, 100 pp.

THE GRAY SQUIRREL (*SCIURUS CAROLINENSIS* GMELIN) IN ITALY: A POTENTIAL PROBLEM FOR THE ENTIRE EUROPEAN CONTINENT

ITALO CURRADO

Dipartimento di Entomologia e Zoologia applicate all'Ambiente 'Carlo Vidano', via Giuria 15, 10126 Torino, Italy

ABSTRACT.—Two pairs of gray squirrels (*Sciurus carolinensis* Gmelin) were introduced near Turin (northwestern Italy) in 1948. Since then, they have increased their numbers and expanded their range, so that gray squirrels now occupy an area of about 250 km² and have almost completely replaced the native red squirrels (*Sciurus vulgaris*). Another small population is present in the park of Nervi, near Genoa, that originated from five specimens introduced in 1966. Frequent damage due to bark-stripping of trees indicates that the gray squirrel is a serious pest in wood plantations, especially of poplars. However, *Corylus avellana* crops also are in danger, because they are grown in a hilly region very close to the range of the gray squirrel. Other damage is caused by the gray squirrel feeding on cereal crops and fruit trees. Interaction with the local edible dormouse (*Myoxus glis*), which is often a pest for hazel, is still unknown. The two Italian gray squirrel populations represent the first successful introductions on the continent of Europe. In a similar way to that in Great Britain, the expansion of the gray squirrel, also facilitated by man, may in future involve all northern Italy and eventually the whole European continent. Research on the rate of range expansion of this rodent in Italy is in progress. In this paper I discuss control and removal strategies, the legal status of the rodent, and the difficulties of persuading people and the local authorities that gray squirrels must be removed.

INTRODUCTION

In 1948 two pairs of gray squirrels (*Sciurus carolinensis* Gmelin) from Washington D.C., were deliberately introduced into the Royal Park of the Castle of Stupinigi, southwest of Turin. Since then the species quickly colonized the deciduous woods of the park and then spread more slowly into the surrounding plain, causing severe damages to plantations and cereal crops (Currado et al., 1987; Currado and Scaramozzino, 1989). Gray squirrels presently occupy an area of about 250 km².

A second Italian population of gray squirrels is found near Genoa, where five specimens from Norfolk (Virginia, U.S.A.) were released in 1966 in the park of Villa Grimaldi at Genova Nervi (Capocaccia Orsini and Doria, 1991).

STUDY AREA AND SURVEY METHODS

Research was initiated in 1983. Periodic surveys have been conducted in the plain surrounding Stupinigi, in the provinces of Torino and Cuneo by searching for squirrels, dreys and damages to trees and cereal crops, and interviewing local residents and hunters, to establish the area colonized, the kind of habitat used, and the rate of range expansion of the gray squirrel. A similar investigation was conducted around Genoa during 1993 and 1994.

DISTRIBUTION OF GRAY SQUIRRELS

The area occupied by the gray squirrel in Piedmont (northwestern Italy) is located South of Turin and is mainly flat, with an elevation ranging from 230 to 260 m (Fig. 1). The 900 ha park of Stupinigi includes 470 ha of mixed woods (mostly *Quercus robur*) with a thick shrub layer (mostly hazel). The wood is fragmented by commercial poplar plantations (180 ha), and adjacent meadows, and fields of maize and wheat. The surrounding plain, interrupted by many canals and rivers, is well cultivated, mostly with cereals and poplars. There are

In M.A. Steele, J. F. Merritt, and D. A. Zegers (eds.). 1998. Ecology and Evolutionary Biology of Tree Squirrels. Special Publication, Virginia Museum of Natural History, 6: 320 pp

a few small natural woods of *Quercus robur*, *Carpinus betulus*, *Alnus glutinosa*, *Robinia pseudacacia*, and *Acer campestre*, generally located along water courses, and thickets distributed throughout the cultivated area.

The park of Racconigi is the farthest point from the release site (over 20 km) where the gray squirrel has been found to date. This site is completely enclosed by a wall; it is a former royal residence of 170 ha, of which 70 ha are comprised of old mixed wood (chiefly 150 years old *Q. robur*), and 80 ha of meadows and clearings (Palenzona et al., 1993). The area occupied by gray squirrels, surrounding the park, is similar to the rest of the remainder of the plain described above. As reviewed elsewhere (Currado et al., 1987; Currado, 1993), bark-stripping of mostly poplars, was reported near to woods, as well as the removal of seeds and ears of maize, and damage to wheat and barley.

The native red squirrels (*Sciurus vulgaris*) have disappeared from a large portion of the area now occupied by the gray squirrel and is present only in the zones of more recent colonization. In the parks of Stupinigi and Racconigi the population density of the gray squirrel appears high (1 individual/2 ha; L. Wauters, pers. comm.). In the re-

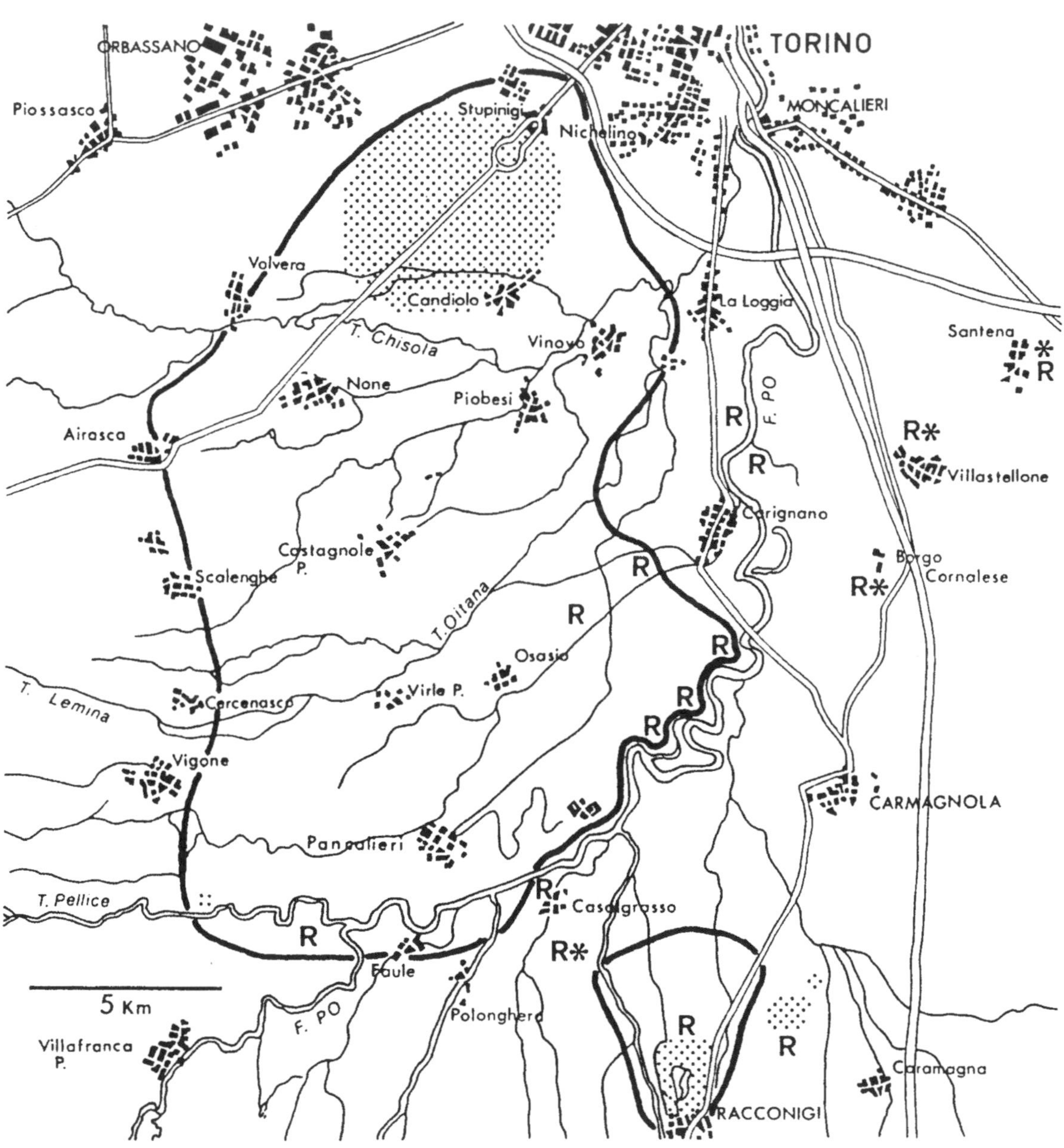

Fig. 1. Distribution of *Sciurus carolinensis* in Northwestern Italy. Solid line delineates area occupied by the gray squirrel in Piedmont by 1994; dotted areas indicate woods, asterisks show private parks, and R = presence of red squirrels.

maining part of the investigated area, the density of gray squirrels appears very low, similar to that of the red squirrels in the areas where it is still found; although this density is not easy to quantify, because of the extremely fragmented habitat.

In Liguria, the park of Villa Groppallo, at Genova Nervi (10 ha, comprised mostly of exotic plants), has a large number of gray squirrels, which rarely cause damage to the plants and is abundantly foraged by the visitors. Even if this park is closed between the sea and the city, it is next to other gardens, thanks to which the gray squirrel has spread eastwards along the coast for 2 km until the village of Bogliasco.

DISCUSSION

It is evident that in Piedmont gray squirrels have spread more rapidly from the release site (Candiolo) southwards (Fig. 1). Their expansion northwards has so far been blocked by the city, and with respect to the latest data published (Currado, 1993), the colonized area to the south is at present 50 km² larger than that in the north.

The zone occupied by gray squirrels around the park of Racconigi does not seem to be linked to the rest of the occupied area; in fact, there are some parks and woods between both areas where the species is absent. This suggests that gray squirrels were introduced into this park some years ago, although it has been known to cross several kilometers of open countryside (Gurnell and Pepper, 1991).

There have been many examples of captures and translocations of gray squirrels in past years and some have been kept as pets. In 1991, five individuals were captured by farmers and were released in a park area in the outskirts of Turin. They remained there for at least two years before disappearing. In the late 1980s, the authorities of Rome bought several gray squirrels from the authorities of Genoa, and introduced them into the park of Villa Celimontana. Some specimens remained in the park until 1993, but they have now disappeared. Many individuals are believed to have been killed by feral house cats, which are very numerous in this area (Amori, 1993 and pers. comm.).

In Liguria, the area occupied by gray squirrels near Genoa has not increased in the last decade, probably because of the less suitable habitat in this region.

Due to the localized nature of damage to trees and crops by gray squirrels in Italy (Currado et al., 1987), the problem has not yet caused concern to local farmers, authorities or the general public. However, this may change as gray squirrels continue to expand their range as they have in Great Britain (Gurnell and Pepper, 1993; Kenward and Holm, 1993) where they are now serious pests to the timber industry and have replaced the native red squirrel.

The bark-stripping of poplars, cultivated for pulpwood and softwood in Italy, is a particular problem. Commercial plantations of Euro-American hybrids, that reach maturity in only 10-14 years, spread throughout the Italian northern plains (80,000 ha; Currado, 1993). These trees produce a thick cambium and are particularly sought after by gray squirrels, which strip trunks and branches in the months of May, June, and July. Wounds often result in girdling of the trunk so that the top of the tree dies and is blown out by the wind.

Further expansion of gray squirrels also would have consequences for the hazelnut crops in the southern Piedmont (7,000 ha), grown on a hilly zone between 250 and 700 m elevation, often in mixed woods. The gray squirrel eats hazelnuts, particularly before they are ripe (Gurnell and Pepper, 1993; Kenward and Holm, 1993). The damage to the crop by squirrels would add to that of the dormouse (*Myoxus glis*), which currently causes a loss of annual yield of 15% (Currado and Scaramozzino, 1990).

The high probability that gray squirrels will spread throughout Italy and other portions of the European continent, both naturally and with the help of humans, makes a removal campaign particularly urgent. At the First European Squirrel Workshop (September 1992) a resolution was written to recommend to the European Community, the Italian Government, and the local governments an immediate action to control and eradicate this species.

In 1993, copies of the resolution were sent to the appropriate ministries and local governments. There are, however, some legal and administrative problems. The recent law 157/92 'Norme per la protezione della fauna selvatica omeoterma e per il prelievo venatorio' (Rules for the protection of wild, warm-blooded fauna and for hunting practices) protects all species of mammals living in Italy, including gray squirrels, even though their introduction was illegal. However, with the approval of the National Institute for Wild Fauna, article 19 enables the local government to control the populations of wild species for the protection of agricultural and forest produce. In addition, article 26 foresees a compensation for damages caused by wild animals to agricultural crops. It therefore appears that control of gray squirrels is lawful. The financing of the control campaign, however, remains a problem.

It will also be necessary to explain to the citizens in general, that gray squirrels in fact exist in Italy, and that they will replace the native red squirrels in the greater part of Italy and other portions of the European continent if they are not immediately removed. The only legal measure currently possible is to prohibit the translocation of gray squirrels within Italy. This should be the first step towards controlling the problem of gray squirrels in Italy.

ACKNOWLEDGMENTS

I thank Giovanni Amori, John Gurnell, Robert Kenward, Harry Pepper, and Luc Wauters for the information, suggestions, and help I received to undertake the removal campaign, Peter John Mazzoglio for the preparation of the English text, and two referees for revising the paper. The research was supported by MURST Scientific Research (60%).

LITERATURE CITED

AMORI, G. 1993. Italian insectivores and rodents: extinctions and current status. Supplemento alle Ricerche di Biologia della Selvaggina, XXI:115-134.

CAPOCACCIA ORSINI, L., AND G. DORIA. 1991. L'utile, il dilettevole, il clandestino: la fauna europea si trasforma. Pp. 33-64, *in* 1492-1992: Animali e Piante dalle Americhe all'Europa (L. Capocaccia Orsini, G. Doria, and G. Doria, eds.). SAGEP Editrice, Genova, 326 pp.

CURRADO, I. 1993. Lo scoiattolo grigio americano (*Sciurus carolinensis* Gmelin), nuovo nemico per l'arboricoltura da legno in Italia (Rodentia: Sciuridae). Pp. 85-94, *in* Arboricoltura da legno e politiche comunitarie, Tempio Pausania, 22-23 giugno 1993 (S. Dettori and M.R. Filigheddu, eds.). Chiarella, Sassari, 342 pp.

CURRADO I., AND P. L. SCARAMOZZINO. 1989. Pet or pest? Piemonte Parchi, 27, Anno IV:21-23.

———. 1990. Modificazioni ambientali e danni da roditori arboricoli in Piemonte. Pp. 254-258, *in* Atti del VI Convegno Nazionale dell'Associazione Alessandro Ghigi per la biologia dei Vertebrati, Torino, 22-24 giugno 1989 (G. Malacarne, L. Levi, and A. Casale, eds.). Museo Regionale di Scienze Naturali, Torino, 367 pp.

CURRADO, I., P. L. SCARAMOZZINO, AND G. BRUSSINO. 1987. Note sulla presenza dello scoiattolo grigio (*Sciurus carolinensis* Gmelin, 1788) in Piemonte (Rodentia: Sciuridae). Annali della Facoltà di Scienze Agrarie della Università degli Studi di Torino, 14:307-331.

GURNELL, J., AND H. W. PEPPER. 1991. Conserving the red squirrel. Forestry Commission Research Information Note 205, Forestry Commission, Edinburgh, United Kingdom, 4 pp.

———. 1993. A critical look at conserving the British Red Squirrel *Sciurus vulgaris*. Mammal Review, 23:125-136.

KENWARD, R. E., AND J. L. HOLM. 1993. On the replacement of the red squirrel in Britain: a phytotoxic explanation. Proceedings of the Royal Society of London, 251:187-194.

PALENZONA, M., F. GRISONI, AND L. GRIBAUDO. 1993. Il recupero del verde storico: l'esperienza in Piemonte del Real parco di Racconigi. Piemonte Ricerca, 147/148:15-24.

AN EXPERIMENTAL RELEASE OF RED SQUIRRELS INTO CONIFER WOODLAND OCCUPIED BY GRAY SQUIRRELS IN SOUTHERN BRITAIN: IMPLICATIONS FOR RED SQUIRREL CONSERVATION

K. H. HODDER, AND KENWARD, R. E.

Institute of Terrestrial Ecology,
Furzebrook Research Station,
Wareham, Dorset,
BH20 5AS, UK

ABSTRACT.—The North American gray squirrel *(Sciurus carolinensis)* has replaced the native Eurasian red squirrel *(Sciurus vulgaris)* in most non-conifer woodland in the United Kingdom (UK). This has been partially attributed to differential feeding ability in deciduous trees. However, previous data collected in the south of the UK showed that red squirrels in conifer woodland on islands survived better than gray squirrels in similar habitat nearby. This work was designed to test whether red squirrels might have a feeding advantage over their congeners in some conifer woodlands and to investigate whether interactions between the two species might contribute to the replacement of red squirrels. Radio-tagged red squirrels were released in conifer woodland in which resident gray squirrels had been radio-tagged. The main findings were 1) that the habitat of the donor site influenced the movements of red squirrels after their release, 2) that the red squirrels may have been avoiding their congeners, and 3) that the survival of translocated red squirrels in conifer woodland was as poor as that recorded for gray squirrels in nearby conifer sites and worse than that of gray squirrels studied concurrently. Red foxes (*Vulpes vulpes*) were probably the most common immediate cause of death for both species in conifer plantations, but the ultimate cause of death may have been related to stress. These results have implications both for further release experiments and for understanding the conservation of squirrels in conifer woodland in Britain.

INTRODUCTION

The native red squirrel (*Sciurus vulgaris*) was once found throughout Britain but is now widespread only in the north; in the south it persists as small, isolated populations in conifer forests and offshore islands. The introduced gray squirrel (Sciurus carolinensis) is established throughout southern Britain and continues to expand its range in the north (Lurz and Garson, 1992; Skelcher, 1993).

The factors responsible for this replacement have yet to be fully resolved. Local epidemics caused by a parapox virus (Keymer, 1983) were associated with the decline of red squirrels in the 1940s, but there is no evidence that gray squirrels can carry or transmit the disease (Gurnell, 1987). Epidemics and local extinctions of red squirrels often preceded the arrival of gray squirrels (Shorten, 1954; Reynolds, 1985), and red and gray squirrels have been able to coexist in other areas for some years (Gurnell, 1987). Relatively conservative breeding in red squirrels could put them at a competitive disadvantage (MacKinnon, 1978), but Kenward and Holm (1993) have shown that habitat, rather than intrinsic factors can account for the demographic differences between populations of the two species.

In M.A. Steele, J. F. Merritt, and D. A. Zegers (eds.). 1998. Ecology and Evolutionary Biology of Tree Squirrels. Special Publication, Virginia Museum of Natural History, 6: 320 pp

In deciduous woods, population densities of gray squirrels correlate well with acorn crops (Gurnell 1983, 1989). Kenward and Holm (1993) showed that foraging behaviour of gray squirrels was also affected by availability of acorns. In contrast, foraging activity and demography of red squirrels correlated with the availability of hazelnuts (*Corylus avellana*). The correlation between tree seed type and red squirrels was still evident when the hazelnuts were much less abundant than acorns. The study suggested that this might be because gray squirrels, but not red squirrels, can tolerate the phytotoxins in acorns. Historical evidence also suggests that availability of tree seeds may have been important in the replacement of red by gray squirrels. The time of most rapid replacement, was a period when oak (*Quercus*) was dominant in woodland in southern Britain (Locke, 1987), and was concurrent with a 79% decline in hazel coppice (Kenward and Holm, 1993). So the replacement of red squirrels in deciduous and mixed woodlands might be explained by differences in feeding niche and competition for food.

The red squirrel is best adapted to the conifer woodlands that predominate over much of its Eurasian range (Kenward and Tonkin, 1986; Wauters and Dhont, 1989*a*, 1989*b*, 1992), and the remaining red squirrel populations in mainland Britain are in woods with a high conifer content (Lurz and Garson, 1992; Gurnell and Pepper, 1993). Kenward and Holm (1989) found that when conifer woodlands with similar cone availability were compared, population densities of the two species were similar, and Gurnell (1991*a*, 1991*b*) found similar population densities of the two species in conifer woodlands. However, Kenward and Rose (1992, 1993), found that red squirrels in Scots pines on an island in southern Britain survived better than gray squirrels in similar mainland habitat. It is possible that, in conifer forests, gray squirrels may be successful during years of good cone crops, but retreat to refuges such as oaks growing in hedges, when less food is available (Kenward and Holm, 1989; Gurnell and Pepper, 1993). In such circumstances, the speed of replacement may be controlled by the availability of refuges in relation to the area of conifer.

If conifer woodland confers an advantage to red squirrels, it may be possible to create reserves for them by habitat management (Kenward and Holm, 1989; Gurnell and Pepper, 1988, 1993), and the conifer plantation which has replaced much oak woodland in southern Britain could be used to restore the native squirrel to some of its former range.

In order to plan for the conservation of red squirrels in Britain, it is important to determine whether red squirrels have a feeding advantage in conifer woodlands and whether gray squirrels might be able to replace their congeners in conifer woodland through interference competition.

METHODS

Red squirrels were obtained for release from two sites in southern Britain (English Nature License SA:141:93). Population densities at the two donor sites were assessed by trapping to ensure that removal of individuals would not reduce populations by more than 10%. Ten squirrels were taken from a plantation of Corsican pine (*Pinus nigra*) with some Scots pine (*Pinus sylvestris*), and four from an area of Scots pine. They were released onto a peninsula on the southern coast of Britain. This site was dominated by 80 ha of mature Scots pine with small numbers of deciduous trees at the periphery, and was adjacent to a 580 ha plantation of Corsican pine. Thirteen gray squirrels were trapped and radio-tagged on the peninsula prior to the release, and an additional 19 in the Corsican pine plantation, following the dispersal of some red squirrels to this area.

Live trapping, transport, husbandry and release.—Squirrels were caught in treadle-operated single-catch traps (Tonkin, 1984; Kenward and Holm, 1993) spaced 60-80 m apart. The trap grids included between 13 and 20 traps. Traps were prebaited for 14 days with a mixture of peanuts, sunflower seeds and flaked maize. This was supplemented with hazelnuts when the traps were set. The traps were set twice for two days, giving four trap days in each session, to produce minimum density estimates. The traps were set again for one day after an interval in order to catch squirrels for removal.

The squirrels were transported in wooden nest boxes insulated with hay. These were placed in weldmesh cages (1.5 by 1.5 by 1.5-m) at the release site. Squirrels were housed separately, except for two males. Dry food (sunflower seeds, peanuts, and hazelnuts) and fresh foods (apple and carrot slices) were provided on trays. Peanuts and sunflower seeds were also given in food hoppers designed to exclude gray squirrels (Gurnell and Pepper, 1993). Fresh water was provided in bottles and shallow pans. Human disturbance was minimized and large mammals were excluded with a four-strand electric fence. The squirrels were caged for 3-6 days in an attempt to familiarise them with the surroundings and the feed hoppers, prior to release. Six additional nest boxes and 2 additional feed hoppers were provided on the peninsula. In an attempt to minimise disturbance, the cage doors were opened before light. Squirrels were released sequentially, in groups of 2-4.

Radio-tagging, tracking and analysis.—Tuned-loop radio collars built by Biotrack (Wareham, BH20 5AJ, UK) were used to tag 32 gray and the 14 red squirrels. Thermistors in the collars gave pulse rates that varied in relation to temperature. This indicated whether the squirrel was dead, active or in a drey. Standard 30-fix ranges were recorded for three red and 16 gray squirrels (Kenward, 1987; Holm, 1990; Kenward and Holm, 1993; Wauters et al., 1994). This included three tracking rounds in each day. These data were analysed for static and dynamic interaction (Macdonald et al., 1980) between the two species using Ranges V software (Kenward and Hodder, 1995).

Four types of range outline were used to estimate static interactions. These were: minimum convex polygons around all the locations (100% MCPs); 75% polygons produced by peeling from the harmonic mean fix (HPPs); 95% harmonic mean contours (HCs); and 85% polygons from cluster analysis (CPs). Respectively, the range outlines gave increasingly precise definition of multinuclear cores (Kenward 1987, 1992; Harris et al., 1990; White and Garrott, 1990).

An index of dynamic interaction was estimated for each pair of animals, by comparing observed and possible distances between them during each tracking round. Observed distances, were calculated from the geometric mean of distances between the pair of animals, and possible distances were calculated from the geometric mean of all possible pairs of distances between the locations of these two animals (Kenward et al., 1993).

To establish whether the spacing of red and gray squirrels was different from spacing of red squirrels alone, range overlaps and indices of dynamic interaction were compared (Mann-Whitney *U* tests; Watt, 1993) for neighboring red and gray squirrels in this study, and data on neighboring red squirrels in conifer woodland in the same season in a previous year (Kenward and Rose, 1992, 1993). The data on red squirrels alone were collected on an offshore site which was close to the release area. Neighboring animals were defined as those whose 100% MCP ranges overlapped.

Causes of death.—All red squirrel remains were retrieved and weighed within 2 days after death, except one animal which may have died five days before discovery. Five carcasses were sent to J. P. Duff at the Ministry of Agriculture Food and Fisheries Veterinary Investigation Centre for post-mortem examination. To investigate whether squirrels eaten by large mammals were likely to have been killed or scavenged after death, 13 gray squirrel carcasses (obtained from control programs) were fitted with radio collars and placed on the ground at least 250 m apart. Six were placed in the Scots pine woodland and seven in the Corsican pine plantation. Signs of scavenging were noted daily for five days and thereafter at 2-5 day intervals for 16 days.

RESULTS

Survival and movements.—Survival between initial capture and release was 100%. All the red squirrels used the nest boxes and the food provided. However, following their release, survival was poor. All of the squirrels were dead after 126 days and only four of 14 animals (28.5%) survived for more than three months after release. Seven carcasses were retrieved intact, another five had been eaten, and two radio signals were lost abruptly. One carcass was found at a fox earth, two appeared to have been cached by foxes, and collars were usually marked by teeth of large mammals.

Eight of the nine squirrels from the donor site with Corsican pine, that survived for more than one day, moved to and settled in the Corsican pine plantation. All four of the squirrels originating from Scots pine either stayed in or moved to areas of Scots pine. No mortality of gray squirrels was recorded among the individuals tagged in the Corsican pine plantation.

Scavenging rates on gray squirrel carcasses.—The experiment with radio-tagged carcasses showed that the scavengers were slow to locate the carcasses. Teeth marks on the collars indicated that the scavengers were probably red foxes (*Vulpes vulpes*) or badgers (*Meles meles*). After five days, none of the carcasses had been eaten in the Corsican plantation, and two had been scavenged in the Scots pine. Between 10 and 16 days, all but two carcasses (one at each site) were eaten.

Range structure and interactions.—As a result of dispersal from the release area and poor survival, only three red squirrels were available for detailed analysis of their spatial interactions with gray squirrels. Static interaction analysis was possible because there were 27 instances of (MCP) ranges of gray squirrels that overlapped with ranges of these three red squirrels. Comparison of range core overlaps between red and gray squirrels with those between red squirrels alone (Kenward and Rose, 1992, 1993) indicated that the overlap of the released red squirrels with gray

Table 1.—*Outcome of the initial release of 10 red squirrels originating from Corsican pine.*

ID	Survival (days)	Weight loss since capture(%)	Remains	Final habitat
AF2	37	N/A	Collar+teeth marks	Corsican
AF5	26	"	"	"
AM1	100	"	"	"
AM3	45	"	"	"
AF3	26	13	Buried carcass with puncture wounds	"
AM5	102	6	"	"
Af1	126	32	Carcass in drey	"
AM4	9	N/A	Lost signal	"
AF4	65	"	Collar	Mixed woods
AM2	1	23	Carcass in nest box	Scots

Table 2.—*Outcome of the second release of four red squirrels originating from Scots pine.*

ID	Survival (days)	Weight loss since capture(%)	Remains	Final habitat
YF6	43	23	Carcass	Scots
AF7	6	3	Carcass	"
AM6	18	N/A	Lost signal	"
YM7	6	2	Carcass	"

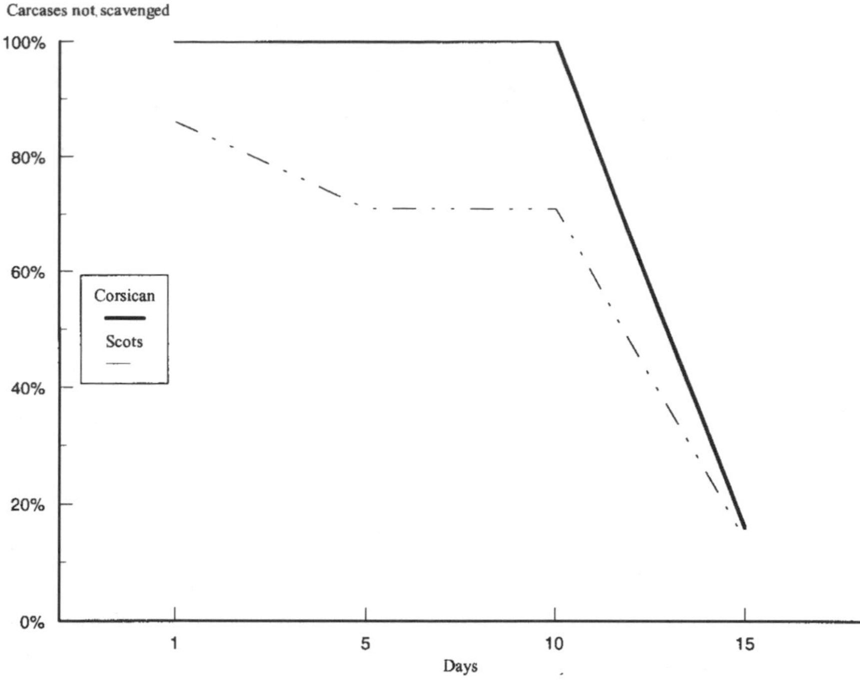

Fig. 1—Scavenging activity on radio-tagged gray squirrel carcasses.

Table 3.—*Percentage of range overlaps and dynamic interaction indices (median and range) for pairs of squirrels with overlapping ranges. Range overlaps for the two species were recorded for red squirrels released in mainland UK and resident gray squirrels. Data for range overlaps for red squirrels with conspecifics was recorded on a nearby island.* P *values are the result of Mann-Whitney* U-*test comparisons.*

	100% MCP	75% HPP	85% HC	95% CP	Dynamic interaction index
Red/Gray	9.5	4.2	0.0	4.8	0.006
(27 pairs)	(0.2 – 65.2)	(0.0 – 59.6)	(0.0 – 30.0)	(0.0 – 74.9)	(0.075 – 0.1)
Red/Red *	15.2	1.1	1.1	5.4	0.021
(21 pairs)	(0.1 – 98.7)	(0.0 – 87.8)	(0.0 – 100.0)	(0.0 – 100.0)	(0.09 – 0.35)
P	0.069	0.413	0.283	0.875	0.802

Kenward et al. (1995)

squirrels tended to be less than overlap between ranges of red squirrels alone. This was particularly clear when range cores produced by cluster analysis were used. With these range cores there was a significant difference between percentage of range overlap of female red squirrels with conspecific females and female red squirrels with female gray squirrels (P = 0.003). There was also a marked difference between range overlaps of male red squirrels with conspecific females and male red squirrels with female gray squirrels (P = 0.2).

Dynamic interactions were generally weak, only two pairs of animals in the red squirrel population had scores greater than 0.2 and none of the interactions between the two species exceeded 0.1. There were no significant differences between levels of interaction between pairs of animals in either the red squirrel population or the mixed population. Range structure was similar for all animals, in that all ranges were multinuclear.

DISCUSSION

In comparison with both red and gray squirrels studied in conifer woodland in southern Britain (Kenward and Rose, 1992, 1993), the red squirrels in this experiment showed poor survival rates. A high proportion of the translocated squirrels were eaten by mammals and the results of the experiment with carcasses of gray squirrels indicated that these squirrels were killed by predators rather than scavenged after death. The carcasses were only found after they had begun to rot; in contrast all but one of the red squirrel deaths were detected by radio-tracking within two days. The predators are likely to have been foxes rather than badgers for three reasons. First, the remains of three red squirrels were found at fox earths or in what appeared to be fox caches. Secondly, foxes were seen hunting by day in the woods concerned and thirdly, foxes have been observed using effective techniques to catch adult squirrels (A. Morris, pers. comm.). Since data from radio-tagging 29 squirrels on a predator-free island showed that these radios are normally very reliable (Kenward and Rose, 1993), we assume that the two animals for which signals were lost were also killed and their tags destroyed by the predator.

The importance of predators should be interpreted with caution because it remains uncertain whether predation was the ultimate cause of death. Post-mortem examination of five squirrels, including the two cached animals, indicated a variety of diseases, some of which may have been debilitating. Enlarged adrenals, occurred in two specimens and weight loss was recorded in all of them. It is unlikely that weight loss could have been associated directly with food supply, because gray squirrels tracked concurrently in the area survived relatively well and cone crops in both Scots and Corsican pine appeared to be good (Kenward et al., 1995). It was also noted that the two females examined post-mortem were anoestrus although both species at Poole harbour were reproductively active at the time. Adrenal hypertrophy, poor reproduction, increased susceptibility to disease and parasitism are recognized as signs of social stress in subordinate animals (Allen and Aspey, 1986). Thus, it is possible that stress may have been a contributory factor in the mortality of the translocated red squirrels. Several factors could have contributed to stress.

Reaction to captivity.—The periods of transport and captivity were brief, and 100% survival during this period indicated that the techniques were effective. A debilitating reaction to captivity was therefore probably not an important factor except in the case of the two males housed together. One male died near the cage shortly after release; its weight loss since capture and enlarged adrenals indicated that stress may have been induced during captivity. This may have been caused by close proximity to another male. We recommend that in the future, squirrels should be housed individually unless the enclosure is large. Gurnell and Pepper (1993) recommend one hectare.

Adverse weather conditions.—Following the first release, the weather conditions were ideal, however severe weather conditions may have contributed to the death of two squirrels following the second release.

Interference competition from gray squirrels.—Comparison of range overlaps suggested that the main foraging areas of the translocated red squirrels might be more separated from those of the gray squirrels than they would have been from other red squirrels. This provides some evidence that the red squirrels may have been avoiding their congeners.

Other evidence might support this suggestion. When traps were laid in the plantation, only gray squirrels were caught. As these individual red squirrels were known to be easy to trap and their ranges included the trap positions, it is possible that they are less likely to enter traps when gray squirrels are in the vicinity. Nevertheless, red squirrels were recorded using dreys built by grey squirrels on several occasions and in other work (Bertram and Moltu, 1986), and red squirrels in other studies are known to enter traps used in control of gray squirrels (S. Pritchard, pers. comm.).

This suggestion of avoidance indicates that interference competition might have been operating. This could be due to agonistic behaviour or more subtle avoidance. Agonistic behaviour was not recorded in this study but Bertram and Moltu (1986) showed that, although red squirrels could displace gray squirrels during agonistic encounters, especially at selective feeding hoppers, the majority of encounters were in favor of gray squirrels.

Our findings on post-release movements and survival have implications for future work. The dispersal and settlement patterns of the translocated red squirrels appeared to be dependent on their habitat of origin. This type of pattern has been noted in translocations of hedgehogs (*Erinaceus europaeus*) (Morris et al., 1993) and in translocations of red squirrels in Europe (Lut Somers, pers. comm.). This suggests that local adaptations may influence the habitat and foraging preferences of red squirrels. A current pilot study is designed to establish whether there are races of squirrels that are genetically adapted to their local environment (Anonymous, 1994).

Radio-tracking indicated that the red squirrels were not using the food hoppers. This may be relevant to future projects although the reasons are unknown. There may have been practical problems associated with the function of the hoppers; recent work in the UK (S. Pritchard, pers. comm.) has shown that the hoppers require modification for a number of reasons. The positive influence that supplemental feeding can have on squirrels has been documented (Sullivan, 1990; Klenner and Krebs, 1991). Thus, the development of a modified food hopper could be worthwhile because the provision of supplemental food to red squirrels may give then a competitive advantage (Gurnell and Pepper, 1993). Nevertheless, the management implications of long-term commitment to supplemental feeding should be considered.

It remains uncertain whether survival of the red squirrels was influenced by unfamiliarity with the release area. This factor could be investigated by releasing red or gray squirrels into different populations of their own species, which should have matching habitats at the donor and recipient sites. However, ethical considerations raised by the poor survival of squirrels in this experiment must be taken into account when considering future releases of red squirrels in southern Britain. The focus of research on the replacement of the native squirrel is now moving to areas where populations of the two squirrel species currently overlap. It is here that the consideration of whether red squirrels might be influenced by interference competition from their congeners could be addressed more easily, by studying their spacing behavior and interactions. This was not included in a recent list of priorities for squirrel research in Britain (Gurnell and Pepper, 1993). However, if such competition does operate it must be crucial to the success of conservation of the red squirrel, and therefore relevant to the way in which it is planned.

ACKNOWLEDGMENTS

Many thanks to British Petroleum plc., and the Rempstone Estate for permission to work in their woods, to J. Murcott, S. Walls and G. Slade for help with fieldwork, and to J. P. Duff for postmortem analyses at the Ministry of Agriculture, Food and Fisheries Veterinary Investigation Centre. We are also grateful to M. Steele and P. Garson for helpful comments on the manuscript. The study was financed by The Rutland Group, British Petroleum plc., the Natural Environment Research Council and sponsorship from Pedigree petfoods through World Wide Fund for Nature (UK) Ltd..

LITERATURE CITED

ALLEN, D. S., AND W.P. ASPEY. 1986. Determinants of social dominance in eastern gray squirrels (Sciurus carolinensis): a quantitative assessment. Animal Behaviour, 34:81-89.

ANONYMOUS, 1994. Red squirrel. English Nature: Species recovery programme newsletter, 6:7.

BERTRAN, B. C. R., AND D. P. MOLTU. 1986. Reintroducing red squirrels into Regent's Park. Mammal Review, 16:81-86.

GURNELL, J. 1983. Squirrel numbers and the abundance of tree seeds. Mammal Review, 13:133-148.

———. 1987. The natural history of squirrels. Christopher Helm, London, 201 pp.

———. 1989. Demographic implications for the control of gray squirrels. Pp.131-143, *in* Mammals as pests (R. J. Putman, ed.). Chapman and Hall, Inc., London, 271 pp.

———. 1991*a*. The red squirrel. Pp.176-186, *in* The handbook of British mammals (G. B. Corbet and S. Harris, eds.). Blackwell Scientific Publications, Oxford, United Kingdom, 588 pp.

———. 1991*b*. The grey squirrel. Pp.186-190, *in* The handbook of British mammals (G. B. Corbet and S. Harris, eds.). Blackwell Scientific Publications, Oxford, United Kingdom, 588 pp.

GURNELL, J., AND H. PEPPER. 1988. Perspectives on the management of red and grey squirrels. Pp. 92-109, *in* Wildlife management in forests (D. C. Jardine, ed.). International Conference on Forestry, Edinburgh, United Kingdom, 123 pp.

———. 1993. A critical look at conserving the British red squirrel. Mammal Review, 23:127-137.

HARRIS, S., W. J. CRESSWELL, P. G. FORDE, W. J. TREWALLA, T. WOOLLARD, AND S. WRAY. 1990. Home range analysis using radio-tracking data-a review of the problems and techniques particularly as applied to the study of mammals. Mammal Review, 20:97-123.

HOLM, J. L. 1990. The ecology of red squirrels Sciurus vulgaris in deciduous woodland. Ph.D. dissertation, University of London, 679 pp.

KENWARD, R. E. 1987. Wildlife radio tagging. Academic Press, London. 222 pp.

———. 1992. Quantity verses quality: programming for collection and analysis of radio tag data. Pp. 231-246, *in* Wildlife telemetry: remote monitoring and tracking of animals. (I. G. Priede, AND S. M. Swift, eds.). Ellis Horwood, Chichester, 708 pp.

KENWARD, R. E., AND K. H. HODDER. 1995. What's new in ranges? The ranges V 1.00 pre-release guide. Institute of Terrestrial Ecology, Furzebrook, United Kingdom, 40 pp.

KENWARD, R. E., K. H. HODDER, AND R. J. ROSE. 1995. Conservation of red squirrels. Final Report to the World Wide Fund for Nature, British Petroleum Exploration Plc. and The Rutland Group of Companies. Furzebrook Research Station, Institute of Terrestrial Ecology, Wareham, Dorset, United Kingdom, 31 pp.

KENWARD, R. E., AND J. L. HOLM. 1989. What future for British red squirrels? Biological Journal of the Linnean Society, 38:83-89.

———. 1993. On the replacement of red squirrels: a phytotoxic explanation. Proceedings of the Royal Society, Series B, 251:187-194.

KENWARD, R. E., M. MARCSTROM, AND V. KARLBLOM. 1993. Post-nestling behaviour in the goshawk, Accipiter gentilis II. Sex differences in sociality and nest switching. Animal Behaviour, 46:371-378.

KENWARD, R.E., AND R.J. ROSE. 1992. Conservation of Red Squirrels. First interim report to British Petroleum Exploration Plc. Furzebrook Research Station, Institute of Terrestrial Ecology, Wareham, Dorset, United Kingdom, 10 pp.

———. 1993. Conservation of Red Squirrels. Second annual report to British Petroleum E x - ploration Plc. Furzebrook Research Station, Institute of Terrestrial Ecology, Wareham, Dorset, United Kingdom, 11 pp.

KENWARD, R. E., AND J. M. TONKIN. 1986. Red and gray squirrels; some behavioural and morphometric differences. Journal of Zoology, 209:279-281.

KEYMER, I. F. 1983. Diseases of squirrels in Britain. Mammal Review, 13:155-158.

KLENNER, W., AND C. J. KREBS. 1991. Red squirrel population dynamics. I. The effect of supplemental food on demography. Journal of Animal Ecology, 60:961-978.

LOCKE, G. M. L. 1987. Census of woodlands 1979-81: a report on Britain's forest resources. Her Majesties' Stationary Office, London, 123 pp.

LURZ, P., AND P. GARSON. 1992. The distribution of red and gray squirrels in Northeast England in relation to available woodland habitats. British Ecological Society Bulletin, 23:133-139.

MACDONALD, D. W., F. G. BALL AND N. G. HOUGH. 1980. The evaluation of home range size and configuration using radio-tracking. Pp. 405-424, *in* A handbook on radiotelemetry and radio-tracking (C. J. Amlaner and D. W. Macdonald, eds.). Pergamon Press, Oxford, United Kingdom, 804 pp.

MACKINNON, K. 1978. Competition between red and grey squirrels. Mammal Review, 8:185-190.

MORRIS, P. A., K. MEAKIN, AND S. SHARAFI. 1993. The behaviour and survival of rehabilitated hedgehogs. Animal welfare, 2:53-66.

REYNOLDS, J. C. 1985. Details of the geographic replacement of the red squirrel (*Sciurus vulgaris*) by the gray squirrel *(Sciurus carolinensis)* in eastern England. Journal of Animal Ecology, 54:149-162.

SHORTEN, M. 1954. Squirrels. Collins (New Naturalist), London, 212 pp.

SKELCHER, G. 1993. North-West red squirrel initiative. Contract report to the "Red Squirrel Initiative." Cumbria and Lancashire Wildlife Trusts, United Kingdom, 32 pp.

SULLIVAN, T. P. 1990. Responses of red squirrel (*Tamiasciurus hudsonicus*) populations to supplemental food. Journal of Mammalogy, 71:579-590.

TONKIN, J. M. 1984. Ecology of red squirrels (*Sciurus vulgaris* L.) in mixed woodland: studies of population dynamics, activity patterns, home range, nest distribution and utilisation and food resources of red squirrels in mixed deciduous/Yew woodland in South Cumbria. Ph.D. dissertation, University of Bradford, 301 pp.

WATT, T. A. 1993. Introductory Statistics for Biology Students. Chapman and Hall, Inc., London, 185 pp.

WAUTERS, L., AND A. A. DHONDT. 1989*a*. Variation in length and body weight of the red squirrel (*Sciurus vulgaris*) in two different habitats. Journal of Zoology, (London), 217:93-106.

———. 1989*b*. Body weight, longevity and reproductive success in red squirrels (*Sciurus vulgaris*). Journal of Animal Ecology, 58:637-651.

———.1992. Spacing behaviour of red squirrels (*Sciurus vulgaris*): variation between habitat and sexes. Animal Behaviour, 43:297-311.

WAUTERS, L., P. CASALE, AND A. A. DHONDT. 1994. Space use and dispersal of red squirrels in fragmented habitats. Oikos, 69:140-146.

WHITE, G. C., AND R. A. GARROTT. 1990. Analysis of wildlife radio-tracking data. Academic Press, New York, 383 pp.

A REVISED BIBLIOGRAPHY OF THE PETAURISTINAE

JAMES H. ROBINS

Department of Biology,
Southeast Missouri State University,Cape Girardeau MO 63701

ABSTRACT.—I updated the bibliography of Lin et al. (1985) to include over seven-hundred references to the Petauristinae. The bibliography is inclusive up to early 1994, and shows that although a large amount has been published recently, the Petauristinae are an understudied group. The majority of the publications deal with the natural history and basic ecology of the group with relatively few references to Old World species. This paper is intended as a research tool for biologists interested in arboreal sciurids.

INTRODUCTION

The purpose of this paper is to update the work of Lin et al. (1985). Their review of the literature produced 166 references. This review includes more than 700 citations, primarily as a consequence of searches through secondary sources.

The Petauristinae are comprised of fourteen modern genera and are distributed throughout Asia, Europe, and North America (Wilson and Reeder, 1993). Relative to other sciurids, they are poorly studied. This bibliography should provide researchers with information on past research, and facilitate future work on this subfamily.

METHODS

Primary sources for the bibliography were scientific indexes such as Biological Abstracts and Zoological Record. Secondary sources were literature cited sections of published books and papers pertaining to the Petauristinae. References were not always complete in the original source material, so efforts were made to include complete bibliographic information.

Where possible, each reference is followed by a genus name or names referred to in the source. General references to the group are indicated with the subfamily name. Multiple species were indicated wherever possible. The indicator "gliding mammals" is used where the emphasis was on gliders as a group and in some cases may not directly relate to specific genera of the Petauristinae.

RESULTS

Three histograms concerning the characteristics of Petauristine publications are given. Figure 1 depicts the number of publications by time period. A four-fold increase in publications is apparent between 1950 and 1980.

Figure 2 shows the number of publications grouped according to subject. This information is biased by my ability to discern the subject of the publication from the title. However, the titles reveal that the majority of the information in the Evolution and Paleontology category deals with fossil locations and descriptions. This is indicative of the few papers that investigate evolutionary trends within the Petauristinae, and should be considered an area in need of research.

Figure 3 illustrates the number of publications dealing primarily with specific genera. Clearly, *Glaucomys* has received the greatest attention in the literature, followed by *Petaurista*. Most genera have not been studied extensively. The extinct category includes those genera and species indicated in the literature as extinct. The extinct genera were not dealt with individually because of discrepancies in taxonomy.

In M.A. Steele, J. F. Merritt, and D. A. Zegers (eds.). 1998. Ecology and Evolutionary Biology of Tree Squirrels. Special Publication, Virginia Museum of Natural History, 6: 320 pp

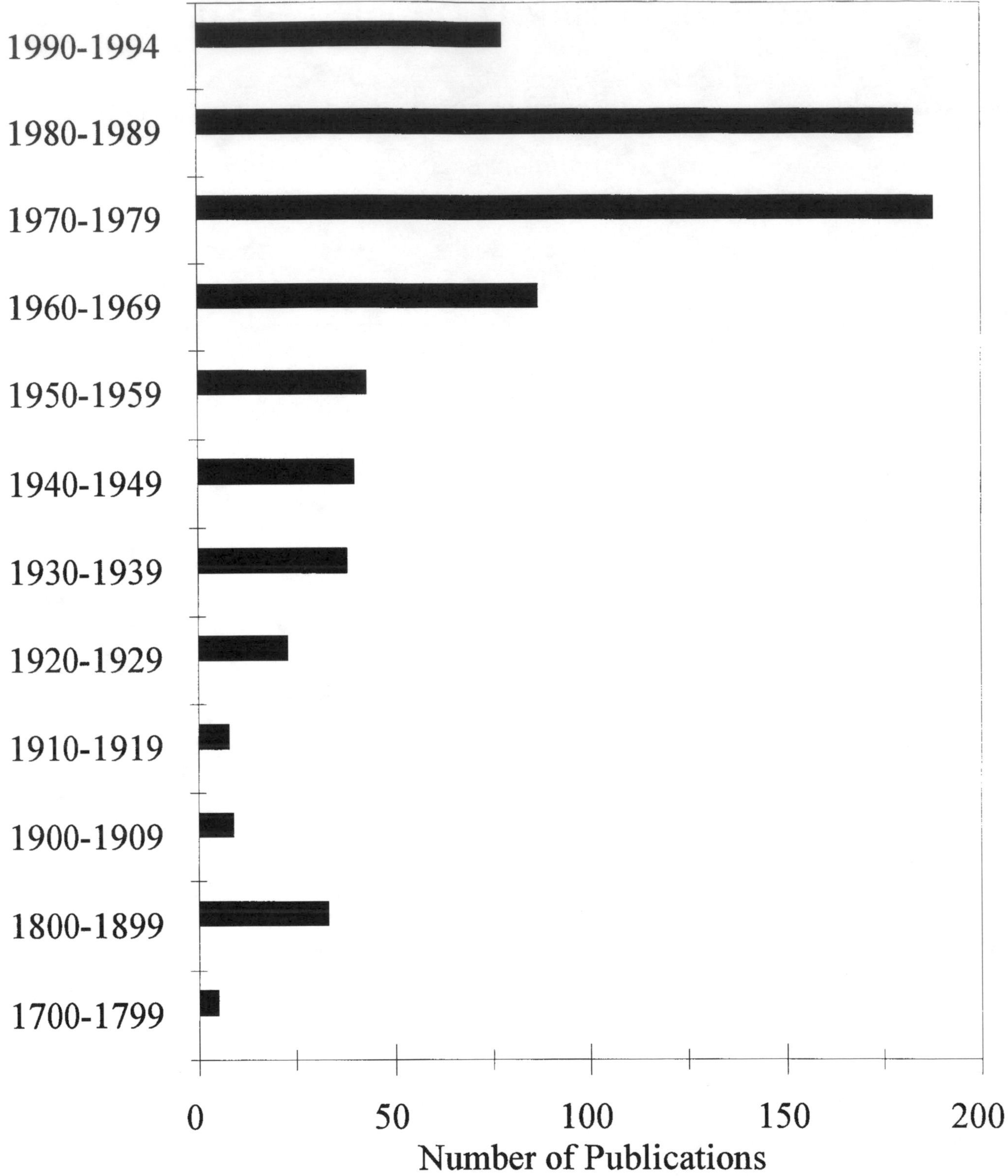

Fig. 1.—The distribution of publications that refer to the Petauristinae, arranged by yearly intervals.

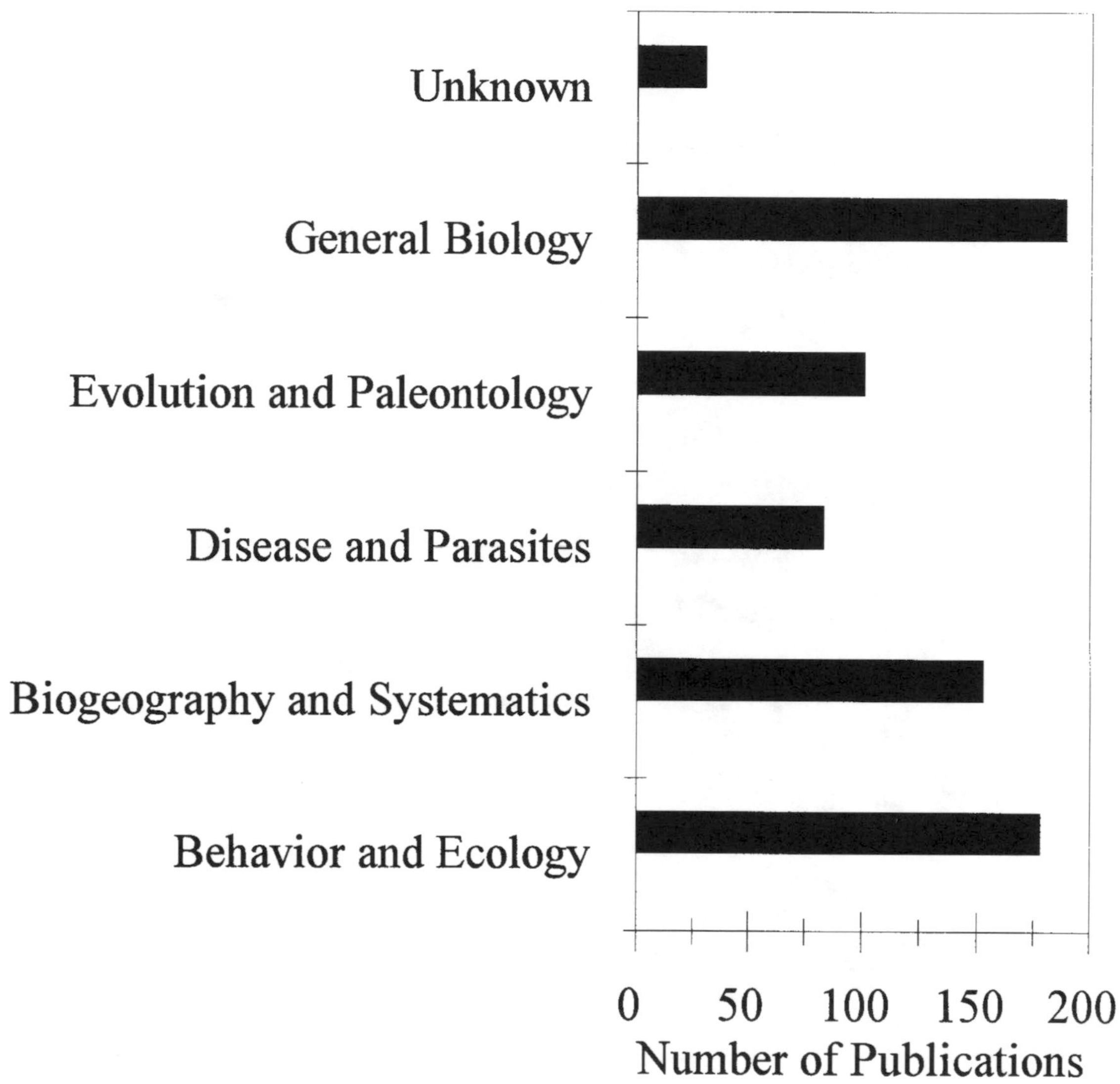

Fig. 2.—The distribution of publications that refer to the Petauristinae, arranged by subject.

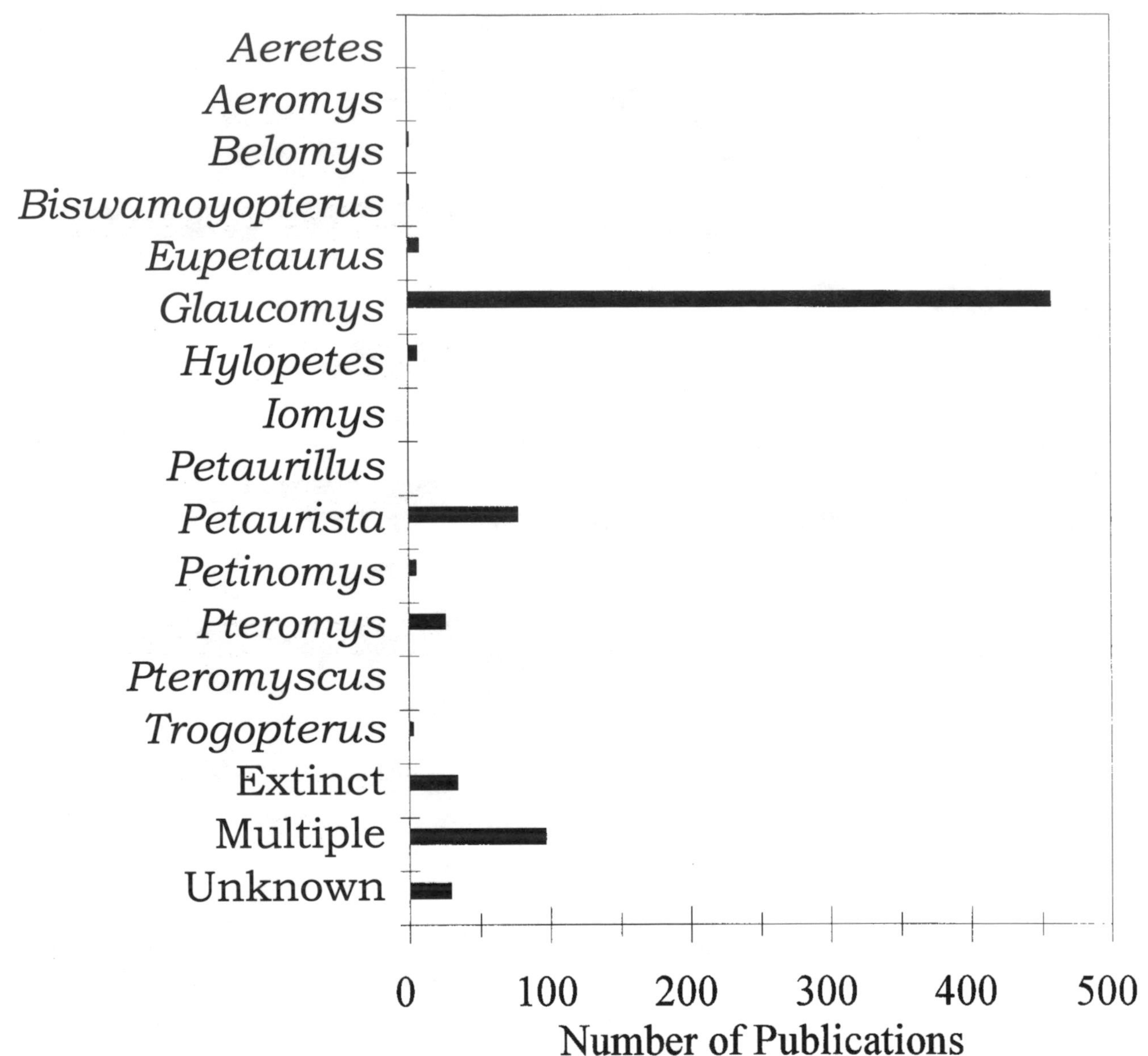

Fig. 3 —The distribution of publications that refer to the Petauristinae, arranged by genus.

BIBLIOGRAPHY

ABBOT, C. C. 1885. A Naturalist's Rambles about Home. New York, D. Appleton and Co., pp. 51-57. (*Glaucomys*)

ABE, M. T. 1989. The use of artificial nesting boxes by some mammal species. Honyurui Kagaku, 29:37-48. (in Japanese with English summary) (*Petuarista leucogenys*)

ADADJANIAN, A. K., AND K. KOWALSKI. 1978. *Prosomys insuliferus* (Kowalski, 1958) from the Pliocene of Poland and of the European part of the U. S. S. R. Acta Zoologica Cracoviensia, 23:29-54. (*Pliopetaurista)*

ADAMS, W. 1958. A flying squirrel that really flew. Malaysian Nature Journal, 13:31.

AGRAWAL, V. C. 1980. Taxonomic notes on some Oriental squirrels. Mammalia, 43:161-172. (Petauristinae)

———. 1986. Rodents—their taxonomy and distribution. Pp. 533-552, *in* Wildlife Wealth of India (T. C. Majupuria, ed.). Tecpress Service, L. P., Bangkok, xii + 656 pp. (*Hylopetes, Petaurista*)

AGRAWAL, V. C., AND S. CHAKRABORTY. 1969. Occurrence of the woolly flying squirrel, *Eupetaurus cinereus* Thomas (Mammalia: Rodentia: Sciuridae) in north Sikkim. Journal of the Bombay Natural History Society, 66:615-616.

AGUILAR, J. P., J. AGUSI, AND J. GILBERT. 1979. Rongeurs miocenes dans le-Valles-Penedes; 2, Les rongeurs de Castell de Barbera. Paleovertebrata (Montellier), 9:17-31 (*Miopetaurista*)

AGUSTI BALLESTER, J. 1978. El Vallesiense inferior de la Peninsula Iberica y su fauna de roedores. Acta Geologica Hispalense, 13:137-141. (*Miopetaurista*)

AH, H. J., J. C. PICKHAM, W. T. ATYES. 1973. *Psorergates glaucomys sp. n.* (Acari: Psorergatidae), a cytogenous mite from the southern flying squirrel (*Glaucomys v. volans*), with histopathologic notes on a mite-induced dermal cyst. Journal of Parasitology, 59:369-374.

AIRAPET'YANTS, A. E. 1963. [Ecology of the volant squirrel (*Pteromys volans*) in Leningrad Oblast.] Vestnik Leningradskogo Universiteta Seriya Biologii, 18(2/4):151-155. (in Russian with English summary)

ALLEN, G. M. 1938. The mammals of China and Mongolia. Part 2. Pp. 631-1350, *in* Natural History of Central Asia, volume 11. New York, the American Museum of Natural History, xxv + 1350 pp. (*Petaurista, Trogopterus, Aeretes*)

ALLENOV, B. V. 1979. Seasonal changes in the reaction of the Russian flying squirrel *Pteromys volans* to the environmental temperature. Zoological Zhurnal, 58:404-408.

ALLRED, D. M., AND D. E. BECK. 1966. Mites of Utah mammals. Bringham Young University Science Bulletin, Biology Series, 8:1-123. (*Glaucomys sabrinus*)

ANDERSON, R. M. 1943. Nine additions to the list of Quebec mammals with descriptions of six new forms. Annual Report of the Provancher Society of Natural History, Canada, 1942:49-62. (*Glaucomys*)

ANDO, M. 1992. [Squirrels - flying and otherwise.] Animal Zoos, 44:8-11. (in Japanese) (*Petaurista, Pteromys*)

ANDO, M., K. FUNAKOSHI, S. SHIRAISHI. 1983. Use patterns of nests by the Japanese giant flying squirrel, *Petaurista leucogenys*. Science Bulletin of the Faculty of Agriculture, Kyushu University, 38:27-43.

ANDO, M., AND Y. IMAIZAMI. 1982. Habitat utilization of the white-cheeked giant flying squirrel (*Petaurista leucogenys*) in a small shrine grove. Journal of the Mammalogical Society of Japan, 9:70-81. (in Japanese with English abstract)

ANDO, M., AND S. SHIRAISHI. 1983. The nest and nest-building behavior of the Japanese giant flying squirrel, *Petaurista leucogenys*. Science Bulletin of the Faculty of Agriculture, Kyushu University, 38:59-69. (in Japanese with English summary)

———. 1984. Relative growth and gliding adaptations in the Japanese giant flying squirrel, *Petaurista leucogenys*. Science Bulletin of the Faculty of Agriculture, Kyushu University, 39:49-57. (in Japanese with English summary)

———. 1985. Development of external characters and behaviour of the Japanese flying squirrel, *Petaurista leucogenys*. Science Bulletin of the Faculty of Agriculture, Kyushu University, 39:135-141. (in Japanese with English summary)

———. 1991. Arboreal quadrupedalism and gliding adaptations in the Japanese giant flying squirrel, *Petaurista leucogenys*. Honyurui Kagaku (Mammalian Science), 30:167-181. (in Japanese with English abstract)

———. 1993. Gliding flight in the Japanese giant flying squirrel *Petaurista leucogenys*. Journal of the Mammalogical Society of Japan, 18:19-32. (in English)

ANDO, M., S. SHIRAISHI, AND T. A. UCHIDA. 1984. Field observations of the feeding behavior in the Japanese giant flying squirrel, *Petaurista leucogenys*. Journal of the Faculty of Agriculture, Kyushu University, 28:161-175. (in Japanese with English summary)

———. 1984. Food habits of the Japanese giant flying squirrel, *Petaurista leucogenys*. Journal of the Faculty of Agriculture, Kyushu University, 29:189-202. (in English)

———. 1985. Feeding behavior of three species of squirrels. Behavior, 95:76-86. (*Petaurista*)

ASANUMA, C., AND D. TAPPER. 1978. The gliding membrane of the flying squirrel: a new proposal for study of neurophysiology and circulatory control in hairy skin. Federation Proceedings, 37:398.

ASHRAF, N. V. K., A. KUMAR, AND A. J. T. JOHNSINGH. 1993. On the relative abundance of two sympatric flying squirrels of Western Ghats, India. Journal of the Bombay Natural History Society, 90:158-162. (*Petaurista, Petinomys*)

ASKINS, R. A. 1988. Family Sciuridae. Squirrels and flying squirrels. Pp. 337-387, *in* Mammals of Thailand (B. Lekagul, and J. A. McNeely, eds.). Saha Karn Bhaet, Bangrak, Bangkok, 758 pp. (in English)

ATUNES, M. T., AND P. MEIN. 1977. Contributions a la paleontologie du Miocene moyen continental du Bassin Tage; III. Mammiferes; Povoa de Santarem, Pero Filho Choes (Secorio); Conclusions generales. Ciencia de la Tierra., 3:143-165. (*Miopetaurista*)

AUDUBON, J. J., AND J. BACHMAN. 1846. Quadrupeds of North America. George R. Lockwood, New York, 1:216-222. (*Glaucomys*)

AUSTAD, S. 1992. On the nature of aging. Natural History, 1992:25-52. (gliding mammals)

AUSTAD, S. N., AND K. E. FISCHER. 1991. Mammalian aging, metabolism, and ecology: evidence from the bats and marsupials. Journal of Gerontology, 46:47-53. (gliding mammals)

AVENOSO, A. C., JR. 1968. Selection and processing of nuts by the flying squirrel *Glaucomys volans*. Ph.D. dissertation, University of Florida, Tallahasse, 126 pp.

BABA, M. 1978. Home range and home utilization of giant flying squirrels (*Petaurista leucogenys*). M.S. thesis, Kyushu University, Fukuoka, Japan, 48 pp.

BABA, M., T. DOI, Y. ONO. 1982. Home range utilization and nocturnal activity of the giant flying squirrel, *Petaurista leucogenys*. Japanese Journal of Ecology, 32:189-198.

BACHMAN, J. 1893. The following species must be added to the list of Mr. Townsend's quadrupeds. Journal of the Academy of Natural Science, Philadelphia, 8:101-103. (*Glaucomys sabrinus*)

BACHMAYER, F., AND R. W. WILSON. 1977. A second contribution to the small mammal fauna of Kohfidisch, Austria. des Naturhistorischen Museums in Wien, Annalen, 81:121-161. (*Pliopetaurista*)

BAILEY, B. 1923. Meat-eating propensities of some rodents of Minnesota. Journal of Mammalogy, 4:129. (*Glaucomys*)

———. 1929. Mammals of Sherburne Co., Minnesota. Journal of Mammalogy, 10:153-164. (*Glaucomys sabrinus*)

BAILEY, V. 1936. The mammals and life zones of Oregon. North American Fauna, 55:1-416. (*Glaucomys sabrinus*)

BAILLIE, J. L., JR. 1930. Outside nests of flying squirrels. Canadian Field-Naturalist, 44:94. (*Glaucomys*)

BAKER, R. H. 1983. Michigan mammals. Michigan State University Press, East Lansing, 642 pp. (*Glaucomys*)

BALLANTYNE, J. 1888. Our squirrels. Ottawa Naturalist, 2:33-44. (*Glaucomys*)

BANFIELD, A. W. F. 1974. The mammals of Canada. University of Toronto Press, Toronto, 438 pp. (*Glaucomys sabrinus*)

BANGS, O. 1896. A review of the squirrels of eastern North America. Proceedings of the Biological Society of Washington, 10:145-167. (*Glaucomys volans*)

———. 1899. Descriptions of some new mammals from western North America. Proceedings of the New England Zoological Club, 1:65-72. (*Glaucomys sabrinus*)

BARBEHENN, K. R. 1978. Concluding comments: from the worm's view, "Eco-pharmodynamics" and 2000 A. D. Pp. 231-236, *in* Populations of Small Mammals Under Natural Conditions (D. P. Snyder, ed.). Special Publications Series, Pymatuning Laboratory of Ecology, Volume 5, University of Pittsburgh, Linesville, Pennsylvania, 237 pp. (*Glaucomys*)

BARKALOW, F. S. 1956. A handicapped flying squirrel, *Glaucomys volans*. Journal of Mammalogy, 37:22-23.

BARNOSKY, A. D. 1986. Arikareean, Hemingfordian, and Barstovian mammals from the Miocene Colter Formation, Jackson Hole, Teton Co., Wyoming. Bulletin of Carnegie Museum of Natural History, 26:1-69. (*Petauristodon*).

BAUDELOT, S. 1972. Etude des chiropteres, insectivores et rongeurs du Miocene de Sansan (Gers). Ph.D. dissertation, University de Toulouse, Toulouse, France. (Available from University Microfilms) (Petuaristine rodent)

BECK, L. R. 1972. Comparative observations on the morphology of the mammalian periovarial sac. Journal of Morphology, 136:247-254. (*Glaucomys sabrinus*)

BENDEL, P. R. 1985. Home range and habitat partitioning by southern flying squirrels. M.S. thesis, Frostburg State University, Frostburg, Maryland, 36 pp. (*Glaucomys volans*)

BENDEL, P. R., AND J. E. GATES. 1987. Home range and microhabitat partitioning of the southern flying squirrel. Journal of Mammalogy, 68:243-255. (*Glaucomys volans*)

BENTON, A. H., AND R. H. CERWONKA. 1960. Host relationships of some eastern Siphonaptera. The American Midland Naturalist, 63:383-391. (*Glaucomys sabrinus*)

BENTON, A. H., O. R. LARSON, AND B. A. VEN HUIZEN. 1971. Siphonaptera from Itasca State Park region. Journal of the Minnesota Academy of Science, 37:91-92. (*Glaucomys sabrinus*)

BENTON, A. H., H. H. TUCKER, JR., AND D. L. KELLEY. 1969. Sipihonaptera from northern New York. Journal of the New York Entomological Society, 77:193-198. (*Glaucomys sabrinus*)

BEQUAERT, J. C. 1945. The ticks, or Ixodoidea, of the northeastern United States and eastern Canada. Annals of the Entomological Society of America, 25:73-232. (*Glaucomys sabrinus*)

BHAT, H. R., M. A. STREENIRASAN, AND S. V. NAIK. 1979. Susceptibility of common giant flying squirrel *Petaurista petaurista philipnensis* to experimental infection with Kyasanur forest disease virus. Indian Journal of Medical Research, 69:697-700.

BLACK, C. C. 1963. A review of the North American Tertiary Sciuridae. Bulletin of the Museum of Comparative Zoology, Harvard University, 130:109-248. (*Glaucomys*)

———. 1972. Holarctic evolution and dispersal of squirrels (Rodentia: Sciuridae). Pp. 305-322, *in* Evolutionary Biology (T. Dobzhansky, M. K. Hecht, W. C. Steere, eds.). Appleton-Century-Crofts, New York, 6. (Petauristinae)

BLACK, C. C., AND K. KOWALSKI. 1974. The Pliocene and Pleistocene Sciuridae from Poland. Acta Zoologica Cracoviensia, 19:461-485. (*Pliopetaurista, Pliopetes*)

BOARDMAN, J. L. 1991. Nest site selection by southern flying squirrels (*Glaucomys volans*) in northeastern Missouri. M.S. thesis, Northeast Missouri State University, Kirksville, 67 pp.

BOISSEAU-LEBREUIL, M. T., H. LAUNAY, AND J. C. BEAUCOURNU. 1984. A diaspiromycose chez de petits mammiferes sauvages captures en Tunisie. Bulletin de la Societe de Pathologie Exotique, 77:369-376. (*Petaurista, Pteromyscus*)

BOND, B. B., AND E. C. BOVEE. 1957. A rediscription of an eimerian coccidian from the flying squirrel, *Glaucomys volans*, designating it *Eimeria parasciurorum nov. sp.* Journal of Protozoology, 4:225-229.

BOOTH, E. S. 1946. Notes on the life history of the flying squirrel. Journal of Mammalogy, 27:28-30. (*Glaucomys*)

BOU, J., A. CASINOS, AND J. OCANA. 1987. Allometry of the limb long bones of Insectivores and Rodents. Journal of Morphology, 192:113-123. (*Petinomys, Hylopetes*)

BOUWENS, P., AND H. DEBRUIJN. 1986. The flying squirrels *Hylopetes* and *Petinomys* and their fossil record. Proceedings of the Koninklijke Nederlandse Akademie van Wetschappen, Series B (Palaeontology, Geology, Physics, Chemistry), 89:113-123.

BOZEMAN, F. M., S. A. MASIELLO, M. S. WILLIAMS, AND B. L. ELISBERG. 1975. Epidemic typhus (Rickettsiae) isolated from flying squirrel. Nature, 255:545-547. (*Glaucomys*)

BOZEMAN, F. M., D. E. SONESHINE, M. S. WILLIAMS, D. P. CHADWICK, D. M. LAUER, AND B. L. ELISBERG. 1981. Experimental infection of ecto-parasitic arthropods with *Rickettsia prowazeke* GVF-16 strain and transmission to flying squirrels (*Glaucomys volans*). American Journal of Tropical Medicine and Hygiene, 30:253-263.

BOZEMAN, F. M., M. S. WILLIAMS, N. I. STOCKS, D. P. CHADWICK, B. L. ELISBERG, D. E. SONESHINE, AND D. M. LAUER. 1976. Ecological studies on epidemic typhus infection in the eastern flying squirrel. Folia Microbiology, 21:507-508. (*Glaucomys volans*)

BRACK, V. J., AND R. E. MUMFORD. 1983. Mist netting: a technique for flying squirrel capture. Indiana Audubon Quarterly, 61:80-81. (*Glaucomys volans*)

BRAUN, J. K. 1988. Systematics and biogeography of the southern flying squirrel, *Glaucomys volans*. Journal of Mammalogy, 69:422-426.

BREWSTER, W. 1937. October farm: from the Concord journals and diaries of William Brewster. Cambridge, Massacheusetts, Harvard University Press, xv + 298 pp. (*Glaucomys*)

BRICKELL, J. 1737. The natural history of North Carolina with an account of the trade, manners, and customs of Christian and Indian inhabitants. J. Carson, Dublin, xv + 408 pp. (*Glaucomys*)

BRIMLEY, C. S. 1923. Breeding habits of small mammals at Raleigh, North Carolina. Journal of Mammalogy, 4:263. (*Glaucomys*)

BRINK, C. H. 1965. Spruce seed as a food of the squirrels Tamiasciurus hudsonicus and *Glaucomys sabrinus* in interior Alaska. M.S. thesis, University of Alaska, Fairbanks, 73 pp.

BRINK, C. H., AND F. C. DEAN. 1966. Spruce seed as a food of red squirrels and flying squirrels in interior Alaska. The Journal of Wildlife Management, 30:503-512. (*Glaucomys sabrinus*)

BROWNELL, L. W. 1923. How our squirrels pass the winter. Nature Magazine, 2:289-291. (*Glaucomys*)

BRYANT, M. D. 1945. Phylogeny of Nearctic Sciuridae. The American Midland Naturalist, 33:257-390. (*Glaucomys*)

BULOT, C. 1974. Recherche de rongeurs fossiles dans les terrains miocenes de la region lectouroise. Bulletin de la Societe d'Histoire Naturelle de Toulouse, 110:245-249. (*Forsythia*)

BURT, W. H. 1940. Territorial behavior and populations of some small mammals in Southern Michigan. Miscellaneous Publications of the Museum of Zoology, University of Michigan, 45:1-58. (*Glaucomys*)

———. 1960. Bacula of North American mammals. Miscellaneous Publications of the Museum of Zoology, University of Michigan, 113:1-76. (*Glaucomys*)

CAHN, A. R. 1937. The mammals of the Quetico Provincial Park of Ontario. Journal of Mammalogy, 18:19-30. (*Glaucomys sabrinus*)

CAMERON, D. M., JR. 1976. Distribution of the southern flying squirrel (*Glaucomys volans*) in Maine. Canadian Field-Naturalist, 90:173-174.

CAPLE, G. P., R. BALDA, AND W. R. WILLIS. 1983. The physics of leaping animals and the evolution of preflight. The American Naturalist, 121:455-467. (gliding mammals)

CAREY, A. B., B. L. BISWELL, AND J. W. WITT. 1991. Methods for measuring populations of arboreal rodents. United States Forest Service General Technical Report, Pacific Northwest, 273:1-24. (*Glaucomys sabrinus*)

CAREY, A. B., AND H. R. SANDERSON. 1981. Routing to accelerate tree cavity formation. Wildlife Society Bulletin, 9:14-21. (*Glaucomys volans*)

CAREY, A. B., AND J. W. WITT. 1991. Track counts as indices to abundances of arboreal rodents. Journal of Mammalogy, 72:192-194.

CARTER, J. H., III. 1982. Flying squirrel found dead at Red-cockaded Woodpecker cavity. Chat, 46:44-45. (*Glaucomys volans*)

CARTER, T. D. 1933. A new flying squirrel of the genus *Petaurista* from northwestern Siam. American Museum Novitates, 674:1.

———. 1942. Three new mammals of the genera *Crocidura, Callosciurus,* and *Pteromys* from northern Burma. American Museum Novitates, 1208:1-2.

CASH, W. A. 1990. PVC plastic elbow attachment: a raccoon, feral cat, flying squirrel deterrent. Sialia, 12:69. (*Glaucomys volans*)

CEBALLOS, G., AND C. GALINDO. 1983. *Glaucomys volans goldmani* (Rodentia: Sciuridae) in central Mexico. The Southwestern Naturalist, 28:375-376.

CEBALLOS, G., AND A. MIRANDA. 1985. Notes on the biology of Mexican flying squirrels (*Glaucomys volans*) (Rodentia: Scuiridae). The Southwestern Naturalist, 30:449-450.

CHAKRABORTY, S., AND V. C. AGRAWAL. 1977. A melanistic example of woolly flying squirrel, *Eupetaurus cinereus* Thomas (Rodentia: Sciuridae). Journal of the Bombay Natural History Society, 74:346-347.

CHANG, W. F. 1985. Ecological study of the flying squirrel in central Taiwan. Proceedings of the Seminar on the Control of Squirrel Damage to Forest Trees, Council of Agriculture Forestry Series, 2:45-68. (in Chinese with English summary) (*Petaurista grandis*)

CHASEN, F. N. 1940. A handlist of Malaysian mammals. Bulletin of the Raffles Museum, 15:1-209. (Petauristinae)

CHATTERJI, K., AND A. MAJHI. 1975. Chromosomes of the Himalayan flying squirrel (*Petaurista magnificus*). Mammalia, 39:447-450.

CHOWATTUKUNNEL, J. T., AND J. H. ESSLINGER. 1979. A new species of *Breinlia* (Nematoda, Filariodea) from the south Indian flying squirrel (*Petaurista philippensis*). Journal of Parasitology, 65:375-378.

CHU, Y. I., AND S. T. YIE. 1970. Some biological notes on the Taiwan squirrel. Bulletin of the Chinese Plant Protection Association, 12:21-30. (in Chinese with English summary) (*Petaurista*)

COLBERT, E. H. 1935. Siwalik mammals in the American Museum of Natural History. Transactions of the American Philosophical Society, new series, vol. 26, i-x + 401 pp. (*Eupetaurus*)

COMSTOCK, A. B. 1914. The pet book. The Comstock Publishing Company, Ithaca, New York, xi + 310 pp. (*Glaucomys*)

CONNER, P. F. 1960. The small mammals of Otsego and Schoharie counties, New York. New York State Museum Science Service Bulletin, 382:1-84. (*Glaucomys*)

———. 1966. The mammals of the Tug Hill Plateau, New York. New York State Museum Science Service Bulletin, 406:1-82. (*Glaucomys sabrinus*)

———. 1971. The mammals of Long Island, New York. New York State Museum, Science Service Bulletin, 416:1-78. (*Glaucomys*)

COOPER, J. E., S. S. ROBINSON, AND J. B. FUNDERBURG, (eds.). 1977. Endangered and threatened plants and animals of North Carolina. North Carolina State Museum of Natural History, Raleigh, xvi + 444 pp. (*Glaucomys sabrinus*)

COOPER, J. G. 1860. Report upon the mammals collected on the survey. Pp. 73-139, *in* Reports of explorations and surveys, to ascertain the most practicable and economical route for a railroad from the Mississippi River to the Pacific Ocean made under the direction of the secretary of war, in 1853, May 31, 1854, and August 5, 1854. Volume 12, Book 2, Part 3:74-139. (*Glaucomys sabrinus*)

CORBET, G. B. 1978. The mammals of the Palaearctic Region: a taxonomic review. British Museum (Natural History), London, 314 pp. (Petauristinae)

CORBET, G. B., AND J. E. HILL. 1986. A world list of mammalian species. British Museum (Natural History), London, 254 pp. (Petauristinae)

COVENTRY, A. F. 1932. Notes on the Mearns flying squirrel. Canadian Field Naturalist, 46:75-79. (*Glaucomys sabrinus*)

COWAN, I. MCT. 1936. Nesting habits of the flying squirrel *Glaucomys sabrinus*. Journal of Mammalogy, 17:58-60.

———. 1937. The distribution of flying squirrels in western British Columbia with the description of a new race. Proceedings of the Biological Society of Washington, 50:77-82. (*Glaucomys sabrinus*)

———. 1942. Food habits of the Barn Owl in British Columbia. The Murrelet, 23:48-53. (*Glaucomys sabrinus*)

CROSS, J. H., J. C. LIEN, AND M. Y. HSU. 1969. *Toxoplasma isolated* from the Formosan giant flying squirrel. Journal of the Formosan Medical Association, 68:678-683. (*Petaurista grandis*)

CROWE, P. E. 1943. Notes on some mammals of the southern Canadian Rocky Mountains. Bulletin of the American Museum of Natural History, 80:391-410. (*Glaucomys sabrinus*)

CRUSAFONT-PAIRO, M., AND J. MA. GOLPE POSSE. 1972. Dos nuevos yacimientos del Vindovoniense en el Valles. Acta Geologica Hispanola, 7:71-72. (*Miopetaurista*)

CRUSAFONT-PAIRO, M., AND J. C. HARTENBERGER. 1976. Complements a la connaissance de la faune de mammifers de Can Ponsic I. gisment type du Vallesian (Espagne). Proceedings of the Congressional-Regulatory Commission of the Mediterranean Neogene Stratigraphy International Union of Geological Science, 6:81-83. International Geological Correlation Programme Project No. 25, Unesco, Paris. (*Miopetaurista*)

CRUSAFONT-PAIRO, M., AND B. KURTEN. 1976. Bears and bear-dogs from the Vallesian of the Valles-Pendes Basin, Spain. Acta Zoologica Fennica, 144:1-29. (*Miopetaurista*)

CUTLER, T. L., AND D. W. HAYES. 1991. Food habits of Northern Spotted Owls in high elevation forests of Pelican Butte, southwestern Oregon. Northwestern Naturalist, 72:66-69. (*Glaucomys sabrinus*)

CUVIER, G. 1850-1856. Anatomie Comparee Recueil de planches de myologie. Paris: Dusacq. Texte et Atlas. (Petauristinae)

DAAMS, R., AND A. VAN DE WEERD. 1980. Early Pliocene small mammals from the Aegean Island of Karpathos (Greece) and their paleogeographic significance. Geologie en Mijnbouw, 59:327-331. (*Petaurista*)

DAAN, S., AND C. S. PITTENDRIGH. 1976. A functional analysis of circadian pacemakers in nocturnal rodents: II. The variability of phase response curves. Journal of Comparative Physiology, 106:253-266. (*Glaucomys*)

DALQUEST, W. W. 1953. Mammals of the Mexican state of San Luis Potosi. Louisiana State University Studies, Biology Series, 1:1-229. (*Glaucomys volans*)

DAO, V. T., AND CAO, V. S. 1990. Six new Vietnamese rodents. Mammalia, 54:233-238. (English with French summary) (*Hylopetes*)

DASCH, G. A., J. R. SAMMS, AND E. WEIS. 1977. Biochemical properties of strains of *Rickettsia prowazekii* isolated from flying squirrels. Abstracts from the Annual Meeting of the American Society of Microbiologists, 77:72. (*Glaucomys*)

DASGUPTA, B. 1967. A new malarial parasite of the flying squirrel. Parasitology, 57:467-474. (*Petaurista*)

DASGUPTA, B., AND A. CHATTERJEE. 1969. Further observations on the malaria parasite of the Himalayan flying squirrel. Parasitology, 59:733-736. (*Petaurista*)

———. 1970. An unusual form of fertilization in the malaria parasite of the Himalayan flying squirrel. Parasitology, 60:431-433. (*Petaurista*)

DASGUPTA, B., A. CHATTERJEE, AND H. N. RAY. 1970. Comparative accounts of the merocysts seen in the Himalayan flying squirrels with a note on the identity of the parasites. Parasitology, 61:411-415. (*Petaurista*)

DAVIS, D. D. 1962. Mammals of the lowland rainforest of north Borneo. Bulletin of the Singapore National Museum, 31:1-129. (Petauristinae)

DAVIS, W. 1963. Reproductive ecology of the northern flying squirrel in Saskatchewan. M.A. thesis, University of Saskatchewan, Saskatoon, 87 pp.

DAWSON, R. M. 1987. The degree and manner of use of artificial nest boxes by the southern flying squirrel (*Glaucomys volans*) in northern Louisiana. M.S. thesis, Louisiana Technical University, Ruston, 22 pp.

DAXNER-HOECK, G. 1975. Sciuridae aus dem. Jungtertiaer von Oesterreich. Paleontologische Zeitschrift, 49(1-2):56-74. (*Miopetaurista*)

DAXNER-HOECK, G., AND P. MEIN. 1975. Taxonomische problems um das Genus *Miopetaurista* (Kretzoi 1962). Paleontologishe Zeitschrift, 49(1-2):75-77.

DAY, J. F., AND A. H. BENTON. 1980. Population dynamics and coevolution of adult Siphonapteran parasites of the southern flying squirrel, Glaucomys volans volans. The American Midland Naturalist, 103:333-338.

DAY, Y.-T., D. R. POGULSKE, P.-F. LEE, Y.-S. LIN. 1992. Morphometrical comparison on bacula of *Petaurista alborufus* and *P. Petaurista* (Rodentia: Sciuridae) from Taiwan. Acta Zoologica Taiwanica, 3:27-33. (in English)

DE BRUIJN, H., A. J. VAN DER MEULEN, AND G. C. KATSIKATSOS. 1980. The mammals from the lower Miocene of Aliveri (Island of Evia, Greece); Part 1, The Sciuridae. Proceedings of the Koninklijke Nederlandse Akademie van Wetschappen, Series B, 83:241-261. (*Miopetaurista*)

DECALESTA, D. S. 1990. Design of rodent and bird-proof exclosures. Journal of the Pennsylvania Academy of Science, 63(1-3):210. (Abstract only) (*Glaucomys*)

DECOURSEY, P. J. 1959. Daily activity rhythms in the flying squirrel, (*Glaucomys volans*). Ph.D. dissertation, University of Wisconsin, Madison, 232 pp.

———. 1960. Daily light sensitivity rhythm in a rodent. Science, 131:33-35. (*Glaucomys*)

———. 1960. Phase Control of Activity in a Rodent. Cold Springs Harbor Symposium, 25:49-55. (*Glaucomys volans*)

———. 1961. Effect of light on the circadian rhythms of the flying squirrel, *Glaucomys volans*. Zeitschrift für Vergleichende Physiologie, 44:331-354.

———. 1984. Stability and precision of circadian rhythms in nocturnal rodents. Bulletin of the South Carolina Academy of Science, 46:89. (Abstract only) (*Glaucomys volans*)

———. 1986. Light-sampling behavior in photoentrainment of a rodent circadian rhythm. Journal of Comparative Physiology, 159:161-169. (*Glaucomys*)

DECOURSEY, P. J., AND S. A. MENON. 1991. Circadian photo-entrainment in a nocturnal rodent: quantitative measurement of light-sampling activity. Animal Behaviour, 41:781-785. (*Glaucomys*)

DEHM, R. 1950. Die Nagetiere aus dem Mittel-Miocan (Burdigalium) von Wintershof-West bie Eichstatt in Bayern. Neues Jahrbuch fuer Mineralogie, Geologie und Palaeontologie, Abhandlungen, Abteilung, 91:321-428. (earliest Petauristinae fossil)

DENNIS, J. V. 1971. Species using red-cockaded woodpecker holes in northeastern South Carolina. Bird Banding, 42:79-87. (*Glaucomys*)

DESMAREST, A. -G. 1827. Sciuroptere. Pp. 138-141, *in* Dictionaire des Sciences Naturelles (F. G. Levrault, ed.). Le Normant, Paris, vol. 48, 572 pp. (*Glaucomys volans*)

DICE, L. R. 1921. Notes on the mammals of interior Alaska. Journal of Mammalogy, 2:20-28. (*Glaucomys sabrinus*)

DICE, L. R., AND H. B. SHERMAN. 1922. Notes on the mammals of Gogebic and Ontonagon counties, Michigan, 1920. Occasional Papers of the Museum of Zoology, University of Michigan, 109:1-47. (*Glaucomys sabrinus*)

DIEN, Z. -M. 1955. A brief account of the Formosan flying squirrel. Taiwan Museum Quarterly Journal, 8:203-206. (*Petaurista grandis*)

DIERSING, V. E. 1980. Systematics of flying squirrels, *Glaucomys volans* (L.), from Mexico, Guatemala, and Honduras. The Southwestern Naturalist, 25:157-172.

DOBY, W. J. 1982. Resource base as a determinant of population parameters in the southern flying squirrel, *Glaucomys volans*. Bulletin of the Ecological Society of America, 63:137. (Abstract only)

———. 1984. Resource base as a determinant of abundance in the southern flying squirrel (*Glaucomys volans*). Ph.D. dissertation, Wake Forest University, Winston-Salem, North Carolina.

DOLAN, P. G. 1975. Thermoregulation and metabolism in two subspecies of the southern flying squirrel (*Glaucomys volans*). M.S. thesis, North Carolina State University, Raleigh, 47 pp.

DOLAN, P. G., AND D. C. CARTER. 1977. Glaucomys volans. Mammalian Species, 78:1-6.

DONAHUE, J., R. STUCKENRATH, AND J. M. ADOVASIO. 1978. Meadowcroft Rockshelter. Pp. 140-180, *in* Early Man in America; from a circum-Pacific perspective (A. L. Bryan, ed.). Occasional Papers of the Department of Anthropology, University of Alberta, 1. (*Glaucomys*)

DORAN, D. J. 1955. A catalogue of the Protozoa and helminths of North American rodents. III. Nematoda. The American Midland Naturalist, 53:162-175. (*Glaucomys sabrinus*)

DORNEY, R. S. 1962. A survey of some Wisconsin Sciuridae with descriptions of three new species. Journal of Protozoology, 9:258-261. (*Glaucomys sabrinus*)

DOUTT, J. K. 1930. *Glaucomys sabrinus* in Pennsylvannia. Journal of Mammalogy, 11:239-240.

DOUTT, J. K., C. A. HEPPENSTALL, AND J. E. GUILDAY. 1977. Mammals of Pennsylvania. Pennsylvania Game Commission, Harrisburg, 283 pp. (*Glaucomys sabrinus*)

DOWNING, K. F. 1992. Biostratigraphy, taphonomy, and paleoecology of vertebrates from the Sucker Creek Formation (Miocene) of southeastern Oregon. Ph.D. dissertation, University of Arizona, Tucson 485 pp. (flying squirrels)

DOYLE, A. T. 1985. Small mammal micro- and macrohabitat selection in streamside ecosystems (Oregon, Cascade Range). Ph.D. dissertation, Oregon State University, Corvallis, 224 pp. (*Glaucomys sabrinius*)

DUDLEY, R., AND P. DEVRIES. 1990. Tropical rain forest structure and the geographical distribution of gliding vertebrates. Biotropica, 22:432-434. (Petauristinae)

DUGGER, D. A. 1990. A comparison of the summer diets of *Glaucomys volans* and *Peromyscus leucopus* in southern New Hampshire. M.S. thesis, University of New Hampshire, Durham, 34 pp.

DUMA, R. J., ET AL. 1981. Epidemic Typhus in United States associated with flying squirrels. Journal of the American Medical Association, 245:2318-2323. (*Glaucomys*)

DURRET-DESSET, M.-C., AND A. G. CHABAUD. 1967. Description of a new nematode Heligmosome parasite of a flying squirrel. Bulletin of the Society of Zoology, France, 92:227-233.

ECKERLINE, R. P., AND H. F. PAINTER. 1986. Species composition of flea populations of southern flying squirrels, *Glaucomys volans*, from different elevations in Virginia. Virginia Journal of Science, 37:62. (Abstract only)

EISENBERG, J. F. 1978. The evolution of the arboreal herbivores in the Class Mammalia. Pp. 135-152, *in* The ecology of arboreal folivores (G. G. Montgomery, ed.). Smithsonian Institution Press, Washington D. C. (*Hylopetes, Petaurista, Petinomys, Pteromyscus*)

ELLERMAN, J. R. 1940. The families and genera of living rodents. Vol. 1. Rodents other than Muridae. British Museum (Natural History), London, xxvi + 689 pp. (Petauristinae).

ELLERMAN, J. R., AND T. C. S. MORRISON-SCOTT. 1966. Checklist of Palaearctic and Indian mammals. British Museum (Natural History), London, 810 pp. (Petauristinae)

ELLIS, L. S. 1987. Nestbox utilization by southern flying squirrels, *Glaucomys volans* Transactions of the Missouri Academy of Science, 21:160. (Abstract only)

———. 1991. Radiotelemetry observations of southern flying squirrels, *Glaucomys volans*. Transactions of the Missouri Academy of Science, 25:16. (Abstract only)

ELLIS, L. S., AND L. R. MAXSON. 1980. Albumin evolution within New World squirrels (Sciuridae). The American Midland Naturalist, 104:57-62. (*Glaucomys*)

EMMONS, L. H., A. GAUTIER-HION, AND G. DUBOST. 1983. Community structure of the frugivorous-folivorous forest mammals of Gabon. Journal of the Zoological Society of London, 199:209-222. (Petauristinae)

EMMONS, L. H., AND A. H. GENTRY. 1983. Tropical forest structure and the distribution of gliding and prehensile-tailed vertebrates. The American Naturalist, 121:513-524. (Petauristinae)

EMRY, R. J., AND R. W. THORINGTON, JR. 1982. Descriptive and comparative osteology of the oldest fossil squirrel, *Protosciurus* (Rodentia: Sciuridae). Smithsonian Contributions to Paleobiology, 47:1-35. (Petauristinae)

EMRY, R. J., AND R. W. THORINGTON, JR. 1984. The tree squirrel *Sciurus* (Sciuridae, Rodentia) as a living fossil. Pp. 23-32, *in* Living Fossils (N. Eldridge, and S. M. Stanley, eds.). Springer Verlag, New York, xi + 291 pp. (Petauristinae)

ENGEL, T. C., M. J. LEMKE, AND N. F. PAYNE. 1992. Live capture methods of sympatric species of flying squirrel. Transactions of the Wisconsin Academy of Science, Arts Letters, 80:149-152. (*Glaucomys*)

———. 1992. Range extension of northern flying squirrels. Transactions of the Wisconsin Academy of Science, Arts Letter, 80:153-154. (*Glaucomys sabrinus*)

ENGESSER, B. 1979. Relationships of some insectivores and rodents from the Miocene of North America and Europe. Bulletin of Carnegie Museum of Natural History, 14:1-68. (*Forsythia*)

ENGESSER, B., A. MATTER, AND M. WEIDMANN. 1981. Stratigraphie und Saeugetier faunen der mittieren Miozaens von Vermes (Kt. Jura). Eclogae Geologicae Helvetiae, 74:893-952. (*Miopetaurista*)

ERONEN, P. 1991. On habitat requirements of flying squirrels (*Pteromys volans*) in southern Finland. Lounais-Hameen Luonto, 78:80-93.

ERXLEBEN, I. CH. P. 1777. Systema regni animalis per classes, ordines, genera, species, varietates cum synonymia et historia animalium. Classis I. Mammalia. Lipsiae, xviii + 636 pp. (*Glaucomys volans)*

EVERMANN, B. W., AND H. W. CLARK. 1920. Lake Maxinkuckee, a physical and biological survey., 1:477-479. (*Glaucomys*)

FAHLBUSCH, V., Z. D. QIU, G. STORCH. 1983. Neogene mammalian faunas of Ertemte and Harr Obo in Nei Mongol, China. 1. Report on field work in 1980 and preliminary results. Scientia Sinica, B26:205-224. (*Pliopetaurista*)

FARJANEL, G., AND P. MEIN. 1984. Une association des mammiferes et de pollens dans la fromation continentale des Marnes de Bresse d'age Miocene superieur, a Amberieu (Ain). Geologie de la France, 1984(1/2):131-148. (*Pliopetaurista*)

FENG, Z.-J, G.-Q CAI, AND C.-L ZHENG. 1986. The mammals of Xizang. Science Press, Bejing, 423 pp. (Chinese with English summary) (*Petaurista*)

FERRIS, G. F. 1951. The sucking lice, Vol. I. Memoirs of the Pacific Coast Entomological Society, 1:1-320. (*Glaucomys sabrinus*)

FERRON, J. 1981. Comparative ontogeny of behavior in four species of squirrels (Sciuridae). Zeitschrift für Tierpsychologie, 55:193-216. (*Glaucomys)*

———. 1983. Comparative activity patterns of two sympatric Sciurid species. Naturaliste Canadien (Quebec), 110:207-212. (*Glaucomys sabrinus*)

———. 1983. Scent marking by cheek rubbing in the northern flying squirrel (*Glaucomys sabrinus*). Canadian Journal of Zoology, 61:2377-2380.

———. 1984. Behavioral ontogeny analysis of Sciurid Rodents, with emphasis on the social behavior of ground squirrels. Pp. 24-42, *in* The biology of ground-dwelling squirrels: annual cycles, behavioral ecology, and sociality (J. O. Murie, and G. R. Michener, eds.). University of Nebraska Press, Lincoln, 459 pp. (*Glaucomys*)

FERRON, J., AND J. -P. OUELLET. 1985. Developpement physique post-natal chez le grand polatouche (*Glaucomys sabrinus*). Canadian Journal of Zoology, 63:2548-2552.

FINDLEY, J. S. 1945. The interesting fate of a flying squirrel. Journal of Mammalogy, 26:437. (*Glaucomys*)

FISHER, J. B. 1829. Synopsis mammalium. J. G. Cottae, Stuttgartiare, xii + 752 pp. (*Glaucomys volans)*

FLYGER, V., AND J. E. GATES. 1982. Fox and gray squirrels and their allies. Pp. 209-229, *in* Wild mammals of North America (J. A. Chapman, and G. A. Feldhamer, eds.). The Johns Hopkins University Press, Baltimore, Maryland, 123 pp. (*Glaucomys*)

FOGEL, F., AND J. M. TRAPPE. 1978. Fungus consumption (mycophagy) by small mammals. Northwest Science, 52:1-31. (*Glaucomys sabrinus*)

FORSMAN, E. D. 1980. Habitat utilization by Spotted Owls in the West-Central Cascades of Oregon. Ph.D. dissertation, Oregon State University, Corvallis, 109 pp. (*Glaucomys sabrinus*)

FORSMAN, E. D., E. C. MESLOW, AND H. M. WIGHT. 1984. Distribution and biology of the spotted owl in Oregon. Wildlife Monographs, 87:1-64. (*Glaucomys sabrinus*)

FOSTER, W. L., AND J. TATE, JR. 1966. The activities and coactions of animals at sapsucker trees. Living Bird, 5:87-113. (*Glaucomys sabrinus*)

FRANZEN, J. L., AND G. STORCH. 1975. Die unter pliozaene (turolische) Wibeltierfauna vonDorn-Duerkheim, Rheinhessen (SW-Deutschland); 1, Entdeckung, Geologie, Mammalia; Carnivora, Proboscidea, Rodentia; Grabungsergebnisse 1972-1973. Senckenbergiana Lethaea, 56(4-5):233-303. (*Miopetaurista*)

FRIANT, M. 1968. Sur les affinites d'un rongeur de l'Eocene D'Europe, Maurimontia. Acta Zoologica, 49:35-46. (*Trogopterus*)

FRIDELL, R. A. 1990. The influence of vegetation composition on habitat use and home range size of southern flying squirrels. M.S. thesis, University of New Hampshire, Durham, 49 pp. (*Glaucomys volans)*

FRIDELL, R. A., AND J. A. LITVAITIS. 1991. Influence of resource distrubution and abundance on home-range characteristics of southern flying squirrels. Canadian Journal of Zoology, 69:2589-2593. (*Glaucomys volans)*

FRYXELL, F. M. 1926. Flying squirrels as city nuisances. Journal of Mammalogy, 7:133. (*Glaucomys)*

FUGIMAKI, Y. 1963. Observations on the Japanese flying squirrel, *Pteromys volans orii* (Kuroda), in captivity. Journal of the Mammalogical Society of Japan, 2:42-45. (in Japanese with English summary)

FUNAKOSHI, K., AND S. SHIRAISHI. 1985. Feeding activities in the Japanese giant flying squirrel, *Petaurista leucogenys.* Journal of the Mammalogical Society of Japan, 10:149-158. (in Japanese with English summary)

GHOSE, R. K., AND T. K. CHAKRABORTY. 1983. A note on the status of the flying squirrels of Darjeeling and Sikkim. Journal of the Bombay Natural History Society, 80:411. (Petauristinae)

GHOSE, R. K., AND S. S. SAHA. 1981. Taxonomic review of Hodgson's giant flying squirrel, *Petaurista magnificus* (Hodgson) [Rodentia: Sciuridae], with a description of a new subspecies from Darjeeling District, West Bengal, Inda. Journal of the Bombay Natural History Society, 78:93-102.

GHOSH, M., AND G. MAJUMDAR. 1978. *Dipetalonema laemmleri* (Nematoda: Dipetalonematidae) from the Himalayan flying squirrel (*Petaurista magnificus*). Zeitschrift fuer Parasitenkunde, 55:195-198.

GIACALONE-MADDEN, J. R. 1976. The behavioral ecology of the southern flying squirrel, *Glaucomys volans*, on Long Island, New York. Ph.D. dissertation, City University of New York, 216 pp.

GIACALON-MADDEN, J. R. 1981. Adaptiveness of social structure in flying squirrels. United States Government Reports, 83:1919. (*Glaucomys volans)*

GILMORE, R. M. 1983. Patterns of habitat use by the southern flying squirrel in a hemlock-northern hardwood ecotone. M.S. thesis, Frostburg State University, Frostburg, Maryland, 47 pp. (*Glaucomys volans)*

GILMORE, R. M., AND J. E. GATES. 1985. Habitat use by the southern flying squirrel at a hemlock-northern hardwood ecotone. The Journal of Wildlife Management, 49:703-710. (*Glaucomys volans)*

GLAZEK, J., L. LINDNER, AND T. WYSOCZANSKI-MINKOWICZ. 1977. Geologiczna interpretacja stanowiska fauny staroplejstocenskiej Kozi Grzbiet w Gorach Swietokrzyskich. Krass, Speleologia, 1:13-28. (*Petauria*)

GOERTZ, J. W. 1965. Late summer breeding of flying squirrels. Journal of Mammalogy, 46:510. (*Glaucomys*)

GOERTZ, J. W., R. M. DAWSON, AND E. E. MOWBRAY. 1975. Response to nest boxes and reproduction by *Glaucomys volans* in northern Louisiana. Journal of Mammalogy, 56:933-939.

GOFF, M. L. 1983. A new species of *Gahrliepia* (*Gahrliepia*) (Acari: Trombiculidae) from Java. International Journal of Entomology, 25:281-284. (*Pteromys*)

GOLDMAN, E. A. 1936. Two new flying squirrels from Mexico. Journal of the Washington Academy of Science, 26:462-464. (*Glaucomys volans)*

GOODWIN, G. G. 1929. Mammals of Cascapedia Valley, Quebec. Journal of Mammalogy, 10:239-246. (*Glaucomys sabrinus*)

———. 1936. A new flying squirrel from Honduras. American Museum Novitates, 898:1-2. (*Glaucomys volans)*

———. 1942. Mammals of Honduras. Bulletin of the American Museum of Natural History, 79:107-195. (*Glaucomys volans)*

———. 1954. Mammals from Mexico collected by Marian Martin for the American Museum of Natural History. American Museum Novitates, 1689:1-16. (*Glaucomys volans)*

———. 1961. Flying squirrels (*Glaucomys volans)* of Middle America. American Museum Novitates, 2059:1-22.

———. 1961. Mammals from the state of Oaxaca, Mexico, in the American Museum of Natural History. Bulletin of the American Museum of Natural History, 141:1-269. (*Glaucomys volans)*

GORDON, D. C. 1961. Adirondack record of flying squirrel above timber line. Journal of Mammalogy, 43:262. (*Glaucomys)*

GOSLING, N. W. 1978. Michigan's night gliders. Out-of-Doors, 32:56-61. (*Glaucomys*)

———. 1978. Night glider nobody notices. Wildlife, 20:460-463. (*Glaucomys)*

———. 1979. Flying squirrel. New England Outdoors, 5:26-30. (*Glaucomys)*

———. 1980. Night glider. Owl, 5:16-21. (*Glaucomys)*

———. 1982. Flying squirrels. The New York Conservationist, 36:34-37. (*Glaucomys)*

GRASSE, P. P., AND P. L. DEKEYSER. 1955. Ordre des rongeurs (Rodents Vicq d'Azyr, 1792, Rodentia Bowdich, 1821). Pp. 1321-1525, *in* Traite de Zoologie (P. P. Grasse, ed.). Paris Masson, 17:1171-2300. (*Eupetaurus*)

GRAY, J. A., AND A. J. SOKOLOFF. 1992. Propatagial innervation in the flying squirrel, *Glaucomys volans*. The American Zoologist, 32:157A. (Abstract only)

GREEN, M. M. 1930. A contribution to the mammalogy of North mountain region of Pennsylvania, Ardmore, Pennsylvannia. Privately published, 19 pp. (*Glaucomys)*

GUILDAY, J. E. 1961. Notes on Pleistocene vertebrates from Wythe County, Virginia. Annals of Carnegie Museum, 36:76-86. (*Glaucomys)*

———. 1962. The Pleistocene local fauna of the natural chimneys, Augusta County, Virginia. Annals of Carnegie Museum, 36:87-122. (*Glaucomys).*

———. 1971. The Pleistocene history of the Appalachian mammal fauna. Pp. 233-262, *in* The distributional history of the biota of the southern Appalachians. Part III: Vertebrates (P. C. Holt, ed.). Virginia Polytechnic Institute and State University, Blacksburg, Virginia, viii + 306 pp. (*Glaucomys)*

———. 1979. Eastern North American Pleistocene Ochotona. Annals of Carnegie Museum, 48:435-444. (*Glaucomys)*

GUILDAY, J. E., AND H. W. HAMILTON. 1973. The late Pleistocene small mammals of Eagle Cave, Pendleton County, West Virginia. Annals of the Carnegie Museum, 44:45-58. (*Glaucomys)*

———. 1978. Ecological significance of displaced boreal mammals in West Virginia Caves. Journal of Mammalogy, 59:176-181. (*Glaucomys)*

GUILDAY, J. E., ET AL. 1978. The Baker Bluff cave deposit, Tennessee and the late Pleistocene faunal gradient. Bulletin of Carnegie Museum of Natural History, 11:1-67. (*Glaucomys)*

GUILDAY, J. E., H. W. HAMILTON, AND A. D. MCCRADY. 1969. The Pleistocene vertebrate fauna of Robinson Cave, Overton County, Tennessee. Palaeovertebrata, 2:25-75. (*Glaucomys)*

GUILDAY, J. E., P. S. MARTIN, AND A. D. MCCRADY. 1964. New Paris No. 4: a late Pleistocene cave deposit in Bedford County, Pennsylvania. Bulletin of the National Speleological Society, 26:121-194. (*Glaucomys)*

GUPTA, B. B. 1966. Notes on the gliding mechanism in the flying squirrel. Occasional Papers of the Museum of Zoology, University of Michigan, 645:1-7. (*Glaucomys)*

———. 1971. Mandible of some flying squirrels and the relationship between anatomy and taxonomy. Pp. 38-40, *in* International Symposium on Bionomics and Control of Rodents. Proceedings and Recommendation of the Symposium. Science and Technology Society, Kanpur, India, 184 pp. (Petauristinae)

GURNELL, J. 1987. The Natural History of Squirrels. Facts on File Publications, New York, 201 pp. (*Glaucomys)*

HAAS, G. E., L. JOHNSON, AND R. E. WOOD. 1982. Siphonaptera from mammals in Alaska. Suppliment IV. Revised checklist for southeastern Alaska. Journal of the Entomological Society of British Columbia, 79:54-61. (*Glaucomys sabrinus*)

HAAS, G. E., AND N. WILSON. 1973. Siphonaptera of Wisconsin. Proceedings of the Entomological Society of Washington, 75:302-314. (*Glaucomys sabrinus*)

HAFNER, D. J. 1984. Evolutionary relationships of the Neararctic Sciuridae. Pp. 3-23, *in* The biology of ground-dwelling squirrels: annual cycles, behavioral ecology, and sociality (J. O. Murie, and G. R. Michener, eds.). University of Nebraska Press, Lincoln, 459 pp. (*Glaucomys)*

HALL, D. S. 1991. Diet of the northern flying squirrel at Sagehen Creek, California. Journal of Mammalogy, 72:615-617. (*Glaucomys sabrinus*)

HALL, E. R. 1934. Two new rodents of the genera *Glaucomys)* and *Zapus* from Utah. Occasional Papers of the Museum of Zoology, University of Michigan, 296:106.

———. 1981. The mammals of North America. John Wiley & Sons, New York, 1083 pp. (*Glaucomys)*

HALL, F. G. 1965. Hemoglobin and oxygen: affinities in seven species of Sciuridae. Science, 148:1350-1351. (*Glaucomys)*

HALL, J. S., AND C. H. BLEWETT. 1964. Bat remains in owl pellets from Missouri. Journal of Mammalogy, 45:303-304. (*Glaucomys volans)*

HAMILTON, W. J., JR. 1943. The mammals of eastern United States. Comstock Publishing Co., Ithaca, N. Y., 236 pp. (*Glaucomys)*

HAMILTON, W. J., JR., AND J. O. WHITAKER, JR. 1979. Mammals of the eastern United States, 2nd ed. Cornell University Press, Ithaca, New York, 343 pp. (*Glaucomys)*

HAMPSON, C. G. 1966. Locomotion and some associated morphology in the northern flying squirrel. Ph.D. dissertation, University of Alberta, Calgary, 229 pp. (*Glaucomys sabrinus*)

HANDLEY, C. O., JR. 1953. A new flying squirrel from the southern Appalachian Mountains. Proceedings of the Biological Society of Washington, 66:191-194. (*Glaucomys)*

———. 1980. Mammals. Pp. 513-516, *in* Endangered and threatened plants and animals of Virginia (D. W. Linzey, ed.). Center for Environmental Studies, Virginia Polytechnic Institute and State University, Blacksburg, 665 pp. (*Glaucomys)*

HARESTAD, A. S. 1990. Nest site selection by northern flying squirrels and Douglas squirrels. Northwest Naturalist, 71:43-45. (*Glaucomys sabrinus*)

HARLOW, R. F., AND M. R. LENNARTZ. 1983. Interspecific competition for red-cockaded woodpecker cavities during the nesting season in South Carolina. Pp. 41-41, *in* Red-cockaded Woodpecker Symposium II (D. A. Woods, ed.). Florida Game and Fresh Water Fish Commission, Tallahassee, iv + 112 pp. (*Glaucomys volans)*

HARLOW, R. F., AND A. T. DOYLE. 1990. Food habits and southern flying squirrels (Glaucomys volans) collected from red-cockaded woodpecker (Picoides borealis) colonies in South Carolina. The American Midland Naturalist, 124:187-191.

HARPER, F. 1961. Land and fresh-water mammals of the Ungara Peninsula. Miscellaneous Publications of the Museum of Natural History, University of Kansas, 27:1-178. (*Glaucomys)*

HARRIS, W. P. 1951. A substitute name for *Petaurista petaurista rufipes* Sody. Journal of Mammalogy, 32:234.

HARRISON, J. L. 1960. Evolution of flying membranes. Malayan Nature Journal, 14:132-134. (gliding mammals)

HASTABACKA, H. 1990. The flying squirrel - a glider from the taiga. Fauna Flora (Stockholm), 85:260-265. (in Swedish) (*Pteromys volans*)

HATT, R. T. 1931. Habits of a young flying squirrel (*Glaucomys volans)*. Journal of Mammalogy, 2:233-238.

HATTEN, I. S. 1992. Population ecology of the southern flying squirrel (*Glaucomys volans)* in Alabama. M.S. thesis, University of Southern Alabama, Mobile, 114 pp.

HATTEN, S., AND D. NELSON. 1992. Nestbox use by southern flying squirrels (*Glaucomys volans)* in Alabama. Journal of the Alabama Academy of Science, 63:66. (Abstract only)

HATTEN, S. D., D. NELSON, AND D. BIGGS. 1993. Population ecology of the southern flying squirrel (*Glaucomys volans)* in Alabama. Journal of the Alabama Academy of Science, 64:95. (Abstract only)

HAVEMAN, J. R., AND W. L. ROBISON. 1976. Northward range extension of the southern flying squirrel in Michigan. Jack-Pine Warbler, 54:40-41. (*Glaucomys volans)*

HAYWARD, G. D., P. H. HAYWARD, AND E. O. GARTON. 1993. Ecology of boreal owls in the northern Rocky Mountains, U. S. A. Wildlife Monographs, 10(124):1-59. (*Glaucomys sabrinus*)

HEALY, W. M., AND R. T. BROOKS. 1988. Small mammal abundance in northern hardwood stands in West Virginia. The Journal of Wildlife Management, 52:491-496. (*Glaucomys volans)*

HEIDT, G. A. 1977. Utilization of nest boxes by the southern flying squirrel, *Glaucomys volans*, in central Arkansas. Proceedings of the Arkansas Academy of Science, 31:55-57.

HEINOLD, L. R. 1973. Flying squirrels - treetop gliders. Science Digest, 74:36-38. (*Glaucomys)*

HEINRICHS, J. 1983. The winged snail darter. Journal of Forestry, 81: 212-215, 262. (*Glaucomys)*

HESSIG, K. 1979. Die fruehesten Flughoernchen und primitive Ailuravinae aus dem sueddeutschen Oligozaen. Mitteilungen der Bayerischen Staatssammlung fuer Palaeontologie und Historische Geologie, 19:139-169. (The earliest flying squirrels and primitive Ailurarinae from Oligocene of southern Germany) (*Oligopetes*)

HEUDE, P. 1898. On *Trogopterus*. Etudes odontologiques; troisieme partie, Rongeurs. Memoires Concernant l'Histoire Naturelle de l'Empire Chinois, 1898:44-89.

HIBBARD, C. W. 1935. Breeding seasons of gray squirrel and flying squirrel. Journal of Mammalogy, 16:325-326. (*Glaucomys)*

HIGHT, M. E. 1972. The use of serum proteins in studying phylogenetic relationships of the Scuiridae. Ph.D. dissertation Wayne State University, Detroit, Michigan, 200 pp. (*Glaucomys)*

HIGHT, M. E., M. GOODMAN, AND W. PRYCHODKO. 1974. Immunological studies of the Sciuridae. Systematic Zoology, 23:12-25. (*Glaucomys)*

HILL, J. E. 1935. The cranial foramina in rodents. Journal of Mammalogy, 16:121-129. (Petauristinae)

———. 1964. Notes on flying squirrels of the genera *Pteromyscus, Hylopetes* and *Petinomys*. Annals of Natural History, 13:721-738.

HOI-SEN, Y., AND S. S. DHALIWAL. 1976. Variations in the karyotype of the red giant flying squirrel (*Petaurista petaurista*; Rodentia, Sciuridae). Malaysian Journal of Science, 4:9-12.

HOKKANEM, H., T. TORMALA, AND H. VUORINEN. 1977. Seasonal changes in the circadian activity of *Pteromys volans* L. in central Finland. Annales Zoologici Fennici, 14:94-97.

———. 1982. Decline of the flying squirrel *Pteromys volans* L. populations in Finland. Biological Conservation, 23:273-284.

HOLLAND, G. P. 1949. The Siphonaptera of Canada. Canada Department of Agriculture, Publication 817, Technical Bulletin, 70:1-306. (*Glaucomys*)

HOLLAND, G. P., AND A. H. BENTON. 1968. Siphonaptera from Pennsylvania mammals. The American Midland Naturalist, 80:252-261. (*Glaucomys*)

HOLLIMAN, D. C. 1963. The mammals of Alabama. Ph.D. dissertation, University of Alabama, Tuscaloosa, 504 pp. (*Glaucomys*)

HOLMES, D. J., AND S. N. AUSTAD. 1994. Fly now, die later: life-history correlates of gliding and flying in mammals. Journal of Mammalogy, 75:224-226.

HONACKI, J. H., K. E. KINMAN, AND J. W. KOEPPL, EDS. 1982. Mammal species of the world: a taxonomic and geographic reference. Allen Press, Inc., and the Association of Systematics Collections, Lawrence, Kansas, ix + 694 pp. (Petauristinae).

HONE, B. 1937. Chebuba - the flying squirrel that moved across the continent. Nature Magazine, 30:296-298. (*Glaucomys*)

HOOGSTRAAL, H., S. GABER, P. F. DIRK VAN PEENEN, J. F. DUNCAN, AND S. KADARSAN. 1972. *Haemaphysalis (Rhipistoma) bartelsi* Schule (Ixodoidea: Ixodidae); immature stage from a treehole of the Indonesian red giant flying squirrel. Journal of Parasitology, 58:989-992. (*Petaurista petaurista*)

HOOGSTRAAL, H., AND G. M. KOHLS. 1965. Description, host and ecology of *Ixodes kuntz*, n. sp., Kuntz's Taiwan Flying Squirrel Tick (Ixodea: Ixodidae). Journal of Medical Entomology, 2:209-214. (*Petaurista grandis*)

HOOPER, E. T. 1952. Records of the flying squirrels (*Glaucomys volans*) in Mexico. Journal of Mammalogy, 33:109-110.

HOWELL, A. H. 1915. Descriptons of a new genus and seven new races of flying squirrels. Proceedings of the Biological Society of Washington, 28:109-114. (*Glaucomys*)

———. 1918. Revision of the American flying squirrels. North American Fauna, 44:1-64. (*Glaucomys*)

———. 1934. Description of a new race of flying squirrel from Alaska. Journal of Mammalogy, 15:64. (*Glaucomys sabrinus*)

———. 1938. Revision of the North American ground squirrels, with a classification of the North American Sciuridae. North American Fauna, 56:1-226. (*Glaucomys*)

HRUBAN, Z., J. MARTAN, AND I. ASCHENBRENNER. 1971. Polarized cylindrical body in the epididymis of the flying squirrel. Journal of Morphology, 135:87-98. (*Glaucomys volans*)

HSU, T. C., AND K. BENIRSCHKE. 1973. *Glaucomys volans* (southern flying squirrel). Folio 312. Atlas of Mammalian Chromosomes. Vol. 7, Springer-Verlag, New York.

HUANG, W.-B 1979. Characteristics and age of the cave faunas of South China. Vertebrata Palasiatica, 17:327-343. (Petauristinae)

HU C., AND T. QUI. 1978. Pleistocene mammalian fauna from Gongwangling, Lantian County, Shaanxi Province. Zhongguo Gushengwo Zhi. Xin Bing Zhong.—Paleontologia Sinica, New C Series, 21:1-64. (*Petaurista*)

HU, J.-Z, AND Y.-Z WANG, EDS. 1984. Sichuan fauna economica, Volume 2. Publisher and place unknown, xxxiv + 365 pp. (in Chinese) (Petauristinae: key to species, p. 202)

HULTKRANTZ, J. W. 1897. Das Ellbogengelenk und seine Mechanik. Fischer, Jena. (gliding mammals)

IMAIZUMI, Y. 1983. Locomotion in *Petaurista leucogenys*. Anima, 121:56-63. (in Japanese)

INGLES, E. 1937. Mac—the flying squirrel. Nature Magazine, 30:229. (*Glaucomys*)

INGLES, L. G. 1954. Mammals of California and its coastal waters. Stanford University Press, Stanford, California, 396 pp. (*Glaucomys*)

———. 1965. Mammals of the Pacific states: California, Oregon, and Washington. Stanford University Press, Stanford, California, 506 pp. (*Glaucomys*)

ISRAEL, S., AND T. SINDAIR, EDS. 1988. Indian Wildlife. Apa Publications (HK), Ltd., 363 pp. (Petauristinae)

IVEY, R. D. 1959. The mammals of Palm Valley, Florida. Journal of Mammalogy, 40:585-591. (*Glaucomys volans*)

IVEY, T. L., AND J. E. FRAMPTON. 1987. Use of nest boxes by squirrels in the South Carolina Piedmont. Proceedings of the Annual Conference of the Southeastern Association of Fish and Wildlife Agencies, 41:279-287. (*Glaucomys volans*)

JACKSON, H. H. T. 1961. Mammals of Wisconsin. University of Wisconsin Press, Madison, 504 pp. (*Glaucomys*)

JACKSON, J. A. 1978. Competition for cavities and red-cockaded woodpecker management. Pp. 103-112, *in* Endangered Birds: management techniques, for preservation of threatend species (S. A. Temple, ed.). University of Wisconsin Press, Madison, xxiii + 466 pp. (*Glaucomys*)

JACOBS, G. H., AND M. S. SILVERMAN. 1976. Electrophysiological evidence for rod and cone based vision in the nocturnal flying squirrel. Journal of Comparative Physiology, A: Sensory, Neural, and Behavioral Physiology, 109:1-16. (*Glaucomys*)

JAMES, G. T. 1963. Paleontology and nonmarine stratigraphy of the Cuyama Valley badlands, California. Part 1. Geology, faunal interpretation, and systematic descriptions of Chiroptera, Instectivora, and Rodentia. University of California Publications in Geological Science, 45:iv + 154 pp. (Petauristinae)

JANOSSY, D. 1978. Larger mammals from the lower most Pleistocene fauna, Osztramos, Location 7 (Hungary). Annales Historico-Naturales Musei Nationalis Hungarici, 70:69-76. (*Pliopetaurista*)

JENTINK, F. A. 1890. Observations relating *Eupetaurus cinereus*, Oldfield Thomas. Notes from the Leiden Museum, 12:143-144.

JOHNSON, M. L. 1968. Application of blood protein electrophoretic studies to problems in mammalian taxonomy. Systematic Zoology, 17:23-30. (*Glaucomys)*

JOHNSON-MURRAY, J. L. 1977. Myology of the gliding membranes of some Petauristine rodents (genera: *Glaucomys) Pteromys, Petinomys,* and *Petaurista*). Journal of Mammalogy, 58:374-384.

———. 1980. Comparative and functional morphology of selected genera of non-gliding and gliding mammals (Phalangeridae, Sciuridae, Anomaluridae, and Cynocephalidae). Ph.D. dissertation, University of Massachusetts, Amherst, 222 pp. (Petauristinae)

———. 1987. The comparative myology of the gliding membranes of *Acrobates, Petauroides* and *Petaurus* contrasted with the curaneous myology of *Hemibelideus* and *Pseudocheirus* (Marsupialia: Phalangeridae) and with selected gliding rodentia (Sciuridae and Anomaluridae). Australian Journal of Zoology, 35:101-113. (Petauristinae)

JONES, G. S. 1973. Albinistic and melanistic mammals from Taiwan. Quarterly Journal of the Taiwan Museum, 26:369-372. (Petauristinae)

———. 1975. Notes on the status of *Belomys pearsoni* and *Dremomys pernyi* (Mammalia, Rodentia, Sciuridae) on Taiwan. Quarterly Journal of the Taiwan Museum, 28:403-405.

JONES, M. L. 1982. Longevity of captive mammals. Zoological Garten, 52:113-128. (*Glaucomys)*

JORDAN, J. S. 1948. A midsummer study of the southern flying squirrel. Journal of Mammalogy, 29:44-48. (*Glaucomys volans)*

———. 1956. Notes on a population of eastern flying squirrels. Journal of Mammalogy, 37:294-295. (*Glaucomys volans)*

KAMIYA, A., K. ISHIGAKI, AND Y. YAMASHITA. 1974. *Citellina petrovi* new record from the Japanese flying squirrel, *Pteromys volans orii.* Japanese Journal of Veterinary Research, 22:116-120.

KAWAMICHI, T. 1984. Socio-ecology of the Japanese giant flying squirrel (1). Shizen, 39:18-26. (*Petaurista leucogenys*)

KAWAMICHI, T. 1984. The world of giant flying squirrrels gliding in the dark (2). Shizen, 39:64-72. (in Japanese) (*Petaurista leucogenys*)

KAWAMURA, Y. 1988. Quaternary rodent faunas in the Japanese islands (part 1). Memoirs of the Faculty of Science at Kyoto University, Series of Geology and Mineralogy, 58(1-2):31-348. (in English) (*Petaurista*)

KEEGAN, H. L. 1951. The mites of the subfamily Haemogamasinae (Acari: Laelaptidae). Proceedings of the United States National Museum, 101:203-268. (*Glaucomys)*

KEITH, L. B., AND E. C. MESLOW. 1966. Animals using runways in common with snowshoe hares. Journal of Mammalogy, 47:541. (*Glaucomys)*

KEITH, L. B., AND J. R. CARY. 1991. Mustelid, squirrel, and porcupine population trends during a snowshoe hare cycle. Journal of Mammalogy, 72:373-378. (*Glaucomys sabrinus*)

KELKER, G. 1931. The breeding time of the flying squirrel (*Glaucomys volans volans*). Journal of Mammalogy, 12:166-167.

KENNICOTT, R. 1857. The quadrupeds of Illinois injurious and beneficial to the farmer. United States Patent Office Report, 1856:52-110. (*Glaucomys volans)*

KHUN, D. Z., AND L. S. KAN. 1991. Population of some mammals in the sclerophylous evergreen tropic forests near Konhkanyng (South Vietnam). Zoological Zhurnal, 70:114-118. (in Russian with English summary) (*Petaurista*)

KIM, K. C. 1977. *Atopophthirus emersoni*, new genus, new species (Aoplura: Hoploppleuridae) from *Petaurista elegans* (Rodentia: Sciuridae) with a key to the genera of *Enderleinellinea.* Journal of Medical Entomology, 14:417-420.

KING, F. H. 1883. Instinct and memory exhibited by the flying squirrel in confinement, with a thought on the origin of wings in bats. The American Naturalist, 17:36-42. (*Glaucomys)*

KITTREDGE, J., JR. 1928. Can the flying squirrel count? Journal of Mammalogy, 9:251-252. (*Glaucomys)*

KLOCKE, B. J. 1992. Aggregation and lowering of body temperature as overwintering strategies in the southern flying squirrel, *Glaucomys volans*. M.S. thesis, Northeast Missouri State University, Kirksville, 64 pp.

KLUGH, A. B. 1924. The flying squirrel. Nature Magazine, 3:205-207. (*Glaucomys)*

KNYSTAUTAS, A. 1987. The Natural History of the U.S.S.R. McGraw-Hill Book Co., New York, 157 pp. (*Pteromys*)

KOOPMAN, K. F., AND P. S. MARTIN. 1959. Subfossil mammals from the Gomez Farias region and the tropical gradient of eastern Mexico. Journal of Mammalogy, 40:1-12. (*Glaucomys volans)*

KOWALSKI, K., AND Y. HASEGAWA. 1976. Quaternary Rodents from Japan. National Science Museum (Tokyo), Bulletin, Series C, 12:31-66. (*Petaurista*)

KRASNEKOV, R. V., AND A. K. AGADZHANYAN. 1976. Discovery of Roussillon (Kuchurgan) small mammals in the central European part of the U.S.S.R. Doklady Academii of Sciences U.S.S.R., Earth Sciences Section, 203(1-6):126-128. (English Translation) (*Pliopetaurista*)

KRETZOI, M. 1959. Insectivorem, Nagetiere und Lagomorphen der junstpliozaenen fauna von Csarnota im Villanyer Gebirge (Sudungarn). Vertebrata Hungarica, 1:137-246. (*Pliopetes*)

KRETZOI, M. 1965. Die Nager und Lagomorphen von Voigtstedt in Thurigen und ihre chronologische Aussage. Palaontologische Abhandlungen, Abt A Palaozoologie (2):585-661. (Petauristinae)

KULIKOV, V. F. 1988. [Morphology and functional significance of the vibrissae apparatus of certain rodents.] Pp. 68-80, *in* Ekologo-funktsionalnaya Morfologiya Kozhnogo Pokrova Mlekopitayushchikh [Ecological and functional morphology of mammalian skin] (V. E. Sokolov, and R. P. Zhenevskaya, eds.). Nauka, Moscow, 205 pp. (in Russian) (*Pteromys*)

KUNTZ, R. E., AND Z. M. DIEN. 1970. Vertebrates of Taiwan taken for parasitological and biomedical studies by U. S. Naval Medical research Unit No. 2, Taipei, Taiwan, Republic of China. Quarterly Journal of the Taiwan Museum, 23:1-38. (*Petaurista grandis*)

KUNZ, T. H., J. R. CHOATE, AND S. B. GEORGE. 1980. Distributional records for three species of mammals in Kansas. Transactions of the Kansas Academy of Science, 83:74-77. (*Glaucomys volans)*

KURODA, M. N. 1935. Formosan mammals preserved in the collection of Marquis Yamashina. Journal of Mammalogy, 16:271-291. (Petauristinae)

———. 1940. A monograph of the Japanese mammals. The Sanseido Company, Ltd., Tokyo, Japan, 311 pp. (in Japanese) (*Petaurista*)

KURTA, A. 1979. Southern flying squirrel caught in a mist net. The Jack Pine Warbler, 57:170. (*Glaucomys volans)*

KURTEN, B., AND E. ANDERSON. 1980. Pleistocene Mammals of North America. Columbia University Press, New York, 442 pp. (*Glaucomys)*

LABUTIN, YU. V. 1988. Commensalism in the nests of large prey-birds in the north-east of Siberia. Ekologiya (Sverdlovsk), 1988:61-62. (in Russian, serial normally translated in the Soviet Journal of Ecology) (*Pteromys*)

LAMBERT, F. 1990. Some notes on fig-eating by arboreal mammals in Malaysia. Primates, 3:453-458. (*Petaurista*)

LANDWER, M. F. 1935. An outside nest of a flying squirrel. Journal of Mammalogy, 16:67. (*Glaucomys)*

LANGDON, F. W. 1880. The mammalia of the vicinity of Cincinnati, a list of species with notes. Journal of the Cincinnati Society of Natural History, 3:23. (*Glaucomys)*

LANGE, D. 1920. Notes on flying squirrels and gray squirrels. Journal of Mammalogy, 1:243-244. (*Glaucomys)*

LARSON, O. R. 1983. North Dakota fleas, VIII. Two new geographic records from the northern flying squirrel (Siphonaptera). Entomological News, 94:53-54. (*Glaucomys sabrinus*)

LAUER, D. M., AND D. E. SONESHINE. 1978. Bionomics of the squirrel flea *Orchopeas howardii* (Siphonaptera: Ceratophyllidae) in laboratory and field colonies of the southern flying squirrel *Glaucomys volans* using radio labelling techniques. Journal of Medical Entomology, 15:1-10.

LAURANCE, W. F., AND T. D. REYNOLDS. 1984. Winter food preferences of captive-reared northern flying squirrels. The Murrelet, 65:20-22 (*Glaucomys sabrinus*)

LAYNE, J. N. 1954. The Os clitoridis of some North American Sciuridae. Journal of Mammalogy, 35:357-67. (*Glaucomys)*

———. 1958. Mammals of southern Illinois. The American Midland Naturalist, 60:219-254. (*Glaucomys volans)*

———. 1974. The land mammals of South Florida. Pp. 386-413, *in* Environments of south Florida: present and past (P. J. Gleason, ed.). Miami Geological Society, Florida, 452 pp. (*Glaucomys*)

LAYNE, J. N., AND M. A. V. RAYMOND. 1994. Communal nesting of southern flying squirrels in Florida. Journal of Mammalogy, 75:110-120. (*Glaucomys volans*)

LEE, D. S. 1969. Flying squirrels feeding on the cones of the sand pine, Florida Naturalist, 42:41. (*Glaucomys*)

LEE, K.-C., F.-Z. ZENG, Y.-C. ZENG. 1987. A new species of *Macrostylophora* Ewing from Guangxi (Siphonoptera: Ceratophyllidae). Acta Zootaxonomica Sin, 12:415-417. (in Chinese with English summary) (*Petaurista petaurista*)

LEE, P. F. 1983. Reproduction and ecology of the giant flying squirrel (*Petaurista petaurista*). M.A. thesis, Taiwan University, Taipei, 73 pp. (in Chinese)

LEE, P. F., Y. S. LIN, AND D. R. PROGULSKE. 1993. Reproductive biology of the red giant flying squirrel, *Petaurista petaurista*, in Taiwan. Journal of Mammalogy, 74:982-989.

LEE, P. F., D. R. PROGULSKE, Y. T. DAY, AND Y. S. LIN. 1992. Growth pattern of the red-giant flying squirrel, *Petaurista petaurista*, in Taiwan. Acta Zoologica Taiwanica, 3:165-170.

LEE, P. F., D. R. PROGULSKE, AND Y. S. LIN. 1986. Ecological studies on two sympatric *Petaurista* species in Taiwan. Bulletin of the Institute of Zoology, Academia Sinica, 25:113-124.

———. 1993. Spotlight counts of giant flying squirrels *Petaurista petaurista* and *P. alborufus* in Taiwan. Bulletin of the Institute of Zoology, Academia Sinca, 32:54-61.

LEE, T. M., AND I. ZUCKER, 1990. Photoperiod synchronizes reproduction and growth in the southern flying squirrel, *Glaucomys volans*. Canadian Journal of Zoology, 68:134-139.

LEIN, J. C., AND J. H. CROSS. 1968. *Plasmodium* (Vinckeia) *watteni* sp. n. from the Formosa giant flying squirrel, *Petaurista petaurista grandis*. Journal of Parasitology, 54:1171-1174.

LEKAGUL, B., AND J. A. MCNEELY. 1977. Mammals of Thailand. Sahakarnbhat, Bangkok, vi + 758 pp. (Petauristinae)

LENNARTZ, M. R., AND D. G. HECKEL. 1987. Population dynamics of a red-cockaded woodpecker population in Georgia Piedmont loblolly pine habitat. Pp. 48-55, *in* Proceedings of the third southeastern nongame and endangered wildlife symposium (R. Odum, ed.). Georgia Department of Natural Resources, Athens, 253 pp. (*Glaucomys volans*)

LENNARTZ, M. R., AND P. W. STANGEL. 1989. Few and far between. Living Bird, 8: 14-20. (*Glaucomys*)

LEWIS, R. E. 1971. A new genus and species of flea from the lesser giant flying squirrel in Nepal (Siphonaptera: Ceratophyllidae). Journal of Parasitology, 57:1354-1361. (*Petaurista elegans caniceps*)

LI, C., L. YIPU, G. YUMEN, H. LIANHAI, W. WENYU, AND Q. ZHUDING. 1983. The Middle Miocene vertebrate fauna from Xiacaowan, Shiong Co., Jiangsu Province, 1. A brief introduction to the new materials from the fossil localities discovered up to the current year. Gu Jizhui Dongwe yu Bu Renlei.--Vertebrata Palasiatica, 21:313-327. (*Miopetaurista*)

LI, C. Y., AND C. MASER. 1986. New and modified techniques for studying nitrogen-fixing bacteria in small mammal droppings. United States Forest Service Research Note, Pacific Northwest No., 441:1-4. (*Glaucomys sabrinus*)

LI, C. Y., C. MASER, Z. MASER, AND B. A. CALDWELL. 1986. Role of three rodents in forest nitrogen fixation in western Oregon: another aspect of mammalian-mycorrhizal fungus-tree mutualism. The Great Basin Naturalist, 46:411-414. (*Glaucomys sabrinus*)

LIM, B. L. 1965. The Malayan whiskered flying squirrel *Petinomys genibarbis malaccanus*. Proceedings of the Zoological Society of London, 144:565-568.

LIM, B. L., AND I. MUUL. 1978. Small mammals. Pp. 403-457, *in* Kinabalu, Summit of Borneo. Sabah Society, Kota Kinabalu, Malaysia, 486 pp . (*Petaurista, Aeromys, Pteromyscus, Hylopetes, Petinomys*)

LIN, Y. S., AND P. F. LEE. 1986. Debarking on *Cryptomeria* trees by the red-giant flying squirrel (*Petaurista petaurista*) in Chitou. Quarterly Journal of Chinese Forestry, 19:55-64.

LIN, Y. S., D. R. PROGULSKE, P. F. LEE, AND Y. T. DAY. 1985. Bibliography of the Petauristinae (Rodentia, Sciuridae). Journal of the Taiwan Museum, 38:49-57.

LIN, Y. S., L. Y. WANG, AND L. L. LEE. 1988. The behavior and activity pattern of giant flying squirrels (*Petaurista p. grandis*). Quarterly Journal of Chinese Forestry, 21:81-94. (in Chinese with English Abstract)

LINNAEUS, C. 1758. Systema naturae per regna tria naturae, sucundum classes, ordines, genera, species, cum characteribus, differentiis, synonymis, locis. Tomus I. Editio decima, reformata. Stockholm, Laurentii Salvii, 1:1-824. (*Glaucomys*)

LINZEY, A. V., AND D. W. LINZEY. 1971. Mammals of Great Smoky Mountains National Park. University of Tennessee Press, Knoxville, 114 pp. (*Glaucomys)*

LINZEY, D. W. 1983. Distribution and status of the northern flying squirrel and the northern water shrew in the southern Appalacians. U. S. National Park Service Resources Management Report, SER-71:193-200. (*Glaucomys sabrinus*)

LINZEY, D. W., AND A. V. LINZEY. 1979. Growth and development of the southern flying squirrel (*Glaucomys volans volans*). Journal of Mammalogy, 60:615-620.

LOEB, S. C. 1993. Use and selection of red-cockaded woodpecker cavities by southern flying squirrels. The Journal of Wildlife Management, 57:329-335. (*Glaucomys volans)*

LOTTRIDGE, S. A. 1906. Familiar wild animals. Henry Holt and Co., New York, 115 pp. (*Glaucomys)*

LOWE, D. W., J. R. MATTEWS, AND C. J. MOSELEY, EDS. 1990. Carolina northern flying squirrel, *Glaucomys sabrinus* coloratus, Virginia northern flying squirrel, *Glaucomys sabrinus* fuscus. Pp. 480-482, *in* The Official World Wildlife Fund Guide to Endangered Species of North America, Volume 1. Beacham Publishing, Inc., Washington D.C, xxiii + 560 pp.

LOWERY, G. H., JR. 1974. The mammals of Louisiana and its adjacent waters. Louisiana State University Press, Baton Rouge, 565 pp. (*Glaucomys)*

LUTHER, W. 1952. Beobachtungen am nordamerikanischen Gleitflughornchen *Sciuropterus* (*Glaucomys) volans* (Thomas). Zeitschrift für Tierpsychologie, 9:402-411.

LUTTICH, S., D. H. RUSCH, E. C. MESLOW, AND L. B. KEITH. 1970. Ecology of red-tailed hawk predation in Alberta. Ecology, 51:190-203. (*Glaucomys)*

MACALISTER, A. 1872. The myology of the Chiroptera. Philosophical Transactions of the Royal Society of London, 162:125-171. (Petauristinae)

MACCLINTOK, D. 1963. Gliders of the night. Pacific Discovery, 16:11-15.

———. 1970. Squirrels of North America. Van-Nostrand Reinhold Co., New York, vii + 184 pp. (*Glaucomys volans)*

MACKINNON, K. S. 1978. Stratification and feeding differences among Malayan squirrels. Malaysian Nature Journal, 30:593-608. (Petauristinae)

MADDEN, J. R. 1974. Female territoriality in a Suffolk Co. Long Island, population of *Glaucomys volans*. Journal of Mammalogy, 55:647-652.

MADDEN, R. C., AND J. GIACALONE-MADDEN. 1982. A method for radio-tagging flying squirrels. The Journal of Wildlife Management, 46:525-527. (*Glaucomys)*

MAJOR, C. J. F. 1893. On some Miocene squirrels with remarks on the dentition and classification of the Sciurinae. Proceedings of the Zoological Society of London, 1893:179-215. (Petauristinae)

MANVILLE, R. H. 1942. Notes on the mammals of Mount Desert Island, Maine. Journal of Mammalogy, 23:391-398. (*Glaucomys)*

———. 1948. The vertebrate fauna of the Huron Mountains, Michigan. The American Midland Naturalist, 39:615-640. (*Glaucomys)*

———. 1949. A study of small mammal populations in northern Michigan. Miscellaneous Publications of the Museum of Zoology, University of Michigan, 73:1-83. (*Glaucomys)*

MARALDI, A. F. 1975. Food preferences of captive flying squirrels, *Glaucomys volans*. Transactions of the Illinois State Academy of Science, 68:205.

MANVILLE, R. H., AND S. P. YOUNG. 1965. Distribution of Alaskan mammals. United States Fish and Wildlife Service, Circulation, 221:1-74. (*Glaucomys sabrinus*)

MARTAN, J., AND Z. HRUBAN. 1970. Unusual spermatozoan formations in the epididymis of the flying squirrel (*Glaucomys volans)*. Journal of Reproducitve Fertility, 21:167-170.

MARTELL, A. M., R. E. YESCOTT, AND D. G. DODDS. 1969. Some records for Ixodidae of Nova Scotia. Canadian Journal of Zoology, 47:183-184. (*Glaucomys)*

MARTIN, R. A. 1974. Fossil mammals from the Coleman IIA fauna, Sumter Co. Pp. 35-99, 114-145, *in* Pleistocene mammals of Florida (S. D. Webb, ed.). University of Florida, Gainsville, 270. (*Glaucomys)*

MASER, C., R. ANDERSON, AND E. L. BULL. 1981. Aggregation and sex segregation in northern flying squirrels in northeastern Oregon, an observation. The Murrelet 62: 54-55. (*Glaucomys sabrinus*)

MASER, C., Z. MASER, J. W. WITT, AND G. HUNT. 1986. The northern flying squirrel: a mycophagist in southwestern Oregon. Canadian Journal of Zoology, 64:2086-2089. (*Glaucomys sabrinus*)

MASER, C., B. R. MATE, J. F. FRANKLIN, AND C. T. DRYNESS. 1981. Natural history of Oregon Coast mammals. United States Department of Agriculture, Forest Service General Techniques Report, Pacific Northwest, 133:1-495. (*Glaucomys sabrinus*)

MASER, C., J. M. TRAPPE, AND R. A. NUSSBAUM. 1978. Fungal-small mammal interrelationships with emphasis on Oregon coniferous forests. Ecology, 59:799-809. (*Glaucomys sabrinus*)

MASER, Z., C. MASER, AND J. M. TRAPPE. 1985. Food habits of the northern flying squirrel in Oregon. Canadian Journal of Zoology, 63:1084-1085.

MASER, Z., R. MOWREY, C. MASER, AND W. YUN. 1985. Northern flying squirrel: the moonlight truffler. Pp. 269, *in* Proceedings of the Sixth North American Conference on Mycorrhizae (R. Molina, ed.). Forest Research Laboratory, Oregon State University, Corvallis, 269 pp. (*Glaucomys sabrinus*)

MASLOWSKI, K. H. 1939. The story of Woolly, a flying squirrel. Nature Magazine, 32:441-444. (*Glaucomys*)

MAYER, W. V. 1941. Variation and systematic position of the flying squirrel of Idaho. The Murrelet, 22:30-31. (*Glaucomys sabrinus*)

MAYR, H., AND V. FAHLBUSCH. 1975. Eine unterpliozaene Kleinsaeunger fauna aus der Oberen Suesswasser-Molasse Bayerns. Mitteilungen der Bayerischen Staatssammlung für Palaeontologie und Historische Geologie, 15:91-111. (*Miopetaurista*)

MCALLEN, I. A. W., AND M. D. BRUCE. 1989. Some problems in vertebrate nomenclature. 1. Mammal. Museo Regionale di Scienze Naturali Bolletino, (Turin), 7:443-460. (in English with Italian summary) (*Petaurista*)

MCATTEE, W. L. 1950. The squirrel that flies and buzzes. Nature Magazine, 43:152. (*Glaucomys*)

MCCABE, R. A. 1947. Homing of flying squirrels. Journal of Mammalogy, 28:404. (*Glaucomys volans*)

MCCLULLOUGH, D. R. 1974. Status of Larger Mammals in Taiwan. Tourism Bureau, Taipei, Taiwan, 36 pp. (*Petaurista*)

MCGRATH, G. L. 1987. Relationships of Nearctic tree squirrels of the genus *Sciuris*. Ph.D. dissertation, University of Kansas, Lawrence, 109 pp. (*Glaucomys*)

MCINTYRE, P. W., AND A. B. CAREY. 1989. A microhistological technique for analysis of food habits of mycrophagous rodents. Research Paper, Pacific Northwest United States Department of Agriculture, Forest Service, Pacific Northwest Resarch Station, Portland Oregon, 404:1-16. (*Glaucomys sabrinus*)

MCINTYRE, R. N. 1950. The "panda bear" of the squirrel world. Yosemite Nature Notes, 29:36-41. (*Glaucomys sabrinus*)

MCKEEVER, S. 1960. Food of the northern flying squirrel in northeastern California. Journal of Mammalogy, 41:270-271. (*Glaucomys sabrinus*)

MCKENNA, M. C. 1962. *Eupetaurus* and the living petauristine sciurids. American Museum Novitates, 2104:1-38.

MCLAUGHLIN, C. A. 1967. Aplodontoid, Sciuroid, Geomyoid, Castroid, and Anomaluroid rodents. Pp. 210-225 *in* Recent mammals of the world (S. A. Anderson, J. K. Jones, Jr., eds.). Ronald Press Co., New York, viii + 453 pp. (Petauristinae)

MEARNS, E. A. 1898. Notes on the mammals of the Catskill Mountains, New York, with general remarks on the fauna and flora of the region. Proceedings of the United States National Museum, 21:341-360. (*Glaucomys*)

MEDWAY, L. 1977. Mammals of Borneo. Malaysian Branch of the Royal Asiatic Society, Kuala Lumpur, xiv + 193 pp. (Petauristinae)

———. 1978. The wild mammals of Malaya and Offshore islands including Singapore. Oxford University Press, London, xix + 127 pp. (Petauristinae)

MEIER, P. T. 1983. Relative brain size within the North American Sciuridae. Journal of Mammalogy, 64:642-647. (*Glaucomys*)

MEIN, P. 1970. Les Sciuropteres (Mammalia, Rodentia) Neogenes d'Europe Occidentale. Geobios, 3:7-77. (*Glaucomys*).

MENON, S. A. 1985. Circadian photoentrainment: % of light schedule viewed by a nocturnal rodent. The American Zoologist, 25:77. (Abstract only) (*Glaucomys volans*)

MERRIAM, C. H. 1884. The mammals of the Adirondack region. L. S. Foster, New York, 316 pp. (*Glaucomys*)

———. 1897. Description of a new flying squirrel from Ft. Klamath, Oregon. Proceedings of the Biological Society of Washington, 11:225. (*Glaucomys sabrinus*)

———. 1900. Descriptions of two new mammals from California. Proceedings of the Biological Society of Washington, 13:151-152. (*Glaucomys sabrinus*)

MICHAUX, J. 1973. Les rongeurs du Languedoc et de l'Espagne, dan leurs rapports avec la faune et la climat de l'Europe, de l'"Austien" au debut du Pleistocene moyen in Le Quarternaire; Geodynamique, Stratigraphie et environment; 9e. Congr. int. INQUA; Christchurch; 1973. Association francaise pour l'Etude du Quaternaire, Suppliment No. 36:24-30. (*Petinomys*)

MILLER, G. S., JR. 1912. Catalogue of the mammals of Western Europe (exclusive of Russia) in the collection of the British Museum. The British Museum, London, 1019 pp. (Petauristinae)

———. 1914. The generic name of the common flying-squirrels. Proceedings of the Biological Society of Washington, 27:216. (*Glaucomys*)

———. 1936. A new flying squirrel from West Virginia. Proceedings of the Biological Society of Washington, 49:143-144. (*Glaucomys*)

MILLER, G. S., JR., AND J. W. GIDLEY. 1918. Synopsis of the suprageneric groups of rodents. Journal of the Washington Academy of Science, 8:431-448. (Petauristinae)

MILNE-EDWARDS, H., AND A. MILNE-EDWARDS. 1868-1874. Memoire sur la faune mammalogique du Tibet Oriental et principalement de la Princepaute de Moupin. Pp. 231-271, *in* Researches pour servir a l'Histoire Naturelle des Mammiferes, Volume 1. Masson, Paris, 394 pp. (*Petaurista*)

MINETT, F. C. 1947. Notes on flying squirrels (*Petaurista sp.*). Journal of the Bombay Natural History Society, 47:52-56.

MITCHELL, R. M. 1979. The sciurid rodents (Rodentia: Sciuridae) of Nepal. Journal of Asian Ecology, 1:21-28. (Petauristinae)

MITTAL, O. P., AND B. KAUL. 1976. Chromosomes in two species of flying squirrels with comments on their phylogenetic relationships. Chromosome Information Service, 20:18-20. (*Hylopetes, Petaurista*)

MIYAO, T. 1972. The length of the intestines in the Japanese giant flying squirrel. Pp. 39-40, *in* Notes on Japanese Mammals (T. Miyao, ed.). Shinshu-Honyurui-Kenkyukai, Matsumoto. (in Japanese) (*Petaurista leucogenys*)

MIYAO, T., H. HANAMURA, AND T. NISHIZAWA. 1978. The relative weight of the mandible in Japanese mammals. Growth, 17:14-27. (in Japanese) (*Petaurista*)

MO, C. F. 1979. *Hirstionyssus chungwalii* n. sp. (Acarina, Laelapidae) from flying squirrels in South China. Acarologia (Paris), 20:39-43.

MOORE, J. C. 1946. Mammals from Welaka, Putnam County, Florida. Journal of Mammalogy, 27:49-59. (*Glaucomys volans*)

———. 1947. Nests of the Florida flying squirrel. The American Midland Naturalist, 38:248-253. (*Glaucomys volans*)

———. 1959. Relationships among living squirrels of the Sciurinae. Bulletin of the American Museum of Natural History, 118:157-206. (Petauristinae)

MOORE, K. L. 1965. Chromatin patterns in various rodents, with special reference to sexual dimorphism in interphase nuclei. Acta Anatomy (Basel), 61:448-501. (*Glaucomys*)

MORI, T. 1923. New names for a Korean flying squirrel. Journal of Mammalogy, 4:191. (*Pteromys*)

MOROZUMI, Y., AND T. MOROZUMI. 1978. Mammals. Pp. 29-168, *in* Natural History of Suwa (Suwa-Kyoikukai, ed.). Suwa-Kyoikukai, Matsumoto. (in Japanese) (*Petaurista*)

MORRISON, P. R., F. A. RYSER. 1951. Temperature and metabolism in some Wisconsin mammals. Proceedings of the Society for Experimental Biology and Medicine, 10:93-94. (*Glaucomys volans*)

MOWBRAY, V. 1939. Notes on the Sierra Nevada flying squirrel. Journal of Mammalogy, 20:379. (*Glaucomys sabrinus*)

MOWREY, R. A., G. A. LAURSEN, AND T. A. MOORE. 1981. Hypogeous fungi and small mammal mycophagy in Alaska taiga. Proceedings of the Alaska Scientific Conference, 32:120-121. (*Glaucomys sabrinus*)

MOWREY, R. A., AND J. C. ZASADA. 1984. Den tree use and movements of northern flying squirrels in interior Alaska and implications for forest management. Pp. 351-356, *in* Fish and wildlife relationships in old-growth forests (W. R. Meehan, T. R. Merrell, Jr., and T. A. Handley, eds.). American Institute of Fishery Research Biologists, vi + 425 pp. (*Glaucomys sabrinus*)

MULHERN, F. 1985. Magellan. American Forests, 91:40-41. (*Glaucomys*)

MUMFORD, R. W., AND C. O. HANDLEY, JR. 1956. Notes on the mammals of Jackson County, Indiana. Journal of Mammalogy, 37:407-412. (*Glaucomys volans*)

MURIE, A. 1961. Some food habits of the marten. Journal of Mammalogy, 42: 516-521. (*Glaucomys*)

MUSSER, G. G. 1961. A new subspecies of flying squirrel (*Glaucomys sabrinus*) from southwestern Utah. Proceedings of the Biological Society of Washington, 74:119-126.

MUUL, I. 1962. Behavior of Michigan flying squirrels. Jack-Pine Warbler, 40:120-124. (*Glaucomys volans*)

———. 1965*a*. Behavioral and physiological influences on the distribution of the flying squirrel, *Glaucomys volans*. Ph.D. dissertation, University of Michigan, 141 pp.

———. 1965*b*. Day length and food: photoperiods cue the flying squirrel. Natural History Magazine, 74:22-27.

———. 1968. Behavioral and physiological influences on the distribution of the flying squirrel, *Glaucomys volans*. Miscellaneous Publications of the Museum of Zoology, University of Michigan, 134:1-66.

———. 1969*a*. Mating behavior, gestation period, and development of *Glaucomys sabrinus*. Journal of Mammalogy, 50:121.

———. 1969*b*. Photoperiod and reproduction in flying squirrels, *Glaucomys volans*. Journal of Mammalogy, 50:542-549.

———. 1970. Intra- and inter-familial behaviour of *Glaucomys volans* (Rodentia) following parturition. Animal Behaviour, 18:20-25.

———. 1974. Geographic variation in the nesting habits of *Glaucomys volans*. Journal of Mammalogy, 55:840-844.

———. 1980. An additional species of squirrel *Petinomys vodermanni* in Thailand. Natural History Bulletin of the Sian Society, 28:135-136.

———. 1989. Rodents of conservation concern in the Southeast Asian region, *in* Rodents: a world survey of species of conservation concern (W. Z. Lidicker, Jr., ed.). Occasional Papers of the International Union of Conservation and Nature, Species Survival Commission, 4:iv + 60 pp. (Petauristinae)

MUUL, I., AND J. W. ALLEY. 1963. Night gliders of the woodlands. Natural History, 72:18-25. (*Glaucomys*)

MUUL, I., AND L. B. LIAT. 1978. Comparative morphology, food habits and ecology of some Malaysian arboreal rodents. Pp. 361-369, *in* The ecology of arboreal folivores (G. G. Montgomery, ed.). Smithsonian Institution Press, Washington D.C., 574 pp. (*Aeromys, Hylopetes, Iomys, Petaurillus, Petinomys, Pteromyscus*)

MUUL, I., AND B. L. LIM. 1971. New locality records for some mammals of West Malaysia. Journal of Mammalogy, 52:430-437. (Petauristinae)

———. 1973. Medical ecological considerations of a collection of mammals from East Malaysia. Southeast Asian Journal of Tropical Medicine and Public Health, 4:285-286. (*Hylopetes, Petaurista*)

———. 1974. Reproductive frequency in Malaysian flying squirrels, *Hylopetes* and *Pteromyscus*. Journal of Mammalogy, 55:393-400.

MUUL, I., B. L. LIM, AND L. F. YAP. 1970. Arboreal mammals and their red cell protozoa in various habitats in West Malaysia. Southeast Asian Journal of Tropical Medicine and Public Health, 1:421-422. (*Aeromys, Petaurista*)

MUUL, I., AND K. THONGLONGYA. 1971. Taxonomic status of *Petinomys morrisi* (Carter) and its relationship to *Petinomys setosus* (Temminck and Schlegel). Journal of Mammalogy, 52:362-369.

MUUL, I., L. F. YAP, AND B. L. LIM. 1973. Ecological distribution of blood parasites in some arboreal rodents. Southeast Asian Journal of Tropical Medicine and Public Health, 4:377-381. (*Aeromys, Petaurista*)

NADLER, C. F., AND D. M. LAY. 1971. Chromosomes of the Asian flying squirrel *Petaurista petaurista* (Pallas). Experimentia, 27:1225.

NADLER, C. F., AND D. A. SUTTON. 1962. Mitotic chromosomes of some North American Sciuridae. Proceedings of the Society of Experimental Biology and Medicine, 110:36-38. (*Glaucomys*)

———. 1967. Chromosomes of some squirrels (Mammalia: Sciuridae) from the genera *Sciurus* and *Glaucomys*) Experientia, 23:249-251.

NAKANO, S., T. HINO, S. NATSUME, M. HAYASHIDA, Y. INABA, AND A. OKUDA. 1991. Notes on nesting trees of Japanese flying squirrel, *Pteromys volans* orii, in Hokkaido during winter. Research Bulletin of the College of Experimental Forestry, Hokkaido University, 48:183-190. (in Japanese with English summary)

NEAL, J. C. 1992. Factors affecting breeding success of red-cockaded woodpeckers in the Ouachita National Forest, Arkansas. M.S. thesis, University of Arkansas, Fayetteville, 96 pp. (*Glaucomys volans*)

NELLIS, C. H., S. P. WETMORE, AND L. B. KEITH. 1972. Lynx-prey interactions in central Alberta. The Journal of Wildlife Management, 36:320-329. (*Glaucomys*)

NELSON, E. W. 1904. Descriptions of new flying squirrels from Mexico. Proceedings of the Biological Society of Washington, 17:147-150. (*Glaucomys volans*)

———. 1918. The flying squirrel (*Glaucomys volans*) and its relatives. National Geographic Magazine, 32:466-468. (*Glaucomys*)

NEUMANN, R. L. 1967. Metabolism in the eastern chipmunk (*Tamias striatus*) and the southern flying squirrel (*Glaucomys volans*) during the winter and summer. Pp. 64-74, *in* Mammalian Hybernation, Volume 3 (K. C. Fisher, A. R.

Dawe, C. P. Lyman, E. Schonbaum, and F. E. South, Jr., eds.). American Elsevier Publishing Company, New York, 535 pp.

NICELY, R. L. 1976. Comparative brain morphology of *Glaucomys volans* and *Spermophilus tridecemlineatus.* M.S. thesis, Stephen F. Austin State University, Nacogdoches, Texas, 65 pp.

NIETHAMMER, J. 1990. Flying squirrels. Pp. 96-103, *in* Grzimek's Encyclopedia of Mammals, Volume 3 (S. P. Parker, ed.). McGraw-Hill Publishing Company, New York, 643 pp.

NORBERG, R. A. 1981. Why foraging birds in trees should climb and hop upwards rather than downwards. The Ibis, 123:281-288. (gliding mammals)

———. 1983. Optimal locomotion modes of foraging birds in trees. The Ibis, 125:172-180. (gliding mammals)

NORBERG, U. M. 1985. Evolution of vertebrate flight: an aerodynamic model for the transition from gliding to active flight. The American Naturalist, 126:303-327. (gliding mammals)

OAKS, E. V. 1982. Identification and characterization of *Rickettsia prowazekii* proteins involved in *Rickettsia*-host interactions. Ph.D. dissertation, University of Maryland, Baltimore, 240 pp. (*Glaucomys)*

OBER, L. D. 1978. The monkey jungle: a late Pleistocene fossil site in southern Florida. Plaster Jacket, 28:1-13. (*Glaucomys)*

OGNEV, S. I. 1940. Mammals of the U.S.S.R. and adjacent countries. Vol. IV, Rodents. Israel Program for Scientific Translations Ltd., 1966, IPST Catalogue No. 1254, S. Monson Binding, Wiener Bindery Ltd., Jerusalem, 429 pp. (Petauristinae)

OGNEV, S. I. 1947. Mammals of the U.S.S.R. and adjacent countries. Vol. V, Rodents. Israel Program for Scientific Translations Ltd., 1963, IPST Catalogue No. 745, S. Monson Binding, Wiener Bindery Ltd., Jerusalem, 662 pp. (Petauristinae)

OSGOOD, D. W. 1980. Temperature sensitive telemetry applied to studies of small mammal activity patterns. Pp. 525-528, *in* A handbook on biotelemetry and radio tracking (C. J. Amlaner, Jr., and D. W. Macdonald, eds.). Pergamon Press, New York, xix + 804 pp. (*Glaucomys sabrinus*)

OSGOOD, F. L. 1935. Apparent segregation of sexes in flying squirrels. Journal of Mammalogy, 16:231. (*Glaucomys)*

OSGOOD, W. H. 1900. Results of a biological reconnaissance of the Yukon River region. North American Fauna, 19:1-100. (*Glaucomys)*

———. 1905. A new flying squirrel from the coast of Alaska. Proceedings of the Biological Society of Washington, 18:133-134. (*Glaucomys sabrinus*)

OSHIDA, T., AND Y. OBARA. 1991. Karyotypes and chromosome banding patterns of a male Japanese giant flying squirrel, *Petaurista leucogenys* Temminck. Chromosome Information Service, 50:26-28.

OXLEY, D. J., AND J. M. GALL. 1977. Additional record of the southern flying squirrel from Quebec, Canada. Canadian Field-Naturalist, 91:424. (*Glaucomys volans)*

OXNARD, C. E. 1968. The architecture of the shoulder in some mammals. Journal of Morphology, 126:249-290. (*Glaucomys, Hylopetes, Petaurista*)

PAAKKONEN, J. 1991. The occurance of the flying squirrel (*Pteromys volans*) in the metropolitan area in the years 1988-1990. Lounais-Hameen Luonta, 78:94-105. (in French with English summary)

PADIAN, K. 1983. A functional analysis of flying and walking in pterosaurs. Paleobiology, 9:218-239. (*Glaucomys)*

PAGELS, J. F., R. P. ECKERLIN, J. R. BAKER, AND M. L. FIES. 1990. New records of the distribution and the intestinal parasites of the endangered northern flying squirrel, *Glaucomys sabrinus*, in Virginia. Brimleyana, 16:73-78.

PAINTER, H. F., R. P. ECKERLIN, AND D. E. SONESHINE. 1984. Seasonal variations in species compostion of Siphonapteran parasite populations on southern flying squirrels, *Glaucomys volans* in Virginia. Virginia Journal of Science, 35:88. (Abstract only)

PAL, N. L., AND B. DASGUPTA. 1976. Malarial parasites in the Hodgsons flying squirrel *Petaurista magnificus.* Proceedings of the Zoological Society (Calcutta), 29:51-60.

PALLAS, P. S. 1778. Novae species quadrupedum e glirium ordine... W. Walther, Erlangae, vii + 388 pp. + 27 pls. (Petauristinae)

PATRICK, M. J. 1991*a*. Distribution of enteric helminths in *Glaucomys volans* L. (Sciuridae): a test of competition. Ecology, 72:755-758.

———. 1991*b*. Occurrence of *Stronglyloides robustus* (Rhabditata: Stronglyloididae) in squirrels (Sciuridae) from Indiana County, Pennsylvania. Journal of the Pennsylvania Academy of Science, 65:48-50. (*Glaucomys volans)*

PAYNE, J., C. M. FRANCIS, AND K. PHILLIPS. 1985. A field guide to the mammals of Borneo. Sabah Society with World Wildlife Fund, Malaysia, 332 pp. (*Aeromys, Hylopetes, Petaurillus, Petaurista, Petinomys, Pteromyscus*)

PAYNE, J. L. 1987. Habitat variation among montane island populations of the flying squirrel, *Glaucomys sabrinus*, in the southern Appalachian Mountains. M.S. thesis, Virginian Commonwealth University, Richmond, 54 pp.

PAYNE, J. L., D. R. YOUNG, J. F. PAGELS. 1989. Plant community characteristics associated with the endangered northern flying squirrel, *Glaucomys sabrinus*, in the southern Appalachians. The American Midland Naturalist, 121:285-292.

PEARSON, P. G. 1954. Mammals of Gulf Hammock, Levy County, Florida. The American Midland Naturalist, 51:468-480. (*Glaucomys volans)*

PENG, H., AND Y. WANG. 1981. New mammals from the Gaoligong Mountains. Acta Theriologica Sinica, 1:167-169. (*Petaurista*)

PENNYCUICK, C. 1972. Animal flight. Studies in Biology, Volume 33. Edward Arnold (Publishers) Limited, London, 68 pp. (gliding mammals)

PERKINS, B. L. 1974. A study of the epididymis of the flying squirrel, *Glaucomys volans.* Ph.D. dissertation, Southern Illinois University, Carbondale, 117 pp.

PERKINS, G. H. 1879. *Sciuropterus volucella.* On its osteology. Proceedings of the American Association for the Advancement of Science, 27:289. (Petauristine anatomy)

PETERKA, H. E. 1936. A study of the myology and osteology of tree squirrels with regard to adaptation to arboreal, glissant, and fossorial habits. Transactions of the Kansas Academy of Science, 39:313-332. (Petauristinae)

PETERSON, B. AND G. GAUTHIER. 1985. Nest site use by cavity-nesting birds of the Caribou Parkland, British Columbia. The Wilson Bulletin, 97:319-331. (*Glaucomys sabrinus*)

PHILLIPS, W. W. A. 1980. Manual of the mammals of Sri Lanka, Part II. Wildlife and Nature Protection Society of Sri Lanka, Colombo. (*Petaurista, Petinomys*)

PIRLOT, P., AND T. KAMIYA. 1982. Relative size of brain and brain components in three gliding placentals (Dermoptera, Rodentia). Canadian Journal of Zoology, 60:565-572. (*Glaucomys)*

PITTS, T. D. 1992. Reproduction of southern flying squirrels (*Glaucomys volans)* in Weakley County, Tennessee. Journal of the Tennessee Academy of Science, 67:81-83. (Abstract only)

POCOCK, R. I. 1922. On the external characters of the beaver (Castoridae) and of some squirrels (Sciuridae). Proceedings of the Zoological Society of London, 1922:1171-1212. (*Glaucomys)*

———. 1923. The classification of the Sciuridae. Proceedings of the Zoological Society of London, 1923:209-246. (Petauristinae)

POLYAKOVA, R. R., AND A. S. SOKOLOV. 1965. Structure of locomotor organs in the volant squirrel, *Pteromys volans* (L.), in relation to its plane flight. Zoological Journal, XLIV:902-916. (In Russian)

QUAY, W. B. 1965. Comparative survey of the sebaceous and sudoriferous glands of the oral lips and angle in rodents. Journal of Mammalogy, 46:23-37. (*Glauromys volans*)

QUENTIN, J. C. 1970. Description of a new Oxyurinae *Sypharista kamegaii* n. gen., n. sp., a parasite of a flying squirrel of Japan. Bulletin of the Museum of Natural History, Paris, 42:989-995.

QUI, L.-C., F.-Y. SONG, AND L.-H. WANG. 1980. Brief news concerning the unearthing of cultural remains in Dushizi Cave, Yang Chun County, Guangdong Province. Vertebrata Palasiatica, 18:26. (Petauristinae)

QUI, Z. D. 1981. A new sciuroptera from the middle Miocene of Linqu, Shandong. Vertebrata Palasiatica, 19:228-238. (*Meinia*)

QUI, Z. 1991. The Neogene mammalian faunas of Ertemte and Harr Obo in inner Mongolia (Nei Mongol), China. 8, Sciuridae (Rodentia). Senckenb Lethaea, 71(3-4):223-255. (in English with German summary) (*Petinomys aucotor, Pliopetaurista rugosa*)

QUI, Z., D. HAN, G. QUI, AND Y. LIN. 1985. Micromammalian fossils from the ancient ape locality of Lufeng, Yunnan. Acta Anthropologica Sinica, 4:13-32. (*Forsythia, Hylopetes*)

QUI, Z., C. LI, AND S. HU. 1984. A late Pleistocene fauna from Sanjia Village, Chenggong County, Kunming Municipality, Yunnan Province. Vertebrata Palasiatica, 22:281-293. (*Petaurista*)

QUI, Z., Y. LIU, Y. LEI. 1986. The middle Miocene vertebrate fauna from Xiacaowan, hiong County, Jiangsu Province. 5. The squirrel family (mammals, rodents). Vertebrata Palasiatica, 24:195-209. (*Parapetaurista, Shuanggouia*)

RABOR, D. S. 1939. *Sciuropterus mindanensis sp. nov.*, a new species of flying squirrel from Mindanao. Philippine Journal of Science, 69:389-393. (*Petinomys*)

RADVANYI, A. 1959. Inherent rhythms of activity of the northern flying squirrel in relation to illumination and to lunar and solar photoperiodism. Ph.D. dissertation, University of British Columbia, Vancouver, 162 pp. (*Glaucomys sabrinus*)

RAKHILIN, V. K. 1968. Biology of the Russian flying squirrel *Pteromys volans.* Zoological Zhurnal, 47:312-313.

RALLS, K. 1976. Mammals in which females are larger than males. Quarterly Review of Biology, 51:245-276. (*Glaucomys)*

RAND, A. L., AND P. HOST. 1942. Results of the Archbold Expeditions. No. 45: mammal notes from Highland County, Florida. Bulletin of the American Museum of Natural History, 80:1-21. (*Glaucomys volans)*

RAPHAEL, M. G. 1984. Late fall breeding of the northern flying squirrel, *Glaucomys sabrinus*. Journal of Mammalogy, 65:138-139.

RAPHAEL, M. G., C. A. TAYLOR, AND R. H. BARRETT. 1986. Smoked aluminum track stations record of flying squirrel occurrence. Pacific Southwest Forest and Range Experiment Station, United States Department of Agriculture, Forest Service, Berkeley, California, Research Note Pacific Southwest- 384. (*Glaucomys sabrinus*)

RASMUSSEN, D. L. 1974. New Quaternary mammal localities in the upper Clark Fork River valley, western Montana. Northwest Geology, 3:62-70. (*Glaucomys*).

RAUSCH, R. 1947. *Andrya sciuri* n. sp., a cestode from the northern flying squirrel. Journal of Parasitology, 33:316-318. (*Glaucomys sabrinus*)

RAUSCH, R., AND J. D. TINER. 1948. Studies on the parasitic helminths of the North Central states. I, Helminths of Sciuridae. The American Midland Naturalist, 39:728-747. (*Glaucomys)*

———. 1981. Cestodes in mammals: zoogeography of some parasite-host assemblages. Symposium, La Specificite Parasitaire des Parasites de Vertebres. Museum National d'Histoire Naturelle, Paris, 13-17, April 1981. (*Glaucomys)*

RAUSCH, R. L., C. MASER. 1977. *Monoecocestus thomasi* sp. n. (Cestoda: Anoplocephalidae) from the northern flying squirrel, *Glaucomys sabrinus* (Shaw), in Oregon. Journal of Parasitology, 63:793-799.

RAUSCH, V. R., AND R. L. RAUSCH. 1982. The karyotype of the Eurasian flying squirrel (*Pteromys volans*), with a consideration of karyotypic and other distinctions in *Glaucomys)* sp. (Rodentia: Sciuridae) Proceedings of the Biological Society of Washington, 95:58-66.

RAYMOND, M., AND J. LAYNE. 1988. Aspects of reproduction in the southern flying squirrel in Florida. Acta Theriologica, 33:505-518. (*Glaucomys volans)*

RAYNER, J. M. V. 1981. Flight adaptations in vertebrates. Pp. 137-172, *in* Vertebrate Locomotion (M. H. Day, ed.). Symposium 48, Zoological Society of London, Academic Press, New York, xvii + 471 pp. (*Glaucomys)*

REDINGTON, B. C. 1971. Studies on the morphology and taxonomy of *Haemogamasus reidi*, Ewing, 1925 (Acari: Mesostigmata). Acarologia, 12: 643-667. (*Glaucomys)*

RHOADS, S. N. 1897. A revision of the west American flying squirrels. Proceedings of the Academy of Natural Science, Phiadelphia 1897:314-327. (*Glaucomys)*

RHODES, G. 1993. Microhabitat selection around winter nestsites by southern flying squirrels (*Glaucomys volans)*. Bios, 64:102. (Abstract only)

RICHARDSON, J. 1828. Short characters of a few quadrupeds procured on Captain Franklin's late expedition. Zoological Journal, 3:516-520. (*Glaucomys)*

RITER, R. A., AND H. H. VALLOWE. 1978. Early behavioral ontogeny in the southern flying squirrel *Glaucomys volans volans*. Proceedings Pennsylvania Academy of Science, 52:169-175.

ROBERT, S., AND J. M. BERGERON. 1977. Les Siphonapteres de la region de Sherbrooke, Quebec. Canadian Entomolologist, 109:1571-1582. (*Glaucomys)*

ROBERTS, T. J. 1977. The Mammals of Pakistan. Ernest Benn, London, xxvi + 361 pp. (*Eupetaurus, Petaurista*)

ROBERTSON, B. L. 1982. A continuation study of a population of southern flying squirrels (*Glaucomys volans)* in a Middle Tennessee woodlot. Tennessee Tech Journal, 17:79. (Abstract only)

ROBERTSON, J. S., JR. 1976. Latest Pliocene mammals from Haile XV A, Alachua County, Florida. Bulletin of the Florida State Museum of Biological Science, 20:111-186. (*Glaucomys)*

ROSENBERG, D. K. 1990. Characteristics of northern flying squirrel and Townsend's chipmunk populations in second- and old-growth forests. M.S. thesis, Oregon State University, Corvallis, 61 pp.

ROSENBERG, D. K., AND R. G. ANTHONY. 1992. Characteristics of northern flying squirrel populations in young second- and old-growth forests in western Oregon. Canadian Journal of Zoology, 70:161-166. (*Glaucomys sabrinus*)

———. 1993. Differences in trapping mortality rates of northern flying squirrels. Canadian Journal of Zoology, 660-663. (*Glaucomys sabrinus*)

ROUDABUSH, R. L. 1937. Two Emeria from the flying squirrel, *Glaucomys volans*. Journal of Parasitology, 23:107-108.

ROSENTRETER, R. 1991. The role of lichens in the ecology of the northern flying squirrel. Northwest Science, 65:74. (Abstract only)

RUDOLPH, D. C., R. N. CONNOR, AND J. TURNER. 1990. Competition for red-cockaded woodpecker roost and nest cavitites: effects of resin age and entrance diameter. The Wilson Bulletin, 102:23-36. (*Glaucomys volans)*

RUE, L. L. 1967. Pictoral guide to the mammals of North America. Crowell Publishing, New York, 299 pp. (*Glaucomys)*

RUST, H. J. 1946. Mammals of northern Idaho. Journal of Mammalogy, 27:308-327. (*Glaucomys sabrinus*)

SAHA, S. S. 1981. A new genus and a new species of flying squirrel (Mammalia: Rodentia: Sciuridae) from northeastern India. Bulletin of the Zoological Survey of India, 4:331-336. (*Biswamoyopterus biswasi*)

SAUNDERS, J. J. 1977. Late Pleistocene vertebrates of the western Ozark Highlands, Missouri. Illinois State Museum Report of Investigation, 33:1-118. (*Glaucomys)*

SAVILE, B. B. O. 1962. Gliding and flight in the vertebrates. The American Zoologist, 2:161-166. (gliding mammals)

SAWYER, S. L. 1983. Homing and ecology in the southern flying squirrel, *Glaucomys volans* in southeastern Virginia. M.S. thesis, Old Dominion University, Norfolk, Virginia, 71 pp.

SAWYER, S. L., AND ROSE, R. K. 1985. Homing in and ecology of the southern flying squirrel Glaucomys volans in southeastern Virginia. The American Midland Naturalist, 113:238-244.

SCHAUB, S. 1953. Remarks on the distribution and classification of the "Histricomorpha." Verhandlungen der Naturforschenden Gesellschaft in Basel, 64:389-400. (*Eupetaurus*)

SCHEIBE, J. S., D. FIGGS, AND J. HEILAND. 1990. Morphological attributes of gliding rodents: a preliminary analysis. Transactions of the Missouri Academy of Science, 24:49-55. (Petauristinae)

SCHINDLER, A.-M., R. L. LOW, AND K. BENIRSCKE. 1973. The chromosomes of the New World flying squirrels (*Glaucomys volans)* and *Glaucomys sabrinus*) with special reference to autosomal heterochromatin. Cytologia, 38:137-147.

SCHMIDT, F. J. W. 1931. Mammals of western Clark County, Wisconsin. Journal of Mammalogy, 12:99-117. (*Glaucomys)*

SCHOLEY, K. 1986*a*. The evolution of flight in bats. Biona Report, 5:1-12. (Petauristinae)

———. 1986*b*. The climbing and gliding locomotion of the giant red flying squirrel *Petaurista petaurista* (Sciuridae). Biona Report, 5:187-204.

SCHOLTEN, T. H., K. RONALD, AND D. M. MCLEAN. 1962. Parasite fauna of the Manitoulin Island region, I. Arthropoda parasitica. Canadian Journal of Zoology, 40:605-606. (*Glaucomys)*

SCHWARTZ, W. W., AND E. R. SCHWARTZ. 1959. The wild mammals of Missouri. University of Missouri Press and Missouri Conservation Commission, Kansas City, Missouri, 341 pp. (*Glaucomys)*

SEN, S., AND M. MAKINSKY. 1983. Nouvelles de micromammiferes dan les faluns Miocenes de Thenay (Loir-et-Cher). Geobios Paleontology, Stratigraphy, Paleoecology, 16:461-469. (Petauristinae)

SETON, E. T. 1929. Lives of game animals, Volume 4. Doubleday, Doran Co., New York, 440 pp. (*Glaucomys)*

SHARMA, T., AND G. S. GARG. 1973. Karyotype and autosomal heterochromatin of a flying squirrel *Hylopetes alboniger alboniger.* Indian Scientific Congress Association, Proceedings, 160:424.

SHARNOFF, S. 1992. Use of lichens by wildlife in North America. Northwest Science, 66:130. (Abstract only) (*Glaucomys sabrinus*)

SHAW, G. 1801. General zoology. Theomas Davison, London, 2:1-266. (*Glaucomys)*

SHELDON, W. G. 1971. Alopecia of captive flying squirrels. Journal of Wildlife Disease, 7:111-114. (*Glaucomys volans)*

SHELDON, W. G., W. C. BANKS, AND C. A. GLEISER. 1971. Osteomaloacia in captive flying squirrels, *Glaucomys volans.* Laboratory Animal Science, 29:229-233.

SHEVYREVA, N. S. 1974. Historical development of some rodents of the suborder Sciuromorpha in Asia. Paleontological Journal, 8:84-93. (*Belomys, Glaucomys) Hylopetes*)

SHOOK, R. A. 1976. Maternal retrieving and reproduction in the southern flying squirrel, *Glaucomys volans.* M.S. thesis, Cornell University, Ithaca, New York, 83 pp.

SIEG, C. H. 1991. Ecology of bur oak woodlands in the foothills of the Black Hills, South Dakota (*Quercus macrocarpa*, riparian). Ph.D. dissertation, Texas Tech University, Lubbock, 198 pp. (*Glaucomys)*

SIMPSON, G. G. 1945. The principles of classification and a classification of the mammals. Bulletin of the American Museum of Natural History, 85:1-350. (Petauristinae)

SKINNER, S. 1991. Squirrel in the sky. Wyoming Wildlife, 55:16-21. (*Glaucomys sabrinus*)

SMILEY, R. L., AND J. O. WHITAKER, JR. 1981. Studies on the idisomal and leg chaetotaxy of the Cheyletidae (Acari) with descriptions of a new genus and four new species. International Journal of Acarology, 7:109-128. (*Glaucomys)*

SMITH, C. C. 1978. Structure and function of the vocalizations of tree squirrels (*Tamiasciurus*). Journal of Mammalogy, 59:793-808. (*Glaucomys)*

SMITH, C. F., AND S. E. ALDOUS. 1947. The influence of mammals and birds in retarding artificial and natural reseeding of coniferous forests in the United States. Journal of Forestry, 45:361-369. (*Glaucomys)*

SNYDER, L. L. 1921. An outside nest of a flying squirrel. Journal of Mammalogy, 2:171. (*Glaucomys volans)*

SOLLBERGER, D. E. 1938. Notes on the life history of the small eastern flying squirrel *Glaucomys volans)*volans (L.). Ph.D. dissertation, Cornell University, Ithaca, New York, 56 pp.

———. 1940. Notes on the life history of the small eastern flying squirrel. Journal of Mammalogy, 21:282-293. (*Glaucomys volans)*

———. 1943. Notes on the breeding habits of the small eastern flying squirrel, *Glaucomys volans volans*. Journal of Mammalogy, 24:163-173.

SONESHINE, D. E., ET AL. 1978. Epizootiology of epidemic typhus *Rickettsia prowazekii* in flying squirrel. American Journal of Tropical Medicine and Hygene, 27:339-349. (*Glaucomys)*

SONESHINE, D. E., D. G. CERRETANI, G. ENLOW, AND B. L. ELISBERG. 1973. Improved methods for capturing wild flying squirrels. The Journal of Wildlife Management, 37:588-590. (*Glaucomys)*

SONESHINE, D. E., D. M. LAUER, T. C. WALKER, AND B. L. ELISBERG. 1979. The ecology of *Glaucomys volans* (Linnaeus, 1758) in Virginia. Acta Theriologica, 24:363-377.

SONESHINE, D. E., AND D. M. LAUER. 1976. Radio-ecological studies of the squirrel flea *Orchopeas howardii* in laboratory and field colonies of the southern flying squirrel (*Glaucomys volans).* Virginia Journal of Science, 27:50.

SONESHINE, D. E., AND G. F. LEVY. 1981. Vegetative associations affecting *Glaucomys volans* in Central Virginia. Acta Theriologica, 26:359-371.

SOON, B. L., AND R. S. DORNEY. 1969. Observations on a Coccidium (*Eimeria dorneyi*) from the northern flying squirrel in Ontario. Bulletin of the Wildlife Disease Association, 5:37-38. (*Glaucomys sabrinus*)

SOPER, J. D. 1923. The mammals of Wellington and Waterloo Counties, Ontario. Journal of Mammalogy, 4:244-252. (*Glaucomys)*

———. 1942. Mammals of Wood Buffalo Park, northern Alberta and District of Mackenzie. Journal of Mammalogy, 23:119-145. (*Glaucomys sabrinus*)

———. 1970. The mammals of Jasper National Park, Alberta. Canadian Wildlife Service Report, Series 10:1-80. (*Glaucomys sabrinus*)

———. 1973. The mammals of Waterton Lakes National Park, Alberta. Canadian Wildlife Service Report, Series 23:1-55. (*Glaucomys sabrinus*)

SORNBORGER, J. D. 1900. The Labrador flying squirrel. Ottawa Naturalist, 14:48-51. (*Glaucomys)*

SPARKS, J. 1992. Realms of the Russian Bear. Little, Brown, and Company, Boston, 288 pp. (*Pteromys volans*)

SPENCER, G. J. 1956. Some records of ectoparasites from flying squirrels. Proceedings of the Entomological Society of British Columbia, 52:32-34. (*Glaucomys)*

STABB, M. A. 1987. The status of the southern flying squirrel (*Glaucomys volans)* in Canada. Ontario Ministry of Natrual Resources, Toronto.

STABB, M. 1988. The sweet tooth of flying squirrels. Trail Landscape, 22:162-164. (*Glaucomys)*

STABB, M. A., M. E. GARTSHORE, AND P. L. AIRD. 1989. Interactions of southern flying squirrels, *Glaucomys volans,* and cavity-nesting birds. Canadian Field-Naturalist, 103:401-403.

STACK, J. W. 1925. Courage shown by a flying squirrel, *Glaucomys volans,* Journal of Mammalogy, 6:128-129.

STAPP, P. 1990. The energetics of winter nest aggregations of southern flying squirrels. M.S. thesis, University of New Hampshire, Durham, 43 pp. (*Glaucomys volans)*

———. 1992. Energetic influences on the life history of *Glaucomys volans,* Journal of Mammalogy, 73:914-920.

———. 1994. Can predation explain life-history strategies in mammalian gliders? Journal of Mammalogy, 75:227-228. (Petauristinae)

STAPP, P., AND W. W. MAUTZ. 1991. Breeding habits and postnatal growth of the southern flying squirrel (Glaucomys volans) in New Hampshire. The American Midland Naturalist, 126:203-208.

STAPP, P., P. J. PERKINS, AND W. W. MAUTZ. 1991. Winter energy expenditure and the distribution of southern flying squirrels. Canadian Journal of Zoology, 69:2548-2555. (*Glaucomys volans)*

STARK, H. E. 1959. The Siphonaptera of Utah: Their taxonomy, distribution, host relations, and medical importance. United States Department of Health, Education, and Welfare, Public Health Service, Atlanta, Georgia, 239 pp. (*Glaucomys)*

STEHLIN, H. G., AND S. SCHAUB. 1951. Die Trigonodontie der simplicidentaten Nager. Schweizerische Palaeontologische Abhandlungen, 67:1-385. (*Eupetaurus, Iomys*)

STIHLER, C. W., K. B. KNIGHT, V. K. URBAN. 1987. The northern flying squirrel in West Virginia. Proceedings of the Southeastern Nongame Endangered Wildlife Symposium, 3:176-183. (*Glaucomys sabrinus*)

STODDARD, H. L. 1920. The flying squirrel as a bird killer. Journal of Mammalogy, 1:95-96. (*Glaucomys volans)*

STOJEBA, R. C. 1978. Nest box utilization by the southern flying squirrel, *Glaucomys volans* (L.), and related life history information in relation to habitat factors. M.S. thesis, University of Arkansas, Fayetteville, 84 pp.

STONE, K. D., G. A. HEIDT, P. T. CASTER, AND S. HARGIS. 1992. Winter home range of female southern flying squirrels (*Glaucomys volans)* in the Ouachita Mountains of central Arkansas. Journal of the Tennessee Academy of Science, 67(1-2):20. (Abstract only)

STONE, K. D., G. A. HEIDT, W. H. BALTOSSER, AND P. T. CASTER. 1993. Microhabitat characteristics affecting nest-box use by the southern flying squirrel (*Glaucomys volans*). Journal of the Tennessee Academy of Science, 68:57. (Abstract only)

STRICKEL, D. W. 1963. Interspecific relations among red-bellied and hairy woodpeckers and a flying squirrel. The Wilson Bulletin, 75:203-204. (*Glaucomys)*

STORMER, F. A., AND N. SLOAN. 1976. Evidence of the range extension of the southern flying squirrel in the upper Peninsula of Michigan. Jack-Pine Warbler, 54:176-177. (*Glaucomys volans)*

SULIMSKI, A. 1964. Pliocene Lagomorpha and Rodentia from Weze-1 (Poland). Acta Palaeontologica Polonica, 9:149-224. (*Pliopetaurista*)

SUMNER, E. L. 1927. Notes on the San Bernadino flying squirrel. Journal of Mammalogy, 8:315-316. (*Glaucomys sabrinus*)

SVIHLA, R. D. 1930. A family of flying squirrels. Journal of Mammalogy, 11:211-213. (*Glaucomys)*

SWENK, M. H. 1915. On a new species of flying squirrel from Nebraska. University of Nebraska Studies, 15:151-154. (*Glaucomys volans)*

SWINHOE, R. 1862. On the mammals of the Island of Formosa (China). Proceedings of the Zoological Society of London, 5:209-246. (Petauristinae)

TACHIBANA, S. 1955. Ecology of the Japanese giant flying squirrel. Yacho, 20:446-447. (in Japanese) (*Petaurista leucogenys*)

TANNER, V. M. 1927. Some of the smaller mammals of Mount Timpanogos, Utah. Journal of Mammalogy, 8:250-251. (*Glaucomys sabrinus*)

TAVROVSKII, V. A., O. V. EGOROV, V. G. KRIVOSHEEV, M. V. POPOV, AND I. V. LABUTIN. 1971. Mlekopitaiushchie Lakutii. Nauka, Moskva. 660 pp. (Petauristinae)

TAYLOR, E. H. 1934. Philippine land mammals. Philippine Bureau of Science Monographs, 30:1-548. (*Hylopetes*).

TEHSIN, R. H. 1980. Occurrence of the large brown flying squirrel and mouse deer near Udaipur, Rajasthan. Journal of the Bombay Natural History Society, 77:498. (*Petaurista*)

TERZEA, E. 1980. Deaux Micromammiferes du Pliocene de Roumanie. Institutul de Speologie "Emile Racovittha", Travaux, 19:191-201. (*Pliopetaurista*)

TEVIS, L., JR. 1953. Stomach contents of chipmunks and mantled squirrels in northeastern Colorado. Journal of Mammalogy, 34:316-324. (*Glaucomys)*

THALER, L. 1966. Les rongeurs fossils du Bas-Languedoc dans leus rapports avec l'histoire des faunes et la stratigraphie du Tertiaire d'Europe. Memoirs of the Museum of National History, Nature, Paris, series C, 17:1-296. (*Hylopetes*)

THENIUS, E. 1972. Grundzuge der Verbreitungsgeschichte der Saugetiere. Eine historische Tiergeographie. Gustav Fischer Verlag, Jena, 345 pp. (Petauristinae)

THOMAS, O. 1888. On *Eupetaurus*, a new form of flying squirrel from Kashmir. Journal of the Asiatic Society, Bengal, 57:256-260.

———. 1907. A new flying squirrel from Formosa. Annals and Magazine of Natural History, 7:171-172.

———. 1908. The genera and subgenera of the Sciuropterus group, with descriptions of the new species. Annual Magazine of Natural History, Series 8, 1:1-8.

———. 1923. Geographical races of *Petaurista alborufus*. Annual Magazine of Natural History, 20:522-523.

THOMPSON, I. D. 1986. Diet choice, hunting behavior, activity patterns, and ecological energetics of marten in natural and logged areas.

Ph.D. dissertation, Queen's University, Kingston, Ontario, 226 pp. (*Glaucomys)*

THOMPSON, R. S., AND J. I. MEAD. 1982. Late Quaternary environments and biogeography in the Great Basin. Quaternary Research (New York), 17:39-55. (*Glaucomys)*

THORINGTON, R. W., JR. 1984. Flying squirrels are monophyletic. Science, 225:1048-1050. (Petauristinae)

THORINGTON, R. W., JR., AND L. R. HEANEY. 1981. Body proportions and gliding adaptations of flying squirrels (Petauristinae). Journal of Mammalogy, 62:101-114.

TIEDMAN, F. 1808. Zoologie. Zu seinen Vorlesungen entworfen. Landshut, 1:451. (*Glaucomys volans)*

TIMM, R. M. 1975. Distribution, natural history, and parasites of mammals of Cook County, Minnesota. Occasional Papers of the Bell Museum of Natural History, University of Minnesota, 14:1-56. (*Glaucomys)*

TINER, J. D., R. AND RAUSCH. 1949. *Syphacia thompsoni* (Nematoda: Oxyuridae) from the red squirrel. Journal of Mammalogy, 30:202-203. (*Glaucomys)*

TIPTON, V. J., H. E. STARCK, AND J. A. WILDIE. 1979. Anomiopsyllinae (Siphonaptera: Hystrichopsysllidae). II. The genera *Callistopsyllus, Conorhinopsylla, Megathroglosus*, and *Stenstonera.* The Great Basin Naturalist, 39:351-418. (*Glaucomys)*

TOMES, R. F. 1862. Report of a collection of mammals made by Osbert Salvin, Esq. F. Z. S., at Duenas, Guatemala; with notes on some of the species, by Mr. Fraser. Proceedings of the Zoological Society of London, 1861:278-288 (*Glaucomys volans)*

TONER, G. C. 1956. House cat predation on small mammals. Journal of Mammalogy, 37:119. (*Glaucomys)*

TORMALA, T., H. HOKKANEN, AND H. VUORINEN. 1978. Outdoor activity of young flying squirrels, *Pteromys volans*, in central Finland. Saeugetierkundliche Mitteilungen, 26:250-251. (in English)

———. 1980. Activity time in the flying squirrel, *Pteromys volans*, in central Finland. Saeugetierkunde, 45:225-234.

TORMALA, T., H. VUORINEN, AND H. HOKKANEN. 1980. Timing of circadian activity in the flying squirrel in central Finland. Acta Theriologica, 25:461-474. (*Pteromys volans*)

TSUCHIYA, K. 1979. A contribution to the chromosome study in Japanese mammals. Proceedings of the Japanese Academy, (B)55:191-195. (Petauristinae)

TSEYTLIN, S. M. 1979. Geologiya paleolita Severnoy Azii. Izd. Nauka, Moscow, Union of Soviet Socialist Republics, 287 pp. (*Petinomys*)

TULLBERG, T. 1899. Uber das system der Nagethiere: eine phylogenetische Studie. Akademischen Buchdruckerei, Uppsala. (Petauristinae)

TURNER, R. W. 1972. Mammals of the Black Hills of South Dakota and Wyoming. Ph.D. dissertation, University of Kansas, Lawrence, 402 pp. (*Glaucomys sabrinus*)

UGDAGAWA, T. 1954. The damage of forests by the giant flying squirrel, and a new method of extermination. Bulletin of Governmental Forest Experiment Station, Japan, 68:133-144. (in Japanese with English summary) (*Petaurista*)

UHLIG, H. G. 1956. Reproduction in the eastern flying squirrel in West Virginia. Journal of Mammalogy, 37:295. (*Glaucomys volans)*

UNAY, E. 1981. Middle and upper Miocene rodents from the Bayraktepe section (Canakkale, Turkey). Proceedings of the Koninklijke Nederlandse Akademie van Wetschappen, Series B: Palaeontology, Geology, Physics, and Chemistry, 84:271-238. (*Miopetaurista*)

UNKNOWN AUTHOR. 1949. Flying squirrels in flight. Life, 27(22):16-18.

———. 1985. Red-cockaded woodpecker recovery plan. United States Fish and Wildlife Service, Atlanta, Georgia, 88 pp. (*Glaucomys volans)*

URBAN, V. K. 1988*a*. Home range and activity of the endangered northern flying squirrel. Transaction of the Northeast Section of the Wildlife Society, 45:79. (Abstract only) (*Glaucomys sabrinus*)

———. 1988*b*. Home range, habitat utilization, and activity of the endangered northern flying squirrel. M.S. thesis, West Virginia University, Morgantown, 117 pp. (*Glaucomys sabrinus*)

VAN DER WEERD, A. 1979. Early Ruscinian rodents and lagomorphs from the lignites near Ptolemais (Macedonia). Proceedings of the Koninklijke Nederlandse Akademie van Wetschappen, Series B: Palaeontology, Geology, Physics, and Chemistry, 82:127-170. (Petauristinae)

VAN DER WEERD, A., AND R. DAAMS. 1978. Quantitative compostion of rodent faunas in the Spanish Neogene and paleoecological implications. Proceedings of the Koninklijke Nederlandse Akademie van Wetschappen, Series B: Palaeontology, Geology, Physics, and Chemistry, 81:448-473. (*Miopetaurista*)

VAN TIEN, D., AND C. VANSUNG. 1990. Six new Vietnamese rodents. Mammalia, 54:233-238. (*Hylopetes pharei*)

VANVOORHEES, D. A. 1976. Feeding energetics and winter survival in the southern flying squirrel, *Glaucomys volans.* M.S. thesis, Wake Forest University, Winston-Salem, North Carolina, 131 pp.

VAUGHAN, T. 1970. The skeletal system, *in* The biology of bats, Volume 1 (W. A. Wimsatt, ed.). Academic Press, New York, 406 pp. (*Glaucomys*)

VENTERS, H. D., AND W. L. JENNINGS. 1962. Epidemiologic note: rabies in a flying squirrel. Public Health Reports, 77:200. (*Glaucomys volans*)

VOIGT, D. R., G. B. KOLENOSKY, AND D. H. PIMLOTT. 1976. Changes in summer foods of wolves in central Ontario. The Journal of Wildlife Management, 40: 663-668. (*Glaucomys*)

VON KOENIGSWALD, W. 1973. Fossil-Bergesellschaftugen Nr. 15; Husarenhof 4, eine alt-bis mittelpleistozaene Kleinsaeugerfauna aus Wuerttemberg mit *Petauria.* Neus Jahrbuch fuer Geologie und Palaeontologie Abhanlung, 143:23-38.

———. 1974. Solnhofen 5, eine villa frachische Spaltenfuellung aus Bayern. Mitteilungen dcr Bayerischen Staatssammlung fuer Palaeontologie und Historische Geologie, 14:39-48. (Petauristinae)

VOORHIES, M. R. 1981. Medial and late Barstovian fossil vertebrate faunas in direct superposition, Devil's Nest area, Knox County, Nebraska. Proceedings of the Nebraska Academy of Science, 91:36-37 (abstract). (Petauristinae).

WALKER, E. P. 1947. "Flying" squirrels, nature's gliders. National Geographic Magazine, Washington, D.C., 91:662-674. (*Glaucomys*)

———. 1949. More about animal behavior. The Smithsonian Report, 1949:261-292. (*Glaucomys*)

———. 1951*a.* Glimpses of flying squirrels. Nature Magazine, 44:81-84. (*Glaucomys*)

———. 1951*b.* Unusual pets that are readily tamed, "Flying" squirrels. Illustrated London News, 281:302-303. (*Glaucomys*)

WANG, F. 1985. Preliminary study of the complex-toothed flying squirrel. Pp. 67-69, *in* Contemporary Mammalogy in China and Japan (T. Kawamichi, ed.). Mammalogical Society of Japan, Osaka, 195 pp. (in English) (*Trogopterus*)

WANG S., C. ZHENG, AND K. TSUNEAKI. 1989. A tentative list of threatened rodents in China and Japan with notes on their distribution, habitat, and status. Pp. 42-44, *in* Rodents: a world survey of species of conservation concern (W. Z. Lidicker, Jr.). Occasional Papers of the International Union for the Conservation of Nature, Species Survival Commission, 4:iv + 60 pp. (*Petaurista*)

WEIGL, P. D. 1969. The distribution of the flying squirrels, *Glaucomys volans* and *G. sabrinus*: an evaluation of the competitive exclusion idea. Ph.D. dissertation, Duke University, Durham, North Carolina, 247 pp.

———. 1977*a.* The northern flying squirrel, *Glaucomys sabrinus. In,* endangered and threatened vertebrates of the Southeastern United States. Miscellaneaous Research, Bulletin, Tall Timbers Research Station 4, Tallahasse, Florida.

———. 1977*b.* Status of the northern flying squirrel, *Glaucomys sabrinus* coloratus, in North Carolina. Pp. 398-400, *in* Endangered and threatened plants and animals of North Carolina (J. E. Cooper, S. S. Robinson, and J. B. Funderburg, eds.). North Carolina State Museum of Natural History, Raleigh, 444 pp.

———. 1978. Resource overlap, interspecific interactions and the distribution of the flying squirrels, Glaucomys volans and G. sabrinus. The American Midland Naturalist, 100:83-96.

WEIGL, P. D., T. W. KNOWLES, AND A. C. BOYNTON. 1992. Parasite-mediated "competition" in the flying squirrels (*Glaucomys*) of the southern Appalachians. The American Zoologist, 32:102A. (Abstract only)

WEIGL, P. D., AND D. W. OSGOOD. 1974. Study of the northern flying squirrel, Glaucomys sabrinus by temperature telemetry. The American Midland Naturalist, 92:482-486.

WELLS-GOSLING, N. 1982. Distribution of flying squirrels (*Glaucomys*) in Michigan. Michigan Academician, 14:209-216.

———. 1985. Flying Squirrels: Gliders in the dark. Smithsonian Institution Press, Washington, D.C., 128 pp. (*Glaucomys*)

WELLS-GOSLING, N., AND L. R. HEANEY. 1984. Glaucomys sabrinus. Mammalian Species, 247:1-8.

WETZEL, E. J., AND P. D. WEIGL. 1994. Ecological implications for flying squirrels (Glaucomys)sp.) of effect of temperature on the *in* vitro development and behavior of Stronglyloides robustus. The American Midland Naturalist, 131:43-54.

WHITAKER, J. O., JR., E. A. LYONS, M. A. SMITH, AND C. MASER. 1983. Nest inhabitants and ectoparasites of northern flying squirrels, *Glaucomys sabrinus* (Shaw), from northeastern Oregon. Northwest Science, 57:291-295.

WHITLOW, W. B., AND E. R. HALL. 1933. Mammals of the Pocatello region of southeastern Idaho. University of California Publications in Zoology, 40:235-275. (*Glaucomys*)

WILLIAMS, D. F. J. VERNER, H. F. SAKAI, AND J. R. WATERS. 1992. General biology of major prey species of the California Spotted Owl. U.S. Forest Service General Technical Report, Pacific Southwest, 133:207-224. (*Glaucomys sabrinus*)

WILLIAMS, M. S., AND F. M. BOZEMAN. 1978. Isolation and characterization of a new *Herpesvirus* from the southern flying squirrel. Abstracts of the Annual Meeting of the American Society of Microbiologists, 78:256. (*Glaucomys volans*)

WILSON, D. E. AND D. M. REEDER (EDS.). 1993. Mammal species of the world: A taxonomic and geographic reference, 2nd ed. Smithsonian Institution Press, Washington, D.C., 1206 pp. (Petauristinae)

WILSON, N., H. HOOGSTRAAL, AND G. M. KOHLS. 1968. Studies on southeast Asian *Haemaphysalis* ticks (Ixodoidea: Ixodidae) redescription of *H.* (*Rhipistoma*) *bartelsi* Shule (resurrected) the Indonesian flying squirrel Haemaphysalid. Journal of Parasitology, 54:1223-1227.

WILSON, R. W. 1972. Evolution and extinction in early Tertiary rodents. Proceedings of the 24th International Geological Congress, section 7:217-224. (Petauristinae)

WILSON, T. M., AND A. B. CAREY. 1992. Nest sites of northern flying squirrels in managed second-growth forests. Northwest Science, 66:129. (Abstract only) (*Glaucomys sabrinus*)

WITT, J. W. 1991. Fluctuations in the weight and trap response for *Glaucomys sabrinus* in western Oregon. Journal of Mammalogy, 72:612-615.

———. 1992. Home range and density estimates for the northern flying squirrel, *Glaucomys sabrinus*, in western Oregon. Journal of Mammalogy, 73:921-929.

WON, P-O. 1968. Notes on the first propagation record of the Palaerctic flying squirrel, *Pteromys volans* aluco (Thomas) from Korea. Journal of the Mammalogy Society of Japan, 4:40-43.

WOOD, A. E. 1955. A revised classification of rodents. Journal of Mammalogy, 36:165-187. (Petauristinae)

———. 1962. The Early Tertiary rodents of the family Paramyidae. American Philosophical Society, Transactions, 52:1-261. (Origins of Petauristinae)

WOOD, A. E., AND R. W. WILSON. 1936. A suggested nomenclature for the cusps of the cheek teeth of rodents. Journal of Paleontology, 10:388-391. (Petauristinae)

WOOD, F. E. 1910. A study of the mammals of Champaign County, Illinois. Bulletin of the Illinois State Laboratory of Natural History, 8:524-536. (*Glaucomys volans*)

WOOD, T. J., AND G. D. TESSIER. 1974. First records of eastern flying squirrel, *Glaucomys volans*, new record from Nova Scotia. Canadian Field-Naturalist, 88:83-84.

WOODMAN, D. R., E. WEISS, G. A. DASCH, AND F. M. BOZEMAN. 1977. Biological properties of *Rickettsia prowazekii* strains isolated from flying squirrels. Infection and Immunity, 16:853-860. (*Glaucomys*)

WRIGLEY, R. E. 1969. Ecological notes on the mammals of southern Quebec. Canadian Field-Naturalist, 83:201-211. (*Glaucomys*)

———. 1975. Poplar bud in subcutaneous tissue of a northern flying squirrel. Canadian Field-Naturalist, 89:466. (*Glaucomys*)

YANAGAWA, H. 1993. [The difference between Ezo flying squirrel and southern flying squirrel.] Animal Zoos, 45:30-31. (in Japanese) (*Pteromys* and *Glaucomys*)

YANAGAWA, H., M. TANAKA, T. INOUE, AND M. TANIGUCHI. 1991. Annual and daily activities of the flying squirrel, *Pteromys volans* orii, in captivity. Honyurui Kagaku, 30:157-166.

YAP, L. F., I. MUUL, AND B. L. LIM. 1970. A *Plasmodium* sp. from the spotted giant flying squirrel in West Malaysia. Southeast Asian Journal of Tropical Medicine and Public Health, 1:418. (*Petaurista elegans*)

YONG, H. S., AND S. S. DHALIWAL. 1976. Variations in the karyotype of the red giant flying squirrel *Petaurista petaurista* (Rodentia, Sciuridae). Malaysian Journal of Science, 4:9-12.

YOUNG, B. L., AND I. J. STOUT. 1984. Diets of small rodents in the Florida sand pine scrub: are rodents food-limited? Bulletin of the Ecological Society of America, 65:97. (Abstract only) (*Glaucomys volans*)

———. 1986. Effects of extra food on small rodents in a south temperate zone habitat: demographic responses. Canadian Journal of Zoology, 64:1211-1217. (*Glaucomys volans*)

YOUNGMAN, P. M. 1975. Mammals of the Yukon Territory. National Museum of Natural Science Canada, Publications in Zoology, 10:1-192. (*Glaucomys sabrinus*)

YOUNGMAN, P. M., AND D. A. GILL. 1968. First record of the southern flying squirrel, *Glaucomys volans volans* from Quebec. Canadian Field-Naturalist, 82:227-228.

YU, Z.-Z., G.-R. YANG, AND Z.-D. GONG. 1986. Seven new species of chigger mites belonging to the genera of *Leptotrombibium* and *Ascoschoengasta* from Yunnan Province (Acarina: Trombiculidae). Acta Zootaxonomica Sinica, 11:166-178. (in Chinese with English summary) (*Petaurista petaurista*)

ZHOLNEROVSKAIA, E. I., N. N. VORONTSOV, AND O. K. BARANOV. 1980. [Immunological analysis of taxonomic interrelationships of Russian flying squirrels *Pteromys volans* arsenjevi with five genera of Palearctic Sciuridae (Rodentia)]. Zoologicheskii Zhurnal, 59:750-754. (in Russian)

ZIELINSKI, W. J., W. D. SPENCER, AND R. H. BARRETT. 1983. Relationship between food habits and activity patterns of pine martens. Journal of Mammalogy, 64:387-396. (*Glaucomys*)

ACKNOWLEDGMENTS

I thank J. Scheibe and two anonymous reviewers for constructive criticism. Denise Dowling, K. Fahey, J. Hurych, and J. Sadler assisted with collection and arrangement of materials.

CLOSING COMMENTS AND FUTURE DIRECTIONS: RESEARCH ON THE ECOLOGY AND EVOLUTIONARY BIOLOGY OF TREE SQUIRRELS

JOHN L. KOPROWSKI AND MICHAEL A. STEELE

Department of Biology, Willamette University, Salem, OR 97301 (JLK)

Department of Biology, Wilkes University, Wilkes-Barre, PA 18766 (MAS)

The most important question that emerges from a volume that synthesizes the efforts of scientists from 11 countries throughout the world must be "Where do we go from here?" The 27 works included in this volume provide an overview of the state of current research and, as well, hint at the direction of future studies. Our objective in this closing chapter is to glean a sense of what is to come and attempt to provide some indications of fruitful areas for future studies.

We first emphasize our strong belief—and the premise on which this volume was first organized—that tree squirrels represent model organisms for many areas of research in ecology, conservation, behavior, and evolutionary biology. In many parts of the world tree squirrels are among our most easily observed mammals and as such represent ideal subjects for studies involving direct observations of social behavior, foraging and food-hoarding behavior, and many types of interspecific interactions. Moreover, as arboreal granivores, the tree squirrels occupy a unique ecological niche that is often characterized by a close interdependence on their food resources and, as shown in several papers in this volume, a potentially dominant role in their environments. It is our hope that many of the papers in this volume will draw attention to the ecological importance of these mammals as well as their utility as subjects for many types of ecological and evolutionary investigations.

While the TABLE OF CONTENTS accurately portrays the breadth of current research activity on tree squirrels, the opportunities for future research are far greater than represented here. Twenty-eight species of *Sciurus,* two species of *Glaucomys*, and three species of *Tamiasciurus*, are currently recognized in addition to dozens of species of African, Asian and South American arboreal squirrels (Wilson and Reeder, 1993). However, only seven of these species are addressed in any detail by researchers in this volume. Obviously, any conclusions that can be drawn on the ecology of tree squirrels to date result from a very limited subset of studies, principally focused on Nearctic and Palearctic regions. The ecological patterns that we at present view as characteristic of tree squirrels may in fact only be indicative of adaptation to resource limitation in Holarctic regions. A broader understanding will likely result from an increase in the taxonomic breadth of future studies. For example, we know very little about tropical tree squirrels and how their behavior and ecology is impacted by the more diverse set of competitors in this region. Furthermore, we do not know how differences in seasonality and resource dispersion influence tree squirrels in the tropics relative to temperate areas. Virtually nothing is known about the impact of tree squirrels on forest regeneration in the tropics.

In M.A. Steele, J. F. Merritt, and D. A. Zegers (eds.). 1998. Ecology and Evolutionary Biology of Tree Squirrels. Special Publication, Virginia Museum of Natural History, 6: 320 pp

The phylogenetic relationships of many of the tree squirrels are yet to be resolved and the list of currently recognized species may also change significantly with a thorough systematic study. E.R. Hall (1981) noted that even a satisfactory key to the 28 members of the genus *Sciurus* did not exist. Nearly 20 years later this is still the case! The interpretation of life-history and behavioral traits in light of phylogenetic relationships can provide significant insight into the ecology of tree squirrels; however, the broader application of species-specific findings is currently limited by the lack of a modern systematic treatment of tree squirrels. Molecular, morphological, and comparative behavioral studies are likely to provide significant approaches for resolving important systematic relationships.

Finally, the conservation of tree squirrels and their importance in understanding habitat loss in many temperate and tropical forests is rapidly emerging as a critical area of research. The conservation status of 8 of 13 Holarctic tree squirrels (*Glaucomys sabrinus, Sciurus anomalus, S. arizonensis, S. navaritensis, S. niger, S. vulgaris, Tamiasciurus hudsonicus*) is recognized as precarious in at least part of each of these species' ranges. Tropical squirrels have received so little study that the conservation status of many of these species also may be a significant issue-we simply do not know. The dependence of tree squirrels on mature forests that produce significant amounts of seeds and provide suitable nest cavities predispose these arboreal species to rarity, especially at current rates of non-sustainable deforestation. Natural fragmentation of suitable habitat or other factors that result in relic or otherwise isolated populations within a species' range contribute to an increased risk of extinction. Such range reductions are in part responsible for the precarious status of species such as *S. anomalus, S. arizonensis, S. nayaritensis, S. richmondi,* and *G. sabrinus.* The great majority of the basic and applied ecological studies in this volume provide important information on the life-history of tree squirrels that is valuable to current and future conservation efforts. Given current trends in habitat loss, such studies are only likely to become more valuable and necessary as many tree squirrels become recognized as important indicators of habitat quality.

These are only a few areas in which future research will likely focus. There is, no doubt, a diversity of other important research questions yet to be uncovered. We hope that the papers contained in this volume serve as an important impetus for future research; however, we also believe that additional research directions can be found by taking a keen look at what is missing in this volume. Finally, it is our goal that this volume serves to stimulate collaboration among researchers to gain a better understanding of **"The Ecology and Evolutionary Biology of Tree Squirrels,"** and their important role in nature.

LITERATURE CITED

HALL, E.R. 1981. The Mammals of North America, Second ed., John Wiley & Sons, New York, 1:1-600 + *90*.

WILSON, D.E., AND D.M. REEDER. (EDS.) 1993. Mammal species of the world: a taxonomic and geographic reference, Second ed. Smithsonian Institution Press, Washington D.C., 1206 pp.